A Writer's Diary

A Writer's Diary

FYODOR DOSTOEVSKY

Volume One 1873–1876

Translated and Annotated by
KENNETH LANTZ

With an Introductory Study by
GARY SAUL MORSON

Northwestern University Press · Evanston, Illinois

Northwestern University Press
Evanston, Illinois 60208-4210

This translation was funded with the assistance of the National Endowment for the Humanities.

ISBN 0-8101-1094-6

Contents

1 8 7 3

1 8 7 6

[ANNOUNCEMENT]

January

CHAPTER ONE

CHAPTER TWO

CHAPTER THREE

Contents

Contents

June

July and August

September

October

November

Contents

6 A Dreadful Recollection   698

CHAPTER TWO

1 A Dream of Pride   701
2 Suddenly the Shroud Fell Away   706
3 I Understand All Too Well   710
4 I Was Only Five Minutes Late   714

December

CHAPTER ONE

1 More about a Case That Is Not as Simple as It
   Seems   721
2 A Belated Moral   729
3 Unsubstantiated Statements   732
4 A Few Words about Young People   737
5 On Suicide and Arrogance   740

CHAPTER TWO

1 A Story from the Lives of Children   743
2 An Explanation Regarding My Participation in the
   Forthcoming Publication of the Magazine *Light*   748
3 Where Does the Matter Stand at the Moment?   749
4 A Short Comment on "Pondering Peter"   753

NOTES   755

Translator's Preface

The eminent Soviet scholar Dmitry Likhachev, in an article significantly entitled "'Stylistic Negligence' in Dostoevsky," remarked that "Dostoevsky flaunts before the reader the rawness of his style and the seemingly improvised nature of his narrative; at the same time he does not conceal his quest for general and maximum accuracy, despite the deliberate and even shocking inaccuracy in specific details. He lays bare the structures of his works and his behind-the-scenes techniques."[1] Likhachev is speaking of Dostoevsky the novelist, but the observation holds true for Dostoevsky's writing generally. His prose is not elegant: it is often convoluted, frequently repetitious, and is full of qualifications such as "perhaps," "rather," "somewhat," "as if," "partly," "a certain," "some sort of," "evidently." Certain favorite phrases—"the main thing," "the most important thing," "above all," "on the contrary," and, of course, "suddenly"—recur with dismaying regularity. Some of these traits may derive from the tradition of nineteenth-century Russian journalistic writing: all journalists wrote with the censor looking over their shoulders, so circumlocutions and qualifications were safer than simple and unambiguous statements. And the weight of an article was, I suspect, often equated with its length. But it would be quite wrong to dismiss Dostoevsky's expository prose as merely a product of a journalistic milieu; it is powerful and distinctive, a deliberately chosen vehicle to convey his sense of life, as Likhachev argues.

Another discerning critic, P. M. Bitsilli, has noted that Dostoevsky's style reveals his "awareness of the impossibility of finding any comprehensive formula to express all the complexity and inner contradictions of this or that element of reality."[2] The truth, in other words, is elusive and incredibly complex; Dostoevsky does

not capture it, but circles around it and approximates it. He himself
often commented on the difficulty of transferring his own insights
into words. "We all know," he wrote, "that entire trains of thought
can sometimes pass through our heads in an instant, like sensations
of some sort, without being translated into human language, never
mind into literary language."[3] "Your idea, even though it may be
a bad one, is always more profound when it is within you, but
when you put it into words it is more ridiculous and less honest. . . ."[4] At the same time, he was wary of making himself too
clear: in July 1876, he complained that his June *Diary*, which
contained a fairly unambiguous statement of his views on Russia's
mission, had been a mistake:

> In my writings I had never yet permitted myself to bring *certain*
> of my convictions to their conclusion, to say *the very last* word. . . .
> Set forth any paradox you please, but do not bring it to a conclusion,
> and you'll have something witty and subtle and *comme il faut*, but
> bring some very speculative statement to a conclusion. . .directly and
> not merely by suggestion, and no one will believe you, precisely
> because of your naiveté, precisely because you have brought it to its
> conclusion and said your final word. On the other hand, however, if
> many of the most famous wits—Voltaire, for instance—had, instead
> of gibes, hints, innuendos and insinuations, suddenly resolved to state
> everything they believed in and revealed all their innermost reality,
> their essence—then, believe me, they would never have gained a tenth
> of the effect they did. Even more: people would only have laughed
> at them. Indeed, people in general somehow do not like the last word
> in anything, the "expressed" thought; they say that "the thought
> expressed is a lie."[5]

I have tried, therefore, to respect Dostoevsky's text, to preserve
the oddities, the complexities, the ambiguities, and even the "sud-
denlys." Although they may be grammatically and logically superfluous, they convey the contradictions and complexities of his
view of life and of his own personality. If one hopes to understand
or, more accurately, to experience that personality (and I think that
Dostoevsky's personality is revealed more fully in the *Diary* than
in his novels and stories), the rawness and rough edges of his prose
must be preserved. This also means attempting to preserve his
long and torturous sentences. Russian can, without any violation
of stylistic norms, create "run-on" sentences, and many of Dostoevsky's fall into this category. English is not so tolerant, so I

Introductory Study: Dostoevsky's Great Experiment

Gary Saul Morson

Part 1: Origin of an Anomaly

Instead of a Preface on Loose and Baggy Monsters, on Clausewitzian Poetics, and on the "Herzenification" of Russian Literature

Dostoevsky's *Writer's Diary* immediately strikes the reader as one of the strangest works of world literature.[1] In the Russian tradition of "loose baggy monsters," the *Diary* may be the loosest and baggiest—as if it were designed to test the limits of the Russian literary mania for formally anomalous works.[2] In issue after issue of the *Diary*, Dostoevsky stresses that Russian history is and must be different from that of any other country, and his strange work seems to match this Slavophile sense of history with a radical "Slavophilism" of literary form.

Nineteenth-century Russian writers and critics of all camps never tired of stressing the distinctiveness of Russian history and the formal anomaly of Russian literature. Near the beginning of Russian literature's great flowering, the epoch's most revered critic, Vissarion Belinsky, insisted that Russianness was to be found in the denial of all "European" cultural norms and patterns. "It is precisely one of the greatest intellectual achievements of our age," Belinsky proclaimed,

> that we have at last begun to realize that Russia had a history of her

1

own that in no way resembled the history of a single European state, and that it should be studied and judged on its own merits and not in the light of the history of European nations, with which it has nothing in common. The same applies to the history of Russian literature. . . . It has been in existence for a mere *hundred and seven years*, yet it already possesses several works whose only interest for foreigners is that they strike them as being unlike the works of their own literature, hence, as being original, independent, i.e., nationally Russian.[3]

This passage, which voiced what was to become a cliché of Russian criticism, expresses a number of noteworthy ideas. Most obviously, Belinsky denies that all nations follow the same historical steps; here, he is evidently responding to the Hegelian view of history as one grand unfolding story, to which Russia is incidental. Instead of History, Belinsky insists on histories, from which it follows that one can recognize an event or artifact as Russian, rather than as a mere imitation, to the extent that it departs from European norms.

Note also Belinsky's keen sense of the *belatedness* of Russian literature.[4] Which other major European country's literature began a century ago, and which one could actually date, to the year, its literature's origin? For Belinsky and others, this sense of belatedness, and therefore of cultural inferiority that must be overcome even more rapidly than economic backwardness, lent a tone of urgency. Criticism was expected to monitor year by year, perhaps even month by month, Russian progress in producing timeless masterpieces. Russian literature, focused on its "thick journals," became a periodical quest for cultural immortality.

No less characteristic of the Russian tradition is the assumption that it is in *literature*, rather than any other of the arts, sciences, or industries, that Russia's genius is to be expressed. We sense these same assumptions operating when, in *A Writer's Diary*, Dostoevsky praises *Anna Karenina*, the last installment of which had just appeared, as not just a literary event but a historical "fact of special significance" (7-8/77, 2.3). It is, he declared, the justification of Russia's existence and the proof of its special character: "If the Russian genius could give birth to this *fact*, then it is not doomed to impotence and can create; it can provide something *of its own*, it can begin *its own* and finish uttering it when the times and seasons come to pass." The very need to point to a great writer—to Tolstoy—as the justification of a whole people is itself characteristic of Russian culture. With his familiar tone of wistful doubt, Dostoevsky

concludes that perhaps Russians can someday contribute to some
other cultural field as well: "It would be absurd simply to suppose
that nature has endowed us only with literary talents."

Tolstoy himself wrote the most famous description of Russian
literature's distinctiveness, which he identified explicitly with its
tradition of *formal* anomaly. Responding to critics who were mys-
tified by the aberrant shape of *War and Peace* and to readers who
could not recognize the genre to which it belonged, Tolstoy boldly
answered that his book was, like all Russian masterpieces, sui
generis. "What Is *War and Peace?*" he asked, and then answered
by specifying what it is not:

> It is not a novel, still less a *poema*, still less a historical chronicle.
> *War and Peace* is what the author wished to express and was able to
> express in that form in which it is expressed. Such a statement of the
> author's disregard for the conventional forms of an artistic prose work
> might seem presumptuous if it were not deliberate and if there were
> no precedents for it. But the history of Russian literature since the
> time of Pushkin not only affords many examples of such a departure
> from European form, but does not offer so much as one example to
> the contrary. From Gogol's *Dead Souls* to Dostoevsky's *Dead House*,
> in the recent period of Russian literature there is not a single work
> of artistic prose, at all rising above mediocrity, that quite fits the form
> of a novel, a poem, or a story.[5]

Tolstoy was no doubt exaggerating in stating that all Russian masterpieces were formally defiant, but this exaggeration itself both typ-
ified and influenced the tradition it described. In *A Writer's Diary*
Dostoevsky went so far as to criticize *War and Peace* as too conservative—as not formally daring *enough*.[6]

In the twentieth century the great Russian Formalist critic Victor
Shklovsky echoed the many descriptions of Russian literature as
an antitradition when he described *War and Peace* as not only the
greatest but also the most *typical* (because *a*typical) work of Russian
literature. With the exaggeration so familiar in Russian criticism,
Shklovsky warned that Tolstoy's masterpiece will never be understood so long as it is read according to the thoroughly alien laws
of European art:

> The novel *War and Peace* is founded on its own laws, the laws of the
> Russian novel, which were being worked out for decades in Russian
> art. The novels of Tolstoy will be incomprehensible if we come to
> judge them according to the norms of old poetics, which would be

like judging Kutuzov's actions according to Clausewitz's rules of war.... His novel has been compared with West European novels of the first half of the nineteenth century. But the frames of these novels had long become [too] narrow for Russian artistic thought.[7]

Like so many of his predecessors, Shklovsky then sketches a history of Russian literature to justify this description. "Great Russian prose was belated in its appearance when compared to West European," Shklovsky argues, "but, having appeared, it conceived of itself and of the world in its own way."[8] What most fascinates Shklovsky is the Russian tendency to combine within a single work fiction and nonfiction, novel and essay, or story and polemical article. Such combinations were for Shklovsky the hallmark of Russian literature and constituted the most radical anomaly of *War and Peace.*

Shklovsky suggests that the origin of Tolstoy's experiment is to be found in Gogol's *Arabesques,* a collection of essays and stories that, Shklovsky believes, should be read not merely as an anthology of Gogol's writings but as an integral literary work. Shklovsky also stresses the importance of Alexander Herzen's *From the Other Shore,* which juxtaposed essays to fictional dialogues; Shklovsky calls this whole combinatory trend the "Herzenification" of Russian literature. "The inclusion of philosophy in a great new form— this was the concern not only of Gogol and Herzen but also of Tolstoy, in such a work as *War and Peace....* Toward the middle of the nineteenth century, elements of 'science' and art converged in Russian prose" (*Povesti o proze,* 6). Shklovsky himself combined scholarship and art in his own works (most notably *Zoo*), and his colleague Boris Eichenbaum actually produced one issue of a literary work in periodical form that is eerily reminiscent of *A Writer's Diary.*[9]

By the 1920s *A Writer's Diary,* which was infamous for its reactionary politics, could not be seriously praised in Bolshevik Russia. But as Shklovsky and Eichenbaum were doubtless aware, it, even more than *War and Peace,* exemplified "Herzenification." Indeed, the opening essay of the 1873 *Diary* explicitly cites Herzen's success in *From the Other Shore* as a key inspiration for the *Diary* itself.

Turning the Periodical into Literature;
Plan of the Present Essay

Considered as a daring experiment in form, *A Writer's Diary* seems even more extreme than *War and Peace.* It resembles most literature so little that many readers have not recognized it as a literary work at all. The *Diary* has usually been treated as a mere anthology, a random collection of Dostoevsky's writings during a given period, with no integrity of its own. It is commonplace to analyze the stories that appear in the *Diary* as if they had originally been published as entirely independent works, whereas no serious scholar would think of interpreting (or anthologizing) his Grand Inquisitor legend without acknowledging how its meaning is conditioned by its place in *The Brothers Karamazov*. Many parts of the *Diary* are quite well known, but not *as* parts of the *Diary*. Only recently have scholars and readers begun to be fascinated by the *Diary* itself.

The relative neglect of the *Diary* (as opposed to its most famous sections) apparently resulted from three causes. First, the *Diary* is so remarkably odd, and so unlike other works, that it is hard to recognize as an integral work. Second, large portions of it are deeply offensive, and so a method that allows for excerpting has obvious advantages. Third, and perhaps most important, Dostoevsky did not always keep to the plan of this already difficult work. If it is hard to limn the outlines of a radically new structure when realized according to plan, it is even harder to do so when the plan is set aside and the structure obscured. One might say that however bold and interesting the experiment of the *Diary*, the work itself may perhaps be regarded as Dostoevsky's most brilliant and intriguing failure.

What was the intended design of the *Diary*? In the work itself irritated "readers" occasionally interrupt the author with this very question, only to receive wry, ambiguous answers. Nevertheless, a number of key characteristics were evidently central to Dostoevsky's plan. I should like to devote the remainder of this introduction's first part to one strange feature of the *Diary*, its periodical format. Part 2 will explore its other most remarkable anomaly, its combination of dramatically diverse literary genres. In the course of describing the work's makeup, I shall also discuss its most significant parts. Part 3 will examine how these diverse elements, published in a periodical form, were designed to cohere as an integral work of art. The fourth part of my introduction will then explain how the ideological changes Dostoevsky underwent while publishing the *Diary* led him to neglect its original plan, which had been designed to express views evidently irreconcilable with his new convictions. In this way, we will see what the *Diary* was supposed to be, how it works when it fulfills that design, and what happened to obscure the already odd shape of Dostoevsky's great experiment.

An Author Gives a Valuable Idea to a Character,
and Then Places Himself in the Position of a Character

One is struck first of all by a literary work that takes the form of a monthly journal. In contrast to most nineteenth-century novels that were published *in* periodicals, the *Diary* in its mature form *was itself* a periodical. Readers were invited to subscribe to a one-person publication for which Dostoevsky served as editor, publisher, and sole contributor. They received monthly (or occasionally double bimonthly) issues, in which the author updated readers on his impressions of public events since the last issue. In his announcement of the *Diary*, Dostoevsky indicated that at the end of each year a book would be made from the monthly issues, which were designed to have lasting, rather than ephemeral, interest. Nevertheless, even in book form the monthly format was to be maintained. Sections would still be labeled "January 1876," "February 1876," and so on. So essential was this format to Dostoevsky's design that he maintained it even when, in 1880, only a single issue appeared. Thus we have the "August" number, even though there was none for any other month.

Dostoevsky's plan was evidently to make the topical timeless. The author would comment on current events but in such a way as to reveal what was of general, artistic significance in them. This was, after all, not a newspaper but an art work, not a diary but a *writer's* diary.

Periodical timelessness presented quite a challenge. Because the author evidently could not know in advance what public events might occur in any given month, he placed himself in the position of having to improvise art out of material he could not fully control—something like the improvisatore in Pushkin's *Egyptian Nights*.[10] The other form on which Dostoevsky's work draws—the diary—also suggests this continual openness to whatever might happen. But unlike literary works that merely imitate the form of diaries, this one really places its author *in the position of a character* not knowing what is to come.

The idea of publishing a work as a periodical seems to have occurred to Dostoevsky long before he found the opportunity to realize it. His earliest reference to the project occurs in a letter of 1865 that he wrote to Baron A. E. Wrangel. Sensitive from the outset to the commercial possibilities of his venture, Dostoevsky confided, "I have in mind a certain periodical publication, though

not a journal. Both useful and profitable. It could come into existence in a year."[11] Two years later he wrote from abroad to his
niece S. A. Ivanova, "When I return [to Russia] I would certainly
like to publish something like a newspaper (I even recall mentioning
it to you in passing, but here both the form and the purpose have
now become completely clear). But for this it is necessary to be at
home and to see and hear everything with my own eyes" (*Pis'ma*
2:44). After another two weeks he wrote to his brother's widow,
"I dream of beginning to publish a weekly journal of my own
type, which I have invented. I hope for success, only for God's
sake don't tell *anyone anything* about it in advance" (*Pis'ma* 2:53).

The idea continued to evolve. He wrote again to Ivanova in 1869
to tell her that he intended to produce a new, special kind of
"enormous useful *annual* . . . to be issued without fail in a large
number of copies and to appear without fail every year in January."
This annual would require compilatory and "editorial" work, but
this would be an active, creative editorship "with an idea, with
great study" (*Pis'ma* 2:161–62). We see here Dostoevsky trying to
base a new work on openness to whatever events might occur in
a given time period, from which he would—with "great study"—
discover something of general import and lasting significance. At
this stage of his thinking, creativity would be less a matter of
composition than of selection and vision.

Despite his fear that someone might steal this profitable idea,
Dostoevsky actually gave a version of it to one of his characters in
The Possessed, thereby, of course, revealing it to his readers as well.
Near the beginning of the novel, Liza Nikolaevna asks Shatov's
help in publishing an annual that would distill the key events in
Russian culture. Such a compilation, she contends, "might reflect
the characteristics of Russian life for the whole year, even though
the facts published are only a small fraction of the events that take
place."[12] Shatov at first voices skepticism: "Instead of a number
of newspapers there would be a few fat books, that's all," he
observes (*Possessed*, 127).

But when Liza explains further, Shatov changes his mind. She
stresses that this would be no simple chronicle, for "the great point
would be the plan and character of the presentation of facts" (*Possessed*, 127). The idea is not to publish everything, nor even everything striking and newsworthy, but instead those incidents that are

   more or less characteristic of the moral life of the people, of the

personal character of the Russian people at the present moment. . . .
everything would be put in with a certain view, a special significance
and intention, with an idea that would illuminate the facts looked at
in the aggregate, as a whole. And finally the book ought to be interesting even for light reading, apart from its value as a work of
reference. It ought to be, so to say, a presentation of the spiritual,
moral, inner life of Russia for a whole year. (*Possessed*, 127–28)

Shatov assumes that Liza wants the selection to be guided by a
political tendency, but Liza replies that "we must not select with
a particular bias. . . . Nothing but impartiality—that will be the only
tendency" (*Possessed*, 128). She does not deny, however, that the
very selection of the facts will necessarily reflect some point of
view, even if not an articulated political program. Shatov concludes
that the work could and should be done, but that it will prove
much more difficult than Liza understands. "One can't work it out
on the spur of the moment. We need experience. And when we
do publish the book I doubt whether we shall find out how to do
it. Perhaps after many trials; but the thought is alluring" (*Possessed*,
128).

Monitoring the Spiritual Life of Russia, Month by Month, and a Compromise

Like Liza's proposed publication, Dostoevsky's *Diary* evidently was
also designed to monitor the moral life of the Russian people as it
evolved, though not year by year but month by month. Missing
from Liza and Shatov's plan was another defining feature of the
Diary: the personal imprint of the author.[13] That is what makes it
truly a *diary*, Dostoevsky wrote to Vsevolod Soloviev: "I am not
a chronicler: this, on the contrary will be a perfect *diary* in the
full sense of the word, that is, an account of what has most interested
me personally—here there will even be caprice" (*Pis'ma* 3:201–2).
Thus the *Diary* had the double and apparently contradictory task
of discovering the real moral development of Russia and yet capriciously indulging whatever happened to strike the author's fancy.
How were these two purposes to be realized together?

Dostoevsky's wife informs us how he first got the chance to try
out his idea, albeit with some compromises. After he finished *The
Possessed*, she writes,

Fyodor Mikhailovich was very undecided for a while as to what to
take up next. He was so exhausted by his work on the novel that it

seemed impossible to him to set to work right away on a new one. And yet, the realization of the idea conceived while we were still living abroad—namely, the publication of a monthly journal, *A Writer's Diary*—presented problems. Quite substantial means were needed for putting out a journal and maintaining a family, not to mention the settlement of our debts. And there was also the question of whether such a journal would have much success, since *it was something entirely new in Russian literature at that time, both in form and in content.*[14]

Evidently Dostoevsky had decided by this point that the *Diary* should be a monthly and was excited by its "entirely new" character "both in form and in content." Dostoevsky's wife reports that it was at just this time that Prince Meshchersky offered Dostoevsky the editorship of the conservative journal *The Citizen.* He would be able to include a version of the *Diary* as a column within *The Citizen,* and so, without assuming financial risk, be paid separately and generously as both editor and contributor. In exchange for these advantages, he would have to surrender temporarily the idea of a one-person publication as well as the monthly format. As Dostoevsky's wife paraphrased his conclusion, "The idea of *A Writer's Diary* might be realized in the pages of *The Citizen,* even though in a different format from the one given it subsequently" (Anna Dostoevsky, 213).

This first trial of Dostoevsky's new genre contains the columns for *The Citizen* written during 1873 under the title *A Writer's Diary.* In 1874 Dostoevsky gave up his editorship and turned his attention to his next novel, *A Raw Youth.* When he finished that book, he at last established *A Writer's Diary* in the form he had intended. Toward the end of 1875 he published an "announcement," invited subscriptions, and added a subtitle to the new work: *A Writer's Diary: A Monthly Publication.*

Part 2: An Encyclopedia of Genres

The Announcement: All That I Have "Seen, Heard, and Read"

The "announcement" of the *Diary* turned out to be an integral part of it. A sort of contract with the reader, it was often cited, sometimes seriously but usually ironically, in the text itself. It purports to outline the rules governing the work, but, like the rules of Rabelais's Abbey of Thélème, the announcement's provisions

seem so expansive as to exclude nothing. Nevertheless, it is typically
mentioned when the author "apologizes" for violating it.

Although several passages in the *Diary* depend on the reader's
awareness of the announcement, the present edition is the first to
include it as part of the text.[15] Earlier editions therefore render
unintelligible several self-referential discussions of the work's odd
form.

The "contract" specifies price, monthly appearance, Dostoevsky's sole authorship, and, with ostentatious vagueness, the kind
of material to be included: "It will be a diary in the literal sense
of the word, an account of impressions actually experienced each
month, an account of what was seen, heard, and read. Of course,
some stories and tales may be included, but preeminently it will
be about actual events." Despite the loophole he had left himself,
when Dostoevsky included the 1876 *Diary*'s first story, he begged
the readers' forgiveness for including something other than "actual
events."

Everything the writer experienced each month in all possible
genres and modes: this seems to be the puzzling format of the new
work. The *Diary* in fact constitutes an encyclopedia of fictional
and nonfictional genres. As we have seen, it is this diversity of
material that apparently fascinated Victor Shklovsky. For most readers, it has obscured any sense of the work's integrity. What whole
could possibly embrace such heterogeneous parts?

To answer this question, it would be helpful to consider first the
particular kinds of writing included in the *Diary*. Although lines
are fluid, we may identify five broad classes of material: fiction
(short stories), what I call "semifiction," autobiography, journalism,
and self-referential articles. The journalism itself includes a variety
of genres. After surveying these forms and considering their connection with each other, we may then inquire into the structure of
the whole. How were these radically heterogeneous parts designed
to cohere into something other than a mere anthology, and how
does one make a generic encyclopedia into an integral work of art?

The Four Short Stories: An Author on the
Verge of Insanity

Most famously, the *Diary* contains Dostoevsky's greatest short stories. In the 1873 *Diary* we find "Bobok" (73.6), a weird tale in
which a narrator overhears corpses talking to each other in their

graves; they indulge in scandal, petty spite, and fantasies of sepulchral debauchery. Mikhail Bakhtin has described this story and
"The Dream of a Ridiculous Man" (from the 1877 *Diary*) as almost
perfect realizations of an ancient literary genre, the menippean
satire. "We would hardly be mistaken," Bakhtin declares, "in
saying that 'Bobok,' in all its depth and boldness, is one of the
greatest menippea [menippean satires] in all world literature."[16]
One need not accept Bakhtin's characterization of this story as the
key to Dostoevsky's work as a whole to recognize its great literary
power.

The story begins with a few lines from Dostoevsky: "On this
occasion I shall include 'The Notes of a Certain Person.' That
person is not I, but someone else entirely." But as this hint suggests,
the "certain person" does resemble Dostoevsky in some interesting
ways, to the point where he may be taken as a peculiar exercise
in self-parody.

Almost immediately, the "certain person" relates how someone
flattered him, as a "literary man," into posing for a portrait. "And
now I read: 'Go and look at this sickly face that seems to border
on insanity.'" Kenneth Lantz's notes to the present edition make
clear that these lines allude to comments in a rival publication, *The
Voice*, about Perov's portrait of Dostoevsky himself, which was
then being exhibited. After comparing the author of *A Writer's
Diary* to the insane narrator of Gogol's "Diary of a Madman," the
commentator in *The Voice* suggested that Perov's "is a portrait of
a man exhausted by a serious ailment."[17]

Moreover, many of the "certain person's" comments—on the
degradation of realism, on aesthetics, on materialism, on the spiritual poverty of intellectuals so sure of their theories that they cannot
experience surprise—echo Dostoevsky's own articles in the *Diary*.
Much as the narrator of *Notes from Underground* spitefully exaggerates some of Dostoevsky's favorite philosophical views, so the
"certain person" gathers the *Diary*'s own repeated concerns into
a mad meditation. Dostoevsky employs his favorite technique of
placing his own ideas in the mouth of a distinctly unappealing
character. Along with this character's other contribution, "A Half-
Letter from 'A Certain Person'" (73.8), the story becomes a complex parodic focus of the 1873 *Diary*'s recurrent themes.

The "Half-Letter" begins with Dostoevsky's account of his conversations with its author, whose work Dostoevsky publishes simply

to get rid of him. The contribution, a vituperative attack on vituperative journalism, itself goes so far beyond the bounds of decency that Dostoevsky cuts off the first half of it, and so it begins
in mid-sentence. Of course, the *Diary* itself was engaged in fierce
exchanges with other publications, and Dostoevsky adds a footnote
to the certain person's text in which he takes some of its criticisms
personally. In effect, he writes himself into his character's text as
his character becomes part of his.

Apparently, it is Dostoevsky's portrait that has brought these
two suffering literary men together. At the end of "Bobok," the
certain person declares that he "will bring this [account] to *The
Citizen*. One of the editors there has also had his portrait exhibited.
Perhaps he'll print this" (73.6). "Bobok" usually appears in anthologies of Dostoevsky's fiction, but it is difficult to see what
readers unaware of the larger context of the *Diary* could make of
this concluding sentence.

The Stories: Joints

The January 1876 issue of the *Diary* features a brief but well-known
story, "The Boy at Christ's Christmas Party" (1/76, 2.2). Following
a sketch about Russian street urchins, Dostoevsky offers this tale
of a boy whose mother has died, leaving him to wander the streets.
The boy finds himself at a Christmas party that (we know from
an earlier sketch in the same issue of the *Diary*) Dostoevsky attended; but the freezing child is not admitted. Returning to the
street, he begins to look for a warm place to stay. He eventually
freezes to death and goes to the other world, where Christ has his
own Christmas party for all such orphans.[18]

This tale, too, changes when read in the context of the *Diary*.
Readers of the story in translation know it from anthologies of
Dostoevsky's fiction, but even to print "The Boy" separately it
was necessary to round off the opening, which proceeds directly
from the preceding sketch. That is why in the *Diary* (though not
in most translations) the story begins on a conjunction.

> A wild creature such as this [street urchin] sometimes knows nothing
> at all—neither where he lives, nor what nation he comes from; whether
> God exists, or the tsar. There are even stories told about them that
> are hard to believe, yet they are facts.

> 2. The Boy at Christ's Christmas Party

But I am a novelist and one "story," it seems, I made up myself. Why do I say "it seems" when I know very well that I made it up? Yet I keep imagining that it really happened somewhere, sometime, and happened precisely on Christmas Eve in *a certain* huge city during a terrible cold spell.[19]

This opening stands as a particularly clear example of how Dostoevsky exhibits the "joints" of the *Diary*, the connections where the nonfiction shades into the fiction. These are the moments where the *Diary*'s own strange poetics, which merge discrepant kinds of material, comes to the center of our attention. Such moments fade from view when the story is read separately. The end of "The Boy" once again brings us back to the context of the *Diary* as a whole:

So why did I make up a story like that, so little in keeping with the usual spirit of a sober-minded diary, and a writer's diary at that? All the more since I promised stories preeminently about actual events! But that's just the point: I keep imagining that all this could really have happened—I mean the things that happened in the cellar and behind the woodpile; as for Christ's Christmas party—well, I really don't know what to say: could that have happened? That's just why I am a novelist—to invent things.

This frame, of course, alludes to the "announcement," with its promise to write "preeminently about actual events." The story thereby both draws upon and sheds light upon the surrounding text. I do not wish to say that it cannot be read with profit on its own, only that it functions rather differently within the *Diary*, whose narrator and techniques we gradually come to know.

The Stories: Reading Horizontally and Vertically

Perhaps the greatest short story Dostoevsky ever wrote occupies the November 1876 issue of the *Diary*. In "The Meek One: A Fantastic Story," a pawnbroker, whose wife has just committed suicide, reflects on their history in order to "focus his thoughts" and understand why her corpse is now before him. The events he recounts, though he only intermittently realizes it, constitute a tale of psychological torture of a poor, meek, and Christian soul—one of those who, as the reader of the *Diary*'s many millenarian passages may understand, will "inherit the earth" at the world's finale.[20] The story's "fantastic" element, which Dostoevsky explains in the

"Author's Foreword" to this issue, lies in its stream of consciousness form, its rough-edged meditation, filled with emotional and
logical contradictions that we watch unfolding moment by moment.
With its structure of chapters and subchapters perfectly fitting the
format of other monthly issues, the story seems to accelerate and
concentrate the "spontaneous" meditations of the work's diaristic
form.

The reader of the *Diary* will also trace numerous other links
between the story and the surrounding articles. The pawnbroker's
thoughts about feminism and the abilities of women allude to Dostoevsky's several articles on the topic; his ethic of self-sufficiency
seems to incarnate the moral sin of "dissociation" that the diarist
elsewhere describes at length; and the heroine's suicide with an
icon in her hand necessarily recalls a similar, real suicide that
Dostoevsky reports earlier in the *Diary*.[21]

Here, as so often in the *Diary*, our attention is focused not only
on the tale itself but also on the story of its making. Readers of
the *Diary* often witness a characteristic sequence of steps. First
Dostoevsky retells a story from the Russian press, then muses upon
it, returns to it in a later issue, and perhaps imagines how it might
be developed into a story. At last, a finished story may follow. Part
of the excitement of *A Writer's Diary* is to be found in this self-
conscious, rather stylized, and yet undeniably riveting dramatiza-
tion of the creative process, with its fits and starts, its multiple
possibilities realized or unrealized, and its occasional, unexpected
conclusion in a polished narrative. We read these finished stories
not just "horizontally," for their internal plot, but also "vertically,"
as the denouement of a second story, the account of their own
creation. That "second story" depends entirely on the context of
the work as a whole.

The Stories: An Epitome

"The Dream of a Ridiculous Man" (4/77, 2.1), which appears in
the April 1877 issue, reads like a response—a counterstory—to
"Bobok." In the earlier menippean satire, a journey to the under-
world (a classic menippean theme) leads to a sense of total despair;
in "The Dream," a voyage through space, guided by an angel,
results in a belief in salvation.[22] As if echoing the *Diary*'s several
articles on suicide out of indifference and materialism, the narrator
of "The Dream" recalls how he decided to kill himself because
"absolutely nothing matters." Shortly after making this decision,

he is accosted on the street by a young girl—a sort of sister to the boy at Christ's Christmas party?—who begs him in despair for help. Although he rebuffs her, he is both surprised and annoyed to discover that he feels ashamed. Why should he have such feelings, he asks himself, when he is about to commit suicide and therefore knows there can be no consequences of his callous act? He soon finds himself wondering whether he would feel shame if he had committed a heinous crime on the moon that no one could ever know about.[23] These paradoxical questions in effect make the point so often argued by Dostoevsky elsewhere in the *Diary*: that morality can never be reduced to mere self-interest, and that an inborn sense of transcendent right and wrong—of "immortality"— is essential to being human.

Instead of actually killing himself, the ridiculous man falls asleep and dreams he has done so. The dreamer is taken from the grave by an angel who flies him through infinite space to a world that is an exact geographical duplicate of our own. But that other world has a different temporality: its people live before the fall, in paradise. This vision of perfect communion gives the ridiculous man the "living image" of a meaningful life, the reason for living that he has missed. After sharing the joy of these prelapsarian people, he himself corrupts them all by his mere presence and so comes to learn his responsibility for all human suffering. When he awakes, he resolves to preach the ideal, even though he knows it may never be realized and that people will laugh at him; and he finds the little girl who has unwittingly saved him.

Critics have disputed whether this tale should be regarded as utopian or anti-utopian.[24] Is the hero's claim to have discovered "the truth" at a precise moment to be taken as a sign of his madness or as an example of a true conversion, recommended to Dostoevsky's readers? The *Diary* itself contains numerous utopian sketches as well as a few anti-utopian ones; we find both essays in praise of that other ridiculous idealist, Don Quixote, and ironic portrayals of dreamers who indulge such mad hopes. From this perspective, the ambiguities of "The Dream" seem to epitomize those of the *Diary* as whole.

Semifiction: Liminal Poetics

The *Diary* seems constantly concerned with moments of transition, uncertain boundaries in life and between life and art. Its most characteristic material, therefore, may be its many pieces of "semifiction"—that is, works that somehow seem to lie between fact and fiction or between reportage and finished stories. "Reality is transfigured, *passing through art*," Dostoevsky once wrote.[25] These sketches seem designed to dramatize the liminal moment of "passing through."

The semifictions vary considerably in technique, but all work by straddling and calling attention to the boundary between fiction and nonfiction. Quite characteristic is "A Hundred-Year-Old Woman," which appears in the March 1876 issue (3/76, 1.2). Dostoevsky begins this entry with a real incident from daily life, recounted to him by a "lady" (it was in fact his wife). The lady has described meeting a woman of a hundred and four who was slowly making her way to her grandchildren. Meditating dreamily on the character of the old woman, Dostoevsky "sketched in an ending to the story of how she reached her own folks to have dinner: there emerged another, perhaps quite plausible little scene." As in other semifictions of *Diary*, a real incident shades into a "plausible" continuation, and so a story is made by drawing "dotted lines" from an "actual event." We have here yet another interpretation of the contract ambiguously outlined in the "announcement."

The story itself culminates in a liminal moment between life and death, as the lady, who has reached her relations, dies in mid-sentence and mid-action, with the precise moment of her passing between two worlds left uncertain. Focusing on the experience of the old lady's great-grandson, the author draws a moral crucial to the *Diary*'s thematics:

> No matter how long Misha lives he will always remember the old woman and how she died, forgetting her hand on his shoulder. And when he dies not a single person on the whole earth will remember or will realize that once upon a time there was such an old woman who lived out her hundred and four years, how and why no one knows. Why remember anyway? It doesn't matter. Millions of people pass away like this: they live unnoticed and they die unnoticed.... May God bless the lives and deaths of simple, good people!

The diarist notices what would otherwise go unnoticed but which is supremely important—what the *Diary* elsewhere calls the "isolated cases" of familial closeness and ordinary kindness that, taken together, shape good lives. As we shall see in sections 3 and 4, Dostoevsky frequently contends that it is ordinary families and the simple goodness of unremarkable people that alone can save a society. Bedeviled by theories and abstractions, the intelligentsia never notices what is always before its eyes. That is one reason that the *Diary* is needed.

In later issues Dostoevsky often pauses on such prosaic scenes, which he has heard about, and then, as in this case, extended by an act of imagination. He stresses that these little narratives are anything but grand: "In short, with our People the result will never be an epic poem, will it? They are the most prosaic people in the world, so that one is almost ashamed of them in that respect" (10/76, 1.1). After describing one such prosaic family, Dostoevsky wonders why it is that "our novelists have to go off looking for material.... Why not just describe the whole [prosaic] truth, step by step? And yet, it seems, I forgot the old rule: what matters is not the subject but the eye" (10/76, 1.1). The truths hidden in plain view are the hardest ones to see. In "A Hundred-Year-Old Woman" and many later pieces, the diarist's eye discerns the meaningfulness that is always there for the seeing.

In such passages Dostoevsky seems to suggest a viewpoint often associated with Tolstoy: that it is ordinary people living prosaic lives, rather than heroes or dramatic "historical" figures known to all, who are truly important. As Dostoevsky hints at the end of "A Hundred-Year-Old Woman," what makes a good life does not usually make a good story. But somehow these trivial incidents, when discerned correctly, might "well turn out better than any of our poems and novels with heroes 'with deep insight and lives torn asunder'" (10/76, 1.1). Here, in effect, is the answer to the Raskolnikovism of the intelligentsia. What truly shapes life, what makes it meaningful, is always taking place unnoticed before us. The *Diary* is designed to teach a special kind of prosaic vision.

To this prosaic, Tolstoyan moral, repeated often in the *Diary*, Dostoevsky adds a motif marked with his own inimitable signature: the importance of childhood memories in shaping a life. We learn the most important moral lessons through glowing memories of early childhood, which guide us through a lifetime. As the author of the *Diary* often explains, morality can never be formalized, and no theory spun from the brain of an intellectual will ever be adequate to the complexities of ethical decisions; but good childhood memories represent the surest guide we have.

Elsewhere in the *Diary* Dostoevsky often reflects on the quite different memories developed by troubled children from "accidental families." When he reports on narcissistic suicides (for example, in his article on Herzen's daughter), he traces them to childhood homes infected with materialism and fashionable skepticism, homes incapable of producing the good memories necessary for later life (10/76, 1.3). This theme was, of course, to become central to *The Brothers Karamazov*. Guided by his memory of his mother holding him before the icon, Alyosha tries, in the novel's conclusion, to create good if unremarkable memories in "the boys." As he has learned from Father Zosima and from his own experience, good memories work better than the best of theories.

The final paragraph of "A Hundred-Year-Old Woman" therefore wryly comments on the utterly prosaic and ordinary nature of its events. Ironically, the author regrets that he has not told a good story. Judged by the usual dramatic standards, his account has failed. As the opening of "The Boy at Christ's Christmas Party" emerges from the preceding article, so the ending of "A Hundred-Year-Old Woman" shades into the next piece of nonfiction. Pausing on the boundary, the author again mentions his contract with the reader:

> Well, still, this is just an inconsequential little scene without a story. True enough, one sets out to recount something with a bit of interest in it from the things heard in the course of a month, but when you sit down to write it turns out to be quite impossible to retell or is irrelevant, or it's simply a case of "not telling everything you know," and so in the end you're left with only little things such as this with no story to them . . .

3. Dissociation

> But still, I'm supposed to be writing about "the things I have seen, heard, and read." At least it's a good thing that I didn't limit myself with a promise to write about *everything* I have "seen, heard, and read." And I keep hearing things that are stranger and stranger. How can I convey them, when they all go off on their separate ways and simply refuse to arrange themselves into one neat bundle! Indeed, I keep thinking that we have begun the epoch of universal "dissociation."

Dostoevsky's point is that such inconsequential events of ordinary private life do indeed contain the "vital forces" by which both individuals and societies live. By contrast, public life seems increasingly riven by "stranger and stranger" new forces, worlds away from the prosaic family of the story. Thus we have the diarist's paradox, about which he also remarks elsewhere: the real world has become more fantastic than the author's fiction. In a world torn from the soil and the family, the ordinary is becoming increasingly extraordinary.

One purpose of the *Diary*, as we have seen, was to find some guiding thread, something approaching a unifying theme, in the immense diversity of Russian life. But how is that to be done if individuals and social forces are so "dissociated" from each other that "they all go off in their own separate ways"? Could the unifying theme be "dissociation" itself? But what sort of unity is that, and how can the *Diary* achieve any wholeness on the basis of utter fragmentation? The ending of "A Hundred-Year-Old Woman" turns into another meditation on the *Diary*'s own poetics.

Semifiction: A Field of Plots

In "Vlas" (73.5), Dostoevsky intertwines fact and fiction with amazing complexity as he attempts to probe the spiritual state of the Russian people at the present moment. He begins by paraphrasing Nekrasov's poem "Vlas," which describes the conversion of a peasant criminal into a godly figure, and then reports that he has recently heard a quite similar story from real life. In this second narrative, one peasant accepts a dare from another to do the most shocking thing possible. Without revealing his plan, the "tempter" instructs the first peasant to steal the Eucharist. The victim, it turns out, is to shoot the Eucharist, thereby becoming Christ's murderer. At the last possible moment, however, the peasant preparing for deicide sees a vision of Christ on the cross and relents. Swearing he is damned forever, he goes crawling on his knees to the monk who has told Dostoevsky the story.

Dostoevsky swears that the story is true and that its whole interest depends on its truth, because, he claims, it distills the essence of the Russian people's life at the present transitional moment after the liberation of the serfs. Read in this allegorical fashion, the story describes the current crisis of the people: like the peasant, they may be saved or damned, may either yield finally to the terrible "urge for negation," as they at present seem to be doing, or else experience an "impulse backward . . . to restore and save oneself" at the last possible moment. It appears that this true story contains the key to Russia's future. The real incident thereby achieves the status of myth.

And which end will the story of the Russian people have, repentance or damnation? To answer this question, Dostoevsky probes the psychology of the two peasants, "Vlas" and "Mephistopheles." Imagining the prehistory of the story, Dostoevsky sketches several possible paths that may have led to the temptation. Adding details between the known events, he retells the monk's tale in various ways, each of which allow for different endings. Is it possible that Vlas might not have repented? And what happens to Mephistopheles? Each version could be the story of Russian history.

Thus Nekrasov's poem, which has found a real-life echo, bifurcates into a multitude of related stories, a field of possibilities all shadowing each other. This *sideshadowing*, as it might be called, becomes quite characteristic of the diarist's method of narration: as we shall see, he often views reality not as a single story but as a field of possibilities with multiple paths to multiple conceivable outcomes.[26] "Vlas" concludes without choosing a single ending: "long ago we entered into a period of complete uncertainty."

Semifiction: A Plan That Is Not a Plan

The semifictional "Plan for a Satirical Novel of Contemporary Life" (5–6/77, 1.3) works by a quite different method. Here Dostoevsky offers a story in the form of a plan for a story that he *might* someday write. He cannot actually write the story because, he concedes, Gogol would be needed to do it justice. At crucial moments of the narrative, which he appears to be making up on the spot, he turns to Gogol's tales to inspire him with events for his plot in progress. The story constantly denies that it is a story, and it concludes with the wish that even though he is not Gogol, Dostoevsky might someday actually write this story.

This "plan" may be understood in two distinct ways. We may regard it as it explicitly offers itself, as an outline for a possible story not yet composed, or we may see it as a finished story that happens to take the form of a plan. The idea of a "plan" may be a mere narrative convention, as, in fact, it typically was in the genre of the sketch (*ocherk*). That genre was quite well developed in Russia, and Dostoevsky was one of its best-known practitioners. The sketch played on its dual status as draft and finished work, which is why Gorky was later to stress the derivation of *ocherk* from *chertit'* (to draw) and from *ochertit'* (to outline). The literary sketch therefore resembles a pictorial one, Gorky reasoned, because both present an outline that is paradoxically a completed work.

Korolenko made much the same point when he observed that, by convention, the reader of a sketch is asked to live with the author through his search for a finished work that turns out to be the report of the search itself, "as if apartments were let out when the wood for their construction had not yet been gathered."[27]

It is worth noting that not only Dostoevsky but also his character Ivan Karamazov was to use this technique. "The Legend of the Grand Inquisitor," Ivan tells Alyosha, is merely the idea for a poem that has not been versified or even written down. As he narrates his new legend, Ivan repeatedly calls attention to its status as a mere plan: "Well, my poem would have been of that kind if it had appeared at that time."[28] When Jesus appears to the people, they instantly recognize him: "That might be one of the best passages in the poem. I mean, why they recognized Him" (*BK*, 295). As this example illustrates, Ivan uses the technique of the plan to achieve a powerful literary effect. In this case, it hints at ineffability, at the impossibility of describing moral beauty that is beyond human words.

The ambivalent status of the "Plan for a Satirical Novel" should illustrate why it is ultimately impossible to count the number of short stories in the *Diary*, for many of them simultaneously claim and deny that they are stories. Indeed, we have already seen something similar with "The Boy at Christ's Christmas Party," which, if paired with the preceding article (as in some anthologies), resembles one of the *Diary*'s semifictional sketches. It begins with reportage, shades into possibility, and then wryly reflects on its own ambiguous status. With their great diversity of forms that straddle fictional boundaries and of frames that represent the author as both reporter and creative writer, the *Diary*'s semifictions seem to define the essential moments of this work's peculiarly liminal poetics.

Autobiography: The Text's Penumbra

By the time he embarked on *A Writer's Diary*, Dostoevsky's biography was already a legend, a "literary fact" in its own right.[29] He exploited it practically and aesthetically. In the early 1860s he counted on it to afford him protection against attacks from the radical left, which hesitated to criticize someone who had suffered mock execution and Siberian exile for his political activities. And any reader of his work soon becomes aware that he exploited his biography for considerable literary power. The shadow of his amazingly dramatic experiences formed a special background to his fiction, and Dostoevsky took considerable pains to let the aura of his life lend vibrancy to his art. The reader becomes aware of a region beyond the novel's story where the work seems to extend into a penumbra of textuality. In that penumbra, autobiographical events, though not mentioned as such and so requiring the reader's external knowledge, nevertheless operate as part of the work.

One thinks not only of the quasi fictionalization of his Siberian experiences in *Notes from the House of the Dead* but also of the frequent descriptions of the last moments of a person condemned to execution. When Raskolnikov experiences a sensation that "might be compared to that of a man condemned to death who has suddenly been pardoned," readers of *Crime and Punishment* respond, and were evidently intended to respond, as they would not if another author had written this passage. We cannot help thinking that this author knows what he is talking about. Prince Myshkin's several detailed descriptions of executions characterize both himself and his creator, and the two together form a peculiar double character. Dostoevsky is sometimes close to explicit about this doubling. In describing an execution he has seen, Myshkin muses: "Perhaps there is some man who has been sentenced to death, been exposed to this torture and has been told 'you can go, you are pardoned.' Perhaps such a man could tell us." Of course, as readers knew, that man *is* telling us.[30]

Encountering such passages, readers almost inevitably wonder about the degree and kind of self-revelation involved, as they also do when following the remarkable accounts of Myshkin's epileptic fits (Dostoevsky was himself an epileptic). There can be little doubt that Dostoevsky meant to exploit this almost voyeuristic interest for his writer's *diary*, a title that intimates confidential recollections. In fact, the *Diary*'s autobiographical sections compel attention and form an intrinsic part of its mix of genres.

The classic versions of many famous stories about Dostoevsky's life can be traced to the *Diary*'s autobiographical articles. He provides what became the canonical account of his "discovery" by the poet and publisher Nekrasov and the critic Belinsky, several allusions to his mock execution, and, in an article on the psychology of political subversives, an analysis of his state of mind as a member of the radical Petrashevsky circle. Many of these reminiscences are offered with polemical intent: my liberal opponents like to blather

on about their love for "the people," Dostoevsky observes, but it
is I, not they, who have lived with criminals and peasants, eaten
with them, labored with them, and slept alongside them in close
quarters for years. The radicals, who wish the Russian people
resembled a revolutionary Parisian mob, regard them as an inert
mass to be civilized by the intelligentsia, but I know *from direct
experience* that the people are, if anything, morally superior to their
would-be saviors. There is no doubt that Dostoevsky was entirely
sincere in expressing these views, and that they represent the principal legacy and constitute the most lasting effect of his time in
Siberia.[31] But it is equally clear that he assiduously used his life
to literary as well as polemical effect.

The tone of the *Diary*'s autobiographical passages varies considerably. In a voice of intimacy, Dostoevsky confides his most cherished memories of the experiences that have made him the person
and writer he is. Such passages, which Konstantin Mochulsky aptly
describes as "half-confession, half-diary," combine well with those
in which the reader is apparently initiated into the mysteries of the
creative process.[32] Dostoevsky tells us events from his life that he
has never before revealed and invites us into the ostensibly private
world of the author at his desk. Much of the extraordinary popular
(and financial) success of the *Diary* was doubtless due to this special
and unusual relation to the readers. Such confidentiality was suggested by the work's status as a diary, that is, a personal document
made available only to intimates.

Of course, readers are not really initiated into the writer's laboratory; one need only compare the published *Writer's Diary* with
its notebooks to see how much processing was necessary to present
the illusion of spontaneity.[33] When the diarist is for some reason
suddenly struck by a recollection, twentieth-century readers of his
truly private notebooks can trace the careful preparation, often
extending over months, for the introduction of an "unplanned"
reminiscence or revealing digression.

Nevertheless, I do not mean to cast doubt on the sincerity of
these reminiscences. On the contrary, they seem to reflect Dostoevsky's deepest beliefs, as well as his understanding that their
considerable power *as literature* depends precisely on their truthfulness. In the *Diary* and elsewhere, Dostoevsky often stresses—it
was one of his favorite insights—that it is often much harder to tell
the truth convincingly than to invent an effective fiction. The author
of *War and Peace* also never tired of making the same point, and

this shared sense of the near impossibility of sincerity and truthfulness constitutes one of the most important connections between
the two Russian geniuses. Dostoevsky's novels are filled with characters' apparently true but actually false confessions, in which the
very spirit of the revelation conflicts with its ostensible purpose.
Those novels repeatedly dramatize the ways in which the dynamics
of self-deceit and self-justification distort efforts at self-knowledge.
In the *Diary*, these dynamics create the shape of the story "The
Meek One." So difficult are they to attain that truthfulness and
sincerity, when actually achieved, can therefore exhibit considerable
literary power. This insight underlies several passages in the *Diary*.

Autobiography: The Imitation of Dostoevsky

The *Diary*'s best-known autobiographical account, "The Peasant
Marey" (2/76, 1.3), is so well crafted that it is often included in
collections of Dostoevsky's fiction. With it anthologized in this
way, its author becomes a fictional narrator, which of course changes
the story considerably. Readers who encounter it in collections of
Dostoevsky's fiction may be surprised to learn that it has been
taken, with good reason, as a generally accurate account of Dostoevsky's conversion experience.[34]

In fact, "The Peasant Marey" seems deliberately to invite both
readings. Such double encoding was not unique in Dostoevsky's
work: *The House of the Dead* also invites reading as both a novel
and a memoir. Whichever way it is taken, not everything fits.[35]
Thus it is first offered as an account from the memoirs of a fictional
character, Goryanchikov, who has been sent to Siberia for mur-
dering his wife; but in the course of the story the narrator is also
described as a political prisoner, which was Dostoevsky's, but not
Goryanchikov's, status. So glaring is this contradiction that it seems
inconceivable to attribute it to mere carelessness. Although difficulties with the censorship led several authors to use a dispensable
fictional cover for actual recollections, that does not seem to be the
whole story in this case.[36]

Rather, *The House of the Dead* seems to play quite deliberately
on its double status. Depending on how we take it, the parts fit
into two different wholes, and the two readings conflict with each
other. If we read the book as Goryanchikov's memoirs, we will
focus on the editor's opening account of Goryanchikov's life after
prison, a life of tortured isolation and perhaps madness. The shadow of that later life is cast over the narrative as a whole and seems

to deprive the tale of any sense of redemption. But if we read the story as Dostoevsky's memoirs, attention focuses on the optimistic conclusion, on freedom and the symbolic promise of resurrection. Two novels subsist within the same covers, and the reader is given a choice, as are we all, between despair and hope, between the suffering that deforms and the suffering that ennobles: "Except a corn of wheat fall into the ground and die, it abideth alone; but if it die, it bringeth forth much fruit."[37]

"The Peasant Marey" directly alludes to the earlier work's interpretive difficulties: "Many people supposed and are even now quite firmly convinced that I was sent to hard labor for the murder of my wife." This teasing passage is perhaps designed to call attention to this story's own complex encoding. That complexity seems to derive from Dostoevsky's purpose, here as elsewhere in the *Diary*, to transform his real experiences into a collective myth of the Russian people as he is simultaneously transforming journalism into art.[38]

Like "The Boy at Christ's Christmas Party" in the preceding issue, "The Peasant Marey" follows directly from a nonfictional article with which it is closely linked (2/76, 1.2). That article had begun with a "riddle," a "contradiction" demanding reconciliation.

> I wrote, for instance, in the January issue of the *Diary* that our People are coarse and ignorant, devoted to darkness and depravity, "barbarians, awaiting the light." Meanwhile, I've only just read . . . in an article by the late and unforgettable [Slavophile] Konstantin Aksakov, a man dear to every Russian—that the Russian people have long been enlightened and "educated." What can I say? Was I troubled by my apparent disagreement with the opinion of Konstantin Aksakov? Not in the least; I completely share that view, and have had warm sympathy for it for a long time. So how can I reconcile such a contradiction?

Dostoevsky initially solves this contradiction with another, no less perplexing one: that "diamonds" may be found in the "filth" of the people. His initial resolution of these antithetical statements is itself antithetical: "Judge the Russian People, not by the abominations they so frequently commit, but by those great and sacred things for which, even in their abominations, they constantly yearn." In advancing these puzzles, Dostoevsky stresses that his readers will deem them untenable paradoxes, riddles that cannot be answered.

After a series of digressions whose significance becomes clear

only later, Dostoevsky begins "The Peasant Marey" with a self-
deprecating opening: "But reading all these *professions de foi* is a
bore, I think, and so I'll tell you a story; actually, it's not even a
story, but only a reminiscence of something that happened long
ago and that, for some reason, I would very much like to recount
here and now." The narrative, which is offered as both a story and
a reminiscence, turns out to be the solution to the initial riddle.
"Now tell me," he asks near the narrative's end, "is this not what
Konstantin Aksakov had in mind when he spoke of the advanced
level of development of our Russian People?" When "The Peasant
Marey" is published separately, the meaning of this key sentence
is necessarily obscured, as is the underlying riddle structure of
which "Marey" forms an intrinsic part.[39]

The story begins in Siberia, where Dostoevsky finds it impossible
to endure the other convicts' hideous depravity, which "had worn
me out to the point of illness." The coarseness, drunkenness, and
violence of these former peasants leads Dostoevsky to appreciate
the judgment of a Polish prisoner: "*Je hais ces brigands!*" Thinking
of these words, the author lies down and loses himself in memories,
which come to him without effort of will. "For some reason" he
suddenly remembers an incident from his childhood that has never
crossed his mind since it happened. He recalls how one summer,
as a nine-year-old child on his father's estate, he regretted having
to return soon to Moscow for his tedious French lessons and went
for a walk. Suddenly he hears (or rather imagines he hears) someone
cry out that a wolf is on the loose, and, without thinking, he runs
to a peasant in terror. In his kindly, almost womanly way, with
his "almost maternal smile," the coarse serf Marey, who like all
serfs has no reason to love his master, comforts the master's boy,
even though no one will ever find out about it. And now, twenty
years later in Siberia, Dostoevsky remembers the incident, which
comes as an answer to the Pole's terrible words. "I remembered
that encounter so vividly, right to the last detail. That means it
had settled unnoticed in my heart, all by itself with no will of
mine, and had suddenly come back to me at a time when it was
needed."

As we have seen, this is in fact how childhood memories are
supposed to work: in the *Diary* (as later in *Karamazov*), they acquire
the power and significance of myth, of a fundamental story capable
of resolving tormenting questions that are unresolvable in any other
way. In the *Republic*, Plato also uses story to resolve problems that

exceed rational solution, and within the structure of the *Diary* the recollection resolves much more than autobiographical problems. It is at this point in the story that Dostoevsky reframes his account not as a mere story, or even as just a reminiscence, but, in a third characterization, as the solution to Aksakov's riddle. And in fact it solves much more than that.

As we read further in the *Diary*, the story and preceding article turn out not only to contain the solution to a riddle and the key transforming event of the author's life but also to embody the central myth of Russian history. "The Peasant Marey" tells the story of an intellectual who has been torn from the native soil but then recovers his connection to his people, their past, and his own true identity as one of them; this pattern is revealed as the fundamental story of Russian history and the key to the country's salvation. In an account constantly repeated in the *Diary*, the Russian educated classes were "divorced from the native soil" and from the people by Peter the Great's reforms; they have lived in European isolation from the people ever since; and they now face a total drying up of all vital forces. As Dostoevsky the prisoner found himself in despair, so the Russian educated classes are experiencing an epidemic of suicides, a key motif of the *Diary*. In one of the *Diary*'s most cited lines, Dostoevsky observes apocalyptically that "the Russian land seems to have lost the capacity to hold people on it" (5/76, 2.2). These suicides are in fact a symptom of a fatal choice facing Russia: either its educated classes will return to the People, as Dostoevsky did, or the country will quickly perish.

Dostoevsky makes the hidden pattern—to him no mere allegory—explicit. The story of his own life and of Russian history is the parable of the prodigal son. "We must bow down before the People's truth," he writes in the article preceding "Marey." "We must bow down like prodigal children who have been away from home for two hundred years but who, however, have returned still Russians."

The *Diary* offers several applications of this story. In a number of articles, Dostoevsky writes that not just the educated but even some of the Russian people are being torn from their roots; that is his explanation for the rise of Protestant sects in the countryside. But the Russian people, like Vlas, will soon return to their Orthodox roots. Retrospectively, we recognize that the plot of the tempted peasant in "Vlas" also repeats the pattern of the prodigal son parable. We repeatedly encounter versions of the same story throughout the *Diary*. Not just Russian but all world history repeats the plot. Here Russia plays the role of home, and Europe, which has abandoned true Christianity for the pursuit of materialism and earthly power, becomes the prodigal son. Having reached the nadir of despair (the imminent threat of proletarian revolution and world war), Europe may return to the true Christianity of Russia.

"The Peasant Marey" achieves mythic power by offering a solution to all the world's most pressing problems. The story of the author's conversion is also the story of the world's salvation. Humanity will be saved by the imitation of Dostoevsky.

Journalism: The Prophetic Articles

Most of the *Diary* consists of journalistic articles, but they too exhibit great variety. We encounter a diversity of genres, tones, and themes. Among these articles, the greatest number of pages is devoted to political pieces concerned with foreign policy. This weighting toward war and diplomacy appears all the more striking when we consider that such articles are entirely absent from the 1873 *Diary* and appear infrequently during the first issues of 1876. By June of that year, however, readers witnessed Dostoevsky in the process of changing the *Diary* quite substantially. What had been at most only one of several elements at the beginning of 1876 soon became the dominant theme.

Evidently, the catalyst for change was the intensification of the "Eastern Question"—the complex of issues surrounding the revolt of Slavic nationalities in the Balkans against Turkish rule. Russian volunteers joined the Serbs, who gave command of their army to the Russian general Cherniaev. When Cherniaev was defeated, the *Diary*'s emphasis on foreign policy temporarily diminished. But Dostoevsky's enthusiasm was rekindled when Russia herself entered the war in 1877 (an event breathlessly reported in the April 1877 issue).

Through the ups and downs of the Balkan conflict, Dostoevsky's new literary genre was often transformed into a mere mouthpiece for the Pan-Slavist cause. It was doubtless this change, which Dostoevsky was never able to reconcile with the initial idea of the *Diary*, that led to its literary failings and the not entirely unjustified dismissal of the work (or large parts of it) as jingoistic propaganda. For a time, Dostoevsky managed to find a place for these articles within the original frame of the *Diary*, but if the outlines of the work were at first merely obscured they eventually disappeared completely.

The foreign-policy polemics exhibit a special narrative voice, quite different from most of the work's journalism. When Dostoevsky speaks of the Eastern Question, he usually adopts the voice of the prophet. Citing several passages from the Book of Revelation and even an obscure sixteenth-century book of prophecies, Dostoevsky forecasts destruction for Europe and calls upon all faithful Russians to adhere to "the Russian idea" of universal salvation based on Russian Orthodoxy.[40] Dostoevsky believed that the prophecy of Moscow as the Third Rome destined to establish true brotherhood on earth was about to be fulfilled, if only various enemies could be defeated.

The registers of Dostoevsky's prophetic voice contrast markedly with the gentle, intimate tone of many other *Diary* articles. In 1873 and the first part of 1876, Dostoevsky spoke as someone seeking some sort of guiding thread amid the chaos of Russian life. It was evidently this tone of perplexed wonder that originally was intended to define the whole. By contrast, the speaker in the prophetic articles no longer seeks because he has already found the inner story of world and Russian history.

Confidently tracing that story from the ancients to the present, Dostoevsky explains even the most trivial current events. He possesses the key to history. Where others see merely local political conflicts, he reads the latest chapter in a drama lasting from the beginning of history to the "final denouement" now at hand.

To prove the power of his method, Dostoevsky "risks" making predictions for the immediate future, and so an assessment of his earlier predictions soon became a regular feature of the *Diary*. They are, of course, usually confirmed, albeit by "facts" that (as Dostoevsky is well aware) are such only to those who accept Dostoevsky's interpretive schema to begin with. He predicts that the Jesuits will seize control of France, and then some speech by a French leader "proves" that they have in fact gained power; but, of course, Dostoevsky's critics regard his interpretation of the speech as no less "ecstatic" than his initial prediction. Repeatedly, "wiseacres," skeptics, and "caustic voices" "interrupt" these articles to mock Dostoevsky's use of evidence, and some of the most interesting articles in these sections of the *Diary* are devoted to dialogues about verification. The influence of these articles may easily be found in *Karamazov*, which devotes considerable attention to the nature of evidence and belief.[41]

The Prophetic Journalism: Metternich and Don Quixote

In contending with real and imagined opponents, Dostoevsky argues most forcefully against those who appeal to calm reason and common sense. The real question for him is not whether this or that interpretation is correct but whether prophecy itself is viable. Dostoevsky explains repeatedly that his own ability to read the inner story of history (evidently based on his novelist's eye) makes his commentary more reliable than those based on conventional methods and considerations, which must be regarded as mere substitutes for real insight. Moreover, whatever value such methods might have had in the past, they cannot work at a time when the apocalypse is upon us. Dostoevsky insists that the closer the end of history draws, the less reliable traditional political analysis becomes.

In normal historical periods, Dostoevsky explains, past events are the best guide to current events. But at moments of catastrophe, when "the past is split in two," conventional analyses will *necessarily* mislead. Revelation tells us that in one instant riches will come to naught, so how can the relative health of European economies be relevant to assessing their power in an apocalyptic age? At such times, Dostoevsky repeats, it is not "Metternich" but "Don Quixote" who turns out to be the supreme political realist.[42]

Dostoevsky asks us to imagine some wily diplomat just before the French revolution using "common sense" to plan for the future. Basing his views on experience, he would see none of the unprecedented cataclysms to come. It is periods like these, Dostoevsky insists, that reveal the shortcomings of "Diplomacy Facing World Problems" (5–6/77, 2.2) and of ordinary practicality at moments of sudden universal upheaval. "If you make it a rule to judge all world events, even those that the most superficial view can see as being of the greatest importance, according to the principle: 'today as yesterday, and tomorrow as today'—then isn't it clear that this rule goes utterly contrary to the history of nations and of humanity?" (9/77, 1.5). In the great nineteenth-century controversy between uniformitarianism and catastrophism, Dostoevsky makes an explicit plea for the catastrophist view of time.

For Dostoevsky, the proper way to understand history, at least current history, is *mythically.* Beyond his specific predictions and political solutions, Dostoevsky urges and exemplifies a particular kind of thinking in these articles. In this respect the *Diary* resembles its great utopian predecessor, *The Republic*, which apart from its political prescriptions praises the philosophical process by which Socrates arrives at them—a process, Socrates maintains, "which anyone who is to gain happiness must value both for itself and for its results."[43] In the *Diary*'s utopian articles, Dostoevsky-as-Socrates instructs readers placed in the role of Glaucon.

It cannot be denied that a large number of these articles are eminently forgettable. Dostoevsky as Don Quixote tortures fact and logic to turn windmills into giants. We read endless attempts to discover the hidden pattern of world history in the twists of French politics, the machinations of German diplomacy, and the shifting allegiances of the Russian intelligentsia. In most cases, the very events to which Dostoevsky attributes such timeless significance proved to be of fleeting interest, known now only to the specialist historian. But a few articles in which Dostoevsky outlines his mythic and quixotic approach in general terms remain of abiding interest, if only as a concentrated sample of this kind of thinking.

Chapter 2 of June 1876 offers the *Diary*'s first comprehensive reading of history. Dostoevsky begins, characteristically, by posing a "paradox" (6/76, 2.1): why is it that Russian Westernizers, when they go abroad, immediately identify with Western radicals, that is, with those who want to destroy European civilization? As Westernizers, after all, they might be expected to want to preserve European civilization. Dostoevsky's answer is that these Russian radicals are unconsciously expressing their own Russianness. In fact, they are even displaying their unwitting Slavophilism. "In short, we are revolutionaries, so to say, out of some internal necessity, even out of conservatism" (6/76, 2.2). Had the radical critic Belinsky lived longer, Dostoevsky opines, he would have become a Slavophile. If only today's radical intelligentsia could become aware of this unconscious impulse, he pleads, the rifts between Slavophiles and Westernizers and between the intelligentsia and the people would be healed. That development would in turn allow all other Russian "questions" to be solved once and for all. One reason the Eastern Question is so significant, Dostoevsky argues, is that it may lead to just such healing by bringing the radicals' unconscious Russianness into plain view.

Dostoevsky then supplements this utopian hope with a fully developed "Utopian Conception of History" (6/76, 2.4). Before Peter

the Great's reforms, he instructs, "the Russian idea"—Orthodoxy—
remained unsullied. Russia was the only remaining Christian country in the world, and so Russia preferred to isolate herself from the
West. Had this isolation continued, however, Russia would not have
preserved but ultimately betrayed its Christianity, the meaning of
which lies precisely in its universality. Thus Peter's reforms, despite
their apparently secular motivation, were in fact providential.

By bringing Russia into its two-century contact with Europe,
Dostoevsky reasons, Peter created an immeasurable "broadening of
outlook" among Russians. As a result of this broadening, Russians
came to develop "something characteristic of the Russian People
alone. . . . it is our acquired capacity to discover the truth contained
in each of the civilizations of Europe or, more correctly, in each of
the personalities of Europe." From here on, Dostoevsky was to repeat constantly his idea that whereas other nations possess a specific
personality and carry a particular, local "idea," a true Russian is
"pan-human" in that he or she can intuitively understand and embrace the personalities and ideas of all peoples. That is why the capa-
cious and all-reconciling Russian idea is destined to contain all others
and resolve their contradictions once and for all.

If the first step of Russian history was the period of Orthodox
isolation, and the second was Russia's "broadening," then the third
and final stage is now upon us.[44] The world will soon witness the
utopian solution to all its problems and the advent of universal
brotherhood. Collapsing Europe, doomed to extinction, will be
saved at the last possible moment by the Russian idea. The first
step toward this utopian solution—"the beginning of the end"—
will be Russia's liberation of the Slavic peoples under Turkish rule.
Russia will undertake this mission utterly selflessly, without any
motives of territorial seizure of the sort that always motivates England and Austria. The liberation of the Slavs will lead immediately
to the Russian occupation of Constantinople, the traditional center
of Eastern Christianity; and with true Christianity at last made
whole, it will "speak its word" to the rest of the world and solve
all world problems forever.

It follows that the skeptics are mistaken in regarding the Balkan
conflict as just another war. It does not in the least resemble all
those petty European wars of the last century. As Dostoevsky writes
in a later article, the Eastern Question pertains not just "to the
seas and the straits, access and egress" but also to something "much

deeper, more fundamental, more elemental, more necessary, more primary" (5–6/77, 2.2).

At a number of points in the June 1876 *Diary*, Dostoevsky imagines what some ironic European, some two-bit Metternich, would reply: "Heavens, what a mocking smile would appear on the face of some Austrian or Englishman if he had the opportunity to read all these *daydreams* I have just written down" (6/76, 2.4). Later in the *Diary* he will state that not counterarguments but events will best answer these mocking Europeans: "If not we, then our children will see how England ends. Now, for everyone in the world 'the time is at hand.' And it's about time, too" (4/77, 1.3; citation from Revelation 1:3).

Adopting another tactic, Dostoevsky replies in the June 1876 *Diary* by exposing the skeptics' questions as self-implicating, as revealing the naïveté and moral corruption of those who pose them. In their habitual turpitude, the skeptics can only conceive of a mere political union, like the North American states. They lack the nobility to appreciate that in Russia's union with the other Slavs "there *truly* will be something special and unprecedented" (6/76, 2.4), just as they cannot believe that anyone could take real Christianity seriously. Questions have presuppositions, and the presuppositions of these "Austrians" demonstrate atheism and selfishness.

The culminating passage of "The Utopian Conception of History" contains Dostoevsky's best-known statement of his apocalyptic hopes. Whatever the "Austrians" think, the Russian mission has nothing to do with the usual political goal of empire or seizure of territory.

> No, it will be a true exaltation of the truth of Christ, which has been preserved in the East, a true, new exaltation of the cross of Christ and the ultimate word of Orthodoxy, at whose head Russia has long been standing. It will be a temptation for all the mighty of this world who have been triumphant until now and who have always regarded all such "expectations" with scorn and derision and who do not even comprehend that one can seriously believe in human brotherhood, in the universal reconciliation of nations, in a union founded on principles of universal service to humanity and regeneration of people through the true principles of Christ. And if believing in this "new word," which Russia at the head of a united Orthodoxy can utter to the world—if believing in this is a "utopia" worthy only of derision, then

you may number me among these utopians, and leave the ridicule to me. (6/76, 2.4)

The *Diary's* utopian passages typically unfold dialogically because they are usually addressed to a scornful opponent. The essential stance of these articles is that of the prophet ridiculed, both at home and abroad, even though he speaks the timeless truth.

The Prophetic Journalism: Nineteen Hundred Years of Protestantism and the Principle of Simultaneity

Dostoevsky offers his next comprehensive myth of world history in the opening essay of 1877. The article "Three Ideas" (1/77, 1/1), on which he expands throughout the year, describes European history since its beginnings as a conflict among three fundamental principles, each associated with a particular people and its corresponding type of personality. In this way, the fate of nations is transformed into ideomachia and psychomachia.

"Three ideas rise up before the world and, it seems, are already in their final stage of formulation," Dostoevsky proclaims. The first idea is Catholicism, by which Dostoevsky means *not* merely "the Catholic religion alone but the entire *Catholic idea*." As he explains in this article and elsewhere, this idea was first formulated by the Romans. Fusing a materialist view of mankind with the concept of universality, the Romans arrived at the idea of *world rule*, of universal earthly power.

Before it could realize this idea, however, the Roman Empire encountered Christianity with its nonmaterialist view of humanity: "The man-god encountered the God-man, Apollo Belvedere encountered Christ" (8/80, 3.3). A compromise was worked out, in which the empire accepted Christianity and the church (the Western church) accepted the Roman idea of universal rule. Ever since, the pope has tried to put this idea into practice. He has attempted to assert earthly power by deposing emperors and by ruling states. The Catholic idea belongs to the Latin peoples, and its principal representative today is France.

In addition to the Roman church, the modern world has generated another form of the Catholic idea: socialism, whose home, appropriately, is also France. However much it might seem to superficial observers that socialism and Catholicism are antithetical, and however much these two ideologies may currently be at odds, they maintain essentially the same ideal: "the *compulsory* union of humanity" (1/77, 1.1). One of two things will happen: either the

Jesuits will succeed in gaining control of France in order to launch a *final* war against Germany (this is the point of Dostoevsky's endless articles on French politics) or, having failed, they, with the pope at their head, will *join* the socialists and proclaim to the world what has always been true, that the two are the same. That is why Bismarck, whom Dostoevsky imagines to be the only person in the world to view politics just as he does, recognizes France, socialism, and the Catholic church not just as annoyances or political rivals but as mortal enemies fighting until the end of the world.

Dostoevsky regards Bismarck as the present pope of the second world idea, Protestantism. Again, by Protestantism he does not mean the ecclesiastical movement that began with Luther but an idea that for nineteen centuries has been "protesting" against Rome and her idea. He speaks of "Protestantism . . . protesting since the time of Arminius and the Teutoburger Wald. This is the German, believing blindly that the renewal of humanity is to be found only in him and not in Catholic civilization." The Reformation did not initiate but expressed the Protestant idea.

This Protestant idea, unlike its timeless opponent, contains not a substantial promise but a fundamental void. It is the embodiment of pure emptiness. It therefore lives parasitically, by *protesting* against its enemy, so that if Catholicism should be defeated once and for all, Protestantism too would soon die because "*she would have nothing to protest against.*" This idea tends to atheism and nihilism, that is, to pure negation.

Of course, Russia carries the third idea, the "Slavic idea." In article after article Dostoevsky repeats his "pan-human" thesis and defends the apocalyptic significance of the Eastern War, which would unite all Orthodox Slavs. (Dostoevsky never mentions that not all Balkan Slavs are Orthodox.)

The conspicuous presence of these three ideas before the world leads to an inevitable question:

> What is awaiting the world, not only in the remaining quarter of this century but even (who can tell?) in the current year, perhaps? Europe is restless, of this there is no doubt. But is this restlessness only temporary, a thing of the moment? Certainly not: it is evident that the time is at hand for the fulfillment of something eternal, something millenarian, something that has been in preparation in the world since the very beginning of its civilization.

But how can we be sure that the final conflict, which has been in

the making for millennia, is at last at hand? The answer is to be
found in another principle of mythic analysis that Dostoevsky introduces in "Three Ideas" although he names it only later: *synchronism* (the principle of "simultaneity").

Dostoevsky observes that each of the three ideas is just now
achieving its "final formulation" at precisely the same moment.
This simultaneity cannot be explained by any direct causal interaction. No, separate causal lines are each governed by the same
clock, which has led each of them to its concluding form and to
a final conflict with the others.

Thus, within a few short years the pope proclaimed infallibility,
Bismarck planned to interfere in the election of the next pope, and
the Eastern Question reached a critical stage. To understand these
events, we must solve "one riddle. . . . why does it always happen,
and particularly lately . . . that the moment some issue in the world
touches on something general and universal, *all the other* world
problems at once come up parallel to it?" (5–6/77, 2.2). Dostoevsky's solution is that history manifests a well-plotted story; when
Dostoevsky refers to a "denouement" he is not speaking merely
metaphorically. History is shaped like a novel, which is presumably
why only a novelist, not a diplomat, could discover its hidden plot
and foresee the coming first of catastrophe and then of utopia.

In September 1877 Dostoevsky feels confident enough to outline
the precise steps leading to Armageddon. In an article entitled
"Who's Knocking at the Door? Who Will Come In? Inescapable
Fate" (9/77, 1.5), he offers a list—"for the record so that it may
later be verified"—of four predictions. First, "the road begins at
Rome, in the Vatican," where the pope, whose Jesuits have covertly
seized control of France, will order the final war against Germany—
"this last battle for survival that *papal Catholicism in its ultimate
death throes* will certainly offer to the whole world in the very near
future."

Second, although this battle might be postponed briefly, it "is
inevitable and near at hand." Third, the battle will instantly become
an "all-European" one and will include the apparently separate
Eastern Question. Thus Roman Catholicism will be over as "by
the will of Providence a reborn Eastern Christianity will take its
place." It will be revealed once and for all why the Eastern Question
is "a world-wide, universal question with an extraordinary, preordained significance, even though this preordination may occur
before eyes that . . . are incapable until the last minute of seeing the

obvious and comprehending the meaning of what has been preordained." Finally—"and you may call this the most hypothetical
and fantastic of all my predictions, I'll admit that beforehand"—
Russia will win this final war: "Now again someone is knocking;
someone, a new man, with a new word, wants to open the door
and come in... But who will come in? That's the question. Will it
be an entirely new man, or will it once more be someone like all
of us, the old homunculi?"

Perhaps the most revealing foreign policy essays occur when
Dostoevsky attempts to explain why Russian armies did not in fact
succeed in occupying Constantinople. An unforeseeable accident—
it was not a "mistake," Dostoevsky insists—intervened. The Turks'
use of a new rifle, it seems, made Russia's assault tactics ineffective.
What is noteworthy about this explanation is that here Dostoevsky
abandons his mythic style of argument in an attempt to counter
the obvious fact of its failure in practice. For what has new military
technology to do with the timeless conflict of eternal principles or
with patterns revealed in apocalyptic writing? Concern with better
rifles figures in the analyses of traditional diplomats and historians.
It is, so to speak, an "Austrian" explanation. But Dostoevsky never
explicitly acknowledges this self-contradiction.

The Prophetic Journalism: Dostoevsky's Moral Nadir

The danger of mythic politics like Dostoevsky's becomes especially
clear in several articles that must be taken as the moral nadir of
his career. The constant reference to "the universal Catholic conspiracy" (a phrase repeated like a mantra) leads to abhorrent essays
accusing Poles in the Russian empire of being secret agents of the
Vatican conspiracy. It also leads to anti-Semitic articles that were,
even by Russian standards of the day, particularly poisonous. Once
Dostoevsky sees history in terms of a single story he adopts conspiracy logic to explain all resistance to his utopian dreams. And
so it appears that the Jews, too, work behind the scenes to impede
the progress of Christian Russia. Carrying their own secret idea of
world domination, the Jews already rule over all of Europe, and
"they are all faithfully awaiting the Messiah, every one of them,
from the very lowest Yid to the very highest and most learned
among them, the philosopher and cabalist-rabbi . . . they all believe
that the Messiah will gather them together in Jerusalem once more
and will use his sword to bring down all the other peoples to sit
at their feet" (3/77, 2.3).

Dostoevsky thus advances a second apocalyptic myth: the final
conflict will be between Jews (representing materialism) and Christians (representing brotherhood). That is the real reason that Disraeli, directing British foreign policy in part from the perspective
of a "Spanish Yid," opposes Russian attempts to liberate the Balkans. This perfidy is only the first terrible plot of the Jews: "Their
reign, their complete reign is drawing nigh! Coming soon is the
complete triumph of ideas before which feelings of love for humanity, the longing for truth, Christian feelings, the feelings of
nationhood and even the national pride of European peoples must
give way. What lies ahead, on the contrary, is materialism, a blind,
carnivorous lust for *personal* material security" (3/77, 2.3). If the
Jews ruled Russia, Dostoevsky contends, we could expect them to
enslave everyone, to skin them, or to "massacre them altogether,
exterminate them completely, as they did more than once with alien
peoples in times of old in their ancient history" (3/77, 2.2). How
this myth of a final conflict of Jews and Christians is to be reconciled
with the battle of three ideas, none of which is Jewish, is something
that Dostoevsky never explains.

Earlier in his career the Jews never occupied much of a place in
Dostoevsky's thinking, and as editor of *Time* he attacked the Slavophile journal *Day* precisely for its anti-Semitic tirades. It seems
to me the fanatic anti-Semitism of the 1877 *Writer's Diary* may
serve as an excellent illustration of Norman Cohn's celebrated thesis
that fanatic anti-Semitic thought in Europe is closely linked to
millenarianism.[45] Cohn's point is that utopian and millenarian
thought should be regarded as highly dangerous. For all his sins,
Metternich makes a better ruler than Don Quixote.

Journalism: Literary Criticism and the Pushkin Speech

The *Diary* also contains a good deal of literary criticism, which
varies in tone and purpose. The death of George Sand occasions
an appreciative, almost sentimental, account of her importance to
Dostoevsky's generation. Dostoevsky responds to the death of Nekrasov with a psychological explanation of the contradiction between
the poet's business sense and his verse about human suffering. The
most interesting essays consider the work of Tolstoy and Pushkin.
Later in this introduction I shall consider the Tolstoy essays, in
which Dostoevsky's assessments of that writer reflect the inner
conflicts of the *Diary* itself. The most important Pushkin criticism
forms the pivot of the August 1880 issue, which includes the text

of Dostoevsky's famous Pushkin speech. This issue of the *Diary* transforms literary criticism into yet another form of apocalyptic politics.

Strictly speaking, the August 1880 *Diary* is devoted not to the speech itself but to the occasion of its delivery and the nature of its reception. Its purpose is not just to reprint the text of the speech but to tell a story about a key *event* in Russian culture. It just so happens that the hero of that story is Dostoevsky himself.

The issue therefore has a plot, consisting of three incidents. The earliest is the delivery of the speech, the text of which is given in the second chapter. The speech attributes to Pushkin Dostoevsky's own diagnosis of Russian society, the tragic contradictions between the intelligentsia and the people and between Slavophiles and Westernizers. Dostoevsky's Pushkin also foresaw what would resolve the split, an appreciation of the Russian spirit as "pan-human." Unique among the great poets of the world, Pushkin could describe Englishmen as Englishmen and Italians as Italians, whereas Shakespeare's or Goethe's foreigners were nothing more than Englishmen or Germans with foreign names.[46] Thus Pushkin was the first to embody the universality that is the distinguishing mark of Russians. In this respect he was both Slavophile (understanding the Russian spirit) and Westernizer (able to include Western peoples within Russianness). If only our intelligentsia could accept Pushkin's idea of Russians as a universal people, all their conflicts would be resolved and brotherhood would reign.

The story's second incident, described in the issue's first chapter (and a part of the third), consists of the audience's immediate response to the speech. The audience's enthusiasm seems to confirm Dostoevsky's hope that his speech could be the catalyst for utopia. With breathless excitement, Dostoevsky informs his readers that the speech inspired the audience to join hands, set aside old quarrels, and serve the Russian cause of universal reconciliation.

> I'm not recalling this to earn praise, and not out of pride: I'm merely recording the seriousness of the moment.... this single, ardent suggestion united everyone in a single thought and a single feeling. Strangers embraced each other and swore to be better in the future. Two old men came up to me and said: "We have been enemies for twenty years and have done much harm to one another, but hearing your words we have made peace." (8/80, 3.4)

Dostoevsky wonders whether this promising beginning will in fact lead to utopia. The issue's first chapter therefore sketches out two possibilities: either the Westernizers will respond with mockery or they will in fact accept Dostoevsky's recipe for reconciliation. On this note of suspense, the chapter ends. This was supposed to be the last event recorded in the August 1880 *Diary.*

Unexpectedly, however, Dostoevsky adds a third chapter, which contains the third incident of the story. It appears that after the first two chapters were written but before the issue could be published, important responses to the speech appeared in rival publications. "I was about to conclude my *Diary,* having limited it to the speech I gave in Moscow on June 8 and the foreword that I wrote to it, foreseeing the row that was, in fact, raised. . . . But after reading your criticism, Mr. Gradovsky, I stopped the printing of the *Diary* so as to append to it a reply to your attacks" (8/80, 3.1). Like others reporting on the speech, Gradovsky mocked Dostoevsky's appeal, just as Dostoevsky had feared some would. Dostoevsky therefore devotes the issue's final pages to an angry reply. It appears that his hopes for the speech, no less than his earlier expectations about the Eastern War, were disappointed.

Carefully dated, each chapter of this issue appears (or is said to appear) *as written,* that is, without benefit of the knowledge recorded in chapters composed later. The August 1880 Diary does not just describe a sequence of events but *enacts* a story. It is this temporal layering that gives the issue its dramatic quality and allows it, in miniature, to reproduce the periodical quality of earlier years. It repeats the drama of utopian hope and disappointment that in 1877 was focused on the Eastern War.

Journalism: Crime and the Environment, Suicides and Trials

Dostoevsky sought to trace the spiritual development of Russia by reporting on sensational events, such as suicides and trials. These two themes each led to a sequence of articles that were closely connected with the *Diary*'s stories. As we have seen, "The Dream of a Ridiculous Man" begins with a contemplated suicide, which is then enacted in a dream. "The Meek One" combines both motifs, as the narrator addresses an imagined court to explain why his wife has killed herself.

Dostoevsky selects suicides that, in his view, reveal fundamental spiritual crises in Russian life. In *Notes from Underground,* Dostoevsky's narrator observes, "I have only, after all, in my life carried

to an extreme what you have not dared to carry halfway."[47] The
suicide cases of the *Diary* also carry to an extreme the despair
facing all educated Russians.

Typically, Dostoevsky focuses on the suicide note (or some spoken
substitute), which he first examines *stylistically.* As Tikhon, the
holy man of *The Possessed*, deduces Stavrogin's state of mind from
the way he writes his confession, Dostoevsky applies his special
stylistics to the last words of those who have condemned themselves.
Under his analysis, style betrays psychology, which in turn reveals
ideology. The suicide's ideology then serves as a key to the "unconscious" spiritual conflicts of millions. Because many of the cases
were already widely known, Dostoevsky's revelation of new meaning in apparently exhausted incidents proved particularly
compelling.

Eventually, Dostoevsky felt confident enough that his guesses
were correct to offer his "formula" of a materialist's suicide note
(in his sketch "The Sentence" [10/76, 1.4]). Here again we witness
how a process of research, guesswork, and correction have eventually led to a short "semifiction," which in turn provided the basis
for the finished story, "The Dream of a Ridiculous Man."

The new Russian law courts, reformed along Western lines and
open to the public, also allowed Dostoevsky to examine crimes as
symptoms of Russia's moral state. Because he is interested not only
in the criminal but also in the public, Dostoevsky reports on trials
as public events. As in *Karamazov*, they are a form of unwitting
theater in which the audience may be the most important actors.

As Dostoevsky covers these cases, not only the defendant is on
trial, but so are the other actors in the judicial process. He calls
attention to the approving response of the press when clever lawyers
get obviously guilty people acquitted, inquires into the motivation
of juries that turn in unjust verdicts, and focuses on the sentiments
that lead audiences at trials to cheer the release of child abusers.
Above all, Dostoevsky dwells on the often tacit *ideas* that "float
about in the air" (73.3) and guide public thought about crime and
about right and wrong. "Some ideas exist that are unexpressed and
unconscious but that simply are strongly felt" (73.3), he remarks,
and one purpose of the *Diary* is to make those ideas explicit and
so available to scrutiny.

The 1873 *Diary* initiates the sequence of articles on crime with
one of Dostoevsky's best-known essays, "Environment" (73.3).
Justly praised for its profundity and rhetorical power, this essay

employs methods central to the *Diary*'s basic conception. It begins
with reflections about why the new Russian juries let the guilty go
free, whereas in England, which invented this institution, jurors
generally do not yield to sentimentality or the intoxication of power.
In Russia, however, a particular idea seems to have "seized all
Russian jurors," not just peasants but "even those from the uppermost classes such as noblemen and university professors." This
idea is "the environment": the theory that all crime is caused not
by morally responsible people but by social evils. It follows that
"there is no crime whatsoever" and so how can anyone be convicted
of anything? Proponents of "the environment" demand: first reform society, and then ask people to behave properly! It is evident
that such an idea contradicts the very basis of trials, for it makes
everyone automatically innocent.

In the first half of the article, Dostoevsky argues "inefficiently."
Digressing into numerous apparently irrelevant issues, he is repeatedly interrupted by various voices representing distinct currents
of Russian thought.[48] They force Dostoevsky to explain his own
outmoded sense of morality, which, he acknowledges, is not only
passé but also somewhat inconsistent. When the voices argue with
each other, Dostoevsky seems to lose control of his own article.
This technique in fact characterizes many *Diary* articles, which
alternate exposition with a sort of eccentric drama.

In this indirect manner Dostoevsky first deepens our understanding of the issues. No less important, he also reveals the character,
not just the logic, of positions—the way ideas feel and are lived.
Along the way he manages to state, if not to defend, key points,
which will turn out to be essential to his refutation of the "environmental" doctrine. He lays the groundwork, too, for examining
the doctrine's effects. What sort of moral environment does the environmental doctrine itself create? Throughout the *Diary,* Dostoevsky
turns the environmental doctrine against itself. For example, he
questions what sort of families are produced by parents who believe
not in individual responsibility but in social determinism.

In "Environment," Dostoevsky suggests that this "progressive"
view of crime and responsibility takes away our very humanity by
denying human freedom. It turns us into what the underground
man calls "piano keys" and "organ stops." "In making the individual dependent on every flaw in the social structure, however,
the doctrine of the environment reduces him to an absolute nonentity, exempts him totally from every personal moral duty and

from all independence, reduces him to the lowest form of slavery imaginable." The doctrine of freedom liberates, the idea of determinism enslaves. But Dostoevsky does not proceed to deny the environmental doctrine altogether, as some less than careful readers have assumed. He argues rather that the truly Christian perspective is to acknowledge that corrupting environment does play a role and may indeed be a mitigating factor, provided that this reasoning is not pushed too far. The problem with the environmental doctrine lies in its categorical formulation. For Christianity, which both allows for mercy and makes people responsible, the question becomes one of locating "the line where the environment ends and duty begins." However, if everything is entirely determined by social conditions, then no line need be drawn.

This question of "the line" suggests a second argument that is central to the 1873 *Diary*: one must be suspicious of Theory, of categorical reasoning, per se. Any ethical theory, not just the doctrine of the environment, will produce grotesque results when formulated as a universal law. Real moral judgment demands fine discrimination among apparently similar cases, and in such a process of judgment generalities play their proper role not as laws but as maxims, as reminders of earlier cases that may or may not be applicable to the one under consideration. The complexities of concrete cases are too numerous, too fine, and too unpredictable for any theory to encompass in advance. For Dostoevsky, it is a characteristic mistake of the intelligentsia (the principal target of the 1873 *Diary*) to yield to fashionable generalities of this sort.

In advancing these arguments, Dostoevsky develops the "prosaic" idea typically associated with Tolstoy. Like Pierre in *War and Peace* (and later Levin in *Anna Karenina*), Dostoevsky defends a *casuistical* approach to ethics in the root sense of that term: morality is not reducible to a theory but depends on sensitivity to particular cases.[49] The questions of whether and to what degree a set of circumstances might mitigate a given crime are ones that must always be raised but never answered *either way* in advance or by a theory. Later in the *Diary*, Dostoevsky himself will discover grounds to attribute diminished responsibility to a convicted criminal. Accused by a rival publication of contradicting himself, he will insist (correctly) that his argument against "the environmental doctrine" was never advanced categorically but, precisely the opposite, as an attack on categorical thinking where only sensitivity to particulars will do. What is needed is training in drawing fine distinctions and in noting telling particulars, which is the sort of education that *A Writer's Diary* repeatedly attempts to provide.[50]

Dostoevsky illustrates the complexity of these moral questions and the need to be suspicious of general theories "in the air" with yet another consideration. What if the environmental theory, which now "floats in the air," should itself come to figure in the deliberations of a person *contemplating* crime? "The criminal and the person planning to commit a crime are two different people, but they belong to the same category. What if the criminal, consciously preparing to commit a crime, says to himself: 'There is no crime!'" Here again, intellectuals invoke their theories as a way of *explaining* events, but they fail to consider the possibility that theories may also *cause* them. Precisely because the environment does contribute to crime, they should not forget that ideas themselves form a part of the environment. Here Dostoevsky sharpens his paradox: the grain of truth in this theory itself constitutes a reason to reject it.

What the environmental theory should lead us to do is not to excuse crime—at least not categorically—but bit by bit, effort by small effort, to improve the environment. We should recognize that the criminal is indeed responsible for his crime, but we should not forget that we have the responsibility for changing the environment that contributed to it, even if our individual efforts at improvement only change the environment a small amount. It is this prosaic concept of responsibility for small improvements, and not its perversion into the "environmental doctrine," that the Russian people, when left uncorrupted by fashionable ideas, truly believe:

> No, the People do not deny there is crime, and they know that the criminal is guilty. The People know that they also share the guilt in every crime. But by accusing themselves, they prove that they do not believe in "environment"; they believe, on the contrary, that the environment depends completely on them.... Energy, work, and struggle—these are the means through which the environment is improved. Only by work and struggle do we attain independence and a sense of our own dignity. "Let us become better, and the environment will be better." This is what the Russian People sense so strongly but do not express in their concealed idea of the criminal as an unfortunate.

Later in the *Diary*, Dostoevsky discusses how, in *Anna Karenina*, Levin arrives after long and futile theorizing at a pretheoretical understanding of ethics. Dostoevsky's praise for this scene (and for some similar passages in Tolstoy's novel) probably reflects his awareness of the sense of prosaic and casuistical morality he shares with his great rival.

Dostoevsky's article does not develop any of these arguments rigorously; they appear briefly, only to be laughed down by "sarcastic voices." The author is on the defensive when he at last switches tactics and, as if following his own advice, considers a particular case. It seems that a peasant beat his wife over a period of many years. Treating her worse than a dog, he drove her, already scarcely in her right mind, to seek refuge in a village court, which sent her away with the recommendation: "Learn to live together." We all read in the papers what happened next, Dostoevsky reminds his readers: "Plainly and simply, the wife who suffered from her husband's beatings hanged herself; the husband was tried and found deserving of mercy." As for me, Dostoevsky writes, I kept thinking about the case and "fancied I could see all the circumstances . . . I see them even now."

What follows is an imaginative reconstruction of the woman's life, a piece of semifiction (in this respect) similar to "A Hundred-Year-Old Woman." "I keep imagining his figure. . . . I would add another touch": Dostoevsky weaves an admittedly imaginary story around the known facts of the case. He then asks the reader to consider whether his story is plausible and, if so, whether the jury's recommendation of mercy based on the doctrine of the environment makes moral sense. Here is the novelist as casuist (in the positive sense), using his psychological sensitivity to understand people and their actions. And here is *A Writer's Diary* in its essential mode of combining fiction and nonfiction, of projecting, interrogating, and imagining real events in order to arrive at their spiritual meaning.

The story that Dostoevsky constructs, like the most horrifying incidents in his novels, remains unforgettable for its stark terror, all the more so *because it is probably true.* In this respect, it resembles the most compelling narratives in *The House of the Dead.* "Have you seen how a peasant beats his wife?" Dostoevsky asks his readers. "I have." As in the novel, and as in the *Diary*'s autobiographical sketches, Dostoevsky relies on his own legendary and true biography to lend his account greater plausibility than mere fiction would have.

Based on some generally overlooked incidents that emerged in the trial, Dostoevsky imagines how the peasant would thrust the woman into a hole in the floor and beat her for hours, with their

ten-year-old child watching. Here as elsewhere in Dostoevsky, wit-
nessing becomes a second torture and the compulsion to witness
becomes a second crime. What has been approached as a case of
cruelty to the wife was also child abuse.

The peasant would leave food out but forbid the wife and child
to eat it, so they would go begging to neighbors and, upon returning, the wife would be beaten again. And remember, Dostoevsky muses, since people are born in various circumstances,
this woman "might have been some Juliet or Beatrice from Shakespeare, or Gretchen from *Faust*" or at least "something no worse,
perhaps, than what could be found in a woman of noble birth."
From this point on, his narrative describes how "Beatrice or
Gretchen" begs inhumanly for her husband to stop the beating,
again with her daughter looking on. "The little girl, all atremble
and huddled on the stove, would steal a wild glance at her mother
hanging by her heels and try to hide again."

It is here that Dostoevsky returns to the bare facts with which
he began the story: that the woman at last went to the village court,
which told her to learn to live together, and then hanged herself,
on "a bright spring day, probably." He imagines the child watching
the hanging body for hours, and then repeats the jury's verdict of
"Guilty, but with *recommendation for clemency*." Dostoevsky then
makes explicit the implications of his second story, the child abuse
case, which the jury and press had not even considered. Dostoevsky
asks: what happens to the child, who testified against her father,
when, because of "clemency," she goes back to live with him in
a few months? "Clemency to whom, and for what? You feel as if
you are in some sort of whirlwind that's caught you up and twists
and turns you around."

Dostoevsky then adds another story. It appears from the press
that a woman used to torture her noisy child by pouring scalding
water on her. Well, let us imagine this case in court, Dostoevsky
suggests; and he reconstructs the defense attorney's argument and
the jury's "recommendation for clemency." But that's just a fiction!
the "sarcastic voice" interrupts. Perhaps, Dostoevsky answers, but
the woman who hanged herself and the girl who witnessed it, those
are not fictions. "'Backwardness, ignorance, the environment—
have some pity,' the peasant's lawyer insisted. . . . Enough contortions, gentlemen of the bar. Enough of your 'environment.'"

If this fourteen-page essay had appeared when the *Diary* was a
monthly, Dostoevsky would probably have made it one of an issue's

two chapters and divided it into two or three articles; there is a break in the text as it is. Much as "The Boy at Christ's Christmas Party" follows a nonfictional article, so the reconstruction of the wife's story follows the purely factual account that precedes it. This is precisely how Dostoevsky uses fiction and semifiction within the *Diary*, to illuminate the moral meaning of well-known facts. These stories and sketches depend on their ambiguous status as fictions that may very well not be fictions at all. For that matter, one could easily excerpt the account of the peasant's wife in "Environment" and publish it as a separate story; it would in fact work quite well, much as "The Boy" and "The Peasant Marey" can stand on their own. But in both of those cases, although we have a powerful story, it is—even if verbally identical—nevertheless a different story from the one that appears in *A Writer's Diary.*

Journalism about Trials: Child Abuse and a Case Not As Simple As It Seems

The Kroneberg trial, a notorious child abuse case, occupies the second chapter of the February 1876 issue. Concerned above all with the social implications of the case, Dostoevsky focuses less on Kroneberg than on his talented liberal lawyer, Spasovich, and on the arguments used to gain acquittal. To be sure, lawyers are supposed to use all available means in defense of their clients, but that is precisely the problem. The court turns into theater, while jury, audience, and the press respond primarily to performance. (Dostoevsky later reworked these themes in *Karamazov*, where Spasovich served as the model for the lawyer Fetyukovich.)

One case in which Dostoevsky became involved extends for over a year. The Kornilova case—"A Case That Is Not as Simple as It Seems" (10/76, 1.1)—concerned a young stepmother who was reproached by her stern husband for not measuring up to his first wife. One day when he was out, she threw his daughter out a fourth-story window; miraculously, the child was unharmed. Kornilova immediately turned herself in, was tried, convicted, and sentenced to Siberia. By Russian law, the sentence also dissolved her marriage.

Dostoevsky first mentions the case in passing in his May 1876 issue. Imagining how some "talented" lawyer would argue for this attempted murderer's acquittal, Dostoevsky then observes, rather cryptically, that this case is indeed "truly bizarre; perhaps it really should be given a detailed and deep analysis that might even serve to lighten the case against this criminal woman" (5/76, 1.5). In the October 1876 issue, Dostoevsky does just that.

As in his articles on other cases, Dostoevsky argues that the available evidence sustains *another story* that others have not detected. In contrast to the Kroneberg case, though, this time the other story exonerates the accused. Focusing on the "bizarre" aspects of the story, Dostoevsky at last concludes that while throwing the girl out the window Kornilova suffered from "an affect of pregnancy"; she was conscious and sane, but she did something she would not have done otherwise and that she would never repeat. Dostoevsky's articles proved instrumental in getting the verdict reexamined and set aside on a technicality. Kornilova was then retried and acquitted on the grounds Dostoevsky had suggested.

In his most fascinating pieces on the case, Dostoevsky employs the techniques we have seen elsewhere to reconstruct the prior life of the family, the incidents leading to the crime, and the likely outcome of them. Moreover, he visits the Kornilovs in order to evaluate his own predictions about them, which prove generally correct. In the December 1877 issue, the last before the publication was suspended, Dostoevsky describes the family as faring well, much as he had expected. Explaining that he in fact delayed this article, which might have appeared earlier, he evidently placed it to provide the *Diary* with something like closure.

As Dostoevsky was obviously well aware, the Kornilova case in effect constitutes a little novella within the *Diary*. He evidently used it to create a unifying narrative thread and genuine suspense within the periodical. In this respect, it serves as a structural parallel to the story of the Eastern War: both extend over the better part of the 1876–77 *Diary*, contain enough twists and turns to create suspense, and conclude more or less when the *Diary* is suspended.

Moreover, although the author takes an active role in both stories, his exhortations cannot determine either outcome. Both stories involve the special excitement, different from that of a novel, created by an author's intermittent attempts to shape events in which he himself is involved and whose outcome is still undecided. Dostoevsky figures as both character and author. That, of course, is true in all genuine diaries, the potentials of which are exploited in this new genre of *A Writer's Diary*.

Journalism: Feuilletons and Chapter Titles

Before prophetic journalism begins to dominate the *Diary*, Dostoevsky positioned the feuilleton as the work's central journalistic genre. Indeed, he appears to have invented the form of the monthly *Diary* by radically expanding and adapting the feuilleton. "Without doubt, *A Writer's Diary* will resemble a feuilleton," he wrote to Vsevolod Soloviev, "with the difference that a monthly feuilleton, naturally, cannot resemble a weekly feuilleton."[51] In the course of the *Diary*, he refers to it a few times as a sort of feuilleton.[52] What precisely was this form for Dostoevsky, and how did he exploit it in his new publication?

By the 1840s the feuilleton had emerged as a major literary genre practiced by many of Russia's most talented writers, including Turgenev, Goncharov, Druzhinin, and Dostoevsky himself. Historically, it began as a mere journalistic miscellany listing disconnected bits of information in a single sheet (hence the term feuilleton). Gradually, the custom evolved of linking the separate items as the haphazard observations of a particular narrator, who wandered digressively from topic to topic and sometimes, in the conventional role of the flâneur, from place to place as well.

Thus we see at the core of this form, both historically and poetically, the problem of finding some sort of connection between radically diverse pieces. For this reason, the feuilleton lent itself to the design of Dostoevsky's new genre, which was to dramatize the search for some kind of underlying trends amid the amazing variety of Russian life. Dostoevsky's notebooks confirm that he planned to use feuilletons often within the *Diary*, where they would enable him to include heterogeneous observations and topics. The *Diary* as a whole would be a sort of feuilleton squared.

Small feuilletons were to be embedded in some sort of large feuilleton. And as the traditional feuilleton included an endless variety of topics, the new monthly version would include a wide variety of *genres*. By including material other than feuilletons, therefore, the *Diary* would be paradoxically true to the genre that inspired it. In this way, and as the pivot of each issue, the feuilleton would set the tone for the whole.

Traditionally, a conventional narrator figured in the feuilleton, as Dostoevsky's own earlier efforts in the genre illustrate. Dreamy, capricious, digressive—originally to justify the diversity of included topics—the feuilletonistic narrator typically finds it hard to concentrate on his announced theme because he is perpetually distracted by stray incidents that cross his path. Yorick in Sterne's *Sentimental Journey* evidently influenced Russian feuilletons, and so we witness in them a speaker occasionally indulging in epigrams or stinging insinuations within a generally lighthearted discourse governed by the spirit of whimsical parody. "I began my remarks about the feuilleton seriously enough," wrote the feuilletonist I. Panaev, "but then I saw that there is no way to talk seriously about the Russian feuilleton."[53] In his notebooks for the first monthly issue of the *Diary*, Dostoevsky reminds himself to maintain this playful tone. Criticizing unsuccessful feuilletonists, he remarks that "they want to talk playfully and simply . . . but then, to our surprise, no playfulness is visible. . . . Some resemble Mr. Turgenev, who has been writing himself out for the last ten years and who keeps . . . milking the humble cow of his wit, with its dried up teats."[54]

One generic formula that rapidly emerged (for example, in Druzhinin's "Dramatic Feuilleton about the Feuilleton and about Feuilletonists") was metaliterary play on the conventions of feuilletons themselves. For example, the narrator would confide to the reader his inability to honor the genre's conventions, including the convention of such confidences. This formula figures prominently in Dostoevsky's feuilletons. Inasmuch as the feuilleton was supposed to tie together the most diverse topics, mock apologies for including irrelevant or inappropriate material became standard. The *Diary*'s announcement, which promises to talk about everything the author has "seen, heard, and read," is clearly indebted to the feuilleton, as are Dostoevsky's "apologies" for violating this almost inviolable promise.

The reader who can mentally bracket the later issues of the *Diary* and focus on 1873 or the first numbers of 1876 will immediately become aware that the feuilletonistic tone extends far beyond the feuilletons proper. We have already seen how the frame of "The Boy at Christ's Christmas Party" whimsically calls attention to its own "inappropriateness"; no less feuilletonistic is its whole presentation as a dreamer's fancy. A similar, though more serious, combination of wistfulness and self-reference characterizes both "The Peasant Marey" (as we have seen, an "unexpected" reminiscence of an unexpected reminiscence of a nonexistent threat) and "A Hundred-Year-Old Woman" (with its conclusion dismissing the account as "inconsequential" and "not even a story"). These two narratives fill the same structural place in the February and March issues that "The Boy" fills in January. Before prophecy comes to dominate the *Diary*, indeed, virtually all its genres—

fiction, semifiction, autobiography, and journalism—continue the tone and method of the feuilleton.

It seems to me that another trademark of the *Diary* also derives from the feuilleton. Anyone who reads the monthly issues will be struck by the long and perplexing chapter titles. In January 1876, for instance, we encounter headings that, whatever else they do, do not help the reader understand in advance the article he or she is about to read:

> 1.3: The Christmas Party at the Artists' Club. Children Who Think and Children Who Are Helped Along. A "Gluttonous Boy." "Oui" Girls. Jostling Raw Youths. A Moscow Captain in a Hurry.
> 3.1: The Russian Society for the Protection of Animals. The Government Courier. Demon-Vodka. The Itch for Debauch and Vorobev. From the End or from the Beginning?

Almost miniature feuilletons themselves, these titles seem to continue the genre's impulse to diversity and spontaneity. They call attention to a narrator unable to stick to the topic or even, retrospectively, to describe concisely and coherently what he has been talking about. The titles evidently are written—and could only be written—*after* the article they introduce, and they are comprehensible only after it has been read. They pose problems for the reader to solve, and many of their elements are riddles: one may guess, but there is no way to know what a "'Oui' Girl" is until one reads the article. Composed of several puzzling parts, the title as a whole, tracing a perplexing sequence of thoughts, also works like a riddle. The reader is implicitly asked to ascertain what the different elements have to do with each other. (They are, in fact, thematically connected, so there is a special pleasure in solving the more interesting titles.) We have seen that in "The Peasant Marey" the diarist casts himself as a riddle solver, and that the author continually tries to solve puzzles of Russian life. In effect, the chapter titles encourage the reader to repeat the author's defining activity of discovering unity within a perplexing diversity.

Self-Referential Material and the 1873 *Diary*: A Periodical Has No Readers, So It Hires One

The metaliterary aspects of the feuilleton, its tendency to parody and self-parody, also lead to another sort of material in the *Diary*:

self-referential essays discussing the *Diary*'s own form and its relations with readers. Whimsical chapter titles composed in this
mode refer to what the author has *not* been able to do, and introductory paragraphs announce in advance that the *Diary* will make
promises as a mere cover for their violation. The January 1881
issue, which was to revive the monthly *Diary* after a three-year
intermission, begins with such a self-canceling promise:

> *1. Finances. A Citizen as an Offended Thersites. Crowing from below
> and the Musicians. A Refuge for Windbags and the Windbags.*
>   Good Lord! Can it be that after three years of silence I now resume
> my *Diary* with an article on economics? What sort of an economist
> and financial expert am I? I've never been either of these things.
> Despite the current epidemic, I have not been infected with the virus
> of economism, yet here I am, following all the others, and coming
> out with an article on economics. That there is a regular epidemic of
> economism these days is beyond doubt. (1/81, 1.1)

Of course, the author immediately digresses into other topics (as
the chapter title intimates he will). The chapter's next article begins
with the reader demanding that the author return to his topic, at
which point, in true metaliterary spirit, Dostoevsky "bares the
device":[55]

> *2. Can We Expect European Finances in Russia?*
>   "So what about finances? Where's your article on finances?" I'll
> be asked. But, again, what sort of an economist am I? What kind of
> an expert on financial matters? In fact, I don't think I even have the
> nerve to write about finances. So why, then, did I embark on such
> a venture and start writing such an article? I did so precisely because
> I'm sure that once I've begun to talk of finances I'll change the subject
> to something else entirely and the result will be an article not about
> finances but something altogether different. That's the only thing that
> encourages me. (1/81, 1.2)

In the third and fourth articles, self-reference has been removed
to the title:

> 1.3. Forget Immediate Problems So That the Roots Can Be Re-
> stored. Through Lack of Ability I Enter into Something Spiritual.
>   1.4. The First Root. Instead of an Authoritative Financial Tone I
> Lapse into Old Words....

The opening articles of 1873 and 1876 employ this technique to introduce *A Writer's Diary*. In so doing, they intimate the work's central themes and methods while denying the author's competence to accomplish any defined purpose. Thus the *Diary*'s feuilletonistic tone is heard from the very start.

"Introduction" (73.1) begins by contrasting the informal procedure by which Dostoevsky was named editor of *The Citizen* with the formality, governed by "two hundred volumes of ceremonial," developed over a thousand years, of the Chinese emperor's recent wedding. How delightful it would be to publish *The Citizen* in China, Dostoevsky muses, because there everything would be specified in advance. Why, in China absolutely no inventiveness would be needed inasmuch as every idea would have been specified long ago! But how am I to publish articles in Russia, Dostoevsky asks, where, on the one hand, there is no volume of ceremonial, but, on the other, the intelligentsia has such a rigid code of beliefs on every conceivable subject that independent thought is impossible?

For example, Dostoevsky confides, I would like to engage in sober reflection, but instead the leaders of the intelligentsia expect me to employ "a few very simplified and purely scientific techniques," preeminently those of a nihilistic sort:

> Formerly, for instance, the words "I don't understand a thing" meant only that the person who uttered them was ignorant; now they bring great honor. One need only say, proudly and with a frank air, "I don't understand religion; I don't understand anything about Russia; I don't understand anything about art," and immediately you place yourself above the crowd. And it's especially good if you really don't understand anything.

Members of the intelligentsia now identify themselves as such by sharing "ready-made ideas. They are sold everywhere, and even given away; but the ones that come free of charge prove to be even more expensive." And so "woe to the writer and publisher who in our time begins to think soberly . . . and to understand things on his own."

This, then, is what makes it impossible to publish *The Citizen*: to be a true *citizen*, one must endeavor to think independently, but then one will have no readers, and what is a publication without readers?

> The only thing he [the publisher] can do is to seek out some suitable individual, or even hire one, and simply talk to him and to him alone.

Perhaps he could publish a magazine for that one individual. It's a loathsome situation, because it amounts to talking to yourself and publishing a magazine only for your own amusement. I strongly suspect that for a long time yet *The Citizen* will have to talk to itself and appear only for its own amusement. Remember that medical science considers talking to oneself a sign of predisposition to insanity. *The Citizen* certainly must speak to citizens, and that is precisely the whole dilemma!

We see here why Dostoevsky's column is a *diary*: a diary does not require any readers. "I shall talk to myself and for my own amusement, in the form of this diary, whatever may come of it."[56]

In this wry way, the opening article defines the 1873 *Diary*'s key motifs. The idea of madness and conversations with oneself reappears most dramatically in the two contributions of the "certain person," "Bobok" (73.6) and "A Half-Letter from 'A Certain Person'" (73.8). As we have seen, these works filter several of the *Diary*'s favorite themes—about art, about materialism—through the thought of a madman. In "Dreams and Musings" (73.11), Dostoevsky compares himself to the mad diarist Poprishchin, the narrator of Gogol's "Diary of a Madman."

The "Introduction" also introduces what turns out to be the central theme of the 1873 *Diary*, the mentality of the intelligentsia. From a variety of angles and in a diversity of genres, Dostoevsky evokes the intelligentsia's shallow conformity, its adherence to a rigid code that makes real exchange of ideas impossible, its belief that it has at last found the final truth, its smug superiority to all the wisdom of the past, and, above all, the danger that it may someday achieve the power it seeks. As the author wanders from topic to topic, he finds unexpected opportunities to contrast the close-mindedness of the intelligentsia with the openness of genuine thought.

For example, the second article, "Old People," presents a complex picture of the generation of Belinsky and Herzen, which was far more appealing than the one that followed. On the one hand, Dostoevsky conveys their serious concern for ideas and their interest in thinking problems through without the aid of ready-made formulas. On the other hand, he dwells on the danger of the ideas they often embraced, such as the purely materialist interpretation of human nature.

The qualified hero of this essay is Herzen, who, unlike the

intelligentsia of the 1870s, maintained a sense of self-irony and therefore a capacity for real dialogue: "Self-reflection—the ability to make of his own deepest feelings an object which he could set before him, pay it tribute and, in the next breath perhaps, ridicule it—was a thing he had developed to the highest degree" (73.2). Self-reflection of this sort characterizes the *Diary* itself.[57] Belinsky, however, tended to be more dogmatic, and the discussion of his materialism leads directly into "Environment," with its attack on the intelligentsia's dangerous "ideas in the air."

In "Something Personal" (73.4), Dostoevsky describes a commonly held opinion among radicals that his story "The Crocodile" was intended to be a vicious allegory on the fate of their hero, Chernyshevsky. This article therefore focuses on this very way of reading, the impoverishing habit among the politically committed of turning art into a narrow-minded or tendentious statement. Of course, one can make any work into whatever allegory one wishes if one is only sufficiently determined and single-minded. This common interpretive method not only reflects a lack of literary sensitivity but also entirely distorts the works under analysis.

After all, Dostoevsky asks, what happens to art if it is read, and still worse, written, as a mere political allegory? According to "Apropos of the Exhibition" (73.9), real art cannot be produced by applying a tendency. What is more, even the tendency will then be debased.[58] In this article Dostoevsky criticizes art produced by people "wearing a uniform." He regrets the waste of talent that inevitably takes place when young writers who might produce real art succumb instead to mouthing the pieties of "common, official, liberal, and social opinion." The fear of being independent, and of being called reactionary or out of step with the times, is mistaken for a sense of social responsibility, a mistake that turns fledgling artists into hacks.

Even mature artists often fall victim to such tendentiousness. In "Vlas" (73.5), Dostoevsky ascribes the flaws of that poem, both aesthetic and moral, to Nekrasov's fear of independently pursuing his subject. As if dramatizing the deadening effect of the intelligentsia's dogmas, the corpses in "Bobok" become especially grotesque when they preen themselves on currently fashionable ideas. Real writers seek artistic immortality, but here the dead themselves hunger to be up-to-date—an ultimate horror later repeated by Ivan Karamazov's devil, who describes the other world as just another

fashionable salon. In "Bobok," the newly dead at last formulate a
progressive plan "to organize our life here, so to say, on new and
rational principles."

Returning to the 1873 *Diary*'s theme of the intelligentsia, the
article "Something about Lying" (73.15) explores how educated
Russians, devoured by *ressentiment* and demanding the respect that
only real scientific knowledge could provide, adopt spurious all-
purpose theories as shortcuts. With a few general nihilist maxims
at their disposal, they talk smugly about sciences they have not
studied. In the article's most memorable passage, Dostoevsky imagines one such Russian, who knows nothing about chemistry, explaining the science to its greatest living representative, the German
scientist Liebig.[59]

The year's final essay, "One of Today's Falsehoods" (73.16),
contains the most extended, and most remarkable, critique of the
intelligentsia mentality. It therefore completes the trajectory begun
in the "Introduction." Dostoevsky replies to another publication
that, guided by an "accepted rule" of "our pseudoliberal times,"
offered a highly dubious argument about student revolutionaries.
It argued that such radicals include only a few lazy students, not
serious ones devoted to their work and to high ideals. Thus they
cannot be used to impugn the ethos of Russian students in general.

Making frequent reference to his own revolutionary past, Dostoevsky describes this defense as in reality something like slander
and as, in any case, utterly false. It is precisely the best and most
idealistic students who are seduced by dangerous revolutionary
ideas, Dostoevsky contends. "I myself am an old 'Nechaevist'; I
also stood on the scaffold condemned to death, and I assure you
I stood in the company of educated people." Such youths adopt
heinous beliefs and commit crimes not because of any moral lapses
but because of the "environment"—not poverty but the "cycle of
ideas" propagated by liberal and radical publications.

There is something about the Russian intellectual milieu that
corrupts even the best ideas. That "something" is what Dostoevsky,
in his article's most memorable passage, calls "the Russian aspect"
of the problem. He explains that among Russians, who in this
respect are utterly unlike Europeans, ideas are inevitably taken to
their most radical conclusions, and so Europeans would not recognize their favorite theories after they have been reprocessed by
the Russian intelligentsia:

> Please allow me this funny phrase "the Russian aspect of their teach-
> ings" because a Russian aspect of their teachings really does exist.
> It consists of those conclusions drawn from their teachings that take
> on the form of an invincible axiom, conclusions that are drawn only
> in Russia; in Europe, as people say, the possibility of these conclusions
> is not even suspected. . . . [And so] obvious, brazen villainy of the
> crudest sort can be considered no more than greatness of soul, no
> more than the noble courage of humanity tearing itself free from its
> chains.[60]

If we are to save Russian youth from dangerous ideas and wasted
lives, Dostoevsky suggests, the leaders of the intelligentsia must
become more responsible. It is necessary to change the very mentality of the Russian intelligentsia. In passages like these, the *Diary*
looks forward to that great sociological and psychological critique
of the intelligentsia, *Landmarks: A Collection of Essays on the Russian Intelligentsia* (1909). This article, and thus the 1873 Diary,
ends self-referentially, with a plea "not to be ashamed when someone calls us on occasion a citizen and . . . once in a while to tell the
truth, even though, to your way of thinking, it may be insufficiently
liberal."

The theme of the intelligentsia provided a loose thematic center
for the articles of 1873. In 1876 Dostoevsky was able to publish
the *Diary* in the form he intended, and because that form was much
more complex, a much more sophisticated design was needed to
create the unity of an art work. What was the design Dostoevsky
had in mind?

Part 3: The New Design

Two Approaches to the *Diary*

There are at least two ways to approach the problem of the *Diary*'s
unity. First of all, in accord with the tenets of numerous critical
schools, one might treat the text as a whole from its beginnings in
1873 (or 1876) to its last issue in 1881. One would then inquire
into the principle that was supposed to tie together such discrepant
material over so many years. Any such interpretation would have
to discover the place of the prophetic articles, which occupy so
large and conspicuous a position, and explain their relation to the
numerous, apparently antithetical, anti-utopian sketches in the
work. Numerous questions of literary theory (such as the poetics

of encyclopedic works) and literary history (the genres to which
the *Diary* might belong) would prove important. This approach
was the one I followed in my earlier study of the *Diary*, *The Boundaries of Genre*, which concluded that the *Diary* belonged to a long
tradition of "meta-utopian" literature—works in which utopia and
anti-utopia were designed to enter into an ultimately inconclusive
dialogue.

The second approach, which I follow in the present analysis,
differs considerably. Instead of assuming that all parts fit the whole
as it was designed, one takes seriously the possibility that the work
may have essentially changed in the course of publication. In the
first approach, the years of publication simply realized the initial
design, whereas in the second approach, time becomes an active
force. It may both cause and record the abandonment of the original
design. In this case, one would seek to discover the *Diary*'s original
design and then to explore how and why Dostoevsky's new concerns
and purposes conflicted with it. Thus, only some parts of the text
reveal the plan with which the author began. The prophetic articles,
which are absent from the early issues and which seem so inartistic
to many readers, might be part of the deviation rather than of the
design.

Both approaches need to explain why relatively few people have
perceived the *Diary* as an integral work of art. The first attributes
this misreading to the complexity of the *Diary*'s design, to its failure
to inspire many imitators, and, perhaps, to the fact that the *Diary*,
though immensely interesting in its conception, was much less so
in its execution. The second approach acknowledges all these reasons—and adds one more: the work as a whole does not reflect
Dostoevsky's design, and it is therefore not surprising that careful
readers should have failed to discern it.

Following the second approach, I will sketch the *Diary*'s initial
design (part 3) and then explain the new philosophical convictions
that proved incompatible with it (part 4).[61]

The *Diary*'s First Unifying Principle:
Synchronic Structure and Frozen Time

Dostoevsky once wrote to his friend Stefan Yanovsky that "the
Diary has at last developed to the point where even the slightest
change in its form is impossible" (*Pis'ma* 3:284)—a remarkable
claim for a work that to many readers has seemed formless.[62] We
know from Dostoevsky's letters and notebooks that the proper use

of the periodical form and the preservation of a great diversity of genres were both essential to the new genre's design. He worried about his tendency to become so concerned with a single topic that "the issue suffers and becomes insufficiently heterogeneous" (*Pis'ma* 3:206). And he was also concerned that readers would not discern anything to unify that heterogeneity.

We have seen that the *Diary* contains fiction, many kinds of semifiction, autobiography, self-referential material, and diverse forms of journalism. How were these genres to be integrated? To comprehend Dostoevsky's idea for *A Writer's Diary* is to identify the design that was supposed to make a whole out of unprecedented heterogeneity. Dostoevsky's experiment depends on a special kind of unity.

In order to create an artistic whole, Dostoevsky developed two key methods, one to assure unity in each monthly issue and one to create a sense of the whole as the publication evolved month by month. Let us examine these two methods in turn before considering (in part 4) how and why Dostoevsky's design eventually failed. A brilliant experiment eventually lost its focus, to the point where readers were generally unable to perceive anything more than an anthology, brilliant in many of its pieces but lacking in any sense of a whole.

If readers were to concentrate on the *Diary*'s first few monthly issues, they would have much less difficulty in detecting the work's intended unity. In these months, Dostoevsky had the time to realize his design. Moreover, the considerations that eventually led him to modify his plan beyond recognition had not yet emerged. It would be helpful to consider the January 1876 *Diary*—his first opportunity to use the form to which he had devoted so much thought.

Just as this issue was about to appear, Dostoevsky wrote his revealing letter about it to Vsevolod Soloviev:

> In issue No. 1 there will be, first of all, the very littlest *preface*, then something or other about children—about children in general, about children with fathers, especially about children without fathers, about children at Christmas parties, without Christmas parties, about child criminals..... Of course, these will not be strict studies or accounts, but only some hot words and indications. Then about *what has been heard or read*—anything and everything that strikes me each month. Without doubt, *A Writer's Diary* will resemble a feuilleton, with the difference that a monthly feuilleton naturally cannot resemble a weekly feuilleton. Here the account will be not so much about events or news

as about what from an event remains most constantly, most connected
with the general, whole idea. Finally, I do not at all want to bind
myself with the task of rendering an account. I am not a chronicler:
this, on the contrary, will be a perfect *diary* in the full sense of the
word, that is, an account of what has most interested me personally—
here there will even be caprice. (*Pis'ma* 3:201–2)

When we compare this remarkable document with the notebooks
for the January issue and with the issue itself, Dostoevsky's idea
becomes considerably clearer. As we have seen, the *Diary* was to
exhibit feuilletonistic qualities: a light and personal tone, a dreamy
and capricious narrator, digressions around a set of loosely related
themes, and discussions of current events not in the objective form
of a chronicle but as they strike the author personally. And yet
from these personal impressions the reader should be able to tease
out something beyond ephemera, something "most connected with
the general, whole idea" of the present moment. This general idea
will not be stated directly but will emerge whimsically, capriciously,
through "hot words" subject to a complex, feuilletonistic layering
of ironies. Everything that this idiosyncratic author has seen, heard,
and read—the allusion is of course to the *Diary*'s "announcement"—will, for all its apparent formlessness, adumbrate a special
poetics of the topical. The result will be an art work that (to use
the words of one of Dostoevsky's characters) finds an image in
what apparently has no image.[63]

As Dostoevsky's letter suggests, each article of the January 1876
issue does indeed resemble a brief, weekly feuilleton. A diversity
of topics is tied together by a common tone and implicit idea. But
a longer monthly feuilleton demands a structure more complex than
that of a traditional weekly one. Thus Dostoevsky organizes a
hierarchy that extends the principle of the parts to the whole. Each
article loosely unites a diversity into a whole, and, in the same
way, the separate articles form chapters with a common focus. The
three chapters in turn join to form an issue.[64] The reader practiced
in discerning a thematic core in an apparently wandering feuilleton
will be able to use the same technique to understand each monthly
issue of the *Diary.*

If written as Dostoevsky intended, each month of the *Diary* would
engage the reader in the author's project of discovering some sort
of "guiding thread" in the vast diversities and possibilities of ongoing Russian life. The experience of interpreting each issue would

teach the readers the skills the author used to "form an image" of the moment. Readers would be enriched both aesthetically and sociologically.

Separate monthly issues therefore did not depend on a common plot or plots to achieve unity. In this respect, the *Diary* differs from Dostoevsky's novels. To be sure, the *Diary* includes some narratives and, in a loose sense, one may regard the narrator's wanderings as tracing a kind of story. Nevertheless, the "clamps" holding an issue together are not narrative but essentially synchronic.[65] The reader understands an issue by attending to the *resonances*—of themes, images, motifs, and tones—among the parts. The diverse elements within and among articles are not chosen at random. They interact, comment on each other, and invite diverse perspectives on the same set of issues, much as the Christmas party that the narrator attends is then seen by the freezing boy shut out of it. Something like a genre painting (a form that Dostoevsky discusses at length), the *Diary* seizes on a moment out of the flux and "unexpectedly" finds an image in it.

Not just the boy, but time itself is frozen at one of those revealing moments when the world is most like itself. It takes a poetic eye to find and describe such moments, Dostoevsky often observes. A synchronic structure of resonances, each monthly issue of the *Diary* creates a sort of poem out of the most unlikely elements. The subtle wit of the *Diary* depends on this shaping of apparently recalcitrant material.

Taken this way, an issue yields not so much a social "tendency" (annoyed "readers" often interrupt the author to demand just that) but a set of open-ended questions. The author gives us some key themes to consider; in the January 1876 issue, children are obviously a central focus. But instead of specific recommendations or programs, we are presented with a field of possibilities, an interaction of perspectives, and the beginnings of inconclusive dialogues.

A diversity of perspectives is created by treating the same theme or events in diverse genres, each of which yields a different vision. The narrator's own voice contributes to this open-endedness through its complex play of tonalities. Views are advanced both seriously and as the idle comments of an impractical, unsociable dreamer, perhaps even a madman. The author may say something "sublime," which is somehow also so naive as to invite readers' well-deserved skepticism or irony; but that irony may turn back on itself, as it seems to reflect a desiccated heart. Statement, parody of statement, and parody of parody play off each other interminably. The intelligentsia demands a simple tendency or program, but readers of the *Diary* receive an education in moral complexity.

The Unity of the January 1876 Issue: Porcelain Utopia

The "very littlest *preface*" that opens chapter 1 of the January 1876 issue is, as Dostoevsky's letter to Soloviev intimates, a wry and feuilletonistic one, resembling the "Introduction" of 1873. The author begins in mid thought: Nowadays young people seem eaten up with vanity and boredom, a combination that derives from a belief in nothing at all, and so they lie, brag, and sometimes shoot themselves out of unsatisfied pride. Some suicides derive from an even more explicit materialism, as young men despair simply because they have no money for a mistress. The newspapers assure us that such deaths come from "thinking too much" and so find something liberal in all this waste, but there is nothing liberal at all, Dostoevsky opines. In this way, the *Diary* returns us to the key themes of 1873. The present moment is much more complex than the intelligentsia allows, which is implicitly why *A Writer's Diary* is needed.

Do you remember, Dostoevsky then asks his readers, that when Goethe's young Werther killed himself, he regretted that he would never again see his favorite constellation, the Great Bear? This sublime thought expressed his appreciation of "*his image as a human being*" (1/76, 1.1) fashioned by God. But our up-to-date young suicides would probably not even bid farewell to the Small Bear, because that would be "too embarrassing" (that is, somehow reactionary).

By this point, the "astonished reader" from the intelligentsia has become sufficiently provoked to invade the text and inquire just what the author is aiming at:

> "You'd better make clear what your tendency is and what your convictions are. Explain: what sort of man are you, and how did you make so bold as to announce this *Writer's Diary?*"
> But that's very difficult, and I can see that I'm not much of a hand at writing forewords.... As far as liberalism is concerned (instead of the word "tendency" I'll simply use the word "liberalism")... our [Russian] liberalism lately has been transformed everywhere into either a trade or a bad habit.

Because most liberalism comes from habit, perhaps the greatest liberals are those who do not profess liberalism at all. Dostoevsky's rivals in the intelligentsia have "bound themselves up with liberalism as with ropes," and so he may be more liberal (in the sense of open-minded) than they. Thus we arrive at the first of the issue's several paradoxes, illiberal liberals and liberal antagonists of liberalism.

Of course, Dostoevsky concedes, readers are bound to find this foreword unsatisfying, not only because it violates current wisdom but also because it does not conform to conventional forewords for new publications. Only too true, Dostoevsky concedes, but that is all I am capable of doing. And "with that I finish my foreword. I only wrote it for the sake of form, anyway." This metaliterary ending, of course, draws on a different set of conventions, those of the feuilleton, in which playfulness predominates and ideas are qualified by a complex, self-deprecating irony. If we turn from this inconclusive conclusion to the article's title, we will be able to solve the riddle of its separate parts and of the whole uniting them: "In Place of a Foreword. On the Great and Small Bears, on Great Goethe's Prayer, and, Generally, on Bad Habits."

In the next article Dostoevsky informs us that he went to the Christmas party at the artists' club in order "to have a look at the children" (1/76, 1.2). He immediately digresses to tell us of his fascination with children, the theme of his recent novel *A Raw Youth* and of a "future novel" as well. What interests Dostoevsky is children *today*, the ones who grow up in broken, "accidental families" and who may eventually commit murder or suicide out of emptiness.

The author arrives at the Christmas party in the third article, which he describes explicitly as a feuilleton.[66] As is conventional for that form, the author presents himself as a dreamer who, before this party, "had not been to a single social event anywhere for far too long and had been leading a solitary life for a considerable time" (1/76, 1.3). Because he is apt to become overstimulated by this otherwise ordinary experience, the author warns us that he may say something eccentric. In this way, we are both prepared for some sort of visionary experience and given grounds to treat it ironically. Indeed, after offering several impressions of the party, the author yields to two quite contradictory waking dreams. The first projects the hellish possibility perceptible beyond the celebration's ordered forms: suddenly all of this European civilization will be cast to the winds and a good old Russian brawl will begin, because that is what the essence of our lives, and ourselves, really is.

The second vision occupies the chapter's final article, "The Golden Age in Your Pocket" (1/76, 1.4). At the parents' ball following the children's party, the author, reflecting on the vain artifice of the entertainment, has a vision of utopia that might be realized at any moment if only people believed it possible. With dreamy enthusiasm, perhaps traceable to his unaccustomed presence in society, the author exclaims to himself: "Oh, dear guests, I swear that each lady and gentleman among you is cleverer than Voltaire, more sensitive than Rousseau, incomparably more alluring than Alcibiades or Don Juan, or any Lucretia, Juliet, or Beatrice!" If you only could believe and wish it, you all have the power to make everyone happy. "Do you really think that the golden age exists only on porcelain teacups?"

Of course, the author realizes that everyone will laugh at this "paradox," and they are right to do so. On the other hand, perhaps their scorn is as mistaken as his hope: "Don't frown at the words *golden age*, Your Excellency: I give you my word of honor that you won't be compelled to walk around in the costume of the golden age wearing only a fig leaf." On this ambiguous utopian note, the chapter ends. It has moved from images of despair (suicide, accidental families, brawls) to probably impossible hopes, and, in a half-serious tone, it has sketched out a dialogue of responses to ultimate questions as they arise at present.

The issue's second chapter focuses entirely on the suffering of children, a theme that (as in *Karamazov*) comes to stand for all evil. We have already considered the opening sketch about child beggars and the following story, "The Boy at Christ's Christmas Party." In the chapter's third article the author visits a colony of abandoned delinquent children and reports in some detail on the experiments for reforming them. He considers their psychology and wonders about their prospects and future sense of themselves. The article's crucial passage concerns the author's reflections on such experimental institutions, which are so unlike the radical reforms proposed by the intelligentsia. For charity of this sort is routinely held in contempt by those who, guided by a theory, demand nothing less than total, revolutionary change. In response, Dostoevsky suggests that, on the contrary, improvements can only be accomplished prosaically, bit by tiny bit.

To illustrate his point, he tells a story that is key to the argument of the early *Diary*. In the days of serfdom, a certain "humble and quiet little fellow," deeply affected by the evil of serfdom, devoted a lifetime to saving every penny so that, after many years, he could buy a single serf's freedom. By the end of his life he had liberated perhaps three or four people. A member of today's intelligentsia would doubtless dismiss this quixotic project as nonsensical, if not positively harmful: "He's 'an idealist of the forties' and nothing more; perhaps even ridiculous and not very skillful, because he thought that he could struggle against all this evil with only his own petty, individual effort" (1/76, 2.3). But in his feuilletonistic voice Dostoevsky asks us to entertain the opposite possibility, that perhaps this "ridiculous" method for combating evil may, for all its shortcomings, prove more effective than the intelligentsia's radical alternative:

> Yet these are the sort of people we need! I am terribly fond of this ridiculous type of petty official who seriously imagines that he, with his microscopic efforts and stubborn persistence, is capable of aiding the common cause without waiting for some widespread campaign and general initiative. That's the sort of little man who might be very useful in a colony of young offenders as well ...

We note the characteristic play of tones in which Dostoevsky praises an idea he calls "ridiculous."[67] The last article of the second chapter deepens the "paradox" that concludes the first: Is the way to radical change perhaps not radical at all, but prosaic? Is utopia to be achieved by entirely ordinary means, and is "nowhere" to be found right here—"in your pocket"—as the closing article of chapter 1 suggests? The contrast between grand plans and "microscopic efforts" resonates throughout this issue (and later ones).

Unity of the January 1876 Issue: Crafty Devils and Their Advocate

The first two chapters, therefore, both begin with an image of despair and end with a debate about utopia. The issue's third chapter reverses this order and, beginning with utopian speculation, ends where the issue began, on the sterile quarreling of the intelligentsia. Taken as a whole, the January 1876 *Diary* describes a circle, as the reader, having returned to the starting point, has come to understand the present moment more profoundly, if not conclusively.

The first article of chapter 3 contains a series of short vignettes.

They describe cruelty and the current "itch for debauchery" inspired by various materialistic "ideas in the air." Some passages comment on recent institutions (the Russian Society for the Protection of Animals), others draw on Dostoevsky's childhood memories of idealistic dreaming shattered by horrible brutality enacted before his eyes. He at last confides his own utopian hopes: "I do not wish to think and live in any other way than with the belief that all our ninety million Russians (or however many will subsequently be born) will all someday be educated, humanized, and happy" (1/76, 3.1).

The author stresses "someday," not immediately, because the process that could lead to such a result must be gradual. No intelligentsia theory will do it: what is needed is "microscopic efforts." Or, as this article phrases the hope, it will happen bit by bit as each person learns to "image himself" (*obrazit'*), a folk expression meaning to establish the human shape in oneself.[68] Implicitly, we must learn to do what the *Diary* does, examine chaos (*bezobrazie*) and humanely shape ourselves by countless tiny efforts. The last item in this article's long title asks, "From the End or from the Beginning?" This question turns out to refer to the need "to begin taking action not always from the end but, partly at least, from the beginning." That is, it is best not to work backward from the theorist's utopia but forward from prosaic efforts at self-improvement and "self-imaging."

The chapter's second article may well be considered the *Diary*'s most interesting piece of semifiction: "Spiritualism. Something about Devils. The Extraordinary Cleverness of Devils, If Only These Are Devils." Anticipating the devil chapter in *Karamazov*, this article employs a dizzying range of tones to recast the monthly issue's key themes—belief and skepticism, utopia and despair, lost children, open time—and numerous other echoes of earlier motifs. Characteristically for the *Diary*, an ostensible topic, the aristocratic craze for table turning, becomes a superb starting point for understanding the driving concerns of the present moment.

So many people seem to believe in spiritualism nowadays that there must be something to it, Dostoevsky muses; why, "Gogol writes to Moscow from the next world and states positively that devils exist. I read the letter, and the style is his" (1/76, 3.2). At least, something vital must be at stake, or why would a whole scientific committee, headed by the chemist Dmitri Mendeleev, have been established to discredit spiritualism? This committee is itself paradoxical, Dostoevsky observes, because if its method were truly empirical it would have to be able to keep an open mind about the question while investigating it, or else its members would be as prejudiced and unscientific as the spiritualists themselves. Yet it is unlikely that even a single member of the committee could even entertain the possibility that devils exist, "despite the fact that a terrific number of people who do not believe in God still believe in the Devil, readily and happily."[69]

As for me, Dostoevsky observes with irony upon irony, I cannot believe in the spirits, but, at the same time, I have developed a wonderful and convincing theory in defense of them. With this ambiguous introduction, Dostoevsky embraces the traditionally paradoxical role of devil's (or devils') advocate. According to Dostoevsky, who assures us too often that he is only joking, the antispiritualists place great weight on the fact that these supposed spirits never seem to reveal anything not known before, whereas real devils, they say, would prove their existence by imparting some great discovery. And so, the antispiritualists conclude, there cannot be spirits, just some sort of fraud, because any spirits who did not prove their existence would have to be awfully stupid. But this conclusion, Dostoevsky observes, depends on a significant mistake. It is precisely out of great intelligence that shrewd devils would confine themselves to trivialities. The poor devils are being abused for nothing!

For what if the devils were to tell us where to dig for coal— "firewood, incidentally, is such a price these days"—or reveal to humanity every conceivable great invention? What if they were to make possible the most utopian dreams? At first, of course, everyone would be in raptures and bless the devils, for we would have everything that "our Russian socialists" dream of. "Corrupting environment" would be at an end, and with it, all misery and all crime. Alas, these raptures would rapidly turn into bitterness. People would realize that with everything given to them, with nothing produced by their own efforts, and with no uncertainty left in the world, life itself would have been taken away. Without freedom, people would have lost their "human image":

> People would realize that there is no happiness in inactivity, that the mind which does not labor will wither, that it is not possible to love one's neighbor without sacrificing something to him of one's own labor, that it is vile to live at the expense of another, and that *happiness lies not in happiness but only in the attempt to achieve it.*

Even if we could have it, utopia provided from above—from the end—would resemble hell. Whatever our socialists or skeptics say, an improved society must come, if at all, "from the beginning," by our own gradual effort. What is more, time must remain open. There must be genuine uncertainty for freedom to exist, for work to be meaningful, and for people to live a human existence. Dostoevsky's anti-utopian article here returns to the issue's key themes.

It follows for Dostoevsky that people provided with such a utopia sooner or later would rebel (like Dostoevsky's underground man) and would renounce the baneful gift. The devils would at last be rejected, this time forever. Foreseeing all this, the extraordinarily crafty spirits will not make such a grave tactical error. Instead, they perform just a few trivial tricks. By inducing some to believe and others to ridicule the believers, the devils set people at odds with each other, for nothing so advances their plan as discord. The more people are mocked (by Mendeleev and his kind) for believing in devils, the more they will insist on believing in them.

Returning to the theme of children, Dostoevsky then tells a story about a person who would not accept definitive proof that pictures of his dead children's spirits were frauds, because, the disconsolate parent explains, these are the only pictures of them that he has. The more he is ridiculed, the more irrational things he will say, Dostoevsky observes. It is a strange psychological fact, which the devils understand, that nothing inclines one to belief more than public scorn or persecution. "Every such persecuted idea is like that petroleum which the arsonists poured over the floors and walls of the Tuileries before the fire. . . . Oh, the devils know the force of a forbidden faith . . . !"

Here Dostoevsky delineates another implicit theme of the issue, one that lies behind all approaches to evil: what is it that compels belief? For the most fundamental beliefs—what inclines people to atheism or religion, socialist change "from the end" or prosaic reform "from the beginning"—have nothing to do with evidence, nothing that a Mendeleev could address. Whatever shapes our way of seeing the world, it resists argument. Indeed, Dostoevsky muses, that is true of Mendeleev's own faith in materialist science, too. In one of his most whimsical musings, the author wonders what would happen if, for instance, the devils were to levitate Mendeleev himself? How would he then maintain his prior beliefs? The empiricist would be confronted by an actual fact and on scientific grounds would be called upon to renounce science itself, a sort of version of the Cretan liar's paradox. The implication, of course, is that Mendeleev would find some way to deny the fact and maintain his irrational faith in the rational.

Throughout this entire sequence of paradoxes, Dostoevsky keeps insisting that he is joking in every word, only to concede that, perhaps, there may be something serious here. After all, if people's basic ideas cannot be changed by argument, then what is the point of a monthly, or any other publication? Immune to disconfirmation, are all beliefs, perhaps, unreliable? As if to illustrate this point, the chapter's third article points out a series of egregious errors in a recent biographical account of Dostoevsky composed by one of his radical opponents.

The chapter's fourth article, which concludes the January 1876 issue, mirrors the opening. The foreword that is no foreword is answered by a concluding promise that is no promise, as the author once again "fails" to define his publication:

> 4. A Turkish Proverb
>
> Just in passing, I will insert a Turkish proverb (a real one—I haven't made it up): If you set off to a certain goal and keep stopping along the way to throw stones at every dog that barks at you, you will never reach your destination.
>
> As far as possible, I'll follow the advice of that wise proverb in my *Diary*, although I wouldn't want to tie myself down with promises beforehand. (1/76, 3.4)

In short, the first monthly issue of the *Diary* creates complex resonances among a number of themes, which are refracted through the sensibilities of diverse genres. Children are treated in feuilleton, reportage, and story. Utopian and anti-utopian sketches enter into dialogue with each other. Through an array of voices and across a variety of topics, author and "readers" frame a complex debate about evil and its cures. No sooner do we identify the author's position than he qualifies and requalifies it with unexpected applications or unstable ironies. Cross-references and thematic echoes interact with a hierarchical structure to produce a complex poetic artifact. A set of questions is defined and a field of possibilities evoked; we sense a direction, but no conclusive answers.

It appears that, as originally designed, the *Diary* was to produce such an odd unity of heterogeneous tones and forms in each monthly issue. The February *Diary* creates a similar structure, in which "The Peasant Marey" corresponds to "The Boy," while an opening article, which comments on the reception of the January issue, introduces the author's inconclusive, self-referential narrative voice. The first chapter, in which the reminiscence of "Marey" solves Aksakov's riddle, contrasts theories about the people with Dostoevsky's own experience of them; in the second chapter, on the Kroneberg case, a lawyer's all-purpose rhetoric obscures the truth about a particular child. On the whole, the February issue traces a complex dialogue about theories, abstractions, and their all-too-frequent abuse. In the March *Diary* a series of variations on "dissociation" defines the thematic dialogue, while "A Hundred-Year-Old Woman" provides the fictional pivot. All three issues filter related concerns through a diversity of genres, held together in a hierarchical structure and a series of often surprising resonances.

The Brothers Karamazov = *A Writer's Diary* + Plot

When Dostoevsky suspended the *Diary* to write the promised "future novel," *Karamazov,* he brought his new way of organizing heterogeneous material with him. In many respects, *Karamazov* may be viewed as a combination of the plotting techniques developed in his earlier novels with the *Diary*'s essentially poetic hierarchy of resonances. Like the *Diary,* Dostoevsky's last novel explicitly includes a great diversity of genres, often labeled by their traditional names in the table of contents. As in the *Diary,* each theme is filtered through radically divergent traditional forms, which are all linked together and set in dialogue with each other. And as in the *Diary,* it is not just people but whole genres, each conveying a distinct sense of the world, that speak to each other. Each traditional form, understood as a view of experience and a particular way of speaking, enters into the novel's ideological symposium.

Thus *Karamazov* includes a formal disputation ("The Controversy"), a sermon, a family chronicle, various kinds of speeches, a parable ("An Onion"), "confessions" in verse and in anecdote, "exhortations," a dream vision, and a menippean satire (Ivan's conversation with the devil), to name just a few of the most obvious examples. The Grand Inquisitor story, as we have seen, begins with a lengthy "preface" about the various genres to which it might belong. The novel's foreword, "From the Author," which apologizes for its failure as a proper foreword, recalls the feuilletonistic anti-prefaces of the *Diary*'s opening articles of 1873 and 1876. "Well, there is the whole foreword," the narrator of *Karamazov* concludes.

"I completely agree that it is needless, but since it has already been written, let it stand" (*BK*, xviii).

Karamazov resembles *A Writer's Diary* with a plot. If one turns to the novel's table of contents, one will see four "parts," each divided into three "books," which are in turn broken into several separately titled chapters. As in the *Diary*, this hierarchical organization encourages the reader to find thematic connections among the particular chapters that make up a book, and then among the books. Each book resembles an issue (or chapter) of the *Diary*, as various incidents, often told in distinct tones or genres, develop resonances among a common theme or set of motifs.

For example, Book 4, "Lacerations," invites us to trace the symbolic parallels among diverse kinds of wounds: physical lacerations (Alyosha's bitten finger, Father Ferapont's mortified flesh) echo with diverse psychological "lacerations" (proud, self-destructive self-indulgence). The fourth book of *Karamazov* creates a kind of prose poem about the wounded human body and spirit. As we have seen, this organizational method, which is used in no earlier novel of Dostoevsky's, was developed in *A Writer's Diary*.[70]

To link its twelve books with each other, *Karamazov* relies on a carefully paced plot. That option was not available for *A Writer's Diary*, which, designed as a periodical, was supposed to be open to whatever might happen in the real world. Dostoevsky surrendered his control over the future of his publication to genuine contingency, a kind of openness that in fact constituted part of the work's appeal. What, then, was to take the place of a preplanned plot in ensuring unity among the issues?

The *Diary*'s Second Unifying Principle: Literature As Heuristic, or Why Success Requires Failure

Across issues, the unity of the *Diary* was to be ensured in a quite different way. Because a poetic design clearly could not work across time on unpredictable material, the synchronic unity of each issue was to be combined with a different principle, which might best be understood as a unity of *procedure*. It was a set of techniques that was to remain constant, and the reader would witness the author trying to apply those techniques to the world's contingency.

As the author tried to build a coherent structure out of unpredictable events, he would adapt the devices exhibited in the opening issues to new material drawn from the changing current of Russian life. Time would provide challenges for the author, and the reader would be admitted to a sort of contest between art and time. Contingency would set problems, and the *Diary* would be the record of their attempted solution. Considerable excitement would be generated by the uncertainty of the contest itself, inasmuch as it was by no means guaranteed that the author would always win.

I once called this technique "literature as algorithm," but I now regard that terminological choice as less than optimal.[71] Strictly speaking, an algorithm is a method guaranteed to yield a correct solution, but no such guarantee exists for the author of the *Diary*. On the contrary, a kind of suspense results from the *resistance* that reality offers to the artist's methods. Perhaps a better term for the work's procedural regularity would be *literature as heuristic*. (A heuristic is a method well adapted to solving a problem but not certain to do so. It is, like Dostoevsky's set of techniques, a shrewd guess based on experience.)

It follows that not every issue of the *Diary* had to be perfect for the work to fulfill its design. Suspense, indeed, requires some imperfection, or where is the contest? This, then, is another oddity of *A Writer's Diary*: to succeed it had to fail sometimes. Unlike other literary forms, the *Diary* not only could tolerate occasional failures but demanded them. They provide the excitement that makes the author's successes all the more interesting. I know of no Russian work whose *design* incorporates flaws in this way. Of course, the failures would have to be interesting in their own right. Moreover, they would have had to be flaws of a certain sort, specified by the design itself. Still more important, they could not occur *too* frequently, or the design itself would be obscured.

This, then, is the formal radicalism of *A Writer's Diary*: it was designed to be a real, not merely a represented, series of difficult encounters of artistic insight with genuine contingency.

Part 4: How and Why Dostoevsky Abandoned His Design

Time as a Field: The Extraordinary Variety of Events, If Only They Are Events

The *Diary* was designed to accommodate only a certain kind of "failure," which its design would lead one to expect. But it could not succeed if readers were unable to perceive the design itself, and, unfortunately, they usually did not. As we have seen, it is a lot easier to perceive the lineaments of Dostoevsky's new genre if one does not read too far beyond the first half dozen issues or so. After that, the *Diary* does indeed often look less like an integral literary work than a record of its author's obsessions. Readers, therefore, understandably have treated it as a grab bag and, extracting its best parts, have read them out of the context of the work. Although these parts are compelling, the *Diary* as a whole turned out to be a failure. Why?

The main reason, I think, is that Dostoevsky himself did not keep to his original plan. He abandoned it because he came to reject the very ideas that gave rise to it. The *Diary*'s design was not fulfilled because of a change in Dostoevsky's philosophy. What remained was the empty shell of the work as originally conceived.

A Writer's Diary grew out of a quite specific sense of time and of social experience. To use Bakhtin's phrase, it was shaped by a complex "form-shaping ideology."[72] But in the course of 1876 and 1877, Dostoevsky came to reject the outlook for whose expression the *Diary* was invented. He accepted in its place a sense of time and social experience radically incompatible with the work's original design, and he was apparently unable to adapt the *Diary*'s form to alien purposes. It is no wonder, then, that even perceptive readers have been unable to read the work as a coherent whole. Bakhtin calls such an unresolvable conflict between an author's purposes and a genre's form-shaping ideology the "tragedy of a genre."[73] As the term tragedy implies, such a defeat is itself both riveting and instructive.

Let us consider in turn the two core ideas of the *Diary* that Dostoevsky came to abandon. Neither *sideshadowing* (a way of imagining time as open) nor the *prosaic* (a particular vision of everyday experience) could be accommodated to the apocalyptic mentality that gripped Dostoevsky when the Eastern Question intensified. Both these ideas run counter to apocalypticism in every important respect.[74]

We have seen that the January 1876 issue, which first realized Dostoevsky's design, displays an encyclopedia of genres and tones. But one voice that is notably absent from it is that of the convinced prophet, seriously predicting the historical future and the end of history. Inasmuch as the *Diary* embraces so many voices, it might have included some element of prophecy, so long as the prophetic remained but one element among many and was conditioned by

the larger ironies of the whole. But when the prophetic voice came
to predominate, the *Diary* as originally designed disappeared from
view.

Let us first consider sideshadowing and the *Diary*'s original conception of time. The temporality that shaped the *Diary*'s design
was above all open. Time was understood as rich in diverse potentials and as allowing for many possible outcomes. Of course,
not just anything could happen in the world or to particular people.
But it is clear that at least several possibilities always present themselves. To understand a moment is to recognize a multiplicity of
trajectories.

In Dostoevsky's view, the intelligentsia commits a grave mistake
when it imagines time as singular (having only one path) and linear
(leading directly to its inevitable outcome). By "linearity," a term
of reproach that appears often in the *Diary*, Dostoevsky means the
sort of determinism or fatalism so brilliantly mocked by the narrator
of *Notes from Underground*. Like the diarist in the spiritualism
sketch, the underground man maintains that if all-explanatory historical laws do exist, as his fashionable opponents contend, then
meaningful human life becomes impossible. True life depends on
choice and real effort demands uncertainty, but deterministic linearity leaves no room for either. If the underlying laws of time
should ever be discovered, then people will foresee the inevitable
future, and if that happens, events to come will in effect have
already happened. If the linear thinkers should prove correct, then
what lies in our future is no future at all: "All human actions will
then, of course, be tabulated according to these laws, mathematically, like tables of logarithms up to 108,000, and entered in a
table; or, better still, there would be published certain edifying
works like the present encyclopedic lexicons, in which everything
will be so clearly calculated and designated that there will be no
more incidents or adventures in the world" (*NFU*, 22). "Logarithmic" time necessarily destroys human responsibility and freedom. Whether reflected in the theory of "the corrupting
environment" or in the dreams of the socialists, the denial of time's
openness takes away our "human image."

The underground man and the author of the *Diary* also argue
that the image of "one possibility" grossly oversimplifies the world
we actually experience. "One may say anything about the history
of the world—anything that might enter the most disordered imagination," declares the underground man. "The only thing one cannot say is that it is rational" (*NFU*, 27). The assumption that

history is rational leads people to overlook whatever does not fit a preconceived pattern and so to misconstrue the world in front of them. Though ostensibly derived from "science," linearity leads one to overlook crucial empirical facts. For this reason, Dostoevsky characteristically constructs *Diary* articles about perplexing social events by first providing the received "linear" description favored by the intelligentsia and then offering a contrasting, infinitely richer, "nonlinear" account. Dostoevsky's description, as he frequently observes, depends on seeing multiple possibilities.

As previously noted, the January 1876 issue begins by raising the question of suicide in this contrasting way. In his articles on specific suicide cases, crimes, and ongoing trials, Dostoevsky typically argues that all the important facts, whether psychological, moral, or social, become visible only when one sees time and people as open to multiple possible developments.

Between the concepts of sheer randomness and of pure linearity lies a sense of time as allowing for many, though not all, outcomes. To comprehend a moment is to discern the *field* of possibilities it contains. It is to see the multiple *potentials* that may *or may not* be developed. The future will develop some potentials but not others, and it is impossible to know in advance which direction time will take. Indeed, it is exceedingly difficult even to perceive the set of possible directions. But that is the defining purpose of *A Writer's Diary*.

The *Diary* enacts a process of temporal discernment practiced monthly. Its status as a periodical (and as a diary) derives from its central concern with time. The author assumes the role of investigator into the potentials of each present moment. He therefore locates telling phenomena, passes them through diverse genres, and imagines possible continuations. He explores the "might-have-beens" and "might-bes": that is the role of fictions and semifictions, which describe *other possibilities*. In his commentary on recent events, Dostoevsky explicitly stresses the conceivability of multiple stories that could emerge from the same set of incidents.

This method, first imagined by Shatov and Liza Nikolaevna in *The Possessed* and at last realized in the complex form of the *Diary*, makes sense only if time is in fact genuinely open. To be meaningful, the *Diary*'s method also presupposes that reality is so elusive and chaotic that discernment of the moment's potentials must be difficult. Temporal astuteness demands keen insight and the ability to take risks. The *Diary* therefore dramatizes a form of shrewd guesswork.

Longing for the Present

Dostoevsky defends this view of the present in several *Diary* articles. In fact, it was of central concern to him more generally. The idea of time as an elusive field of possibilities appears in his notebooks and surfaces prominently in his novel *A Raw Youth*, which was written between the 1873 and 1876 portions of the *Diary*. Dostoevsky thought of his willingness to tackle the unformed present, where lines of development had not set, as the distinguishing mark of his work.

While Dostoevsky was publishing the *Diary*, he responded to a letter that accused him of wasting his gifts on mere trifles from current life (*Pis'ma* 3:205). Dostoevsky replied that such "trifles" were essential to his activity as a writer, both in the novel he was planning (*Karamazov*) and in the *Diary* itself. He then digresses to describe a recent meeting with Goncharov, in which that writer disclaimed any interest in "current reality" because great art, according to Goncharov, cannot be made out of what is still formless. But that is precisely what Dostoevsky tried to do.[75]

In Dostoevsky's view, the reason that present reality is likely to appear formless is that it is open: one does not know which of its possibilities will be realized, and what social forms will emerge from this multiplicity. For such knowledge, one needs to contemplate a moment from a temporal distance. That is one reason that the tutor to whom Arkady, the hero of *A Raw Youth*, sends his narrative advises him to write on historical themes, especially the life of the Russian nobility. Aristocratic forms of life have long been set, the tutor points out, and it is consequently easy to write beautiful or edifying descriptions of them. But if one focuses on a current hero, who may come from an "accidental family," then the narrative

> can have no beauty of form. Moreover, these types are in any case transitory, and so a novel about them cannot have artistic finish. One may make serious mistakes, exaggerations, misjudgments. In any case one would have to guess too much. But what is the writer to do who doesn't want to confine himself to the historical form, and is possessed by a longing for the present? To guess...and make mistakes.[76]

This passage, and Dostoevsky's dialogue with Goncharov, are often interpreted as Dostoevsky's defense of his favorite subject matter: characters from classes other than the nobility who display a precarious sociopsychological identity. Robert Louis Jackson has also

brilliantly pointed to Dostoevsky's project of creating a special
"kind of beauty" out of the "image of imagelessness," which led
to a quintessentially Dostoevskian aesthetics of the ugly and "poetics of the underground." These readings are surely correct, but
they do not exhaust the matter. In speaking of the transitional and
the historical, Dostoevsky was concerned as well with *temporality*
itself—with the "guesses" necessarily involved in comprehending
the present moment.

The writer "possessed by a longing for the present" must understand *presentness.* He must grasp the moment in all its openness
and formlessness, without imposing an "inevitable" future or sub-
stituting a finished picture from the past. In the *Diary*'s article
"The Boy Celebrating His Saint's Day" (1/77, 2.5), Dostoevsky
contrasts a scene from Tolstoy's *Boyhood,* in which a child contem-
plates suicide, with a recent case in which a boy actually killed
himself. After dismissing the usual sort of linear and liberal interpretation of the recent incident, Dostoevsky focuses on the difference between the present and the time described by Tolstoy. In
Tolstoy's world, *actually* committing suicide did not belong to a
young person's set of possibilities, but for today's youth it does.
"The fact is that . . . [in the recent case] there are also features of
a new sort of reality quite different from that of the placid, middle-
stratum Moscow landowning family whose way of life had long
been solidly established and whose *historian* is our Count Leo
Tolstoy."

Class is surely part of Dostoevsky's point, but I think he is no
less concerned with time. That is why he italicizes the word *historian,* which takes on pejorative connotations. Twice more in this
article Dostoevsky uses and italicizes this word, with mounting
irony. By choosing to represent the past, the author of *War and
Peace* has avoided the much more difficult task of investigating the
present. From this perspective, indeed, the question of class is
itself one of time, because even the present life of the nobility (say,
of the heroes of *Anna Karenina*) is relatively remote from the seething ferment of unformed possibilities that characterize the openness
of the current moment.[77]

And who, Dostoevsky asks, will be the *"historian"* of the present,
of the chaos reigning in all those "other corners" of life that seem
to shape the ethos of the moment? "And if, within this chaos that
has gone on for so long and that is particularly prevalent in the
life of our society now,—a life in which, perhaps, even an artist

of Shakespearean proportions cannot find a normative law and a guiding thread—who, then, will illuminate even a little part of this chaos, never mind dreaming of some guiding thread?" Of course, the answer to this question is Dostoevsky himself. The form perhaps best adapted to finding the "guiding thread" is implicitly the very work in which this article appears, *A Writer's Diary.*

Presentness and Pastness

To represent the present is for Dostoevsky altogether different from representing the past. We live through the present uncertainly, without knowing where it will lead, but the past is given to us in memory, which makes a radical experiential difference. As Dostoevsky points out, memory necessarily includes knowledge of what happened after the remembered event. Not only do we see the past in temporal perspective but we cannot help doing so, whereas the present cannot be seen that way. It therefore must not be described as if it were already past; it demands a completely different approach. The qualitative difference between the past and the present is central to the design of the *Diary,* conceived as a work monitoring the moment *as* it happens.

In "Apropos of the Exhibition" (73.9), Dostoevsky raises these issues while considering genre painting, a form he regards as close to the *Diary* itself. It might seem that no obstacle exists to genre paintings that depict everyday scenes from the past, but in fact such efforts necessarily lead to radical incoherence and the confusion of distinct *kinds* of temporality.

> What is genre [painting], in essence? Genre is the art of portraying contemporary, immediate reality that the artist has himself felt personally and has seen with his own eyes, in contrast with historical reality, which cannot be seen with one's own eyes and which is portrayed not in its immediate but in its completed aspect . . . Historical reality in art, for instance, is naturally not that of immediate reality (genre) precisely because the former is completed and not current.

The present is not "completed" in that one does not know what may come of it, and that incompleteness is essential to our experience of presentness. Genre is the art of capturing that sense of the ongoing moment. Quite different techniques must be employed to represent the past, which is necessarily known as "completed."

There can be no more radical distinction than that between open and closed time. To be sure, Dostoevsky concedes, some have tried to paint the past as genre, but such attempts can lead to nothing but a shallow notoriety. For these paintings involve a "confusion of conceptions of reality" and rely on a falsity. This falsity pertains to a past offered as if subsequent events had not followed.

> Ask any psychologist you like and he will tell you that if you imagine some event of the past, especially of the distant past,--one that is completed and historical (and to live without imagining the past is impossible)—then the event will *necessarily* be imagined in its completed aspect, i.e., with the addition of all its subsequent developments that had not yet occurred at the historical moment in which the artist is trying to depict a person or event. And thus the essence of a historical event cannot even be imagined by an artist exactly as it probably happened in reality.

Accurate representation of the past is impossible because each past moment was open: it was actually just another present moment. It had the potential to lead in directions other than the one actually realized. But we do not *experience* the past, we *remember* it, and memory alters the past by closing it down. We remember what did happen, not what might have; we remember what led to where we are now. Events that have happened lose the presentness they had and acquire pastness, which is quite a different thing.

According to Dostoevsky, a remembered event necessarily includes within the event itself the future that had not yet happened and need not have happened. Memory therefore forecloses the possibility that something else might have happened. Our intellect may tell us that time was open then just as it is now, but our actual experience of the past, through memory, includes one and only one subsequent course of events. In short, *memory necessarily involves foreshadowing*, the importing of the future into the past. It must therefore falsify the past, which did not somehow include the future that happened to have resulted from it.[78] Realized possibility is falsely, but unavoidably, perceived as necessity.

Freedom is an attribute of presentness. We cannot imagine the people of the past as truly free, as we directly experience our own freedom, even if we know they were no less free than we are. In Dostoevsky's view, past events cannot be endowed with the attributes of presentness. Any attempt to "combine both realities—the historical and the immediate" therefore creates an "unnatural combination," from which "arises the worst kind of untruth." Dostoevsky's example is Ge's shocking genre painting of "The Last Supper":

> There sits Christ—but is that Christ? It may be a very good young
> man, deeply hurt by his quarrel with Judas ... but this is not the
> Christ we know. ... we must ask the question: where are the eighteen
> centuries of Christianity that followed, and how are they connected
> with the event? How is it possible that from such an ordinary quarrel
> of such ordinary people gathered to have supper, such as Mr. Ge
> depicts, there could arise something so colossal?
>
> Nothing at all is explained here; there is no historical truth here;
> there is not even any truth of genre here; everything here is false. ...
> everything here is disproportionate and out of scale with the future.

As Dostoevsky was well aware, these very questions are discussed
at great length in *War and Peace*, and Dostoevsky's comments on
genre painting implicitly initiate the *Diary*'s several dialogues with
Tolstoy. Up to a point, the two writers agree with each other and
disagree with almost everyone else. In the embedded essays of *War
and Peace*, Tolstoy also distinguishes between our experience of
the present, which is open, and of the past, which memory and
narrative history falsely represent as having led inevitably to where
we are right now. A sort of temporal analogue to an optical illusion
leads us unwittingly to overlook the presentness of each past moment. "It is this consideration," Tolstoy observes, "that makes the
fall of the first man, resulting in the birth of the human race,
appear patently less free than a man's entry into wedlock today.
It is the reason why the life and activity of men who lived centuries
ago and are connected with me in time cannot seem to me as free
as the life of a contemporary, the consequences of which are still
unknown to me."[79] If I examine an action performed a moment
ago, Tolstoy explains, it seems unquestionably free, but if I recall
one performed ten years ago, the consequences may be so plain
that "I find it hard to imagine what would have happened had that
action not been performed" (*W&P*, 1444–45). Thus a contemporary
event appears to us the work of its participants, "but in the case
of a more remote event, we see only its inevitable consequences,
which prevent our considering anything else possible" (*W&P*,
1445). Historical writing magnifies the distortions of memory, according to Tolstoy's famous argument.

In other essays Tolstoy repeatedly contrasts the openness of each
moment of battle, in which "a hundred million chances" and
choices can shape countless outcomes, with the neat narratives
written by "the historians." Almost without exception, historians
read their own present into the past as if only one outcome had

been possible all along. They commit several temporal fallacies, most notably "the fallacy of retrospection, which [mis]represents all the past as a preparation for future events" (*W&P,* 854).

Dostoevsky's argument also coincides with Tolstoy's well-known dramatizations of the effects of memory. In Tolstoy's view, memory "imperceptibly, unconsciously, and inevitably" (*W&P,* 298) leads even the most truthful people into falsehood, and for the very reasons that Dostoevsky was later to repeat. In *War and Peace* Tolstoy often describes events and then, a few hundred pages later, describes characters' recollections of them, which differ considerably from what actually happened. His most brilliant touch is to have his characters introduce the very same distortions that the readers themselves have unconsciously made. Unless we go back to the original passage, we may not notice the character's error. As Tolstoy depicts it, memory reprocesses the messiness of reality, with its loose ends and multiple possible outcomes, by shaping it into a good story.[80]

Tolstoy developed a number of remarkably complex devices to counter the distorting effects of memory. He wanted to represent the past as it was experienced, in all its presentness. For him, the obstacles Dostoevsky mentions served as challenges to be overcome. It would take us too far afield to explore Tolstoy's methods, but it is worth mentioning that at least one of them recalls Dostoevsky's "monthly publication." In an essay published while *War and Peace* was being serialized, Tolstoy explains that he is publishing each part of his book without knowing what will happen next to his fictional characters. For him as for them, the future will be unknown and open to multiple possibilities. Otherwise he would unwittingly impose the subsequent events he has in mind and so be false to the experience of the characters. Serialization was therefore not just the way in which Tolstoy happened to publish *War and Peace*; it was essential to its design. It is quite possible that this idea exercised an important influence on Dostoevsky's *Diary.*

Dostoevsky, however, took Tolstoy's innovation one step further and used periodical publication to portray current, not past, events. The dramatic attempt to discern by reportage the shape of time as it passes and so to fashion stories catching the throb of the present would take place before the readers' eyes, month by month, *even as* society changed. For Dostoevsky, Tolstoy's past-centered device, like Ge's painting, necessarily involved an essential falsity. Thus, although Tolstoy and Dostoevsky agreed about time, they differed about the artistic consequences of their shared position. Tolstoy sought ways to endow the past with presentness; Dostoevsky developed ways of describing the present as it unfolds.

We may perhaps attribute these different solutions to differing conceptions of realism. For Dostoevsky, realism dictated that the past must be represented as we (now) experience it, in all its *pastness*, shaped by memory of what came later. The past has pastness because it is known only through memory. We must be true to our experience, however distorting. For Tolstoy, realism demanded that the past be represented as the people of the past experienced it, in all the *presentness* it then possessed, which meant that the effects of our memories of what came later must somehow be thought away. We must be true to the experience of *others*, however much it differs from our own intuitions. Agreeing about the eternal openness of time as it passes, they disagreed about the artist's proper response.

Sideshadowing

In order to represent the present moment in all its openness and "incompleteness," the *Diary* makes frequent use of the device that I have called *sideshadowing*. Sideshadowing was essential to the work's original design.

Sideshadowing may be understood as an opposite of *foreshadowing*, which embodies a sense of time as closed. When a narrative relies on *fore*shadowing, it establishes a radical divergence between the heroes, who do not know what will happen to them, and the reader, who can read signs of the future unavailable to the characters. The hero experiences a world of choice and chance that allows for many possible futures, but the reader sees the shadow cast by coming events that have already been determined, in a sense already happened. *Oedipus the King* offers only the most dramatic example of the kind of narrative irony made possible by this difference between reader's (or author's) time and characters' time. That irony depends on our awareness that the story is already over, already written down in the text we are reading or seeing performed. Foreshadowing works by reminding us of the structure of the whole that predetermines the significance and outcome of each moment.

In foreshadowing, the reader, though not the hero, understands that the future is already present in the present. To use Dostoevsky's terms, foreshadowing treats present moments as already "completed." Robbed of their presentness, they are viewed as somehow already over, as simply the past of the inevitable future that the author has made available to the reader. When foreshadowing is used, the difference between time in the making and time already made, between "genre" and "history," is obliterated. That is why foreshadowing creates the sense of time as closed.

By contrast, *sideshadowing* treats time as truly open. Wherever we might be tempted to see one path, it projects the possibility of two or more that might just as well have happened. If *fore*shadowing allows the shadow of an inevitable future to be cast on the present, *side*shadowing allows us to see that even the present did not have to be what it is. A shadow is cast from the side, from *another possible present* that might just as well have been. Two or more alternative presents are made visible, the possible and the actual. The actual is therefore understood as just another possibility that somehow came to pass. With sideshadowing, we see not only what did happen but what might have happened. In a peculiar form of simultaneity, time itself acquires a double.

Sideshadowing counters our tendency to view current events as inevitable products of the past. Just because one possibility was realized to the exclusion of incompatible alternatives does not mean that those alternatives *could not* have been realized. In allowing us to catch a glimpse of those unrealized possibilities, sideshadowing demonstrates that our tendency to trace straight lines of causality oversimplifies events, which may allow for *many possible stories*. However coherent and apparently necessary is the sequence we know, that necessity is an illusion. What happened did not have to happen, and whatever exists, including ourselves, might not have existed. Sideshadowing therefore induces a kind of temporally based humility.

To understand a given moment is to understand not just what did happen but what else *might* have happened. Sideshadowing leads us into the subjunctive and the contrary-to-fact conditional; it implicitly insists on the wisdom of those tenses, which correctly project a ramifying temporality. The present we know is one of many possible presents. Many futures may follow from any moment.

Sideshadowing may also be projected backward to suggest that we may be the product of a past different from the one we imagine.

Or at least we could have been. Many routes led here, and they each had their own trajectory, which means that the "same" present may tend to different futures. Varying pasts endow the present with different vectors and different ranges of possibilities to come.

Whether applied to past, present, or future, sideshadowing multiplies stories. Each moment in time is understood as containing not just one but a whole *field of possibilities.* To understand a moment is to understand that whole *field* and not just the particular one of its possibilities that happens to be realized. Sideshadowing creates a sense of time's openness and "incompleteness" by making potentialities visible.

In works that use sideshadowing, the plot that is enacted becomes but one of many possible plots.[81] In the story the author narrates, we glimpse a complexity of myriad stories sustainable by the same material. It as if we were privy to the author's notebooks before he had chosen a particular course of events or as if we could somehow read through the final plot to glimpse all the alternatives simultaneously. Or perhaps it is as if we were somehow admitted to a writer's laboratory or allowed to read a writer's diary.

Sideshadowing inheres in the very conception of Dostoevsky's new genre, which allows us to see stories in the process of creation. *A Writer's Diary* shimmers from the shadows of possible stories, stories not yet written or perhaps never to be written. It hints at the other plots for stories it does include, and we sense, from the detailed descriptions of real events on which the stories are based, the possibility of various outcomes. The *Diary*'s technique of allowing us to see stories in creation, of seeing diverse possibilities emerge from the same material, represents only one type of sideshadowing inherent in Dostoevsky's experimental new form.

Both before and after he published the *Diary,* Dostoevsky made frequent use of sideshadowing. His penchant for this device reflects his deeply held belief in human freedom and his desire to render it *palpable* to the reader. Dostoevsky knew that logical argument would never provide convincing proof that determinism and a linear sense of time are false, just as nothing would ever convince Mendeleev to believe in the supernatural. Determinism was accepted by the intelligentsia on faith, as the only view that made sense. But Dostoevsky hoped to provide a special sort of *novelistic* proof: what he called "a live image" of a different sense of the world.

To do so, he had to jettison the structure of a well-made novel that makes the outcome seem inevitable. He needed the exact opposite, a plot that depended on a directly experienced sense of freedom and uncertainty. In this way, readers would have a palpable alternative to determinism, and they could ask which image of time corresponds more closely to their own experience. The underground man could only raise clever objections to logarithmic time, but Dostoevsky turned to the more powerful technique of a directly experienced alternative.

In his novels Dostoevsky therefore developed complex methods of sideshadowing to create the sense of a world rife with possibilities. The *Diary*, as a new form to be set literally in the ongoing present, was apparently designed to capitalize on these methods by placing them in the foreground and making them the work's defining purpose. In a new genre that took the form of a periodical, the openness of the world would not just be reflected in the work but would directly shape it.

Sideshadowing in Dostoevsky's Fiction: Clouds of Story

Let us first consider some examples of sideshadowing in Dostoevsky's fiction. In order to relieve their boredom, several characters in *The Possessed* go to visit the mad "prophet" Semyon Yakovlevich. Having completed a lengthy description of the journey and the visit itself, the narrator unexpectedly announces that none of these events are important. "At this point, however, there took place, I am told, an extremely enigmatic incident, and, I must own, it was chiefly on account of it that that I have described this expedition so minutely" (*Possessed*, 341). Here as elsewhere, the narrator of *The Possessed* typically gives us "too many facts," including apparently "irrelevant" details. We recognize their presence as characteristic of Dostoevskian narration. Too many facts, presented with no clear explanation and an air of mystery, lead us to construct or intimate many possible stories. Stories also multiply if the facts may not be facts at all or if other "facts" lie behind the ostensible ones, with ever-receding orders of possibility and suspicion. But what was this "extremely enigmatic incident"?

It appears that, as everyone was leaving, Stavrogin and Liza Nikolaevna jostled against each other in the doorway. Or at least, "I am told" they did.

I fancied that they both stood still for an instant, and looked, as it

were, strangely at one another, but I may not have seen rightly in
the crowd. It is asserted, on the contrary, and quite seriously, that
Liza, glancing at Nikolay Vsevolodovich [Stavrogin], quickly raised
her hand to the level of his face, and would certainly have struck him
if he had not drawn back in time. Perhaps she was displeased with
the expression of his face, or the way he smiled, particularly just after
such an episode with Mavriky Nikolaevich. I must admit I saw nothing
myself, but all the others declared they had, though they certainly could
not have seen it in such a crush, though perhaps some may have. But I
did not believe it at the time. I remember, however, that Nikolay
Vsevolodovich was rather pale all the way home. (*Possessed*, 341)

Readers will recognize this rhetoric as quintessentially Dostoevskian. With qualification piled on qualification, tentative judgments
no sooner made than withdrawn and perhaps ambiguously reas-
serted, the narrator claims not to be sure what he himself has seen.
Reports of others are probably even more unreliable, and apparently
contradictory, though not necessarily groundless. Frivolous people
with a taste for scandal say things "quite seriously" that are different from what the narrator himself has seen, although he does
not entirely trust his own eyes, either. Moreover, since the action
in question was checked before it happened, one must distinguish
between an aborted possibility and nothing at all.

Something may or may not have happened, and if it did, it may
have been one thing or another. Liza and Stavrogin may have simply
stared strangely at each other, or, "on the contrary," Liza may have
intended to slap Stavrogin. If that was her purpose, it may have
had various motivations. Of course, nothing at all might have happened. What we are given here is not one but *many possible incidents*.
The real point is that whatever happened, *any* of these incidents
could have happened. What is important is the field of possibilities,
not the one possibility actualized.

We see here one reason that Dostoevsky uses such a chronicler
to tell his story. Conscientious but often unsure, the narrator often
presents various accounts of important and not so important incidents. Rumors therefore predominate, and we are given inconclusive assessments about which (if any) of several contradictory
stories might be true. It might almost be said that rumor is the
prime character of *The Possessed*, and it is certainly the main engine
of its many stories. As a result, our attention is called not only to
actualities but also to possibilities. Clouds of story hover over the

narrative landscape. The novel moves not from point to point but "from smudge to smudge."[82]

Possibilities are multiplied not only by uncertainty over what happened but also by the variety of contexts in which events that clearly did happen might be set. That is another reason that we are repeatedly given "too many facts," which create many sequences leading to any given present. Even if we do know what happened in the present, its significance, and the futures it adumbrates, vary greatly, depending on the paths that might have led to it. In the scene at Semyon Yakovlevich's doorway, both uncertainties—about what did happen and about what might have led to whatever might have happened—add to the "enigma" and multiply sideshadows.

At the beginning of *Karamazov*, the chronicler of that novel reports on what might have happened to Adelaida Ivanovna, old Karamazov's first wife, after she left him and ran away to Petersburg with a divinity student (i.e., a radical intellectual). Fyodor Pavlovich receives news that "she had somehow suddenly died somewhere in a garret, according to some stories—from typhus, but according to others—allegedly from starvation."[83] We note the emphatic use of subjunctives and vague qualifiers in this sentence. The two versions of Adelaida Ivanovna's death evidently contradict each other. Moreover, if Adelaida Ivanovna died of starvation, we would be led to construct a whole different narrative—about her relations with the divinity student, for instance. And how could a wealthy woman have allowed herself to starve to death? From self-lacerating pride? To enact a romance, as she imagined she was doing when she married Fyodor Pavlovich? Out of spite, or from some sort of principle? If she did not die of starvation, who spread the rumor she had, and why; and why did it gain currency?

As the passage continues, a different sort of doubling of possibilities is described:

> Fyodor Pavlovich was drunk when he heard of his wife's death, and it is said that he ran out into the street and began shouting with joy, raising his hands to Heaven: "Lord, now lettest Thou Thy servant depart in peace," but according to others he wept without restraint like a little child, so much so that, they say, people were sorry for him, in spite of the repulsion he inspired. (*BK*, 6)

We again note the frequent use of phrases indicating dubious report. Fyodor Pavlovich's two alleged reactions, each the subject of rumor, differ considerably and would seem to testify to incompatible states

of mind and qualities of character. The reader might be inclined
to think that one of them, weeping without restraint, might have
been an act and therefore not so different from the buffoonish
"shouting with joy," but in one of the novel's most memorable
asides, the narrator immediately insists that the weeping might in
fact have been sincere:

> It is quite possible that both versions were true, that he rejoiced at
> his release, and at the same time wept for her who released him. As
> a general rule, people, even the wicked, are much more naive and
> simple-hearted than we suppose. And we ourselves are, too. (*BK*, 6)

In this case, it is not important which story is true or what actually
happened; what matters is that either version, or both together,
could have been true. The chronicler allows that even Fyodor Pavlovich's character allows for radical alternatives. And the same applies to us.

Even when Dostoevsky does not use a chronicler, he creates many
of the same effects. The omniscient narrator of *Crime and Punishment* frequently pauses to recount that, years later, when Raskolnikov recalled a given incident, he wondered at his state of mind:
why did he do what he did, or go where he went, when some other
alternative, equally plausible, might have led to a different outcome?
Like the chronicler's rumors, these "future recollections" endow
the text with sideshadows. The reader learns not only what Raskolnikov did but also what he might just as well have done.

In Dostoevsky's first-person narratives, a key moment often occurs when the hero who has been constructing one account for
himself recognizes that *something else* might have been going on,
that there was another story aside from the one he was telling. In
the crucial discovery scene of "The Meek One," from the November 1876 *Diary*, the narrator is shocked to find his wife singing.
This apparently trivial incident indicates to him that his wife's
thoughts have been quite different from the ones he attributed to
her. He begins at last to grasp that *other people have other stories*.
"The Dream of a Ridiculous Man" projects a whole other world
in which the narrator can relive his life differently and so become
aware of other possibilities he has overlooked. Contemplating the
alternative earth that he visits, a world like ours but with a different
history and temporality, he asks, "Are such duplicates possible?"
In the world and time of Dostoevsky, they are; and his works force
the duplicates, time's doubles and shadows, into view.

Of course, doubling figures as a key principle of plot construction in most of Dostoevsky's works. Heroes often possess a series of doubles, from highly delineated main characters to a series of degraded caricatures. Each double enacts a latent possibility for the hero. Svidrigailov is the Raskolnikov who might have killed himself, Luzhin the Raskolnikov who wants all his fortune "at once," and Lebeziatnikov the two-bit intellectual who imagines that he is superior to ordinary people. Raskolnikovism, it appears, allows for more lives than one. *The Possessed* seems overpopulated with Stavrogin's many doubles, to the point where he seems trapped in a hall of mirrors and bound by a plot that his other selves have made—an amazing variation on the myth of Narcissus, perhaps. (*The Double* may be another such variation.) In the *Diary* the various suicides, who are often compared with each other, serve as doubles of each other. The feuilletonistic narrator's wanderings and digressions naturally offer "too many facts" sustaining too many stories; his dreamy unreliability creates a haze of possibilities.

The criminal cases that figure in the *Diary* allow Dostoevsky to make the openness of time most explicit. Indeed, it might be supposed that one reason Dostoevsky often based plots on crime is that, as Porfiry Petrovich remarks in *Crime and Punishment*, we tend to imagine crimes as conforming to relatively simple stories "laid down in books," whereas in fact every crime "at once becomes a thoroughly special case and sometimes a case unlike any other that's gone before" (*C&P*, 333). Where others might see one story, Porfiry realizes there may be many others, which are invisible to linear intellect.

To explain why he does not follow prescribed methods, Porfiry Petrovich chooses the example of "the old Austrian Hofkriegsrath . . . on paper they'd beaten Napoleon and taken him prisoner, and there in their study they worked it all out in the cleverest fashion, but look you, General Mack surrendered with his whole army, he-he-he!" (*C&P*, 334). Porfiry evidently derives this striking illustration from *War and Peace*, where it was used to show that in battle there are "a hundred million" possibilities where strategists typically see only one or two. Porfiry, and Dostoevsky, apply this Tolstoyan lesson to crime.[84]

No matter how ironclad the evidence for a given account might seem, the evidence might sustain other possibilities. The plot of *Karamazov*, and of several stories within it, depends on this premise of multiplicity. Up to a point, *Karamazov* resembles all detective

stories in which a second story, found by the detective, lies behind
the obvious one believed by the official police. *Karamazov* differs
in emphasizing that *several* versions, not just one, might be true.
In this respect, *Karamazov* is in part a parody of detective stories
and their fundamental premise. Indeed, the whole moral import
of *Karamazov* involves discovering not only who actually murdered
Fyodor Pavlovich but also who *might* have done so. From a moral
perspective, it is not just the act, but also the field of possible acts,
that matters. That is why Ivan, as he eventually learns, is wrong
to focus on the "act" and ignore the "wish." Father Zosima's belief
that we are all to blame even for the crimes we have not committed,
and that we are all responsible for each other, reflects the novel's
key tenet that responsibility pertains not just to actualities but also
to possibilities.

Sideshadowing in the *Diary*: Kairova Time

In the *Diary* Dostoevsky repeatedly refutes accepted views of well-
known crimes by showing their sideshadows. The Kairova case
offers a telling example. The mistress of a married man, Kairova,
who knew that her lover Velikanov was again living with his wife,
purchased a razor, came to the bedroom where the couple was
sleeping, and attacked the wife. The two awoke and prevented the
mistress from continuing the attack; Kairova was tried and
acquitted.

Dostoevsky deplores the "liberal" reaction of those who applauded
the verdict as somehow progressive, but indicates that the question
put to the jurors was so simplistic that conviction was impossible.
They were asked whether Kairova, "having premeditated her act,"
intended to kill Velikanova "but was prevented from the ultimate
consummation of her intent" by the couple (5/76, 1.3). Even though
Kairova was doubtless guilty of a crime, this question, in Dostoevsky's view, cannot be answered at all, either positively or negatively, and so the jury, faced with an impossible dilemma, properly
chose acquittal. Why was the question unanswerable?

According to Dostoevsky, this case, which he recounts in some
detail, could be one that challenges naive notions of linear intentionality. It may well have happened, he writes, that Kairova's
intention was not fixed at the outset (was therefore not "premeditated") but evolved bit by bit *along with* her behavior. When she
bought the razor, Kairova might still not have known whether she

would attack Velikanova with it, much less whether she would kill her.

> Most likely she hadn't the slightest idea of this even when sitting on the steps with the razor in her hand, while just behind her, on her own bed, lay her lover and her rival. No one, no one in the world could have the slightest idea of this. Moreover, even though it may seem absurd, I can state that even when she had begun slashing her rival she might *still not have known* whether she wanted to kill her or not and whether *this was her purpose* in slashing her.

At each moment, her incomplete intention allowed for many possibilities, and to understand her act one must grasp that multiplicity. Dostoevsky cautions that he does not mean to say that she was insane or that she acted unconsciously. No, she was aware of what she was doing at each moment, but she could not tell in advance what she would do the next moment. To preclude misunderstanding, Dostoevsky also counters the objection that this sort of thinking would make all convictions for *attempted* murder impossible: he admits that sometimes the intention to kill is indeed complete. Even in this case, according to Dostoevsky, Kairova is doubtless guilty of some crime, even if the court's question was so ill-formed as to preclude a proper conviction.

Kairova *might* have done several radically different things, and Dostoevsky sketches out the field of possibilities. She might have passed the razor over her rival's throat "and then cried out, shuddered, and ran off as fast as she could." Or she might have taken fright and turned the razor on herself, and either maimed or killed herself. Or, on the contrary, she might have flown into a frenzy "and not only murdered Velikanova but even begun to abuse the body, cutting off the head, the nose, the lips; and only later, suddenly, when someone took that head away from her, had realized what she had done."

Dostoevsky's point is that the incomplete moment and intention did not predetermine a single outcome. All these very different actions "could have happened and could have been done by this very same woman and sprung from the very same soul, in the very same mood and under the very same circumstances." If identical circumstances could lead to multiple results, then time is open, and to understand it one must imagine a field of possibilities. Whatever happens, one must project the sideshadows. Quite similar passages occur in Dostoevsky's early discussions of the Kornilova case.

The motif of seizing a weapon with no specific intention yet formulated was used again, with remarkable power, in *Karamazov*. It will be recalled that in his frenzied jealousy and pursuit of Grushenka, Dmitri seizes a pestle in the presence of Fenya and rushes off with it. When, after Fyodor Pavlovich has been found murdered, the investigating lawyer asks Dmitri why he seized the pestle, Dmitri is unable to give a coherent motive, precisely because he had none. He was angry, murderously angry, and he suddenly seized a weapon that happened to be in view, but he did not yet have a specific intention. Like Kairova's, his intention was to evolve bit by circumstantial bit. It might have led to murder, although in this case it did not; and even if it had, the murder would not have been premeditated. The intention was not formulated until the last possible moment, when he was standing over his father's head with the weapon in hand. The investigator, working from a naive and legalistic idea of intentionality, insists that Dmitri must have had some purpose in mind *when* he seized the pestle, much as the court in the Kairova case made the same assumption about the razor.

> "But what object had you in view in arming yourself with such a weapon?"
> "What object? No object. I just picked it up and ran off."
> "What for, if you had no object?" . . .
> "Bother the pestle!" broke from him suddenly.
> "But still . . . "
> "Oh, to keep off the dogs. . . . Oh, because it was dark. . . . In case anything turned up."
> "But have you ever on previous occasions taken a weapon with you when you went out, since you're afraid of the dark?" . . .
> "Well, upon my word, gentlemen! Yes, I took the pestle . . . What does one pick things up for at such moments? I don't know what for. I snatched it up and ran—that's all." (*BK*, 571)

As throughout the investigation, Dmitri is being entirely truthful here. He had no specific object in taking the pestle; he does not know why he snatched it, he just snatched it. The investigator assumes, as we generally do, that actions proceed from intentions, but here, as in the Kairova case, Dostoevsky's point is that sometimes actions may, instead of following from intentions, be part of the process by which intentions themselves evolve over time. Throughout this process, the intention may be vague and open.

Dostoevsky is so often interpreted from a Freudian perspective that it is worth stressing that his point is *not* that there is some *sub*conscious intention guiding and preceding Kairova's and Dmitri's actions. Their inability to identify an intention derives not from its repression but from its genuine absence. They did not have an intention, whether conscious or subconscious; rather, they were in a certain disposition. From a Dostoevskian standpoint, subconscious intentionality is really not that different from conscious intentionality, and both are equally inapplicable to Dmitri and Kairova. For them time was open, but a prior intention, whether conscious or unconscious, significantly closes down time. If their only choice was whether to carry out their plan, then time merely enacts or fails to enact what was there from the outset, but it does not itself shape anything and does not possess a developing plurality of possibilities. By contrast, the "prosaic intentionality" of "Kairova time" develops with constant sideshadows, with changes in the evolving state of mind itself, and with a multiplicity of options and potentials that change moment by moment.[85]

The Design and the Prophet

In introducing the Kairova case, Dostoevsky apologizes for taking it up after the trial is already over. "For nothing comes to an end, and so nothing can ever be too late," he writes; "every event continues and takes on new forms, even though it may have finished its initial stage of development" (5/76, 1.2). In fact, the very design of the *Diary* presupposes ramifying, open-ended processes. The lives of people and of nations take place in "Kairova time." That is why the author repeatedly confides his difficulties in finding some sort of guiding thread, tells us of his strenuous attempts to discern even a vague field of possibilities in a world so diverse and rich in potentials. "A novelist could never imagine possibilities such as real life offers every day by the thousands under the guise of the most ordinary things" (3/76, 2.1), he confides. Readers of the *Diary* watch the author marvel at the baffling strangeness of ordinary events and wonder how he might convey them "when they all go off on their separate ways and simply refuse to arrange themselves into one neat bundle!" (3/76, 1.3).

It should now be apparent why the prophetic mode could not be reconciled with the work's original design. When, like Pierre in *War and Peace*, the author thinks he has discovered the key to history, the world's multiplicity disappears. He knows the true story of history—can foresee "how England ends"—and he has discovered how utopia will come to pass. Instead of *side*shadowing, *fore*shadowing governs history and divulges the "denouement" in advance. The present is in effect already over. There is no need to attend to the various conversations of the moment, as he has done before, because events-to-come speak to Dostoevsky: "I once more seemed to hear voices from what may be the very near and perturbing future" (9/76, 2.5).

The author sees signs of the future in the way one might discover foreshadowing in an already written novel. The present only seems incomplete to those who cannot read the entrails of time. To the author, it is already historical, already "complete," like the past—a necessary moment in a story that has been tending for a thousand years to its providential ending.

When Dostoevsky embraces this apocalyptic vision, a singularity of tone dominates the work. Seemingly interminable articles interpret apparently trivial events in light of an inevitable future. The caprice and playful experimentation of a "monthly feuilleton" yield to the prophet's insistent monotone. There is no longer any need to determine an event's potentials by filtering it through diverse genres, and so a generic homogeneity takes over the work. Formally, as well as ideologically, the heterogeneity that defined the work fades from view for long stretches, until some disappointment temporarily shocks Dostoevsky back to a more cautious relation to time.

Vortex Time

In the *Diary*'s apocalyptic sections, Dostoevsky adapts another kind of time that also appears in his novels. I would call this other temporality *vortex time*. Vortex time and sideshadowing work in opposite ways. If in sideshadowing apparently simple events ramify into multiple futures, in vortex time an apparent diversity of causes all converge on a single catastrophe. A hidden clock seems to synchronize these causal lines so that, even though they seem unrelated to each other, they not only lead to the same result but also do so at the same moment.

Vortices shape Dostoevsky's famous "scandalous scenes," in which unexpected synchronicities create cascading crises. In *The Possessed* several causal lines all converge when a series of unexpected guests—Marya Timofeevna, Lebyadkin, Pyotr Stepanovich, and at last Stavrogin—appear in Varvara Petrovna's drawing room. Reflecting on the way everything seems to conspire to produce crisis, the narrator observes that "the utterly unexpected arrival of Nikolay Vsevolodovich, who was not expected for another month, was not only strange from its unexpectedness but from its fateful coincidence with the present moment" (*Possessed*, 179).

Any reader of Dostoevsky's novels will immediately think of many similar examples and will recall the increasing intensity of excitement as the vortex is approached. Quite various motives lead Dmitri to stand over his father's head with a murder weapon in his hand: the money he owes Katerina Ivanovna, the rivalry over Grushenka, resentment over his abandonment as a child, his father's counterclaim over the inheritance, Ivan's recently enunciated theory justifying murder, and the old man's loathsome behavior in the elder's cell. We watch Dmitri in a frenzy grab at straws more and more desperately to get the three thousand rubles he needs. The closer he gets to the catastrophe, the more evidently does any action, no matter to what end it may be directed, draw him to the murder scene. In much the same way, a diversity of contradictory ideologies all direct Raskolnikov to the murder scene, and several theories that cannot be reconciled with each other all converge for Kirillov in suicide. In the vortex all forces, all theories, no matter what their initial direction, are redirected to point toward the catastrophe ahead.

And as the catastrophe or scandal approaches, time speeds up. Crises follow each other with increasing rapidity until a moment of apparently *infinite temporal density* is reached. For Madame Stavrogina, the chronicler remarks, "the present moment might really be . . . one of those in which all the essence of life, of all the past and all the present, perhaps, too, all the future, is concentrated, as it were, focused" (*Possessed*, 183). In such scenes the novel may cite Dostoevsky's favorite line from the Apocalypse, that *there shall be time no longer* (Revelation 10:6).

Of course, Dostoevsky's favorite metaphor for the speeding up of time is "the last moments of a man condemned." The nearer the prisoner gets to execution, the more he experiences in each moment, each second, each fraction of a second, until, perhaps, the speed itself is unbearable and he "longs to be shot more quickly." Readers of Dostoevsky will recall that the same vortex temporality characterizes the epileptic fit. The *Idiot* relies on the temporal similarity of execution and epilepsy, and of both with the idea of approaching apocalypse.[86]

As we have seen, the *Diary* comes to apply this model of time to current events. All diverse causal chains now lead to the same outcome, the vortex of war that will bring utopia. They are all reaching their "final formulation" at the same moment (the theory of "synchronism" or "simultaneity"). And time speeds up. Europe changes year by year, month by month, until at last it is changing "hour by hour" (11/77, 3.1). For Dostoevsky, it makes no sense to negotiate peace terms with foreign powers that may not exist within a few days. When Dostoevsky writes this way, he insists that the predictions he made a few short months ago, predictions that everyone regarded as fantastic, have now been confirmed. As the expected vortex approaches, Dostoevsky starts to record when he has written each part of an issue because predictions are verified before they can even be printed. Issues become temporally labeled and layered:

> When I was beginning this chapter the facts and reports that are suddenly filling the entire European press had not yet appeared, so that everything I wrote here as speculation has now been borne out almost word for word. My *Diary* will come out next month, on October 7, while today is only September 29 and the "soothsayings," if I can call them that, on which I rather riskily embarked in this chapter will look somewhat dated, like established facts from which I merely copied my "soothsayings." (9/77, 1.5)

Such passages could not differ more profoundly from the January 1876 issue.

In his novels Dostoevsky found ways to combine sideshadowing with the vortex to produce the special thrill and suspense we call Dostoevskian.[87] He typically did so by setting a vortex plot within an antithetical world governed by an open, prosaic time. The latter measures the madness of the former, as Pyotr Ilich's prudence contrasts with Dmitri Karamazov's insane attitude to blood and money (and the servant Nastasya's contrasts with Raskolnikov's). The vortex derives from the characters' ideologies and pathologies; it testifies to obsession and reflects illness of body, mind, or spirit. It is something to be exorcised, which is one reason that the epigraph of *The Possessed* is Jesus' driving of the madman's devils into the swine, "who ran violently down a steep place into the lake." Cured, the former madman returns to normal and the people see him "sitting at the feet of Jesus, clothed and in his right mind."[88] Some of Dostoevsky's heroes are cured and some are not, but all live in a world where obsession is demonic and exorcism is possible.

In Dostoevsky's novels vortex time typically possesses main characters (and some minor ones) but does not govern the world. In *The Possessed* Stepan Trofimovich attributes the end of his professorial career to "a vortex of combined circumstances," but, the narrator tells us, "it turned out afterwards that there had been no 'vortex' and even no 'circumstances'" (*Possessed*, 4). For other characters, the vortex surely exists but is of their own making. It is the "disease" that afflicts Raskolnikov, and so Dostoevsky also describes the healthy Razumikhin, who believes not in sudden challenges to fate but in constant small efforts and undramatic exertions. Razumikhin also maintains that history resists all schemes of explanation and never fits a pattern dreamed up by some "mathematical brain." He voices the temporality of the novel. We have already seen that Porfiry Petrovich cites Tolstoy's view of time as maximally open; his unequal contest with Raskolnikov may be viewed as a duel of temporalities in which Raskolnikov's obsessional disease loses.

Each of these and several other solutions effectively combine open and closed time into a coherent aesthetic structure. But that does not happen in the *Diary*, where Dostoevsky just abandons one temporality for the other. He apparently tries to overhaul the machine while it is in motion. To match his new shaping idea, he discards some parts and replaces them with others. The most obvious formal markers of the original design—the monthly format, the division into chapters and articles, and the lengthy chapter titles—remain, but they become an empty shell.

In part, this change reflects a peculiar fact about the *Diary* and about Dostoevsky at this time: he himself quite seriously assumed the obsessional role previously typical of his own characters. In this respect the *Diary* resembles Gogol's *Selected Correspondence*, in which Gogol quite seriously speaks like one of his mad narrators.[89] It is possible, of course, that Dostoevsky could have worked out an aesthetically effective form of apocalyptic prophecy based entirely on vortex time, but he was evidently unable to do so with the material and forms developed to convey a radically different chronicity.

The *Diary*'s Second Form-Shaping Idea: Prosaics

In embracing the apocalypse, Dostoevsky also contradicted a second "form-shaping idea" of the *Diary* as originally designed. The *Diary* was formulated to convey a Dostoevskian version of the "prosaic idea," associated with the great novels of Tolstoy and carried by some earlier Dostoevsky characters, such as Razumikhin and Porfiry Petrovich. What did prosaics mean for the author of *A Writer's Diary*?

(1) First, it meant a relentless hostility to the intelligentsia's belief in a Theory to explain everything. The author insists on the messiness of the world and the complexity of human nature, which can never be reduced to a system. Many of the articles in the 1873 *Diary* and later issues indict the intelligentsia for its foolish beliefs that complexity is illusory and that a relatively simple "formula" might explain history and individual lives. As we have seen, Dostoevsky typically constructs his articles to make the opposite point. Taking an apparently simple phenomenon and paraphrasing the "linear" interpretations favored by the liberals and radicals, he reveals—in reportage, autobiography, sketch, and fiction—layer upon inexhaustible layer of unsuspected and unformalizable complexity.

(2) The *Diary* as originally designed rejected the idea that salvation or social betterment depends on some grand scheme. In the author's real world beyond Theory, improvement comes prosaically, by unremarkable efforts of individual self-betterment and by "isolated cases" of generosity. That is why the author's wanderings were to be a structural pivot of the work: he remarks on the unremarkable. Coming across examples of severe social problems, he discovers or imagines "isolated cases" in which one ordinary person, guided by no Theory, helps another. At times, he may also report chilling incidents in which members of the intelligentsia who disdain anything but total solutions withhold simple person-to-person aid.[90] The work's sequence of small daily incidents directs our attention away from political abstractions. "Don't you see," the author explains, "that loving the universal man means surely to scorn and sometimes even to hate the real man standing next to you?" (73.5).

(3) Progress must be made *gradually*. Neither history nor psychology allow for short cuts. Individual self-improvement is the work of a lifetime. Dostoevsky notes with approval how Levin, in *Anna Karenina*, comes to understand that one cannot achieve integrity by donning a "uniform" or imitating a model. As people get better, their "microscopic efforts" accumulate and their examples may become infectious. By contrast, members of the intelligentsia have defeated their own purposes because "instead of

taking the first nine steps, they immediately took the tenth one" (3/76, 1.3). They try to go right to the end, but society can get better only if people start "from the beginning," with each individual self.

(4) Any attempt to effect change suddenly, on the basis of a formula, will at best delay real improvement and at worst cause considerable harm. Such efforts at radical change have been made before, and the intelligentsia errs in seeing itself as the first generation to apply a "scientific" formula to society. According to Dostoevsky, people have been seeking such a formula for "the whole six thousand years of their history and they cannot find it. The ants know the formula for their ant heap; the bee knows the formula for its hive. . . . but humans do not know their formula" (8/80, 3.3). In his articles on *Anna Karenina*, Dostoevsky (correctly) attributes to Tolstoy a belief that evil has no single source and therefore allows for no single solution: "[In *Anna*] It is clear and intelligible to the point of obviousness that evil lies deeper in human beings than our socialist-physicians suppose; that no social structure will eliminate evil" (7-8/77, 2.3). It is equally clear to Dostoevsky that many of Russia's social diseases are iatrogenic, exacerbated by the "socialist-physicians" themselves.

Consequently, the more influence the intelligentsia wields, and the more Russian thinkers come to accept total solutions "from the end," the worse things will become. At the extreme, utopians in power would create hell on earth because they would rapidly become impatient with the recalcitrance of human nature. Love of Humanity would lead to the elimination of countless individual people:

> If there were brothers, then there would be brotherhood. If there are no brothers, then you will not achieve brotherhood through any sort of "institution." What sense is there in setting up an institution and inscribing on it: *"Liberté, egalité, fraternité"*? You will achieve nothing at all worthwhile here through an "institution," so that it will be necessary—absolutely, inescapably necessary—to add to these three "institutional" words a fourth: *"ou la mort,"* *"fraternité ou la mort"*— and brother will go off to chop the head off brother so as to achieve brotherhood by means of this "civic institution." (8/80, 3.3)

It is in passages like these that Dostoevsky, read a century later, does indeed seem prophetic.

(5) Collectively and individually, ethics can never be reduced to

a system of rules. Instead, it is a matter of an educated sensitivity to individual cases. By showing the fine distinctions between apparently similar cases, Dostoevsky demonstrates concretely the crudeness of generalizations in the face of life's dizzying complexity. The *Diary*'s method of treating the same story from diverse perspectives and in different genres also serves to exhibit the unexpected depths contained in real particular cases but missing from rule-bound formulations.

In the root sense of the word, The *Diary* preaches *casuistry*, reasoning by cases. Real ethical consciousness never reasons from the top down but from the bottom up. It proceeds from the particularities of each incident and not from the system of norms into which the case might be made to fit. "Cutting off heads is easy if one follows the letter of the law, but it is always much more difficult to settle a matter in accordance with the truth, in a humane and paternal fashion" (12/76, 1.5), he observes. Even the theory of "the corrupting environment" "in *some* specific instances and in *some* certain categories is dazzling in its truth, but . . . is absolutely mistaken when applied as a whole and in general" (10/76, 1.1). In England, where the theory is applied on a case-by-case basis, it favors ethical decisions, Dostoevsky contends. But among us it has the opposite effect because of that most lamentable characteristic of Russia's educated people, the tendency to take all theories to the extreme and make all judgments categorical.

(6) Although life exhibits endless complexity, the moral truths needed to grasp it are profoundly ordinary. Educated Russians constantly but mistakenly "feel that the truth is something far too dull and prosaic for us and much too ordinary," but ordinary and prosaic is what it is. "The truth can lie on the table right in front of people for a hundred years but they won't pick it up; they go chasing after fabrications precisely because they consider truth to be fantastic and utopian" (73.15). The truths we seek are hidden in plain view. Of course, the idea of prosaic truth forms the philosophical core of *Anna Karenina*, and Dostoevsky singles out for special praise Levin's discovery of moral foundations in a peasant's simple comment. Tolstoy's point, as Dostoevsky observes, was not that the peasant had some special insight but that he reminded Levin of *what he already knew*. Abstruse theories had concealed the moral sense that Levin had absorbed in childhood.

(7) It follows for Dostoevsky that the most important social institutions are the most prosaic ones, especially the family. Levin

finds his way because of what he learned as a child, and Dostoevsky the prisoner was saved by childhood memories. But what about those products of "accidental families" who have not had such a childhood? For Dostoevsky, Tolstoy's failure to address this question of *contemporary* children represents the main shortcoming of his work. That is one reason the *Diary*'s first monthly issue takes children as its central theme and why that theme recurs in subsequent issues.

Child beggars, child abuse cases, suicides of the young—these related themes lead to a diversity of stories, sketches, and articles, as well as an occasional sermon. True families, Dostoevsky tells us, cannot be produced by command, by theory, or by occasional attention. They form bit by bit, prosaically, at countless ordinary moments when "we continue to grow into one another's souls every day, every hour. . . . A family, after all, is also *created*, not provided ready-made" (2/76, 2.5).

The 1876 *Diary* begins with a description of Dostoevsky's earlier exploration of this family idea in his novel *A Raw Youth* and then announces plans for a future novel that will be his *Fathers and Children*. The monthly *Diary* is at last suspended so Dostoevsky can write that work, *The Brothers Karamazov*, an extension of both the earlier novel and the *Diary*. Dostoevsky also often cites *The Possessed* when introducing sketches about the reasons that bad contemporary fathers (who rely on progressive ideas rather than daily prosaic attention) produce worse children. It is almost as if Dostoevsky's many experiments of the 1870s, the three novels and the intermittent *Diary*, constituted one long work about Russia's spiritual progress as reflected in its decaying families.

A Debate with Tolstoy, and an Inverse Square Law of Ethics

This complex of prosaic ideas could not be reconciled with Dostoevsky's apocalypticism. According to Dostoevsky's prophetic articles, utopia was not only possible but immediately realizable. It could be achieved not gradually but suddenly, not by microscopic efforts but by massive military force. Rather than prosaic truth, Dostoevsky offers an obscure key to history that he alone understands. History's messiness could be resolved into a neat story after all. Although Dostoevsky's millenarian Theory differed from the ideologies of the intelligentsia, it shared the same characteristics that Dostoevsky himself had rejected as profoundly dangerous.

Particularly remarkable are those passages in which Dostoevsky abandons his concern for the family. In one essay Dostoevsky, with astonishing blindness to anything but his "cause," encourages a young woman who, against the understandable wishes of her family, wanted to serve with the volunteers in Serbia (6/76, 2.5). And without a trace of irony, Dostoevsky enthusiastically reports a "typical" incident:

> A father—an old soldier—instead of living at his ease, suddenly takes up arms and sets off on foot for thousands of miles, asking directions along the way, to go fight the Turks and support his brethren, and he takes his nine-year-old daughter along with him (this is a fact): "There'll be good Christians to be found who'll look after my daughter while I'm off wandering." And he goes . . . And there are thousands of cases like his! (10/76, 2.4)

We could not be farther from the *Diary*'s articles describing what happens to children, especially young girls, who lose their families and fall into the hands of strangers.

The *Diary*'s articles on the Eastern War contain no finely delineated descriptions of its participants. We get no semifictional musings about what might actually happen to the soldiers or those they leave behind. Evidently, the work's original design of exploring individual cases might well yield narratives incompatible with utopian politics. The form elaborated for one purpose could not be adapted for another, radically different one.

Perhaps the most telling example of Dostoevsky's changed perspective occurs in his critique of the eighth part of Tolstoy's *Anna Karenina*. Tolstoy's publisher, Katkov, had refused to run the novel's last section, in which the author satirized enthusiasm for the Eastern War. On prosaic grounds similar to those that Dostoevsky himself had defended, the novel's hero, Levin, rejects the ideologically based enthusiasm for a cause remote from home. Dostoevsky reacted with anger that probably reflects the inner conflicts of his own thought and of the *Diary*.

In a key passage of the novel, Levin is asked whether he would kill a Turk about to torture a child before his eyes, and he replies that he cannot decide such a question in advance. Particulars would be too important and the consequences of a wrong decision, either way, would be too terrible to allow for a prior decision based on generalities. In any case, the war is not before our eyes but at a distance, and that makes a great difference to Levin. Quite mistakenly, people tend to feel most confident in making judgments about distant events precisely because particularities and complexities tend to be obscured in proportion to our distance from them. Levin's morality, and the novel's, works by a sort of inverse square law, in which responsibility diminishes rapidly with distance. We owe our debt to particular people, not to Humanity.

Dostoevsky replies to Tolstoy with all the perspicacity of someone answering a side of himself. The implications of Dostoevsky's argument extend far beyond the immediate topic at hand, the Eastern War. After citing Tolstoy's novel at length and paraphrasing it with great sensitivity, Dostoevsky's article elevates the disagreement into a timeless dialogue on fundamental and perhaps unresolvable ethical questions.

There may be merit to Levin's argument that the reliability of moral judgments is greatest when particulars are visible. But this prosaic argument itself has a moral weakness, according to Dostoevsky. For surely there is something wrong with Tolstoy's apparent dismissal of all responsibility for anything we cannot touch with our own hands. Apparently echoing the ridiculous man of the April 1877 *Diary*, Dostoevsky asks whether we should feel no pity if we knew that on Mars infants' eyes were being pierced. And what if it were in the next hemisphere? In short, "if distance really does have such an influence on humaneness, then a new question arises of itself: At what distance does love of humanity end?" (7-8/87, 3.4).

For Levin, the reluctance to judge at a distance is all the greater when the judgment would involve violence and killing. It is to sort out the issue of violence from that of distance that the proponents of the war ask Levin what he would do if the Turks were torturing someone right in front of him. Would he use violence then? Citing Levin's refusal to answer, Dostoevsky re-creates a parodic version of such an eventuality.

> Imagine such a scene: Levin is standing right there, with rifle and fixed bayonet, and two paces away a Turk is voluptuously holding a needle, ready to pierce the eyes of the child already in his arms. The boy's seven-year-old sister screams and rushes madly to tear him away from the Turk. And here stands Levin, thinking and hesitating: "I don't know what I'll do. I don't feel anything. I'm one of the People myself. There isn't any immediate feeling for the oppression of the Slavs and there can't be any."
>
> But seriously, what would he have done after all the things he's told us? How could he not save the child? Would he really let the child

be tortured? Would he really not snatch him from the hands of the villainous Turk?

"Well, yes, I'd snatch him away, but suppose I had to give the Turk a good hard push?"

"Then push him!"

"Push him, you say! And if he doesn't want to let the child go and draws his saber? Why, suppose I had to kill the Turk?"

"Well then, kill him!"

"But how can I kill him? No, I mustn't kill the Turk. No, it's better to let him pierce the child's eyes and torture him; I'll go home to Kitty." (7–8/77, 3.4)

In part, Dostoevsky's satire impugns Levin's great reluctance to see that violence must sometimes be resisted by violence, or one becomes responsible for what one could have prevented. But the reach of Dostoevsky's satire extends further, to the very bases of prosaic morality.

In "going home to Kitty," Dostoevsky's Levin resembles the ridiculous man's indifferent rejection of the little girl's pleas for help: Dostoevsky allows the shadow of that story to be cast over Tolstoy's novel. Dostoevsky understands that in Levin's prosaic perspective, the distance that affects responsibility is not only physical but relational. In prosaics, we owe our greatest debt to our families, to those who live with us, and only then, in concentric circles of greater compass and descending importance, to others— first to our nearest friends, then perhaps to our employees or fellow workers, next to those with whom we are barely acquainted, and perhaps finally to someone one just happens to meet. We are not responsible for everyone equally, and from a prosaic standpoint it would be morally perverse to treat one's immediate family no differently from someone one has just met. In this respect, distance does indeed "have an influence on humaneness."

The irony of returning to Kitty is of course magnified by what Kitty is doing, namely, taking care of their infant. How can Levin let one infant be tortured so he can go and play with another, even if it is his own? Elsewhere in the *Diary*, Dostoevsky has himself pointed to the danger of thinking in terms of Humanity; here he presents the other side of the question, the danger of beginning, and perhaps almost ending, at home.[91]

Of course, Dostoevsky's critique, like most parodies, distorts Levin's argument. Levin does not utterly renounce the use of force, or even of killing, when necessary. (Though skeptical of the Eastern

War, Tolstoy was not yet a pacifist.) What Levin renounces is making such a decision *in advance* and on the basis of *a principle*. He insists on taking account of all the particularities of the moment and on trusting his educated ethical sensibility over any abstract rule. No rule can simply *derive* or *forecast* a future moment, with a rich enough sense of its presentness and ethically relevant facts. Dostoevsky's example, like the hypothetical situation proposed by Koznyshev to Levin in the novel, is notably weak in particulars, a caricature of a real situation. Levin also implicitly rejects the unspoken assumption behind Dostoevsky's parody and Koznyshev's example. In projecting this torture of a child, they assume that the test of a moral outlook is how well it functions in extreme situations, whereas for Levin (and Tolstoy) the best test is ordinary life. An ethics based on extreme situations is likely to be of no use, or of positive harm, in anything but extreme situations, and Levin's whole education has been to see the importance of prosaic circumstances as the basis for morality. The Turkish example, we might say, is set in vortex time, in which everything converges on one irreversible catastrophe, after which nothing of importance is left to consider: but most decisions of life take place in a continuum of time, in an open time of sideshadowing, where imponderable long-term effects in multiple possible futures also need to be taken into account and answered for.[92]

Dostoevsky's dialogue with Tolstoy, and with himself, reflects the terrible conflict that tore his new work apart. That conflict was simultaneously moral and aesthetic. Could Dostoevsky's two radically different perspectives somehow be joined in a work that would be both morally convincing and aesthetically coherent? That seems to be the problem that Dostoevsky set for himself when he suspended the *Diary* to write his greatest masterpiece, *The Brothers Karamazov.*

The Interest of the *Diary*

True to its own diversity, *A Writer's Diary* compels interest for various reasons. Everyone has recognized the brilliance of many of its parts: it contains Dostoevsky's greatest short fiction, as well as brilliant semifiction, sketches, and articles. As a source of problems, motifs, themes, and forms, it exercised decisive influence on *Karamazov.* Beyond that, the *Diary* was itself a remarkable experiment with a new literary form. If one attends to the sections where Dostoevsky was able to realize his design, his new genre seems, to this reader at least, quite successful. Even the ideological shift that conflicted with its design and obscured its outlines is itself interesting. It tells us a great deal about the inner conflicts that shaped Dostoevsky's character, thought, and art.

Notes

All references to *A Writer's Diary*, which are to the present Lantz translation, are given by month and year, chapter and article. Thus a quote ascribed to "6/76, 2.1" is drawn from the June 1876 issue, chapter 2, article 1 ("My Paradox"). Articles in the 1873 *Diary* are identified by year and article only, so that 73.3 is "Environment."

Dostoevsky frequently uses ellipses (three dots); they are an important part of his style. I indicate Dostoevsky's ellipses by three *unspaced* dots (...) and my own omissions with spaced dots (. . .).

My thanks to Nikolai Aristides, Caryl Emerson, Jane Morson, and Andrew Wachtel for their help with this study.

Part 1: Origin of an Anomaly

1. For more information on the *Diary*, see Morson, *The Boundaries of Genre: Dostoevsky's "Diary of a Writer" and the Traditions of Literary Utopia* (Austin: University of Texas Press, 1981; Evanston, Ill.: Northwestern University Press, 1988). A bibliography of criticism on the *Diary* appears on p. 189, n. 5.

The present interpretation of the *Diary* differs substantially from the one advanced in *Boundaries*. These differences reflect changes in both my methodological approaches and my reading of the text itself. See the opening to part 3 of the present essay.

2. The phrase, of course, belongs to Henry James, Preface to *The Tragic Muse*, in *The Art of the Novel: Critical Prefaces by Henry James* (1934; New York: Scribner's, 1962), p. 84. James was not referring to Russian novels alone, but American Slavists have often used his characterization as a starting point for examining the great Russian novels, which are long and, apparently, "loose and baggy."

3. V. G. Belinsky, *Selected Philosophical Works* (Moscow: Foreign Languages, 1956), pp. 373, 386–87.

4. The Russian reaction to belatedness was notably quite different from the reaction of English poets as described in the classic study by W. Jackson Bate, *The Burden of the Past and the English Poet* (1970; New York: Norton, 1972). The Russian reaction to belatedness was not a sense that resources were exhausted but a feeling that it was necessary to hurry up to produce masterpieces.

5. Lev Tolstoi, "Neskol'ko slov po povodu knigi 'Voina i mir'" (Some words about the book *War and Peace*), from the ninety-volume Jubilee edition, vol. 16, p. 7. The article first appeared in *Russian Archive* in 1868.

6. See part 4 of the present study.

7. Viktor Shklovskii, "Roman-poema i roman pokhozhdenie," *Povesti o proze: Razmyshleniia i razbory,* vol. 2, *V kotorom rasskazyvaetsia o russkoi proze* (Moscow: Khudozhestvennaia literatura, 1966), p. 280.

8. Viktor Shklovskii, "O russkom romane i povesti," *Povesti o proze,* p. 3.

9. On the Formalist idea of turning a journal into a literary work of its own kind, see Morson, *Boundaries,* pp. 56–58.

10. In Pushkin's story Charsky asks the improvisatore, "How can it be that someone else's idea, which had only just reached your ear, immediately became your own property, as if you had carried, fostered, and nurtured it for a long time? Does this mean that you never encounter either difficulty, or a dampening of spirit, or the restlessness that precedes inspiration?" The improvisatore responds: "No one except the improvisatore himself can comprehend this alacrity of impressions, the close tie between one's own inspiration and another's will." Alexander Pushkin, *Complete Prose Fiction,* trans. Paul Debreczeny (Stanford, Calif.: Stanford University Press, 1983), p. 255. Of course, Dostoevsky, unlike Pushkin's improvisatore, could select his topics from among *several* themes and events presented by Russian society each month.

11. All citations from Dostoevsky's letters, which will be given in the text, are drawn from the four-volume edition edited by A. S. Dolinin (Moscow and Leningrad: Gosizdat, 1929–58), henceforth *Pis'ma.* This citation is from *Pis'ma,* vol. 1, p. 424.

12. Fyodor Dostoevsky, *The Possessed,* trans. Constance Garnett (New York: Modern Library, 1936), p. 127.

13. As Bakhtin correctly observed, Dostoevsky tended to avoid using what Bakhtin called "no man's thoughts"—"separate thoughts, assertions, propositions that can be themselves true or untrue, depending on their relationship to the subject and independent of the carrier to whom they belong." Mikhail Bakhtin, *Problems of Dostoevsky's Poetics,* ed. and trans. Caryl Emerson (Minneapolis: University of Minnesota Press, 1984), p. 93. Further references are to *Problems.*

14. Anna Dostoevsky, *Dostoevsky: Reminiscences,* trans. and ed. Beatrice Stillman (New York: Liveright, 1977), pp. 212–13 (italics mine).

Part 2: An Encyclopedia of Genres

15. In the recent thirty-volume edition of Dostoevsky's works (1972–90), and in the earlier thirteen-volume edition of Boris Tomashevsky and K. Khalabaev (Moscow and Leningrad: Gosudarstvennoe izdatel'stvo, 1926–30), the announcement appears in the appended notes. It is omitted from the twelve-volume edition published by Marks (1894–95) and from the earlier English translation.

16. Bakhtin, *Problems,* p. 138. With considerable exaggeration, Bakhtin, in defending the importance of "Bobok," maintains that menippean satire "sets the tone for Dostoevsky's entire work" (p. 138). On the other hand,

I do believe that menippean satire is one of the key elements shaping
Dostoevsky's work, and that, if Bakhtin has overestimated the genre's
importance, his critics have in response underestimated it.

17. See also the note in the thirty-volume edition of Dostoevsky's notes,
vol. 21, p. 402.

18. For a superb new interpretation of this story, which links it to
Dickens and the genre of the Christmas story as well as to "The Dream
of a Ridiculous Man" (which appears later in the *Diary*), see Robin Feuer
Miller, "Dostoevsky's 'Dream of a Ridiculous Man': Unsealing the Generic
Envelope," forthcoming in *Freedom and Responsibility in Russian Literature:
A Festschrift for Robert Louis Jackson*, ed. Elizabeth Cheresh Allen and
Gary Saul Morson (Evanston, Ill.: Northwestern University Press). Miller's
article develops Robert Louis Jackson's subtle reading of the story, which
sets it in the context of the January 1876 *Diary*, in Jackson's "The Fourth
Window: 'A Boy at Christ's Christmas Party,'" in *The Art of Dostoevsky:
Deliriums and Nocturnes* (Princeton, N.J.: Princeton University Press,
1981), pp. 260–71.

19. The Garnett version of this story, translated as "The Heavenly
Christmas Tree," begins: "I am a novelist, and I suppose I have made
up this story." Constance Garnett, trans., *The Short Stories of Dostoevsky*,
ed. William Phillips (New York: Dial, 1946), p. 537.

20. Thus I prefer the title "The Meek One" to other versions, such as
Garnett's "A Gentle Spirit."

21. See "Two Suicides" (10/76, 1.3); the "icon" suicide is the second
of the two.

22. Robert Louis Jackson concludes that "Bobok" gives us the vision
of "The Dream" in "reverse perspective." See Jackson, "Some Considerations on 'The Dream of a Ridiculous Man' and 'Bobok' from the
Aesthetic Point of View," in *Art of Dostoevsky*, p. 303.

23. In the chapter "Night" in *The Possessed*, Stavrogin poses the same
question (*Possessed*, 238–39).

24. On these two readings, see Morson, *Boundaries*, 177–82. See also
Miller, "Dostoevsky's 'Dream of a Ridiculous Man.'"

25. From "Otvet 'Russkomu vestniku'" in the thirty-volume edition of
Dostoevsky's works, vol. 19, p. 134.

26. Sideshadowing is discussed in greater detail in part 4 of the present
essay. For further commentary on the concept, see Gary Saul Morson's
articles, "Bakhtin, Genres, and Temporality," *New Literary History* 22,
no. 4 (Autumn 1991): 1071–92; "For the Time Being: Sideshadowing,
Criticism, and the Russian Counter-Tradition," in *After Post-Structuralism*,
ed. Nancy Easterlin and Barbara Riebling (Evanston, Ill.: Northwestern
University Press, forthcoming); and "Anna Karenina's Omens," in *Freedom and Responsibility in Russian Literature*, ed. Allen and Morson. The
topic will be discussed at length in a book I am writing, *Narrative and
Freedom: The Shadows of Time*. See also Michael André Bernstein's forthcoming study, *Foregone Conclusions*.

27. The Gorky quotation as cited by E. I. Zhurbina, *Teoriia i praktika*

khudozhestvenno-publitsisticheskikh zhanrov: Ocherk, Fel'eton (Moscow: Mysl', 1969), p. 56, from vol. 30 of Gorky's collected works (1956); the Korolenko quotation as cited by Zhurbina, p. 70, from V. G. Korolenko, *Sobranie sochinenii v desiati tomakh*, vol. 8 (1955), p. 70. For more information on these matters, and their relation to the essay and Montaigne, see Morson, *Boundaries*, pp. 14–17.

28. Fyodor Dostoevsky, *The Brothers Karamazov*, trans. Constance Garnett (New York: Modern Library, 1950), p. 293. References in the text are to *BK*; the translations have occasionally been modified for accuracy or style.

29. The classic essay on how a version of a writer's life can itself become a literary fact in some periods belongs to the Russian Formalist Boris Tomashevsky. See Boris Tomashevskij, "Literature and Biography," in *Readings in Russian Poetics: Formalist and Structuralist Views*, ed. Ladislav Matejka and Krystyna Pomorska (Cambridge, Mass.: MIT Press, 1971), pp. 49–51.

30. From *Crime and Punishment*: Fyodor Dostoevsky, *Crime and Punishment*, trans. Constance Garnett (New York: Modern Library, 1950), p. 184. Further references are to *C&P*. From *The Idiot*: Fyodor Dostoevsky, *The Idiot*, trans. Constance Garnett (New York: Modern Library, 1962), pp. 20–21. On "penumbral textuality," see Gary Saul Morson, *Hidden in Plain View: Narrative and Creative Potentials in "War and Peace"* (Stanford, Calif.: Stanford University Press, 1987), pp. 176–88.

31. Joseph Frank's already authoritative biography of Dostoevsky stresses the centrality and sincerity of these convictions learned from the Siberian experience. See Frank, *Dostoevsky: The Stir of Liberation*, 1860–65 (Princeton, N.J.: Princeton University Press, 1986).

32. Konstantin Mochulsky, *Dostoevsky: His Life and Work*, trans. Michael A. Minihan (Princeton, N.J.: Princeton University Press, 1967), p. 474.

33. For the notebooks to the *Diary*, see *The Unpublished Dostoevsky: Diaries and Notebooks (1860–81)*, ed. Carl R. Proffer, vol. 2, trans. Arline Boyer and Carl Proffer (Ann Arbor, Mich.: Ardis, 1975) and vol. 3, trans. Arline Boyer and David Lapeza (Ardis, 1976). The Russian text is *Nieizdannyi Dostoevskii: Zapisnye knizhki i tetradi*, 1860–1881, ed. V. R. Shcherbina et al., Literaturnoe nasledstvo no. 83 (Moscow: Nauka, 1971).

34. For a sensitive interpretation of Dostoevsky's conversion experience in terms set by "The Peasant Marey," see Joseph Frank, *Dostoevsky: The Years of Ordeal, 1850–59* (Princeton, N.J.: Princeton University Press, 1983), pp. 116–27.

35. Joseph Frank offers a different sort of double reading of Dostoevsky's novel *The Insulted and the Humiliated* in which two novels, which Dostoevsky did not succeed in stitching together, compete in the final version. "One may of course attribute such dissonance to artistic oversight (and Dostoevsky's own admission that he wrote the book too hastily seems to confirm such a judgment), but it can also be diagnosed as part of an internal evolution that had not yet completed its course." See Frank, *Stir*

of Liberation, p. 118. Frank's reading of this novel is the best I know, and I think that his conclusions about it are correct. In other cases, however, it seems to me that Dostoevsky learned to make a virtue of the forms produced by "haste" and found creative methods that deliberately exploited effects that previously and otherwise would be artistic lapses (as they are in *The Insulted and the Humiliated*).

36. Frank makes the case for the explanation in terms of censorship (*Stir of Liberation*, p. 219).

37. John 12:24, the epigraph to *The Brothers Karamazov*. Frank correctly explains why it is wrong to regard Dostoevsky as believing that all suffering is positive (*Stir of Liberation*, pp. 129-30).

38. On this narrative's controlling analogy between individual conversion and the creation of an artistic image, see Robert Louis Jackson, "The Triple Vision: 'The Peasant Marey,'" in *Art of Dostoevsky*, pp. 20-32.

39. In order to sever the story from the rest of the *Diary*, Garnett omits its entire first paragraph. In her version the story begins, "It was the second day in Easter week" (*Short Stories of Dostoevsky*, p. 529). In this way, the story's triple vision—the diarist, the prisoner, the child—becomes, without the diarist, a double vision. The sentence about Aksakov is kept, but its allusion to the previous article is of course lost.

40. For the obscure book of prophecy, see 5-6/77, 1.1, and Lantz's notes to the article. If Dostoevsky's tone here is noncommittal, he later, with no apparent irony, quotes Lichtenberger's book as evidence in support of his views (7-8/77, 2.2).

41. On evidence in *Karamazov*: I refer not only to the misleading information about the murder, and to the varied interpretations at the trial, but also to the inability of Zosima's "mysterious visitor" to get people to accept his genuine evidence of guilt.

42. In apocalyptic thought the end is often understood as the realization of paradoxes: it is the time when there shall be no more time, when death shall die, when hell freezes over, etc.

43. *The Republic of Plato*, trans. Francis Macdonald Cornford (New York: Oxford University Press, 1945), p. 43.

44. The idea of three stages of history, with the third the age of utopia (or the reign of the Holy Spirit), is a trope of apocalyptic thought. The prophet announces the third age. See Norman Cohn, *The Pursuit of the Millennium: Revolutionary Millenarians and Mystical Anarchists of the Middle Ages*, rev. and expanded ed. (New York: Oxford University Press, 1970).

45. See ibid.; also Norman Cohn, *Warrant for Genocide: The Myth of the Jewish World-Conspiracy and the "Protocols of the Elders of Zion"* (New York: Harper, 1969).

46. It seems not to have occurred to Dostoevsky that his own perspective as a Russian reader might affect his perception, or that an English reader might regard Pushkin's Italians as Russians in Italian dress.

47. Fyodor Dostoevsky, *"Notes from Underground" and "The Grand Inquisitor,"* the Garnett trans., rev. Ralph Matlaw (New York: Dutton, 1960), p. 115. Further references are to *NFU*.

48. See Bakhtin's remarkable analysis of the rhetoric of this essay (*Problems*, pp. 94–95). He concludes that here, as in Dostoevsky's journalism generally, "everywhere his thought makes its way through a labyrinth of voices, semi-voices, other people's words, and other people's gestures. He never proves his positions on the basis of other abstract positions, he does not link thoughts together according to some referential principle, but juxtaposes orientations and amid them constructs his own orientation. . . . His path leads not from idea to idea, but from orientation to orientation. To think, for him, means to question and to listen, to try out orientations."

49. For a recent defense of ethical reasoning by cases, and a call for a revival of casuistry in this sense, see Albert R. Jonsen and Stephen Toulmin, *The Abuse of Casuistry: A History of Moral Reasoning* (Berkeley and Los Angeles: University of California Press, 1988). On prosaics and Tolstoy, see Morson, *Hidden in Plain View*; Morson, "Prosaics: An Approach to the Humanities," *American Scholar*, Autumn 1988, pp. 515–28; Morson, "Prosaics and *Anna Karenina*," *Tolstoy Studies Journal* 1 (1988): 1–12; and Morson and Caryl Emerson, *Mikhail Bakhtin: Creation of a Prosaics* (Stanford, Calif.: Stanford University Press, 1990).

50. Thus Dostoevsky defended arguing for the release of Kornilova and answered charges of inconsistency by asserting that temporary mental aberration and the "corrupting environmental" are *sometimes* relevant. The "environmental" theory, he says, is "a notion that in *some* specific instances and in *some* certain categories is dazzling in its truth, but which is absolutely mistaken when applied as a whole and in general" (10/86, 1.1).

51. *Pis'ma* 3:201–2; the full passage is quoted in part 3 of this introduction.

52. For example, in response to one critic of the *Diary*, Dostoevsky wrote: "As far as my feuilleton is concerned…By the way, I don't know why the Moscow columnist, my fellow writer, thinks that I am ashamed to be called a feuilletonist. . . . If my Moscow teacher absolutely must call my *Diary* a feuilleton, then he's free to do so; I'm quite content with that" (73.14).

53. As cited in Zhurbina, *Teoriia i praktika*, p. 252.

54. *Unpublished Dostoevsky*, 2:87.

55. I of course use the term in the Russian Formalist sense of a device that announces itself as one.

56. This passage may serve as a good example of a favorite rhetorical device of Dostoevsky's, which Bakhtin would describe in terms of "double-voicing" and which Joseph Frank has recently called "inverted irony." As Frank explains, inverted irony "turns back on the writer as a means of turning *against* an imagined judge and critic in the person of the reader." It is used by both Dostoevsky (or his journalistic persona) and his characters (e.g., the underground man). See Frank, *Stir of Liberation*, p. 236.

57. In *Boundaries of Genre*, I stressed the deep formal and ideological affinity of the *Diary* and Herzen's *From the Other Shore*. For a remarkable new reading of the relation between these two works, see Aileen Kelly,

"Irony and Utopia in Herzen and Dostoevsky: *From the Other Shore* and *Diary of a Writer,*" *Russian Review* 50, no. 4 (October 1991): 397-416.

58. This point was not new to Dostoevsky. Long before he wrote the *Diary,* he viewed art as both having a social purpose and yet demanding absolute freedom, even to realize that purpose. That is why one cannot dictate themes to art, as the radical critics tried to do. In Dostoevsky's view, dictation in the name of utility destroys utility itself. Moreover, the utilitarians misconstrue usefulness by unduly limiting it to immediate needs; this misconstrual derives from their misunderstanding of time, which they view as closed. The utility of art is not to be limited to immediate needs, or by the demands of an ideology, because—and this is the main mistake of the radicals—the future is radically uncertain, and no ideology will ever fathom the future (or rather, futures). Even if we limit ourselves to the problem of utility, it must be said that we do not know what future needs will be. But beauty—Apollo Belvedere and Pushkin, both rejected by the radicals—will always be useful, in Dostoevsky's view. Thus, although the aesthetic (beauty) and the useful were regarded as opposite demands, they are the same when utility is properly understood. Dostoevsky presented this argument as a middle ground between the two camps, but it is plain that it is a sophisticated version of the anti-utilitarian position. I paraphrase Dostoevsky's position as expressed in his classic article, "Mr. ——bov and the Question of Art." For an English version, see *Dostoevsky's Occasional Writings,* ed. and trans. David Magarshack (New York: Random House, 1963), pp. 86-137.

59. The most profound interpretation of *ressentiment* in Dostoevsky is Michael André Bernstein, "Lacerations: The Novels of Fyodor Dostoevsky," in *Bitter Carnival: "Ressentiment" and the Abject Hero* (Princeton, N.J.: Princeton University Press, 1992), pp. 87-120. Like Dostoevsky, Bernstein is himself concerned with the role of *ressentiment* in the inscape of the intellectual's mentality and with the spread of a dangerous complex of ideas to society at large. See esp. his book's introduction, "Murder and the Utopian Moment," pp. 3-10, and its concluding chap., "Those Children That Come at You with Knives: Charles Manson and the Modern Saturnalia," pp. 157-84. Bernstein's book ends with a passage from *The Idiot.*

60. Cf. Ivan Karamazov's comment to Alyosha in the chapter "The Brothers Make Friends": "And I won't go through all the axioms laid down by Russian boys on that subject [atheism], all derived from European hypotheses; for what's a hypothesis there, is an axiom with the Russian boy, and not only with the boys but with their teachers too, for our Russian professors are often just the same boys themselves" (*BK,* 278-79). The *Diary*'s passage on "the Russian aspect of their teachings" serves as the epigraph to Joseph Frank, *Through the Russian Prism: Essays on Literature and Culture* (Princeton, N.J.: Princeton University Press, 1990). See esp. chap. 6, "The Search for a Positive Hero," pp. 75-82.

Part 3: The New Design

61. I have come to agree with a version of the thesis advanced by Aileen Kelly that the *Diary* is riven by inconsistencies between two visions. Kelly calls those two visions "irony" and "utopia." Her "irony" corresponds roughly to my "prosaics" (see part 4). "Herzen had argued with great cogency that one cannot be both an ironist and a utopian. *Diary of a Writer* can be seen as an evasion of that choice" (Kelly, "Irony and Utopia," p. 407). It seems to me that something close to what Kelly calls the ironic vision gave birth to the original design of the *Diary*; the utopian vision, when it overcame Dostoevsky, led to the design's abandonment. He "evaded" the choice by making both in turn and never reconciling them.

62. All the more remarkable because the letter was written at the end of 1877, when the *Diary* no longer seemed to possess formal unity. The passage seems to express Dostoevsky's original desire to make the *Diary* a new kind of literary form even while he attempted to persuade himself that somehow, despite all the changes the work had undergone, the formal unity was undamaged, if not perfected. For a reading of another key passage in this letter—Dostoevsky's hope that the *Diary* itself might become one genre in a still larger and more heterogeneous work(!)—see Andrew Wachtel's *An Obsession with History* (Stanford: Stanford University Press, forthcoming). Wachtel argues that *Karamazov* itself might be regarded as a work embedded in (or should we say *embedded out* of?) the *Diary*.

63. I refer, of course, to Ippolit Terentiev in *The Idiot*. Garnett renders the line: "Can anything that has no shape appear as a shape?": Constance Garnett, trans., *The Idiot* by Fyodor Dostoevsky (New York: Modern Library, 1935), p. 389. Robert Louis Jackson has seen in this line the key to Dostoevsky's poetics. See his classic study, *Dostoevsky's Quest for Form: A Study of His Philosophy of Art* (New Haven, Conn.: Yale University Press, 1966), esp. the chap. "Two Kinds of Beauty," pp. 40–70.

64. In the monthly *Diary*, issues range from two to four chapters. Most have two. There are three double issues (issues for two months), two of which have four chapters (July–August 1876 and May–June 1877) and one of which has three chapters (July–August 1877). January 1876, March 1877, October 1877, November 1877, and August 1880 have three chapters each.

65. Bakhtin uses the term *clamps* in this sense. See, e.g., *Problems*, p. 72.

66. I am not going to describe this Christmas party, he begins, because "I read about it myself with much pleasure in other feuilletons" (1/76, 1.3).

67. Or consider this marvelous sample of this kind of rhetoric, which occurs in the same article: speaking about clergymen-teachers who have engaged in work stoppages for more pay, Dostoevsky comments, "Our newspapers take the side of the whiners, as I do myself" (1/76, 2/3).

68. See the note in Dostoevsky's notebooks (*Unpublished Dostoevsky*

2: 114-15). The concepts *obraz* (image), *obrazit'*, *bezobrazie* (ugliness, shapelessness) are central to Robert Louis Jackson's reading of Dostoevsky's aesthetics; see *Dostoevsky's Quest for Form*. Caryl Emerson uses the difference between Jackson, who focuses on the image, and Bakhtin, who focuses on the word, to present two views of Dostoevsky's work and to create a dialogue between two critical visions. See Emerson, "Readings of Dostoevsky that Bakhtin Couldn't Do (Toward a Typology of Loopholes in His Thesis)," in *Freedom and Responsibility in Russian Literature*, ed. Allen and Morson.

69. Believing in the devil without believing in God: this puzzling statement also appears in *The Possessed*, where it is glossed as the position of worldly people who really have no convictions at all, as distinguished from passionate atheists, who disbelieve passionately in both God and the devil. "Is it possible to believe in the devil without believing in God?" asks Stavrogin. The monk Tikhon replies, "That's quite possible. It's done right and left." Both Tikhon and Stavrogin then equate the worldly people who believe not in God but in the devil with the "lukewarm" mentioned in the Apocalypse: "I know thy works, that thou art neither cold nor hot; I would thou wert cold or hot. So then because thou art lukewarm, and neither cold nor hot, I will spue thee out of my mouth" (Revelation 3:15-16). See the chapter "At Tikhon's" in *The Possessed*, pp. 698-99.

70. Garnett's title "Lacerations" preserves this poetic structure for the book, but it is lost in the recent translation by Pevear and Volokhonsky, who render the title as "Strains." See Richard Pevear and Larissa Volokhonsky, trans., *The Brothers Karamazov: A Novel in Four Parts with Epilogue* by Fyodor Dostoevsky (San Francisco: North Point, 1990). See Caryl Emerson's review of this version: Emerson, "The Brothers, Complete," *Hudson Review* 44, no. 2 (Summer 1991): 309-16.

71. See Morson, *Boundaries*, pp. 30-33. Of course, in a looser sense, the term algorithm is used this way.

Part 4: How and Why Dostoevsky Abandoned His Design

72. The important concept of "form-shaping ideology" (or "idea" or "force") appears intermittently in Bakhtin. See, e.g., *Problems*, pp. 103, 110. For a gloss on this concept, see Morson and Emerson, *Mikhail Bakhtin*, chaps. 6 and 7.

73. See Mikhail Bakhtin, "Epic and Novel: Toward a Methodology for the Study of the Novel," in *The Dialogic Imagination: Four Essays by M. M. Bakhtin*, trans. Caryl Emerson and Michael Holquist (Austin: University of Texas Press, 1981), p. 28. For a gloss on the concept, see Morson and Emerson, *Mikhail Bakhtin*, p. 276.

74. In "Irony and Utopia" Kelly observes: "The *Diary*, like *The Brothers Karamazov*, is ambivalent because it operates between two sets of criteria for making sense of reality and human conflict that are never reconciled. Dostoevsky the utopian believes that history derives its meaning from the transcendent purpose it is designed to accomplish, while Dostoevsky the

ironist sees human freedom threatened by attempts to impose a single coherent pattern on the chaotic multiplicity of contingent reality" (p. 410). Allowing for a difference in terminology, I think that Kelly is quite right about the *Diary*. From an aesthetic point of view, the relevant fact is that one of the two irreconcilable ideas proved incompatible with the design developed to express the other. I believe that in writing *Karamazov*, Dostoevsky set himself the task of finding both ideological and aesthetic reconciliation. That is, he sought to combine the idea that inspired the *Diary*'s design with the contradictory one that proved irreconcilable with it. Aesthetically, he surely succeeded in *Karamazov*. Ideologically, he produced an intriguing, pleasing, and unstable amalgam, which I prefer to call "the mythic prosaic."

75. On Dostoevsky's debate with Goncharov and Tolstoy, and on the problem of describing the present moment, see Robert Louis Jackson, "The Problem of Type," in *Dostoevsky's Quest for Form*, pp. 92–123. Agreeing with Dostoevsky that realist artists represent types (characteristic of certain aspects of society), Goncharov observes in a letter to Dostoevsky: "You say yourself that 'such a type is being born'; forgive me if I permit myself to note a contradiction here: if it is being born, then it is still not a *type*. . . . A work of [realist] art . . . can only appear, in my opinion, after life has set; it does not harmonize with life that is coming into existence" (cited ibid., p. 109). Goncharov also once observed that "art, a serious and strict one, cannot depict chaos, disintegration" (cited ibid., p. 111).

76. Fyodor Dostoevsky, *A Raw Youth*, trans. Constance Garnett (New York: Dell, 1961), p. 607.

77. The association of class with time is made by Arkady's tutor in *A Raw Youth*, who refers with disparagement to those who write what are in effect historical novels set in the present. They do so by simply choosing some representative of a class that has lost its former importance, some aristocratic "grandson of those heroes" of historical novels set in the past. The allusion is evidently to Konstantin Levin (in Tolstoy's *Anna Karenina*) as a sort of "grandson" of some hero in *War and Peace*.

It is worth noting that in ruling out the aristocracy from the cutting edge of presentness, Dostoevsky is drastically limiting the field of possibilities for history. For how does he know that the aristocracy could not still have an effect? Here Dostoevsky may be charged with some sort of historical hubris, which may be seen as a symptom of the sort of thinking that would lead him to imagine that he had found *the* key to history.

78. This falsification would seem to be a version of what George Kline has called "the fallacy of the actual future." See George L. Kline, "'Present,' 'Past,' and 'Future' as Categoreal Terms, and the 'Fallacy of the Actual Future,'" *Review of Metaphysics* 40 (December 1986): 215–35.

79. Leo Tolstoy, *War and Peace*, trans. Ann Dunnigan (New York: Signet, 1968), p. 1444. Further references are to *W&P.*

80. On memory in Tolstoy, see Natasha Sankovitch, "Creating and Recovering Experience: Repetition in Tolstoy" (Ph.D. diss., Stanford University, 1992).

116   A Writer's Diary

81. In *Problems* Bakhtin observes that in the polyphonic novel the plot is "conceived as only one of many possible plots and is consequently in the final analysis merely accidental for a given hero" (p. 84). In "Epic and Novel" he observes that "reality as we have it in the novel is only one of many possible realities" (p. 34). For Bakhtin, this view of time also justified ethical responsibility: in the present, we have choice, and so are accountable. And once an event has happened, once it has become past, it is irrevocable, and so our actions have real consequences. (If events were revocable after they had happened—if the past were changeable—then responsibility would disappear along with the sentiment of regret.)

82. I owe this phrase to Caryl Emerson (conversation). On the temporality of chroniclers and on rumors, see Emerson, *Boris Godunov: Transpositions of a Russian Theme* (Bloomington, Ind.: Indiana University Press, 1986), chapters 2 and 3.

83. I have retranslated this and other lines from *Karamazov*, inasmuch as Garnett (like other translators) has a tendency to soften Dostoevsky's seemingly obsessive hypotheticals. In Garnett, this sentence occurs on p. 6 (end of bk. 1, chap. 1).

84. *War and Peace* and *Crime and Punishment* were being serialized at the same time in the same journal. Porfiry refers to a recently published part of Tolstoy's novel. A network of ongoing interrelations developed between the two works as they were being serialized.

85. At the crucial moment, Dmitri does not kill his father. A Freudian might be inclined to describe these events as a successful resistance of the repressed wish that has become manifest. There would be some merit in such a description, although one might also point out that Dmitri's wish is not at all repressed but fully conscious and frequently verbalized. In general, Freudians have not faced the difficulty that Dostoevsky presents by making what should be difficult to speak (from a psychoanalytic perspective) the subject of endless commentary by everyone from wise monks to gifted buffoons.

A more substantial objection might also be raised from a Dostoevskian standpoint. The psychoanalytic account assumes incorrectly that it is the evil wish that is somehow most "original" and most genuine, whereas Dostoevsky describes Dmitri's sense of nobility as no less original and genuine. Whichever choice Dmitri made, he would be denying a deep and powerful wish. Psychology here is fundamentally Manichaean: as Dmitri says, "God and the devil are fighting there and the battlefield is the heart of man" (*BK*, 127). This is another way of saying that time is open and we have choice. The psychoanalytic assumption that only the vicious is likely to be honest and truthful would seem to Dostoevsky an appalling *reverse sentimentality.* It also gives new meaning to Tikhon's statement that it is entirely possible to deny God but to believe readily in the devil. (My thanks to Caryl Emerson for her help in formulating this point.)

86. On time and the apocalypse in *The Idiot*, see Robert Hollander, "The Apocalyptic Framework of Dostoevsky's *The Idiot*," *Mosaic* 7 (1974): 123-39; and David M. Bethea, "*The Idiot:* Historicism Arrives at the

Station," in *The Shape of Apocalypse in Modern Russian Fiction* (Princeton, N.J.: Princeton University Press, 1989), pp. 62–104.

87. Bethea describes the *Idiot* as a "duel of temporalities" between historical chronicity and apocalypse (*"The Idiot,"* p. 93). He describes a decisive victory for apocalyptic temporality in this novel. It is worth noting that in *War and Peace* sideshadowing dominates the book's temporality because (unlike Dostoevsky) Tolstoy does not counterbalance it with vortex time. But in *Anna Karenina,* one mark of Anna's misperception of reality and her increasing illness is that she believes in omens, fate, and the vortex time of certain romances.

88. The epigraph is Luke 8:32–37.

89. For a recent reading of the Gogol of *Selected Passages* as a Gogolian character, see Alexander Zholkovsky, "Rereading Gogol's Miswritten Book: Notes on *Selected Passages from Correspondence with Friends*" in *Essays on Gogol: Logos and the Russian Word*, ed. Susanne Fusso and Priscilla Meyer (Evanston, Ill.: Northwestern University Press, 1992), pp. 172–84.

90. In "An Isolated Case" (3/77, 3.2), Dostoevsky tells a story about a doctor who, "in a hurry to get home to have his coffee," refused to help a drowned man just pulled out of the water. And yet this doctor "was, perhaps, an educated man with new ideas, a progressive, but one who 'rationally' demanded new, common laws and rights for all and paid no heed to isolated cases. He may have supposed, rather, that isolated cases damage the cause by postponing general solutions to the question and so far as isolated cases are concerned, 'the worse, the better.'"

91. I call this debate timeless because it seems to apply to our own epoch as well. Looking back on the carnage of the twentieth century, one recognizes the truth of Dostoevsky's (and Tolstoy's) idea that nothing causes greater suffering than schemes to save Humanity, or a favored portion of it, once and for all. From the Thousand-Year Reich to the Bolsheviks and the Khmer Rouge, we have witnessed the unprecedented horror of utopias in practice. And yet we have also become aware of the moral culpability of nations that could intervene to prevent terrible sufferings elsewhere but neglect to do so. But again, the record of such interventions, when they have been attempted, also calls attention to the dangers, both practical and moral, of judging at a distance. There seem to be no easy answers. It is hard to imagine a time when these questions would not be relevant.

92. On the ethically misleading character of extreme situations, see Bernstein, "Those Children That Come at You with Knives" and Bernstein, *Foregone Conclusions*.

A Writer's Diary

1 8 7 3

1

Introduction

On the twentieth of December I learned that everything had been settled and that I was the editor of *The Citizen*. This extraordinary event—extraordinary for me at least (I don't wish to offend anyone)—came about in a rather simple fashion, however. On the twentieth of December I had just read in the *Moscow News* the account of the wedding of the Chinese emperor; it left a strong impression on me. This magnificent and, apparently, extremely complex event also came about in a remarkably simple fashion: every last detail of the affair had been provided for and decreed a thousand years ago in nearly two hundred volumes of ceremonial. Comparing the enormity of the events in China with my own appointment as editor, I felt a sudden sense of ingratitude to our Russian practices, despite the ease with which my appointment had been confirmed. And I thought that we, that is, Prince Meshchersky and I, would have found it incomparably more advantageous to publish *The Citizen* in China. Everything is so clear over there.... On the appointed day we both would have presented ourselves at China's Main Administration for Press Affairs. After kowtowing and licking the floor, we would rise, raise our index fingers, and respectfully bow our heads. The Plenipotentiary-in-Chief for Press Affairs would, of course, pretend to take no more notice of us than he would of an errant fly. But the Third Assistant to the Third Secretary would rise, holding the warrant of my appointment as editor, and would pronounce in an impressive but gentle voice the admonition prescribed by the ceremonial. It would be so clear and so comprehensible that we both would be immensely pleased to hear it. Were I in China and were I stupid and honest enough, when taking on the editorship and acknowledging my own

limited abilities, to experience fear and pangs of conscience, someone would at once prove to me that I was doubly stupid to entertain
such feelings and that from that very moment I would have no
need of intelligence at all, assuming I had had any in the first
place; on the contrary, it would be far better if I had none at all.
And without a doubt, this would be a most pleasant thing to hear.
Concluding with the fine words: "Go thou, Editor; henceforth thou
mayest eat rice and drink tea with thy conscience newly set at rest,"
the Third Assistant to the Third Secretary would hand me a beautiful warrant printed in gold letters on red silk. Prince Meshchersky
would pass over a substantial bribe, and the two of us would go
home and immediately put out such a magnificent edition of *The
Citizen* as we could never publish here. In China we would put
out an excellent publication.

I suspect, however, that in China Prince Meshchersky would
certainly have tricked me by inviting me to be editor; he would
have done it mainly so that I could stand in for him at the Main
Administration of Press Affairs whenever he was summoned to
have his heels beaten with bamboo sticks. But I would outsmart
him: I would at once stop publication of *Bismarck* and would myself
commence writing articles so excellent that I would be summoned
to the bamboo sticks only after every other issue. I would learn to
write, however.

I would be an excellent writer in China; here, that sort of thing
is much more difficult. There, everything has been anticipated and
planned for a thousand years ahead, while here everything is topsy-
turvy for a thousand years. There I would have no choice but to
write clearly, so that I'm not sure who would read me. Here, if
you want people to read you it's better to write so that no one
understands. Only in the *Moscow News* do they write column-and-
a-half editorials and—to my astonishment—they are written clearly,
even if they are the products of a well-known pen. In *The Voice*
such editorials go on for eight, ten, twelve, and even thirteen columns. And so you see how many columns you must use up in
order to win respect.

In Russia, talking to other people is a science; at first glance,
at least, it seems just the same as in China. Here, as there, there
are a few very simplified and purely scientific techniques. Formerly,
for instance, the words "I don't understand a thing" meant only
that the person who uttered them was ignorant; now they bring
great honor. One need only say, proudly and with a frank air, "I

don't understand religion; I don't understand anything about Russia; I don't understand anything about art," and immediately you place yourself above the crowd. And it's especially good if you really don't understand anything.

But this simplified technique proves nothing. In essence, each one of us in Russia, without thinking much about it, suspects that everyone else is ignorant and never asks, conversely, "What if I'm the one who's ignorant, in fact?" It's a situation that ought to please us all, and yet no one is pleased and everyone gets angry. Indeed, sober thought in our time is all but impossible: it costs too much. It is true that people buy ready-made ideas. They are sold everywhere, and even given away; but the ones that come free of charge prove to be even more expensive, and people are already beginning to realize that. The result is benefit to none and the same old disorder.

We are, if you like, the same as China, but without her sense of order. We are barely beginning the process that is already coming to an end in China. No doubt we will reach that same end, but when? In order to get a thousand volumes of ceremonial so as at last to win the right not to think deeply about anything, we must experience at least another thousand years of sober thought. And there you have it—no one wants to hasten this term because no one wants to think.

Something else that is true: if no one wants to think, then, it would seem, so much the easier for the Russian writer. Indeed, it really is easier; and woe to the writer and publisher who in our time begins to think soberly. It's even worse for one who decides to study and to understand things on his own, and still worse for one who makes a sincere declaration of his intention. And if he declares that he has already managed to understand a tiny smidgen and wants to express his ideas, then everyone quickly drops him. The only thing he can do is to seek out some suitable individual, or even hire one, and simply talk to him and to him alone. Perhaps he could publish a magazine for that one individual. It's a loathsome situation, because it amounts to talking to yourself and publishing a magazine only for your own amusement. I strongly suspect that for a long time yet *The Citizen* will have to talk to itself and appear only for its own amusement. Remember that medical science considers talking to oneself a sign of predisposition to insanity. *The Citizen* certainly must speak to citizens, and that is precisely its whole dilemma!

And so this is the sort of publication with which I have become involved. My situation is as uncertain as it can be. But I shall talk to myself and for my own amusement, in the form of this diary, whatever may come of it. What shall I talk about? About everything that strikes me and sets me to thinking. If I should find a reader and, God forbid, an opponent, I realize that one must be able to carry on a conversation and know whom to address and how to address him. I shall try to master this skill because among us, that is to say, in literature, it is the most difficult one of all. Besides, there are different kinds of opponents: one cannot strike up a conversation with every one. I'll tell you a story I heard the other day. They say it is an ancient fable, perhaps even of Indian origin, and that's a very comforting thought.

Once upon a time the pig got into a quarrel with the lion and challenged him to a duel. When the pig came home he thought the matter over and lost his nerve. The whole herd assembled to consider the matter and announced their decision as follows: "Now then, brother pig, there is a wallow not far from here; go and have a good roll in it and then proceed to the duel. You'll see what happens."

The pig did just that. The lion arrived, took a sniff, wrinkled up his nose, and walked away. And for a long time thereafter the pig boasted that the lion had turned tail and fled the field of battle.

That's the fable. Of course we don't have any lions here—we don't have the climate for them and they're too grand a thing for us in any case. But in place of the lion put an honest person, such as each of us is obliged to be, and the moral comes out the same.

Apropos of that, I'll tell you another little story.

Once when speaking with the late Herzen I paid him many compliments on his book *From the Other Shore*. To my great pleasure, Mikhail Petrovich Pogodin heaped praise on this same book in his excellent and most curious article about his meeting abroad with Herzen. The book is written in the form of a dialogue between Herzen and his opponent.

"What I especially like," I remarked in passing, "is that your opponent is also very clever. You must agree that in many instances he backs you right to the wall."

"Why that's the essence of the whole piece," laughed Herzen. "I'll tell you a story. Once when I was in St. Petersburg, Belinsky dragged me off to his place and sat me down to listen to him read an article, 'A Conversation Between Mr. A and Mr. B,' that he had written in some heat. (You can find it in his *Collected Works*.) In this article, Mr. A., who is Belinsky himself, of course, is made out to be very clever, while his opponent, Mr. B., is rather shallow. When Belinsky had finished reading, he asked me with feverish anticipation:

"'Well, what do you think?'

"'Oh, it's fine, very fine, and it's obvious that you are very clever. But whatever made you waste your time talking to a fool like that?'

"Belinsky threw himself on the sofa, buried his face in a pillow, and shouted, laughing for all he was worth:

"'Oh, you've got me there, you really have!'"

2

Old People

That story about Belinsky put me in mind of my debut in literature, God knows how many years ago. It was a sad and fateful time for me. I recall Belinsky in particular, as he was when I knew him then and as he then knew me. I often recall these old people now because, of course, I'm encountering the new people. Belinsky was the most intense person I have ever met. Herzen was something else altogether: he was a product of our aristocracy, *gentilhomme russe et citoyen du monde* above all, a type that appeared only in Russia and which could appear only in Russia. Herzen did not emigrate and he did not lay the foundation for other Russian emigrés; no, he was simply born an emigré. They all, those people like him, were just born emigrés, even though the majority of them never left Russia. In one hundred and fifty years of the life of the Russian gentry that preceded him, with only a few exceptions, the last roots rotted and the last links with the Russian soil and the Russian truth were shaken loose. History itself seemed to predestine Herzen as its most vivid illustration of how the huge majority of our educated classes split themselves off from the People. In that sense he is a historical type. When they broke with the People, they naturally lost God as well. The restless ones among them became atheists; the listless and quiescent ones became indifferent. They bore only contempt for the Russian People, all the while imagining and believing that they loved the People and wished the best for them. They loved the People negatively, imagining in their stead some sort of ideal, a Russian People as they ought to be according to their conceptions. This ideal people, through an involuntary process in the minds of certain leading representatives of the majority, took the form of the Paris mob of 1793. This was the most alluring ideal of a people at that time. Herzen, of course,

126

had to become a socialist and to become one exactly in the manner
of a young Russian nobleman, that is, without any need or aim
but simply out of the "logical progression of ideas" and the emptiness he felt in his heart when in Russia. He renounced the very
foundations of the old society; he denied the family, and was, it
seems, a good husband and father. He denied private property but,
pending the new order, contrived to put his own affairs in good
order and was pleased to enjoy financial independence while abroad.
He worked to foment revolutions and incited others to them, and
at the same time he loved comfort and family peace. He was an
artist, a thinker, a brilliant writer, a remarkably erudite man, a
wit, a marvelous conversationalist (he spoke even better than he
wrote), and had a superb capacity for self-reflection. Self-reflection—the ability to make of his own deepest feelings an object
which he could set before him, pay it tribute and, in the next breath
perhaps, ridicule it—was a thing he had developed to the highest
degree. Certainly, he was an unusual man; but whatever he was—
whether he wrote his memoirs or published a journal with Proudhon
or went out to the barricades of Paris (which he described so
amusingly in his memoirs); whether he suffered or rejoiced or
doubted; whether, to please the Poles, he sent to Russia, in 1863,
his appeal to Russian revolutionaries, even though he did not trust
the Poles and knew that they had deceived him, knew that his
appeal would be the doom of hundreds of these unhappy young
people; whether he, with incredible naiveté, admitted this himself
in one of his last articles, not even suspecting in what light his
admission cast him—always, everywhere, throughout his life, he
was above all a *gentilhomme russe et citoyen du monde*, simply a
product of the old system of serfdom which he hated and from
which he emerged, not just by his birth but by his very rupture
with his native land and its ideals. Belinsky, on the contrary, was
no *gentilhomme* at all—oh, no. (God knows what his origins were.
I think his father was an army doctor.)

For the most part, Belinsky was not a self-reflective person; he
was always, throughout his life, a wholehearted enthusiast. He was
delighted with my first work, *Poor People* (subsequently, a year
later, we went our separate ways for various reasons which, however,
were altogether trivial); but at the time of our first acquaintance
he attached himself to me with all his heart, and at once, with the
most straightforward rashness, he threw himself into converting
me to his faith. I am by no means exaggerating his ardent attraction

to me, at least in the first months of our acquaintance. I found him to be a passionate socialist, and in speaking to me he began directly with atheism. That was very significant, I thought, and revealed his amazing intuition and his unusual capacity to become totally inspired by an idea. The Internationale, in one of its proclamations about two years ago, began directly with the significant declaration: "We are above all an atheistic society," i.e., they began with the very essence of the matter. Belinsky began in the same way. While cherishing reason, science, and realism above all, he also understood better than anyone that reason, science, and realism alone could only create an antheap and not the social "harmony" in which man could create a life for himself. He knew that moral principles are the basis of everything. He believed in the new moral principles of socialism (which to date, however, have shown nothing but vile distortions of nature and common sense) to the point of folly and with no reflection at all; here there was only enthusiasm. But as a socialist he first had to dethrone Christianity. He knew that the revolution must necessarily begin with atheism. He had to dethrone the religion that provided the moral foundation of the society he was rejecting. He radically rejected the family, private property, and the moral responsibility of the individual. (I would note that he, like Herzen, was also a good husband and father). Certainly he understood that in denying individual moral responsibility he was also denying personal freedom; but he believed with all his being (much more blindly than Herzen, of course, who, it seems, had his doubts near the end) that socialism not only would not destroy personal freedom but would, to the contrary, restore it to unheard-of grandeur, but on a new and adamantine foundation.

There remained, however, the radiant personality of Christ himself, which was most difficult to contend with. Belinsky, as a socialist, was absolutely bound to destroy Christ's teachings; to label them false and uninformed philanthropy, proscribed by contemporary science and by economic principles. Still there remained the most radiant image of the God-man, its moral unattainability, its marvelous and miraculous beauty. But Belinsky, in his continuous, unflagging enthusiasm, did not pause even before this insurmountable obstacle, as did Renan when he proclaimed in his *Vie de Jésus*, a book filled with unbelief, that Christ is still the ideal of human beauty, an unattainable type, never to be repeated in the future.

"But do you know," Belinsky screeched one evening (sometimes, if he was very excited, he would screech) as he turned to me, "Do you know that man's sins cannot be counted against him and that he cannot be laden down with obligations and with turning the other cheek when society is set up in such a mean fashion that a man cannot help but do wrong; economic factors alone lead him to do wrong, and it is absurd and cruel to demand from a man something which the very laws of nature make it impossible for him to carry out, even if he wanted to...."

We were not alone that evening; one of Belinsky's friends, a man whom he highly respected and whose advice he often followed, was present, as was a certain young novice writer who later won fame in literature.

"It's touching just to look at him," said Belinsky, suddenly breaking off his furious exclamations and turning to his friend as he pointed to me. "I no sooner mention the name of Christ than his whole face changes, just as if he were going to cry.... But believe me, you naive fellow," he said, attacking me again, "Believe me, that your Christ, were he born in our time, would be the most undistinguished and ordinary of men; he would be utterly eclipsed by today's science and by those forces that now advance humanity."

"Oh, I think not," interrupted Belinsky's friend. (I recall that we were sitting, while Belinsky was pacing back and forth around the room). "I think not. If Christ appeared now he would join the socialist movement and take his place at its head...."

"He would indeed," Belinsky agreed suddenly with surprising haste. "He certainly would join the socialists and follow them."

These forces that advanced humanity, which Christ was destined to join, were then all Frenchmen: George Sand, the now totally forgotten Cabet, Pierre Leroux, and Proudhon, who was then only beginning his work. As far as I can recall, Belinsky held these four in the greatest respect. Fourier's reputation had slipped a good deal by then. Belinsky would discuss these four for whole evenings at a time. There was one German to whom Belinsky then paid great tribute, and that was Feuerbach. (Belinsky, who all his life could never master a single foreign language, pronounced it "Fierbach"). Strauss was spoken of very reverently.

Given such a warm faith in his ideas, he was, of course, the happiest of men. People were wrong in writing later that had Belinsky lived longer he would have joined the Slavophiles. He would never have ended up a Slavophile. Belinsky might have ended by emigrating had he lived longer and succeeded in getting out of

the country. And now, as a small and rapturous old man whose
former warm faith never permitted him the slightest doubt, he
would be making the rounds of various congresses in Germany and
Switzerland; or he might have taken a post as adjutant to some
German Mme. Högg, and be running errands on behalf of the
women's movement.

Still, this most blessed among men, who possessed a remarkably
tranquil conscience, had his occasional sad moments. But his sad-
ness was of a special kind: it came not from doubts or disillusionments—oh, no—but from the questions "Why not today, why not
tomorrow?" In all of Russia there was no one in a bigger hurry.
Once I met him near the Znamensky church at three o'clock in
the afternoon. He told me that he had gone out for a stroll and
was on his way home.

"I often drop by here to take a look at how the construction is
progressing" (the station for the Nikolaevsky railway was still being
built). "It makes my heart rest a bit easier to stand and watch the
work: at long last we'll have one railway at least. You'll never
believe how that comforts my heart at times."

This was said well and with passion; Belinsky never put on airs.
We set off together. I recall that on our way he said, "And when
they've laid me in my grave" (he knew that he had consumption),
"only then will they realize whom they've lost."

In his last year of life I no longer visited him. He had taken a
dislike to me; but I had passionately accepted all his teaching. A
year later, in Tobolsk, while we were in the cells of the transit
prison awaiting our further fate, the wives of the Decembrists
managed to persuade the prison superintendent to arrange a secret
meeting with them in his apartment. We saw these great martyr-
esses who had voluntarily followed their husbands to Siberia. They
gave up everything: their social position, wealth, connections, relatives, and sacrificed it all for the supreme moral duty, the freest
duty that can ever exist. Guilty of nothing, they endured for twenty-
five long years everything that their convicted husbands endured.
Our meeting went on for an hour. They blessed us on our new
journey; they made the sign of the cross over us and gave each of
us a copy of the Gospels, the only book permitted in the prison.
This book lay under my pillow during the four years of my penal
servitude. I read it and sometimes read it to others. I used it to
teach one convict to read. The people around me were precisely
those who, according to Belinsky's beliefs, *could not help* but commit

crimes; accordingly, they were justified but were merely less fortunate than others. I knew that the whole Russian People also
called us "unfortunates," and I heard this term used many times
and coming from many lips. But this was something different,
certainly not what Belinsky was talking about and what we hear
now in some verdicts brought down by our juries, for example. In
this word "unfortunate" and in this verdict of our People there
was the reflection of a different idea. Four years of penal servitude
was a long school; I had the time to become convinced.... And
that is just what I would like to talk about now.

3

Environment

I think that all jurors the whole world over, and our jurors in particular, must share a feeling of power (they have other feelings as well, of course); more precisely, they have a feeling of autocratic power. This can be an ugly feeling, at least when it dominates their other feelings. Even though it may not be obvious, even though it may be suppressed by a mass of other, nobler emotions, this sense of autocratic power must be a strong presence in the heart of every juror, even when he is most acutely aware of his civic duty. I suppose that this is somehow a product of the laws of nature themselves. And so, I recall how terribly curious I was, in one respect at least, when our new (just) courts were instituted. In my flights of fancy I saw trials where almost all the jurors might be peasants who only yesterday were serfs. The prosecutor and the defense lawyers would address them, trying to curry favor and divine their mood, while our good peasants would sit and keep their mouths shut: "So that's how things are these days. If I feel like lettin' the fella off, I'll do it; and if not, it's Siberia for him."

And yet the surprising thing now is that they do not convict the accused but acquit them consistently. Of course, this is also an exercise, almost even an abuse of power, but in one direction, toward an extreme, a sentimental one, perhaps—one can't tell. But it is a general, almost preconceived tendency, just as if everyone had conspired. There can be no doubt how widespread this "tendency" is. And the problem is that the mania for acquittal regardless of the circumstances has developed not only among peasants, yesterday's insulted and humiliated, but has seized all Russian jurors, even those from the uppermost classes such as noblemen and university professors. The universality of this tendency in itself presents a most curious topic for reflection and leads one to diverse and sometimes even strange surmises.

Not long ago one of our most influential newspapers briefly set forth, in a very modest and well-intentioned little article, the following hypothesis: perhaps our jurors, as people who suddenly, without rhyme or reason, sense the magnitude of the power that has been conferred upon them (simply out of the blue, as it were), and who for centuries have been oppressed and downtrodden—perhaps they are inclined to take any opportunity to spite authorities such as the prosecutor, just for the fun of it or, so to say, for the sake of contrast with the past. Not a bad hypothesis and also not without a certain playful spirit of its own; but, of course, it can't explain everything.

"We just feel sorry to wreck the life of another person; after all, he's a human being too. Russians are compassionate people"—such is the conclusion reached by others, as I've sometimes heard it expressed.

However, I have always thought that in England, for instance, the people are also compassionate; and even if they do not have the same softheartedness as we Russians, then at least they have a sense of humanity; they have an awareness and a keen sense of Christian duty to their neighbor, a sense which, perhaps, taken to a high degree, to a firm and independent conviction, may be even stronger than ours, when you take into account the level of education over there and their long tradition of independent thought. Over there, such power didn't just tumble down on them out of the blue, after all. Indeed, they themselves invented the very system of trial by jury; they borrowed it from no one, but affirmed it through centuries; they took it from life and didn't merely receive it as a gift.

Yet over there the juror understands from the very moment he takes his place in the courtroom that he is not only a sensitive individual with a tender heart but is first of all a citizen. He even thinks (correctly or not) that fulfilling his civic duty stands even higher than any private victory of the heart. Not very long ago there was a clamor throughout the kingdom when a jury acquitted one notorious thief. The hubbub all over the country proved that if sentences just like ours are possible over there, then all the same they happen rarely, as exceptions, and they quickly rouse public indignation. An English juror understands above all that in his hands rests the banner of all England; that he has already ceased to be a private individual and is obliged to represent the opinion of his country. The capacity to be a citizen is just that capacity to elevate oneself to the level of the opinion of the entire country. Oh, yes, there are "compassionate" verdicts there, and the influence of the "corrupting environment" (our favorite doctrine now, it seems) is taken into consideration. But this is done only up to a certain limit, as far as is tolerated by the common sense of the country and the level of its informed and Christian morality (and that level, it seems, is quite high). Nonetheless, very often the English juror grudgingly pronounces the guilty verdict, understanding first of all that his duty consists primarily in using that verdict to bear witness to all his fellow citizens that in old England (for which any one of them is prepared to shed his blood) vice is still called vice and villainy is still called villainy, and that the moral foundations of the country endure—firm, unchanged, standing as they stood before.

"Suppose we do assume," I hear a voice saying, "that your firm foundations (Christian ones, that is) endure and that in truth one must be a citizen above all, must hold up the banner, etc., etc., as you said. I won't challenge that for the time being. But where do you think we'll find such a citizen in Russia? Just consider our situation only a few years ago! Civic rights (and what rights!) have tumbled down on our citizen as if from a mountain. They've crushed him, and they're still only a burden to him, a real burden!"

"Of course, there's truth in what you say," I answer the voice, a bit despondent, "but still, the Russian People...."

"The Russian People? Please!" says another voice. "We've just heard that the boon of citizenship has tumbled down from the mountain and crushed the People. Perhaps they not only feel that they've received so much power as a gift, but even sense that it was wasted on them because they got it for nothing and aren't yet worthy of it. Please note that this certainly doesn't mean that they really aren't worthy of the gift, and that it was *unnecessary* or *premature* to give it; quite the contrary: the People themselves, in their humble conscience, acknowledge that they are unworthy, and the People's humble, yet lofty, awareness of their own unworthiness is precisely the guarantee that they are worthy. And meanwhile the People, in their humility, are troubled. Who has peered into the innermost secret places of their hearts? Is there anyone among us who can claim truly to know the Russian People? No, it's not simply a matter here of compassion and softheartedness, as you, sir, said so scoffingly. It's that this power itself is frightful! We have been frightened by this dreadful power over human fate, over the fates of our brethren, and until we mature into our citizenship, we will show mercy. We show mercy out of fear. We sit as jurors and think, perhaps: 'Are we any better than the accused? We have money and are free from want, but were we to be in his position we might do even worse than he did—so we show mercy.' So maybe it's a good thing, this heartfelt mercy. Maybe it's a pledge of some sublime form of Christianity of the future which the world has not yet known!"

"That's a partly Slavophile voice," I think to myself. It's truly a comforting thought, but the conjecture about the People's humility before the power they have received gratis and that has been bestowed upon them, still "unworthy" of it, is, of course, somewhat neater than the suggestion that they want to "tease the prosecutor a bit," although even the latter still appeals to me because of its realism (accepting it, of course, more as an individual case, which indeed is what its author intended). But still . . . this is what troubles me most of all: how is it that our People suddenly began to be so afraid of a little suffering? "It's a painful thing," they say, "to convict a man." And what of it? So take your pain away with you. The truth stands higher than your pain.

In fact, if we consider that we ourselves are sometimes even worse than the criminal, we thereby also acknowledge that we are half to blame for his crime. If he has transgressed the law which the nation prescribed for him, then we ourselves are to blame that he now stands before us. If we were better, then he, too, would be better and would not now be standing here before us. . . .

"And so now we ought to acquit him?"

No, quite the contrary: now is precisely the time we must tell the truth and call evil evil; in return, we must ourselves take on half the burden of the sentence. We will enter the courtroom with the thought that we, too, are guilty. This pain of the heart, which everyone so fears now and which we will take with us when we leave the court, will be punishment for us. If this pain is genuine and severe, then it will purge us and make us better. And when we have made ourselves better, we will also improve the environment and make it better. And this is the only way it can be made better. But to flee from our own pity and acquit everyone so as not to suffer ourselves—why, that's too easy. Doing that, we slowly and surely come to the conclusion that there are no crimes at all, and "the environment is to blame" for everything. We inevitably reach the point where we consider crime even a duty, a noble protest

against the environment. "Since society is organized in such a vile
fashion, one can't get along in it without protest and without
crimes." "Since society is organized in such a vile fashion, one
can only break out of it with a knife in hand." So runs the doctrine
of the environment, as opposed to Christianity which, fully recognizing the pressure of the environment and having proclaimed
mercy for the sinner, still places a moral duty on the individual to
struggle with the environment and marks the line where the environment ends and duty begins.

In making the individual responsible, Christianity thereby acknowledges his freedom. In making the individual dependent on
every flaw in the social structure, however, the doctrine of the
environment reduces him to an absolute nonentity, exempts him
totally from every personal moral duty and from all independence,
reduces him to the lowest form of slavery imaginable. If that's so,
then if a man wants some tobacco and has no money, he can kill
another to get some tobacco. And why not? An educated man, who
suffers more keenly than an uneducated one from unsatisfied needs,
requires money to satisfy them. So why shouldn't he kill an uneducated man if he has no other way of getting money? Haven't
you listened to the voices of the defense lawyers: "Of course," they
say, "the law has been violated; of course he committed a crime
in killing this uneducated man. But, gentlemen of the jury, take
into consideration that...." And so on. Why such views have
almost been expressed already, and not only "almost.". . .

"But you, however," says someone's sarcastic voice, "you seem
to be charging the People with subscribing to the latest theory of
the environment; but how on earth did they get that theory? Sometimes these jurors sitting there are all peasants, and every one of
them considers it a mortal sin to eat meat during the fasts. You
should have just accused them squarely of harboring social
tendencies."

"Of course, you're right—what do they care about 'environment,'
the peasants as a whole, that is?" I think to myself. "But still,
these ideas float about in the air; there is something pervasive about
an idea...."

"Listen to that, now!" laughs the sarcastic voice.

"But what if our People are particularly inclined toward this
theory of the environment, by their very nature, or by their Slavic
inclinations, if you like? What if they are the best raw material in
Europe for those who preach such a doctrine?"

The sarcastic voice guffaws even louder, but it's a bit forced.

No, this is still only a trick someone is pulling on the People, not a "philosophy of the environment." There's a mistake here, a fraud, and a very seductive fraud.

One can explain this fraud, using an example at least, as follows:

Let's grant that the People do call criminals "unfortunates" and give them pennies and bread. What do they mean by doing that, and what have they meant over the course of perhaps some centuries? Is it Christian truth or the truth of the "environment?" Here is precisely where we find the stumbling block and the place where the lever is concealed which the propagator of "the environment" could seize upon to effect.

Some ideas exist that are unexpressed and unconscious but that simply are strongly felt; many such ideas are fused, as it were, with the human heart. They are present in the People generally, and in humanity taken as a whole. Only while these ideas lie unconscious in peasant life and are simply felt strongly and truly can the People live a vigorous "living life." The whole energy of the life of the People consists in the striving to bring these hidden ideas to light. The more obstinately the People cling to them, the less capable they are of betraying their instincts, the less inclined they are to yield to diverse and erroneous explanations of these ideas—the stronger, more steadfast, and happier they are. Among such ideas concealed within the Russian People—the ideas of the Russian People—is the notion of calling a crime a misfortune and the criminal an unfortunate.

This notion is purely Russian. It has not been observed among any European people. In the West it's proclaimed only by some philosophers and thinkers. But our People proclaimed it long before their philosophers and thinkers. It does not follow, however, that the People would never be led astray at least temporarily or superficially by some thinker's false interpretation of this idea. The ultimate interpretation and the last word will remain, undoubtedly, always the People's, but *in the short term* this might not be the case.

To put it briefly, when they use the word "unfortunate," the People are saying to the "unfortunate" more or less as follows: "You have sinned and are suffering, but we, too, are sinners. Had we been in your place we might have done even worse. Were we better than we are, perhaps you might not be in prison. With the retribution for your crime you have also taken on the burden for all our lawlessness. Pray for us, and we pray for you. But for now, unfortunate ones, accept these alms of ours; we give them that you might know we remember you and have not broken our ties with you as a brother."

You must agree that there is nothing easier than to apply the doctrine of "environment" to such a view: "Society is vile, and therefore we too are vile; but we are rich, we are secure, and it is only by chance that we escaped encountering the things you did. And had we encountered them, we would have acted as you did. Who is to blame? The environment is to blame. And so there is only a faulty social structure, but there is no crime whatsoever."

And the trick I spoke of earlier is the sophistry used to draw such conclusions.

No, the People do not deny there is crime, and they know that the criminal is guilty. The People know that they also share the guilt in every crime. But by accusing themselves, they prove that they do not believe in "environment"; they believe, on the contrary, that the environment depends completely on them, on their unceasing repentance and quest for self-perfection. Energy, work, and struggle—these are the means through which the environment is improved. Only by work and struggle do we attain independence and a sense of our own dignity. "Let us become better, and the environment will be better." This is what the Russian People sense so strongly but do not express in their concealed idea of the criminal as an unfortunate.

Now imagine if the criminal himself, hearing from the People that he is an "unfortunate," should consider himself only an unfortunate and not a criminal. In that case the People will renounce such a false interpretation and call it a betrayal of the People's truth and faith.

I could offer some examples of this, but let us set them aside for the moment and say the following.

The criminal and the person planning to commit a crime are two different people, but they belong to the same category. What if the criminal, consciously preparing to commit a crime, says to himself: "There is no crime!" Will the People still call him an "unfortunate"?

Perhaps they would; in fact they certainly would. The People are compassionate, and there is no one more unfortunate than one who has even ceased to consider himself a criminal: he is an animal, a beast. And what of it if he does not even understand that he is an animal and has crippled his own conscience? He is only doubly unfortunate. Doubly unfortunate, but also doubly a criminal. The People will feel compassion for him but will not renounce their own truth. Never have the People, in calling a criminal an "unfortunate," ceased to regard him as a criminal! And there could be no greater misfortune for us than if the People agreed with the criminal and replied to him: "No, you are not guilty, for there is no 'crime'"!

Such is our faith—our common faith, I should like to say; it is the faith of all who have hopes and expectations. I should like to add two more things.

I was in prison and saw criminals, hardened criminals. I repeat: it was a hard school. Not one of them ceased to regard himself as a criminal. In appearance they were a terrible and a cruel lot. Only the stupid ones or newcomers would "put on a show," however, and the others made fun of them. For the most part they were a gloomy, pensive lot. No one discussed his own crimes. I never heard a protest of any kind. Even speaking aloud of one's crimes was not done. From time to time we would hear a defiant or bragging voice, and all the prisoners, as one man, would cut the upstart short. Talking about *that* was simply not acceptable. Yet I believe that perhaps not one of them escaped the long inner suffering that cleansed and strengthened him. I saw them lonely and pensive; I saw them in church praying before confession; I listened to their single, unexpected words and exclamations; I remember their faces. Oh, believe me, in his heart not one of them considered himself justified!

I would not like my words to be taken as harsh. Still, I will risk speaking my mind and say plainly: with strict punishment, prison, and hard labor you would have saved perhaps half of them. You would have eased their burden, not increased it. Purification through suffering is easier—easier, I say, than the lot you assign to many of them by wholesale acquittals in court. You only plant cynicism in their hearts; you leave them with a seductive question and with contempt for you yourselves. You don't believe it? They have contempt for you and your courts and for the justice system of the whole country! Into their hearts you pour disbelief in the People's truth, in God's truth; you leave them confused. . . . The criminal walks out of the court thinking: "So that's how it is now;

they've gone soft. They've gotten clever, it seems. Maybe they're afraid. So I can do the same thing again. It's clear enough: I was in such a hard pinch, I couldn't help stealing."

And do you really think that when you let them all off as innocent or with a recommendation for mercy you are giving them the chance to reform? He'll reform, all right! Why should he worry? "It looks like I didn't do anything wrong at all"—this is what he thinks *in the final analysis.* You yourselves put that notion in his head. The main thing is that faith in the law and in the People's truth is being shaken.

Not long ago I spent several years living abroad. When I left Russia the new courts were only in their infancy. How eagerly I would read in our newspapers there everything concerning the Russian courts. With real sorrow I also observed Russians living abroad and their children, who did not know their native language or who were forgetting it. It was clear to me that half of them, by the very nature of things, would eventually become expatriates. I always found it painful to think about that: so much vitality, so many of the best, perhaps, of our people, while we in Russia are so in need of good people! But sometimes as I left the reading room, by God, gentlemen, I became reconciled to the temporary emigration and emigrés in spite of myself. My heart ached. I would read in the newspaper of a wife who murdered her husband and who was acquitted. The crime is obvious and proven; she herself confesses. "Not guilty." A young man breaks open a strongbox and steals the money. "I was in love," he says, "very much in love, and I needed money to buy things for my mistress." "Not guilty." It would not be so terrible if these cases could be justified by compassion or pity; but truly I could not understand the reasons for the acquittal and I was bewildered. I came away with a troubled feeling, almost as if I had been personally insulted. In these bitter moments I would sometimes imagine Russia as a kind of quagmire or swamp on which someone had contrived to build a palace. The surface of the soil looks firm and smooth, but in reality it is like the surface of some sort of jellied green-pea aspic, and once you step on it you slip down to the very abyss. I reproached myself for my faintheartedness; I was encouraged by the thought that, being far away, I might be mistaken and that I myself was the kind of temporary emigré I spoke of; that I could not see things at first hand nor hear clearly. . . .

And now I have been home again for a long while.

"But come now—do they really feel pity?" That's the question! Don't laugh because I put so much stress on it. At least pity provides some sort of explanation; at least it leads you out of the darkness, and without it we comprehend nothing and see only gloomy blackness inhabited by some madman.

A peasant beats his wife, inflicts injuries on her for many years, abuses her worse than his dog. In despair to the point of suicide and scarcely in her right mind, she goes to the village court. They send her away with an indifferent mumble: "Learn to live together." Can this be pity? These are the dull words of a drunkard who has just come to after a long spree, a man who is scarcely aware that you are standing in front of him, who stupidly and listlessly waves you away so you won't bother him; a man whose tongue doesn't work properly, who has nothing in his head but alcohol fumes and folly.

The woman's story, by the way, is well known and happened only recently. We read about it in all the newspapers and, perhaps, we still remember it. Plainly and simply, the wife who suffered from her husband's beatings hanged herself; the husband was tried and found deserving of mercy. But for a long time thereafter I fancied I could see all the circumstances of the case; I see them even now.

I kept imagining his figure: he was tall, the reports said, very thick-set, powerful, fair-haired. I would add another touch: thinning hair. His body is white and bloated; his movements slow and solemn; his gaze is steady. He speaks little and rarely and drops his words like precious pearls, cherishing them above all else. Witnesses testified that he had a cruel nature: he would catch a chicken and hang it by its feet, head down, just for his own pleasure. This amused him—a most characteristic trait! For a number of years he had beaten his wife with anything that was at hand—ropes or sticks. He would take up a floorboard, thrust her feet into the gap, press the board down, and beat and beat her. I think he himself did not know why he was beating her; he just did it, probably from the same motives for which he hung the chicken. He sometimes also starved her, giving her no bread for three days. He would place the bread on a shelf, summon her, and say: "Don't you dare touch that bread. That's *my* bread." And that's another remarkably characteristic trait! She and her ten-year-old child would go off begging to the neighbors: if they were given bread they would eat; if not, they went hungry. When he asked her to work she did everything with never a hesitation or a murmur, intimidated, until finally she became a virtual madwoman. I can imagine what she looked like: she must have been a very small woman, thin as a rail. It sometimes happens that very large, heavy-set men with white, bloated bodies marry very small, skinny women (they are even inclined to choose such, I've noticed), and it is so strange to watch them standing or walking together. It seems to me that if she had become pregnant by him in her final days it would have been an even more characteristic and essential finishing touch; otherwise the picture is somehow incomplete. Have you seen how a peasant beats his wife? I have. He begins with a rope or a strap. Peasant life is without aesthetic pleasures such as music, theaters, and magazines; it is natural that this void be filled with something. Once he has bound his wife or thrust her feet into an opening in the floorboards, our peasant would begin, probably methodically, indifferently, even sleepily; his blows are measured; he doesn't listen to her cries and her pleading; or rather, he does listen, and listens with delight—otherwise what satisfaction would there be in beating her? Do you know, gentlemen, people are born in various circumstances: can you not conceive that this woman, in other circumstances, might have been some Juliet or Beatrice from Shakespeare, or Gretchen from *Faust*? I'm not saying that she was—it would be absurd to claim that—but yet there could be the embryo of something very noble in her soul, something no worse, perhaps, than what could be found in a woman of noble birth: a loving, even lofty, heart; a character filled with a most original beauty. The very fact that she hesitated so long in taking her own life shows something so quiet, meek, patient, and affec- tionate about her. And so this same Beatrice or Gretchen is beaten and whipped like a dog! The blows rain down faster and faster, harder and harder—countless blows. He begins to grow heated and finds it to his taste. At last he grows wild, and his wildness pleases him. The animal cries of his victim intoxicate him like liquor: "I'll wash your feet and drink the water," cries Beatrice in an inhuman voice. But finally she grows quiet; she stops shrieking and only groans wildly, her breath catching constantly; and now the blows come ever faster and ever more furiously. . . . Suddenly he throws down the strap; like a madman he seizes a stick or a branch, anything he can find, and shatters it with three final, terrible blows across her back—enough! He steps away, sits down at the table, heaves a sigh, and sets to drinking his kvass. A small girl, their daughter (and they did have a daughter!) trembles on the stove in the corner, trying to hide: she has heard her mother crying. He walks out of the hut. Toward dawn the mother would revive and get up, groaning and crying with every movement, and set off to milk the cow, fetch water, go to work.

And as he leaves he tells her in his slow, methodical, and serious voice: "Don't you dare eat that bread. That's *my* bread."

Toward the end he also liked hanging her by her feet as well, the same way he had hung the chicken. Probably he would hang her, step aside, and sit down to have his porridge. When he had finished his meal he would suddenly seize the strap again and set to work on the hanging woman. . . . The little girl, all atremble and huddled on the stove, would steal a wild glance at her mother hanging by her heels and try to hide again.

The mother hanged herself on a May morning, a bright spring day, probably. She had been seen the night before, beaten and completely crazed. Before her death she had also made a trip to the village court, and there it was that they mumbled to her, "Learn to live together."

When the rope tightened around the mother's neck and she was making her last strangled cries, the little girl called out from the corner: "Mamma, why are you choking?" Then she cautiously approached her, called out to the hanging woman, gazed wildly at her. In the course of the morning she came out of her corner to look at the mother again, until the father finally returned.

And now we see him before the court—solemn, puffy-faced, closely following the proceedings. He denies everything. "We never spoke a sharp word to each other," he says, dropping a few of his words like precious pearls. The jury leaves, and after a "brief deliberation" they bring in the verdict: "Guilty, but with *recommendation for clemency.*"

Note that the girl testified against her father. She told everything and, they say, wrung tears from the spectators. Had it not been for the "clemency" of the jury he would have been exiled to Siberia. But with "clemency" he need spend only eight months in prison and then come home and ask that his daughter, who testified against him on behalf of her mother, be returned to him. Once again he will have someone to hang by the heels.

"A recommendation for clemency!" And this verdict was given in full cognizance of the facts. They knew what awaited the child. Clemency to whom, and for what? You feel as if you are in some sort of whirlwind that's caught you up and twists and turns you around.

Wait a moment, I'll tell you one more story.

Once, before the new courts were established (not long before, however), I read of this particular little incident in our newspapers: a mother was holding in her arms her baby of a year or fourteen months. Children of that age are teething; they are ailing and cry and suffer a good deal. It seems the mother lost patience with the baby; perhaps she was very busy, and here she had to carry this child and listen to its heart-rending cries. She got angry. But can such a small child be beaten for something like this? It's a pity to strike it, and what can it understand anyway? It's so helpless and can't do a thing for itself. And even if you do beat it, it won't stop crying. Its little tears will just keep pouring out and it will put its arms around you; or else it will start to kiss you and just go on crying. So she didn't beat the child. A samovar full of boiling water stood in the room. She put the child's little hand right under the tap and opened it. She held the child's hand under the boiling water for a good ten seconds.

That's a fact; I read it. But now imagine if this happened today and the woman was brought to trial. The jury goes out and, "after a brief deliberation," brings in the verdict: "Recommendation for clemency."

Well, imagine: I invite mothers, at least, to imagine it. And the defense lawyer, no doubt, would probably start twisting the facts:

"Gentlemen of the jury, this is not what one could call a humane act, but you must consider the case as a whole; you must take into account the circumstances, the environment. This woman is poor; she is the only person working in the household; she puts up with a lot. She had not even the means to hire a nurse for her child. It is only natural that at a moment when, filled with anger caused by the corroding environment, so to say, gentlemen, it is only natural that she should have put the child's hand under the samovar tap..., and so...."

Oh, of course I fully appreciate the value of the legal profession; it is an elevated calling and a universally respected one. But one cannot help sometimes looking at it from a particular point of view—a frivolous one, I agree—but involuntary nonetheless: what an unbearable job it must be at times, one thinks. The lawyer dodges, twists himself around like a snake, lies against his own conscience, against his own convictions, against all morality, against all humanity! No, truly, he earns his money.

"Come, come!" exclaims suddenly the sarcastic voice we heard before. "Why this is all nonsense, nothing but a product of your imagination. A jury never brought in such a verdict. No lawyer ever contorted the facts like that. You made it all up."

But the wife, hung by her heels like a chicken; the "This is *my* bread, don't you dare eat it"; the girl trembling on the stove, listening for half an hour to her mother's cries; and "Mamma, why are you choking?"—isn't that just the same as the hand under the boiling water? Why it's *almost* the same!

"Backwardness, ignorance, the environment—have some pity," the peasant's lawyer insisted. Yet millions of them do exist and not all hang their wives by their heels! There ought to be some limit here. . . . On the other hand, take an educated person: suppose he hangs his wife by her heels? Enough contortions, gentlemen of the bar. Enough of your "environment."

4

Something Personal

A number of times people have urged me to write my literary memoirs. I don't know whether I should, and in any case my memory is weak. Besides, I find that recalling the past makes me sad; on the whole, I don't like reminiscing. Yet certain episodes from the beginning of my literary career come to me of their own accord and with amazing clarity, despite my weak memory. Here, for example, is one anecdote.

One spring morning I dropped in on the late Egor Petrovich Kovalevsky. He had a very high opinion of my novel *Crime and Punishment*, which at that time had only just appeared in *The Russian Messenger*. He praised it with much enthusiasm and passed on a comment that I greatly valued from a certain person whose name I cannot reveal. Meanwhile, two publishers of two magazines entered the room one after the other. One of these magazines later acquired a circulation unprecedented among our monthly publications, but at that time it was only just becoming established. The second magazine, on the other hand, was coming to the end of a remarkable life that had had so much influence on both literature and the public at large. But then, on that morning, its publisher still did not know that his journal was already so close to the end of its career. This publisher and I went into another room and were left by ourselves.

Without giving his name I will say only that our first meeting had been a very lively one, an exceptional encounter which I have always remembered. Perhaps he remembers it as well. At that time he was not yet a publisher. Subsequently, we had a good many misunderstandings. We very rarely met after my return from Siberia, but once in passing he paid me a very warm compliment, and in connection with some other matter he drew my attention to a poem—the best he had ever written. I'll add that there could be no one whose appearance and manner are less like those of a poet, never mind a "suffering" poet. And yet he is one of the most passionate, gloomy, and "suffering" of our poets.

"Well," he told me, "we've just given you a dressing-down," (he meant in his magazine and on account of *Crime and Punishment*).

"I know," I said.

"And do you know why?"

"As a matter of principle, I should think."

"For Chernyshevsky."

I was struck dumb with astonishment.

"N.N., who wrote the review," the publisher continued, "told me, 'His novel is good, but since he stooped to mocking and caricaturing this poor exiled Chernyshevsky in a tale he wrote two years ago, I'm going to tear his novel to pieces.'"

"Do you mean it's still that stupid gossip about 'The Crocodile?'" I cried, when I made the connection. "Don't tell me that you believe that too! Have you read 'The Crocodile?'"

"No, I haven't."

"Well, it's all gossip, the vilest kind of gossip there can be. Only someone with the intellect and the poetic instincts of a Bulgarin could find a 'civic' allegory between the lines of this little comic story—but an allegory about Chernyshevsky! If you only knew how absurd such an accusation is! In fact I'll never forgive myself for not protesting this vile slander two years ago, just when people started spreading it!"

This conversation with the editor of a magazine which has now long faded happened seven years ago, and yet I haven't protested this "slander" until now: either I ignored it or "just didn't have the time." Meanwhile, this mean act attributed to me simply remained in the memories of certain individuals as an undisputed fact; it has made the rounds in literary circles; it has reached the public; and it has caused me unpleasantness more than once. It is time to say at least a few words about it, the more so that it is now apropos. And although what I have to say is unsubstantiated, it is intended to refute a slander which is itself utterly unsubstantiated. My long silence and my neglect up to this point have only seemed to give it credence.

The first time I met Nikolai Gavrilovich Chernyshevsky was in 1859, the first year after my return from Siberia. I don't remember where and how we met. We met subsequently but not very often and exchanged a few words, but only a few. We always shook hands, however. Herzen told me that Chernyshevsky made an unpleasant impression on him by his appearance and manner. As for me, I liked Chernyshevsky's appearance and manner.

One morning I found attached to the doorknob of my apartment one of the most remarkable of those proclamations that were appearing at the time—and quite a lot of them were appearing then. This one was entitled "To the Young Generation." You could imagine nothing more foolish and absurd. Its contents were quite outrageous, and it was couched in the most ridiculous terms, which only a villain could devise so as to cause maximum offense. I was angry and downcast for the whole day. All this was still a new thing then and it was so close at hand that it was difficult to get an accurate picture of the people who wrote it. It was difficult simply because one somehow couldn't believe that beneath this confused bluster lay something utterly trivial. I'm not talking about the whole movement of that time, only about the people involved in it. As far as the movement is concerned, it was a perverse and unhealthy phenomenon, yet an inevitable product of historical development; it will constitute a solemn page in the Petersburg period of our history. And this page, it seems, is still a long way from being written.

And so I, who in heart and in soul had long been at odds both with these people and with the intentions of their movement—I suddenly felt annoyed and almost ashamed at their clumsiness: "Why do they do things in such a stupid and clumsy way?" And what concern of mine was this cause? But it wasn't their ineffectiveness that I regretted. I did not know a single one of the people who ran around distributing proclamations, nor do I know any now. But I was saddened when I realized that this was not merely an isolated phenomenon, not a silly little prank of certain people who were of no concern to me. One feeling was overwhelming: their level of education, their mentality, and their utter lack of understanding of reality oppressed me terribly. Although I had already lived in St. Petersburg for three years and had closely followed certain events, I was still shocked by the proclamation that morning. For me it was an utterly new and surprising revelation: until that day I had never suspected such pettiness could exist! I was frightened precisely by the degree of pettiness. Toward evening I suddenly got the notion to go off to see Chernyshevsky.

I had never ever called on him before, nor thought to do so, any more than he had called on me.

I recall that this was five o'clock in the afternoon. I found Nikolai Gavrilovich quite alone; not even his servants were home, and he let me in himself. He gave me a most cordial welcome and led me into his study.

"Nikolai Gavrilovich, what on earth is this?" I said when I took out the proclamation.

He took it as something utterly unfamiliar and read it. There were only about ten lines.

"Well, what about it?" he asked with a faint smile.

"Are they really so stupid and ridiculous? Is there really no way of stopping them and putting an end to this abomination?"

He gave an impressive and very serious reply.

"Do you really suppose that I support them? Do you think that I could have had a hand in putting together this wretched leaflet?"

"No, I do not," I answered, "and I hardly think it necessary to assure you of it. But in any case they must be stopped somehow. Your word means something to them, and of course they're afraid of what you might say."

"I don't know any of them."

"I'm sure you don't. But you certainly don't need to know them or speak to them personally. You need only express a word of censure publicly, and they'll hear about it."

"That may not have any effect. And, indeed, things like this, as extraneous facts, are inevitable."

"Yet they are damaging to everyone and everything."

At this point another visitor, I don't remember who, rang the bell. I left. I consider it my duty to note that I spoke sincerely with Chernyshevsky and I fully believed then, as I believe now, that he did not support those who ran around distributing proclamations. It seemed to me that Nikolai Gavrilovich was not displeased at my visit; he confirmed this when, a few days later, he himself called on me. He spent an hour with me, and I must confess that rarely have I met a kinder and more cordial person, so that even then I was surprised to hear some people claim that he was harsh and unsociable. I realized that he wanted to get to know me and I recall being pleased at that. I visited him once more, and he returned my call. Shortly thereafter my circumstances compelled me to move to Moscow, where I spent nine months.

Our acquaintance, which had only begun, was thus broken off.
Thereafter came Chernyshevsky's arrest and his exile. I was never
able to learn anything about his case; I know nothing even now.

A year and a half later I got the notion to write a fantastic tale,
modeled somewhat on Gogol's "The Nose." I had never tried
writing in a fantastic vein before. This was a purely literary prank,
done solely for fun. Several comic situations had presented themselves, in fact, and these I wanted to develop. Although it doesn't
merit a retelling of the plot, I will do so so that it may be clear
what people made of it. At the time in Petersburg some German
had a crocodile, which he was exhibiting in the Arcade for an
admission fee. A certain Petersburg official, before going on a trip
abroad, takes his young wife and their inseparable friend to the
Arcade and the three of them happen to stop by to see the crocodile.
This clerk is of the middling sort, but one of those with a certain
independent means; he is still young but is corroded by vanity;
above all, he is a fool, like the unforgettable Major Kovalev who
lost his nose. He is comically confident of his great virtues; semi-
educated, but considers himself almost a genius; people in his own
department look on him as utterly worthless, and he is constantly
offended by the fact that no one pays attention to him. As if in
revenge for this, he bullies and tyrannizes his weak-charactered
friend, flaunting his intellect before him. His friend hates him but
tolerates everything because he is secretly attracted to the wife.
This young and quite pretty lady, a purely Petersburg type—a silly
flirt of the middle class—gapes at the monkeys displayed along
with the crocodile in the Arcade. Meanwhile, her brilliant husband
has teased the crocodile, which hitherto had been sleepy and lying
like a log. The crocodile suddenly opens its maw and swallows
him whole, leaving not a shred behind. It is soon evident that the
great man has suffered not the slightest damage from the crocodile;
on the contrary, with his characteristic obstinacy he declares from
within the beast that he is quite comfortable there. The friend and
the wife go off to urge the authorities to free the husband. To
accomplish this the authorities consider it absolutely essential to
kill the crocodile, cut it open, and free the great man. Of course,
they would also have to recompense the German owner and his
inseparable *Mutter* for the crocodile. The German at first is both
irate and afraid that his crocodile, having swallowed *ein ganz* government official, might die. But soon he realizes that this member
of the Petersburg administration, swallowed by a crocodile but still

alive, could subsequently have great appeal at box-offices all over
Europe. He demands an enormous sum for the crocodile and the
rank of colonel as well. The authorities, on the other hand, are
thoroughly nonplussed by this sort of incident, which is new to
the Ministry and entirely without precedent. "If there had been
even some tiny little precedent we could act; but as it stands it's
awkward." The authorities also suspect that the clerk crawled into
the crocodile as a result of some forbidden, liberal tendencies.
Meanwhile, his spouse finds her status as "a widow, more or less"
not without a certain interest. Her swallowed husband, meanwhile,
tells his friend flatly that staying inside the crocodile is incomparably better than working at his job since now, at least, people
have to pay attention to him—something he could never get them
to do before. He insists that his wife give parties and that he and
the crocodile be taken along in a trunk. He is certain that the
whole of Petersburg society and all the high officials will come
rushing to these parties to look at this new phenomenon. And here
he intends to carry the day: "I will proclaim the truth and teach
them; I will give advice to the statesman and display my talents
before the minister," he says, considering himself a creature not of
this earth, already entitled to give advice and to pronounce judgments. The friend asks, delicately but not without malice: "And
what if, through some unexpected process which, however, must
be expected, you were to be digested into something which you
might not expect?" The great man answers that he has already
considered that, but he will indignantly struggle against this phenomenon, even though, in accordance with the laws of nature, it
is highly probable. His wife, however, does not agree to give parties
for such a purpose, even though she is attracted to the idea: "How
would it look, having my husband brought to me in a trunk?" she
says. Besides, her status as more or less a widow becomes increasingly appealing. She comes into fashion; people take an interest
in her. Her husband's superior begins visiting and plans to use
her for his own ends. . . . Such is the first half of this farcical story;
it is unfinished. I will certainly finish it one day, although I had
already forgotten it and had to reread it to refresh my memory.

But here is what people made out of that little thing. Scarcely
had the story appeared in the magazine *Epoch* (in 1865) when
suddenly *The Voice* made a strange observation in a feuilleton. I
don't remember it literally, and it happened too long ago to check,
but its sense was something like the following: "It is in vain that

the author of "The Crocodile" sets out on such a path; this will
bring him neither the honor nor the advantage he expects," and
so forth. Then followed several most obscure and unfriendly barbs.
I glanced over them and understood nothing; I saw only that there
was a good deal of poison in them, but did not know why. The
vague remark in *The Voice* could do me no harm in itself, of course;
a reader would have no more understanding of it than I had. But
suddenly, a week later, N. N. Strakhov told me: "Do you know
what they think there? They're sure that your "Crocodile" is an
allegory—the history of Chernyshevsky's exile—and that you wanted to lampoon him." Although I was surprised, I was not very
worried: people interpret things in all sorts of ways, after all. This
interpretation seemed to me to be too isolated and too farfetched
to gain much currency, and I thought it utterly unnecessary to
protest. I shall never forgive myself this, because that interpretation
took hold and spread widely. *Calomniez, il en restera toujours quelque
chose.*

However, I'm convinced even now that there was no intention
of slandering me; why would there be, and for what? I had quarreled
with almost no one in the literary world, at least not quarreled
seriously. Now, at this moment, for the second time in the twenty-
seven years of my literary career, I am speaking about myself
personally. This was simply a matter of obtuseness, gloomy, suspicious obtuseness that had settled in the mind of some person
with a "tendency." I am convinced that this mind, so full of
thoughts, is even now certain that it was not mistaken and that I
deliberately ridiculed the unfortunate Chernyshevsky. I even believe
that none of my explanations and excuses will alter that view in
my favor even now. And yet this is a mind filled with thoughts.
(Of course, I am not speaking of Andrei Aleksandrovich; in his
capacity as editor and publisher of his newspaper he played no
role here, as usual).

Where is the allegory? Well, of course the crocodile represents
Siberia; the self-confident and frivolous official is Chernyshevsky.
He's fallen into the maw of the crocodile but still cherishes the
hope to give instruction to the whole world. The weak-charactered
friend whom he treats so despotically represents all of Chernyshevsky's Petersburg friends. The pretty but none-too-intelligent
wife who relishes her status as a "widow, more or less," is. . . . But
at this point things become so messy that I don't wish to soil myself
by continuing to interpret the allegory. (Yet that interpretation has

become firmly entrenched, and that last suggestion has perhaps become particularly entrenched—I have definite evidence of that.)

This means that people assumed that I, a former exile and convict, would rejoice in the exile of some other "unfortunate"; and, even more, that I would write a gleeful lampoon about it. But tell me, where is the proof? Is it in the allegory? You can bring me whatever you like—"Notes of a Madman," the ode "God," "Yury Miloslavsky," the poetry of Fet—whatever you like—and I will at once set to proving to you from the first ten lines you care to show me that here is an allegory of the Franco-Prussian War or a lampoon of the actor Gorbunov; in short, on anyone you like. Remember how in the old days, at the very end of the forties, for example, the censor would examine manuscripts and black-liners? There was not a line or a dot where he did not suspect an allegory of some sort. Let them produce at least something from my life to show I resemble the malicious, heartless writer of lampoons who could be expected to write such stories.

On the other hand, the very haste and carelessness of such groundless conclusions testify to a certain mean spirit in the accusers themselves and reveal their coarse and inhumane views. That their conclusion is simple-minded is no excuse—what of it? One can be simple-minded and vile, and nothing more.

Perhaps I bore some personal hatred of Chernyshevsky? To discount such an accusation I deliberately told you of our brief and cordial acquaintance. People will say that this is not enough and that I bore a secret hatred. But let them present some causes for this hatred if they have any to present. There were none. On the other hand, I am convinced that Chernyshevsky himself would confirm the accuracy of my account of our meeting if he ever had a chance to read it. And God grant him that opportunity. This I wish as warmly and passionately as I sincerely regretted and still regret his misfortune.

But perhaps there was hatred because of convictions?

Why should there be? Chernyshevsky's convictions never offended me. One can have a good deal of respect for a man even when one has radically different opinions from him. Here, incidentally, I can speak not entirely without substantiation and even have some small evidence to offer. One of the very last issues of the magazine *Epoch*, which ceased publishing at that time (it might have been the very last issue), contained a long critical article on Chernyshevsky's "famous" novel *What Is To Be Done?* This is a remarkable article and it is the product of a well-known author. And what do we find here? It pays proper tribute to Chernyshevsky's intellect and talent. The novel itself earns fervent praise. No one ever doubted his remarkable intellect. Our article only remarked on the specific features and the errantry of this intellect, but the very seriousness of the article testified that our critic also paid due respect to the author's merits. Now you must agree: if I had hated Chernyshevsky because of his convictions, I would, of course, naturally not have allowed the journal to publish an article that spoke of him with due respect; and in fact it was I and no one else who edited *The Epoch*.

Perhaps in printing a malicious allegory I hoped to gain something somewhere *en haut lieu*? But can anyone ever say of me that I sought or gained anything in that sense in any *lieu* whatsoever, i.e., that I sold my pen? I believe that the one who made that conjecture did not himself have that idea, despite his naiveté. And it would certainly not have gained currency in the literary world had that been all I was accused of.

What of the possible accusation that I lampooned certain domestic arrangements of Nikolai Gavrilovich in my "allegory?" I repeat once more that I do not even wish to touch upon that in my "defense" so as not to soil myself. . . .

It's a shame that I have to speak about myself this time. But that's what it means to write literary memoirs. I shall never write them. I deeply regret that I have undoubtedly bored the reader; but I am writing a diary, a diary which consists partly of my personal impressions, and just recently I had one "literary" impression which indirectly reminded me of this forgotten anecdote about my forgotten "Crocodile."

The other day one of the people I respect most and whose opinion I value highly said to me: "I've only just read your article on 'Environment' and on the sentences handed down by our jurors (*The Citizen*, No. 2). I agree with you fully, but your article can cause an unpleasant misunderstanding. People will think that you are in favor of abolishing the jury system and that you support renewed interference from some administrative overseer. . . . "

I was astonished and saddened. This was the voice of a man who was most impartial and who stood outside any literary parties and "allegories."

"Do you really think that people will interpret my article that

way? After this I won't be able to talk about anything. The economic and moral condition of the People after their liberation from
the yoke of serfdom is dreadful. The facts continually testifying to
that are indisputable and highly alarming. The decline of morality,
the fall in prices, the Yid tavern-keepers, thievery, banditry in
broad daylight—all these facts are indisputable, and they grow more
ominous every day. And what are we to do? If someone, troubled
in spirit and in heart, takes up a pen and writes—what then? Will
they cry out that he is a proponent of serfdom and stands for a
return to the enslavement of the peasants?"

"In any case we must hope that the People have complete freedom
to emerge from their lamentable situation on their own, without
any patriarchal supervision or turning back."

"Of course we must; that's my idea precisely! And even if this
national decadence (and here and there the People themselves, when
they look at what they are doing, are now saying: 'It's true enough,
we've gone weak!')—even if it, I say, were to cause some sort of
real, indisputable calamity among the People, some sort of mon-
umental collapse, some great disaster—even then they would save
themselves, themselves and us as well, as they have already done
more than once; their whole history can testify to that. That is my
idea. An end to interference is just what's needed! . . . But how
many different ways can one's words be interpreted. You might
even stumble upon another allegory here!

5

Vlas

Do you remember Vlas? He comes to mind for some reason.

> In open coat of homespun thread
> Through town you see him slowly pass;
> No hat to cover his gray head,
> This peasant pilgrim called Old Vlas.
> A copper icon on his breast,
> He gathers offerings for God's church....

As you know, at one time this Vlas "had no God."

> ...his heavy hand
> Dispatched his wife while in her prime;
> Thieves, bandits, and their contraband
> Found refuge with him many a time.

He even gave refuge to thieves, says the poet, trying to frighten us and adopting the tone of a pious old woman. Goodness, the sins he committed! But then came the clap of thunder. Vlas fell ill and saw a vision, after which he vowed to become a beggar and collect money to build a church. It was Hell itself he saw in his vision, no more and no less:

> He saw the world of vanities crumble,
> He saw the sinners roast in Hell,
>
> Where nimble devils, unrelenting,
> Attack the wretched here within.
> A restless witch, skilled in tormenting,
> With Ethiops as black as sin...

. . . .
Some are impaled on rods of iron
While others lick the red-hot floor. . . .

In short, there are inconceivable horrors, so dreadful that one is
frightened to read about them. "But," the poet continues, "not all
can be described: 'Pious pilgrims, clever women,/Can tell you
better tales than this.'"

Oh, poet! (You are, unfortunately, our genuine poet.) If only
you would stop approaching the People with your rapturous outpourings about which "Pious pilgrims, clever women,/Can tell you
better tales—," you would not offend us by concluding that it is
only through such paltry doings of old women that we "See Godly
temples rising up/All o'er the face of our own land." Yet even
though it is only his own "foolishness" that leads Vlas to wander
with his beggar's sack, you still have understood the full gravity
of his suffering; you were still struck by the grandeur of his figure.
(You are a poet, after all, and could scarcely react differently). "All
the might of this great soul,/Devoted to this Godly cause,—" as
you so grandly put it. I would like to think, however, that you
mock him unwittingly, as a result of your liberal fear, because this
awesome, even frightening force of Vlas's humility, this urge of his
to save himself, this passionate thirst for suffering has struck even
you, a universal man and Russian *gentilhomme,* and this majestic
image from the People has wrung rapture and respect even out of
your ultraliberal soul!

Vlas gave away all that he owned
And for himself he kept but naught;
And, gathering alms, the world he roamed;
To build God's temple here, he sought.
And so it is this peasant lives—
Full thirty years it soon will be—
Feeding himself on what God gives
And keeping his vow most rigidly.

. . . .
Filled with grief past consolation,
Dark of face, erect and tall,

(That's truly marvelous!)

He passes on with gait unhurried
Through the village, through the town.

. . . .
But never a word passed o'er his lips.
A book, an icon at his side,
Strong chains of iron round his hips
To overcome his sinful pride.

That really is wonderfully said! It's so good, in fact, that it's just
as if you were not its author; as if it were not you but some other
person who later gave a performance "on the Volga" in verses
about the barge-haulers' songs that were likewise magnificent. Well,
perhaps you didn't really give a performance "on the Volga," or
maybe just a small one: even on the Volga you were in love with
the universal man within that barge-hauler, and you truly suffered
for him—not for the barge-hauler himself, that is, but for what we
might call the universal barge-hauler. Don't you see that loving the
universal man means surely to scorn and sometimes even to hate
the real man standing next to you? I deliberately picked out the
incomparably beautiful verses in this farcical (you'll pardon me,
but I mean the thing as a whole) poem of yours.

I recalled this poetical Vlas because the other day I heard an
utterly fantastic story about another Vlas—about two of them, in
fact—but these Vlases were quite special and unprecedented. This
is a true incident and its exceptionality alone makes it remarkable.

In the monasteries of Holy Russia there are, even now, people
say, certain ascetics and monks who are confessors and who cast
their light on us all. Whether this is a good thing or bad, and
whether we need monks or do not—these are things I choose not
to discuss at present, nor did I take up my pen for that purpose.
But since we are living in the real world as given, one cannot throw
even a monk out of the story if the whole thing is based on him.
These monks who illuminate the lives of others are sometimes,
apparently, men of great education and intellect. That is what
people say, at least; I know nothing about it. I have heard that
there are some who have an amazing ability to penetrate the human
heart and to gain mastery over it. Several such people, apparently,
are known all over Russia, or at least are known to those who are
concerned with such things. Such an elder lives, let's suppose, in
Kherson Province, and people come to him, some even on foot,
from Petersburg, from Arkhangelsk, from the Caucasus, and from
Siberia. They come, of course, with souls weighed down by despair,
souls that no longer expect recovery; or they come bearing such a

terrible burden in their hearts that the sinners can no longer speak about it to their own priest and spiritual father—not because of fear or mistrust, but simply out of utter despair for their own salvation. But then they hear about some such remarkable monk and they go to see him.

"And so it is," such an elder once said in friendly conversation with a certain listener, "that I have been listening to people for twenty years now, and you can believe how many things I have heard during these twenty years of my acquaintance with the most secret and complex ailments of the human soul. But even after twenty years I sometimes shudder and grow angry when I hear some secret confessions. You lose the spiritual calm that's needed to give comfort and have to restore your own humility and tranquility. . . . "

And then he told me this remarkable tale from the life of the People that I mentioned above.

It happened once that a peasant came crawling into my cell on his knees. I had already seen him through the window, crawling on the ground. The first thing he said to me was: "There's no salvation for me; I'm damned! Say what you like—I'm damned all the same!"

I managed to calm him down. I could see that he had been crawling for the sake of the suffering and had crawled a great distance.

"A few of the lads got together in the village," he began, "and we set to arguing among ourselves as to which of us could do the most daring, shocking thing. I'm a proud fellow, and so I said I'd do worse than any of them. One of the lads took me aside and told me, face-to-face, 'You'd never ever do what you said; you're just bragging.'

"I told him I was ready to swear to it.

"'Just wait now,' he says, 'You have to swear by your own salvation in Heaven that you'll do everything I tell you.'

"I swore to it.

"'It'll soon be Lent,' he says, 'so make your fast. When you go to Holy Communion, take the Eucharist but don't swallow it. When you step back, take it out of your mouth and keep it. Then I'll tell you what else to do.'

"That's what I did. He took me straight from the church into a garden. He took a stick, drove it into the earth, and said 'Put the Eucharist on the stick.' I did that.

"'Now,' he says, 'get a gun.'

"I brought one.

"'Load it.'

"I did that.

"'Take it up and shoot.'

"I raised the gun and aimed it. And just as I was about to fire I suddenly saw before me a cross and, on it, the crucified Christ. Then I fell down, unconscious."

This had happened a few years before he came to the elder. Who was this Vlas? Where did he come from? What was his name? None of that, of course, did the elder reveal, nor did he tell what penance he had imposed on him. He probably burdened his soul with some terrible load even beyond human strength, considering that, in this case, the heavier the burden, the better. He came crawling in looking for suffering, after all. Now isn't this a very typical incident that suggests a great deal, so that it's worthy of a few minutes of close examination? I still hold that these very same and sundry "Vlases," repentant and unrepentant, will say the last word; they will say it and will show us a new path and a new way out of all those apparently insoluble tangles we find ourselves in. Our Russian destiny will not be finally resolved by Petersburg. And therefore every *new* feature, even the smallest, that serves to characterize these "new people" may be worthy of our attention.

In the first place, I am amazed—and amazed most of all—by the very origin of this affair, namely, that such an argument and contest as to who could do the most daring thing could even occur in a Russian village. This is a fact that has many implications, and for me it was almost a total surprise; and I have seen a good many of the People, including some who were most willful. I would also note that the apparent singularity of the fact in itself testifies to its veracity: when people tell lies, they invent something much more mundane and in keeping with everyday life so as to be believed.

Then, the purely medical aspect of the case is quite remarkable. A hallucination is predominantly a pathological phenomenon, and such an illness is very rare. The possibility of a person, in good health but highly distraught, having a sudden hallucination may be unprecedented. But that's a medical problem, and I know little about it.

The psychological aspect of the case is another matter. We have before us two national types that represent with full clarity the

Russian People in their entirety. We see, first, the complete loss of a sense of measure in everything (and note that this is nearly always something temporary and passing that seems like the work of some evil power). There is an urge to go beyond the limit, an urge for that sinking sensation one has when one has come to the edge of an abyss, leans halfway over it, looks into the bottomless pit itself, and—in some particular but not infrequent cases—throws oneself headlong into it like a madman. We see this urge for negation in a person who may be the most inclined toward belief and reverence—the urge to negate everything: those things his heart holds most sacred, all those things the People cherish in totality, a thing which only a moment earlier had been an object of worship but which now suddenly seems an unbearable burden. What is especially striking is the haste and impetuosity with which the Russian reveals himself—in his good or his evil aspects—in certain characteristic moments of his own life or the life of the nation. Sometimes he simply can't be held back. Whether it is a matter of love or of drink, of debauchery, egoism, or envy—some Russians will surrender themselves utterly and totally, ready to break their links with everything and renounce everything: family, custom, God. The kindest man may suddenly be transformed into a vile reprobate and criminal; he needs only to be caught up by this whirlwind, this fateful maelstrom of violent and momentary negation and destruction of self that is so typical of the Russian national character at certain fateful moments in its existence. On the other hand, it is with the same force, the same impetuosity, the same urge for self-preservation and repentance that the Russian, like the Russian People as a whole, saves himself; he does this usually when he reaches the outermost limit, that is, when he has nowhere farther to go. Especially characteristic is the fact that this impulse backward, the impulse to restore and save oneself, is always more serious than the former urge to deny and destroy the self. Accordingly, the urge to destroy can be charged to a petty meanness of spirit; but the Russian sets about restoring himself with the most enormous and serious effort, and has only contempt for himself in his former movement toward negation.

I think that the principal and most basic spiritual need of the Russian People is the need for suffering, incessant and unslakeable suffering, everywhere and in everything. I think the Russian People have been infused with this need to suffer from time immemorial. A current of martyrdom runs through their entire history, and it flows not only from external misfortunes and disasters but springs from the very heart of the People themselves. There is always an element of suffering even in the happiness of the Russian People, and without it their happiness is incomplete. Never, not even in the most triumphant moments of their history, do they assume a proud and triumphant air; they have an air of tenderness that almost reaches the point of suffering; the People sigh and attribute their glory to the mercy of the Lord. The Russian People seem to take delight in their sufferings. What is true of the entire People is also true of individuals, generally speaking at least. Consider, for example, the many types of Russian wrongdoers. Here one finds not only debauchery taken to an extreme, debauchery that is sometimes amazing in its bold sweep and in the abominable depths to which a human soul can sink. The wrongdoer is, first of all, a suffering person himself. There is no naively gloating self-satisfaction in the Russian, even if he is a fool. Compare a Russian drunkard with a German one, for example: the Russian is far more foul than the German, but the German is certainly the more stupid and ridiculous of the two. The Germans are predominantly a complacent people who are proud of themselves. These basic national traits stand out the more strongly in the drunken German in proportion to the amount of beer consumed. The drunken German is definitely a happy man and he never weeps; he sings songs boasting of his prowess and is proud of himself. He comes home drunk as a cobbler, but still proud of himself. The Russian likes to drink from grief and to weep. And if he does put on airs, it's not because he's gloating; he only wants to raise a ruckus. He'll always recall some past insult and hurl reproaches at the one who insulted him, whether that person is present or not. He may brazenly insist that he's the next thing to a general; he'll swear like a trooper if you don't believe him, and finally he'll shout for someone to come and help him convince you. Yet the reason he presents such an ugly spectacle, the reason he wants someone to help him, is that in the depths of his drunken soul he knows very well that he's not a general but only a vile drunkard who has sunk to a level lower than any animal. What's true of one tiny instance is also true of much more important ones. The worst wrongdoer, even the one whose brazen and refined vices seem so attractive that other fools follow his example, still has some secret sense, in the depths of his deformed soul, that in the final analysis he's nothing more than a wretch. He's not complacent; reproach wells up in his heart, and he takes his revenge for it on those around him; he rages and attacks everyone. So it is that he pushes himself to the limit as he grapples with the suffering that is constantly building up in his heart; at the same time he seems to revel with delight in his suffering. If he has the capacity to rise up out of his fallen state, then he exacts a terrible vengeance on himself for his past fall, an even more painful vengeance than he had exacted on others for the secret torments his own dissatisfaction with himself caused him while befogged in his degradation.

Who provided the impulse to set both these peasant lads to disputing which could commit the most brazen sin? What were the' reasons that led to such a contest? These things remain a mystery, but there can be no doubt that both lads suffered—one by accepting the challenge, the other by offering it. Of course there must have been some prior cause: either some concealed enmity between them or a hatred that began in childhood, of which they themselves were unaware and which suddenly erupted at the moment of their dispute and challenge. The latter is the more likely; and it's likely that they were friends until that moment, living in an accord that became harder to bear the longer it went on. But at the moment of the challenge, the tension of mutual hatred and the victim's envy of his Mephistopheles was already something extraordinary.

"I'm not afraid of anything; I'll do whatever you say; let my soul be damned, but I'll put you in disgrace!"

"You're bluffing. You'll run away like a mouse to the cellar. I'll have the last laugh. The soul be damned!"

They could have found some other deed—something very shocking—for their contest: a robbery, a murder, open rebellion against some powerful person. The lad swore, after all, that he was ready for anything, and his tempter knew that a serious promise had been made, one that would be kept.

But no. The tempter thinks the most dreadful acts are too ordinary. He invents some unthinkable sin, unprecedented and inconceivable, and his choice reveals the People's whole outlook on life.

Inconceivable? Yet the very fact that he had decided on this, specifically, shows that he had perhaps been considering it already. This fanciful notion had crept into his soul long ago, perhaps even in his childhood; he was struck by the horror of it, yet also found it agonizingly delightful. That he had conceived of it all—the gun,

the garden—long before and had kept it as an awful secret—of this
there can be scarcely any doubt. Of course, he did not conceive
this with the intent of carrying it out himself, and indeed, he would
perhaps never have dared do it on his own. It was only that this
vision appealed to him; from time to time it would stir his soul,
beckoning him on, while he would shrink back, cold with horror.
One moment of unheard of audacity and then—let everything be
damned! And of course he believed that this would be the cause
of his eternal perdition, but: "All the same, what heights I
reached!"

There are many things one cannot conceive but only feel. There
is a great deal one can know unconsciously. Yet, in truth, this is
a curious soul, particularly coming from the environment it does.
Indeed, that's the whole point of the matter. It would also be good
to know how he regarded himself: did he feel more to blame than
his victim? As far as we can judge by his mentality, we must suppose
that he regarded himself as more to blame, or at least equally to
blame, so that when challenging his victim to this "brazen act,"
he was challenging himself as well.

We hear that the Russian People know the Gospels poorly and
that they do not know the fundamental principles of our faith.
That's true, of course, but they do know Christ and they have
borne Him in their hearts from time immemorial. There can be
no doubt of that. How can one have a genuine conception of Christ
without religious instruction? That's another question. But a heartfelt knowledge of Christ and a genuine conception of Him are fully
present. It is passed on from generation to generation and has
become a part of the People's hearts. Perhaps the only love of the
Russian People is Christ, and they love His image in their own
fashion, that is, to the point of suffering. Above all else the People
take pride in the name "Orthodox"—namely, those whose concept
of Christ is truer than any others'. I repeat: there is much one can
know unconsciously.

And so to make a mockery of something the People hold so
sacred, and thus to break one's links with the whole land; to destroy
oneself forever through negation and pride solely for the sake of
one moment of triumph—why the Russian Mephistopheles could
invent nothing more daring! The prospect of such an extreme of
passion, the prospect of such dark and complex sensations within
the soul of a common, simple man is astounding! And remember
that all this developed almost to the point of a conscious idea.

The victim, however, does not give in, is not humbled, is not frightened. At least he pretends that he isn't frightened. The lad accepts the challenge. Days pass, and he keeps to his promise. And now it is no longer a fanciful notion but a reality: he attends church; he hears the words of Christ every day, yet he does not shrink back. There are terrible murderers who are not daunted even by the sight of their victim. One such murderer, caught at the scene of the crime and guilty beyond any doubt, would not confess but kept lying to the investigating magistrate. And when the magistrate rose and ordered the man taken to prison, the murderer, with an air of utter tenderness, asked as a favor to be allowed to bid farewell to the woman he had murdered and whose body was still lying there (she was his former mistress, and he had killed her out of jealousy). He bent down, kissed her tenderly, and began to weep; still on his knees, he stretched his hands over her body and said once more that he was not guilty. I simply want to note that a man's feelings can atrophy to a brutish level.

But in the case in point there is no question of atrophy of feelings. Moreover, there is also something quite peculiar—mystical horror, the most colossal power over the human soul. This certainly was present, at least judging by the outcome of the affair. Yet the young lad's powerful spirit was still capable of grappling with this horror; he proved that. But is this really strength, or is it only an extreme of pusillanimity? Probably it is both these things combined in the meeting of opposite extremes. Nevertheless, this mystical horror not only did not bring an end to the struggle but prolonged it even more; and it probably was the very force that brought the struggle to an end by banishing every tender feeling from the sinner's heart: the more strongly the horror oppressed him, the less possible it became for him to feel. A sense of horror is something pitiless; it withers the heart and hardens it toward any lofty or tender feeling. And that is why the criminal was able to endure the moment before the communion chalice even though he may have been utterly paralyzed by fear. I also think that the mutual hatred of victim and tormentor totally vanished during these days. The tormented victim may have had pathological fits of hatred toward himself, those around him, and those who were praying in church, but least of all he hated his Mephistopheles. They both felt that they had need of one another so that together they might put an end to the affair. Each probably felt himself powerless to end it alone. Why, then, did they carry on? Why did they assume such a burden of torment? Yet they simply were unable to break their alliance. Had their contract been broken, they would at once have become inflamed with a mutual hatred ten times stronger than before, and there probably would have been a murder: the victim would have killed his tormentor.

This could well have happened. Even murder would be nothing compared to the horror endured by the victim. The point is that deep within the souls of each of them there must have been some sort of infernal delight in their own perdition, the breath-catching urge to lean over the abyss and peer into it, a stupendous rapture at one's own temerity. It's almost impossible that they could have brought the affair to its conclusion without these passionate sensations to stimulate them. They were not a couple of stupid, dull youngsters or simple lads playing pranks—not when they began with a competition to see who could commit the worst sin and ended with the despair in the elder's cell.

Note also that the tempter did not reveal the whole secret to his victim: when he left the church he did not know what he was to do with the Eucharist until the very moment his tempter ordered him to get the gun. So many days of such mystical uncertainty again testify to this sinner's terrible obstinacy. On the other hand, our village Mephistopheles reveals himself as a fine psychologist.

But perhaps when they came into the garden neither was aware of what he was doing? Still, the victim remembered loading and aiming the gun. Could he have only been acting mechanically, even though fully aware, as sometimes really happens when one is truly terrified? I do not think so: had he been transformed into a virtual machine that continues its operation only through force of inertia he would certainly not have had the vision that followed. He would simply have fallen down senseless once the full force of inertia had been exhausted—not *before*, but after shooting. No, it's most likely that he was in a state of complete and extraordinarily lucid consciousness the whole time, despite the mortal dread that kept growing with every second. And the very fact that the victim endured such pressure of progressively growing horror is, I repeat, proof of his immense spiritual strength.

Let us also keep in mind, in any case, that loading a gun is a process that demands a certain amount of concentration. I think that the most difficult, unbearable thing at a moment like this is the capacity to detach oneself from one's horror, from the idea that continues to oppress. Usually, people who are stricken by such an extreme of horror are no longer able to pull themselves away from contemplating it; they cannot detach themselves from the object or idea that has struck them. They stand transfixed before it and stare, as if enchanted, directly into the face of the object of horror. But the young lad carefully loaded the gun, and he remembered doing it; he remembered taking aim, and remembered everything, right to the very last moment. It is also possible that the process of loading the gun was a relief, a release for his suffering soul, and he was happy to concentrate but for a brief moment on some external object that provided this release. This is what happens at the guillotine to those about to be decapitated. Mme. Dubarry cried to the executioner: "Encore un moment, monsieur le bourreau, encore un moment!" Her sufferings would have been multiplied twentyfold during this extra moment, had she been granted it, yet still she cried out and begged for it. But if we suppose that for our sinner the loading of the gun was something like Dubarry's "encore un moment," then of course after such a moment he could not once more have faced the horror from which he had detached himself and continued to aim and fire. Now his hands would simply have grown numb and refused to move, and the gun would have dropped from them, despite the consciousness and willpower that had not left him.

And now, at the very ultimate moment, all the falsehood, all the baseness of his act, all the cowardice that he took for strength, all the disgrace of his fall—all these things burst forth from his heart in an instant and stood before him in dreadful accusation. An incredible vision appeared to him, and it was all over.

The thunderous voice of judgment came out of his own heart, of course. Why was it not expressed consciously? Why was there not a sudden parting of the clouds that had obscured his mind and his conscience? Why did it appear in an image that seemed entirely external, as a fact independent of his own spirit? We find here an immense psychological problem and an act of God. The criminal certainly saw this as an act of God. Our Vlas became a beggar and demanded suffering.

And what of the other Vlas, the tempter who was left? The story does not say that he came crawling after repentance; it says nothing about him. Perhaps he, too, came crawling; but perhaps he stayed on in his village and lives there now, still drinking and scoffing on church holidays: he did not see the vision, after all. But is that what really happened? I would very much like to know his story, just for the sake of information, as a subject for a sketch.

This is why I would like to know: what if he really and truly is a village nihilist, a homegrown cynic and thinker, an unbeliever who decided on such a contest with haughty mockery on his face, who did not suffer and tremble with his victim, as I suggest in this sketch, but who followed his victim's trembling and writhing with cold curiosity, solely out of a need to see someone else suffer, to see another man humiliated—who knows, perhaps even for the sake of scientific enquiry?

If indeed such traits are present even in the character of the People (and nowadays we may assume anything) and in our villages, then this is a new revelation, and a surprising one at that. I think we never heard of such traits before. Mr. Ostrovsky's tempter, in his fine comedy *Don't Live as You Choose*, is not well done at all. It's a shame we have no accurate information about these things.

Of course, the interest in the story I have told—at least if it contains any interest—lies only in the fact that it is genuine. But peering into the soul of our contemporary Vlas may sometimes be not without benefit. Our contemporary Vlas is quickly changing. The same seething ferment is going on in the depths where he lives as it is higher up, where we dwell, and it has been going on since February 19. Our epic hero has awakened and is stretching his arms; perhaps he will have the urge to go on a spree, to dash off somewhere beyond the limit. People say that he's already gone on a spree. Dreadful things are told and described in print: drunkenness, banditry, drunken children, drunken mothers, cynicism, destitution, corruption, godlessness. Some serious but rather rash people consider, on the basis of facts, that if such a "spree" continues for only ten years more, the consequences from an economic standpoint alone will be beyond imagining. But let us remember "Vlas" and be calm: at the critical moment all the falsehood, if indeed it is falsehood, will burst forth from the People's hearts and confront them with incredible accusatory power. Vlas will come to his senses and will set about doing God's work. In any case, he will save himself should things have reached the point of disaster. He will save himself and us as well, for once more the light and the salvation will come radiating from below (in a form that our liberals may find entirely surprising; and there will be a good deal of amusement in this). We even have a few hints about this surprise, and facts are appearing even now. . . . However, we can talk about that later. In any case, our bankruptcy as "fledglings from Peter's nest" is now beyond doubt. The Petrine period of Russian history was truly ended by the 19th of February, so that long ago we entered into a period of complete uncertainty.

6

Bobok

On this occasion I shall include "The Notes of a Certain
Person." That person is not I, but someone else entirely.
I think no further foreword is needed.

NOTES OF A CERTAIN PERSON

The other day Semyon Ardalonovich up and said to me, "Ivan
Ivanych, tell me, for Heaven's sake, will there ever be a day when
you'll be sober?"

That's a strange thing to ask. I'm not offended; I'm a timid
fellow. But just the same, they made me out to be a madman. An
artist once happened to paint my portrait. "You're a literary man,
after all," he says. So I let him have his way, and he put the portrait
on exhibit. And now I read: "Go and look at this sickly face that
seems to border on insanity."

My face may well be like that, but do they have to say it right
in print? Everything that appears in print should be noble; we
need some ideals, but this. . . .

He could at least have said it indirectly—that's the whole point
of style. But no, he won't say it indirectly. Humor and elegance
of style are disappearing nowadays, and abuse is taken for witticism.
But I don't take offense: I'm not some distinguished man of letters
who'll go off his head over a thing like that. I wrote a story, but
they wouldn't publish it. I wrote an article, but it was rejected.
I've taken a lot of articles around to various publishers, but they
always turn me down: "There's no salt in it," they say.

"What sort of salt do you want, then?" I ask, with sarcasm in
my voice. "Attic?"

He doesn't even understand. Mostly I do translations from the

French for booksellers. I also write advertisements for shopkeepers: "A rare item! The finest tea from our own plantations. . . . " I made a pile of money writing a eulogy for His Excellency the late Piotr Matveevich. I put together *The Art of Appealing to the Ladies* on commission from a bookseller. I've put out about six of these little books in my lifetime. I want to do a collection of Voltaire's bon mots, but I fear that people here may find them a bit too tame. What's Voltaire nowadays? These days we need an oak cudgel, not a Voltaire! We ought to be knocking one another's teeth out! Well, that's my entire literary output. From time to time I'll send letters to the editor, fully signed, but for which I'm not paid. I'm always giving advice and admonitions, criticizing things and pointing out the way. Last week I sent my fortieth letter in two years to the same newspaper; they've set me back four rubles in postage stamps alone. I have a nasty disposition, that's what it is.

I don't think the artist painted me on account of my literary work; it probably was on account of the two symmetrical warts on my forehead: that's a phenomenon of nature, he says. They don't have any ideas, you see, so now they go on about these phenomena. But what a job he did on my warts in the portrait—they're as good as life! That's what they call realism.

As far as madness is concerned, we've had a lot of people reckoned among the insane in the past year. And it's done in such a fine literary style: "Given such an original talent . . . and then, at the very end, we see that . . . however, it should have long been apparent. . . . " It's done very slyly—in fact from the point of view of pure art one might even admire it. But yet these "lunatics" come back even more clever than they were before. That's just how it is: we can drive people mad, but we've never yet made anyone more clever.

I think the cleverest of all is the one who calls himself a fool at least once a month. Now that's something we never hear of these days! There was a time when a fool realized that he was a fool once a year at the very least, but now it never happens. Everything's so muddled now that you can't tell a fool from a clever man. They've done that on purpose.

I recall the witty saying of the Spaniards, some two hundred and fifty years ago, at the time the French built their first madhouse: "They have locked up all their fools in a special building to make people think that they themselves are wise." Just so: you can't

prove your own intelligence by shutting someone else up in a
madhouse. "Mr. K. has gone mad, so now we are wise." No, that's
not how it works.

But damn it, why have I started carrying on about my own
intelligence? All I do is grumble. Even my maid is fed up with it.
A friend of mind dropped in yesterday. "Your style is changing,"
he says. "It's like mincemeat. You chop things finer and finer. You
put something in parentheses with other parentheses inside and
then insert something else in brackets, and start chopping it some
more. . . ."

He's right. Something queer is happening to me. My character
is changing, and my head aches. I'm beginning to see and hear
some strange things. Not voices, exactly, but it's as if someone
right beside me is saying: "Bobok, bobok, bobok!"

What is this bobok? I must find some distraction.

I was walking around looking for some distraction when I came
upon a funeral. It was a distant relative of mine. He was a Collegiate
Councilor, however. A widow, five daughters, none of them married.
Think what it must cost in shoes alone! The deceased earned a
regular salary, but now there's only a miserable little pension.
They'll have to tighten their belts. They always received me coldly.
And I wouldn't have gone now, had it not been such a special
occasion. I joined the others in the procession to the cemetery;
they kept apart from me and looked down their noses. My uniform
coat really is rather shabby. It must be twenty-five years since I've
been to a cemetery. What a place it is!

First of all, there's the smell. About fifteen corpses had arrived.
Funeral palls of various prices. There were even two catafalques:
one for a general and one for a lady. A lot of mournful faces, a lot
of faces pretending to mourn, and a lot of obviously happy faces
as well. The clergy have nothing to complain about: it's an income
for them. But the smell, the smell! I wouldn't want to be a clergyman here.

I took a cautious look at the faces of the corpses, unsure of my
own impressionability. Some of them have soft expressions, others
unpleasant ones. On the whole their smiles aren't nice, and some
of them are particularly not nice. I don't like them; I'll have dreams
about them.

During the service I went out of the church to get some air. It
was overcast but dry. Cold, too; but it's October, after all. I took

a walk round the graves. They have various categories. The third category costs thirty rubles; it's decent and not too expensive. The first two categories mean burial inside the church or in the entry; they make you pay through the nose for those. This time they buried six, including the general and the lady, in the third category.

I took a look in these wretched graves, and it was dreadful: water, and what water! It was quite green and ... but why go on about it? The gravedigger was constantly bailing it out with a bucket. While the service was still going on I went out the gate to stroll around a bit. There's an almshouse there, and a restaurant a little farther along. Not a bad little place; you can get a bite to eat and everything. Quite a few of the mourners had come in here as well. I could see a lot of good cheer and genuine liveliness. I had a snack and a drink.

Then I lent a hand in carrying a coffin to the grave. Why is it these corpses get so heavy when they're in the coffin? I've heard it's some sort of inertia, that the body can't manage itself any more, it seems ... or some such nonsense. It goes against common sense and the laws of mechanics. I don't like it when people with only a general education butt in to try to solve specialized problems, but it's done all the time in Russia. Civilians love to make judgments on military matters—even on things only a field marshal should decide, while people trained as engineers more often talk of philosophy and political economy.

I didn't go to the Litany afterward. I'm a proud man, and if they are going to receive me only because of special circumstances, then why bother trudging off to their dinners, even if they are funeral dinners? I just don't understand why I stayed at the cemetery. I sat down on a tombstone and fell into an appropriate reverie.

I began thinking about the Moscow Exhibition and ended thinking about astonishment; I mean astonishment in general, as a topic. This is what I concluded about "astonishment."

It's ridiculous, of course, to be astonished at everything, while being astonished at nothing is much more attractive and for some reason is considered good form. But, practically speaking, it's hardly like that. I think it's far more ridiculous to be astonished at nothing than to be astonished at everything. Besides, to be astonished at nothing is almost the same as to respect nothing. And a stupid man isn't even capable of respect.

"Above all I want to feel respect. I *long* to feel respect," an acquaintance of mine told me just the other day.

He longs to feel respect! My God, I thought, what would happen to you if you ventured to say that in print!

At this point my mind began to wander. I don't like reading inscriptions on gravestones; you always see the same thing. On the stone next to me lay a half-eaten sandwich: stupid and inappropriate. I threw it on the ground, since it wasn't bread, only a sandwich. However, I think it's not a sin to throw bread crumbs on the ground; it's only a sin when it's on the floor. I must check it in Suvorin's *Almanac*.

I imagine I must have sat there for a long time, perhaps too long; I mean to say that I even lay down on a long stone carved like a marble coffin. And how was it that suddenly I began hearing various things? At first I didn't pay any attention and tried to ignore the voices. But the conversation went on. I could hear some muffled sounds, as if the mouths were covered with pillows; and yet they were audible and seemed quite near. I came to life, sat up, and began listening carefully.

"That's simply not possible, Your Excellency. You declared in hearts, sir; I'm your partner, and now, suddenly, you have seven in diamonds. We should have agreed about the diamonds beforehand, sir."

"What, then, are we to play entirely by memory? What charm is there in that?"

"It's absolutely impossible, Your Excellency, without stipulations of some sort. We must have a dummy, and we must have one hand not turned up."

"Well, you won't find any dummy here."

What presumption! Both strange and surprising. One voice was very weighty and authoritative, the other sounded soft and saccharine; I wouldn't have believed it, had I not heard it myself. I didn't think I could be at the Litany. But how can they be playing preference here, and who is this general? The sounds were coming from the grave; that was certain. I bent down and read the inscription on the headstone: "Here lies the body of Major-General Pervoedov . . . Chevalier of this order and that." Hmm. "Passed away in August of this year . . . fifty-seven . . . Rest, beloved ashes, until the joyous morn."

Well, damn it, he really was a general! On the other little grave, where the obsequious voice came from, there was still no monument, only a stone slab; a newcomer, no doubt. A Court Councilor, by the sound of his voice.

"Oh-ho-ho!" said a new voice, about thirty feet away from the general's place and coming from a fresh grave. This was a rough, masculine voice, but softened by a sanctimonious touch.

"Oh-ho-ho!"

"Oh, he's hiccuping again!" suddenly came the fussy and haughty voice of an irritated lady, apparently one from high society. "What a punishment to lie next to this shopkeeper!"

"I wasn't hiccuping at all; I've had nothing to eat in any case; it's just my nature. Anyhow, madam, it's your own fussiness about things here that keep you from settling down."

"Then why did you have to lie next to me?"

"It was my wife and little ones who put me here; it wasn't my wish. The mystery of death! I wouldn't have lain next to you for anything, not for gold of any color. I'm here because of my means—it's a matter of price, ma'am. Because that's something we can always manage, to pay for a third-class grave."

"You must have piled up a good bit with your overcharging."

"How can we overcharge you when you haven't paid a thing on your account since January? You've a tidy little bill in the shop."

"That's ridiculous. In my opinion it is utterly ridiculous to try to collect debts here! Go up above. Ask my niece; she inherited it all."

"There's not much chance of asking anywhere, or going anywhere now. We've both come to the end of our days, and we are equal in sin before God's judgment."

"Equal in sin," the deceased lady mimicked scornfully. "Don't you dare say another word to me!"

"Oh-ho-ho!"

"Still, the shopkeeper is doing as the lady says, Your Excellency."

"And why should he not do as she says?"

"As we all know, Your Excellency, because of the new order down here."

"What new order do you mean?"

"Well, you see, Your Excellency, we have, so to say, died."

"Ah, yes! But still, the order...."

Well, I was obliged to them; they certainly cheered me up! If that is the state of affairs down there, what can we expect of the upper floor? But the things that were going on down there! I went on listening, however, but it was with real irritation.

"No, I wish I could have lived a bit longer! No ... you know ...

I wish I could have lived a bit longer!" said a new voice, coming from somewhere in the space between the general and the irritated lady.

"Listen to that, Your Excellency, our neighbor is at it again. He doesn't say a word for three days, and suddenly: 'I wish I could have lived a bit longer; no, I wish I could have lived!' And he says it with such appetite, he-he-he!"

"And without thinking of what he's saying."

"It gets the better of him, Your Excellency, and he falls asleep, fast asleep. He's been here since April, you know, and all of a sudden: 'I wish I could have lived!'"

"It is a bit dull, though," remarked His Excellency.

"It does get dull, Your Excellency. Shall we tease Avdotia Ignatevna again, he-he-he?"

"No, please, spare me that. I cannot abide that twittering busybody."

"And I cannot abide either one of you," replied the woman with disgust. "You are both extremely boring and have no capacity for discussing elevated matters. You needn't put on airs, Your Excellency; I know a little story about how a servant swept you out from under the bed of a married lady one morning."

"Wretched woman!" muttered the General.

"Avdotia Ignatevna, ma'am," the shopkeeper muttered again suddenly, "tell me, dear lady, and don't bear me a grudge: are these my forty days of torment, or is it something else . . . ?"

"Oh, he's on about that again. I just knew it, because I can smell the stench of him, and that means he's tossing and turning!"

"I'm not tossing and turning, ma'am, and I don't have any stench because my body is still whole and sound. But you, my lady, have already begun to turn bad, because the stench is truly unbearable, even for a place like this. It's only out of politeness that I haven't mentioned it."

"Oh, you are a nasty creature to insult me so. He reeks to high heaven, but he talks about me."

"Oh-ho-ho-ho! If only my forty-day memorial would come. I can hear the tearful voices up there, the wailing of my wife and the quiet weeping of my children!"

"Much they have to weep about: they'll stuff themselves full of rice porridge and go home. Oh, I wish someone would wake up!"

"Avdotia Ignatevna," the unctuous official spoke up. "Just wait a wee while and the newcomers will begin to talk."

"Are there any young people among them?"

"There are, Avdotia Ignatevna. There are even some young men."

"Isn't that just what we need!"

"Well, haven't they begun yet?" the general inquired.

"The ones from the other day haven't even come to yet, Your Excellency. I'm sure you are aware that sometimes they don't say a word for a week. It's good that they brought a lot of them all at once yesterday, the day before, and again today. Aside from them, almost everyone for twenty-five yards around is from last year."

"Yes, it should be interesting."

"Just today, Your Excellency, they buried the Actual Privy Councilor Tarasevich. I recognized the voices. I know his nephew who helped lower the coffin."

"Hmm, where is he, then?"

"Only about five paces from you, Your Excellency, on your left. Almost at your very feet. . . . You ought to make his acquaintance, Your Excellency."

"Hmm, perhaps not. . . . I don't think I should make the first move."

"He'll take the initiative himself, Your Excellency. He'll even be flattered. Let me look after things, Your Excellency, and I. . . . "

"Ah, ah . . . oh, what's happening to me?" groaned the thin, frightened voice of a newcomer.

"A newcomer, Your Excellency, a newcomer, thank God, and how quickly! Sometimes they don't say a word for a week."

"A young man, it seems!" squealed Avdotia Ignatevna.

"I . . . I . . . I had complications, and so suddenly!" the young man babbled again. "Schultz told me just last night: 'You have complications,' he said, and I was dead by morning. Ah, ah!"

"There's nothing to be done, young man," said the General kindly, evidently delighted by the presence of someone new. "You must stop grieving! Welcome to our Vale of Jehoshaphat, as it might be called. We are good people, and you'll get to know us and like us. Major-General Vasily Vasilievich Pervoedov, at your service."

"Oh, no, no! I won't accept this! I'm being treated by Schultz; I developed complications, you see; first I had chest pains and a cough, and then I caught a cold; chest congestion and influenza . . . and then suddenly, quite unexpectedly . . . that's the main thing, it was quite unexpected."

"You say it was your chest first," the official joined in gently, as if wishing to raise the spirits of the newcomer.

"Yes, my chest, with a lot of phlegm; then suddenly, no more phlegm, just my chest. I couldn't breathe . . . and, you know. . . .

"I know, I know. But with chest problems you should have gone to Ekk right away, not to Schultz."

"I kept intending to go to Botkin, you know . . . and suddenly. . . ."

"Well, Botkin will skin you," remarked the General.

"Botkin doesn't skin you, not at all. I've heard he's got such a fine manner and he can tell you everything beforehand."

"His Excellency was remarking about Botkin's fees," the official corrected.

"What do you mean? He only charges three rubles, and he gives you such an examination, and a prescription. . . . And I certainly wanted to consult him, because I was told that. . . . So, gentlemen, what should I do: go to Ekk or to Botkin?"

"What? To whom?" The General's corpse shook with friendly laughter. The official's falsetto joined in.

"My dear boy, my dear, delightful boy, how I love you!" squealed Avdotya Ignatevna with delight. "How I wish they would put someone like you next to me!"

No, I cannot put up with this! Is this what corpses are like today? But I must listen to more of this and not jump to any conclusions. This whining newcomer—I remember seeing him in his coffin not long ago and he looked like a frightened chicken, an absolutely repulsive expression on his face! But let's hear what comes next.

But next there developed such a row that I couldn't even keep it all in my memory, since very many of them woke up all at once. An official, a State Councilor, awoke and immediately, without a moment's hesitation, began taking up with the General a proposal for a new subcommittee in the Ministry of —— Affairs and for the probable transfer of various functionaries connected with this subcommittee; and the General was utterly carried away by this discussion. I confess that I myself learned many a new thing and was amazed at the ways one can glean news of officialdom in this capital city of ours. Then a certain engineer awoke; but he went on mumbling utter nonsense for a long time, so that our friends paid him no heed and simply let him work it out of his system. At last the prominent lady who had been buried under the catafalque that

morning began to display signs of sepulchral animation. Lebeziatnikov (for the name of the obsequious Court Councilor whom
I so despised and who was located near General Pervoedov was in
fact Lebeziatnikov) began fussing and expressing his astonishment
that they were awakening so quickly this time. I confess that I was
amazed as well. However, some of those who were waking up had
been buried two days earlier, such as a certain very young girl of
about sixteen who could, however, only giggle in a most vile and
rapacious manner.

"Your Excellency, the Privy Councilor Tarasevich is awakening!"
Lebeziatnikov announced suddenly and hastily.

"Eh? What?" mumbled the newly awakened Privy Councilor in
a fussy, lisping voice. There was something capriciously imperious
in the sound of that voice. I listened with curiosity, since I had
heard some things about this Tarasevich of late, things that were
highly suggestive and alarming.

"It is I, Your Excellency, for the moment it is only I, sir."

"What is your problem? How may I help you?"

"I wish only to inquire about Your Excellency's health. At first,
everyone here, being unaccustomed to the place, feels somewhat
cramped. . . . General Pervoedov would like to have the honor of
making Your Excellency's acquaintance and hopes. . . . "

"Never heard of him."

"Surely, Your Excellency—General Pervoedov, Vasily Vasilevich. . . . "

"Are you General Pervoedov?"

"Indeed not, Your Excellency, I am only Court Councilor Lebeziatnikov at your service, sir; but General Pervoedov. . . . "

"Nonsense! I must ask you to leave me in peace."

"Let him be," said General Pervoedov with dignity, at last putting an end to the vile overzealousness of his sepulchral minion.

"He hasn't quite awakened yet, Your Excellency, and you must
keep that in mind. It's only that he's unaccustomed to things here;
once he wakes up fully he'll receive you properly. . . . "

"Let him be," repeated the General.

"Vasily Vasilevich! Hallo, Your Excellency!" came the sudden
exclamation of a new voice, loud and excited, from the vicinity of
Avdotia Ignatevna. This was an impertinent, aristocratic voice with
a fashionably weary tone and impudent intonation. "I've been
listening to you all for the past two hours; I've been here for three

days now. Do you remember me, Vasily Vasilevich? Klinevich: we
met at the Volokonskys' where you—I can't imagine why—were
also received."

"What? Count Piotr Petrovich? Have you really . . . at such tender
years. . . ? I am truly sorry!"

"And I am sorry as well, yet what does it matter? I want to get
all that I can from this place. And I'm not a count but a baron,
only a baron. We're merely some mangy little family of barons
who originated in the servants' quarters; how we came to be barons
I don't know, nor do I care. I'm only a good-for-nothing from the
pseudo-upper class and consider myself a charming rascal. My
father is a general of some sort, and my mother was once received
en haut lieu. Sieffel the Yid and I passed off fifty thousand rubles'-
worth of false banknotes last year, but I informed on him, and
Julie Charpentier de Lusignan went off to Bordeaux with all the
money. And just imagine—I was already quite properly engaged
to Miss Shchevalevsky, who's three months short of being sixteen
and still at school. She was bringing ninety thousand with her.
Avdotia Ignatevna, do you remember how you seduced me fifteen
years ago when I was fourteen and still in the Corps of Pages?"

"Ah, it's you, wretch. Well, God sent you, at least, otherwise
there would be no one here. . . ."

"You were wrong when you thought it was your neighbor, the
merchant, who was smelling bad. . . . I just kept quiet and laughed.
That was me; they had to bury me in a sealed coffin."

"What a vile creature you are! Still, I'm glad; you will simply
not believe, Klinevich, what lack of life and wit there is here."

"Yes, indeed, and I have some original ideas to try out. Your
Excellency—not you, Pervoedov—the other Excellency, Mister Tarasevich, Privy Councilor! Answer me! It's Klinevich, who took
you to see Mlle. Furie last Lent. Do you hear me?"

"I hear you, Klinevich. I'm very pleased, and you have my
assurance that. . . ."

"I don't have any assurance of anything, and don't give a hang.
I would only like to give you a big kiss, you dear old fellow, but
I can't, thank God. Do you know, gentlemen, what this *grand-père*
cooked up? He died three or four days ago and—can you imagine?—
he left a deficit of some four hundred thousand in government
funds. The sum was supposed to support widows and orphans,
but it seems for some reason he was the sole administrator and so
his accounts hadn't been audited for eight years. I can imagine

what long faces they're all wearing up there and how they'll remember him. The very thought makes one's mouth water, doesn't
it! All last year I was amazed at how a seventy-year-old fellow like
him, with gout and rheumatism, could have such stores of energy
for dissipation; but now we have the answer! It was those widows
and orphans: the very thought of them must have warmed his
blood! I've known about it for a long time, and I was the only
one who knew; Charpentier told me, and when I found out I at
once leaned on him, the blessed man, in friendly fashion: 'Let's
have twenty-five thousand, unless you'd like your accounts audited
tomorrow.' But he could only scrape up thirteen thousand, and so,
it seems, he died just in time. *Grand-père*, hey, do you hear me?"

"*Cher* Klinevich, I am fully in agreement with you, and you
need not . . . enter into such details. Life contains so much suffering,
so many torments, and so little retribution. . . . I wanted some peace
at last and, as far as I can see, I have hopes of deriving something
from this place as well. . . ."

"I'll wager he's already sniffed out Katish Berestova!"

"Who? . . . Which Katish?" came the trembling, rapacious voice
of the old man.

"Ah, which Katish indeed? She's here, not more than five paces
from me, on the left, and ten paces from you. This is her fifth
day here, and if you had known, *grand-père*, what a wicked little
creature she is . . . a good home, a good education, and a monster
to the tips of her fingers! I didn't show her to anyone up there; I
was the only one who knew. . . . Katish, say something!"

"Hee-hee-hee!" responded a cracked, girlish voice; but in that
voice one felt something like the prick of a needle. "Hee-hee-hee!"

"And is she a nice little blo-onde?" babbled the *grand-père*,
drawing out the last word.

"Hee-hee-hee!"

"For a long time now . . . a long time," babbled the old fellow,
trying to catch his breath, "I've loved to dream about a nice little
blonde . . . about fifteen . . . in circumstances just like these. . . ."

"Monster!" exclaimed Avdotia Ignatevna.

"Enough!" Klinevich announced flatly. "I see that I have excellent material to work with. We shall at once set to arranging
things here in a better fashion. The main thing is that we pass our
remaining time here happily. But how much time have we? Hey,
you, the official of some sort—Lebeziatnikov, was it, that someone
called you?"

"Lebeziatnikov, Semyon Evseeich, Court Councilor, at your service, and absolutely delighted to be so."

"I couldn't give a damn if you're delighted, but you seem to know everything about this place. Tell me, first (and I've been amazed at it since yesterday), how is it that we can speak here? We've died, after all, and yet we're speaking; we seem to be able to move, and yet we shouldn't be able to speak and move. What sort of hocus-pocus is this?"

"If you please, baron, Platon Nikolaevich could explain it better than I."

"Who is this Platon Nikolaevich? Just answer my question!"

"Platon Nikolaevich, our local homegrown philosopher, natural scientist, and Master of Arts. He's published several little books of philosophy, but for the past three months he's gone right off to sleep so that there's no way we can rouse him now. Once a week he mutters a few irrelevant words."

"Get to the point!"

"He explains it all by a very simple fact, namely, that up above, while we were still alive, we were wrong in thinking that death up there was really death. Here the body more or less comes to life again; the remnants of life are concentrated, but only in the consciousness. This is—I don't quite know how to put it—a continuation of life as if by inertia. In his view, everything is concentrated somewhere in the consciousness and continues for two or three months . . . sometimes even for half a year. . . . We have one person here, for instance, whose body has almost entirely decomposed, but every six weeks or so he will still suddenly mumble one word—meaningless of course—about a bean or something: 'Bobok, bobok.' So that means there is still a faint spark of life glowing in him. . . ."

"Quite silly. But how is it that I have no sense of smell, and yet I can smell the stench?"

"That's . . . he-he! Well, at this point our philosopher got completely lost in a fog. He remarked specifically about the sense of smell, that the stench here was a moral one, so to say—he-he! Apparently the stench is from the soul, so that after two or three months it can reach a new awareness . . . this being, so to say, the final concession of mercy. . . . Yet it seems to me, baron, that these are all mystical ravings, quite understandable in his circumstances. . . ."

"That's enough; I'm sure the rest is all nonsense. The main thing is that we have two or three months of life and then, finally, bobok. I propose to you that we spend these two months as pleasantly as possible and to do so, that we arrange things on an entirely new basis. Ladies and gentlemen! I propose that we abandon all sense of shame!"

"Oh, indeed, let us abandon all sense of shame!" came the sound of many voices; strangely enough, there were entirely new voices among them, meaning that they belonged to people who had only just awakened. The bass voice of the engineer, who had now completely awakened, rumbled among them with special eagerness. The girl Katish burst into a fit of joyous giggles.

"Oh, how I long to lose my sense of shame!" exclaimed Avdotia Ignatevna rapturously.

"Do you hear that? If even Avdotia Ignatevna wants to abandon her sense of shame...."

"No, no, Klinevich. I used to feel shame; I was still ashamed up there, but here I have a terrible urge to be ashamed of nothing!"

"As I understand it, Klinevich," growled the engineer's bass voice, "you want to organize our life here, so to say, on new and rational principles."

"I really don't give a damn about that. We should wait for Kudeiarov for that; they brought him in yesterday. Once he wakes up he'll explain it all to you. What a personality he is—a giant among men! I think they'll be hauling in another one of your natural scientists tomorrow, and probably an officer and, if I'm not mistaken, a certain newspaper columnist in three or four days and his editor, too, I think. But never mind them! We're getting a nice little group together and everything will take shape of itself. But meanwhile, I don't want any lying. That's the only demand I make, because it's the most important thing. It's impossible to live on earth without lying, for life and lies are synonymous; but down here, just for fun, let's not lie. The grave means something after all, damn it! We'll each tell our stories to the others and be ashamed of nothing. I'll tell you about myself first of all. I'm a carnivore in essence, you see. Up there, all such things were held together with rotten ropes. Down with ropes! Let's live these two months in the most shameless truth! Let us bare our bodies and our souls!"

"Let us bare ourselves!" cried all the voices.

"I'm terribly, terribly eager to bare myself," squealed Avdotia Ignatevna.

"Ah...ha...I can see that we are going to have a very fine time here. I don't want to go see Ekk!"

"No, I wish I could live a bit longer, just a bit longer, you know!"

"Hee-hee-hee!" giggled Katish.

"The main thing is that no one can stop us, and even though Pervoedov may get angry, as I can see, he still can't touch me. *Grand-père*, do you agree?"

"I agree, absolutely and with the greatest pleasure, but on condition that Katish begin her autobiography first."

"I protest; I protest with every ounce of my strength!" said General Pervoedov forcefully.

"Your Excellency!" babbled the wretched Lebeziatnikov in a flurry of excitement, lowering his voice to coax the General. "Your Excellency, it would be much better for us if we agreed. That girl is right here, you know . . . and finally, there are all those other things. . . ."

"To be sure, there is the girl, but. . . ."

"It would be better, Your Excellency, it truly would be better! Let's at least give it a try; let's at least have an example. . . ."

"Even in the grave they don't give you any peace!"

"In the first place, General, you play cards in the grave, and in the second place, we don't give a damn about you," intoned Klinevich with measured emphasis.

"My dear sir, I must ask you not to forget yourself."

"What? You can't get your hands on me, and I can tease you from here just as I used to tease Julie's lapdog. In any case, ladies and gentlemen, what sort of a general is he down here? He was a general up there, but down here he's not even small potatoes!"

"No, I'm not small potatoes . . . even here I'm. . . ."

"Down here you'll rot in your coffin, and six brass buttons will be all that's left."

"Bravo, Klinevich!" howled several voices.

"I served my emperor. . . . I have a sword. . . ."

"Your sword is fit only for killing mice, and besides, you've never drawn it from its scabbard."

"All the same, I was a part of the whole."

"There was no shortage of parts of the whole."

"Bravo, Klinevich, bravo, ha-ha-ha!"

"I don't understand what significance the sword has," announced the engineer.

"We shall flee from the Prussians like mice, and they'll smash us to smithereens!" cried a new voice from far away, literally choking with delight.

"A sword, my dear sir, signifies honor!" the General tried to shout, but only I heard him. Thereupon began a long and furious uproar with riotous shouting and racket; only Avdotia Ignatevna's squeals, impatient to the point of hysteria, could be recognized.

"Quickly, quickly! Oh, when are we going to give up our sense of shame?"

"Oh-ho-ho! In truth my soul is going through its torment!" came the voice of the shopkeeper, and. . . .

And at this point I suddenly sneezed. It happened unexpectedly and unintentionally, but the effect was striking: everything fell silent as the grave and vanished like a dream. A real sepulchral silence ensued. I do not think that they were shamed by my presence: they had resolved to be ashamed of nothing, after all! I waited about five minutes and heard not a word and not a sound. I cannot suppose, either, that they feared I would denounce them to the police, for what could the police do in this case? I cannot help but conclude that they still had some sort of secret, unknown to mortal men, which they carefully concealed from every mortal.

"Well, dear friends," I thought, "I'll come and visit you again." And with this I left the cemetery.

No, I cannot accept this, in truth, I cannot! Bobok does not trouble me (that's what it turned out to be, this bobok)!

Debauchery in a place like that, debauchery of one's final hopes, debauchery among sagging, decomposing bodies, debauchery that does not even spare the final moments of consciousness! These moments are given to them as a gift and. . . . And the main thing—in a place like that! No, this I cannot accept. . . .

I shall visit other "categories" in the graveyard and listen everywhere. That's just what has to be done—to listen everywhere, not just at one end of the cemetery, so as to form an understanding. Perhaps I'll stumble on something to give comfort as well.

But I'll certainly come back to these people. They did promise to tell their autobiographies and various other little stories. Foo! No, I won't go, certainly not; it's a matter of conscience!

I'll bring this to *The Citizen*. One of the editors there has also had his portrait exhibited. Perhaps he'll print this.

7

A Troubled Countenance

I've been reading a thing or two from our current literature and feel that *The Citizen* should include some mention of this on its pages. But what sort of a critic am I? I truly had intended to write a proper critical article, but it seems I can only say something "à propos." The things I read were "The Sealed Angel," by Mr. Leskov, a poem by Nekrasov, and an article by Mr. Shchedrin. I've also read the articles by Mr. Skabichevsky and N. M. in *Notes of the Fatherland*. Both these articles were revelations to me, in a way, and I certainly must talk about them sometime. But now I shall begin from the beginning, i.e., in the order in which I read the works—with "The Sealed Angel."

This is a story by Mr. Leskov in *The Russian Messenger*. I know that many people here in Petersburg liked this work and that very many people read it. In truth, the story deserves this attention: it is distinctive and entertaining. It is a tale told by a former dissenter, an Old Believer, at a posting station one Christmas night, of how he and a whole worker's artel of some hundred and fifty other dissenters were converted to Orthodoxy through a miracle. These workers were building a bridge in a large Russian city and had spent three years living in their own separate barracks on the bank of the river. They had their own chapel and in it a large collection of ancient icons that had been consecrated before the time of Patriarch Nikon. Mr. Leskov relates in a very interesting manner how one gentleman—a not altogether unimportant official—wanted to extract a bribe of some fifteen thousand rubles from the artel. Making a sudden incursion into the chapel with troops to back him up, he demanded a hundred rubles ransom for each icon. The dissenters were unable to provide this money. Thereupon he confiscated their icons. Holes were drilled in the icons and they were strung on iron rods like so many bagels and then taken away to some cellar. But among them was an icon of an angel, ancient and particularly revered, and considered by the artel to have miraculous powers. The official, angered by the stubborn refusal of the dissenters to pay the ransom, decided to impress them in a striking manner, gain revenge, and offend them deeply: he took a stick of sealing wax and in the presence of the whole group dripped the wax on the angel's face and applied an official seal to it. When the local bishop saw the sealed face of the holy image he declared, "A troubled countenance," and had the desecrated icon placed on a window in the cathedral. Mr. Leskov assures us that the bishop's words and his placing of the desecrated icon in the cathedral rather than in the cellar pleased the group of Old Believers.

Thereupon followed the complex and interesting story of how this "Angel" was stolen from the cathedral. An Englishman, a gentleman and apparently the contractor for the bridge, became involved with the dissenters and took a liking to them; since they were frank and honest with him, he undertook to help them. The dissenters' conversations with the Englishman about icon painting are particularly noteworthy. This part is truly good, the best in the whole story. The story ends with the description of how the icon was at last stolen from the cathedral during the midnight service, the seal removed from the angel, and a new icon—still unconsecrated and which the Englishman's wife undertook to "seal up" in the manner of the old one—substituted for the original. And so at the critical moment the miracle happened: light was seen emanating from the newly sealed icon (true, it was seen only by one person), and when the icon was brought to the cathedral it turned out to be unsealed; that is, there was no wax on the face of the angel. The dissenter who had brought the icon was so struck by this that he at once went to the bishop in the cathedral and confessed everything; the bishop forgave him, saying: "This should be an inspiring demonstration to you of where the faith is more efficacious. You," he said, "removed the seal from your angel through a knavish trick, while ours removed his own seal and led you here."

The miracle so struck the dissenters that the whole artel of them, a hundred and fifty men or so, embraced the Orthodox faith.

But at this point the author made a slip and ended his tale rather awkwardly. (Mr. Leskov is inclined to such slips: just recall the end of Deacon Akhilla in his *Cathedral Folk*.) It seems he got frightened of being accused of favoring superstitions, so he made haste to demystify the miracle. He has the narrator himself, a little peasant and former dissenter, "merrily" confess that the day after their conversion to Orthodoxy they discovered how the seal had been removed from the angel. The Englishwoman had not dared to pour wax over the face of the angel, even though the icon was yet unconsecrated, so she fastened the seal to a piece of paper which she slipped under the edge of the mounting. The paper, of course, slid free while the icon was being taken to the cathedral, and the angel thus became "unsealed." Thus it is not entirely comprehensible why the dissenters remained faithful to Orthodoxy despite the explanation of the "miracle." Of course, they were touched by the kindness of the bishop who forgave them. But taking into account the firmness and the purity of their former beliefs; taking into account the desecration of their sacred objects and the insult offered to the sacredness of their own feelings; taking into account, finally, the general nature of our dissenters as a whole, one can hardly explain the conversion of dissenters by an appeal to their tender feelings: tender feelings for what and for whom? Was it gratitude merely for the *forgiveness* of the bishop? But surely they—better than anyone—should have been aware of the extent of a bishop's authority in the church, and they would thus be unlikely to have many tender feelings toward that same church in which a bishop, after such an unprecedented, public, shameless, and arbitrary sacrilege by a bribe-seeking official (a sacrilege that touched the dissenters and *all Orthodox believers* in equal measure), allowed himself only to sigh, "A troubled countenance!"; a bishop who could not even prevent a minor official from taking actions so bestial and offensive to religion.

And, on the whole, in this regard Mr. Leskov's tale left me with a queasy feeling and a certain skepticism toward the truth of his story. Of course, the story is marvelously narrated and merits much praise, but the question remains as to whether it is all true. Could all that really happen in Russia? And that is just the point, since the story is supposed to be based on actual fact. Let's imagine a case like this: let's suppose that in some Orthodox church somewhere there now is an ancient icon of miraculous powers revered by all Orthodox everywhere. Imagine that some artel of dissenters, as a group, steals that icon from the cathedral specifically in order to keep that ancient holy thing in their own chapel. All that could happen, of course. Imagine that some ten years thereafter an official finds this icon and haggles with the dissenters to extract a sizable bribe. They aren't able to raise such a sum, and so he takes some sealing wax, drips it on the face of the holy image, and applies an official seal to it. Does he do that simply because the icon has been in the hands of the dissenters for a time and its sacred essence has been lost? The "Angel" Mr. Leskov tells us about was also an Orthodox icon, consecrated in ancient times and revered by all Orthodoxy before the schism, was it not? And surely in such circumstances the local bishop could and would have the right at least to raise a finger in defense of the icon and not simply sigh, "A troubled countenance." Our educated people may regard these *disturbing* questions of mine only as petty superstitions; but I am convinced that offenses to the People's feelings in regard to the things they revere as sacred is a terrible outrage and an act of extraordinary inhumanity. Would the thought never have occurred to the dissenters: "So how would this Orthodox bishop have stood up for the church had the offender been some even more prominent person?" Could they have had any respect for a church in which the highest spiritual authority, as described in the story, has so little actual power? For how can one explain the action of the bishop if not through his lack of power? Is it really a matter of his laziness and indifference, and the unbelievable suggestion that he, having forgotten the duties of his office, has become merely a government official? For such nonsense to get into the heads of his spiritual flock would be the very worst thing of all: his Orthodox children would then gradually lose all their energy for matters of faith; their devotion and love for the church would disappear, and the dissenters would regard the Orthodox church with scorn. A spiritual pastor must mean something, mustn't he? Don't the dissenters realize that?

And so those are the sorts of thoughts that come into my head after reading Mr. Leskov's lovely story. And thus once more I say that I am inclined to regard this story—at least in certain details—as almost implausible. Meanwhile, I read the following news item in one of the recent issues of *The Voice:*

> One of the village priests from Orel Province writes to the newspaper *Contemporary Life:* "I have been engaged in teaching the children of my parishioners to read and write almost since the abolition of serfdom, and I abandoned that duty only when our local *zemstvo* took on the cost of teaching and expressed the desire to have teachers who

were free from other duties. But at the beginning of the current school year of 1872–73 there was a shortage of village schoolmasters in our district. Not wishing to see our village school closed, I decided to declare my wish to take on the position of teacher and applied to the school board to be confirmed in that position. The school board replied that 'I would be officially given the post of schoolmaster when the peasants' community expressed its agreement.' The community did agree and drew up a resolution to that effect. In accordance with the wishes of the school board, I applied to the county administration for the resolution to be endorsed. The county administration, headed by an ignorant clerk, one M.S., and a warden who is completely under his thumb, declined to endorse the resolution on the grounds that I had no time to teach; but in reality their motives were quite different. I applied to the mediator. He made the following remarkable statement straight to my face: '*In general the government is not disposed to have peasant education in the hands of the clergy.*' 'Why would that be?' I asked. 'Because,' the mediator replied, '*the clergy promote superstitions.*'''

What do you think of that piece of news, ladies and gentlemen? It almost reestablishes the veracity of Mr. Leskov's story, upon which I cast so much doubt and which I stubbornly continue to doubt. What is important here is not that such a mediator happened to exist: what does it matter if some fool idly makes a foolish remark? And what do we care about his convictions? What is important is that this was expressed so frankly and with such authority, with such deliberate authority and with such cool lack of ceremony. He expresses his wise conviction frankly and without a moment's hesitation, right *to the face* of the priest, and aside from that has the impudence to attribute his convictions to the government and to speak *in the name of* the government.

Now tell me, would anyone—never mind a mediator, but someone having ten times his authority—venture to tell that to a pastor in the Baltic provinces, say? Heavens, what a noise this pastor would make, and what a row would have ensued! In Russia the priest humbly writes to the newspaper to draw attention to the arrogant person. But the thought occurs that had this person been of higher rank than a mediator (which could very well happen, because anything can happen in Russia), then perhaps the good shepherd from Orel Province might not have even tried to accuse him, knowing that all that would come of it would be "a troubled countenance" and nothing more. And one cannot demand from him the zeal of the first centuries of Christianity even though we might like to have it. On the whole we are inclined to accuse our clergy of indifference toward their sacred cause; but what can they do, given their circumstances? And meanwhile the clergy's help to the People has never been so urgently needed. We are living through the most troubled, the most awkward, the most transitory, and the most fateful moment, perhaps, in the whole history of the Russian People.

A very strange phenomenon came to light recently in one corner of Russia: German Protestantism in the midst of Orthodoxy, the new sect of Stundists. *The Citizen* wrote about the sect at the time. It is an almost grotesque phenomenon, but one seems to sense something prophetic in it.

In the province of Kherson a certain Pastor Bonecktberg, seeing the local Russian peasants as unenlightened and spiritually abandoned, took pity on them out of the kindness of his heart and began preaching the Christian faith to them but maintaining an Orthodox view and urging them not to deviate from the Orthodox faith. But the matter developed differently: his preaching had complete success, yet the new Christians began by leaving Orthodoxy at once, making that their first and categorical condition; they turned away from ritual and icons and began to congregate in the Lutheran fashion, singing psalms from a book; some of them even learned German. The sect is spreading with fanatical speed and is moving into other districts and provinces. The sectarians have changed their way of life and no longer drink. Their reasoning is as follows.

"They (the German Lutheran Stundists, that is) live so well, so honestly, and in such a decent fashion because they don't have to fast in the Lenten seasons...."

It's wretched logic, but it does have a certain sense, particularly if you regard fasting as merely a ritual. And where is a poor man to learn the salutary and profound purpose of Lent? And, indeed, the whole of his former faith he regarded merely as ritual.

Thus it was the ritual he was protesting.

This, I suppose, is understandable. But why did he start protesting so suddenly? Where can we find the reason that compelled him to do it?

The reason, perhaps, is a very general one: it is the fact that since the Emancipation of February 19, 1861, the light of a new life has been shining on him. He might have stumbled and fallen when he took his first steps on the new road, but there was no doubt he would recover; and when he recovered he saw at once how "poor and wretched, naked, blind and base" he was. The most important thing was that he longed for truth—whatever that truth might cost, even if it meant sacrificing all that he had formerly held sacred. Because one cannot—neither through depravity nor pressure nor humiliation of any sort—wipe out, extinguish, or eradicate in the hearts of our People the thirst for truth, for that thirst is more precious to them than anything. The People may sink to terrible depths; but at the moments when they are most despicable they will always remember that they are only despicable and no more, and that somewhere there exists a higher truth and this truth stands above all else.

So that is the phenomenon. It is, perhaps, still a unique phenomenon on the periphery of things, but it is scarcely an accidental one. It may die down and solidify in its early stages and again be transformed into some sort of ritualism, as in the case of most of the Russian sects, especially when they are left alone. But whatever you think, I want to repeat that this phenomenon, perhaps, still contains something almost prophetic. At the present time, when everything in the future appears so enigmatic, it is sometimes permissible to believe even in prophecies.

What would happen if something of this sort were to spread all over Russia? I don't mean exactly the same thing—not the Stundists (especially as I have heard that appropriate measures have already been taken)—but just something along the same lines? What if the entire People, having sunk to the depths of their degradation and perceived their own wretchedness, should suddenly say to themselves: "I do not want degradation; I do not want to drink liquor. I want truth and the fear of God; but truth most of all, truth above all."

That the thirst for truth will come upon him, of course, is cause for joy. And yet instead of truth the result may be the most outlandish lies, as in the case of the Stundists.

In fact, what kind of Protestants, what kind of Germans are our People anyway? And why should they learn German in order to sing psalms? Isn't everything, everything that they are seeking, to be found in Orthodoxy? Does not Orthodoxy, and Orthodoxy alone, contain the truth and the salvation of the Russian People, and in ages yet to come the salvation of the whole of humanity? Has not

Orthodoxy alone preserved the divine image of Christ in all its purity? And perhaps the principal, preordained mission of the Russian People, within the destiny of humanity as a whole, is simply to preserve within it this divine image of Christ in all its purity, and when the time comes, to reveal this image to a world that has lost its way!

Indeed; but before all this comes to pass, our pastor has awakened early, with the birds, and has come to the People to tell them the truth—the Orthodox truth, since he was very conscientious. But the People followed him, and not Orthodoxy—not from gratitude alone, but because it was through him that they first glimpsed the truth. And so it turned out that "life is good with him because there is no fasting." One can understand a conclusion like that when a strong personality has become involved.

By the way, what about our priests? What do we hear about them?

Our priests are also beginning to rouse themselves, we hear. Our clergy have for some time now been showing signs of life, apparently. We were touched to read the bishops' admonitions in churches regarding preaching and an exemplary way of life for clergy. Our clergy, according to all accounts, are resolutely setting themselves the task of writing sermons and are preparing to deliver them.

But will they manage to arrive in time? Will they manage to awaken with the birds? Our pastor is a bird of a different feather, a bird of passage, and he has another kind of backing. His service is of a different kind, in any case; his church hierarchy is different, and so on. All that is true, of course, but our priest isn't a government official either, after all! And is he not the one who preaches the unique great Truth which has the power to save the whole world?

The pastor arrived before our priest, that's true. But what could our priest have done in the case of, say, the Stundists? We are all inclined to blame our priests, but let us look closely into the problem: could they have limited themselves merely to reporting the matter to the authorities? Oh, of course not: we have many good spiritual leaders among us—more, perhaps, than we expect or more than we ourselves deserve. But still, what would our good priest have preached about in this case? (I, as a layman unfamiliar with the matter, sometimes wonder about this.) About the superiority of Orthodoxy to Lutheranism? But the peasants are a dark people, after all: they will understand nothing, and probably will not be swayed by this. About good behavior and good moral standards, speaking generally and not going into too many details? But what kind of "good moral standards" can there be when the People are drunk from morning until night? In that case, abstention from liquor so as to eliminate the evil at its very source? No doubt that would be the thing to do, although without entering into too many details, for . . . for one still has to take into account Russia's importance as a great power which costs us so dearly. . . . Well, this, in a sense, is almost the same thing as "a troubled countenance," you see. And so all there is left to preach about is that the People should *drink just a bit less*. . . .

But what does our pastor care about Russia's importance as a great European power? And he's not afraid of any "troubled countenance," and his service is of quite a different kind. And that is why he won the day.

8

A Half-Letter from "A Certain Person"

I am printing below a letter, or more precisely a half-letter, from "a certain person" to the editor of *The Citizen;* it was quite impossible to print the whole letter. This is still that same "person," the very one who has already once distinguished himself in *The Citizen* on the subject of graves. I must confess that I am printing this simply in order to be rid of him. The editor's office has received literally stacks of his articles. In the first place, this person appears as my resolute defender against my supposed literary enemies. On my behalf he has already written three "anticriticisms," two "notes," three "marginal notes," one article "apropos," and finally "an admonition on behavior." In this latter polemical composition of his he purports to admonish my "enemies" but in fact attacks me, and even does it in a tone whose energy and fury I have never encountered, even among my "enemies." And he wants me to print it all! I made it very plain to him that, in the first place, I have no "enemies" and that he is only imagining the whole thing; and, in the second place, he is too late, for all that journalistic racket we heard after the appearance of the first issue of *The Citizen* this year—all the fury unprecedented in literature, the intolerance and the simple-minded methods of attack—stopped two or three weeks ago just as suddenly and inexplicably as it began. Finally, if I were to take it into my head to answer anyone, I could manage to do it myself, without his help.

He got angry, quarreled with me, and left. I was relieved. He is not a well man. . . . In the article that he already published here, he revealed a few features of his biography: he is a man in distress who "distresses" himself every day. But what frightens me most is the excessive force of the "civic energy" of this contributor. Imagine that from the very beginning he made it plain that he

expected no honorarium whatsoever but was writing simply out of
his "civic duty." He even confessed, with a proud but self-damaging
frankness, that he was not writing to defend me at all but only
wanted to use the opportunity to expound his own ideas, since not
a single periodical would accept his articles. Plainly and simply,
he was cherishing the fond hope of creating his own little corner
for himself in our journal from which—even without pay—he would
have the opportunity to expound his ideas on a regular basis. What
sort of ideas does he have? He writes about everything; he expresses
opinions about everything with bitterness, with rage, with venom,
and with "a tear of tenderness." "Venom for ninety percent and
a tear of tenderness for one percent," he himself declares in one
of his manuscripts. If a new magazine or newspaper should begin
publication, he is there at once: he imparts his wisdom and offers
his admonitions. It's absolutely true that he sent off as many as
forty letters full of advice to one newspaper: advice on publishing,
on how to behave, on what to write about, and on what to pay
attention to. In the course of two and a half months some twenty-
eight of his letters have accumulated in our editor's office. He always
writes over his full signature so that he is known everywhere; he
spends his last kopecks on postage stamps and even encloses return
postage in his letters, supposing that he will at last achieve his end
and manage to begin correspondence on civic matters with various
editors. What amazes me most is that even after twenty-eight letters
I am completely unable to discover what his views are and exactly
what he is aiming at. It's all a great muddle. . . . Along with crude
methods, red-nosed cynicism, and the "aggrieved aroma" of a
frenzied style and worn-out boots, there are flashes of a certain
covert longing for tenderness, for some ideal; there is faith in beauty,
Sehnsucht for something lost, and the result of it all is something
quite revolting. I'm quite fed up with him. True, he's open about
his rudeness and expects no payment for his efforts, so in that
sense he is an honorable person; but I've had enough of him and
his honor! No more than three days after our quarrel he appeared
again with his "final attempt," and brought this "Letter of a Certain
Person." What could I do but take it? And now I'd better print
it.

It's quite impossible to publish the first half of the letter. Here
he writes only of personalities and abuses beyond all limits almost
all the Petersburg and Moscow press. Not one of the periodicals
he reproaches ever reached the level of shameless mockery of his
abuse. And yet his own main point is to abuse them solely for the

vulgarity and sneering tone of their polemics. I simply took a scissors, cut off the first half of his letter, and returned it to him. The concluding part of his letter I am printing only because it contains what one might call a general topic: here he exhorts some imaginary columnist, and his exhortation is general enough to be applicable to columnists of all periods and all nations. The style is very elevated, and the force of the style is equalled only by the simple-mindedness of the ideas expressed. When he addresses his exhortation to the columnist he uses the "thou" form, as in the classical odes. The author was very firm in his wish that I should not begin his half-letter after a full stop but insisted that it begin right in the middle of a sentence, just where I had cut it off with the scissors, as if to say, "Let them see how they mutilated me!" He also insisted on the title: I wanted to print "A Letter from 'A Certain Person,'" but he absolutely insisted that it be entitled "A Half-Letter from 'A Certain Person.'"

And so, here is this half-letter:

A HALF-LETTER FROM "A CERTAIN PERSON"

... and does the word "swine" truly contain such magical and alluring meaning that you at once take it to apply inevitably to yourself? I have observed for a long time that in Russian literature this little word has always had a certain special and even mystical meaning, as it were. Dear old Krylov himself realized that and used the word "swine" with particular fondness in his fables. The literary man who reads this word, even when he is completely alone, will shudder forthwith and at once commence to thinking: "Could that be me? Does that refer to me?" Granted, it is a powerful little word, but why must you always assume that it refers to yourself and yourself alone? There are others besides you. Or perhaps you have your own private reasons for thinking this? For how else can I explain your suspicious cast of mind?*

★This is certainly an exaggeration, but it does contain a measure of truth. There is a hint here specifically at the fact that in the first issue of *The Citizen* I had the misfortune to cite an ancient Indian fable about the duel of the lion and the pig; in doing so, however, I carefully eliminated even the possibility of supposing that I was immodestly using the word "lion" to refer to myself. And what happened? In fact, many people expressed extreme and hasty suspicions about it. It was a regular phenomenon: a letter to the editor arrived from a subscriber in a remote border region of Russia; the subscriber brazenly and recklessly accused the editors of referring to their subscribers as "swine"—an assumption so absurd that even certain Petersburg columnists did not venture to make use of it when casting their aspersions ... and of course that is the measure of everything. *The Editor.* [Dostoevsky's note]

The second thing I wish to point out to you, my columnist friend, is that you lack restraint in preparing your columns. The pages you write are so crammed with generals, wealthy stockholders, and princes who need you and your witty words that on reading you I have to conclude that their excessive number suggests rather that you do not know even one of them. At one point you are present at an important meeting and utter some bon mot, carelessly and haughtily, but in doing so you cast a ray of light on the proceedings, and the meeting at once takes a turn for the better. At another point you ridicule a certain wealthy prince to his face, in exchange for which he promptly invites you to dinner; but you pass him by and proudly, yet in proper liberal fashion, decline the invitation. And then, in an intimate salon conversation you jokingly reveal the whole secret inner workings of Russia to a visiting foreign lord: in trepidation and delight he at once telegraphs London, and on the following day Victoria's whole cabinet is turned out. And again, while taking your stroll from two to four on the Nevsky, you propose the solution to a thorny problem of state to three retired cabinet ministers who are, nonetheless, running after you; you encounter a captain of the Guards who has lost everything at cards and toss him a loan of two hundred rubles; you go with him to Finfina to express your noble (supposedly) indignation. . . . In short, you are here, you are there, you are everywhere: you move through all society; people are always plucking at your sleeve; you gobble up truffles and sample bonbons, drive here and there in cabs, are on intimate terms with the waiters at Palkin's—in a word, without you nothing can happen. A position as lofty as yours at last begins to seem suspicious. The unassuming reader in the provinces may indeed take you for one who has been passed over for some honor, or at least for a retired minister who wants to regain his office by means of a free, but opposition, press. But the experienced reader in either of the capitals knows otherwise: for he knows that you are no more than a pen-pusher hired by a publisher determined to make a profit; you have been hired, and you are obliged to defend the interests of your employer. It is he (and no other) who sets you against any person he chooses.

And so all your anger and passion and barking is nothing more than the work of a hireling who attacks in whatever direction his employer's hand points. If you would at least stand up for yourself! But it is quite the contrary: what surprises me most about you is that you really do grow heated and take things to heart as if they really meant something to you; you abuse a rival columnist supposedly over some cherished idea or matter of principle which is truly precious to you. Meanwhile you know very well that you have no ideas of your own, never mind principles. Or have you, perhaps, after so many years of excitement and savoring the stench of your success, at last imagined that you have an idea or are capable of having principles? If such is the case, then how can you count on my respect?

There was a time when you were an honest and decent young man.... Oh, recall Pushkin's verse—a translation from the Persian, if I am not mistaken: a venerable old man speaks to a youth who is avid to go off to battle:

> I fear amidst war's strident clamor
> Thou canst but lose and ne'er reclaim
> Thy modesty, thy timid manner,
> Thy tender charm, thy sense of shame.

Alas, you have lost all these things, lost them long ago, and lost them forever! Just look at how you have quarreled with your columnist-enemy and try to comprehend the depths to which you both have sunk in your abuses! For neither of you is as despicable as you paint each other. Remember that in their early years children fight with one another largely because they have still not learned how to express their ideas intelligently. And you—a child with gray hair—from a lack of ideas use all the words you know to abuse someone else. A bad method! It is precisely your lack of convictions and genuine learning that leads you to try to pry into your rival's private life. You are avid to learn of his failings; you exaggerate them and expose them to salutary publicity. Neither do you spare his wife and children. You both pretend the other is dead and you write one another lampoons in the form of obituaries. Tell me, who will ever believe you in the end? As I read your column, spattered with your saliva and ink, I cannot help but be led to think that you are not right, that there must be some special, secret meaning to your article, that you and your rival must have come to blows at a dacha somewhere and neither of you can forget the incident. I cannot help but find in favor of your rival, and the effect of your case is ruined. Is that really what you were setting out to do?

How childishly clumsy you are! Having heaped abuse on your rival, you end your column as follows: "I can see you now, Mr. N. N.: after you have read these lines you rush about your room in a fury; you tear your hair; you shout at your wife who has come running into the room in alarm; you drive your children away; grinding your teeth, you pound the wall with your fist in impotent rage...."

Oh, my friend, you are only a naive but overwrought victim of your own fictitious fury affected for your employer's benefit! My columnist friend! Tell me: when I read in your column the lines that supposedly describe your rival, do you not realize that I see this is you—you yourself, and not your rival—who is rushing about the room tearing your hair; that it is you who beats your servant who rushes in, frightened (that is, if you have a servant and if he has not lost his primitive innocence since February 19th); it is you who, with shrieking and gnashing of teeth, flings yourself against the wall and beats it with your fists until they are bloody! For who will believe that you can send such lines to your rival unless you have first pounded the wall until your own fists were bloody? In such a manner you betray yourself.

Come to your senses; show some compunction. And when you show some compunction, you will also acquire some ability to write a column. That is the benefit you can derive from this.

Let me give you an allegory. Out of the blue you suddenly put up posters announcing that next Thursday or Friday (imagine the day on which you write your column) in Berg's Theater or in some facility specially set up for the purpose, you will display yourself naked, right down to the last detail. I believe that you will find willing spectators; such spectacles are particularly attractive to today's society. I believe that a crowd will assemble—even a large crowd. But will they come to show their respect for you? And if not, then what have you accomplished?

Consider, now, if you are able: are your columns not doing this very same thing? Do you not come out on the very same day every week, naked to the last detail, and display yourself to the public? And for what, and for whom do you do this?

The most amusing thing here is that all your readers know the secret behind your war; they know, yet they don't wish to know and pass by you indifferently, while you both rush about in fury and think that everyone is following your doings. Oh, simpleminded man! The public knows all too well that the owner of a newspaper in the capital, seeing another newspaper established on the same lines as his own, pats the pocket where he keeps his wallet and says to himself: "This wretched new paper may do me out of a couple of thousand subscribers. I'll hire myself a shaggy great mongrel and set him on my rival." That mongrel is you!

The owner is pleased with you; he strokes his whiskers and, after breakfast, thinks with a smile, "Yes, indeed, I've hounded him, and no mistake!"

Do you recall Turgenev's Antropka? This is truly a brilliant piece by a favorite writer. Antropka is a little urchin in a village—or, more correctly, he is the brother of another village urchin (whose name, let's say, is Nefed)—who has disappeared from the hut one dark

summer night on account of some misdeed. The strict father has sent
the older boy to bring his miscreant little brother home. And so, on
the bank of a ravine we hear the shrill cries:

"Antropka! Antropka!"

For a long time the guilty little scamp does not reply, but at last,
"as if from another world," a quavering, meek little voice is heard
from the other side of the ravine:

"Wha-a-t?"

"Daddy wants to be-e-at you!" says the older brother, with malicious, eager joy.

The voice "from another world" is not heard again, of course. But
in the dark night the strained, tormented, malicious cries still
continue:

"Antropka-a! Antropka-a-a!"

This brilliant little picture of crying out to Antropka and—most
important—its impotent but angry distress is heard again, not only
among village urchins but also among adults who have attained hoary
venerability, members of today's society who, however, have been
upset by the reforms. And isn't there a thing or two in our capital
that reminds you of these Antropkas? For do you not see something
of Antropka in the relationship between these two owners of city
newspapers? Have not you and your rival both been sent out by your
masters to find Antropkas? And the Antropkas—aren't these the new
subscribers who you assume might believe in your innocence? You
both know that all your rage, all your strained efforts will be in vain
and that Antropka will not answer, that you will not manage to steal
away a single subscriber from the other, that each of you will have
enough subscribers in any case. But you have both become so wrapped
up in this game of yours and enjoy this impotent journalistic laceration
so much that you cannot restrain yourselves! And so every week, on
the established days, there come the furious, strained cries: "Antropka-a! Antropka-a!" And we listen to them.

I'll permit myself one more allegory.

Imagine that you have been invited into proper society (for I suppose
that you too move in proper social circles). You are one of the invited
guests at an evening party for the name day of a State Councilor (one
as high in rank as that). The host has already informed the guests
that you are a very witty man. You enter politely, well dressed; you
pay your respects to the hostess and compliment her graciously. You
sense with pleasure that people are looking at you, and you prepare
to distinguish yourself. And suddenly—oh, horrors!—in the corner of
the room you notice your literary rival who has arrived before you;

until now you never even suspected he knew your hosts. Your expression has changed, but the host, assuming this is due to a passing indisposition, naively hurries to introduce you to your literary enemy. You both mutter something and at once turn your backs on one another. The host is embarrassed but takes courage, supposing that this is no more than a new literary fashion of which he is unaware, being always caught up in official business. In the meantime, card games are arranged and the hostess, with her usual graciousness, invites you to play whist. To get away from your rival you happily choose a card. A new horror: it turns out that you are to share his table. You cannot refuse since as partners you have two congenial and agreeable society ladies. They both quickly take their seats, while various relatives and friends gather around, all eager to listen to two literary men, all staring fixedly at your mouths, ready to seize upon your first words. Your rival turns to one of the ladies and calmly says, "You have the opportunity to make a good deal, madam." Everyone smiles and exchanges glances: his witty remark has gone over well, and your heart contracts with envy. The lady deals the cards. You pick up your cards and find deuces, threes, sixes; the highest card is a jack. You grind your teeth while your rival smiles. He has a good hand and proudly declares a slam. Your eyes grow dim. You seize a heavy bronze candlestick, a family heirloom and the pride of the host (the hostess keeps it locked in a cupboard all year, exhibiting it only on name days). You seize this candlestick and fling it violently at your rival's head. Screams and confusion! Everyone jumps to his feet, but you two have already leapt at each other, mouths foaming with rage, and are pulling at each other's hair.* Judging by the lack of patience and self-restraint exhibited in your writing, I am justified in concluding that you have a similar lack of patience in private society. Your partner, the young lady who was expecting such witty conversation from you, screams and takes refuge under the wing of her husband, an important lieutenant-colonel of engineers. He, pointing at the two of you twisting each other's hair, tells her, "I warned you what to expect from contemporary literature, my dear!" But the two of you have already been dragged down the stairs and kicked out onto the street. The host, whose name day is being celebrated, feels responsible and apologizes to his guests, suggesting they forget about Russian literature and continue with whist. You have deprived yourself of a social evening, some pleasant yet innocent moments with a Petersburg lady, and a supper. But neither of you is concerned about that: each of you takes a cab and rushes away through the malodorous

*The editor finds this picture somewhat exaggerated. [Dostoevesky's note]

Petersburg streets, each to his own apartment to sit right down and compose a column. You urge your driver on, with a fleeting moment of envy of his innocence; but you are already mulling over your article. You arrive, seize your pen, and relate exactly, down to the last detail, what happened to you at the home of the Councilor!

You denounce your host; you denounce his wife and the refreshments; you inveigh against the custom of celebrating name days; you criticize the engineer lieutenant-colonel and the lady, your partner; and at last you come to your rival. And now you set it all down to the last detail in your well-known, usual, current fashion of revealing all inside information. You tell of how he beat you and how you beat him; you vow that you will beat him again in the future and that he has promised to beat you. You want to append to your article the handful of his hair that you have torn out. But it's already morning. . . . You rush around the room, waiting for the editorial offices to open. You arrive at the editor's office, and suddenly he, with a calm air, announces that on the previous night he has made up with his rival publisher, who has closed down his newspaper, transferring the subscribers to him, your employer; the two of them have celebrated their peace with a bottle of champagne at Dussault's. Then he thanks you for your services and announces that he no longer needs you. Now tell me what a spot you are in!

What I like least of all are the last days of the pre-Lenten carnival, when the common people are drinking themselves into the last stages of ugliness. The dull, ugly faces of besotted figures in torn coats crowd around the taverns. Two of them stop on the street: one claims he is a general, while the other shouts, "Liar!" The first curses in rage, while the second again shouts, "Liar!" The first works himself up still more furiously, while the second goes on with his "Liar!" And so it continues for perhaps two hundred times! It is beauty that they both find in this impotent and endless repetition of the same words, wallowing, as it were, in the enjoyment of the impotence of their own degradation.

When I read your columns I cannot help but imagine a kind of endless, drunken, senseless carnival that has gone on in our literature for much too long already. For aren't you two doing the same thing as these two mindless drunkards in peasant coats standing on the street corner? Does your rival not claim in each of his columns that he is a general, and do you not reply to him, like the peasant on the corner, "Liar!"? And it all goes on a countless number of times without even the least suspicion that the whole thing has at last made us sick to death. I imagine you both just as if you were on the last day of Carnival (the day of forgiveness!), deprived of your senses by intoxication; I picture you both on the street in front of the offices of your respective editors, wallowing in the dirty brown snow of our capital, thrashing about and shouting hoarsely at each other with all your might: "Help! Police! He-e-elp!"

But I say nothing and hurry past. . . .

                                                        A Silent Observer.

N.B. "Silent Observer" is the pseudonym of "A Certain Person"; I neglected to mention this before.

9

Apropos of the Exhibition

I went in to see the exhibition. Quite a number of paintings by our Russian artists are being sent off to the Vienna International Exhibition. It's not the first time this has happened, and contemporary Russian artists are beginning to become known in Europe. But still the question arises: can they understand our artists there, and from what point of view will they judge them? In my opinion, if you were to make the best possible French or German translation of a comedy by Mr. Ostrovsky—*Our Own Folk, We'll Settle It,* say, or any other one—and were to stage it somewhere in Europe, I truly don't know what the result would be. Something would be understood, of course; and—who knows?—perhaps people there would even find some enjoyment in it; but at least three-quarters of the comedy would remain totally inaccessible to the European mentality. I recall in my youth how terribly interested I was to learn that Mr. Viardot (the husband of the famous singer who was then performing here in the Italian opera), a Frenchman who knew not a word of Russian, was translating our Gogol under the guidance of Mr. Turgenev. Viardot, of course, had some critical and artistic ability and in addition a sensitivity to the poetry of other nationalities, which he proved with his excellent translation of *Don Quixote* into French. Mr. Turgenev, of course, understood Gogol down to the finest subtleties; I suppose that, like everyone in those days, he was in raptures over him; and beyond that he himself was a poet, although at that time he had still scarcely stepped over the threshold of his poetic career. (N.B. He had written only a few verses—I forget which ones—besides the tale "Three Portraits," a work of importance.) And so something could have come of it. I note that Mr. Turgenev probably has an excellent knowledge of French. And what happened? The result of this translation was something so strange that even though I had previously suspected it was impossible to translate Gogol into French, I still never expected anything like this to emerge. You can find this translation even now; have a look and see what it is like. Gogol has literally disappeared. All the humor, everything comic, all the individual details and principal turns of the plot which, even now, when you sometimes recall them by chance while alone (and often during the most unliterary moments of your life) cause you suddenly to burst out laughing to yourself in an utterly unrestrained fashion—all this has disappeared as if it had never existed. I don't know what the French could have made of Gogol on the basis of this translation; I suppose that they didn't think anything at all, however. "The Queen of Spades" and *The Captain's Daughter*, which were also translated into French at the time, have also doubtless been diminished by half, although there was much more in them that could be understood than in Gogol. In short, all that is characteristic, all that is ours and predominantly national (and thus all that is truly artistic) is, in my opinion, incomprehensible to Europe. Translate Turgenev's short novel *Rudin* (and I speak of Mr. Turgenev because he has been the most translated of Russian writers, and of his novel *Rudin* because of all his works it is the one that most closely approaches something in the German mentality) into any European language you like and even it will not be understood. There will not be even the slightest hint of the real essence of the thing. *A Hunter's Sketches* will not be understood any more than Pushkin or any more than Gogol. And so all of our major talents, I think, are perhaps fated to remain completely unknown to Europe for a long time; and the greater and more original the talent, the less it will be recognized. Yet I believe that we understand Dickens in Russian almost as well as the English do, perhaps even with all the subtleties; we may even love him no less than do his own countrymen. And yet how typical, original, and national Dickens is! What can we conclude from this? Is such an understanding of other nationalities a special gift the Russians have which the Europeans do not? Perhaps there is a particular gift, and if such a gift exists (just as does the gift of speaking foreign languages, which is really greater in the Russians than in other Europeans), then it is something of great significance, promises much for the future, and means that the Russians are destined to do many things, although I don't know whether this is a wholly good gift or whether it contains something harmful as well.... It is more likely (many people will say) that Europeans know little about Russia and Russian life because until now they have not had the need to come to know them in any great detail. It is true, indeed, that in Europe until now there has been no particular necessity to get to know us in any detail. But still it seems certain that a European of any nationality can always learn another European language and enter into the soul of any other European nationality more easily than he can learn Russian and comprehend our Russian essence. Even Europeans who have made a point of studying us for some particular purpose (and there have been such), and who applied great effort to their study, left us having surely learned a great deal, perhaps, but still not fully understanding certain facts; one may even say that it will be a long time—a generation or two at least—before they do understand. All this suggests that we may still suffer a long and unhappy alienation from the European family of nations; that the Europeans will continue to make a long series of errors in their assessments of Russia; that they will evidently be inclined always to think the worst of us. And perhaps it also explains that constant, general hostility of Europe toward us, a hostility founded on some very powerful and immediate sense of loathing; it is a loathing of us as if we were something repulsive; it is partly even a superstitious fear of us; and it is the eternal, familiar, ancient judgment pronounced on us: that we are not Europeans at all. . . . We, of course, take offense at this and try with all our might to prove that we are Europeans. . . .

Of course, I'm not saying that our landscape painters, for instance, will not be understood in Europe: the views of the Crimea, the Caucasus, and even of our steppes will arouse interest there too, naturally. But our Russian, predominantly national landscapes, i.e., those of the northern and central regions of our European Russia, will create no great effect in Vienna, I think. "This barren landscape," whose whole character consists in its lack of character, so to say, is charming and dear to us, however. But what do the Germans care about our feelings? Take those two birch trees in Mr. Kuindzhi's landscape, for instance ("A View of Valaam"): in the foreground there is a marsh and swamp grass; in the background, a forest; rising from the forest we see not really a cloud but a mist, dampness; dampness seems to penetrate everything; you can almost feel it; and in the center, between you and the forest, stand two white birch trees, bright and strong—the most powerful point in the picture. What is special about this? What is

characteristic? Yet how fine it is!...Perhaps I am mistaken, but
I think this isn't likely to appeal to a German.

About historical painting there's nothing to be said: we've long
been far from brilliant in purely historical genres, so we won't
cause any astonishment in Europe; we won't even cause much
astonishment with our paintings of battles; even the resettlement
of the Circassians (a huge, highly colored painting that may have
great merit—I can't judge) will not produce a very strong impression
abroad, I think. But genre painting, our own genre painting—will
they understand any of it? Yet it has reigned almost exclusively
here for so many years; and if we have something to be proud of
and something to show off, then of course it is our genre painting.
Take, for example, the little painting by Makovsky, "The Lovers
of Nightingales' Singing"—I'm not sure what it's called. Just look
at it: the little room of some townsman or retired soldier, a dealer
in songbirds and, probably, one who traps birds as well. You can
see several bird cages, benches, a table on which a samovar is
standing; around the samovar sit the guests, two merchants or
shopkeepers, admirers of the nightingale's singing. The nightingale
is in a cage hanging in the window and is probably whistling,
chattering, and trilling out its song while the guests listen. They
are obviously both serious people, dour shopkeepers concerned
mainly with their profits, well on in years, and perhaps tyrants in
their own families (it seems somehow accepted that this entire "dark
kingdom" must absolutely consist of family tyrants who rule their
households with an iron fist), and yet they have obviously both
melted from delight—a most innocent, almost touching delight.
Something touching to the point of absurdity is going on here. The
one sitting by the window has bowed his head a little; he has raised
one hand and holds it suspended, listening intently, melting, a
blissful smile on his face; he is listening to the last sounds of the
trill. . . . He wants to capture something; he's afraid of losing something. The other is sitting at the table, drinking tea, with his back
almost toward you. But you know that he is "suffering" no less
than his friend. The host is sitting in front of them; he has invited
them to listen and, of course, to sell them the nightingale. He is
a rather wizened and tall fellow somewhat past forty, dressed very
casually (what need is there for formality here in any case?); he is
saying something to the merchants, and you sense that he speaks
with authority. In terms of social status (meaning financial status),
he is an insignificant person before these shopkeepers, of course;

but now he has a nightingale, and a good one, and therefore he looks proud (as if he were singing himself); he treats the merchants even with a certain arrogance and severity (don't disturb the birds, gentlemen). . . . It's interesting that the shopkeepers sit and never question that it is only appropriate for the host to talk a bit harshly to them because "that nightingale he's got is a really fine bird!" When they've finished their tea the bargaining will begin. . . . Well, I ask you, what will a German or a Viennese Yid (Vienna, they say, is full of Yids, just like Odessa) understand in this picture? Someone may explain what is going on, and he will learn that the Russian merchant of fair-to-middlin' means has two passions: race horses and nightingales, and so this picture is all terribly funny; but what will come of that? That is a piece of abstract knowledge, and a German will find it very difficult to imagine why it's so amusing. But we look at the picture and smile; we recall it later, and again for some reason we find it amusing and pleasant. You may laugh at me, but truly I believe that in little pictures such as these one even finds love for humanity, not only for the Russians in particular but even for humans in general. I chose this little picture only to give one example. But what's most annoying is that we would understand a similar picture from German life just as well as they themselves and would even take as much delight in it as they and experience almost the same German feelings as they; but they would understand absolutely nothing of one of our Russian paintings. In one sense, however, we may be better off for that.

Then we see a game of cards going on in an Estonian or Livonian cabin; now that, of course, can be understood, especially the figure of the boy who is taking part in the game. Everyone is playing cards and telling fortunes, so that "The Ten of Spades" (that is the name of the painting) will be quite comprehensible. But I don't think that Perov's "Hunters" would be understood. I am deliberately picking out one of the most accessible paintings of our national genre school. This painting, "Hunters at a Campsite," has been well known for a long time now. One of the hunters is excitedly telling some very tall tale; another listens to him, utterly convinced; the third doesn't believe a word of it and lies there laughing. . . . What a charming thing! Of course, if it were explained, the Germans would also understand, but they wouldn't understand as we do that this is a purely Russian yarn spinner and he's concocting his story in purely Russian fashion. Why, we can almost hear him and know what he's talking about; we know every twist and turn in his line of fibs, the words he uses and the emotions he expresses. I'm sure that if Mr. Perov (and he would certainly have the ability to do it) were to portray French or German hunters (in another manner, of course, and with different characters), then we Russians would understand German and French yarn-spinnings as well, with all their subtleties and all their specifically national characteristics, their style and their subject; we would grasp all this from merely looking at the picture. But a German, no matter how he tried, wouldn't understand our Russian manner of lying. Of course this is not a great loss to the German, and once again, perhaps, we have an advantage; still, the German wouldn't understand the painting completely and so would not be able to appreciate it properly; and that's a pity, because we are going there to have our paintings applauded.

I don't know how people in Vienna will react to Makovsky's "Psalm-Singers." In my view this is no longer a genre painting but a historical one. I'm not quite serious, of course; but just study the picture carefully: it's only a group of singers—an official church choir of sorts—performing at a service. They're all gentlemen with carefully shaven chins and wearing official costumes. Look carefully at this gentleman with the side-whiskers, for instance: it's clear that he is camouflaged, as it were, in this costume which doesn't suit his personality at all and which he wears only as part of his official function. It's true that all choristers wear such costumes only as part of their official function and that such has been the practice since time immemorial, since the days of the Patriarchs; but here this "camouflage" seems to be particularly noticeable. You are used to seeing such a fine-looking official only in uniform in a government office; he's a modest, solid, well-groomed fellow of the middle class. He's in the middle of drawing out his song— something like the famous "Affli-i-cted!"—but even the "Afflict-ed!" is transformed into something official when you look at him. In fact there's nothing funnier than to suppose that this totally loyal fellow who has settled comfortably in government service could be "afflicted" by anything! If you don't look at them but simply turn away and listen, you will be charmed; but when you look at these figures you feel that the psalm is being sung just for the sake of form . . . that the picture is really about something quite different. . . .

I have a great fear when "tendency" takes hold of a young artist, especially at the beginning of his career; and what do you think causes me the most concern? Precisely that the purpose of this tendency will not be achieved. There is a certain dear critic whom I have been reading recently and whose name I don't wish to mention here. Will he believe that any work of art without a pre-conceived tendency, a work created exclusively out of the demands of art and even on an entirely noncontroversial subject which doesn't contain the least hint of anything "tendentious"—will this critic believe that such a work contributes far more *for his purposes* than all the "songs about the shirt," for instance (not Hood's, but those of our own writers), even though superficially the work may appear to belong to the category called "satisfaction of idle curiosity"? If even scholars, apparently, have still not realized this, then what may sometimes happen in the hearts and minds of our young writers and artists? What a muddle of conceptions and preconceived notions they must have! To satisfy social demands, the young poet suppresses his own natural need to express himself in his own images, fearing that he will be censured for "idle curiosity"; he suppresses and obliterates the images that arise out of his own soul; he ignores them or leaves them undeveloped, while extracting from himself with painful tremors the images that satisfy common, official, liberal, and social opinion. What a terribly simple and naive mistake, what a serious mistake this is! One of the most serious mistakes is that the denunciation of vice (or what liberal opinion accepts as vice) and the arousal of feelings of hatred and vengeance is considered the only possible way to achieve the purpose! But even with such a narrow approach as this, a powerful talent could still wriggle free and not suffocate at the very beginning of his career; he need only keep in mind the golden rule that a word spoken may be silver, but one unspoken is gold. There are so many significant talents who promised so much but who were so badly corroded by "tendency" that it essentially put them into uniform. I have read the two latest poems by Nekrasov, and this honorable poet of ours is now certainly wearing a uniform. Yet even in these poems there are some good things that hint at Mr. Nekrasov's former talent. But what is to be done? His subject is also "wearing a uniform"; his technique, his ideas, his vocabulary, his verisimilitude are uniformed . . . yes, even verisimilitude itself has donned a uniform. Does our esteemed poet know, for instance, that no woman, not even one overflowing with the finest of civic sentiments and who has gone to such efforts in order to see her unfortunate husband by traveling four thousand miles in a cart "and coming to know its delights"; who has, as you tell us, fallen "from the lofty heights of the Altai" (which, by the way, is quite impossible)— do you know, sir, that this woman would never kiss the chains of her beloved husband first of all? She would first kiss him, and only then, if seized by such a powerful and noble upsurge of civic feeling, would she kiss his chains; and any woman certainly would act that way. Of course, this is only a minor observation, and it would not be worth mentioning since the poem itself was written for no particular reason except, maybe, to toss off something for January 1st. Mr. Nekrasov, however, still has a solid reputation in literature, one that is established and almost complete, and has produced many excellent verses. He is a poet of suffering, and has almost earned this appellation. But I can't help feeling sorry for the new poets: not a single one of them has a talent strong enough to keep him from submitting to "uniformed" ideas at the beginning of his career and thus saving himself from literary consumption and death. What is to be done? A uniform is a pretty thing, after all, with its embroidery and glitter.... And what an advantage to wear one! These days, especially advantageous.

No sooner had I read in the newspapers of Mr. Repin's barge-haulers than I got frightened. Even the subject itself is terrible: we have accepted somehow that barge-haulers are the best means of representing the well-known social notion of the unpaid debt of the upper classes to the People. I came expecting to see these barge-haulers all lined up in uniforms with the usual labels stuck to their foreheads. And what happened? To my delight, all my fears turned out to be vain: they are barge-haulers, real barge-haulers and nothing more. Not a single one of them shouts from the painting to the viewer: "Look how unfortunate I am and how indebted you are to the People!" And in that alone we can credit the artist with a great service. They are marvelous, familiar figures: the two foremost haulers are almost laughing; at any rate they are certainly not crying, and aren't thinking at all about their social status. A little soldier is slyly trying to conceal the fact that he wants to fill his pipe. The little boy has put on a serious face; he is shouting, even arguing. He is a wonderful figure, almost the best in the picture and equal in conception to that of the very last hauler, a wretched, drooping little peasant who is trudging along on his own and whose face isn't even visible. One simply can't imagine that any notion of the politicoeconomic and social debts of the higher classes to the People could ever penetrate the poor, drooping

head of this little peasant, oppressed by perpetual grief . . . and—
and do you know, my dear critic, that the very humble innocence
of thought of this peasant achieves your purpose far more readily
than you think?—precisely your tendentious, liberal purpose! More
than one spectator will walk away with pain in his heart and with
love (and with what love!) for this poor little peasant, or for this
boy, or for this sly scoundrel, the soldier! Why, you can't help but
love them, these defenseless creatures; you can't walk away without
loving them. You can't help but think that you are indebted, truly
indebted to the People. . . . You will be dreaming of this whole group
of barge-haulers afterward; you will still recall them fifteen years
later! And had they not been so natural, so innocent, and so simple,
they would not have produced such an impression and would not
have composed such a picture. Why, it's almost complete! Anyway,
all these uniform collars are disgusting, no matter how much gold
embroidery they have! Still, what need is there to go on about this?
One can't recount a painting; they're far too difficult to convey in
words. I will say only that the figures are Gogolian. That is a large
thing to say, but I am not claiming that Mr. Repin is a Gogol in
his own medium. Our genre painting still has not reached the level
of Gogol and Dickens.

One can see, though, that even Mr. Repin overdoes it a bit: this
is noticeable specifically in the costumes, and there only in two
figures. It's quite impossible for rags like that even to exist. That
shirt, for instance, must have accidentally fallen into a bowl where
meat was being chopped for cutlets. To be sure, barge-haulers are
not noted for wearing finery. We all know where such people come
from: at home at winter's end, at least according to a number of
reports, they subsist on bark and in the spring go off to find a
boss who'll hire them to haul barges, some of them, at least, only
for the porridge they eat, with scarcely any formal contract. There
have been some cases where a barge-hauler died of eating porridge
on his first days on the job; he would fall upon it in his hunger,
choke to death, and "burst." Doctors doing autopsies, it is said,
found such people stuffed with porridge right up to their throats.
So there are some subjects of this sort. But still, an unspoken word
is golden, the more so that one couldn't even put on a shirt like
that once it had been taken off: you'd never get into it again.
However, in comparison with the merits and the independent conception of the painting, this minor exaggeration in costumes is
insignificant.

It's a pity that I know nothing of Mr. Repin. It would be interesting to know if he is a young man. How I wish he were still a young man who is only beginning his artistic career. A few lines above I was quick to stipulate that he is still not a Gogol. Yes, Mr. Repin, it's a long, long trip to reach Gogol; don't let your well-earned success go to your head. Our genre painting has made a good start and we have talented people, but it lacks something to enable it to broaden and expand. Why, even Dickens is genre and nothing more, but Dickens created Pickwick, *Oliver Twist*, and the grandfather and grand-daughter in *The Old Curiosity Shop*. No, our genre painting is a long way from that; it is still at the stage of "Hunters" and "Nightingales." Dickens has a lot of "Hunters" and "Nightingales" on the periphery of his works. So far as I can tell from various indicators, it seems that at the present moment in our art our genre painting regards Pickwick and the grand-daughter even as something ideal, and as far as I could gather from conversations with certain of our major artists, they fear the ideal like some kind of unclean spirit. No doubt this is a noble fear, but it is a prejudicial and unjust one. Our artists need a bit more boldness, a bit more independence of thought, and, perhaps, a bit more education. And that's why I think our historical painting is not strong and is somehow languishing. Evidently our contemporary artists are afraid of historical subjects and have fastened upon genre as the sole true and legitimate outlet for any real talent. I think that an artist seems to sense that (in his conception) he will certainly have to "idealize" in historical painting, and thus, to lie. "One must portray reality as it is," they say, whereas reality such as this does not exist and never has on earth because the essence of things is inaccessible to man; he perceives nature as it is reflected in his ideas, after it has passed through his senses. Accordingly, more scope must be given to the idea, and the ideal should not be feared. A portraitist, for example, seats his subject to paint its portrait; he prepares; he studies the subject carefully. Why does he do that? Because he knows from experience that a person does not always look like himself, and therefore he seeks out "the principal idea of his physiognomy," that moment when the subject most resembles his self. The portraitist's gift consists in the ability to seek out and capture that moment. And so what is the artist doing here if not trusting first his own idea (the ideal) more than the reality before him? The ideal is also reality, after all, and just as legitimate as immediate reality. Many artists in

Russia don't seem to realize that. Take Bronnikov's "Hymn of the Pythagoreans," for instance. Some genre painter (even one of our most talented) might even be surprised at how a contemporary artist could pick such subjects. And yet subjects such as these (almost fantastic ones) are just as real and just as essential to art and to humans as is immediate reality.

What is genre, in essence? Genre is the art of portraying contemporary, immediate reality that the artist has himself felt personally and has seen with his own eyes, in contrast with historical reality, for instance, which cannot be seen with one's own eyes and which is portrayed not in its immediate but in its completed aspect. (Let me make a *nota bene* here: I said "seen with his own eyes." But Dickens never saw Pickwick with his own eyes; he perceived him only in a variety of forms of reality that he had observed; he created a character and presented him as the result of his observations. Thus this character is every bit as real as one who really exists, even though Dickens took only an ideal of the reality.) But what happens here is a confusion of conceptions of reality. Historical reality in art, for instance, is naturally not that of immediate reality (genre) precisely because the former is completed and not current. Ask any psychologist you like and he will tell you that if you imagine some event of the past, especially of the distant past—one that is completed and historical (and to live without imagining the past is impossible)—then the event will *necessarily* be imagined in its completed aspect, i.e., with the addition of all its subsequent developments that had not yet occurred at the historical moment in which the artist is trying to depict a person or event. And thus the essence of a historical event cannot even be imagined by an artist exactly as it probably happened in reality. And so the artist is overcome by a kind of superstitious fear of the fact that he will perhaps have to "idealize" despite himself, which to his mind means to lie. So, to avoid this imaginary error, he tries (and there were cases of this) to combine both realities—the historical and the immediate; from this unnatural combination arises the worst kind of untruth. In my view this pernicious error can be seen in certain of Mr. Ge's paintings. For instance, he took his "Last Supper," which once created such a stir, and made a regular genre painting out of it. Look at it more carefully: this is an ordinary quarrel of some very ordinary people. There sits Christ—but is that Christ? It may be a very good young man, deeply hurt by his quarrel with Judas, who is standing there getting dressed to go off and denounce him, but this is not the Christ we know. His friends have crowded around the Teacher to comfort him; but we must ask the question: where are the eighteen centuries of Christianity that followed, and how are they connected with the event? How is it possible that from such an ordinary quarrel of such ordinary people gathered to have supper, such as Mr. Ge depicts, there could arise something so colossal?

Nothing at all is explained here; there is no historical truth here; there is not even any truth of genre here; everything here is false.

No matter from which point of view you judge, this event could not have happened this way: everything here is disproportionate and out of scale with the future. Titian, at least, would have given this Teacher a face like the one he gave him in his famous picture "Render unto Caesar"; then many things would have become clear at once. In Mr. Ge's picture some good people have simply gotten into a quarrel; the result is something false, a preconceived idea. And falsity is always a lie and not realism at all. Mr. Ge was trying for realism.

Well, it seems I have forgotten about the exhibition. However . . . what sort of a reporter am I? I only wanted to make a few remarks "apropos." Nevertheless, the editors promise to publish a detailed account of our artists' paintings that are being sent to the Vienna Exhibition; or, perhaps, still better, to try to talk about them from the Exhibition itself, with an account of the impression they produce, in turn, on the foreigners who come to see them.

10

An Impersonator

Who asked you in!??

A little note abusing me has appeared in *The Russian World*, no. 103. I don't reply to abusive articles, but I shall reply to this one because of certain reasons that will become clear in the course of my reply.

First of all, the fact is that the one who vilifies me is a clergyman; that was the last area from which I expected an attack. The "Note" is signed "Pr. P. Kastorsky." What is this "Pr."? Priest? What can this abbreviation mean if not "priest"? The more so that the note concerns a church matter. In numbers 15 and 16 of *The Citizen* Mr. Nedolin's tale "The Deacon" was published. And that's what the note is about.

Here is the "note":

UNMARRIED NOTIONS OF A MARRIED MONK

Clergymen and others associated with the church are in our time not infrequently chosen by our writers as heroes of their literary works; even oftener they appear as incidental or "accessory" characters. It is certainly a fine thing that they are portrayed in literature: the clerical world has a good many characteristic types, so why not portray them with their good and bad qualities? The recent success of "Notes of a Psalm-reader" in *Notes of the Fatherland,* and then the still greater success of *Cathedral Folk* in *The Russian Messenger* show how much interest the literary portrayal of the everyday life of our clergy can arouse in society. Both the aforementioned works presented our clergy from different points of view, and both were read with attention and with pleasure. And why was this? Because they were written well, were artistic, and showed a knowledge of their subject. But the result is quite different when, as a result of imitation or some other reason—presumption or frivolity, for instance—people with absolutely no conception of the subject undertake such a task. They only embarrass themselves and damage the cause by presenting mistaken views; and therefore one cannot pass unheeding such ill-disposed attempts to caricature the life of our clergy. I, following in the footsteps of "Psalm-reader," who in *The Russian World* not long ago drew attention to the writer Dostoevsky's ignorance of choristers, cannot remain silent about an even more serious, ludicrous, and unforgivable act of ignorance which again was made manifest in the same magazine, *The Citizen*, beneath which the signature of this same Mr. Dostoevsky appears as editor.

We shall pause here for a moment. What does he mean, "following in the footsteps of 'Psalm-reader,'" who revealed the ignorance of the writer Dostoevsky"? I never read that article. (And again, it's *The Russian World*!) When I look it up (in no. 87), I find there really is a charge against me signed by "Psalm-reader." Let's have a look at what it is:

ON CHORISTERS' UNIFORMS

(A Letter to the Editor)

In issue no. 13 of *The Citizen* (March 26) I happened to read Mr. Dostoevsky's article about the exhibition at the Academy of Arts. Discussing the psalm-readers portrayed by the painter Makovsky, Mr. Dostoevsky wrote the following lines: "They're all gentlemen with carefully shaven chins and wearing *official costumes*. It's true that *all choristers wear such costumes* only as part of their official function and *from time immemorial have worn such costumes, and such has been the practice from time immemorial, since the days of the Patriarchate. . . .,*"

Let me interrupt for a moment: in the first place, there is certainly no such stupid sentence in my article. I wrote: "It's true that all choristers wear such costumes only as part of their official function and that such has been the practice since time immemorial, since the days of the Patriarchate . . . ," which is something quite different. Let's continue the quotation:

This is without foundation: neither *from time immemorial* nor *since the days of the Patriarchate* have members of choirs in the Russian church ever worn such costumes as we see them wearing nowadays and in which they are portrayed in Mr. Makovsky's painting. This uniform is a recent borrowing from the West—from Poland, to be more precise—and among the esteemed leaders of our church there have been and still are more than a few who find this liveried masquerade to be inappropriate; the choristers in their choirs sing in ordinary black frock-coats which, of course, are much more modest and decorous than the broad-sleeved Polish gown. "From time immemorial" and since the days of the *"Patriarchate"* choristers have sung standing in long black caftans, and always holding rosaries; this is precisely how the choristers stand even now in the churches of the dissenters and the prayer houses of the Old Believers.

N.B.: It would seem from this, perhaps, that in Orthodox churches today the choristers sing while seated. It is always useful to listen to an informed person.

> Fearing [he has a lot to fear!] lest Mr. Dostoevsky's ill-informed remarks establish an erroneous view on these uniforms [will this cause an earthquake or something?], which should have been remodeled in Russian fashion long ago, I have the honor to ask the editor of *The Russian World* to provide space for these brief lines of mine.
>
> Psalm-reader.

This is the note of the Psalm-reader to which the priest Kastorsky refers. Before continuing with Kastorsky, let us finish with the Psalm-reader.

What made you so angry, Mr. Psalm-reader? You point out an error and try to teach us a lesson, but meanwhile you fall into error yourself. You say: "This is without foundation: neither *from time immemorial* nor *since the days of the Patriarchate* have members of choirs in the Russian church ever worn such costumes. . . . " Is that so? Why is that "without foundation"? Why can one not say *from time immemorial* and *since the days of the Patriarchate*? What, was it only yesterday they started wearing these clothes? Hasn't it been at least since great-great-great-grandfather's day? With the solemn frown of a great historian you come to correct us, but you yourself say nothing precise. One expects the great historian to determine accurately the time, the year, maybe even the day when the choristers first donned this garb, but after you have finished blowing your trumpet you content yourself with only a feeble supposition: "We got this from Poland," and nothing more! But what a grand ringing of bells you indulged in!

Just tell us, Mr. Psalm-reader, what you think: was this Polish influence, which was felt in Russia in many areas at once—and even on the clergy—something that occurred a long time ago, in your opinion, or did it happen just the other day? Then why can't one, for the sake of making sense, say that this has been the case *from time immemorial* and *since the days of the Patriarchate*? It goes back not only to the time of the Patriarchate but almost to the time of the *patriarchs*.

These costumes (or ones like them) appeared at the time of Peter the Great; accordingly, they go back almost to the time of the patriarchs, or very nearly so. Is that recent? Can't one say *from time immemorial*, after all? Or "since the days of the Patriarchate"? And if in my article I myself did not specify with historical accuracy just when our choristers began wearing these costumes, then it was because I had no intention or aim in so doing but wanted only to say that this was begun a very long time ago—so long ago that one could say "*from time immemorial*," and everyone who read my article would understand. I was not talking about the time of Dmitry Donskoi and I was not talking about Yaroslav's time. I meant "a very long time ago" and nothing more.

But enough of the learned Psalm-reader. He jumped up, waved his arms a lot, and—nothing came of it. At least he expressed himself politely: "Fearing," he says, "lest Mr. Dostoevsky's *ill-informed* remarks . . ." and so on. But Pr. Kastorsky at once goes beyond the limits set by the Psalm-reader. He's a frisky fellow! . . . "The writer Dostoevsky's ignorance of choristers. . . ." "I cannot remain silent about an even more serious, ludicrous, and unforgivable act of ignorance which again was made manifest in the same magazine, *The Citizen*, beneath which the signature of this same Mr. Dostoevsky appears as editor."

Just think what dreadful crimes this Dostoevsky has committed: one can't even *forgive* them! A man of the cloth who, it would seem, ought to be love incarnate but who is incapable of forgiveness! . . . But what sort of "ignorance" does he have in mind? What's the matter here? There's nothing to be done but to quote the whole of Kastorsky; we'll give the readers a treat. Why should we content ourselves with only "half a loaf"? The more, the better; that's my idea.

In issues 15-16 of *The Citizen*, which came out on the 16th of April, there appeared "The Deacon: A Story Told to a Group of Friends," by Mr. Nedolin. This story has a most erroneous and impossible basis: it portrays a deacon most vociferous who is *beaten* by his wife, and *beaten* so energetically and cruelly that he flees to a monastery to escape her blows; here he "consecrated himself to the Lord and could no longer think of worldly matters." He stands inside the walls of the monastery, while the wife who had been beating him stands outside; here he sings an adaptation of the psalm:

> Holy, O God, is Thine anointed!
> To do Thy will is he appointed.
> The giant, foe of Christians all
> Beneath his sword shall surely fall.

And his abandoned wife again "stands outside the monastery; pressing her burning forehead to the wall she weeps" and begs that her husband, who has been accepted into the monastery, can be sent out so that she can be "his slave and his dog." But the husband did not come out and remained in the monastery until his death.

What a wretched, impossible, and absurd cock-and-bull story this is! Who this Mr. Nedolin is we do not know; but certainly he is someone who is totally ignorant of Russian legislation or Russian life—ignorant to the point that he supposes that in Russia a married man can be accepted into a monastery and be permitted to stay there; but how could the editor, Mr. Dostoevsky, not know that? He was the one who not long ago was proclaiming at such length that he was a great Christian and an Orthodox one as well, with an orthodox faith in miracles of the most singular kind. Does he, perhaps, number the acceptance of a married man into a monastery among his miracles? If so, then that is a different matter; but anyone who knows even the least bit about the laws and regulations of our church could easily show Mr. Dostoevsky that such a miracle could never happen here because it is strictly forbidden and can be prosecuted under specific laws which no monastic authority can violate, and that a man who has a living wife cannot be admitted to a monastery.

The extremely impoverished and clumsily constructed plot of the story "The Deacon" could still have been improved somewhat, of course, had it been given a plausible ending, and this could well have been done by a writer or an editor with even a sketchy knowledge of the milieu depicted. The story could have been developed, for instance, to the familiar dramatic situation in which the deacon, to hide from his shrewish wife, flees to various monasteries; but he is evicted by the authorities of some of them because he is married, while from others his wife demands he be returned to her, and again, perhaps, she beats him. . . . Then, seeing no way to save himself from his wife in his own country but still longing for monastic life, the unfortunate deacon might run away to Mount Athos, say, where under the Moslem rule of the Turkish Sultan the Orthodox Church in many ways functions more independently than it does in Russia. There, as we know, monasteries sometimes are not afraid to take in even married people who wish to become monks; there the Russian deacon who had been so mercilessly abused by his wife might find refuge and pray and sing, but in any case he would certainly not sing the adaptation into verse which the deacon of *The Citizen* sings because, *first*, as is very well known, this adaptation enjoys no popularity among men of the cloth; *second*, it is not adapted to singing and is not sung; and *third*, adaptations of secular verses are not permitted to be sung within the walls of a monastery, and no one who lives in the monastery is allowed to violate that prohibition lest the silence appropriate to the place be disturbed.

Pr. P. Kastorsky.

Now let me reply to this point by point and, first, let me assure the perturbed priest Kastorsky about his main point by explaining to him that the story "The Deacon" was never intended as a study of manners and mores. Its esteemed author, Mr. Nedolin (not a pseudonym), who spent a part of his life in very active government service, had in this instance no concern at all with clerical life. Mr. Nedolin could, with no loss at all to himself or to the story, have just as well made his hero, the "*deacon*," a postal clerk, for instance, and if he was a deacon in the story then it is only because this is an actual incident. This poem in prose is something exceptional, almost fantastic. Do you know, priest Kastorsky, that when one describes actual events by scrupulously observing all their random nature they nearly always take on a fantastic, almost improbable character? The task of art is not to portray the random bits of daily life but their general idea, perceptively read and faithfully drawn out from the entire broad range of similar phenomena of life. Mr. Nedolin's story generalizes on quite a different manifestation of the human spirit. If he had had intentions of portraying manners and mores, for instance, then from that point of view this one anecdote of his would certainly have entered into the exceptional. Recently (several months ago, I mean), I heard that in one of our most distinguished monasteries one stupid and malicious monk killed a ten-year-old boy in school with his cruel beatings, and did so in the presence of witnesses. Now, doesn't this seem quite fantastic at first glance? And yet it apparently is quite true. But if someone were to write a story about that, people would at once begin to shout that it was improbable, exceptional, presented with some preconceived intention—and they would be right, at least judging from the point of view of only an accurate portrayal of the ways of our monasteries. There would be no accuracy with only such an anecdote; even today one finds in our monasteries an angelic life for the glory of God and the church, and the incident of the cruel monk will remain forever an exception. But for the storyteller, for the poet, there may be other tasks beyond the aspect of genre; there are the depths of the human spirit and character— general, eternal, and, I think, never to be fully explored. But you seem to think that once the word *deacon* has appeared in print there must absolutely follow some special description of clerical life; and if it's to be a description of clerical life then we have writers with patents who have already staked out this territory, and woe to anyone else who ventures to tread on it: this is our corner, our area to exploit, our source of income. Tell me the truth, Priest Kastorsky: isn't that what really upset you? For heaven's sake, surely someone can write the word *deacon* without intending to take anything away from Mr. Leskov. So please calm down.

Now that I've soothed you somewhat, I must ask you to direct your attention to the title of your polemical article, "Unmarried Notions of a Married Monk."

Let me ask in passing: what do you mean by "unmarried" here? How would these notions be changed if they were "married" ones? Are there, in fact, "married" and "unmarried" notions? Well, of course, you're not a literary man, and this is all a lot of nonsense; you are the excited priest Kastorsky, and we shouldn't expect fine style from you, particularly in the state you're in. The main point here is this: who told you that our deacon became a monk? Where in Mr. Nedolin's entire story did you find that he took monastic vows? Yet this is a vital point; when you put such a title on your article you plainly mislead the reader unacquainted with Mr. Ne- dolin's story: "True enough," he thinks, "a married deacon can't become a monk! How is it *The Citizen* didn't know that?" And so, after distracting the reader with the word *monk* you exclaim triumphantly in the middle of your article: "What a wretched, impossible, and absurd cock-and-bull story this is!... How could the editor, Mr. Dostoevsky, not know that..." and so on.

You have stacked the deck, plainly and simply, and I am quietly exposing your cheating. But you have made a small error, Father, and didn't think too carefully about what you were doing. A married man *cannot take monastic vows*, that is true; but why will "no monastic authority admit a married man into a monastery," as you claim with such excitement? Where did you find such information? Should someone, for instance, have a notion to take up residence in a monastery (one that had proper facilities, for example) but had a wife somewhere in the capital or abroad, would he be thrown out of the monastery simply because he was married? Is that how it is? You do not know such things, Father, and you a clergyman! I could even mention several persons, whom all Petersburg society knows well and still remembers, who very late in life moved into monasteries and have been living there a long time even though they are married and have wives who are alive even now. It was all arranged by mutual consent. In just such a manner Mr. Nedolin's deacon *took up residence* in the monastery. All you have to do is take away the distortion you deliberately concocted about monastic vows (which does not appear at all in Mr. Nedolin's story) and everything will at once be clear to you. In the story it was even better than a matter of mutual consent; it happened directly with the permission of the authorities. I have the means to pacify you most effectively on this account, Father. Suppose that I made some enquiries and received the following information.

First, some six months before his *admission* to the monastery, the artist-deacon had first revealed to the landowner, as he was bidding him farewell, that he intended to go *take up residence* in the monastery; even then he knew what he was talking about, because he had already made known his intention to Father John, the abbot, who was very fond of him (or at least was fond of his singing, because he was a great music lover and had done his best to support Sofron.) It seems that the abbot himself had even been encouraging him to come and *live* in the monastery. The deacon hesitated in taking up the landowner's offer to go abroad, and that was why he waited another six months or so; but when his patience ran out he did go off to the monastery. This was a very simple matter to arrange: Father John was a bosom friend of the superior of the diocese, and when two such personages agree on something then no further pretexts are needed. But probably a pretext was found whereby the deacon was "posted," so to say, to the monastery. The vow the deacon made to "consecrate himself to the Lord" (which makes you particularly angry) was an entirely free, unofficial, and

inner one, made to himself and as matter of his own conscience.
Moreover, in Mr. Nedolin's story it is stated very clearly that the
deacon was only *residing* in the monastery and had by no means
taken monastic vows; that, Father, is your own quite brazen concoction. Here is some specific evidence: the landowner, who had
returned, continued to urge Sofron to leave the monastery and go
abroad, and the deacon even considered that on the first day of
their talks. Now could that have happened had Sofron already taken
vows? And, finally, don't conceal the fact that he was an extraordinary artist—uncommonly gifted, at least—and that is how he
appears in the story from the very beginning. And if such is the
case, then it is understandable why Father John, the great music
lover, should take such an interest in him. . . .

"But that isn't explained in the story!" you will shout in a fit
of anger. But no, it is explained in part; one can deduce a good
deal from the story even though it is brief and can be read quickly.
But suppose that not everything is explained: why should it be?
It need only be plausible; and if you take away the obfuscation of
monastic vows, then it all becomes plausible. True, Mr. Nedolin's
story is a little too compact; but then you aren't a literary man,
Father, and have proved it; yet I can tell you frankly that a huge
number of the stories and novels we see today would profit by
some abbreviation. What is the point of the author dragging you
through some four hundred and eighty pages and then suddenly,
on page four hundred and eighty-one, inexplicably dropping the
narrative in Petersburg or Moscow and dragging you off to somewhere in Moldavo-Wallachia for the sole purpose of telling you how
a flock of ravens and owls flew off some Moldavo-Wallachian roof;
and having told you that, he again suddenly abandons the ravens
and Moldavo-Wallachia as if they had never existed and never
returns to them again for the rest of the story so that, at last, the
reader is left in total bewilderment? Some authors write for money,
simply to produce more pages! Mr. Nedolin did not do that and
perhaps he was right.

"But the wife, the wife!" I hear you exclaim as you roll your
eyes. "How could the wife allow that and not complain? Why didn't
she make a legal 'demand' that he be returned to her, by force?"
But it was precisely on this point about the wife that you truly
misfired, Father. Your imagination took such flight in your article
that you even began composing a novel of your own: how the wife
at last had her deacon returned to her, again began thrashing him,

and how he fled to another monastery and was again brought back until he at last fled to Mount Athos where he settled peacefully under the "*Mohammedan*" administration of the Sultan (imagine that: I had always assumed the Sultan was a Christian!).

Joking aside, Father, you should realize that your office alone demands at least a little knowledge of the human heart, but you don't know it at all. You might be a poor fictionist, but if you were to take pen in hand you might still be able to describe the everyday lives of the clergy more accurately than Mr. Nedolin; but in matters of the human heart Mr. Nedolin knows more than you do. A woman who spends whole days standing outside a monastery wall, weeping, will not go to court and will not resort to force. She's had enough of force! But your version is just one beating after another; in an outburst of authorial enthusiasm you continue the novel, and again you have beating. No, enough beating, for heaven's sake! Do you recall, Father, the last scene of Gogol's *Marriage?* After Podkolesin has jumped out the window Kochkarev shouts: "Bring him back! Bring him back!"—imagining that the absconded bridegroom is still fit for the marriage. Well, that's just the way you judge matters here. The matchmaker stops Kochkarev by saying: "Ah, you know nothing about the marriage business: it's one thing if he'd gone through the door, but when he flew out the window it's good-bye forever." If you take away the comic aspects of Podkolesin's case, he fits exactly the situation of the poor deacon's wife abandoned by her husband. No, Father, the beatings are finished! This woman—this exceptional character, a passionate and powerful creature who, by the way, has much greater spiritual strength than her artist-husband—this woman, under the influence of her environment, habits, and lack of education, might truly begin by beating her husband. The very realism of the events here would appeal to a man of sense and understanding, and Mr. Nedolin acted like a master in not toning down the reality. Women who have an excess of spirit and character, especially passionate women, can love no other way than despotically and even have a particular inclination toward such weak, childish characters as the artist-deacon. And why did she come to love him so deeply? Can she really know? He weeps; she cannot help but look scornfully on his tears; but she does it like a cat watching a mouse, herself tormented and enjoying his tears. She is jealous: "Don't you dare sing in front of gentlemen!" It seems she could swallow him whole out of love. And then he runs away from her; she never believed he could do it! She is proud and presumptuous; she knows that she is beautiful, and (this is a strange psychological fact) she was convinced all the while that he loved her as totally as she loved him and could not live without her, despite the beatings! Why, that was her whole faith; moreover, she never had any doubts about it. And suddenly everything is revealed to her: this child, this artist does not love her at all, has long ceased loving her, and, perhaps, never even loved her formerly! She is at once humbled, downcast, crushed, but still does not have the strength to renounce him; she loves him madly, even more madly than before. But since she is a powerful, noble, and exceptional character, she grows and rises far above her former way of life and her former environment. No, now she will certainly not resort to force to get him back. She would never take him now even if it could be done by force; she still has her immense pride, but now it is a different kind of pride; it has become en-nobled: she would rather die of grief right there on the grass by the monastery wall than use violence, write petitions, and try to prove her rights. Ah, Father, don't you see that the whole point of the story is in this and not at all in the details of the daily lives of the clergy? No, Father, this little story is a lot more significant than it seems to you, and a good deal deeper. I repeat: you would not write it this way and you do not even understand what it is about. You have the soul of a Kochkarev in part (I mean in a literary sense, of course—I won't go further than that), as I had the honor of pointing out to you. . . .

As far as your own authorship and artistic sense are concerned, I think that Pushkin's well-known epigram can be applied to you entirely:

A painting once a cobbler stopped to view,
And pointed out an error in one shoe;
The artist took the brush and made it right.
"There!" said the cobbler, "Now I think you might
Correct that bosom: it's a bit too bare;
The face as well requires some repair."
To these complaints Apelles put an end:
"Judge not above the boots, my cobbler friend!"

You, Father, are that very same cobbler, the only difference being that you failed to show Mr. Nedolin any errors even in matters of footwear, something which I trust I have proved to you very clearly. And you won't gain anything by manipulating the evidence. In a case like this, you see, to be able to understand anything about the human soul and "judge above the boots," you need more development in another direction and less of that cynicism, that "spiritual materialism"; there must be less scorn for people, less disrespect and indifference toward them. Let us have less of that carnivorous greed and more faith, hope, and charity! Just look at the crude cynicism with which you treat me personally and the indecency, so inappropriate to your office, with which you speak of miracles. I didn't want to believe it when I read the following lines you wrote about me: "But how could the editor, Mr. Dostoevsky, not know that? He was the one who not long ago was proclaiming at such length that he was a great Christian and an Orthodox one as well, with an orthodox faith in miracles of the most singular kind. Does he, perhaps, number the acceptance of a married man into a monastery among his miracles? If so, then that is a different matter...."

In the first place, Father, this is something you made up (what a passion for making up stories you have, after all!). Nowhere did I ever say anything about my *personal* faith in miracles. All that you have invented, and I challenge you to show me where you found it. Let me say one thing more: had I, F. Dostoevsky, said that about myself (which I never did), then believe me I would not have disavowed my remarks out of any fear of liberals or of Kastorskys. Plainly and simply, there was never anything of the sort, and I am simply stating that fact. But had there been, why would my faith in miracles be any business of yours? What relevance do they have to this matter? And what are singular miracles and nonsingular ones? How do you explain such distinctions to yourself? On the whole, I wish you would not bother me in such matters, if only because pestering me with such things does not suit you at all, despite all your contemporary enlightened views. A man of the cloth, and so irritable! You ought to be ashamed, Mr. Kastorsky.

But, you know, you're really not Mr. Kastorsky, and certainly not the priest Kastorsky; that's all fraud and nonsense. You're an *impostor*, wearing a disguise like the mummers at Christmas. And do you know what else? I wasn't taken in by you for even a tiny moment; I recognized you as an impostor immediately, and that pleases me, for I can see your long nose even from here: you were quite convinced that I would take the clown's mask with its gaudy colors for a real face. You should also know that I replied to you rather too impolitely only because I at once recognized you as an impostor. If you really had been a priest I—despite your crude remarks, which at the end of your article reach the level of a boastful seminarian's whinnying—would have answered you within the bounds of decorum, not out of personal respect for you but out of respect for your high office and the high idea contained in it. But since you are just an impostor, then you must suffer a penalty. I shall begin the punishment by explaining to you in detail how it was that I recognized you (between you and me, I had even guessed beforehand who was hiding behind the mask, but I will not say your name aloud, at least for the time being), and of course you must find that very annoying. . . .

"But if you guessed beforehand, then why did you address your reply to a priest?" you may ask. "Why did you first write so many unnecessary things?"

"Because one treats a man by the way he is dressed," I reply. And if I wrote something unpleasant to Mr. "Priest" then the gentleman who thought up and used such an unworthy device as to dress himself in priestly garb should have that on his conscience. Yes, it was a shabby trick, and he realized it himself. Moreover, he did his best to shield himself. He did not sign the letter "P. Kastorsky, Priest" but used an abbreviation, "Pr." "Pr." doesn't mean priest, strictly speaking at least. One could always say that it meant "prince," or something of the sort.

I recognized you by your style, Mr. Mummer. This is the main thing here, you see: critics today sometimes praise contemporary writers for that, and even readers are satisfied (because what are they to read, after all?). But our criticism has long been in a sad state, and our artists for the most part are closer to sign painters than genuine artists. Not all of them, of course. There are some who have talent, but most are pretenders. In the first place, Mr. Mummer, you overdid it in your letter. Do you know what it means to speak in essences? No? Let me explain it to you. The contemporary "artist-writer" who creates certain types and who stakes off a certain speciality for himself in literature (portraying merchants, say, or peasants, and so on) usually spends his whole life walking around with a pencil and notebook, eavesdropping and writing down characteristic words and phrases; at last he manages to collect several hundred of such characteristic little words. Then he begins to write a novel, and as soon as one of his merchants or clergymen is to say something, the writer puts together a speech for him from the phrases written in his notebook. The readers laugh and admire the work because it seems so authentic: it's copied straight from nature, but it proves to be worse than a lie precisely because the merchant or the soldier in the novel speaks in *essences*, that is, in a manner in which no merchant or soldier ever speaks in real life. In real life, for instance, he may use one such expression as you have written down out of every eleven. This word may be characteristic and malapropos, but the other ten words that preceded it are quite correct, like those of anyone else. But in the works of the artist who creates types, such a character uses only the characteristic words which had been written down, and the result is something false. The character thus depicted speaks *like a book*. Readers admire it, but you can't deceive an old experienced literary man.

Work like this, for the most part, is the work of a sign painter or house painter. But eventually the "artist" begins to regard himself as a Raphael and you can't convince him otherwise! Writing down characteristic little phrases is a fine and useful thing, and one can't get by without it; but one mustn't use them in a completely mechanical fashion. It's true that there are shades of difference between such "stenographer-artists" as well; some are certainly more talented than others, and therefore they use these phrases with some caution, taking into account the mood of the era, the locale, the character's educational level, and maintaining a sense of measure. But they still cannot avoid this "essence-ism." The very valuable rule that an uttered word is silver but an unuttered one golden has long ceased to be a habit among our artists. They have little faith in their readers. The sense of measure is disappearing altogether. Finally, we should also take into account the fact that our artists (like any group of ordinary people) begin to scrutinize carefully the facts of real life, take note of their characteristic features, and transform a specific type into a work of art at a time when that type is already passing from the scene and is changing into something else in conformity with the nature of the epoch and its development; the result is that we are almost always served stale food as if it were fresh. And they themselves believe that it is fresh and not something stale or ephemeral. An observation of this sort is rather too subtle for our author-artist, however, and he probably will not understand it. But I will still say that only a writer of genius or a very powerful talent can distinguish a type *at the right time* and present it to us *at the right time*; the ordinary writer simply follows in his footsteps more or less slavishly, working from ready-made patterns.

I, for instance, have never once in my life met a single priest—even a most highly educated one—whose manner of speech was entirely without some of those distinctive features linked to his profession. It may be only some tiny detail, but there always is something. Yet if you were to make a stenographic record of his conversation and print it, then probably you would not notice any of those distinctive features, at least in the case of a highly educated priest who had spent a good deal of time in lay society. Naturally, this is not enough for our "artist"; the public as well has been taught to expect something else. For example, most readers think that the uneducated people in Pushkin's tales certainly speak less correctly than those of Grigorovich, who spent his whole life describing peasants. I think that many artists as well will agree with that. Grigorovich would not allow one of his priests, for instance, to speak with scarcely any of the characteristic features of his class and milieu; therefore he would not put such a priest in his story but would have a more characteristic one. And so he would make a contemporary priest in given circumstances and in a given milieu speak something like a priest from the beginning of the century, also in given circumstances and in a given milieu.

Priest Kastorsky begins as do the others, scarcely showing any traces of his own given milieu.

As long as he is praising the artistic merits of the writer Leskov he speaks *like everyone else*, with none of the distinctive expressions and thoughts characteristic of his profession. But that is what the author wanted: he had to leave this aside so that his positive literary assessment might sound more serious and his criticism of Mr. Nedolin more severe, for a comic and characteristic phrase would have spoiled the severe tone. But suddenly the author realized that the reader might not believe that this was a priest writing; he took fright and at once plunged into typicalities—a whole load of them. There's scarcely a word that isn't typical! And naturally the result of all this welter is a counterfeit and disproportional typicality.

The most obvious sign of an uneducated man who for some reason is compelled to speak using language and conceptions that are not of his own milieu is a certain inaccuracy in the use of words whose meaning, let's suppose, he knows but whose nuances of usage in the realm of conceptions of some other profession he does not know. "...And therefore *to pass unheeding* such *ill-disposed* attempts...," "the ignorance once more *made manifest* in this same magazine...," "it portrays a deacon *most vociferous*...," and so on. This last expression, "most vociferous," is rather too crude precisely because Pr. Kastorsky, wishing to express the concept of a person endowed with a beautiful singing voice, thinks that the expression "most vociferous" conveys this notion. The author-specialist forgot that, although even now one can find poorly educated people among the clergy, there are very few indeed who are so ignorant as not to understand the meaning of words. This might do in a novel, Mr. Mummer, but it does not stand up in real life. Such an erroneous expression might be appropriate for a sacristan, but certainly not for a priest. I will not cite any more of these expressions; there are, I repeat, a whole load of them, pulled most crudely out of a notebook. But the worst of all is that the author-typicalist (if one speaks of the author-artist, then the concept of the author-*tradesman* is also possible, and the word *typicalist* defines a trade or a craft)—the author-typicalist has presented his type in such a morally unattractive light. He should have presented Pr. Kastorsky as a man of dignity and virtue, and typicality would not have hindered that at all. But the typicalist himself was put in an awkward position from which he could not extricate himself: he felt absolutely compelled to abuse his fellow author and jeer at him, and so he, like some mummer-impostor, had to attribute his better impulses to a priest. And when it came to miracles, the typicalist lost all self-restraint. The result was something terribly stupid: a man of the cloth, yet he jeers at miracles and divides them into singular and nonsingular ones! That was poorly done, Mr. Typicalist.

I think that the "Psalm-reader" as well is a product of that same pen: the awkward tradesman's naiveté simply overflowed at the end with all the "fears" of the Psalm-reader, which do not sparkle with much wit. In short, gentlemen, all this sign painter's work might do in stories but, I repeat, it will not stand up to an encounter with real life and will at once betray its true nature. Don't try to deceive an old literary man, you author-artists.

What are these, then, simply jokes on their part? No, they're not jokes at all. It's—well, one could say it's Darwinism, the struggle for survival. Don't you dare set foot in our meadow, they say. But what harm could Mr. Nedolin do to you, gentlemen? I assure you that he has no intention whatsoever of describing the clergy from the point of view of their everyday lives; you can rest assured on that. It's true that one peculiar thing confused me for a moment: if the impostor typicalist attacked Mr. Nedolin, then in abusing him he ought conversely to be praising himself. (On this score these people haven't the least bit of self-respect: they are prepared to write and publish praises to themselves in their own hand with utter shamelessness.) And yet, to my great surprise, the typicalist promotes and praises the talented Mr. Leskov and not himself. Something different is going on here, and it, probably, will be clarified. But the fact that we are dealing with an *impostor* is beyond all doubt.

And what is the role of *The Russian World* in this case? I truly don't know. I never had any dealings with *The Russian World* and never intended to have any. Lord knows why people leap out at you.

11

Dreams and Musings

In the last issue of *The Citizen* we again took up the topic of drunkenness or, rather, of the possibility of healing the abscess of widespread drunkenness among the People, of our hopes and our faith in a better future soon to come. But for a long time my heart could not help but be beset by sorrow and doubts. Of course, because of current important affairs (and in Russia everyone looks like such an important man of affairs) one hasn't the time (and it is foolish) to think about what will happen ten years from now or at the end of the century, i.e., when we will no longer be here. The motto of the real man of affairs of our time is *après moi le déluge*. But for idle, impractical people who have no affairs to deal with, truly it is permissible sometimes to dream—if one can dream—of things to come. Didn't Poprischin, in Gogol's "Notes of a Madman," dream of Spanish affairs?—"...all these events have so shattered and shaken me that I..." etc., he wrote forty years ago. I confess that sometimes there are many things that shake me as well, and truly I even get depressed from my musings. I was musing the other day, for instance, about Russia's status as a great European power, and what didn't come into my head on this sad topic!

Just consider our efforts to become a great European power, whatever the price, as soon as possible. Granted, we are already a great power; but I wish only to say that this costs us too dearly—much more dearly than the other great powers, and that is a very bad sign. The whole thing thus becomes somewhat unnatural. I would hasten to make this reservation, however: I am judging exclusively from the Westernerizers' point of view, and such really is the conclusion that emerges from that view. The national and, so to say, somewhat Slavophile point of view is another matter;

here, as we know, there is a faith in certain inner, distinctive forces of the People, in certain principles of the People which are inherent in them and entirely individual and original and which are their salvation and support. But when I read Mr. Pypin's articles I was sobered. Of course, I continue to wish with all my might, as I always have, that the precious, solid, and independent principles inherent in the Russian People exist in reality. But still, you will have to accept his point: what kind of principles are these when even Mr. Pypin himself cannot see, hear, or discern them, when they are hidden away and simply refuse to be tracked down? And therefore even I must manage to get by without these principles that give solace to the soul. So I conclude that we are still barely clinging to the summit of our great power status, doing whatever we can to keep our neighbors from quickly realizing our situation. In this we can find tremendous help from the general European ignorance of all things that concern Russia. At least until now there has been no doubt at all about this ignorance, and this is something we should not regret; to the contrary, it will be very disadvantageous for us if our neighbors look more closely and carefully at us. The fact that until now they understood nothing about us was a great source of our strength. But the point is that now, alas, it seems they are beginning to understand us better; and that is very dangerous.

Our gigantic neighbor is persistently studying us and already sees right through many things. Without entering into the fine points, take even our most obvious features that stand out at once. Take our immense spaces and our border areas (populated by non-Russians and foreigners who year by year grow more strongly individualistic in their own non-Russian elements and in foreign elements borrowed from their neighbors). Take these things and consider: in how many areas are we strategically vulnerable? In order to defend all this (from my civilian's point of view, at least) we need to have a far larger army than our neighbors. Take into account as well the fact that these days war is made not so much with armaments as with brains, and you will agree that in this latter area we are particularly disadvantaged.

Nowadays armaments are changed every ten years or even more often. In fifteen years or so, perhaps, soldiers will no longer shoot with rifles but with lightning of some sort, using a kind of all-consuming electrical current produced by a machine. Tell me, what can we invent in this line so as to set it aside as a surprise for our neighbors? What if, fifteen years from now, every great power has acquired and hidden away in storage one such surprise for any eventuality? Alas, we can only adopt and purchase weapons from others and we do well if we manage to repair them ourselves. To invent machines such as these we need our own independent science, not one we have purchased; our own, not one brought in from abroad; a science that is free and has its roots in our own soil. We still do not have such a science; we do not even have a purchased one. Again, take our railways: consider our distances and our poverty; compare our capital cities with those of the other great powers and try to comprehend: how much would such a railway network, essential for us as a great power, cost? And note that in Europe these networks were built long ago and were done gradually, while we have to hurry and catch up; distances there are short, while ours are on the scale of the Pacific Ocean. Even now, we are painfully aware of what the mere beginning of our railway network has cost us; we know what the substantial diversion of capital into this one area has meant to the detriment of our poor agriculture, say, and to every other industry as well. The point here is not so much the monetary sum as the measure of the nation's effort. However, we will never be able to finish if we try to list point by point our needs and our lack of resources. But take, at last, education—science, that is—and look at how far we have to go to catch up to the others in this area. In my humble opinion, if we want to overtake any one of the great powers we ought every year to be spending at least as much on education as we do on the military. We also have to realize that so much time has already been lost that we do not have the necessary funds, and that in the final analysis all this would serve only as a sudden prod and not as a normal development; it would be agitation and not education.

I'm just musing here, of course; but . . . I repeat, one sometimes cannot help but speculate in this way and so I shall continue. Note that I place a monetary value on everything; but is that really the proper way to calculate things? Money certainly does not buy everything; only some uneducated merchant in one of Mr. Ostrovsky's comedies would argue that. Money will build you schools but won't produce teachers. A teacher is something delicate; a teacher for the People, a national teacher, is produced over the course of centuries and is maintained by traditions and immeasurable experience. But let's suppose that with money you do produce not only teachers but, finally, scientists as well; and what of it?—you still would not produce human beings. What does it matter if he is learned if he cannot truly understand things? He may master pedagogy and teach it superbly from behind his desk but he himself still not become a pedagogue. People—people are the most important thing. People are more valuable than even money. You cannot buy people at any market for any sum of money because they are not bought and sold but, again, are produced only over the course of centuries; and that requires time—some twenty-five or thirty years at least, even in Russia where centuries have long since been devalued. A person of ideas and independent learning, a person who can independently deal with practical matters, is produced only by a prolonged independent life of the nation, by years of its onerous labor; in a word, such a person is produced by the entire historical life of the country. But our historical life over the past two centuries has hardly been independent. To hasten artificially the essential and constant historical phases of the life of the nation is absolutely impossible. We have seen this in our own country, and the problem continues today: two centuries ago we wanted to hurry and to push everything ahead, but instead we got stuck; for despite all the triumphant shouts of our Westernizers we certainly did get stuck. Our Westernizers are the people who today are trumpeting at full volume and with extraordinary malice and satisfaction that we have neither science nor common sense or patience or ability, that we are destined only to crawl behind Europe, slavishly aping her in everything, and that because we are Europe's wards it is criminal for us even to think of our own independence; but tomorrow, should you even try to voice your doubts about the unquestionably wholesome effect of our revolution of two centuries back, they would at once cry out in unison that all your dreams of national independence are only kvass, kvass, and more kvass; two centuries ago, they would say, we emerged from the mob of barbarians and became most enlightened and happy Europeans, and we ought to remember this with gratitude for the rest of our days.

But let's leave the Westernizers and suppose that we can do everything with money—even buy time, even somehow at full steam reproduce the uniqueness of our way of life; the question then arises as to where we are to find this money. Nearly half our present budget is provided by vodka—that is, by the current drunkenness and debauch of the People—and so by the whole future of our People. We are, so to say, funding our grand budget as a great

European power with our own future. We are cutting off the tree at its very root in order to get its fruit more quickly. And who was it who wanted that? It happened involuntarily, of itself, through the strict historical course of events. Our People, liberated by the mighty command of our Monarch, are inexperienced in this new life and are taking their first steps along this new road without having lived independently: this is an enormous and extraordinary turning point, scarcely expected and scarcely precedented in history because of its comprehensiveness and its nature. These initial, independent steps of an epic hero on his new road demanded immense caution and extraordinary care; meanwhile, what did our People encounter on these first steps? Uncertainty on the part of the upper levels of society; the centuries-long alienation of our intelligentsia from the People (this is the main thing); and, to complete the picture, cheap vodka and the Yid. The People took to drink and went off on a spree—first from joy and then from habit. Did anyone ever show them anything better than cheap vodka? Did anyone ever provide them any diversion or teach them anything? Nowadays in some areas—in many areas, in fact—there are taverns not just for hundreds of inhabitants but for dozens and, indeed, for only a few dozen. There are areas with taverns and only fifty inhabitants, or even fewer. *The Citizen* has already published a special article that contained a detailed budget for one of our present-day taverns: one simply cannot suppose that taverns could survive only through the sale of vodka. So how, then, do they stay in business? Through the debauchery of the People, through thievery, receiving stolen goods, usury, banditry, the destruction of the family, and the disgrace of the People—that's how they stay in business!

Mothers drink, children drink, the churches are empty, fathers take to banditry: the bronze arm of Ivan Susanin is sawed off and brought to the tavern; and the tavern accepts it! Just ask the opinion of medicine: what sort of a generation can be born from such drunkards? But never mind; suppose, just suppose (and God grant it is so!) that these are only the musings of a pessimist who exaggerates the trouble by tenfold! We believe, we try to believe, but . . . if in the next ten or fifteen years the propensity of our People for drunkenness (which is still undeniable) does not diminish but persists and so expands even more, then would not my picture of things be justified? And now we must have the budget of a great power and therefore we are greatly in need of money;

who, I ask, is going to supply this money over the next fifteen
years if the present state of affairs continues? Labor? Industry?
For sound financing is provided only by labor and industry. But
what kind of labor can we have when these taverns exist? Genuine,
proper capital accumulates in a country only on the basis of the
general well-being of its labor force; otherwise capital accumulates
only in the hands of kulaks and Yids. And so it will be if things
continue as they are, if the People do not come to their senses,
and if the intelligentsia do not come to their aid. If the People do
not come to their senses, then they all, as a whole, in a very short
time, will find themselves in the hands of all sorts of Yids, and
then no community will be able to help them: there will be only
beggars equal in poverty who have mortgaged themselves and sold
themselves into bondage as a community, while the Yids and the
kulaks will be providing the entire budget on their behalf. We will
have a class of petty, base, and thoroughly depraved bourgeois and
a countless number of beggars enslaved by them—that is the picture! The wretched Yids will be drinking the blood of the People
and feeding themselves on the People's debauchery and humiliation,
but since they will be providing the funds for the budget they will
have to be supported. It is a nasty picture, a terrible picture, and
thank God that it is only a dream! The dream of Titular Councilor
Poprishchin, I agree. But it will not come true! The People have
had to save themselves more than once already! They will find in
themselves a protective force as they have always found it; they
will find within themselves the principles that will preserve and
save them—those very same principles which our intelligentsia simply cannot find in our People. The People will turn their backs
on the tavern; they will choose labor and order; they will choose
honor and not the tavern! . . .

And, thank God, all this seems to be borne out; at least there
are signs that it is. We have already noted the temperance societies.
It's true that they are only just beginning; they are weak attempts,
barely perceptible, but—but let us hope their development is not
hindered because of any special considerations! On the contrary,
it is so necessary to support them! What if they were supported
by all our leading intellects, our literary people, our socialists, our
clergy, and by each one who writes, month after month, of how
he is fainting beneath the burden of his debt to the People. What
if our schoolteachers, who are only now beginning to appear, were
to support them! I know that I am an impractical person (now,

after Mr. Spasovich's recent, well-known speech, it is even flattering
to admit that), but—just think—I can see that even the poorest of
schoolteachers could do so much, and merely through his own
initiative, if only he wanted to! And this is the point: what matters
here is personality, character; what matters is the person who can
work and the one who truly has the desire to do something. For
the most part, teachers' positions are now being taken by young
people who, although they might want to do good, do not know
the People; they are wary and mistrustful; after their first, often
very ardent and noble efforts, they quickly tire and take a gloomy
view of things; they begin to regard their post merely as a step on
the way to something better; then they either take utterly to drink
or, for an extra ten rubles, they abandon everything and run off
wherever they choose; they even run off without pay, even to America "to experience free labor in a free country." This has happened
and, I have heard, is happening even now. There, in America,
some sort of vile entrepreneur can wear out the former teacher with
rough manual labor, cheat him of his pay, and even thrash him
with his fists; and at every blow the teacher exclaims to himself
tenderly: "Lord, how reactionary and ignoble such blows were in
my own country, and how noble, delicious, and liberal they are
here!" And it will seem that way to him for a long time; trifles
such as these will not lead him to change his convictions! But let
us leave him in America; I will continue my idea. My idea, I
remind you, is that even the least significant village schoolteacher
could undertake the whole initiative to liberate the People from the
barbaric passion for drink, if only he so desired. On this subject
I even have the plot for a short novel and, perhaps, I shall risk
passing it on to the reader before the novel is written. . . .

12

Apropos of a New Play

This new play is a drama by Mr. Kishensky, *Strong Drink Every Day Keeps Fortune Away*; we decided to include the whole of the three last acts in this twenty-fifth issue of *The Citizen* despite the fact that they took up nearly half of our space. But we did not want to disturb the totality of the impression they produce, and perhaps the readers will agree that the play merits their particular attention. It was written for the popular stage and written knowledgeably, clearly, and with indisputable talent—and that is the main thing, particularly now, when scarcely any new talents are coming on the scene.

The characters, who are all products of the industrial milieu of a small "factory town," are a most varied lot and are clearly drawn. You can see the plot here for yourselves, and I will not summarize it in any detail. The idea is serious and profound. It is very much a tragedy whose *fatum* is vodka; it is vodka which ties everything together, pervades everything, sets things in motion, and brings about the catastrophe. True, the author, like a genuine artist, could not help but take a broader view of the world he depicts even though he announces in the title of his drama that his subject is "strong drink every day keeps fortune away." We also find reflected here the whole extraordinary economic and moral trauma that followed the wide-ranging reforms of the current reign. The old world and the old order—which, as bad as it was, was still an order—have disappeared forever. And the strange thing is that the dark moral aspects of the old order—egoism, cynicism, slavery, disunity, venality—have not only not disappeared with the abolition of serfdom but seem to have grown stronger, developed, and multiplied; on the other hand, of the good moral aspects of the old way of life—which certainly existed—scarcely anything remains. All this is reflected in the picture presented by Mr. Kishensky, at least in my understanding of it. Everything here is transitory, everything is unstable and, alas, provides not even a hint of something better to come.

The author vigorously makes the point that education is the means of salvation and the only solution; but meanwhile vodka has everything in thrall; it has poisoned everything and turned it wrong; it has invaded the People and made them its slaves. It is a gloomy, terrible picture Mr. Kishensky draws of this new slavery into which the Russian peasant has fallen after emerging from his former slavery.

The play has two different types of characters: people of the old, disappearing world, and those of the new, young generation.

The author knows the young generation. His favorite characters, whom he sees as the hope of the future and who constitute the bright spots in this gloomy picture, have come out rather well (which is very odd, since our poets are scarcely ever successful with "positive" characters). At least, Maria is flawless. Ivan, her fiancé, is not quite so successful, despite the veracity with which he is portrayed. This young lad is handsome, bold, literate; he has seen and learned a good deal about the new life and is kind and honest. His only failing is that the author has come to love him a bit too much and has portrayed him too positively. Had the author taken a somewhat more negative attitude toward him, the reader's impression would have been more favorable toward this favorite hero. True, the author, as a sensitive artist, did not fail also to note the most unfavorable traits in the character of his Ivan. Ivan is a character with great energy and a strong mind, but he is young and arrogant. He has a noble faith in truth and justice but assumes that others have the same faith and unfairly demands the impossible from them. For example, he has some knowledge of the law, so that the clerk "Levanid Ignatych" is reluctant to attack him directly; but he has too naive a faith in his own knowledge and therefore is not equipped to cope with evil; he not only fails to understand the danger he is in but never even suspects it. This is all so natural and would have come off beautifully, because that is how things would happen. Moreover, the author did not leave out a host of very sympathetic details: Vanya is aware of all the infamy of the villains (who are hostile to him as well), but as a healthy and strong young man who still finds everything in life so attractive, he is unwilling to keep away from them; he joins them and *sings songs* with them. This youthful trait makes him very attractive to the reader. But, I repeat, the author grew too fond of him and never once ventured to look at him objectively. It seems to me that it is still not enough to portray faithfully all the given qualities of a character; one must truly illuminate that character with one's own artistic vision. A real artist must under no circumstances remain on the same level as the character he portrays, contenting himself only with a reflection of real life; no truth will emerge from such an impression. Had the author applied a little—even a touch—of irony to the confidence and youthful arrogance of his hero, the reader would have had more fondness for the character. Otherwise one thinks that the author simply wanted to show him as being entirely in the right in the whole calamity that befell him.

The other characters from the young generation—characters who are lost almost from childhood, "the sacrificed generation"—have come off even more truthfully than the "positive" characters. They fall into two groups: the guiltless and the guilty. We have here, for instance, one girl (Matryosha), an unfortunate creature who is sacrificed; and the worst thing is that you sense she is not the only such victim, that you can find as many such "unfortunates" in Russia as you please, that there are whole villages of them, multitudes. The veracity of this description induces a sense of horror in a person who has feelings and who looks carefully at our future. This is the generation which has sprung up after the reforms. In early childhood they encountered a family that was already disintegrating and without ideals; they found wholesale drunkenness; then, directly, they found themselves in the factory. The poor girl! She has practiced debauchery from the age of twelve, perhaps, and she herself scarcely knows that she is debauched. At Christmas she leaves the factory for a short stay in the village and is astonished that her former friend, the village girl Masha, can prefer her honor to fine clothes: "Come on, now, Stepan Zakharych, your ignorance is showing," she says. "What's the harm if some shopkeeper or gentleman wants to play around with a girl?" She makes this remark with total conviction of its truth and justice; moreover, she says this feeling pity for Masha and the villagers. When Masha spurns a wretched scoundrel of a businessman, Matryosha says plainly: "What's the use of trying to talk sense to these people! Ignorant clods! Somebody else in her place would've been glad to do it! She could have charmed him and got a little something for herself; it would have kept her brother happy, too!" And finally, when this unfortunate Matryosha conspires with the wretched businessman to give Masha some sleeping powder so that he can rape the poor, honest girl while she is unconscious, and then when she climbs onto the stove to see whether the victim has fallen asleep, she does these evil things not only unaware of any wrong but fully convinced that she is doing her former friend Masha a favor, a good deed for which the girl will later thank her. In Act Five—the last, terrible catastrophe—Matryosha is not troubled by Masha's despair, nor that of her father or her fiancé, nor by the murder which is about to be committed, nor by anything else. Indeed, she has no heart, for where could she have acquired one? She shrugs her shoulders and utters her favorite word: "Ignorance!" The author uses this exclamation frequently and with it applies the final, artistic touch to this character. A tragic fate! A human being transformed into some rotten worm, utterly pleased with herself and her pitifully limited horizon.

Here we have environment, *fatum*; this unfortunate girl is not to be blamed, and you realize that. But there is another character, the most rounded one in the play; this is Masha's brother, a debauched, wasted, despicable factory lad who eventually sells his sister to the businessman for three hundred rubles and a velvet jacket. Now this is a character from among the guilty of the "sacrificed" generation. Here we have not only the influence of the environment. True, his circumstances and environment are the same: drunkenness, the disintegrating family, and the factory. But he does not place his faith in debauchery naively, as does Matryosha. He is not naively base as she is, but lovingly so; he brings something of his own to his moral squalor. He realizes that vice is vice and knows what virtue is; but he has come consciously to love vice and to despise honor. He already consciously rejects the old order of the family and custom; he is stupid and dull, that's true, but he has a certain enthusiasm for sensuality and for the most base and cynical form of materialism. He is not simply a worm, as is Matryosha, in whom everything is petty and withered. He stands at the meeting of the village commune and you feel that he understands nothing of what is going on and is incapable of understanding, that he is living in a world of his own and has detached himself completely from the real world. He sells his sister without any pangs of conscience and appears the next morning in his father's hut—the scene of despair—in his velvet jacket, carrying a new accordion. The one thing in which he believes as all-powerful is vodka. With a most obtuse yet

assured manner, he serves vodka before each of his undertakings—
plain vodka to the men, sweetened to the women—certain that
everything will happen as he wishes and that vodka can achieve
everything. The finishing touch to the irony with which he is
portrayed is that he has, alongside his utter cynicism, an urge to
observe the polite manners of the past, the traditional "decorum"
of peasant life. Having arrived in the village and not yet having
greeted his mother, he installs himself in the tavern and politely
sends her some sweetened vodka. When he and Matryosha manage
to get the mother to come to the tavern where they can be free to
cajole her into giving permission to sell her own daughter to be
raped by the businessman, he first serves her sweet vodka and
offers her a seat saying, "Be so kind as t' take a chair, dear
mamma." And she is very gratified at this mark of "civility." Some
of those who have read Act One of the play have reproached our
author for his excessively *naturalistic* peasant language, maintaining
that it could be more literary. I, too, am not satisfied with the
naturalism of the language; everything ought to be artistic. But if
you read attentively and read the play a second time you cannot
help but agree that it would be impossible to change the language—
at least in some places—without weakening the distinctive quality
of the play. This "be so kind as t' take a chair, dear mamma"
could not be changed: otherwise it would not sound so common.
And note that the son has as much respect for his "dear mamma,"
this vile, stupid, tipsy old crone, as he does for the sole of his
boot.

Here are the tragic words of the father of this family, a drunken
old man, about this "sacrificed generation":

> *Zakhar* (drinks a glass of vodka): Drunkards! Think about this
> now, my friends: a fella sits at his machine in the factory all week;
> his hands and his feet get numb and he feels just like his head is full
> of fog. It's like they all get a bit crazy! They don't even look like
> humans no more. There ain't a breath of air in the place; the walls
> are bare; you don't even want to look at it! There's never a ray of
> sunlight to brighten it up; that you only see on holidays! And so,
> friends, a holiday comes along: now you, Granddad, can sit and read
> the Bible; another fella will go off to have a look at the crop in the
> field or into the woods or to his beehives, maybe; or maybe he'll go
> have a chat with the neighbors about the zemstvo or a meeting or
> maybe the price of grain. But where's the factory hand to go, tell
> me? What's he got to talk about? Everything in his life is measured

off and weighed. Is he going to talk about the fines they set for Lord knows what? Or about the rotten food they give him? Or that for a ruble's-worth of tea they charge him two and a half, and don't let him out of the gate so he's got to buy his provisions from the owner and so's there'll be even more deviltry going on inside? Is that what he'll talk about? Well then, his only road leads to the tavern, and the only talk is about vodka and filthy goings-on.

Vasily: That's just the way it is!

Zakhar: Think about it, friends. Our factory lad also wants his bit of fun; he's young, too! People get together for a round dance and some songs and laughter—and the factory watchman sends them packing. So the whole lot of them go off to the tavern or some pot-house! And the talk turns to girls and to who can outdrink the others. And just look at the things that go on inside the factories! Girls of twelve are looking out for lovers! The little ones who change the bobbins guzzle vodka like water! And the filthy language in the factory, the yelling and groaning—it's a steady uproar, a regular hell! The children pick it up from the grownups. We send our children there to their doom! You think you can find even one girl there who's not gone wrong, and one lad who's not taken to drink—in those factories?

But the most characteristic of all the scenes in this peasant drama is Act Three, the meeting of the commune. This part of the play contains a powerful idea. This meeting is the *only* thing that has remained solid and fundamental in Russian peasant life; it is its main link with the past and its main hope for the future. And we see that this meeting as well already bears the seeds of its own destruction; its inner workings are already infected! You see that in many ways it is only a matter of form, but that its inner spirit and age-old inner truth have been shaken, shaken along with the shaky people who participate in it.

A scandalous injustice is done at this meeting: contrary to custom and law, the only son of a widow (Ivan, the hero of the play) is sent off to the army in place of another from a wealthy family of three; what is worse, this is done knowingly, with conscious contempt for justice and custom; it is done for vodka and for money. It is not even a case of bribery here; a bribe would not be so serious, after all; a bribe can be an isolated crime that can be set right. No, almost everything here stems from deliberate contempt for oneself, for one's own sense of justice and, accordingly, for one's own traditional way of life. The cynicism already is evident in the fact that, contrary to custom and ancient rule, the commune allows a drinking bout at the beginning of the meeting: "We'll sort things out better if we're a bit stewed," say the leaders of the meeting with a sneer. Half the citizens who gather there have already long lost any faith in the force of the commune's decision and so in the necessity for it: they consider it little more than an unnecessary formality that can always be dispensed with. Justice can and should be ignored for the sake of immediate advantage. Very soon, one feels, the modern "clever fellows" will regard this whole ceremony as mere stupidity, merely another unnecessary burden, because the decision of the commune, whatever it may be, will always turn out to be the one favored by the wealthy and powerful predator who runs the meeting. Instead of empty formalism, then, it is better to go straight into the grip of this predator. And he will treat you with some vodka, as well. You can see that the majority of these autonomous members no longer even assume that their decision could hold against the will of this powerful man; they have all grown feeble; their hearts are flabby; they all want something sweet, some material reward. In essence, they are all slaves already and cannot even conceive of how to resolve something for justice rather than for their own advantage. The young generation is present here and looks at what their fathers are doing not only disrespectfully, not only scornfully, but as at some outdated nonsense; they see it precisely as a stupid, unnecessary form that survives only through the obstinacy of a few stupid old men who, in any case, can always be bribed. This is how Stepan—the drunken, despicable lad who later sells his sister—regards the meeting. The author renders all these episodes of the commune's meeting very well. And the most important thing is that Stepan's view is almost correct: not only does he understand nothing of what is happening at the meeting; he doesn't even think it necessary to understand. He could not help but notice that an outsider, the businessman who has resolved to ruin Vanka and to take away his fiancée, was permitted to influence the meeting. The members of the commune drank his liquor and allowed the businessman's clerk to say out loud that without the businessman, whose factory work supports them, "your whole district would go a-begging on church porches, but if the decision is in favor of his honor, then he'll cancel a lot of the fines imposed on the people." The matter is decided in the businessman's favor, of course, and Vanya is sent off to the army.

At this meeting (which involves a most varied lot of characters) there are two almost tragic figures: one is Naum Egorov, an old man who for twenty years has occupied the first place at the meeting and has directed it; and the other, Stepanida, Ivan's mother. Naum Egorych is a sensible, steady, honest old man with a lofty soul. He has a high regard for the decision of the commune. For him this is not simply a gathering of householders in a certain village; no, he has elevated himself to take the broadest view of things: although the decision may be only that of a meeting of his village, for him it seems a part of the judgment of all peasant Russia, which stands and survives only through the commune and its decision. But, alas, he is too reasonable and cannot help but see the weakened state of the commune and the direction in which it has been pulled for some time. Of course there was injustice and villainy at former meetings twenty years ago; but contempt for the meeting from its very own members and contempt for their own business was not present and was not elevated into a principle. People did bad things, but they knew they were doing bad and that there was good; now, however, they do not believe in good, or even in the necessity for it. Nevertheless, Naum, this last of the Mohicans, maintains his belief in the truth of the commune no matter what the cost; he believes in an almost *compulsory* truth, and therein lies his tragedy. He is a formalist: sensing that the content is slipping out of his hands, he insists all the more stubbornly on the form. When he sees that the members are drunk, he is about to ask that the meeting be postponed; but when they shout that "we'll sort things out better if we're a bit stewed" he submits: "The commune has made its decision; one can't go against it." He is fully and painfully aware that in essence the wretched clerk they have hired, Levanid Ignatych, is the only one who matters and that the meeting will make the decision as ordered by the businessman's clerk. But still the old man maintains his self-deceit despite himself: he dismisses Levanid from the chair of the meeting and takes over himself, giving the clerk a reprimand for his rude remarks about the commune.

A few honest voices are raised on Vanka's behalf, commending him as a good, sensible lad whom the commune needs and who ought to be spared; then the drunken voice of an old man pipes up, "Well, if he's the best we've got, we ought to make him a recruit!" This is now a conscious mockery of justice, a flaunting of injustice, a game.... A judge is making a joke of himself, and in a case that concerns the fate of a man! Naum hears this and of course realizes that his "commune" is coming to its end. Ivan's mother is standing there. She is not yet an old woman and is strong and proud. She has been a widow since she was a young woman. As a widow she has been intimidated and wronged by the commune. But she has endured everything, has set her little house in order, and has raised her only beloved son, Vanya, to be her joy and consolation; now she hears how the commune is taking away her last hope and her last joy, her son. Naum Egorych, foreseeing the drunken, wanton decision of the commune, quickly tells Stepanida: "Ekh, what's to be done! The commune's got the authority! You've got to plead with them, Stepanida; plead with the commune!" But she is not willing to beg. She stubbornly accuses the commune of an unjust decision, taken while drunk and having been bribed, and of envy of her Vanya. "Now, Stepanida, you'll only make them more angry at you!" Naum exclaims in alarm. "Do you think I'd do this if I saw any law or conscience here, Naum Egorych," Stepanida replies. "It's only vodka talking! If I thought I could win any sympathy I'd scrape my knees on the bare ground; I'd wash the floor of the hut with my tears; I'd break my head bowing to the ground to them! But you can't change their minds and get them to take pity! Can't you see: this has all been set up and prearranged. They're a flock of crows who want to get rid of my bright falcon; they'll peck him to death! You people sell your souls for vodka! What do you worship? Vodka! Whoever brings you the most has bought your vote. Don't you see, Vanya, that you've offended that fat merchant? Don't the rest of you know that that merchant sneaked in drunk to bring shame on Vanya's bride? But you don't know about that! The merchant's vodka is good! You've got no shame, you bloodsuckers! You even blamed me for taking in a homeless orphan! But you won't have it your way! It won't happen! That there mediocor knows my Vanya and won't let him be wronged!" (She exits hastily.)

The proud woman is one of the characters our poet is most successful at portraying. Say what you will, gentlemen, but this is a powerful scene. Of course, it's a Russian village and the character is a simple peasant woman who cannot even speak correctly; but, my Lord, this monologue about scraping the skin from her knees "if she thought she could win any sympathy" is worth many an emotional scene from similar tragedies. There are no classical phrases here, no beautiful language, no white coverlet, and no burning

black eyes of a Rachel; yet I tell you that if we had our own Rachel
you would have shuddered in the theater at the unvarnished truth
of this scene of a mother cursing the communal court. The scene
ends with a significant movement: they run off to the "mediocor"
to find justice and to complain to him of the commune's decision,
and this is a depressing warning.

It is scarcely necessary to point out any more of the best scenes
of this work. But I cannot resist sharing my impression and will
say plainly that rarely have I read anything more powerful and
more tragic than the finale of Act Four.

The victim, Masha, who has been sold to the businessman by
her mother and brother, has already been drugged and is lying
unconscious on the stove. Matryosha, this artless criminal, climbs
onto the stove to have a look and—almost joyfully, almost convinced
that she has now made Masha happy—announces to the businessman: "She's ready! She wouldn't move even if you cut her to
pieces!" The clerk Levanid, the businessman's friend, gets up and
leaves. "What a life you merchants have," he says enviously. And
now, before approaching his victim, the businessman is seized by
an almost poetic feeling: "It's 'cause we're a power now!" he
exclaims lasciviously and significantly. "Whatever we want we can
do! If a merchant gets a notion to do something nowadays then he
can do it, 'cause we're a power!" "You're a power, true enough!"
the victim's brother agrees. Then the superfluous characters leave
the hut, the wretched scoundrel creeps toward Masha, while the
drunken mother who has sold her innocent daughter, the unfortunate Vanya's fiancée, falls asleep in a drunken stupor on the floor
at the feet of the utterly drunken father of this happy family. *Strong
Drink Every Day Keeps Fortune Away!*

I will not list all the other features of this terrible picture which
strike you with their truth, such as the criminals who scarcely are
aware of their crime, or those who are aware but who no longer
have the right to condemn their crime, such as the drunken father,
for example, whom the daughter tragically accuses to his face and
whom she curses. . . . There are some remarkably subtle observations here: when Masha comes to her senses, she first wants to kill
herself; then, however, she puts on the silk sarafan which the
businessman has left for her with her mother, but puts it on out
of malignant joy, *to torment herself*, to inflict even more pain on
herself as if to say, "You see, I've become a trollop myself now!"

Here is the conversation of the "innocent" mother and the "innocent" Matryosha on the day after the tragedy:

Matryoshka (enters): Good day to you, Aunt Arina! How are things here? I have to tell you I was scared to call on you yesterday!

Arina: Oh-h, my girl, what a dreadful time we've had! It was awful! When she found out in the morning she grabbed a knife and almost killed us all with her own hand; and then she wanted to do herself in! We had an awful time trying to calm her down! She doesn't even want to set eyes on Styopka now.

Matryoshka: He was telling me!

Arina: Well, toward evening she settled down, you see, and now she's like a stone! "God's punished me for Matryoshka," she says, "and now I'm just like her." Just now I gave her the sarafan—the one that Silanty Savelich bought from you—and she put it on. "I've turned into Matryoshka," she says, "so I should put on her sarafan." That's how things are.

Matryoshka: Where is she now?

Arina: Oh, my girl, she's gone off to the shed and crawled into the straw; *she's laying there with her face buried in it.*

Matryoshka: I hope she doesn't do anything foolish to herself when she's not in her senses!

But the victim did not kill herself: "I got scared," she says later. Our poet has a depth of psychological insight into the People. Take Vanya, who returns unexpectedly from the mediator after a day's absence. For the sake of real truth the poet did not spare his hero: in the first moments Ivan is in a state of bestial rage; he holds Masha alone to be responsible, he is unjust and hateful; but when at last he understands what has really happened, he proposes, as if despite himself, that Masha marry him even *so*. But our author knows all too well that this is almost unthinkable, given the customs of our People, at least if the relationship is an honest one. A girl who has been dishonored, even through deceit and even through no fault of her own, is still considered to be unclean if not completely dishonorable. And Masha herself is proud: "Don't dirty yourself with me, Vanya!" she cries. "Go away! Farewell, Vanya!" And then, in the last monologue, she quickly goes to the table, pours a glass of vodka, casts a burning glance at everyone, and cries with a desperate, malicious, outlandish glee: "Well, why are you so down in the mouth? Be glad—you've done your job! Momma! Daddy! Let's drink and have a good time! You won't have to go hanging about the taverns alone now, Dad, you can go with your daughter! It was lonely for you to drink by yourself, Momma, but now there's the two of us! Let the liquor flow! Let it drown my grief and my conscience!"

And she raises the glass to her lips. So ends the drama.

I'm not saying that there are no flaws here; but this work has so many genuine merits that its flaws are almost without significance. For example, Masha's tone in the monologue of Act Four—which she ends with a beguiling and lofty rush of spirit: "Now it has become so easy!"—is rather too melodic. It's true that this is scarcely even a monologue but a reflection or a feeling—one of those same reflections and feelings whose influence has led Russians with heart and poetry to compose all the songs of the Russian People. Therefore Masha's reflection, which in essence is utterly faithful and natural, could have taken a rather lyrical form. But art has its limitations and rules, and the monologue might have been shorter. Perhaps Masha's tone at the end of the play, after the catastrophe, is not entirely true either: it would have been better had she spoken just a bit less. Her father's terrible words would have had much stronger effect if they had also been fewer and not so melodious. But all that can be remedied; the author can certainly correct that in the second edition, and, I repeat, in comparison with the work's indisputable merits all these things are little more than trifles. It would also be good if the author were to eliminate altogether from his play the appearance at the end (quite unnecessarily) of the virtuous old factory owner who virtually sermonizes about our "debts to the People." His being here is all the more absurd since he is the very same factory owner who has enslaved the entire population of the area, who harasses them with arbitrary fines and feeds his workers rotten food. Finally, the master of the house, Zakhar, has emerged rather ambiguously. There is something false, unexplained, and stiff in his own explanation of why he took to drink; the matter could be conveyed much more simply and naturally.

However, this is only my opinion and I may be wrong; but I am certain that I am not wrong about the solid merits of this serious work. I am only too pleased to share my impressions with the readers. Nothing more serious than this, at least, has appeared recently—and perhaps for quite a long time—in our literature. . . .

13

Little Pictures

I

Summer, school holidays; dust and heat, heat and dust. It is unpleasant to stay in the city. Everyone has left. The other day I was
about to get on with reading the pile of manuscripts that has
accumulated in the editorial office. . . . But I'll postpone my remarks
about manuscripts, although I do have something to say about
them. One wants fresh air, leisure, freedom; but instead of fresh
air and freedom I find myself wandering alone aimlessly along
streets covered with sand and lime, feeling as if insulted by someone—truly, a feeling rather like that. As we all know, half of our
problems vanish if we can only find someone to blame for them,
and it's all the more vexing when there's really no one to be
found. . . .

The other day I was crossing from the sunny to the shady side
of Nevsky Prospect. As you know, you always cross Nevsky Prospect carefully or else you may be run over in a moment; you jockey
for position, look carefully around, and seize the moment before
launching off on the dangerous journey; you wait for a tiny gap in
the rush of carriages two or three lanes wide. In winter—two or
three days before Christmas, for instance—crossing the Prospect is
particularly interesting: you take a great risk, especially if a frosty
white fog has covered the city since dawn so that you scarcely can
make out a passerby three paces away. And so you somehow slip
through the first lanes of carriages and cabs rushing toward the
Police Bridge, happy that you no longer have to worry about them;
the hoofbeats, rumblings, and hoarse cries of the coachmen are
left behind, but there's no time for rejoicing: you have only reached
the midpoint of the dangerous crossing, while risk and the unknown

await you. You cast a hasty, anxious glance and quickly determine how to slip through the second lane of carriages rushing in the direction of the Anichkov Bridge. But you sense that there is no time for thinking, and besides, there is this hellish fog: all you can hear are hoofbeats and shouts and can see no farther than a couple of yards around you. And then—suddenly, unexpectedly—out of the fog come urgent, rapidly approaching, harsh sounds, fearful and ominous at this moment and very like the noise of six or seven people chopping cabbage in a vat. "Where to go? Ahead or back? Will I have time or not?" And lucky for you that you stood still: out of the fog only a pace away from you suddenly emerges the gray snout of a hotly breathing trotting horse, rushing madly with the speed of an express train; there's foam on the bit, the shaft-bow is jutting out, the reins are taut, while the lovely strong legs quickly, evenly, and steadily measure off a *sazhen* at every pace. A moment passes, there is the desperate cry of the coachman, and everything flashes and flies past, from the fog and into the fog again—the hoofbeats, the chopping sounds, the cries have all disappeared again like a vision. An authentically Petersburg vision! You cross yourself and now, almost scorning the second lane of carriages which so frightened you for a moment, quickly reach the welcome sidewalk still all a-tremble from what you have experienced and—oddly enough—deriving at the same time some inexplicable pleasure from it, certainly not because you have escaped the danger, but simply because you were subjected to it. It is a retroactive pleasure, I don't dispute, and one that in our age is useless besides, the more so that one ought to be protesting and not feeling pleasure, for the trotting horse is certainly not some liberal thing; it brings to mind the hussar or the merchant on a spree and, accordingly, notions of inequality, high-handedness, *la tyrannie*, and so on. I know that and don't dispute it; I merely want to finish my thought. And so the other day, with the usual winter caution, I was about to cross the Nevsky Prospect when suddenly, snapping out of my reverie, I stopped in amazement in the very middle of the crossing: there was no one around, not a single carriage, not even some cabbie's rattling droshky! The street was empty for two hundred yards in either direction; one might even stop to discuss Russian literature with a friend, so little was the danger! It was an insult, even! When have we ever seen such a thing?

Dust and heat, astonishing odors, torn-up pavement, and buildings being remodeled. It's more and more common now to touch up the façade to make it look stylish and distinct. I'm amazed by the architecture of our day. In fact, all of Petersburg's architecture is remarkably characteristic and distinct and always impressed me specifically by the fact that it expresses all the lack of character and personality typical of the city over the entire period of its existence. In a positive sense, what is typical and unique to Petersburg are only these little decaying wooden houses, which still survive, sometimes on even the most elegant streets next to enormous mansions, and which stand out as glaringly as a pile of firewood beside a marble palazzo. As far as the palazzi are concerned, it is precisely in them that we see all the lack of character of the idea and all the negativity of the essence of the Petersburg period from its very beginning to its end. In that sense, there is no such city as Petersburg; from the point of view of architecture, it is a reflection of all the architectural styles of the world and of all periods and fashions; everything has been, bit by bit, borrowed and distorted in its own way. In these buildings you can read as in a book all the currents of all the great and trivial ideas that, appropriately or accidentally, have landed here from Europe and that gradually overcame and captured us. Here we see the pallid architecture of churches of the last century; here is a pitiful imitation in Roman style from the beginning of our century; here we see a building that seems to have come from the Renaissance era; and there is an example of the ancient Byzantine style, supposedly discovered by the architect Ton during the reign of Nicholas I. And then we see some more buildings—hospitals, institutes, and even palaces from the first decades of our century; these are in the style of Napoleon I—immense, pseudomajestic and unbelievably boring; there is something labored and contrived in the style which, like the bees on Napoleon's mantle, is supposed to express the majesty of the new epoch that had then just begun and the unprecedented dynasty with its pretentions to existence in perpetuity. And then we see some houses, or palaces almost, belonging to certain of our noble families but products of a much later period. These are built in the manner of some Italian palazzi or in the not entirely pure French style of the prerevolutionary era. But in the Venetian or Roman palazzi in Italy, whole generations of Italian families have lived out their days, one after the other, over the course of centuries. Our palazzi, however, were installed only during the last reign, but also with pretensions to permanence, it seems: the order of things that had been established at that time

seemed only too solid and reassuring, and the appearance of these
palazzi seemed to express all that faith: they, too, were intended
to last for ages. However, this all came almost on the eve of the
Crimean War, and then followed the liberation of the peasants. . . .
I will be very sad if, someday, on one of these palaces I see the
sign of a tavern and pleasure garden or a French hotel for travelers.
And, finally, look at the architecture of this enormous, modern
hotel. Here we see the businesslike approach, Americanism, hundreds of rooms, an immense commercial enterprise; one sees immediately that we, too, have railways and we have suddenly found
ourselves to be businessmen. And now . . . truly, I don't know how
to define our current architecture. We have some sort of disorderly
style here which, however, entirely corresponds to the disorder of
the present moment. We have a vast number of very tall (and above
all, they must be tall) buildings for tenants, buildings with very
thin walls, so they say, and cheaply built, with an amazing variety
of styles of façades: we see Rastrelli and late rococo, doge balconies
and windows which absolutely must be œils-de-bœuf and absolutely
must have five stories—and all this in one single façade. "Now
then, my friend, you've got to put in a doge window for me; I'm
no worse than one of them raggedy doges, am I? And you've got
to build me five stories so's I can take in tenants: a window is one
thing, but I've got to have five stories; I can't go wasting all my
money on playthings." However, I'm not a Petersburg feuilletonist
and this wasn't at all what I started to talk about. I began with
manuscripts in the editor's office and went off on something
unrelated.

2

Dust and heat. I've heard that several parks and amusement centers, where one can get a breath of fresh air, have been opened for
those who are spending the summer in Petersburg. I don't know
if there is any fresh air to breathe there because I still have not
visited any of them. It's better, stuffier, and sadder in Petersburg.
You can walk around, pondering things in utter solitude, and this
is better than the fresh air of the Petersburg amusement parks.
Besides, very many parks and gardens have suddenly been opened
in the city and in places where one never expected them. On almost
every street now you can find a gate which often has a heap of
lime and bricks beside it, with a sign: "Entrance to the tavern
garden." There in the courtyard some forty years ago a little plot

ten paces by five had been fenced off in front of some decrepit outbuilding. And so this is now the "tavern garden." Tell me, why is it so much more melancholy in Petersburg on Sundays than on weekdays? Is it because of the vodka? The drunkenness? Is it because drunken peasants lie about and sleep on Nevsky Prospect in broad daylight—or at least in the evening, as I've seen myself? I don't think so. Working people who are out drinking don't bother me, and, having stayed on in Petersburg, now I've become quite accustomed to them, although formerly I couldn't abide them and even hated them. On holidays they walk around the streets drunk— whole crowds of them at times—pushing people and stumbling into them; and this is not because they want to create a row but just because a drunken man cannot help but stumble into people and push them. They curse out loud despite the crowds of women and children they pass; and this not from rudeness but just because a drunken man can have no other language than a foul one. And this really is a language, a whole language—as I recently became convinced; it is the language most convenient, original, and best suited for one who is drunk or even tipsy, so that it absolutely had to come into being; and if it did not exist—*il faudrait l'inventer.* I'm quite serious here. Just consider. As we know, the first thing that happens to a drunken person is that his tongue becomes tied and moves sluggishly; however, the flow of thoughts and sensations of a drunken man—or at least of anyone who is not as drunk as a cobbler—increases by almost ten. And therefore there is a natural need to find the sort of language that can satisfy both these, mutually contradictory, states. Ages and ages ago this language was found and accepted all over Russia. Purely and simply, it is one noun not found in the dictionary, so that the entire language consists of but one word that can be pronounced with remarkable ease. One Sunday, quite late in the evening, I happened to be walking some fifteen paces away from a group of six drunken tradesmen; suddenly I realized that it was possible to express all thoughts, sensations, and even entire, profound propositions using only this one noun which, besides, has very few syllables. One of the lads first pronounces this noun sharply and forcefully to express his scornful dismissal of something they had been discussing earlier. Another replies by repeating this same noun, but now in quite a different tone and sense—specifically, in the sense that he thoroughly doubts the expediency of the first lad's denial. A third one becomes indignant at what the first has said; sharply and excitedly, he gets into the discussion, shouting out this same noun, but now in the sense of disparagement and abuse. The second fellow again interrupts, angry at the third, who's offended him, and stops him as if to say: "Why do you have to stick your oar in, chum? We've been having quite a discussion here; what d'you mean by getting on to our Filka!" And this whole notion he expressed by using this same forbidden word, this same monosyllabic name of a certain object, and raised his hand to take the third fellow by the shoulder. But then, suddenly, the fourth lad, the youngest of the group, who had kept silent to this point but who probably had found the solution to the original problem that had caused the dispute, raised his arm and shouted. . . . "Eureka!" you might think. "I've got it! I've got it!" No, it wasn't eureka, and he hadn't got it. He only went on repeating this same noun, not found in the dictionary; just one word, only a single word, but with delight, with a scream of rapture, and, it seems, a little too exuberantly, because the sixth, a morose fellow and the eldest of them, didn't like the sound of it and at once put a stop to the youngster's delight by turning to him and repeating in a gloomy, didactic bass . . . that same noun which isn't mentioned in the presence of ladies and which clearly and accurately signified: "What're you bawling about?" And so, without having said anything else at all, they repeated this same little word of theirs six times in succession and understood one another completely. This is a fact that I witnessed myself. "Have mercy!" I shouted at them suddenly, without knowing why (I was in the middle of a crowd of people). "You've not walked more than ten paces and you've used (and I used the word) six times! That's disgraceful! Aren't you ashamed of yourselves?"

They all stared at me as people stare at something utterly unexpected and fell silent for a moment; I thought they would begin abusing me, but they didn't. Only the youngest, after walking some ten paces more, suddenly turned to me and shouted as he walked, "So why'd you have to say it one more time when you've already heard it six times from us?"

A burst of laughter rang out and the group went on, paying no more attention to me.

3

No, it's not such people who've been out drinking that I'm talking about, and it's not those who make me so sad on Sundays. I was most surprised to discover not long ago that there are peasants, townspeople, and tradesmen in Petersburg who are quite sober, who do not "indulge" at all, even on Sundays; and it wasn't specifically that which astonished me, but the fact that there are many more of them, it seems, than I had heretofore suspected. Now these people I find an even more melancholy sight than the drunken revelers, and that's not because I feel sorry for the sober people; there's certainly no reason to feel sorry for them; yet some strange ideas come into one's mind. . . . Toward evening on Sundays (you never see them at all on weekdays) a great many such people, who have been busily working all week and who are absolutely sober, come out onto the streets. They come out specifically to take walks. I have noticed that they never go to the Nevsky but tend to take strolls near their homes or amble along as they and their families return from visiting somewhere. (It seems there are also many tradesmen with families in Petersburg). They proceed sedately with terribly serious faces, looking not at all as if they were out for a stroll; they say little to one another—husbands and wives particularly say scarcely a word to one another—but they are always dressed in their Sunday best. Their clothes are poor and old; the women wear colorful dresses; but everything has been cleaned and washed for the holiday, specifically, perhaps, for this very hour. There are some in Russian dress, but many men wear German clothes and are clean-shaven. What I find most annoying is that it seems they really and truly believe they are enjoying a genuine holiday treat in taking such a promenade. But what sort of a treat could it be on this broad, bare, dusty street where the dust hangs in the air even after sunset? That's just my point: as far as they are concerned, this is paradise; so, to each his own.

Very often they have children with them; there are also very many children in Petersburg, and people still say that terrible numbers of them die off here. As I could see, they are mostly very young and have barely learned to walk or cannot yet walk at all. Could it be that there are so few older children because they do not survive infancy? Here I see among the crowd a single trades-man, but with a child, a little boy; they are by themselves, and both have such a lonely look about them. The man is about thirty and has a haggard and unhealthy face. He is dressed in his Sunday best: a German frock coat, worn at the seams, with shabby buttons and a very greasy collar; his trousers are "accidental" third-hand ones acquired at the flea market but cleaned up as well as can be. A calico shirtfront, a tie, a top hat (very rumpled); he is clean-shaven. Probably he works in some locksmith's shop or does something in a printing office. His expression is doleful and gloomy, pensive, harsh, and almost angry. He holds the child's hand and the child toddles along behind him, scarcely able to keep his balance. He's a little boy a bit more than two years old, very feeble and pale but wearing a little caftan and boots with red trim and a cap with a little peacock feather. He is tired; the father has said something to him; perhaps it was just a remark but it sounds as if he raised his voice. The boy grew quiet. But they went on another five paces and the father bent down, carefully picked up the child, and carried him in his arms. The child clung to the father trustingly, as if this were a matter of habit; he put his right arm around his father's neck and began to stare at me with childish amazement, as if to say, "Why are you following us and staring that way?" I was about to nod to him and smile but he frowned and clung even more tightly to his father's neck. It appears that the two are great friends.

When I wander about the streets I enjoy examining certain total strangers, studying their faces and trying to guess who they are, how they live, what they work at, and what is on their minds at this particular moment. When I looked at the tradesman and his son I got the idea that the wife must have died only a month ago and, for some reason, I thought it must have been of consumption. The motherless little boy (the father works all week in the shop) is looked after for the time being by some old woman who lives in the basement where they rent a wretched little room, or perhaps only a space in the corner. And now, on Sunday, the widower and his son have gone somewhere far away on the Vyborg side to their only remaining relative—most likely the late wife's sister, whom they rather rarely visited before; she's married to some noncommissioned officer with a wound stripe and she certainly must live in some enormous government building, also in the basement but in her own apartment. She, perhaps, heaved a few sighs over her late sister, but not many; the widower also probably did not spend overly long in grieving during his visit but was gloomy all the while, spoke rarely and little; he certainly must have turned the conversation to some particular point concerning his work but soon left off talking of that as well. They must have put on the samovar and drunk their tea in Russian style, sucking little bits of sugar.

The boy sat on a bench in the corner the whole time, frowning and shy, until at last he fell asleep. His aunt and her husband paid little attention to him, but they finally gave him a bit of milk and bread. The host—the sergeant who until now had paid no attention to him—made some joke about the child as a mark of affection, but something very risqué and inappropriate; he himself (and only he) laughed at it, while the widower, on the contrary, at that same moment, for some unknown reason, sternly raised his voice at the boy, the result of which was that the latter felt a sudden need for the toilet; thereupon the father, no longer scolding and with a serious air, carried him out of the room for a moment. . . . They said their goodbyes in the same gloomy and solemn manner as they had carried on their conversation, observing all the polite conventions of decorum. The father took up the child in his arms and carried him home, from the Vyborg side to the Liteiny. Tomorrow he'll again be in the shop and the boy will be with the old woman. And so you walk around and about and imagine all sorts of idle pictures like this for your own diversion. It's a pointless occupation, and "nothing edifying can be derived therefrom." And that is why my spirits sink on Sundays in vacation time on the dusty and gloomy Petersburg streets. What, hasn't it occurred to you that the streets in Petersburg are gloomy? I think that this must be the gloomiest city that can possibly exist in the world!

It's true that on weekdays as well a great many children are brought out, but toward evening on Sundays there are almost ten times as many of them on the streets. How haggard, pale, sickly, and anemic they are, and what gloomy little faces they have, especially those who are still being carried; those who are already walking all have crooked legs and flounder along rocking from side to side. Almost all of them have been carefully dressed, however. But good heavens, a child is like a little flower or a leaf on a tree in spring: it needs light, air, freedom, room to grow, fresh food; but instead of all these things there is the stuffy basement with some odor of kvass or cabbage, a dreadful stench at night, food that does not nourish, cockroaches and fleas, raw dampness that seeps from the walls, and outside only dust, bricks, and lime.

But they love their pale and sickly children. Here's a little three-year-old girl, a pretty little thing in a clean dress; she's hurrying to her mother who is sitting by the gate amid a large group of people who have come out of the building to chat for an hour or two. The mother is busy talking but keeps her eye on the child,

who is playing some ten paces away. The girl bends down to pick
up something—a little pebble of some sort—and accidentally steps
on the hem of her skirt; now she simply can't straighten up. She
tries twice and then falls down and starts to cry. The mother was
about to get up to help her, but I picked up the little girl first.
She straightened, cast a quick and curious glance at me, still with
tears in her eyes, and then, a bit afraid and embarrassed, quickly
ran back to her mother. I approached and politely inquired how
old the girl was; the mother replied affably enough but with great
reserve. I remarked that I had a little girl of the same age, but no
reply followed. "You may very well be a good man," the mother's
silent glance told me, "but what are you doing standing here?
You'd best be on your way." All the people who had been talking
also fell silent and seemed to be thinking the same thing. I touched
my hat and went on.

Here, on a busy intersection, another little girl has lagged behind
her mother, who until now had been holding her hand. True, the
peasant woman suddenly spotted some fifteen paces away a friend
who was coming to visit her and, trusting that the child knew the
way, she let go of her hand and rushed off to meet her visitor. But
the child, thus suddenly abandoned, took fright and began to cry,
running tearfully to catch up with her mother.

A gray-haired and bearded passerby—a total stranger—stopped
the running woman and seized her hand: "Why are you rushing
off so? Can't you see the child crying back there? You mustn't do
that! The girl might get frightened."

The woman wanted to make some sharp reply but thought better
of it; with no sign of annoyance or impatience, she picked up the
little girl who came running to her and now walked sedately toward
her visitor. The man looked on sternly until he saw the outcome
and then went on his way.

Pointless, quite pointless little scenes, which I'm almost ashamed
to set down in my diary. From now on I'll try to be much more
serious.

14

To a Teacher

A Moscow columnist in our Petersburg *Voice* (no. 210) has taken me to task for my last three "little pictures" (*The Citizen*, no. 29). Motivated, apparently, by feelings of delicacy, he objects that in my second scene, when I spoke about the foul language of our people when drunk, I referred to—but of course did not name—a certain indecent object.... "I never imagined the depths to which a columnist could sink when he has no proper material at hand," says my Moscow complainant about me. And so it turns out that I resorted to something indecent solely to enliven my column and give it some zest, some cayenne pepper....

Now that makes me sad; and all the while I was thinking that people would draw the very opposite conclusion from my column, i.e., that from a great deal of material I derived only a little. I thought that the title would save me: little pictures, not large ones; people don't expect so much from little ones. And so I jotted down only a few sad thoughts about the way our Petersburg working classes spend their spare time. The sparseness of their joys and entertainments; the poverty of their spiritual lives; the basements where they raise their pale, scrofulous children; the boring, broad Petersburg streets—straight as arrows—as places for their walks; this young tradesman-widower with his child in his arms (an actual picture)—all that seemed to me material enough for a feuilleton so that, I repeat, I might have been accused of something quite the opposite, i.e., that I did little with such an abundance of material. I was consoled by the fact that I managed at least to suggest my main conclusion: that among the vast majority of our People—even the ones in Petersburg basements, even given the most impoverished spiritual environment—there still is a striving for dignity, for a certain decency, for genuine self-respect; love for the family and

263

for children is being preserved. I was especially struck by the fact
that they so truly and even tenderly love their sickly children; I
was specifically cheered by the thought that disorders and abuses
in our People's family life, even amid circumstances such as those
in Petersburg, are still exceptions—numerous though they may be—
and wanted to share this fresh impression with the readers. Just
at that time I had read in a newspaper column a very frank admission from a highly intelligent man regarding a certain book of
an official nature that had come out. The column argued that to
discuss whether the reform had or had not benefited the People
was essentially a waste of time: even if the reform had been of no
benefit to the People it was no matter—let everything go to blazes,
since the reform had to happen (and there may be a good deal of
truth in that, on the principle of *pereat mundus*, despite the way
the question was put). And finally, as far as the People—the peasants—are concerned, the columnist admitted very plainly that "in
fact it is quite true that our People themselves did not deserve the
reform . . . and that if, before the reform, in literature and journalism
we and Messrs. Marko Vovchok and Grigorovich crowned our peasants with roses and laurels, we know full well that we placed these
crowns on heads infested with lice. . . . But that was necessary at
the time in order to rouse enthusiasm for the cause," etc., etc. That
is the essence of the idea (which I did not quote literally) expressed
in the column with such frankness and without the least trace of
the former polite formulas. I must admit that these remarks are
even too frank; their starkness, which is made evident almost for
the first time with such satisfaction, put me in a most curious
disposition, and I recall that I decided then that though we in *The
Citizen*, for instance, may well agree with the first part of this
notion—the reform was needed no matter what the consequences—
still in no way can we agree with the second part of this fateful
notion, and we are firmly convinced that these lice-ridden heads
were still worthy of the reform and were in no way beneath it. I
think that such a conviction can make up one of the characteristic
features of our own point of view; that is why I mention it now.

As far as my feuilleton is concerned. . . . By the way, I don't know
why the Moscow columnist, my fellow writer, thinks that I am
ashamed to be called a feuilletonist and states in French that I am
"plus feuilletoniste que Jules Janin, plus catholique que le pape."
This bit of French from Moscow is put here to make people think
that the author is a fellow of proper form, but I still don't understand

why he labels me as one of the Roman Catholic persuasion and why he needed to bring the poor pope into it. As far as I am concerned, I only stated that I was not a "Petersburg" feuilletonist; and by this I meant only to indicate for the future that I don't intend to write only about Petersburg life in particular; accordingly, there's no reason to expect very detailed accounts of that life from me whenever I find it necessary to talk about it. If my Moscow teacher absolutely must call my *Diary* a feuilleton, then he's free to do so; I'm quite content with that.

My Moscow teacher assures us that my feuilleton created quite a furor in Moscow "in the market stalls and in Zariade" and calls it a "shopkeeper's" feuilleton. I'm very pleased that I provided so much enjoyment to the readers from those areas of our ancient capital. But the venom of his remarks comes from the assertion that supposedly I sought deliberately for sensation; not having any better educated readers, I sought some in Zariade, and with that in mind I wrote "*about that*" and, accordingly, I am "the most resourceful of all the feuilletonists. . . ."

> "I just can't figure it out [writes the teacher, telling of the effect of my feuilleton in Moscow]—I can't figure it out; it's truly amazing that everybody wants to get his hands on this issue of *The Citizen*," said one of our newspaper sellers in surprise as he answered my question about the demand for *The Citizen*. When I explained the reason to him, the newsboy ran off to Mecklenburg and Zhivarev, our newspaper dealers, to pick up all their remaining issues; but they had also sold out. "People in the market stalls and Zariade keep asking for it. . . . " The fact is that the central shopping district has heard the news that *The Citizen* has printed an article *about that*, and so all the shopkeepers, instead of buying *Entertainment*, have rushed to pick up a *Citizen*.

Listen, that's not bad news at all, and you're wasting your time trying to shame me about having readers among the shopkeepers. Quite the contrary: I would very much like to win their favor since I certainly don't have the same low opinion of them as you. You see, they bought the paper to have a good laugh and also because there was a commotion over it. Everyone pounces on a commotion; it's the nature of every human being, especially in Russia (you, for example, pounced on it at once); so I think that one mustn't reserve any particular scorn for the shopkeepers over that. As far as amusement and having a laugh are concerned, there are various

forms of amusement and various kinds of laughter, even in matters
that may be quite unseemly. My teacher qualifies his remarks,
however; he adds: "I am certain that the pen of the author of the
'little pictures *about that*' was guided by the best of intentions when
it wrote this shopkeeper's feuilleton." In other words, the teacher
gives me credit by allowing that when I mentioned *that*, I was not
motivated directly and principally by a desire to corrupt the People.
I thank him for this, at least; since the author is writing in *The
Voice*, this magnanimous qualification is, perhaps, meaningful,
since I know from experience that its publisher, Andrei Aleksandrovich, would not think twice about accusing me of whatever he
pleases, even of intentions of corrupting the Russian People and
Russian society. (He has, after all, accused me of supporting serfdom.) Andrei Aleksandrovich's influence also showed itself in the
implications of your startling remark: "... and if such 'little pictures' of yours will do nothing to contribute to the reform of in-
ebriated workers...," you say. This thought comes straight from
the head of Andrei Aleksandrovich! Why, he gets the notion that
I was writing with the direct and immediate purpose of correcting
the bad language of our foul-mouthed working people! But, you
see, they've never even heard of you and me, nor even of Andrei
Aleksandrovich—these workers I wrote about in my feuilleton!

No, I had something different in mind when I wrote about that
"noun which is not mentioned in the presence of ladies but which
is most commonly used among drunkards," and I insist that I had
a rather serious and justifiable intention, and I will prove it to you.
My idea was to show the uncorruptedness of the Russian People,
to show that if our People do use bad language when drunk (for
when sober they use it much, much less frequently) then they do
so not out of love for obscene words and not from the pleasure of
profanity but simply from a foul habit which has become almost
a necessity, so that even those notions and feelings which are the
furthest from profanity are expressed in profane language. I went
on to point out that the main reason for this habit of profanity
must be sought in drunkenness. You may think whatever you like
of my surmise on the necessity—when one is drunk and the tongue
does not move freely and yet one has a strong urge to talk—to
resort to the shortest, most conventional, and most expressive
words; but that our People are uncorrupted even when they do use
profanity—that was worth pointing out. I even make so bold as to
affirm that the aesthetically and intellectually developed levels of

our society are incomparably more corrupted in this sense than
our coarse and very backward common People. In masculine society, even of the highest circles—even among gray-haired and
bemedaled old men—it sometimes happens after dinner, when important topics and sometimes even matters of state are discussed,
that little by little the conversation turns to somewhat risqué subjects. These subjects, in turn, soon degenerate into such abomination, such foul language, and such foul thoughts that the
imagination of the People would never conceive of the like. This
happens very often among all groups of this circle that stands so
high above the People. Men who are known as paragons of virtue,
even devoutly religious men, even the most romantic poets—they
all participate eagerly in such conversations. What is most important here is the fact that certain of these men are unquestionably
upright and do many good deeds as well. What appeals to them
is the obscenity of it and the refinement of that obscenity; not so
much the profane word, as the idea which that word contains; they
like the depth of the degradation; they like, specifically, the stench,
just as a refined epicure likes Limburger cheese (something unknown to the People); they have the urge to smear it around, to
inhale and revel in the odor. They laugh; and of course they speak
condescendingly of this abomination; but it is obvious that they
like it and cannot do without it, even if it be only in words. The
People have a different kind of laughter, even when it is about
those same topics. I am sure that in our Zariade people did not
laugh for the sake of the abomination, nor from love of *that and
the art of it*; their laughter was extremely simple-hearted and not
depraved; healthy, though coarse; entirely unlike the laughter of
some of those who spread filth in our society or in our literature.
The People use profanity to no purpose and often when talking
about things that are not at all indecent. Our People are not corrupt
and are *even very pure,* despite the fact that they are unquestionably
the greatest users of profanity in the whole world—and, truly, it
is worth giving a little thought to this contradiction.

My Moscow teacher finishes his remarks in his feuilleton about
me with extraordinary, almost satanic pride:

> I shall utilize the example of my esteemed colleague [he means me]
> when I have to write a feuilleton and have no material and shall try
> then to create some "little pictures" [what contempt!] of my own;
> but at the present moment I have no need to take advantage of the

example he offers [i.e., a clever person always has lots of ideas without *that*], because even though we in Moscow also have "heat and dust," "dust and heat" [the opening words of my feuilleton—quoted to try to shame me once more], still, from out of this dust [Aha! Here he's getting to the point; now he's going to show us what a clever Moscow journalist can find even in "this dust," as compared to Petersburg's] and from beneath this heat [What does that mean—"from beneath this heat"?] one can, with a certain amount of attention [Just listen to him!], perceive that the living pulse of our renowned city, which weakens palpably in the summer, begins to beat stronger so that, ever gaining strength, it reaches in the winter months an intensity which the pulse of Moscow life can no longer surpass.

Now what an idea! That's how it is in our Moscow! And what a lesson for me! And do you know what, teacher? I can't help but think that you deliberately seized upon my remarks about *that* specifically to add some entertainment value to your feuilleton as well (otherwise, why all your intensity?); perhaps you even envied my success in Zariade. This is indeed very possible. Otherwise you would not have dug so deeply into the matter and smeared around so much filth by referring to it so many times. Not only did you mention it and smear it around, you even had a good smell yourself: "... still, we are mature enough at least to be able to smell when we are served up something that pierces the nose and can judge it despite the author's intentions...."
Now what does that smell like?

15

Something about Lying

Why is it that we all—every single one of us—tell lies? I'm convinced that people will stop me right there and shout: "Ah, what a lot of nonsense! Not everybody, certainly not! You don't have a topic and so you've thought that up for an effective opening." I've already been charged with failing to have a topic; but the point is that I truly am convinced of the universality of our lying. You live with an idea for fifty years, you see it and feel it, and suddenly it appears to you in such a light that you think you've never known it at all. Not long ago it suddenly dawned on me that in among our educated classes in Russia there can't be even a single person who doesn't lie. That is just because in Russia even entirely honest people can lie. I am convinced that among other nations, in their vast majority, only worthless people lie; they lie for practical advantage, that is, with direct criminal intent. But in Russia the most honest people can lie for no reason whatsoever and with the most honorable intentions. The vast majority of our lies are told for the sake of sociability. One wants to produce an aesthetic impression on the listener, to make him feel good, and so people lie, even sacrificing themselves to the listener, so to say. Let any one of you try to recall: haven't you, for instance, twenty times or more exaggerated the number of miles you've driven in an hour if you felt that this might please your listener? And wasn't your listener really pleased enough to avow at once that a certain troika he knew about had once outpaced a railway train on a bet, and so on, and so on? And what about hunting dogs, or how you were fitted for false teeth in Paris or how Botkin cured you? And haven't you told such marvels about your own illness that although you naturally began believing them yourself halfway through the story (for halfway through the story you always begin to believe it yourself), still,

when you went to bed that night recalling with satisfaction how
pleasantly impressed your listener had been, you couldn't help
saying, "Eh, what a pack of fibs I told!" However, that's a poor
example, for there's nothing more pleasant than to talk of one's
own illness if you can only find someone to listen; and once you've
begun to speak, it's just impossible not to lie; that even aids the
recovery. But when you've come back from abroad,, haven't you
told about the thousand things you've seen "with your own
eyes . . ."? However, let me take back that example as well: there's
no way a Russian returning from abroad can help exaggerating;
otherwise there would have been no point in going there. But what
about the natural sciences! Haven't you discussed the natural sciences or the bankruptcy and escapes abroad of various Petersburg
and other Yids without understanding anything at all about those
Yids and without the faintest idea about the natural sciences? Tell
me, now, haven't you told a story of something that supposedly
happened to you to the very same person who had once told it to
you, claiming that it had happened to him? Have you really forgotten how, in the middle of the story, you suddenly remembered
this and guessed what was happening and found confirmation of
it in the pained look your listener directed so intently at you (for
in such cases people for some reason stare at one another with ten
times the usual concentration); do you recall how, despite everything
and despite the fact that all the humor had now been lost, you
still—with the courage worthy of a great purpose—continued to
babble out your story and, finishing it hurriedly and with nervously
hasty politeness, handshakes and smiles, you each rushed off on
your separate ways so that when—right out of the blue—something
prompted you in your final paroxysm to shout down the stairs at
your fleeing listener some question about the health of his auntie,
he did not even turn around to reply; and this fact remained in
your memory as the most painful part of the entire incident? In
short, if anyone can answer *no* to all this—that is, that he has never
told any such stories, has never mentioned Botkin, never lied about
the Yids, never shouted down the stairs some question about the
health of auntie, and that nothing of this sort has ever happened
to him—then I simply won't believe it. I know that the Russian
liar very often lies without ever noticing it himself so that one may
not even be aware that he is lying. This is how it happens, you
see: no sooner will a person tell a lie and pass it off successfully,
than he'll take such a liking to it that he'll include the story among

the authentic facts of his personal life; and he acts utterly in good
conscience because he believes it fully himself; indeed, it would
sometimes be unnatural not to believe it.

"Eh, nonsense!" people will say once more. "These are just
trivial things, white lies; they're not of any universal significance."
That may be. I agree that this all seems very innocent and suggests
only noble traits of character—the feeling of gratitude, for instance.
Because if someone has listened to your lies, then you can't help
but let your listener tell you a few as well, if only from a sense of
gratitude.

The genteel mutual relationship that lying involves is virtually
the prime prerequisite of Russian society—of all Russian meetings,
gatherings, clubs, learned societies, and so on. In fact, it is only
some honest blockhead who will stand up for the truth in such
instances and suddenly begin to doubt the number of miles you
have driven or the marvels that Botkin has performed on you. But
these are only callous and hemorrhoidal fellows who are quickly
punished for what they have done and who later wonder why this
punishment befell them. They're mediocre people. Nevertheless,
all this lying, despite its innocent nature, so strongly suggests some
of our significant fundamental traits that we can almost see something universal emerging. For example: first, that we Russians are
above all afraid of the truth, or rather, we are not so much afraid
of it as we constantly feel that the truth is something far too dull
and prosaic for us and much too ordinary, and so, in constantly
evading it, we have at last transformed it into one of the most
unusual and rare things in our Russian world (I'm not talking
about the newspaper of that name). In this way we have entirely
abandoned the axiom that truth is the most poetic thing in the
world, especially truth in its purest form; moreover, it is even more
fantastic than anything the ingenious human mind is capable of
inventing and conceiving. In Russia the truth almost always has
an entirely fantastical character. In fact, people have finally reached
the point where all those things the human mind is forever and
ever lying to itself about are much more understandable than the
truth itself; and this is the case all over the world. The truth can
lie on the table right in front of people for a hundred years but
they won't pick it up; they go chasing after fabrications precisely
because they consider truth to be fantastic and utopian.

The second point that our universal Russian lying suggests is
that we are all ashamed of ourselves. Truly, every one of us carries

within an almost inborn shame of himself and his own face; and as soon as a Russian finds himself in society he at once tries as hard as he can to appear to be anything other than he in fact really is; everyone tries to put on an entirely different face.

Herzen has already said of Russians abroad that they simply do not know how to behave in public: they speak loudly when everyone else is quiet and do not know how to say anything politely and naturally when it is necessary to speak. And he is absolutely right: at once we see some distortion, a lie, a painful strain; at once we see the urge to feel shame for things as they actually are, to camouflage and conceal one's own God-given, Russian face and appear with a different one, as alien and un-Russian as possible. All of this comes from the most complete inner conviction that for every Russian his own face must certainly be insignificant and comic to the point of shame, and that if he puts on a French or English face—one not his own, in short—the result will be something much more respectable and no one will recognize him behind that countenance. In this regard, let me note one very characteristic thing: all this wretched shame of one's self and all this cheap rejection of one's self is unconscious in the majority of cases; it is something involuntary and overpowering; but, consciously, the Russians—even those who are most thorough in rejecting their selves—are still not prepared to accept their insignificance and make no bones about demanding respect: "I'm just like an Englishman, after all," argues the Russian, "and so I, too, must be respected since all Englishmen are respected." This basic social type of ours has been evolving for two hundred years in accord with the explicit principle stated two hundred years ago: never under any circumstances must you be yourself; you must put on a different face and despise your own for all time; always be ashamed of your own self and never be yourself. The results were conclusive. There is not a German nor a Frenchman nor any Englishman in the world who, when meeting other people, would be ashamed of his own face if in his own heart he knew he had done nothing shameful. The Russian knows this full well; and the educated Russian also knows that being unashamed of one's own face, wherever he may be, is precisely the chief and essential feature of one's sense of personal dignity. That is why he wants to appear as a Frenchman or an Englishman: just so that he will quickly be taken for someone who is never, anywhere, ashamed of his own face.

"Innocuous things, old hat; we've heard it a thousand times," people will say again. That may well be, but here is something still more characteristic. There is a point on which any Russian person of the educated category, when appearing in society or in public, is terribly exacting and will not yield an inch. (At home or in his own mind it's another matter.) This point is intellect, the desire to appear more clever than he is and—this is remarkable— it is certainly not a desire to seem cleverer than everybody else or even cleverer than anyone in particular but only *not to be stupider than anyone else.* "Just admit," he says, "that I'm not stupider than anyone else and I'll admit that you're not stupider than anyone else." Once again we have something in the nature of mutual gratitude here. To take an example: as we know, the Russian will happily and eagerly defer to European authority without even permitting himself any analysis of the matter; he particularly does not like to analyze such instances. Oh, it's another matter should the authority of genius come down from his pedestal or simply go out of fashion: then no one is more severe to that authority than the Russian intelligentsia; there is no limit to its arrogance, contempt, and mockery. We stand in naive amazement later if we find out that in Europe they continue to respect the authority who has come down from his pedestal here and that they still pay him his full due. But that very same Russian, although he may have bowed before that fashionable genius without ever analyzing why, will still never ever admit that he is stupider than this genius before whom he has just bowed, no matter how ultra-European he may be. "Well, so there's a Goethe and a Liebig and a Bismarck, we'll say . . . but still, I amount to something too"—this is how every Russian, even the most wretched, if it comes to that, pictures it. In fact, it's not a matter of "picturing," since there is scarcely any conscious thought here; it is more of a spasmodic reaction. It is a kind of continual sensation of idle, random, and quite unjustified self-esteem. In short, the Russian of the higher classes can never, under any circumstances, attain that highest, perhaps, degree of manifestation of human dignity which is to acknowledge oneself less intelligent than another when this truly is the case; I don't even know if there can be exceptions to this. I hope that people don't find my "paradox" too amusing. A rival of Liebig who, perhaps, never finished his high-school course, will naturally not try to argue that he is the better man when he's told that he is in the presence of Liebig himself. He'll hold his peace; but still, something will be urging him on to make a claim, even in Liebig's presence. . . .

It's another matter if, let's say, he were to meet Liebig without
knowing it in a railway car, say. And if the talk turned to chemistry
and our gentleman managed to get into the conversation, then
there's no doubt that he could keep up a most complete, learned
argument, knowing no more about the subject than the single word
"chemistry" itself. Liebig would be astonished, of course, but in
the eyes of the other listeners our gentleman might emerge the
victor. For in terms of boldness the learned language of the Russian
knows scarcely any bounds. Here there arises a phenomenon that
exists only in the soul of the Russian educated classes: in that soul,
as soon as it finds itself in public, not only is there no doubt of its
own intelligence but there is not even any doubt of its own complete
erudition, if the matter comes to erudition. One might understand
the matter of intelligence; but as concerns one's erudition, I should
think that each person ought to have the most accurate information
on the subject. . . .

Of course, all this happens only in public when there are strangers
around. But at home and in his own mind. . . . Well, at home and
in private not a single Russian cares about his own education or
erudition; he never even raises the question. . . . And if he should
raise it, then most likely even in private he would decide the matter
in his favor, although he would have the most complete information
about his own erudition.

Not long ago I myself, in the course of a two-hour trip in a
railway car, happened to hear a whole treatise on classical languages.
One person spoke and everyone else listened. The speaker was a
gentleman whom none of the passengers knew, a portly, middle-
aged man of restrained and lordly manner, whose words came slowly
and weightily. He aroused everyone's interest. It was obvious from
his very first words, not only that was he speaking on this subject
for the first time, but that this was perhaps the first time he had
even thought about it, so that it was merely a brilliant improvisation.
He entirely rejected classical education and called its introduction
into Russia "historical and fatal idiocy." That was the only harsh
expression he permitted himself, however; the tone he chose was
too elevated and did not permit him to become heated, out of
contempt alone for the topic. The bases on which his argument
rested were the most elementary ones, admissible only in a thirteen-
year-old schoolboy, and almost the same ones on which certain of
our newspapers base their campaign against classical languages,
i.e., "Since all works in Latin have been translated we don't need

the Latin language," and so on and so forth. He produced an extraordinary impression in our railway car; many—ladies in particular—thanked him on leaving for the pleasure he had given them. I am convinced that he went away with the greatest respect for himself.

These days in public (whether it be in railway cars or somewhere else) conversations are very different from those of years gone by; now people want to listen and want someone to instruct them on all political and social topics. It's true that public conversations in Russia are begun only with great strain; at first, everyone holds back for a long time before they decide to say anything, but once they begin, they sometimes become so passionate that one almost has to restrain them physically. More restrained and responsible conversations, and those which one might call more elevated and private, revolve for the most part around the stock exchange and matters of government, but from a confidential, "insider's" point of view that claims knowledge of higher secrets and motives unknown to the ordinary public. The ordinary public listens meekly and respectfully, while the windbags rise in their esteem. Of course, scarcely any one of them believes the others, but they part almost always quite content and even a little grateful to one another. You can manage to travel pleasantly and happily on our railways if you have the ability to allow the others to fib and believe them as much as possible; in that case you, too, will be allowed to tell a few with effect should you be tempted to do so; the benefit, thus, is mutual. But as I have already said, there are general, momentous, essential topics of conversation in which everyone takes part, and not only for the purpose of passing time pleasantly. I repeat: people have an urge to learn and to understand contemporary problems; people—particularly women and particularly mothers of families—seek and yearn for someone to teach them. It is remarkable that with all this most curious and significant longing for counselors and guides in public affairs, with all this noble striving, people are too easily satisfied, and sometimes in the most unexpected manner; they believe everything; they are very poorly prepared and equipped—much more poorly than your most vivid imagination could have conceived a few years ago, when it was more difficult to draw a precise conclusion about our Russian society than it is now when we have more facts and information at hand. One can state positively that every windbag with relatively decent manners (our public, alas, still has a prejudiced weakness for decent manners despite the education that is being spread further and further through feuilletons) can gain the upper hand and convince his listeners of whatever he pleases, earning their gratitude and departing with deep respect for himself. The one necessary condition, of course, is that he be a liberal; that goes without saying. On another occasion, also on the train and also not long ago, I happened to hear a whole treatise on atheism. The speaker, a gentleman who might have been an engineer with good social connections but who had a gloomy look and a unhealthy need for listeners, began with monasteries. He did not know the first thing about the question of monasteries: he took the existence of monasteries as something inseparable from the dogmas of faith; he imagined that monasteries were supported by the state and cost the treasury dear, and, forgetting that monks comprise a completely free association of persons just as do other organizations, he demanded in the name of liberalism that they be abolished as tyrannies of some sort. He ended with a complete and limitless atheism based on the natural sciences and mathematics. He kept referring to the natural sciences and mathematics without, however, citing a single fact from these sciences in the entire course of his dissertation. Once again, he was the only one who spoke, while the others only listened. "I shall teach my son to be an honest man and that's all," he stated in conclusion, in the full and obvious assurance that good deeds, morality, and honesty are things that are given and absolute, dependent on nothing, and which you can always find in your pocket when the need arises, without any trouble, doubts, or confusion. This gentleman also had unusual success. In the railway car were officers, elderly men, ladies, and grown children. On parting they thanked him warmly for the pleasure he had afforded them, and one lady—the mother of a family, smartly dressed and quite pretty— declared with a charming giggle that now she was quite convinced that in her soul there was "nothing but vapor." This gentleman also must have departed feeling unusual respect for himself.

This self-respect, now, confuses me. The fact that there are fools and windbags will surprise no one, of course; but this gentleman was obviously no fool. Neither was he a scoundrel or a cheat; it is very possible that he was an honest man and a good father. He simply understood nothing at all of those questions which he undertook to solve. Would he not, surely, an hour or a day or a month later, think to himself: "My friend, Ivan Vasilevich (or whatever his name is), you've been arguing here, but truly you don't understand anything about the subject you've been discussing. Why, you realize that better than anyone. You've just been referring to the natural sciences and mathematics, but you know full well that you've long forgotten the scant bit of math you took in your technical school, and even there you didn't know it very well; and you never did have any notion of the natural sciences. So how could you talk? How could you teach people? Why, you yourself realize that you were only telling tales, and yet you're still proud of yourself. Shouldn't you be ashamed?''

I'm convinced that he might ask himself all these questions, despite the fact that, perhaps, he's wrapped up in "business" and doesn't have any time for idle questions. I'm also thoroughly convinced that these questions, if only in passing, have entered his mind. But *he wasn't ashamed; his conscience didn't trouble him!* And it's that lack of conscience in the educated Russian that for me is truly a phenomenon. Never mind that it is so common and so frequent among us and that everyone has grown accustomed to it and learned to live with it; it still remains a surprising and amazing fact. It testifies to the indifference toward the judgment of one's own conscience, or—which is the same thing—to such exceptional lack of self-respect that you fall into despair and lose all hope that anything independent and beneficial to the nation can ever come from such people and such a society. The public—meaning outward appearance, the European façade, the law given by Europe once and for all—this public crushes every Russian: in public he is a European, a citizen, a knight, a republican, with a conscience and with his own solidly established opinion. At home and in his own mind: "You can whip me if you like, but I don't give a damn for all these opinions!" Lieutenant Pirogov, who forty years ago was whipped by Schiller, the locksmith, was a terribly prophetic figure, the prophecy of a genius who had foreseen the future with dreadful insight, for there are a countless number of these Pirogovs, so many that one cannot whip them all. Remember that immediately after the incident the lieutenant ate a puff-pastry and that same evening made a great impression dancing the mazurka at the birthday party of a certain eminent official. What do you think: when he was cutting capers on the dance floor and straining his so recently abused limbs to perform the steps, was he thinking of how he had been whipped only two hours earlier? Certainly he was thinking of that. And was he ashamed? Certainly he was not! When he woke up the next morning he probably said to himself: "Aw, to hell with it! What's the point of starting anything if no one will find out?" This "What's the point of starting anything" suggests, on the one hand, a great capacity to come to terms with virtually anything and, at the same time, such a breadth of our Russian nature that before such qualities even the Unlimited grows pale and dims. Two hundred years of being unaccustomed to even the slightest independence of character and two hundred years of despising one's own Russian face have stretched the Russian conscience to such fatal dimensions, from which . . . well, what do you think you could expect from it?

I am convinced that the lieutenant was capable of reaching such limits, or such limitlessness, that, perhaps, during the mazurka he declared his love to his lady, the host's eldest daughter, and made her a formal proposal of marriage. The figure of this young miss, fluttering with her cavalier in a charming dance and not knowing that he had been whipped only an hour earlier and that this meant nothing to him at all, is infinitely *tragic*. And what do you think if she had found out and the proposal were made anyway? Would she have married him (under the condition, of course, that no one else would find out)? Alas, she certainly would have married him!

And yet the huge majority of our women can still be excluded from the number of Pirogovs and all the "limitless" ones. One sees more and more prominently in our women the qualities of sincerity, perseverance, seriousness, and honor, a longing for truth and sacrifice. Indeed, all these things were always stronger in Russian women than in men. That is beyond doubt, even despite today's exceptions. Women are less given to lying and many do not lie at all, while there are scarcely any men who do not lie (I am speaking about the present moment in our society). Women are more persevering and patient in work; they are *more serious* than men and want to work in order to do something, not merely to *seem* to do something. Can we not, perhaps, expect that our women will do great things for us?

16

One of Today's Falsehoods

Some of our critics have noted that in my latest novel, *The Devils*, I used the story of the well-known Nechaev affair; but at the same time they stated that I did not include specific portraits in my novel, nor did I make a literal reproduction of the Nechaev story; they said that I took a phenomenon and attempted only to explain how it could arise in our society, and this in the sense of a social phenomenon, not in an anecdotal sense, and not merely as an account of a particular incident in Moscow. For my part, I may say that all of this is quite correct. In my novel I do not touch personally upon the notorious Nechaev or his victim, Ivanov. *My* Nechaev character is, of course, unlike the actual Nechaev. I wanted to pose the question and, as clearly as possible, provide an answer to it in the form of a novel: how is it possible in our changing and astonishing society of today to have not a Nechaev but *Nechaevs*, and how does it happen that these *Nechaevs* eventually acquire their own Nechaevists?

And so, recently—a month ago in fact—I read in *The Russian World* the following curious lines:

> ...we think that the Nechaev case ought to convince us that *students* in Russia do not get mixed up in such lunacy. An idiotic fanatic such as Nechaev could find proselytes only among the idle and underdeveloped and not among young people involved in studies.

And further:

> ...the more so that only recently the Minister of Education (in Kiev) stated that after an inspection of educational institutions in seven districts he could say that *"in recent years our young people regard their studies with incomparably greater seriousness and study much more, and much more diligently."*

By themselves—judging entirely independently—these lines do
not signify very much (I hope the author will pardon me for saying
so). But they contain a distortion and an old, tiresome lie. The
complete and basic idea here is that if Nechaevs occasionally do
surface among us, then they absolutely must be idiots and fanatics;
and if they also manage to find followers, then it absolutely must
be "*only* among the idle and underdeveloped and *not* among young
people involved in studies." I don't know just what the author of
the little article in *The Russian World* meant to prove by this distortion: did he want to flatter our students? Or, to the contrary,
did he, through this sly maneuver, try, by seeming to flatter them,
to trick them a little—but with the most honest intentions, for their
own good; I mean did he use for this end the well-known method
that governesses and nurses apply to little children: "Look, children, how *those* bad creatures are shouting and fighting; they'll
certainly be punished for their bad behavior. But you, now, are
such dear, sweet, good children; you sit up straight while you're
eating; you don't swing your feet under the table; and for that you'll
certainly be given some sweets"? Or, finally, did the author simply
want to "defend" our students from the government and use for
this end a means which, perhaps, he considers extraordinarily sly
and subtle?

Let me say frankly: although I posed all these questions, the
personal aims of the author of the little article in *The Russian World*
do not arouse the slightest interest in me. And so as to make my
point absolutely clear, I will even add that the falsehood and tiresome old distortion in the idea expressed by *The Russian World* I
am inclined to consider in the present instance as something accidental and unpremeditated: I mean that the author of the article
himself believed his own words fully and accepted them for the
truth with that elevated simplicity which in any other case would
be most laudable and even touchingly disarming. But aside from
the fact that a falsehood taken as truth always has a most dangerous
appearance (even though it may appear in *The Russian World*)—
aside from that, one can't help but be struck by the fact that never
before has it appeared in such a stark, precise, and artless form
as in this little article. Truly, there are some people who, if made
to bow down and worship God, would break their foreheads. So
it is from that point of view that it is interesting to trace the
development of this falsehood and clarify it as well as possible, for

we shall wait a long time before finding another example of such
artless candor!

For longer than anyone can remember in our pseudoliberal times
it has been the accepted rule of our newspaper press to "defend
our young people": from whom? from what? The answers to those
questions sometimes remain in a fog of uncertainty, and thus the
matter takes on a most ridiculous and even comic aspect, especially
when it involves attacks on other organs of the press in the sense
that "we're more liberal than you are, you see; you are attacking
young people and so you must be more reactionary." I'll note in
parentheses that that same little article in *The Russian World* contains an accusation plainly directed at *The Citizen*: we are supposedly making a blanket accusation against students in Petersburg,
Moscow, and Kharkov. Leaving aside the fact that the author of
the article *knows full well* himself that we never made any such
wholesale accusation, I would simply ask him to explain what he
means by a wholesale accusation against young people. I don't
understand this at all! It means, of course, to dislike for some
reason all young people as a whole, and not even young people so
much as young people of a certain age! What kind of muddled
thinking is this? Who can put any stock in such an accusation?
It's clear that both the accusation and the defense have been made
off the cuff, as it were, without even taking much thought. It's
worth pondering this: "I've demonstrated that I am liberal, that
I praise our young people and take to task those who don't praise
them—that's enough to keep our subscribers happy, and the matter's done with, thank goodness!" Indeed, "the matter's done
with," for only the bitterest enemy of our young people could
undertake to defend them *in this way* and to come up with such
an astounding distortion (accidentally—I am now more than ever
convinced) as did the naive author of the little article in *The Russian
World*.

The whole importance of this matter lies in the fact that this
technique is not the invention of *The Russian World* alone but one
common to many organs of our pseudoliberal press, and there,
perhaps, it is used in not so naive a fashion. Its essence, *in the
first place*, is in wholesale praise of our young people, in everything
and in every instance, and in crude attacks on all those who may
on occasion permit themselves to take a critical attitude even toward
youth. The technique is based on the absurd assumption that young

people are still so immature and so fond of flattery that they will
not understand and will accept everything at face value. And, in
truth, things have reached the stage where very many of our young
people (I firmly believe not all of them, by any means) really have
come to like this crude praise, demand flattery, and are prepared
to accuse without discrimination all those who do not indulge them
in everything and at every step, particularly in some situations.
The damage done by this is still only temporary, however; with
age and experience the views of our young people will change as
well. But there is also another side to the falsehood, which involves
direct and material damage.

This second aspect of the technique of "defending our young
people from society and from the government" consists in the
simple *denial of the fact*, a denial that is sometimes crude and
brazen: "There is no fact," they say. "There never was and there
never could have been; he who says there was is therefore slandering
our youth and is therefore the enemy of our youth!"

That is the technique. I repeat, the bitterest enemy of our young
people could not have invented anything more prejudicial to their
direct interests. This I certainly wish to prove.

By denying the fact at all costs one can achieve amazing results.

Well, gentlemen, what are you going to prove and how are you
helping the matter when you begin asserting (and why—God only
knows) that young people who are "led astray"—those, that is,
who can be led astray (even by Nechaev)—must absolutely consist
only of "the idle and underdeveloped," those who do not study at
all; in short, that they must be loafers with the very worst tendencies? In such a fashion, by isolating the case and by removing
it from the sphere of those who do study and reducing it only to
"the idle and underdeveloped," you thus indict in advance these
unfortunate people and disavow them once and for all: "You yourselves are to blame; you're rowdy and lazy and haven't learned to
sit quietly at the table." By isolating the case and depriving it of
the right to be examined in the context of the whole (and it is
precisely here that the only possible defense of these unfortunate
"lost sheep" lies), you thus not only sign the final sentence against
them, as it were, but even deprive them of compassion itself, for
you flatly assert that their very errors were caused only by their
despicable qualities and that these youths, even without committing
any crime, must arouse contempt and disgust.

On the other hand, what would happen if we suddenly found

that those involved in some *case* or other were by no means underdeveloped rowdies who swing their feet under the table, were by
no means only idlers but, on the contrary, were diligent, ardent
young people who were in fact studying and who possessed good
hearts but who had only been set off on a wrong tendency? (Please
understand this phrase "set off on a tendency": wherever in Europe
could you now find more uncertain shifting among all sorts of
tendencies than in Russia today?) And so, according to your theory
of "idlers and underdeveloped people," these new "unfortunates"
appear as thrice guilty: "They were given the proper means; they
finished their education; they worked hard—they have no justification! They are three times less deserving of compassion than
idle, underdeveloped people!" That is the result that comes directly
from your theory.

Please, gentlemen (I am speaking in general and not only to the
writer from *The Russian World*), on the basis of your "denial of
the fact" you assert that the Nechaevs absolutely must be idiots,
"idiotic fanatics." Is that really so? Is that just? In the present
instance I set Nechaev aside and say "Nechaevs," in the plural.
Yes, among the Nechaevs there can be creatures who are very
shadowy, very dismal and misshapen, with a thirst for intrigue and
power of most complex origins, with a passionate and pathologically
premature urge to express their personalities, but why must they
be "idiots?" On the contrary, even the genuine monsters among
them may be very well developed, extremely clever, and even educated people. Or do you think that knowledge, a course of training, a few facts picked up in school (or even in university) form
the soul of a youth so thoroughly that with the receipt of his diploma
he at once acquires an unfailing talisman that once and for all
enables him to recognize the truth and avoid temptations, passions,
and vices? And so, by your way of thinking, all these youths who
complete their studies at once become something like a multitude
of little popes with the power of infallibility.

And why do you suppose that the Nechaevs must absolutely be
fanatics? Very often they are simply scoundrels. "I am a scoundrel,
not a socialist," says one Nechaev. True, he says that in my novel
The Devils, but I assure you that he could have said it in real life.
These scoundrels are very crafty and have thoroughly studied the
magnanimous aspect of the human soul—and most often the soul
of youth—so as to be able to play on it as on a musical instrument.

And do you really think that the proselytes whom some such Nechaev could gather in Russia must absolutely consist only of loafers?
I don't believe that; not all of them would be. I myself am an old
"Nechaevist"; I also stood on the scaffold condemned to death,
and I assure you that I stood in the company of educated people.
Almost that whole company had graduated from the highest institutions of learning. Some of them, later on, *when everything had
passed,* distinguished themselves by making remarkable contributions to specialized fields. No, gentlemen, the Nechaevists do not
always come only from idlers who have never studied anything.

I know that you will doubtless reply that I wasn't a Nechaevist
at all but only one of the Petrashevsky Circle (although I think
that name is incorrect, since a far greater number—compared with
those who were standing on the scaffold but who were members
of the circle the same as we—remained absolutely untouched and
undisturbed. True, they never even knew Petrashevsky, but this
long-past story was not at all about Petrashevsky in any case. That
is all I wanted to note).

But let that be; I was a member of the Petrashevsky Circle, then.
How do you know that the members of that circle could not have
become Nechaevists, i.e., set off on Nechaev's path, *in the event
that things had taken such a turn?* Of course, one couldn't even have
imagined that at the time: how could things have ever *taken such
a turn?* Times then were completely different. But let me say one
thing about myself alone: a *Nechaev* I probably could never have
become, but a *Nechaevist*—well, of that I can't be sure; perhaps I
could have become one ... in the days of my youth.

I spoke of myself just now in order to have the right to speak
about others. Nonetheless, I will go on talking only about myself,
and if I do mention others then it is in general, impersonally, and
in a completely abstract sense. The *case* of the Petrashevsky Circle
is such an old one and belongs to such ancient history that probably
no harm will come from my recalling it now, the more so that I
do it in such an elusive and abstract way.

There was not a single "monster" or "scoundrel" among the
Petrashevsky Circle (whether we speak of those who stood on the
scaffold or those who remained untouched—it's all the same). I
think that no one can refute this statement. That there were educated people among us—that, too, as I have already noted, is not
likely to be disputed. But there were not many among us who
could resist that well-known cycle of ideas and concepts that had

then taken such a firm hold on young society. We were infected
with the ideas of the then theoretical socialism. Political socialism
did not exist in Europe at that time, and the European ringleaders
of the socialists even rejected it.

It was in vain that Louis Blanc had his face slapped and his hair
pulled (as if deliberately, he had hair that was very thick and black)
by his colleague-members of the National Assembly, the deputies
of the right, from whose hands Arago (the astronomer and member
of the government, now deceased) tore him on that unhappy morning in May of 1848 when a mob of impatient and hungry workers
broke into the Chamber. Poor Louis Blanc, who had been a member
of the Provisional Government for a time, had certainly not incited
them: he had only given a lecture in the Luxembourg Palace, on
the "right to work," to these wretched and hungry people who
had been deprived of their livelihood as a result of the revolution
and the republic. It is true that since he was still a member of the
government his lectures in that sense were extremely indiscreet
and, of course, absurd. Considérant's journal, just like Proudhon's
articles and pamphlets, tried to spread among these hungry, des-
titute workers a complete loathing for the right of hereditary private
property, among other things. There is no doubt that from all this
(i.e., from the impatience of hungry people inflamed by theories
of future bliss) there later arose political socialism, whose essence,
despite all the goals it proclaims, still consists only in the desire
for the universal robbery of all the property-owning classes by the
have-nots, and then "let things happen as they will." (For as yet
they have not properly decided anything about the kind of society
that will replace the current one; all they are certain of is that the
present has been a total failure—and to date that is the entire formula
of political socialism.) But in those days the matter was still seen
in the rosiest and most blissfully moral light. It is really true that
at the time this nascent socialism was being compared—even by
some of its ringleaders—with Christianity, and was taken as merely
a correction and improvement of the latter, in accordance with the
spirit of the age and civilization. All these new ideas of the time
had tremendous appeal for us in Petersburg; they seemed to be
sacred and moral in the highest degree and, most of all, they seemed
to be universal—the future law of all humanity without exception.
Even well before the Paris revolution of 1848 we were caught up
by the fascinating power of these ideas. Even in 1846 Belinsky had
initiated me into the whole *truth* of this coming "regenerated world"

and into the whole *sanctity* of the future communistic society. All
these convictions of the immorality of the very foundations (Christian ones) of contemporary society and of the immorality of religion
and the family; of the immorality of the right to private property;
of the elimination of nationalities in the name of the universal
brotherhood of people and of contempt for one's fatherland as
something that only slowed universal development, and so on and
so forth—all these things were influences we were unable to resist
and which, in fact, captured our hearts and minds in the name of
something very noble. In any case, the whole topic seemed a majestic one that stood far above the level of the prevailing ideas of
the day, and that was precisely what was so seductive. Those of
us—that is, not only those of the Petrashevsky Circle alone but
those in general who were then *infected* but who later on utterly
rejected all these visionary ravings, all this gloom and horror being
prepared for humanity supposedly to regenerate it and restore it
to life—those of us at the time still did not know the causes of our
illness and therefore were still unable to struggle against it. And
so why, then, do you think that even murder à la Nechaev would
have stopped us—not all of us, of course, but at least some of us—
in those frenetic times, surrounded by doctrines that had captured
our souls, in the midst of the devastating events in Europe at the
time—events that we, neglecting our own country, followed with
feverish anxiety?

There can be no doubt whatever that the murderer Nechaev
portrayed the monstrous and repulsive murder of Ivanov in Moscow
to his victims, the "Nechaevists," as a political matter, useful to
the future "common and *great* cause." Otherwise one simply cannot
comprehend how a few youths (whoever they might have been)
could have agreed to such a dismal crime. Once again, in my novel
The Devils, I attempted to depict those diverse and multifarious
motives by which even the purest of hearts and the most innocent
of people can be drawn into committing such a monstrous offense.
And therein lies the real horror: that in Russia one can commit
the foulest and most villainous act without being in the least a
villain! And this happens not only in Russia but all over the world,
and it has happened since time began, in times of transition when
people's lives are being thoroughly unsettled, when there are doubts
and denials, skepticism and uncertainty in fundamental social convictions. But this is more possible in Russia than anywhere else,
particularly in our time, and this trait is the most unhealthy and

melancholy one of our present age. The possibility of considering oneself—and sometimes even being, in fact—an honorable person while committing obvious and undeniable villainy—that is our whole affliction today!

What, in particular, are young people—in comparison with people of other ages—being defended from which makes you, the people who defend them, demand that almost as soon as they have done something and studied diligently they show a steadfastness and maturity of conviction which even their fathers did not possess and which today is less evident than ever? Our young people of the educated classes, raised in families where one most often encounters dissatisfaction, impatience, crude ignorance (despite the level of education of these classes), and where genuine education is almost everywhere replaced by an insolently negative attitude copied from others; where material concerns hold sway over every higher idea; where children are brought up without any grounding in their native soil, with no natural truth, with that disrespect or indifference toward their native land and that scornful contempt for the People which has become so common in recent times—is it here, from this wellspring, that our young people are to draw the truth and integrity of conviction to guide them on their first steps in life? This is where the source of the evil lies: in the tradition; in the legacy of ideas; in our national, age-old stifling in ourselves of any kind of independent thought; in the notion of the high status of a European, unfailingly with the proviso of disrespect to oneself as a Russian!

But probably you won't put any stock in these very general remarks of mine. "Education," you say; "hard work." "Lazy, underdeveloped people," you repeat. Keep in mind, gentlemen, that all these exalted European teachers of ours—our light and our hope—all these Mills and Darwins and Strausses sometimes have a very strange view of the moral obligations of a person of today. And yet these are not idlers who have learned nothing, and they are not rowdy children who swing their feet under the table. You'll laugh and ask me why I took it into my head to mention these names in particular. It's because when one speaks of our intelligent, ardent young students it's difficult even to imagine that they could escape these names as they take their first steps in life. Can a Russian youth remain indifferent to the influence of these leaders of progressive European thought and others like them, and in

particular to the Russian aspect of their teachings? Please allow
me this funny phrase "the Russian aspect of their teachings" because a Russian aspect of their teachings really does exist. It consists
of those conclusions drawn from their teachings that take on the
form of an invincible axiom, conclusions that are drawn only in
Russia; in Europe, as people say, the possibility of these conclusions
is not even suspected. People will tell me, perhaps, that these
thinkers are certainly not propagating evil notions; that, for example, even if Strauss does hate Christ and has set himself the
life's goal of mocking and despising Christianity, he nevertheless
worships humanity as a whole and his teaching is as elevated and
noble as can be. It's very possible that all this is true and that the
goals of all today's leaders of progressive European thought are
philanthropic and magnificent. But what I believe to be certain is
this: if you were to give all these grand, contemporary teachers full
scope to destroy the old society and build it anew, the result would
be such obscurity, such chaos, something so crude, blind, and
inhuman that the whole structure would collapse to the sound of
humanity's curses before it could ever be completed. Once having
rejected Christ, the human mind can go to amazing lengths. That's
an axiom. Europe, or at least the highest representatives of her
thought, rejects Christ; we, as we know, are obliged to copy Europe.

There are historical moments in the lives of people in which
obvious, brazen villainy of the crudest sort can be considered no
more than greatness of soul, no more than the noble courage of
humanity tearing itself free from its chains. Do you really need
examples of this? Are there not thousands of examples? Tens of
thousands? Hundreds of thousands?...It's a complicated and immense topic, of course, and it's very difficult to take it up in an
article like this; but nevertheless, in the final analysis I think that
my own proposition might also be considered: that even an honest
and open-hearted boy, even one who does well in school, may,
sometimes, become a Nechaevist...again, of course, assuming he
happens to come across a Nechaev; that's a sine qua non....

We of the Petrashevsky Circle stood on the scaffold and listened
to our sentences without the least bit of repentance. Obviously, I
cannot testify for all of us; but I think that I'm not mistaken in
saying that at that moment, if not each one of us, then the great
majority would have deemed it dishonorable to renounce our convictions. This is a matter from the distant past, and therefore,

perhaps, one might also ask the question: could that stubbornness and lack of repentance not be merely the signs of a bad nature, signs of underdeveloped and rowdy children? No, we were not rowdy children and perhaps were not even bad young people. The sentence of death by firing squad that was read to us at first was certainly not pronounced as a joke; almost all the condemned were convinced that the sentence would be carried out and underwent at least ten dreadful, infinitely terrible minutes expecting to die. During these final moments, some of us (I know this for certain) instinctively withdrew into ourselves and, in examining our whole, still so young lives, did repent of certain of our meaner actions (those which lie lifelong in secret on the conscience of every person); but that deed for which we had been condemned, those ideas and those notions which possessed our spirits, we saw as not only requiring no repentance but even somehow as purifying us in a martyrdom for which we would be forgiven much! And so it continued for a long time. It was not the years of exile and not the sufferings which broke us. On the contrary: nothing broke us, and our convictions only supported our spirits by the awareness of a duty fulfilled. No, it was something else which changed our views, our convictions, and our hearts. (I permit myself, of course, to speak only of those of us whose change of conviction became known and who themselves testified to this in one way or another.) This "something else" was the direct contact with the People, the brotherly union with them in common misfortune, the awareness that we ourselves had become as they, equal to them, and even placed on the very lowest of their levels.

I repeat that this did not happen very quickly, but gradually and after a very long, long time. It was not pride and not vanity that stood in the way of confession. And yet I was, perhaps, one of those (I again am speaking only of myself) who found it easiest to return to the root of the People, to discover the Russian soul, to recognize the People's spirit. I came from a family that was Russian and pious. As far back as I can remember I recall my parents' love for me. In our family we knew the Gospels virtually from our earliest childhood. I was only ten years old when I already knew almost all the main episodes from Karamzin's Russian history, which our father read aloud to us in the evenings. Each visit to the Kremlin and the Moscow cathedrals was a solemn event for me. Others, perhaps, did not have the kinds of memories I had.

I very often ponder the question and ask it now: what are the chief impressions that today's young people gain from their childhood? And if even I, who naturally could not haughtily pass by that new, fateful milieu into which misfortune thrust us and could not regard the spirit of the People as it manifested itself before me with only a superficial, haughty glance—if I, I am saying, found it so difficult to convince myself at last of the falsehood and injustice of almost all that we had previously regarded as light and truth, then what of the others, who were even more deeply alienated from the People, whose alienation was hereditary and acquired from their fathers and grandfathers?

It would be very difficult to tell the story of the rebirth of my convictions, the more so because it is not that interesting, perhaps; and somehow it is not appropriate for a feuilleton article....

. . . .

Gentlemen who defend our young people: will you take into account that milieu and that society in which these young people grow up and ask yourselves: can there be anything in our time which is less protected from *certain influences*?

First of all, pose the question: if the very fathers of these young people are not better, not firmer, and not healthier in their convictions; if from their earliest childhood these children have encountered in their own families nothing but cynicism, haughty and indifferent (for the most part) negation; if the words "native land" have only been uttered before them with a mocking intonation and all those who brought them up regarded Russia's cause with scorn or indifference; if the noblest among their fathers and educators spoke only to them of "universally human" ideas; if even in childhood their nurses were dismissed because they read the Prayer to the Virgin Mary over their cradles—then tell me: what can one ask of these children, and is it humane when one is defending them— if any such defense is needed—to escape by a mere denial of the fact?

Not long ago I happened to find the following *entrefilet* in the newspapers: "*The Kama-Volga Gazette* reports that recently three *high-school students* in their third year at the Second Kazan High School *have been charged* with a crime connected with *their proposed flight to America.*" (*St. Petersburg Gazette*, November 13). Twenty years ago the news of some third-year high-school students running off to America would have seemed utter nonsense to me. But the fact alone that *now* this doesn't seem like nonsense but something I can *understand*—in that alone I can see its justification!

Justification! Good Lord, can one use that word?

I know that these are not the first such students and that others have run off even before, and they did so because their elder brothers and fathers had run off. Do you remember Kel'siev's story of the poor officer who fled *on foot*, via Tornio and Stockholm, to Herzen in London, where the latter found work for him as a compositor in his printing shop? Do you remember Herzen's own story of that *cadet* who set off for the Philippine Islands, I think, to set up a commune and who had left Herzen 20,000 francs for future emigrants? And yet all that is already ancient history! Since then, old men, fathers, brothers, young women, and guards officers have run off to America to experience "free labor in a free country.". . . Probably the only ones who haven't tried it are seminary students. Can we blame little children such as these three high-school students if their poor heads were turned by the *grand ideas* of "free work in a free country" and the commune and the common-European man? Can we blame them if all this rubbish seems a religion to them, while emigration and betrayal of one's native land seems a virtue? And if we do blame them, then to what extent? That's the question.

In order to support his idea that *only* layabouts and idling defectives become involved in "such lunacy" in Russia, the author of the article in *The Russian World* cites the well-known and encouraging remarks of the Minister of Education, who said not long ago in Kiev that he had been convinced, after an inspection of educational institutions in seven districts, that *"in recent years our young people regard their studies with incomparably greater seriousness and study much more, and much more diligently."*

These are encouraging words, of course, words in which, perhaps, lies our *only* hope. The educational reform carried out during the present reign contains almost *all* our future possibilities, and we know it. But the Minister of Education himself, if I recall, stated in that same speech that we have long to wait before we shall see the final results of the reform. We always believed that our young people were quite capable of taking a more serious attitude toward their studies. But meanwhile we are still blanketed by such a fog of false ideas; we and our young people are surrounded by so many mirages and prejudices, while our whole social life—the lives of the fathers and mothers of these young people—takes on a stranger and stranger aspect, so that one cannot help but look for any and all ways to lead us out of our confusion. One of those ways is for us to be less callous, not to be ashamed when someone calls us on occasion a citizen and...once in a while to tell the truth, even though, to your way of thinking, it may be insufficiently liberal.

A Writer's Diary

1 8 7 6

[Announcement]

Subscriptions to *A Writer's Diary* for 1876

In the coming year F. M. Dostoevsky's publication, *A Writer's Diary*, will appear monthly in separate issues.

Each issue will be composed of sixteen to twenty-four pages of small print in the format of our weekly newspapers. But this will not be a newspaper; all twelve issues (for January, February, March, etc.) will form a whole, a book written by a single pen. It will be a diary in the literal sense of the word, an account of impressions actually experienced each month, an account of what was seen, heard, and read. Of course, some stories and tales may be included, but preeminently it will be about actual events. Each issue will come out on the last day of the month and will be sold separately in all bookstores for twenty kopecks. But those wishing to subscribe to the whole year's edition will enjoy a discount and will pay only two rubles (not including delivery and mailing); the cost with mailing and home delivery will be two rubles, fifty kopecks.

Subscriptions from local subscribers in Petersburg are being accepted in A. F. Bazunov's bookstore, near the Kazan Bridge, house No. 30, and in M. P. Nadein's "Store for Out-of-Towners," 44 Nevsky Prospect. In Moscow: at the Central Bookstore, Nikolsky Street, Slavyansky Bazaar Building.

Those from outside the capitals are kindly requested to deal solely with the author, who may be reached at the following address: Fedor Mikhailovich Dostoevsky, Apt. 6, Strubinsky House, Greek Street, by the Greek church, St. Petersburg.

January

1

1. In Place of a Foreword. On the Great and Small Bears,
on Great Goethe's Prayer, and, Generally, on Bad
Habits

. . . At least Khlestakov, when he was spinning his lies to the Mayor,
was still just a tiny bit apprehensive that they might grab him and
throw him out of the drawing room. Our contemporary Khlestakovs
are afraid of nothing and lie with complete composure.

Nowadays they all are completely composed. Composed and perhaps even happy. Scarcely anyone takes stock of himself; everyone
acts "naturally," and sees this as complete happiness. Nowadays,
just as before, vanity eats away at everyone, but yesterday's vanity
would enter timidly, casting feverish glances about, looking intently
at others' reactions: "Did I make the right sort of entrance? Did
I say the right thing?" But nowadays when someone enters a room
he is firmly convinced that everything belongs to him alone. And
if it turns out not to be his alone, he doesn't even get angry but
resolves the matter at once. Haven't you heard about notes like
this: "Dear Papa, I am twenty-three years old and I still have
accomplished nothing. I am certain that I will never amount to
anything, so I have decided to end my life. . . ."

And he shoots himself. But here at least we can understand
something: "What is there to live for if not for pride?" he says.
But another fellow will take a look around and go off and shoot
himself in silence, solely because he hasn't the money to acquire
a mistress. And that is the act of a total swine.

The newspapers assure us that this happens because such people
think too much. "He spends a long time thinking quietly, and
suddenly he hits on just the thing he had been aiming for all along."
My conviction is quite the contrary: he doesn't think at all; he

simply isn't capable of formulating an idea; he is as benighted as a savage, and if he conceives a longing for something, it comes from deep within him and not from conscious thought. It's the behavior of an utter swine, and there is nothing liberal about it.

And there is not a moment of Hamlet's pondering "that dread of something after death...."

And there is something terribly strange about this. Is such thoughtlessness really a part of the Russian character? I say thoughtlessness, not senselessness. Don't believe, then; but think, at least. Our suicide doesn't have even a shadow of a suspicion that he is called *I* and is an immortal being. It seems he hasn't even heard a thing about that. And yet he's by no means an atheist. Remember the atheists of times gone by: when they lost their faith in one thing, they at once began to believe passionately in something else. Remember the passionate faith of Diderot, Voltaire.... But among us they are a complete tabula rasa, and it's not a matter of Voltaire at all: our fellow just had no money to acquire a mistress, and nothing more.

When young Werther ends his life, he regrets, in the last lines he left, that he will never again see "the beautiful constellation, the Great Bear," and bids it farewell. Oh, how that little touch reveals Goethe, who was only then beginning his career! Why did young Werther feel so deeply about these constellations? Because every time he contemplated them he realized that he was no mere atom or nonentity before them, and that the whole infinitude of divine, mysterious wonders were by no means beyond his thought, nor beyond his consciousness, nor beyond the ideal of beauty that lay in his soul, and that, accordingly, they were equal to him and revealed his kinship with the infinity of being ... and that for all the happiness of experiencing such a grand idea, an idea that revealed who he was, he was obliged only *to his image as a human being.*

"O Great Spirit, I thank Thee for the human image that Thou hast given me."

And that should have been great Goethe's prayer throughout his life. We, however, take the human image that has been given to us and smash it to pieces, quite simply and without any of these German tricks; and as for the Great Bear, or the Little Bear for that matter—well, no one would think of bidding them farewell; and if anyone did think of it, he wouldn't do it: that would be just too embarrassing.

"Now what are you on about?" an astonished reader asks.

"I just wanted to write a foreword, because you simply can't do without one altogether."

"If that's the case then you'd better make clear what your tendency is and what your convictions are. Explain: what sort of man are you, and how did you make so bold as to announce this *Writer's Diary?*"

But that's very difficult, and I can see that I'm not much of a hand at writing forewords. Writing a foreword is perhaps as difficult as writing a letter. As far as liberalism is concerned (instead of the word "tendency" I'll simply use the word "liberalism")—as far as liberalism is concerned, the well-known "Mr. X," in a recent feuilleton in which he commented on how the press greeted the new year of 1876, recalls in passing, and not without sarcasm, that everything went off rather liberally. I'm pleased that he was sarcastic. In truth, our liberalism lately has been transformed everywhere into either a trade or a bad habit. I mean, in itself it certainly would not be a bad habit, but among us it somehow turned out that way. It's strange, even: our liberalism, it seems, belongs to the category of quiescent liberalisms; quiescent and tranquil which, in my opinion, is not very nice, because quietism least of all, it seems, is compatible with liberalism. And yet, in spite of all this tranquility, there are undeniable signs appearing everywhere that very gradually the notions of what is liberal and what is not are disappearing altogether in our society; and in that respect people are becoming thoroughly confused; there are examples of even extreme cases of such confusion. In a word, our liberals, instead of becoming more free, have bound themselves up with liberalism as with ropes, and so I too, taking advantage of this interesting occasion, can pass over the details of my liberalism in silence. But in general I will say that I consider myself more liberal than anyone, if only because I have no wish whatsoever to become quiescent. Well, that's enough about that. As to the type of man I am, I would say the following about myself: "Je suis un homme heureux qui n'a pas l'air content," i.e., "I am a happy man who isn't satisfied with everything. . . ."

With that I finish my foreword. I only wrote it for the sake of form, anyway.

2. A Future Novel. Another "Accidental Family"

There was a Christmas tree and a children's party at the Artists' Club, and I went to have a look at the children. Even formerly I always watched children, but now I pay particular attention to them. For a long time now I have had the goal of writing a novel about children in Russia today, and about their fathers too, of course, in their mutual relationship of today. The "poem" or "idea" is ready and it was the first thing to be created, as should always be the case with a novelist. I will take fathers and children from every level of Russian society I can and follow the children from their earliest childhood.

A year and a half ago, when Nikolai Alekseevich Nekrasov asked me to write a novel for *Notes of the Fatherland*, I almost began my *Fathers and Sons*; but I held back, and thank God I did, for I was not ready. In the meantime I wrote only *A Raw Youth*, this first attempt at my idea. But here the child had already passed his childhood and appeared only as an unprepared person, timidly yet boldly wanting to take his first step in life as quickly as possible. I took a soul that was sinless yet already tainted by the awful possibility of vice, by a premature hatred for its own insignificance and "accidental" nature; tainted also by that breadth of character with which a still chaste soul already consciously allows vice to enter its thoughts, cherishes it and admires it in shameful yet bold and tempestuous dreams—and with all this, left solely to its own devices and its own understanding, yet also, to be sure, to God. All such are the miscarriages of society, the "accidental" members of "accidental" families.

We read in the newspapers not long ago of the murder of a woman named Perova and of the suicide of her murderer. She lived with him; he worked in a printer's shop but had lost his job; she rented an apartment and took in lodgers. Quarrels began. Perova asked him to leave her. The murderer was a man of thoroughly modern character. "If I can't have her then no one can." He gave her his word that he would leave her, then stabbed her barbarically at night, deliberately and with premeditation; then he cut his own throat. Perova left two children, boys of twelve and nine, whom she had borne illegitimately, but not by the murderer and even before she knew him. She loved them. They both witnessed the terrible scene on the evening of the murder when he tormented their mother with reproaches until she fell into a faint; they begged her not to go to his room, but she went.

The newspaper *Voice* appeals to the public to help the "unfortunate orphans," one of whom, the elder, attends High School No. 5; the other is still at home. Here is yet another "accidental family," yet other children with dark shadows cast over their young souls. This dismal picture will remain in their souls forever and might painfully undermine youthful pride from the very days when "all the impressions of existence were new to us." The result will be an inability to cope with life's problems, early pangs of vanity, a blush of false shame for their past, and a dull, sullen hatred for people; and this, perhaps, may last a lifetime. May the Lord bless the future of these innocent children, and may they never cease to love their poor mother without reproach and shame for their love. And we absolutely must help them. On that score our society will respond nobly and with sympathy. Surely they will not have to leave their school once they have begun it. And the elder, apparently, will not leave school and his future seems already arranged; but what of the younger? Surely we won't just collect some seventy or a hundred rubles and then forget about them? Thanks to *The Voice* for reminding us of these unfortunates.

3. The Christmas Party at the Artists' Club. Children Who Think and Children Who Are Helped Along. A "Gluttonous Boy." "Oui" Girls. Jostling Raw Youths. A Moscow Captain in a Hurry.

Of course I'm not going to describe in detail the Christmas party and the dancing at the Artists' Club: all that was done long ago at the proper time, and I read about it myself with much pleasure in other feuilletons. I will say only that prior to this affair I had not been to a single social event anywhere for far too long and had been leading a solitary life for a considerable time.

First the children, all in charming costumes, performed their dances. It's interesting to observe how the most complex concepts are implanted quite imperceptibly in a child and to realize that one who is still unable to connect two thoughts sometimes may have an excellent grasp of life's most profound matters. One German scholar suggested that when a child completes his first three years of life he has already acquired fully a third of the ideas and knowledge that he will take to his grave as an old man. There were even six-year-olds at the Artists' Club, but I am certain that they already fully understood the reasons they had come here, adorned in such fine costumes, while at home they went about bedraggled (and given the means of the middle class of society today, they certainly would be bedraggled). Besides that, they probably already understand that this is exactly how it must be, that this is by no means an exception but a normal law of nature. Of course, they can't express that in words, but they know it inwardly, even though it is a very complex notion.

The smallest children were my favorites; they were very charming and quite at ease. The older ones were at their ease too, but with a certain boldness. Of course, the most free and easy and cheerful were those who will be mediocre and untalented in the future. This is a general rule: mediocrities are always free and easy, whether as children or as adults. The more gifted and exceptional among children are always more restrained, and if they are spirited, then they are always disposed toward leading the others and taking charge. It's a pity, too, that everything is made so easy for children nowadays—not only all their studies and acquisition of knowledge, but even their games and toys. The child scarcely begins to lisp his first words and at once people begin to make things easy for him. Our whole system of pedagogy these days is concerned with making things easier. There are times when making things easy does nothing for development but, to the contrary, can even promote dullness. Two or three ideas, two or three impressions deeply experienced in childhood through one's own effort (through one's own suffering as well, if you like) will lead the child much more deeply into life than the easiest school, which quite often produces people who are neither this nor that, neither good nor bad, who are not even depraved in their depravity or virtuous in their virtue.

> What, have the oysters come? Oh, joy!
> And off he rushes, gluttonous boy,
> To swallow. . . .

Now this same "gluttonous boy" (Pushkin's only second-rate verse, because he wrote it quite without irony, and almost with praise) must be the result of something, mustn't he? He's a nasty fellow, and one we have no need of, and I am certain that an education made all too easy greatly facilitates the emergence of such a type; and we have more than enough of his sort already!

Girls, still, are easier to understand than boys. Why is it that girls, almost up to the age of their maturity (but no further) are always more developed or seem more developed than boys of the same age? You can gain a particular understanding of girls while watching them dance: in some you can quickly see a future "oui" girl who will never manage to get married despite all her wishes to do so. I call "oui" girls those who, until almost thirty years of age, answer only *oui* or *non*. On the other hand, there are some who, one can already see, will shortly get married, just as soon as they make up their minds to do so.

It is even more cynical, in my view, to dress a girl who is all but grown up in a child's outfit at a dance; it is truly wrong, in fact. Some such girls, in their short little dresses and bare legs, stayed on to dance with the grownups after the children's ball had ended at midnight and the parents had begun to dance.

Still, I found everything very much to my liking, and had I not been jostled about by the "raw youths," it all would have gone most satisfactorily. In fact, the adults were all elegantly polite, in keeping with the holiday, while the youths (not the children, but the raw youths—future young men, hordes of them, in all sorts of uniforms) jostled about intolerably with no apology, passing to and fro as if they had the right to behave this way. I must have been elbowed fifty times; perhaps they are taught to do that as a means of developing a free and easy manner. Nonetheless, having grown unaccustomed to social events, I was pleased with everything, in spite of the stifling heat in the room, the electric illumination, and the frenzied, imperious shouts of the master of ceremonies.

The other day I picked up a copy of the *Petersburg Gazette* and read a report from Moscow about the various disturbances over the holidays in the Noblemens' Club, in the Circle of Artists, in the theater, at the masquerade, and elsewhere. If one is to believe the correspondent (for when a correspondent reports on vice he may intentionally keep silent about virtue), our society has never been more prone to scandal than at present. It is strange indeed: why is it that, since childhood and all through my life, no sooner do I find myself in a large holiday gathering of Russians than I at once begin thinking that they are only making a pretense and suddenly will jump up and commence a first-rate row, just as they might in their own homes. It's an absurd and fantastical notion, and how ashamed I was of it and how I reproached myself for it, even as a child! It's a notion that won't stand up to the slightest analysis. Oh, of course the shopkeepers and captains the honest correspondent writes about (and I have complete faith in him) existed before and have always existed; they are perennial types; but still, they used to be more timid and hid their feelings, while now, every so often, such a fellow will pop up right on center stage, a fellow who is absolutely convinced he is asserting his new rights. Undeniably, in the last twenty years a terrific number of Russians suddenly imagined that, for some reason, they had become fully entitled to act disgracefully and that now it's a good thing and they will be praised for doing so and not thrown out. On the other hand, I also realize that it's remarkably pleasant (oh, for many, many people!) to stand up in the middle of a social gathering where everyone around—ladies, gentlemen, and even authorities—is so sweet-tongued, polite, and treating one another as equals, as if this were really in Europe somewhere—to stand up amid these Europeans and suddenly bellow out something in the purest national idiom, to fetch someone a cuff on the ear, to blurt out some obscenity to a young lady, and, in general, to commit some indecency right there in the middle of the hall: "There you are, that's what you get for two hundred years of Europeanism; but we're still here, just as we were; we haven't disappeared!" It's pleasant. Still, the savage will be wrong: he won't be acknowledged and will be thrown out. Who will throw him out? The police force? Certainly not—not the police force, but some other savages just like him! That's where the force is. Let me explain.

Do you know who probably most enjoys and appreciates this European and festive gathering of Russian society in European style? Why it's precisely the Skvoznik-Dmukhanovskys, the Chichikovs, and even, perhaps, the Derzhimordas; that is to say, those people who, at home and in their private lives are most completely "national." Oh, yes, they have their own social events and dances *there*, at home, but they have little appreciation or respect for them; what they appreciate is the Governor's ball, a ball with high society like the ones Khlestakov has told them about. But why? Precisely because they themselves are not like polite society. That's why our savage treasures European forms even though he knows very well that he, personally, will not change and will come home from the European ball just the same brawler he was before; but he's comforted by the thought that he's paid homage to virtue, even in the form of an ideal. Oh, he knows very well that all this is only a mirage; yet still, having attended the ball, he's assured himself that this mirage continues and is maintained through some invisible but extraordinary force; and that he himself didn't dare to come out to the middle of the hall bellowing something in the national idiom; and the thought that he had not been permitted to do so and will not be in the future he finds remarkably pleasant. You will not believe how much a barbarian can come to love Europe; such love enables him also to participate in a cult, as it were. Doubtless he often cannot even define the meaning of this cult. Khlestakov, for instance, maintained that the cult consisted of the hundred-ruble melons that were served at high-society balls. Perhaps Skvoznik-Dmukhanovsky, even now, keeps his faith in the watermelon, even though he eventually saw through Khlestakov and scorned him; yet he is happy to pay homage to virtue even in the form of the watermelon. This certainly isn't a matter of hypocrisy here but of the most genuine sincerity—a need, moreover. Hypocrisy works well here, for what is hypocrisy? Hypocrisy is that very tribute which vice is obliged to pay to virtue—an enormously comforting thought for one who wants to remain vicious in practice yet still not break his link, in his heart at least, with virtue. Oh, vice is terribly fond of paying tribute to virtue, and that's a very fine thing; we ought to be satisfied with that much for the time being, should we not? And so the captain, bellowing in the middle of the hall in Moscow, continues to be only an exception and a man in a hurry—well, for the time being at least. Even "for the time being" is a comfort in this shaky age of ours.

Thus the ball is something decidedly conservative, in the best sense of the word; and I'm definitely not joking when I say that.

4. The Golden Age in Your Pocket

Still, I also found the ball rather wearisome; not wearisome, exactly, but somewhat annoying. The children's ball ended and the parents' began, and Lord, what a poor thing it was! Everyone in new clothes, and no one knowing how to wear them; everyone celebrating, and no one happy; everyone full of pride, and no one knowing how to make the most of himself; everyone envious, and everyone silent and aloof. They don't even know how to dance. Look at that very short officer twirling over there (you're certain to encounter such a very short, furiously twirling officer at any middle-class ball). The entire technique of his dancing consists only in the almost brutish way he twirls and jerks his lady about and in his capacity to go on twirling thirty or forty ladies in a row and taking pride in it; but is there anything graceful in that? After all, a dance is almost a declaration of love (think of the minuet), while this fellow looks just as if he's in a brawl. And one quite fantastic and utterly improbable thought occurred to me: "What if all these dear and respectable guests wanted, even for one brief moment, to become sincere and honest? How would this stuffy hall be transformed then? What if each of them suddenly learned the whole secret? What if each one of them suddenly learned how candid, honest, and sincere he really was? What if he knew how much heartfelt joy, purity, noble feelings, goodwill, and intellect—never mind intellect, but wit, most subtle and sociable—he had, and that each and every one of them shared these qualities? Yes, ladies and gentlemen, all that exists within every one of you, and no one, not a single one of you knows anything about it! Oh, dear guests, I swear that each lady and gentleman among you is cleverer than Voltaire, more sensitive than Rousseau, incomparably more alluring than Alcibiades or Don Juan, or any Lucretia, Juliet, or Beatrice! You don't believe that you are that beautiful? But I give you my solemn word that neither in Shakespeare nor in Schiller nor in Homer, nor in all of them put together, can you find anything so charming as now, this very minute, you can find here in this very ballroom. What is Shakespeare! Here you would see something of which our wise men have not dreamed. But your trouble is that you yourselves don't know how beautiful you are! Do you know that each of you, if you only wanted, could at once make everyone in this room happy and fascinate them all? And this power exists in every one of you, but it is so deeply hidden that you have long ceased to believe in it. Do you really think that the golden age exists only on porcelain teacups?

Don't frown at the words *golden age*, Your Excellency: I give you my word of honor that you won't be compelled to walk around in the costume of the golden age wearing only a fig leaf; you can keep your full general's uniform. I assure you that even people of general's rank can get into the golden age. You just have to try, Your Excellency, right now even; you're the senior rank, after all, and the initiative is yours. And you will see yourself what Piron's wit, so to speak, you could display, which would be a complete surprise to you. You're laughing; you don't believe it? I'm glad I made you laugh, and yet my whole outburst just now is not a paradox but the complete truth. . . . And your whole trouble is that you don't believe it.

2

1. The Boy with His Hand Out

Children are a strange lot; I dream of them and see them in my fancies. In the days before Christmas and on Christmas Eve itself I kept meeting on a certain street corner a little urchin who could have been no more than seven. In the terrible cold he was wearing clothes more fit for summer, but he did have some sort of old rag wrapped around his neck, which meant that someone had dressed him before sending him out. He was wandering "with hand out"; that's a technical term meaning to go begging, a term coined by such boys themselves. There are many like him; they hang about you, whining some well-rehearsed phrases. But this boy didn't whine; his speech was innocent and unpracticed and he looked trustingly into my eyes; obviously he was only beginning this profession. In answer to my questions he said that he had a sister who was out of work and ill. Perhaps that was true, but only later did I learn that there are hordes of these urchins: they are sent "with hands out" even in the most terrible cold, and if they collect nothing, they probably can expect a beating. Once a boy has collected a few kopecks, he returns with red, numbed hands to some cellar where a band of "dodgers" are drinking. These are people who, "quitting work at the factory on Saturday night, return to work no earlier than Wednesday evening." In the cellars their hungry and beaten wives drink with them; their hungry babies cry here too. Vodka, filth, and depravity, but vodka above all. With the kopecks he has collected in hand, the urchin is at once sent to a tavern and he brings back more vodka. Sometimes, for the fun of it, they pour half a bottle into his mouth and roar with laughter when, his breath catching, he falls to the floor scarcely conscious: "...and pitilessly he poured and poured/The horrid vodka into my mouth...."

309

When he gets older he's quickly packed off to a factory somewhere, but he's forced once again to bring all that he earns back
to the dodgers, and they drink it up. But even before they get
factory jobs these children become fully fledged criminals. They
roam about the city and know places in various cellars into which
they can crawl to spend the night unnoticed. One boy slept several
nights in succession in a basket in the quarters of a janitor who
never even noticed him. It is only natural that they become thieves.
Thievery becomes a passion even among eight-year-olds, who sometimes even have no awareness of the criminality of their actions.
In the end they bear it all—the hunger, cold, beatings—only for
one thing, for freedom. And they run away from the dodgers to
take up a vagrant's life on their own. A wild creature such as this
sometimes knows nothing at all—neither where he lives, nor what
nation he comes from; whether God exists, or the tsar. There are
even stories told about them that are hard to believe, yet they are
facts.

2. The Boy at Christ's Christmas Party

But I am a novelist and one "story," it seems, I made up myself.
Why do I say "it seems" when I know very well that I made it
up? Yet I keep imagining that it really happened somewhere, sometime, and happened precisely on Christmas Eve in *a certain* huge
city during a terrible cold spell.

I dreamed there was a boy—still very small, about six or even
younger—who awoke one morning in the damp and cold cellar
where he lived. He was wearing a wretched wrapper of some sort
and he was trembling. His breath escaped in a white cloud and,
while he sat, bored, in the corner on a trunk, he would let this
white vapor out of his mouth and amuse himself by watching it
billow up. But he was very hungry. Several times that morning he
had approached the bed on which his sick mother lay on a mattress
as thin as a pancake, a bundle beneath her head to serve as a
pillow. How did she come to be here? Probably she had come with
her boy from another city and suddenly fell ill. The landlady of
this wretched tenement had been picked up by the police two days
ago; the other tenants had all gone off, it being the holiday season,
leaving but one dodger who had been lying in a drunken stupor
for the last twenty-four hours, having been unable even to wait for
the holiday. In another corner of the room an old woman of eighty

groaned with rheumatism. She had once worked somewhere as a children's nurse but now was dying alone, moaning, grumbling, and complaining at the boy so that he had become frightened of approaching her corner. In the entry way he managed to find some water to quench his thirst, but nowhere could he find a crust of bread; again and again he went to wake his mother. At last he grew frightened in the darkness; the evening was well advanced, but still no candle had been lit. When he felt his mother's face he was surprised that she made no movement and had become as cold as the wall. "And it's dreadful cold in here," he thought. He stood for a time, absently resting his hand on the dead woman's shoulder; then he breathed on his fingers to warm them, and suddenly his wandering fingers felt his cap that lay on the bed; quietly he groped his way out of the cellar. He would have gone even before but he was afraid of the big dog that howled all day long by the neighbor's door on the stairway above. But the dog was no longer there, and in a thrice he was out on the street.

Heavens, what a city! He had never seen anything like it before. In the place he had come from there was such gloomy darkness at night, with only one lamppost for the whole street. The tiny wooden houses were closed in by shutters; as soon as it got dark you wouldn't see a soul on the street; everyone would lock themselves in their houses, only there would be huge packs of dogs—hundreds and thousands of dogs—howling and barking all night. Still, it was so nice and warm there, and there'd be something to eat; but here—Dear Lord, if only there was something to eat! And what a rattling and a thundering there was here, so much light, and so many people, horses, and carriages, and the cold—oh, the cold! Frozen vapor rolls from the overdriven horses and streams from their hot, panting muzzles; their horseshoes ring against the paving stones under the fluffy snow, and everyone's pushing each other, and, Oh Lord, I'm so hungry, even just a little bite of something, and all of a sudden my fingers are aching so. One of our guardians of the law passed by and averted his eyes so as not to notice the boy.

And here's another street—look how wide it is! I'll get run over here for sure. See how everyone's shouting and rushing and driving along, and the lights—just look at them! Now what can this be? What a big window, and in the room behind the glass there's a tree that stretches right up to the ceiling. It's a Christmas tree, with oh, so many lights on it, so many bits of gold paper and apples; and there's dolls and little toy horses all around it; children are running around the room, clean and dressed in nice clothes, laughing and playing, eating and drinking something. Look at that girl dancing with the boy, how fine she is! And you can even hear the music right through the glass. The little boy looks on in amazement and even laughs; but now his toes are aching and his fingers are quite red; he can't bend them any more, and it hurts when he tries to move them. The boy suddenly thought of how much his fingers hurt, and he burst into tears and ran off, and once more he sees a room through another window, and this one also has trees, but there are cakes on the tables, all sorts of cakes—almond ones, red ones, yellow ones; and four rich ladies are sitting there giving cakes to anyone who comes in. The door is always opening to let in all these fine people from the street. The boy crept up, quickly pushed open the door, and went in. Heavens, how they shouted at him and waved him away! One of the ladies rushed up to him and shoved a kopeck in his hand; then she opened the door to let him out on the street again. How frightened he was! And the kopeck rolled right out of his hand and bounced down the stairs: he couldn't bend his red fingers to hold on to it. The boy ran off as quickly as he could, but had no notion of where he was going. He felt like crying again, but he was afraid and just kept on running, breathing on his fingers. And his heart ached because suddenly he felt so lonely and so frightened, and then—Oh, Lord! What's happening now? There's a crowd of people standing around gaping at something: behind the glass in the window there are three puppets, little ones dressed up in red and green and looking just like they were alive! One of them's a little old man, sitting there like he's playing on a big violin, and the others are standing playing on tiny fiddles, wagging their heads in time to the music and looking at one another; their lips are moving and they're talking, really talking, only you can't hear them through the glass. At first the boy thought that they were alive, but when he finally realized that they were puppets he burst out laughing. He had never seen such puppets before and had no idea that such things existed! He still felt like crying, but it was so funny watching the puppets. Suddenly he felt someone grab him from behind: a big brute of a boy stood beside him and suddenly cracked him on the head, tore off his cap, and kicked at his legs. The boy fell down, and the people around him began shouting; he was struck with terror, jumped to his feet and ran off as fast as he could, wherever his legs would take him—through a gateway into a courtyard where he crouched down behind a pile of wood. "They won't find me here, and it's good and dark as well."

He sat there, cowering and unable to catch his breath from fear, and then, quite suddenly, he felt so good: his hands and feet at once stopped aching and he felt as warm and cozy as if he were next to the stove. Then a shudder passed over him: "Why I almost fell asleep!" How nice it would be to go to sleep here: "I'll sit here for a bit and then go back to have a look at those puppets," he thought, and grinned as he recalled them. "Just like they were alive! . . ." Then suddenly he heard his mother singing him a song as she bent over him. "Mamma, I'm going to sleep; oh, how nice it is to sleep here!"

Then a quiet voice whispered over him: "Come with me, son, to my Christmas party."

At first he thought that it was still his mamma, but no—it couldn't be. He couldn't see who had called him, but someone bent over him and hugged him in the darkness; he stretched out his hand . . . and suddenly—what a light there was! And what a Christmas tree! It was more than a tree—he had never seen anything like it! Where can he be? Everything sparkles and shines and there are dolls everywhere—but no, they are all girls and boys, only they are so radiant and they all fly around him, kissing him, picking him up and carrying him off; but he's flying himself; and he sees his mother looking at him and laughs joyously to her.

"Mamma! Mamma! How lovely it is here, mamma!" cries the boy; and he kisses the children again and wants at once to tell them about the puppets behind the glass. "Who are you, boys and girls?" he asks, laughing and feeling that he loves them all.

"This is Christ's Christmas party," they answer. "On this day Christ always has a Christmas party for those little children who have no Christmas tree of their own. . . ." And he learned that all these boys and girls were children just like him, but some had frozen to death in the baskets in which they had been abandoned on the doorsteps of Petersburg officials, others had perished in the keeping of indifferent nurses in orphans' homes, still others had died at the dried-up breasts of their mothers during the Samara famine, and yet others had suffocated from the fumes in third-class railway carriages. And now they are all here, all like angels, all with Christ; and He is in their midst, stretching out His hands to them, blessing them and their sinful mothers. . . . And the mothers of the children stand apart, weeping; each one recognizes her son or daughter; and the children fly to their mothers and wipe away their tears with their tiny hands, begging them not to weep because they are so happy here. . . .

Down below, the next morning, the porters found the tiny body of the runaway boy who had frozen to death behind the woodpile; they found his mother as well. . . . She had died even before him; they met in God's Heaven.

So why did I make up a story like that, so little in keeping with the usual spirit of a sober-minded diary, and a writer's diary at that? All the more since I promised stories preeminently about actual events! But that's just the point: I keep imagining that all this could really have happened—I mean the things that happened in the cellar and behind the woodpile; as for Christ's Christmas party—well, I really don't know what to say: could that have happened? That's just why I'm a novelist—to invent things.

3. A Colony of Young Offenders. Dark Individuals. The Tranformation of Blemished Souls into Immaculate Ones. Measures Acknowledged as Most Expedient Thereto. Little and Bold Friends of Mankind.

On the third day of the holiday I saw all these "fallen" angels, a whole fifty of them altogether. Please don't think I'm joking when I call them that; there can be no doubt that these are children who have been "wronged." Wronged by whom? Who is to blame, and how, and for what? For the moment these are but idle questions for which I have no answer. We'd best get down to business.

I paid a visit to the colony for young offenders that's located beyond the Powder Works. I had been wanting to go there for a long time but hadn't managed; then, unexpectedly, I had some free time and found some good people who offered to show me everything. We set off on a mild, rather overcast day, and once past the Powder Works we drove right into a forest; in the forest is the colony. How lovely it is in winter in a snow-covered forest; how fresh, how pure the air, and how isolated it is here. Some thirteen hundred acres of forest have been donated to the colony, which consists entirely of a few attractive wooden houses set some distance apart from each other. The whole colony has been built with donated money; each house cost some three thousand rubles, and in each house lives a "family." A family is a group of twelve to seventeen boys, and each family has its tutor. The plan is to have up to seventy boys, judging from the size of the colony, but at present, for some reason, there are only about fifty. I must admit that the colony had been generously endowed, and the yearly expenses for each young offender are considerable. It's odd, too, that the sanitary conditions in the colony, as was recently reported in the newspapers, are not entirely satisfactory: there has been a good deal of illness of late, even though, it would seem, the air is fine and the children are well looked after. We stayed in the colony for several hours, from eleven in the morning right until twilight, but I came to see that one visit was not enough to take in everything and comprehend it all. The director invited me to come and spend two days with them; and that's a very tempting offer.

The director, P. A. R-sky, is known in the world of belles-lettres; his articles appear occasionally in *The European Messenger.* He greeted me most cordially and courteously. The office keeps a book in which visitors enter their names if they choose. I noticed many well-known names among those inscribed; this suggests that people know about the colony and take an interest in it. In spite of all his courtesy, the esteemed director is, it seems, a man of great reserve, even though he emphasized almost with delight the positive features of his colony while somewhat playing down all those things that were not so pleasant or not yet put right. I hasten to add that this reserve—or so it seemed to me—derives from his most ardent love for the colony and for the project he has taken on.

All four tutors (I think there are four—one for each family) are by no means old people; they are young, in fact, and receive some three hundred rubles a year in salary; almost all of them are seminary graduates. They live full-time with their pupils and even wear almost the same clothes—a kind of blouse with a belt. The dormitories were empty when we toured. It was a holiday, and the children were off playing somewhere; but it was all the more convenient to inspect the facilities. There is no luxury, nothing superfluous resulting from the excessive kindness or humane feelings of the donors and founders of the institution. Such a thing could happen very easily, and it would be a major error. The folding iron cots, for instance, are the simplest kind; the sheets are made from rather coarse linen; the blankets are also of the plainest variety, but are warm. The tutors get up early, and they and all the pupils tidy and clean the dormitories and wash the floors when necessary.

I caught a certain scent near some of the beds, and learned something almost incredible: some of the pupils (not many, but some eight or nine), not even the very young ones but those aged twelve or thirteen, simply wet their beds in their sleep. When I asked whether this was the result of some ailment, I was told that it was not; it happened simply because the children were uncivilized; when they are admitted they are in so savage a state that they cannot even comprehend that they can and must behave differently. But if that's the case, then where must they have been before? In what wretched slums must they have been raised, and what people must they have dealt with! There is scarcely a peasant family so impoverished that it would not teach a child how to behave in such a case and where even the smallest child would not know what to do. So what sort of people has such a young offender encountered? How bestially indifferent must they have been toward his very existence! Yet this is an actual fact, and I consider it of the greatest significance. Please don't laugh at my inflating this nasty little detail to such dimensions: it is much more serious that it might seem. It indicates that there truly are individuals so dark and dreadful that every trace of their humanity and civic duty has disappeared. When one realizes that, one can also understand what such a tiny, savage soul will become when forsaken and rejected by the human community this way. Yes, these children's souls have witnessed some gloomy scenes and they are accustomed to strong impressions that will remain with them for ever, of course, and will recur in terrible dreams for the rest of their lives. And so those who would reform and educate such children must struggle with these terrible impressions; they must eradicate them and implant new ones—an enormous task.

"You will not believe the savage state some of them are in when they come here," P.A. told me. "There are some who know nothing of themselves or of their place in society. Such a boy has been wandering around the streets scarcely knowing what he is doing, and the only thing on earth he knows and can make any sense of is his freedom—the freedom to wander about, half dead from cold and hunger, but only to wander freely. There is one small boy here, no more than ten, and even now he is utterly unable to get along without stealing. He steals aimlessly, not for profit, but mechanically, simply to steal."

"So how do you hope to reform such children?"

"Through work, a completely different way of life, and through fair treatment. And finally there's the hope that in three years their old weaknesses and habits will be forgotten of their own accord, simply through the passage of time."

I inquired whether there were not yet other notorious and nasty adolescent habits among the boys. I would remind you, by the way, that the boys here ranged in age from ten to seventeen, even though only children under fourteen are supposed to be admitted for treatment.

"Oh, no; we give no chance for such nasty habits to exist," P.A. quickly replied. "The tutors are always with them and watch constantly for things like that."

But I found this difficult to believe. There are several boys in the colony who are from the division of young offenders, now abolished, that used to be located in the Lithuanian Castle. I visited that prison three years ago and saw these boys. Then I learned from absolutely reliable sources that perversion in the Castle was rampant, and that those vagabond children who were admitted but not yet infected with this perversion and who initially loathed it eventually submitted to it almost against their will because their fellows made fun of their chastity.

"And have you had many recidivists?" I inquired.

"Not so many; there were only eight among all those released from the colony." (Yet this is still a goodly number.)

I note that the pupils are released primarily as tradesmen, and that preliminary accommodation is found for them. Formerly the passports issued by the colony were a great handicap to them. But now the means have been found to issue them passports from which, at first glance at least, one cannot tell that the bearer is from the colony of young offenders.

"On the other hand," P.A. hastened to add, "there are some among those released who even now cannot forget about the colony, and whenever there's a holiday, they'll most certainly come to spend some time and visit us."

And so the surest means of reform, of transforming a soul that has been dishonored and defamed into one that is serene and honest, is work. The day in the dormitory begins with work, and then the pupils go to the workshops. In the metal working and carpentry shops I was shown the things they had crafted. These articles are good, considering everything, and will naturally improve greatly when things are better organized. They are sold for the pupils' benefit, and in such a manner each one accumulates something for the day of his release. The children are busy with their work in the morning and afternoon but they do not tire; it seems that work truly does produce a rather strong effect on them morally: they strive to outdo one another and take pride in their success.

Another means for their spiritual development is, of course, the system introduced in the colony whereby the boys mete out their own justice. Each one guilty of an offense is tried by a court of the whole "family" to which he belongs, and the boys either acquit him or sentence him to punishment. The only punishment is being excluded from games. Those who do not submit to the judgment of their fellows are punished by total exclusion from the colony. For that they have their "Peter-and-Paul Fortress," as the boys call it, a special, isolated hut equipped with cells for those temporarily isolated. However, it seems that confinement in the "Fortress" depends exclusively on the director. We visited this fortress; at that time there were two boys confined in it. I note that this confinement is carried out with great caution and solicitude and is imposed for something particularly serious and inveterate. Each of the two was kept in his own small room under lock and key, but we did not get to see them.

This self-administered justice in essence is a good thing, of course, but it smacks of something literary. There are many proud children—proud in a good sense—who can be hurt by the "democratic" power of boys and offenders like themselves, so that they may not even gain a proper understanding of this power. There may be personalities who are much more talented and clever than the others in the "family," and they may be stung by vanity and hatred of the majority decision; and the majority is almost always mediocre. And do the boys who sit in judgment truly understand what they are doing? On the contrary, isn't it likely that, as always and inevitably happens among children in all schools, childish "parties" will form among them, parties grouped around rival boys who are a bit stronger and smarter than the others and who set the tone and lead the others around as if on a string? They are still children, after all, and not adults. Finally, will those who are convicted and who suffer punishment subsequently regard their former judges in the same simple, brotherly fashion as they did before? Doesn't this self-administered justice destroy the sense of comradeship? Of course, this is a means of educating and developing and is based on and was devised with the notion that these previously delinquent children, by having the right of self-administered justice, will accustom themselves to the law, to self-restraint, and to justice, about which they had hitherto known nothing; that it will ultimately develop a sense of duty in them. These are all beautiful and subtle ideas, but to some extent they can be said to cut both ways. As far as punishment is concerned, of course, the most effective of restraints has been chosen—the deprivation of one's freedom.

Let me insert here, by the way, one odd *nota bene*. The other day I happened to hear a very surprising observation about corporal punishment, which has now been abolished in all our schools: "We've now abolished corporal punishment everywhere in the school, and it's a fine thing we did; but what were the repercussions of that? Just that now we have many more cowards among our young people, as compared with the past. They've begun to fear even the slightest physical pain, the least suffering or deprivation, even any kind of insult, any sting to their vanity, so much so that some of them, as we have seen, hang or shoot themselves when faced with the slightest threat or some difficult lesson or examination." Several actual instances of this can in fact best be explained solely by the cowardice of the young people when faced with something threatening or unpleasant; still, this is a strange point of view on the matter, and the *observation* is original at least. I set it down for the record.

I saw all the boys at dinner. The dinner was very simple but nourishing, abundant, and prepared excellently. We sampled it with pleasure before the boys arrived; and yet the cost of food for each boy is only fifteen kopecks a day. They serve soup or cabbage stew with beef, and have porridge or potatoes for a second course. When they get up in the morning they have tea and bread, and bread and kvass between dinner and supper. The boys are well fed; they take turns serving at the table. Once they had taken their places at the table they sang, extremely well, the prayer "Thy Nativity, O Christ Our Lord." One of the tutors teaches them to sing the prayers.

Here at dinner, when all the boys were gathered together, I was most interested in studying their faces. Their faces were not too bold or brazen; they were simply faces that would not be taken aback by anything. Scarcely a single face could be described as dull (although I was told there were dullards among them; former inmates of the foundling home were most prominent in this category). On the contrary, there were even some very intelligent faces. Some faces were ugly, but not physically so; all their features were nearly handsome, but in some faces there was something that would not reveal itself. There were not very many joyous faces, yet the pupils were very much at ease with their superiors and with anyone else, although not at ease in quite the same way as other children whose hearts are more open. And probably a great number of them wanted to slip away from the colony at once. Many of them, evidently, try not to let their secrets slip out inadvertently—that much can be seen from their faces.

The tutors treat the boys humanely and are courteous to the point of delicacy (although they know how to be strict when necessary); but I think this treatment in some cases does not touch the boys' hearts and of course does not touch their intellects. They address them using the formal *you*, even the smallest boys. This *you* sounded somewhat artificial to me, a little unnecessary. Perhaps the boys who come here see this only as a case of "the gentlemen having a bit of fun." In short, this *you* is perhaps a mistake, even a rather serious one. It seems to me that it puts a certain distance between the children and the tutor; there is something formal and bureaucratic in that *you*, and it is a bad thing if some boy takes it as an expression of contempt. After all, how can he, who has seen such outlandish sights and heard the most unnatural cursing, who has lived by unrestrained thievery—how can he believe that suddenly he merits such treatment from a gentleman? In a word, the familiar *thou* would, in my opinion, more closely reflect the real truth in this case; but as it stands, everyone seems to be playacting a little. It's much better, after all, if the children would finally realize that the tutors are not their instructors but their fathers, and that they themselves are only naughty children who must be reformed. However, this *you* perhaps may not spoil the boys, and when he later winces on hearing a *thou*, or even the curses that he inevitably will hear the very day of his release from the institution, then he will sigh for his colony even more tenderly.

Among the things that still need to be put right, particularly prominent is reading. I was told that the children like reading very much; that is, they like listening to someone read aloud on holidays or when they have spare time. There are, apparently, good readers among them. I heard only one of them, and he read well; they say that he loves to read aloud to the others and have them listen to him. But among them are also those who are barely literate and totally illiterate. And the things they read! In one of the families after dinner I saw a book by some sort of author lying on the table; and they read how a certain Vladimir conversed with some Olga on various profound and strange topics, and how later the inevitable environment "shattered their existence." I saw their "library"; it is a cupboard containing Turgenev, Ostrovsky, Lermontov, Pushkin, and so on; there are several useful travel stories, etc. The whole collection is haphazard and has also been donated. Once reading has been permitted, it can have a remarkable formative influence, of course; but I also know that if all Russia's educative forces, led by all the pedagogical councils, wanted to determine or stipulate what children in such circumstances ought to be given to read, then of course they would have to adjourn before they ever reached a conclusion; for this is a very difficult problem, and its final solution will not come from some meeting. On the other hand, our literature has absolutely no books which the People can understand. Neither Pushkin nor the *Sevastopol Tales* nor *Evenings on a Farm* nor the tale of Kalashnikov or Koltsov (particularly Koltsov) is at all understood by the People. Of course, these boys are not the People but are God only knows who—such human specimens as almost escape classification: to what category and type do they belong? But even if they did understand something, they still would be utterly incapable of appreciating it because all this wealth would drop on them out of the blue, as it were; their past lives have simply not prepared them for this. And what of the muckraking writers and satirists? Is this the sort of spiritual influence needed by these poor children who have seen so much filth already? Perhaps these little people have no wish at all to laugh at others. Perhaps these souls, obscured by darkness, would open themselves with joy and tenderness to the most naive, elementary, and artless impressions; to things utterly childish and simple, at which today's secondary-school student, of the same age as these delinquent children, would smile condescendingly and pull a face.

There is also a school, quite in its infancy, but there are plans to organize it better in the very near future. Drawing and painting are scarcely taught. There is no religious instruction at all: there is no priest. But they will have a priest of their own when their church is completed. This wooden church is now being built. The leaders of the colony and the builders are proud of it. Its architecture is truly not bad, but it is done in the somewhat official, markedly

Russian style that has become boring. I note, by the way, that
religious instruction in schools—whether for delinquents or for our
other primary schools—must certainly be entrusted to no one other
than a priest. But why could not even primary schoolteachers tell
simple stories from the Bible? I won't dispute the fact that one can
find truly bad people among the great multitude of village schoolteachers; but if one of them wants to teach atheism to a boy, he
can do it without teaching church history; he need only tell him
about the duck and "what it is covered with." On the other hand,
what do we hear of our clergy? Oh, I certainly don't want to offend
anyone, and I am sure that the school for delinquents will have
the worthiest of priests to tend it; however, what have almost all
our newspapers been writing about lately with particular zeal? They
have printed the most unpleasant facts about clergy who were giving
religious instruction in schools and who, by the dozens, quit the
schools and refused to teach in them unless they were given extra
pay. I don't dispute that "he who labors is worthy of his payment,"
but this eternal whining about extra pay grates on the ear and
lacerates the heart. Our newspapers take the side of the whiners,
as I do myself; yet I still dream of those ancient zealots and preachers of the Gospel who traveled barefoot and naked, enduring beatings and sufferings and preaching Christ without any additional
pay. Oh, I'm not an idealist; I understand all too well that times
are different now. But would it not be gratifying to hear that our
spiritual educators had increased their goodwill by even an iota
before increasing their salaries? I repeat: please don't be offended.
Everyone knows very well that the spirit has not run dry in the
hearts of our clergy and that there are ardent workers among them.
And I am already convinced that just such a one will work in the
colony. But it would be better if the boys were simply told stories
from the Bible without any "official" moral; for the time being
that would be enough for religious instruction. A series of pure,
holy, beautiful pictures would work powerfully on these souls which
thirst after beautiful impressions....

Still, I said farewell to the colony with a cheerful heart. There
may be things in need of fixing up, yet there are facts which indicate
substantial progress toward achieving its goals. Let me tell you
about two of them by way of conclusion. When I was in the colony
one of the pupils, a lad of about fifteen, was confined in the
"Fortress." Before coming here he had been held for some time
in the prison of the Lithuanian Castle while the division of young

offenders was still located there. He was sentenced to join the colony but tried to escape from it twice, I believe; he was caught both times, once outside the colony itself. At last he stated flatly that he would not submit to the rules of the institution, and for this he was put into solitary confinement. At Christmas his relatives brought him some presents, but he was not allowed to have them because he was being kept in confinement; a tutor confiscated them. The boy was terribly offended and much affected by this, and when the director visited him he began to complain bitterly, harshly accusing the tutor of confiscating the parcel of gifts for his own use; at the same time he spoke angrily and sarcastically about the colony and his fellow pupils, making accusations against all of them. "I sat down and had a serious talk with him," P.A. told me. "He maintained a gloomy silence the whole time. Two hours later he suddenly sent for me again, begging me to come and see him; and what do you think he did? He rushed to me, his eyes full of tears, utterly shaken and transformed; he began to repent and to reproach himself; he also told me things that had happened to him previously and that he had kept hidden from everyone; he told me his secret—that he had long been addicted to a most shameful habit from which he could not free himself, and that this tormented him. In short, it was a complete confession. I spent two hours with him," P.A. added. "We had a real talk; I advised him of certain methods to help him struggle with his habit, and so on."

When P.A. told me this he deliberately passed over the content of their conversation; but you will have to agree that it is a gift to be able to enter into the sick soul of a deeply embittered young offender who has never had any notion of the truth. I confess I would very much like to know all the details of that conversation. Here is another fact: every tutor in every family not only sees that the pupils tidy the dormitory and wash and clean it but also joins them in the work. They wash the floors on Saturdays; the tutor not only demonstrates how this is to be done but himself sets to washing the floor with the boys. This is a most thorough under- standing of one's vocation and one's human dignity. Would you ever find such an attitude to one's work among bureaucrats, for example? And if, indeed, these people resolve to unite the colony's goals with their own private aims in life, then, of course, the matter will be "fixed up," even despite some theoretical errors, if such should occur initially.

A man who has seen a good deal of life said to me the other

day: "Heroes—that's what you novelists are looking for. And when
you can't find any heroes among us Russians, you start to grumble
at the whole country. Let me tell you a little story: once upon a
time, a good while ago now, during the reign of the late emperor,
there lived a government official who served first in St. Petersburg
and then in Kiev, I think, where he died. Now on the surface of
it, that would seem to be his whole life's story. Yet, what do you
think? This humble and quiet little fellow all his life suffered such
inner torments over serfdom, over the fact that in Russia a man
created in the likeness and image of God could be so slavishly
dependent on a man such as himself, that he began to scrape and
save out of his own meager salary, denying his wife and children
almost the necessities of life; and when he managed to accumulate
enough he would buy some serf's freedom from his landowner. Of
course, it would take him ten years to free one man. In the course
of his whole life he managed in this way to redeem about three or
four people, and when he died he left nothing to his family. This
all happened without publicity, quietly, unknown to everyone. What
sort of hero can he be, of course! He's 'an idealist of the forties'
and nothing more; perhaps even ridiculous and not very skillful,
because he thought that he could struggle against all this evil with
only his own petty, individual effort. Yet still, it seems that our
Potugins ought to be a bit more charitable toward Russia and not
throw mud at her for anything and everything."

I am setting down this little story here (it's not entirely relevant,
I suppose) only because I have no reason to doubt its authenticity.

Yet these are the sort of people we need! I am terribly fond of
this ridiculous type of petty official who seriously imagines that he,
with his microscopic efforts and stubborn persistence, is capable
of aiding the common cause without waiting for some widespread
campaign and general initiative. That's the kind of little man who
might be very useful in a colony of young offenders as well....
Oh, naturally, working under better-educated and higher supervisors....

However, I spent only some few hours in the colony, and there
was much that I might have conceived wrongly or missed or been
mistaken about. In any case, I find that the means for making
blemished souls over into immaculate ones are still insufficient.

3

1. The Russian Society for the Protection of Animals. The Government Courier. Demon-Vodka. The Itch for Debauch and Vorobev. From the End or from the Beginning?

In no. 359 of *The Voice* I happened to read of the celebration of the tenth anniversary of the Russian Society for the Protection of Animals. What a kind and humane society this is! As far as I understand, its main idea is almost entirely conveyed in these words from the speech of the Society's president, Prince A. A. Suvorov: "In fact, the task of our new charitable institution seemed all the more difficult because the majority was unwilling to see in the protection of animals those same moral and material benefits for humans as derive from their kind and sensible treatment of domestic animals."

And in fact the Society is concerned not only about poor dogs and horses; man, too—Russian man—needs to humanize and "image himself"[1] and this is something which the Society for the Protection of Animals can undoubtedly promote. Once the peasant has learned to have pity for his animals, he will begin to have pity for his wife. And therefore, although I am very fond of animals, I am delighted that the worthy Society values people even more than animals—people who have become coarse, inhumane, semi-barbaric, and who are seeking the light! Any means of enlightenment are precious, and one can only wish that the Society's idea

1. To image oneself is an expression heard among the People; it means to give an image, to restore in man his human image. One who has been drinking for a long time is told, with reproach: "You ought to image yourself." I heard this from the convicts. [Dostoevsky's note]

in fact becomes one means of enlightenment. Our children are
raised and grow up encountering many disgusting sights. They see
a peasant who has grossly overloaded his cart lashing his wretched
nag, who gives him his living, across the eyes as she struggles in
the mud; or, something I myself saw not very long ago, for instance:
a peasant was hauling calves to the slaughterhouse in a large cart
in which he had loaded about ten of the creatures; he climbed into
the cart with an air of utmost calm and sat down upon a calf. He
found a soft seat there—just like a sofa with springs—but the calf,
its tongue hanging out and its eyes bulging, may have drawn its
last breath even before it reached the slaughterhouse. I am sure
that this scene didn't trouble anyone on the street: "Doesn't
matter—it's going to be slaughtered anyway." But scenes such as
these undoubtedly brutalize and corrupt people, especially children. It's true that the worthy Society has already been attacked;
I have heard people make fun of it more than once. I've heard
mention, for example, of the time about five years ago when the
Society laid charges against a cabman for mistreating his horse.
He was fined fifteen rubles, I think. And that, of course, was a
miscalculation, because after such a heavy fine many people truly
did not know whom to pity: the cabman or his horse. Nowadays,
it's true, the new law provides for a fine of not more than ten
rubles. Then I heard about the Society's allegedly excessive concerns for putting to death by chloroform stray, and thus harmful,
dogs who had lost their owners. People noted that at a time when
people are starving in the provinces struck by famine, such tender
concern for dogs might seem to grate on the ear. But objections
such as these do not stand up to criticism. The aim of the Society
is more enduring than the vicissitudes of day-to-day living. It is
based on something splendid and true which sooner or later must
take root and triumph. Nevertheless, looking at it from another
point of view, it would be extremely desirous that the activities of
the Society and the aforementioned "vicissitudes of day-to-day living" should enter into a mutual equilibrium, so to say; then, of
course, it would be easier to chart that salvational and charitable
course the Society should follow in order to achieve abundant and,
above all, practical results that would truly achieve its purpose. . . .
Perhaps I am not expressing myself clearly; I shall tell you a little
story which really happened and hope that by its graphic account
I can convey more clearly what I want to express.

This happened to me a long, long time ago—in my "prehistoric"

period, as it were—in 1837 to be precise. It happened on the road
from Moscow to St. Petersburg; I was then only fifteen years old.
My elder brother and I and our late father were traveling to St.
Petersburg where the two of us were to enroll in the Chief Engineering School. It was May, and it was very warm. We were
traveling without changing horses, almost at a walking pace, and
we would spend two or three hours at each posting station. I recall
how weary we finally became of this journey, as it dragged on for
almost a week. My brother and I were eager to enter a new life
and were terribly prone to dreaming of the "beautiful and the
sublime" (this phrase was still fresh then and was spoken without
irony). And how many such beautiful phrases existed and circulated
at that time! We believed passionately in something, and although
we both knew very well everything that was required for the mathematics examination, we dreamed only of poetry and poets. My
brother wrote verses—three a day—and even on the road I was
continually composing in my mind a novel from Venetian life. Only
two months earlier Pushkin had died, and my brother and I had
agreed on the road that when we arrived in St. Petersburg we would
at once stop off at the scene of his duel and seek out his former
apartment to see the room in which he had yielded up his spirit.
And so it was that once, before evening, we stopped at an inn by
a posting station—I don't remember the village, but I think it was
in Tver Province; the village was large and prosperous. Within
half an hour we were to make ready to leave, but in the meantime
I was looking out the window and saw the following.

Directly across the street from the inn was the station building.
Suddenly a courier's troika came flying up to the station entrance
and a government courier leapt out; he had on a full-dress coat
with the little narrow flaps on the back that were worn then, and
he wore a large tricornered hat with white, yellow, and, I think,
green plumes (I forget this detail and could check it, but I seem
to recall the flash of a green plume). The courier was a tall, extremely stout, and strong fellow with a purplish face. He ran into
the station and, no doubt, knocked back a glass of vodka there. I
recall that our driver said that such couriers always drink a glass
of vodka at every station, since without it they couldn't stand up
to "the punishment they have to take." In the meantime a new
troika of fresh, spirited horses rolled up to the station and the
coachman, a young lad of twenty or so, wearing a red shirt and
carrying his coat on his arm, jumped onto the seat. The courier

at once flew out of the inn, ran down the steps, and got into the carriage. Before the coachman could even start the horses, the courier stood up and, silently, without any word whatsoever, raised his huge right fist and dealt a painful blow straight down on the back of the coachman's neck. The coachman jolted forward, raised his whip, and lashed the shaft horse with all his might. The horses started off with a rush, but this did nothing to appease the courier. He was not angry; he was acting according to his own plan, from something preconceived and tested through many years of experience; and the terrible fist was raised again, and again it struck the coachman's neck, and then again and again; and so it continued until the troika disappeared from sight. Naturally the coachman, who could barely hold on because of the blows, kept lashing the horses every second like one gone mad; and at last his blows made the horses fly off as if possessed. Our coachman explained to me that all government couriers travel in almost the same fashion and that this particular one was universally known for it; once he had had his vodka and jumped into the carriage, he would always begin by beating, "always in that same way," for no reason whatsoever; he would beat in a measured manner, raising and lowering his fist, and "he'll keep using his fists on the coachman like that for nearly a mile, and then he'll quit. And if he gets to feeling bored, he might take it up again in the middle of the trip; then again, maybe God will prevent it. But he'll always start up again when they're getting close to the station: he'll start about a mile away, and you'll see his fist going up and down, and that's how they'll drive up to the station, so's everybody in the village can marvel at it. Your neck aches for a month afterward." When the young lad comes back people laugh at him: "Didn't that courier whack you across the neck, though!" And the lad, perhaps, that very day will beat his young wife: "At least I'll take it out on you"; and perhaps also because she "looked on and saw it. . . . "

Doubtless it is cruel of the coachman to whip his horses that way: they come galloping into the next station worn out and barely able to breathe. But tell me, in truth, could any member of the Society for the Protection of Animals resolve to bring charges against that peasant for cruel and inhumane treatment of his horses?

This disgusting scene has stayed in my memory all my life. I could never forget the courier, and for a long time thereafter I couldn't help but explain many of the shameful and cruel things about the Russian People in too one-sided a manner. You realize that I am talking about something that happened long ago. This little scene was like an emblem, so to say; something that very graphically demonstrated the link between a cause and its effect. Every blow that rained down on the animal was the direct result of every blow that fell on the man. At the end of the 1840s, in the era of my most selfless and passionate dreams, I suddenly had a notion that if I should ever found a philanthropic society I would certainly have this courier's troika engraved on the society's seal as an emblem and an admonition.

Oh, there's no doubt that times now are not what they were forty years ago, and couriers do not beat the People; but the People beat one another, having retained flogging in their courts. The point is not that, but in the causes that bring effects after them. The courier is gone, but on the other hand there is "demon-vodka." In what way can demon-vodka resemble the courier? It can do so very easily in the way it coarsens and brutalizes a man, makes him callous, and turns him away from clear thinking, desensitizes him to the power of goodness. A drunkard doesn't care about kindness to animals; a drunkard will abandon his wife and children. A drunken man came to the wife he had abandoned and whom, along with her children, he had not supported for many months; he demanded vodka and set to beating her to force her to give him still more vodka; the unfortunate woman, compelled to virtual forced labor (just recall what women's work is and what value we place on it now) and not knowing how to feed her children, seized a knife and stabbed him. This happened recently, and she will be brought to trial. But there is little point in telling you about her because there are hundreds and thousands of such cases—just open a newspaper. But the chief similarity between demon-vodka and the courier is certainly that it, just as fatally and irresistibly, towers over the human will.

The worthy Society for the Protection of Animals comprises 750 members, people who can be influential. Suppose it wanted to help reduce drunkenness among the People even a little and stop the poisoning of a whole generation by liquor! The strength of the People is fading away; the source of our future wealth is drying up; their intellect is becoming impoverished and their development retarded. And what will the children of today's People carry away in their minds and hearts when they grow up in the abominations of their fathers? A fire broke out in a village; there was a church in the village, but the tavernkeeper came out and shouted that if

the villagers abandoned the church and saved his tavern, he would
stand them a barrel of vodka. The church burned down, but the
tavern was saved. These instances are still trivial compared with
the countless horrors yet to come. If the worthy Society wished to
assist, even in a small way, in eradicating these prime causes, it
would, in so doing, both improve its own status and further its
excellent campaign of education. Otherwise, how can they compel
people to be compassionate when things are arranged precisely
with the aim of destroying every trace of humanity in humans?
And is it only liquor that incites and depraves the People in our
remarkable times? It is as if the very atmosphere contains some
sort of intoxicant, a kind of itch for depravity. An unprecedented
distortion of ideas has begun among the People, along with a general
worship of materialism. In this instance what I mean by materialism
is the People's adoration of money and the power of the bag of
gold. The notion has suddenly burst forth among the People that
a bag of gold now is everything, that it holds every sort of power,
and that everything their fathers have told them and taught them
hitherto is all nonsense. It would be a great misfortune if this way
of thinking should become firmly established among the People,
and yet, how else are they to think? For example, the recent railway
disaster in which over a hundred army recruits were killed on the
Odessa line—do you really believe that such power will not have
a corrupting effect on the People? The People see and marvel at
such might—"They do whatever they like"—and they begin to
doubt in spite of themselves: "So that's where the real power is;
and that's where it has always been. Just get rich and you can have
it all; you can do anything you like." There can be no notion more
corrupting than this one. And it is in the very air and gradually
is permeating everything. The People have no defense against this
idea; they have no education, and there is no means whatsoever of
exposing them to other opposing ideas. Over the whole of Russia
there now stretch nearly twenty thousand versts of railways, and
throughout this system even the most minor official stands as one
who spreads these ideas; he appears to have total power over you
and your fate, over your family, and over your honor should you
happen to fall into his clutches on the railway. Not long ago one
stationmaster, on his own authority and by his own hand, dragged
a lady out of the railway carriage in which she was traveling and
delivered her to some gentleman who had complained to this stationmaster that she was his wife and was running away from him—

and this without any judicial process and without any doubt that
he had the right to do it. It is clear that this stationmaster, if he
was in possession of his faculties, still must have become crazed
by the notion of his own authority. All these incidents and examples
burst in on the People in a continual process of temptation; they
see them every day and they draw the inevitable conclusions. In
the past I was ready to condemn Mr. Suvorin for his incident with
Mr. Golubev. I thought then that an innocent man should not be
dragged into disrepute in such a fashion and have all the stirrings
of his soul described in the bargain. But now I have changed my
view somewhat even on this incident. What business is it of mine
that Mr. Golubev is not guilty! Mr. Golubev may be as pure as the
driven snow, but still Vorobev is guilty. Who is this Vorobev? I
have no idea; and I am certain that he does not even exist, but it
is that same Vorobev who charges furiously over all the railway
lines, who arbitrarily sets fares, who forcibly ejects passengers from
railway carriages, who destroys trains, who allows goods to rot at
stations for months on end, who brazenly inflicts damage on entire
towns, provinces, the whole country, and who only shouts in a
wild voice, "Clear the way, I'm coming!" But the chief thing this
pernicious upstart is to be blamed for is that he has placed himself
above the People as a seductive and fatal idea. However, why do
I attack Vorobev? Is he the only such corrupting idea? I repeat:
this new materialism and skepticism seems to be wafting through
the air; we have begun to worship gratuitous gain, pleasure without
labor; all sorts of deceit and villainy are committed in cold blood;
people are murdered for the sake of a ruble in their pocket. I know
very well that the past also had its share of terrible things, but
certainly things are ten times worse now. What is most important
is that this notion is circulating as if it were a doctrine or a faith.
Two or three weeks ago in St. Petersburg a young lad, a cabbie
who was scarcely of age, was driving an old couple at night; when
he noticed that the man had passed out from drink, he drew his
penknife and began stabbing the old woman. He was captured, and
the poor fool confessed at once: "I don't know how it happened
and how the knife got into my hands." And, in truth, he really
did not know. This is specifically a matter of the environment. He
was caught up and drawn in—as if into a machine—by today's itch
for debauchery, by the popular tendency of today: gratuitous gain.
Why not give it a try, even with only a penknife?

"No, we're not interested in the protection of animals these days;

that's only a scheme the gentlemen have thought up." I have heard
that very same statement, but I totally reject it. Not being a member
of the Society myself, I am still ready to serve it and, I think,
already am serving it. I don't know whether I expressed with even
partial clarity my wish for that "equilibrium of the activities of the
Society with the vicissitudes of day-to-day living" which I wrote
of above; but understanding the humane and humanizing purpose
of the Society, I am still deeply devoted to it. I could never understand the notion that only one-tenth of people should get higher
education while the other nine-tenths of people should serve only
as their material and means while themselves remaining in darkness. I do not wish to think and live in any other way than with
the belief that all our ninety million Russians (or however many
will subsequently be born) will all someday be educated, humanized, and happy. I am fully convinced that universal education can
harm none of us. I even believe that the kingdom of thought and
light is possible to achieve here, in our Russia, even sooner, perhaps, than anywhere else, for even now no one here will stand up
for the idea that we must bestialize one group of people for the
welfare of another group that represents civilization, such as is the
case all over Europe. It is here, after all, that serfdom was voluntarily abolished by the upper classes with the will of the tsar at
their head! And therefore, once more, I give a most warmhearted
welcome to the Society for the Protection of Animals; I wanted
only to express the thought that it would be a good thing if we
were to begin taking action not always from the end but, partly at
least, from the beginning.

2. Spiritualism. Something about Devils. The
   Extraordinary Cleverness of Devils, If Only These Are
   Devils

And now, however, I've covered a whole sheet with writing and
there is no more room. And I had wanted to talk a bit about the
war, about our border regions; I wanted to say something about
literature, about the Decembrists, and about at least fifteen other
topics. I see that I must write more succinctly and compress
things—something to keep in mind in the days ahead. A word, by
the way, about the Decembrists before I forget: in announcing the
recent death of one of them, our journals stated that he apparently

was one of the very last of the Decembrists; this is not quite accurate. Among the surviving Decembrists are Ivan Aleksandrovich Annenkov, the one whose original story was told in such distorted fashion by the late Alexandre Dumas-père in his well-known novel *Les Mémoires d'un maitre d'armes*. Matvei Ivanovich Muravev-Apostol, the brother of the one who was executed, is alive, as are Svistunov and Nazimov. Perhaps there are yet other survivors.

In a word, there is much I shall have to put off until the February issue. But I would like to conclude the present January diary with something a bit more cheery. There is one very amusing and, most important, fashionable topic, and that is devils and spiritualism. In fact, something amazing is going on: people write and tell me, for instance, that a young man sits in an armchair, tucks up his feet, and the chair begins to dance around the room—and this is in St. Petersburg, the capital! Now why was it that no one ever did this before—dancing around the room while sitting in a chair with his legs tucked up? Instead, everyone just went on working and meekly earning their ranks. People insist that there's a lady somewhere in the provinces who has a house with so many devils in it that even Uncle Eddy's cabin doesn't have half as many. And don't we have devils of our own! Gogol writes to Moscow from the next world and states positively that devils exist. I read the letter, and the style is his. He urges us not to summon them up, not to turn tables, and not to have anything to do with them: "Do not tease the devils, do not hob-nob with them; it is a sin to tease devils. . . . If nervous insomnia begins to torment you by night, do not grow angry, but pray: this is the work of devils. Make the sign of the cross over your nightshirt and say a prayer." The voices of clergymen are raised advising even scientists to have nothing to do with "witchery" nor to study it scientifically. When even clergymen have spoken out, it means the thing has grown beyond a joke. But the whole problem is: are these really devils? Now this is a question the Committee of Inquiry into Spiritualism recently formed in St. Petersburg ought to resolve! Because if they finally do establish that these things are not the work of devils but of some sort of electricity or other, some new manifestation of universal energy, then total disillusionment would set in at once: "What a marvel," people would say, "and how boring!" They would all drop spiritualism, forget about it at once, and go back to their own business as before. But in order to investigate the question of whether these are devils at work at least one member of the committee must be able and have the opportunity to admit the existence of devils, even as a hypothesis. But it is hardly likely that even one member of the committee can be found who believes in devils, despite the fact that a terrific number of people who do not believe in God still believe in the Devil, readily and happily. And therefore the question is beyond the committee's competence. My whole problem is that I simply cannot believe in devils myself, and so it is a great pity that I have developed a very clear and astonishing theory of spiritualism, but one wholly founded on the existence of devils; without them my whole theory collapses of itself. And it is this theory that I, in concluding, wish to pass on to the reader. The fact is that I am defending devils: this time they are being unfairly attacked and treated as fools. Don't worry, they know what they are doing; that is just what I want to prove.

In the first place, people write that spirits are stupid (by spirits I mean devils, the Unclean Power, for other than devils, what spirits can be at work here?); that when they are summoned up and questioned (through table-turning), they only give silly answers, know no grammar, and have never communicated a new idea or passed on a single new discovery. Thinking that way is a grave mistake. What would happen, for instance, if the devils at once showed their power and overwhelmed humans with their discoveries? What if they suddenly revealed the electric telegraph (i.e., assuming it had not already been invented) or passed on various secrets to people: "Dig in such-and-such a place and you'll find a treasure or find deposits of coal" (firewood, incidentally, is such a price these days). Still, all these things are just trifles! Of course, you understand that human science is still in its infancy and has not done much more than begin its work; about all it has accomplished is to get itself firmly on its feet. And now, suppose, suddenly a whole shower of revelations commences, of the order, say, that the sun stands still while the earth revolves around it (because there are probably many discoveries of that magnitude, things which our wise men have not dreamt of, that still await discovery). Suddenly all this knowledge would simply tumble down on humanity and, the main thing, it would come quite gratuitously, as a gift. What would happen to people then, I ask? Oh, of course, everyone would be in raptures at first. People would embrace one another in ecstasy; they would rush off to study these revelations (and that would take time); they would suddenly feel themselves overcome by happiness

and up to their necks in material blessings; perhaps they would
walk or fly through the air, covering immense distances ten times
faster than they now do by railway; they would extract fabulous
harvests from the earth, create new organisms through chemistry;
and there would be beef enough to supply three pounds per person,
just as our Russian socialists dream—in short, eat, drink, and be
merry. "And now," all the lovers of humanity would cry, "now
that human needs are taken care of, now we will reveal our true
potential! There are no more material deprivations, no more corrupting environment, once the source of all flaws; now humans
will become beautiful and righteous! There is no more ceaseless
labor to try to feed oneself, and now everyone will occupy himself
with sublime, profound thoughts and with universal concerns. Now,
only now, has life in the higher sense begun!" And what clever
and good people, perhaps, would give voice to such words, and
the novelty of it all might attract still others until, at last, they
would raise their voices in a common hymn: "Who can be likened
unto this beast? Praise be to him who has brought fire down from
the heavens!"

But such rapturous outpourings would scarcely be enough for
even one generation! People would suddenly see that they had no
more life left, that they had no freedom of spirit, no will, no
personality, that someone had stolen all this from them; they would
see that their human image had disappeared and that the brutish
image of a slave had emerged, the image of an animal, with the
single difference that a beast does not realize that it is a beast, but
a human would realize that he had become a beast. And humanity
would begin to decay; people would be covered in sores and begin
to bite their tongues in torment, seeing that their lives had been
taken away for the sake of bread, for "stones turned into bread."
People would realize that there is no happiness in inactivity, that
the mind which does not labor will wither, that it is not possible
to love one's neighbor without sacrificing something to him of one's
own labor, that it is vile to live at the expense of another, and that
happiness lies not in happiness but only in the attempt to achieve it.
People would be overcome by boredom and sickness of heart:
everything has been done and there is nothing more to do; everything has become known and there is nothing more to discover.
There would be crowds of people seeking to end their lives, but
not as they do now, in some obscure corner; masses of people
would gather, seizing one another's hands, and suddenly destroy

themselves by the thousands through some new method that they discovered along with all their other discoveries. And then, perhaps, those who remained would cry out to God: "Thou art right, O Lord: man does not live by bread alone!" Then they would rise up against the devils and abandon witchery. . . . Oh, never would God send down such torments on humanity! And the kingdom of the devils would collapse! No, the devils won't make such a grave political error. They are sophisticated politicians and move toward their goal by a most subtle and logical route (I repeat: that is, if devils indeed do exist!).

The fundamental principle of their kingdom is discord; that is, they want to found it on discord. Why do they specifically need discord here? Why, it's obvious: just remember that discord itself is a dreadful force; discord, after a long period of strife, drives people to folly; it dulls and distorts their reason and their feelings. In discord he who gives offense, once he realizes what he has done, does not go to be reconciled with the one he has offended, but says: "I offended him, and so I must take revenge on him." But the main thing is that the devils have the most thorough knowledge of the history of the human race and particularly remember all those things on which discord has been based. They know, for instance, that if in Europe sects exist that have broken away from Catholicism and continue up to now as religions, then this is only because blood was spilled because of them at one time. Should Catholicism, for example, come to an end, then all the Protestant sects would inevitably collapse as well: what would be left for them to protest against? Even now they are almost inclined to move into some sort of "humanism," or even simply to atheism, and people have remarked on that for some time now. And if these sects still continue to cling to life as religions, then it is because they still continue to protest. They protested even last year, and what a protest it was!—they took on the pope himself.

Oh, of course in the final analysis the influence of the devils will prevail and they will crush humanity like a fly with their "stones turned into bread." That is their principal goal, but they will undertake to fulfill it only after having first ensured that their future kingdom will be safe from human rebellion and so guarantee its longevity. But how can humans be subdued? Of course: *divide et impera* (divide the enemy and you will conquer him). And for this they need discord. On the other hand, people will get tired of the stones turned into bread, and so something must be found for them

to do so they won't get bored. And isn't discord a fine occupation
for human beings!

Now please observe how the devils introduce discord among us
and, so to say, from the very first step begin spiritualism with
discord. Our frenzied age makes this so much easier. Just look at
how many believers in spiritualism among us have already been
offended. People shout and laugh at them for believing in table-
turning, as if they had done or planned to do something dishonest;
but still they carry on investigating the question despite the discord.
How can they stop investigating it in any case? The devils start
their work in a very roundabout way: they arouse curiosity but
confuse people instead of explaining; they make people uncertain
and openly laugh in their faces. An intelligent person, worthy of
all respect, stands with a puzzled frown on his face and painfully
seeks an answer: "Whatever can this be?" At last he is ready to
give up and abandon his quest, but the laughter of the crowd grows
louder, and the matter develops to the point where the believer has
to continue despite himself, out of his own sense of pride.

Before us, armed with all the weapons science has to offer, sits
the Committee to Investigate Spiritualism. The public waits in
anticipation, but what happens? The devils have no intention of
offering any resistance; to the contrary, in a most disgraceful manner they decide they will "pass." Seances are unsuccessful; deceit
and trickery are exposed. Malicious laughter rings out from all
sides; the committee retires with scornful glances; believers in spiritualism are thoroughly put to shame; a desire for revenge creeps
into the hearts of both sides. Now, it would seem, the devils are
gone for good, but no! No sooner have the scientists and sober-
minded people turned away than the devils at once perform some
even more supernatural trick for the erstwhile believers, and once
again they are convinced, now even more firmly than before. More
temptation, more discord! Last summer in Paris a certain photographer was brought to trial for various spiritualistic frauds; he would
summon up the dead and take their photographs; he was overwhelmed with orders. But they picked him up, and he made a
complete confession in court; he even brought in the lady who had
been helping him by representing the spirits he summoned up.
And what do you think—were those whom the photographer deceived convinced? Not in the least. One of them, apparently, said:
"Three of my children have died, and I have no photos of them;
but the photographer took their pictures, which all resemble my

children, and I could recognize each one. What do I care if he's confessed to fraud? He has his reasons for doing that, but I'm holding a fact in my hand, so leave me alone." This was in the newspapers. I don't know whether I reported all the details correctly, but the essence is accurate. Now imagine if such a thing happened here. No sooner would the learned committee, its work finished and the wretched fraud exposed, turn its back than the devils would seize one of its most obdurate members—even, say, Mr. Mendeleev himself, who has exposed spiritualism in his public lectures—and catch him up at once in their nets, just as they caught Crookes and Olcott in their time. They would take him aside and lift him into the air for five minutes, materialize before him various dead people he had known, and do it all in such a manner that he could no longer have any doubts. And what would happen then, tell me? As a true scientist he would have to accept actual fact—he, who has been giving lectures! What a picture, what a shame, what an uproar, what shouts and cries of indignation! Of course this is only a joke, and I am sure that nothing of this sort will happen to Mr. Mendeleev, although in England and in America it seems that the devils have acted precisely according to this plan. And what if the devils, having prepared the ground and planted sufficient discord, suddenly want to broaden the sphere of their activities and turn to something genuine and serious? They're an unpredictable lot with a strong sense of irony and could do something of that sort. For instance, what if they suddenly burst into the midst of the People, along with literacy, say? And our People are so defenseless, so given to ignorance and debauchery, and there are so few who can guide them in this sense, it seems! The People might put their faith in these new phenomena with a passion (they believe in Ivan Filippovich, after all). Then how their spiritual development would be delayed! What damage might be done, and for what a period of time! What an idolatrous worship of materialism, and what discord; discord a hundred, a thousand times worse than before; and this is exactly what the devils need. And discord certainly will ensue, especially if spiritualism manages to provoke restrictions and persecution (and persecution would inevitably follow from the rest of the People who do not believe in spiritualism). Then it would spread in an instant, like burning kerosene, and set everything ablaze. Mystical ideas love persecution; they are created by it. Every such persecuted idea is like that petroleum which the arsonists poured over the floors and walls of the Tuileries before the fire and which, in turn, could only feed the blaze in the building that was under guard. Oh, the devils know the force of a forbidden faith and they, perhaps, have already been waiting many centuries for mankind to trip over a turning table! Of course, they are governed by some sort of enormous unclean spirit of awesome power, more clever than the Mephistopheles whom Goethe made famous, as Yakov Polonsky tells us.

I have been most definitely joking and having fun from the first word to the last; but this is what I would like to express in conclusion: if we regard spiritualism as something that bears within it some sort of new religion (and almost all, even the most sober-minded among the spiritualists, are inclined to share even a little of that view), then something of what I have said above might be taken seriously. And therefore, may God grant speedy success to free study of the question from both sides. This alone will help to eradicate quickly the nasty spirit that is spreading about, and will, perhaps, enrich science by some a new discovery. But to shout at one another, to heap scorn on one another and ostracize one another for spiritualism, means, in my view, only to strengthen and disseminate the idea of spiritualism in its worst sense. This is the beginning of intolerance and persecution. That's just what the devils want!

3. A Word Apropos of My Biography

The other day someone showed me a copy of my biography included in *The Russian Encyclopedic Dictionary* (Second Year, Volume 5, Book 2, 1875), published by Professor I. N. Berezin of St. Petersburg University and complied by Mr. V.Z. It is hard to imagine so many mistakes being made on one half-page. I was born not in 1818 but in 1822. My late brother, Mikhail Mikhailovich, the publisher of the journals *Time* and *Epoch*, was my elder brother, not younger than I by four years. After my term of hard labor, to which I was exiled in 1849 as a *state criminal* (Mr. V.Z. mentions not a word about the nature of my crime, saying only that "he was involved in the Petrashevsky affair," i.e., in God knows what sort of affair, since no one is obliged to know and remember the Petrashevsky affair, while the *Encyclopedic Dictionary* is intended for general reference; people might think that I was exiled for robbery). After my term of hard labor, by the will of the late emperor, I directly entered the army as a private soldier and after three years of service was promoted to officer's rank. I was never deported ("settled") to Siberia, as Mr. V.Z. says.

The order of my literary works is mixed up: tales that belong to the very first period of my literary activity are attributed in the biography to the latest period. There are many such mistakes, and I am not listing them all so as not to weary the reader; but I will point them all out if challenged. There are, however, outright fabrications. Mr. V.Z. states that I was the editor of the newspaper *The Russian World*; to that I declare that I was never the editor of *The Russian World*; furthermore, not a single line of mine has ever appeared in that worthy publication. I don't deny that Mr. V.Z. (Mr. Vladimir Zotov?) can have his own point of view and consider it utterly trivial, in a biographical account of a writer, to indicate accurately when he was born, what interesting experiences he has had, where, when, and in what order he published his works, which works can be his earlier and which his later, which periodicals he published, which ones he edited, and which ones he merely worked for. Just the same, one would wish for a little more good sense, only for the sake of accuracy. Otherwise, readers may think that all the articles in Mr. Berezin's dictionary have been put together in such a sloppy fashion.

4. A Turkish Proverb

Just in passing, I will insert here a Turkish proverb (a real one— I haven't made it up): If you set off to a certain goal and keep stopping along the way to throw stones at every dog that barks at you, you will never reach your destination.

As far as possible, I'll follow the advice of that wise proverb in my *Diary*, although I wouldn't want to tie myself down with promises beforehand.

February

1

1. On the Fact That We Are All Good People. How Russian Society Resembles Marshal MacMahon

The first issue of *A Writer's Diary* was well received; scarcely anyone abused it, at least scarcely anyone in literature—beyond that, I don't know. If there was any literary abuse then it passed unnoticed. *The St. Petersburg Gazette* hastened to remind its readers in an editorial that I have no love for children, adolescents, and the young generation, while in their feuilleton later on in the same issue they reprinted a whole story from my *Diary,* "The Boy at Christ's Christmas Party," a story that shows, at least, that I don't hate children totally. Still, none of that matters very much; the only thing I am concerned about is whether it is a good thing that I pleased everyone. Is that a good sign or a bad one? Could it be a bad sign? And yet—why not? Better take it as a good sign rather than a bad one and stop at that.

And truly enough, we are all good people—apart from the bad ones, of course. But let me remark in passing that there may be no bad people among us at all, but only some useless ones. We haven't matured enough to be bad. Don't laugh, but stop and think: through lack of our own bad people (even though, as I've said, we have plenty of useless ones), there was a time when we would go so far as to idealize certain nasty types who appeared among our literary characters and who were largely borrowed from foreign literatures. It's not enough that we esteemed such people—we slavishly tried to imitate them in real life and even bent over backward to model ourselves on them. Just recall: what a crowd of Pechorins we had who did so many nasty things in real life after they read *A Hero of Our Time.* The forefather of all these nasty types in Russian literature was Silvio from the story "The Shot," a character

343

whom the straightforward and beautiful Pushkin borrowed from
Byron. And Pechorin himself killed Grushnitsky only because he
didn't cut a fine enough figure in his dress coat, and wasn't regarded
as a very dashing hero by the ladies at high-society balls in St.
Petersburg. If in the past we valued and respected these evil wretch-
es, then it was only because they appeared to be people whose
hatred was *unfaltering,* as opposed to us Russians, who, as we all
know, are people whose hatred is short-lived; this is a trait we have
always particularly disliked in ourselves. Russian people are incapable of long and serious hatred—not only hatred of others but
even of vices, of the darkness of ignorance, of despotism, obscur-
antism, and all those other retrograde things. We Russians are at
once ready to make peace, even at the first opportunity—isn't that
so? In fact, just stop and think: what do we have to hate one
another about? For the wrongs we commit? Ah, but this is a most
elusive, most delicate, and most unfair cause for hatred; it cuts
both ways, in short; at present, at least, we'd best not take it up.
There remains hatred because of convictions; but here I'm utterly
unconvinced that we can hate with any seriousness. At one time,
for example, we had Slavophiles and Westernizers, and they did a
lot of fighting with one another. But now, with the abolition of
serfdom, the reforms of Peter I have been completed and a general
sauve qui peut has ensued. And now we have the Slavophiles and
the Westernizers suddenly in agreement on the same idea: that now
we must expect everything from the People; that the People have
arisen, are moving, and that they and only they will utter our
ultimate word. The Slavophiles and Westernizers, it would seem,
could have been reconciled at this point, but such was not the case:
the Slavophiles believe in the People because they recognize in
them their own particular principles; the Westernizers, on the other
hand, agree to believe in the People only on condition that the
People have no principles of their own whatsoever. And so the
fight goes on. What do you think of that? In fact, I don't think
there even is a fight: fighting is fighting; love is love. And why
couldn't those who are fighting be loving one another at the same
time? Indeed, this sort of thing happens very often in Russia when
truly good people get into a fight. And how can you say we aren't
good people (once again, aside from the useless ones)? You see,
we fight for the chief and sole reason that the time has now suddenly
become one not of theories and journalistic scuffles but of action
and practical decisions. Suddenly there is the need to say something

positive—about education and pedagogy, about the railways, the zemstvos, the medical services, and so on. There are hundreds of issues, and the main thing is that we must now do this as quickly as possible so as not to delay matters; and since over the past two hundred years we all have become unaccustomed to any work and have all become utterly incapable of even the slightest practical activity, it is only natural that we all suddenly grabbed each other by the hair; and the less capable people felt themselves, the more furiously they entered the fray. What's wrong with this, I ask you? It's merely touching, and nothing more. Look at children: they fight precisely at an age when they haven't yet learned to express their ideas. Isn't that exactly what we are doing? And so? We shouldn't be at all discouraged by this; on the contrary, it only shows, to some extent at least, that we are fresh and, so to say, virginal. To be sure, we heap abuse on one another in every possible fashion in our literature, for instance, because we lack ideas: this is a ridiculous, naive practice one finds only among primitive peoples; but yet, in truth, there is something almost touching here: precisely our lack of experience, our childish inability even to hand out abuse in proper fashion. I'm certainly not making a joke or being sarcastic: there exists everywhere among us an honest and radiant expectation of good (think what you like, but such is the case), a longing for the common cause and the common good, and this takes precedence over any egoism. It is a most naive longing, full of faith and not narrowly exclusive or based on feelings of caste; and if we do find some minor and infrequent examples of such exclusivity, then they are barely perceptible and universally scorned. This is very important, and do you know why? Because not only is it not something trivial, it in fact is a great deal. Well, that ought to be enough: why do we still need some sort of "unfaltering hatred"? No one can doubt the honesty and sincerity of our society; these things are visible at the first glance. Look well and you will see that, first of all, we place our faith in an idea, in an ideal, while personal, earthly benefits come only later. Oh, nasty people manage even among us to get their business done, in quite the opposite sense, and these days more than ever before, it seems. Yet these useless people never shape our public opinion and are not our leaders; on the contrary, even when enjoying honors, they were more than once compelled to conform totally to the image of idealistic, young, impractical, and poor people whom they thought to be ridiculous. In that respect our society resembles the People,

who also value their faith and their ideals above all that is worldly
and transient; and that, in fact, is our society's main point of contact
with the People. This idealism does credit both to society and the
People; lose it and we will not buy it back at any price. Even
though our People are weighed down by vice—now more than
ever—they have never been without ideals, and even the greatest
scoundrel among the People would never say, "One must do as I
do." On the contrary, he always believed and regretted that he was
doing something wrong and knew there was something far better
than he and his deeds. The People do have ideals—firmly held
ones; and that is the most important thing: circumstances will
change, things will improve, and the People, perhaps, will simply
shed their vices, while their radiant principles will remain, even
stronger and more sacred than ever before. Our young people want
to do heroic deeds and make sacrifices. The young lad of today,
about whom so many different things are said, often worships the
naivest kind of paradox and is willing to sacrifice everything on
earth for it—his fate and his very life; but that is solely because
he considers his paradox to be the truth. It is only because he is
not enlightened: when the light comes, other points of view will
appear of their own accord and the paradoxes will disappear; yet
his purity of heart will not vanish; the desire for sacrifices and
heroic deeds that now burns so radiantly in him will not die out.
And this is our strong point. But of course there is another matter
and another question: what precisely do all of us who seek the
common good and who join together in the longing for the success
of the common cause—what do we see as the means to accomplish
our aim? We must admit that here we have not managed to bring
our voices into harmony, and so in that respect our society today
is very much like Marshal MacMahon. On one of his journeys
through France not long ago, the worthy marshal, in one of his
speeches of response to some mayor or other (the French are terribly
fond of all these speeches of welcome and speeches of response),
expressed the view that his entire policy could be summed up in
the words "love of country." This view was voiced at a time when
all France, so to say, was straining in expectation of what he would
say. It was a strange view; a laudable one, to be sure, but sur-
prisingly vague, because that same mayor might reply to the marshal that there are some kinds of love which can drown one's
country. But the mayor made no objection, of course, because he
feared the reply would be:—"J'y suis et j'y reste!" a phrase beyond

which, it seems, the worthy marshal will not go. But even so, this is still just like our society: we all join in love, if not of our country then of the common cause (the words themselves are unimportant). But in what we see as the means to this end, and not only means but the common cause itself—in that we are as vague as Marshal MacMahon. And so, even though I pleased some readers and much appreciate the fact that hands have been extended to me, so to say, I can still see that there will be strong disagreements over details later, for I cannot agree with everyone and everything, no matter how obliging I might be.

2. On Love of the People. An Essential Contract with the People

I wrote, for instance, in the January issue of the *Diary* that our People are coarse and ignorant, devoted to darkness and depravity, "barbarians, awaiting the light." Meanwhile, I've only just read in *Fraternal Aid* (an anthology published by the Slavic Committee in aid of the Slavs fighting for their freedom)—in an article by the late and unforgettable Konstantin Aksakov, a man dear to every Russian—that the Russian people have long been enlightened and "educated." What can I say? Was I troubled by my apparent disagreement with the opinion of Konstantin Aksakov? Not in the least; I completely share that view, and have had warm sympathy for it for a long time. So how can I reconcile such a contradiction? But the point is just that it can be very easily reconciled, I think; but to my astonishment others think that these two notions are irreconcilable. One must know how to segregate the beauty in the Russian peasant from the layers of barbarity that have accumulated over it. Through the circumstances of nearly the whole of Russian history, our People have been so dedicated to depravity, and so corrupt, led astray, and continually tormented, that it is a wonder they have survived preserving their human image at all, never mind preserving its beauty. But, indeed, they have also preserved the beauty of their image. He who is a true friend of humanity, whose heart has even once throbbed for the sufferings of the People—he will understand and overlook all the impenetrable deposits of filth that weigh down our People and will be able to find diamonds in this filth. I repeat: judge the Russian People not by the abominations they so frequently commit, but by those great and sacred things for which, even in their abominations, they constantly yearn.

Yet not all of the People are villains; there are true saints, and
what saints they are: they are radiant and illuminate the way for
us all! I have a kind of blind conviction that there is no such
scoundrel and villain among the Russian People who would not
recognize that he is low and vile; but there are others who can
commit some vile act and even exalt themselves for it, raising their
villainy into a principle and maintaining that in it lies *l'Ordre* and
the light of civilization; such unhappy people end by believing that
sincerely, blindly, even honestly. No, do not judge our People by
what they are, but by what they would like to become. Their ideals
are powerful and sacred; it is these ideals that have preserved our
People through centuries of torment; these ideals have fused with
the People's soul since time immemorial and have conferred upon
it the blessings of frankness, honor, sincerity, and a broad mind,
receptive to everything; and all this is combined in a most attractive,
harmonious fashion. And if, along with this, there is so much filth,
then the Russian himself grieves over it all the more and believes
that it is all only extrinsic and temporary, a delusion of the Devil,
and that the darkness will end and one day the eternal light will
shine forth. I will not remind you of the People's historical ideals,
of their saints—Sergei, Theodosius of Pechersk, even Tikhon of
Zadonsk. Incidentally, are there many of us who know about Tikhon of Zadonsk? Why is it that we know absolutely nothing of
this and take an oath never to read anything? Are we short of time?
Believe me, gentlemen, you would be astonished at the beautiful
things you would learn. But I'll turn, rather, to our literature:
everything in it of true beauty has been taken from the People,
beginning with the meek and simple type, Belkin, created by
Pushkin. Why, everything we have comes from Pushkin. His turning to the People at such an early stage of his career was so
unprecedented and astonishing; it provided a point of view which,
in those days, was so astonishingly novel that it can only be explained, if not by a miracle, then by the remarkable magnitude of
his genius, which, I might add, even now we are incapable of
appreciating. I will not mention the purely national types that have
appeared in our time, but think of *Oblomov*, think of Turgenev's
Nest of Gentlefolk. In the latter, of course, it's not the People, yet
everything that is lasting and beautiful in Turgenev's and Goncharov's characters comes from the fact that through them the
writers came into contact with the People; this contact with the
People gave them exceptional powers. They borrowed the People's

simplicity, purity, meekness, breadth of outlook, and lack of malice, as opposed to all that was twisted, false, extrinsic, and slavishly borrowed. Don't be astonished that I have suddenly begun to speak about Russian literature. The service our literature has performed is that almost all of its best representatives paid homage to the People's truth and acknowledged the People's ideals as truly beautiful even before our intelligentsia did (note that). However, literature often had little choice but to accept these ideas as exemplary. It is true, I think, that artistic feeling rather than goodwill was at work here. But enough of literature for the moment; I took up the topic only apropos of the People in any case.

The question of the People and our view of them, our present understanding of them, is our most important question, a question on which our whole future rests; one might even say it is the most practical question at the moment. However, the People are still a theory for all of us and still stand before us as a riddle. All of us who love the People look at them as if at a theory and, it seems, not one of us loves them as they really are but only as each of us imagines them to be. And even if the Russian people eventually were to turn out to be not as we imagined them, then we all, despite our love for them, would likely renounce them at once with no regrets. I am speaking about all of us, including even the Slavophiles, who, perhaps, would be the first to renounce them. As for me, I won't hide my convictions because I specifically want to define more clearly the further tendency my *Diary* will take and so avoid misunderstandings, so that each one of you might know beforehand whether it is worth extending a literary hand to me or not. This is what I think: we are hardly so good and so beautiful that we could set ourselves up as an ideal for the People and demand that they become absolutely like us. Don't be surprised at hearing the question posed from such an absurd angle. In fact, we have never posed the question any other way: "Who is better, we or the People? Are the People to follow us, or are we to follow them?" This is what everyone is saying now, everyone who has even the tiniest thought in his head and some concern in his heart for the common cause. And so I reply frankly: it is we who ought to bow down before the People and wait for everything from them, both ideas and the form of those ideas; we must bow down before the People's truth and acknowledge it as the truth, even in the terrible event that some of it comes from the *Lives of the Saints*. To put it briefly: we must bow down like prodigal children who have been away from home for two hundred years but who, however, have returned still Russians (and in that, incidentally, is our great merit). But, on the other hand, we should bow down on only one condition, and that is a sine qua non: the People must accept much of what we bring with us. We cannot utterly annihilate ourselves before them and their truth, whatever that truth might be. Let that which is ours remain with us; we will not give it up for anything on earth, even, at the very worst, for the joy of unity with the People. If such does not happen, then let us both perish on our separate ways. Yet certainly it will happen; I am completely convinced that this *something* which we brought with us truly exists—it is not a mirage but has an image and a form and a weight. Nonetheless, I repeat once more: there is much ahead of us that is an enigma, so much that even the expectation is frightening. People predict, for example, that civilization will ruin the People: events supposedly will take such a course that, along with salvation and light, so much untruth and deceit will enter in; there will be so much tumult and such filthy habits will develop that only in generations to come—in two hundred years, if you like—will the good seeds sprout, while something dreadful awaits our children and us, perhaps. Is that how you see it, gentlemen? Are the People consigned to pass through yet a new phase of depravity and falsehood such as we passed through when inoculated with civilization? (I think no one will disagree that we began our civilization directly with depravity.) I would like to hear something more reassuring on this account. I am very much inclined to believe that our People are such an enormity that all such new, muddy torrents, should they burst forth from somewhere and overflow, will simply dissipate by themselves. And on this, give me your hand; let's work together, each through his own "microscopic" actions, so that the cause may advance more directly and with fewer mistakes. It is true that we ourselves have no ideas how to do anything in this area; we only "love our country," will not agree on the means, and will quarrel many times yet; still, if we've already agreed that we are good people, then, whatever may happen, things will finally work themselves out in the end. That's my credo. I repeat: we have here a two-hundred-year period of being unaccustomed to any work and nothing more than that. And through being unused to work we have ended our "period of culture" by everywhere ceasing to understand one another. Of course, I am speaking only of serious

and sincere people—it's only they who fail to understand one another; opportunists are a different matter: they have always understood one another. . . .

3. The Peasant Marey

But reading all these *professions de foi* is a bore, I think, and so
I'll tell you a story; actually, it's not even a story, but only a
reminiscence of something that happened long ago and that, for
some reason, I would very much like to recount here and now, as
a conclusion to our treatise on the People. At the time I was only
nine years old. . . . But no, I'd best begin with the time I was
twenty-nine.

It was the second day of Easter Week. The air was warm, the
sky was blue, the sun was high, warm, and bright, but there was
only gloom in my heart. I was wandering behind the prison barracks, examining and counting off the pales in the sturdy prison
stockade, but I had lost even the desire to count, although such
was my habit. It was the second day of "marking the holiday"
within the prison compound; the prisoners were not taken out to
work; many were drunk; there were shouts of abuse, and quarrels
were constantly breaking out in all corners. Disgraceful, hideous
songs; card games in little nooks under the bunks; a few convicts,
already beaten half to death by sentence of their comrades for their
particular rowdiness, lay on bunks covered with sheepskin coats
until such time as they might come to their senses; knives had
already been drawn a few times—all this, in two days of holiday,
had worn me out to the point of illness. Indeed, I never could
endure the drunken carousals of peasants without being disgusted,
and here, in this place, particularly. During these days even the
prison staff did not look in; they made no searches, nor did they
check for alcohol, for they realized that once a year they had to
allow even these outcasts to have a spree; otherwise it might be
even worse. At last, anger welled up in my heart. I ran across the
Pole M-cki, a political prisoner; he gave me a gloomy look, his
eyes glittering and his lips trembling: "Je hais ces brigands!" he
muttered, gritting his teeth, and passed me by. I returned to the
barrack despite the fact that a quarter-hour before I had fled it
half-demented when six healthy peasants had thrown themselves,
as one man, on the drunken Tatar Gazin and had begun beating

him to make him settle down; they beat him senselessly with such
blows as might have killed a camel; but they knew that it was not
easy to kill this Hercules and so they didn't hold back. And now
when I returned to the barracks I noticed Gazin lying senseless on
a bunk in the corner showing scarcely any signs of life; he was
lying under a sheepskin coat, and everyone passed him by in
silence: although they firmly hoped he would revive the next morning, still, "with a beating like that, God forbid, you could finish
a man off." I made my way to my bunk opposite a window with
an iron grating and lay down on my back, my hands behind my
head, and closed my eyes. I liked to lie like that: a sleeping man
was left alone, while at the same time one could daydream and
think. But dreams did not come to me; my heart beat restlessly,
and M-cki's words kept echoing in my ears: "Je hais ces brigands!"
However, why describe my feelings? Even now at night I sometimes
dream of that time, and none of my dreams are more agonizing.
Perhaps you will also notice that until today I have scarcely ever
spoken in print of my prison life; I wrote *Notes from the House of
the Dead* fifteen years ago using an invented narrator, a criminal
who supposedly had murdered his wife. (I might add, by the way,
that many people supposed and are even now quite firmly convinced
that I was sent to hard labor for the murder of my wife.)

Little by little I lost myself in reverie and imperceptibly sank
into memories of the past. All through my four years in prison I
continually thought of all my past days, and I think I relived the
whole of my former life in my memories. These memories arose
in my mind of themselves; rarely did I summon them up consciously. They would begin from a certain point, some little thing
that was often barely perceptible, and then bit by bit they would
grow into a finished picture, some strong and complete impression.
I would analyze these impressions, adding new touches to things
experienced long ago; and the main thing was that I would refine
them, continually refine them, and in this consisted my entire
entertainment. This time, for some reason, I suddenly recalled a
moment of no apparent significance from my early childhood when
I was only nine years old, a moment that I thought I had completely
forgotten; but at that time I was particularly fond of memories of
my very early childhood. I recalled one August at our home in the
country: the day was clear and dry, but a bit chilly and windy;
summer was on the wane, and soon I would have to go back to
Moscow to spend the whole winter in boredom over my French

lessons; and I was so sorry to have to leave the country. I passed by the granaries, made my way down into the gully, and climbed up into the Dell—that was what we called a thick patch of bushes that stretched from the far side of the gully to a grove of trees. And so I make my way deeper into the bushes and can hear that some thirty paces away a solitary peasant is plowing in the clearing. I know he's plowing up the steep side of a hill and his horse finds it heavy going; from time to time I hear his shout, "Gee-up!" I know almost all our peasants, but don't recognize the one who's plowing; and what difference does it make, anyway, since I'm quite absorbed in my own business. I also have an occupation: I'm breaking off a switch of walnut to lash frogs; walnut switches are so lovely and quite without flaws, so much better than birch ones. I'm also busy with bugs and beetles, collecting them; some are very pretty; I love the small, nimble, red-and-yellow lizards with the little black spots as well, but I'm afraid of snakes. I come across snakes far less often than lizards, however. There aren't many mushrooms here; you have to go into the birch wood for mushrooms, and that's what I have in mind. I liked nothing better than the forest with its mushrooms and wild berries, its insects, and its birds, hedgehogs, and squirrels, and with its damp aroma of rotting leaves that I loved so. And even now, as I write this, I can catch the fragrance from our stand of birches in the country: these impressions stay with you all your life. Suddenly, amid the deep silence, I clearly and distinctly heard a shout: "There's a wolf!" I screamed, and, beside myself with terror, crying at the top of my voice, I ran out into the field, straight at the plowing peasant.

It was our peasant Marey. I don't know if there is such a name, but everyone called him Marey. He was a man of about fifty, heavy-set, rather tall, with heavy streaks of gray in his bushy, dark-brown beard. I knew him but had scarcely ever had occasion to speak to him before. He even stopped his little filly when he heard my cry, and when I rushed up to him and seized his plow with one hand and his sleeve with the other, he saw how terrified I was.

"It's a wolf!" I cried, completely out of breath.

Instinctively he jerked his head to look around, for an instant almost believing me.

"Where's the wolf?"

"I heard a shout. . . . Someone just shouted, 'Wolf'" . . . I babbled.

"What do you mean, lad? There's no wolf; you're just hearing reassuring me. But I was all a-tremble and clung to his coat even more tightly; I suppose I was very pale as well. He looked at me with an uneasy smile, evidently concerned and alarmed for me.

"Why you took a real fright, you did!" he said, wagging his head. "Never mind, now, my dear. What a fine lad you are!"

He stretched out his hand and suddenly stroked my cheek.

"Never mind, now, there's nothing to be afraid of. Christ be with you. Cross yourself, lad." But I couldn't cross myself; the corners of my mouth were trembling, and I think this particularly struck him. He quietly stretched out a thick, earth-soiled finger with a black nail and gently touched it to my trembling lips.

"Now, now," he smiled at me with a broad, almost maternal smile. "Lord, what a dreadful fuss. Dear, dear, dear!"

At last I realized that there was no wolf and that I must have imagined hearing the cry of "Wolf." Still, it had been such a clear and distinct shout; two or three times before, however, I had imagined such cries (not only about wolves), and I was aware of that. (Later, when childhood passed, these hallucinations did as well.)

"Well, I'll be off now," I said, making it seem like a question and looking at him shyly.

"Off with you, then, and I'll keep an eye on you as you go. Can't let the wolf get you!" he added, still giving me a maternal smile. "Well, Christ be with you, off you go." He made the sign of the cross over me, and crossed himself. I set off, looking over my shoulder almost every ten steps. Marey continued to stand with his little filly, looking after me and nodding every time I looked around. I confess I felt a little ashamed at taking such a fright. But I went on, still with a good deal of fear of the wolf, until I had gone up the slope of the gully to the first threshing barn; and here the fear vanished entirely, and suddenly our dog Volchok came dashing out to meet me. With Volchok I felt totally reassured, and I turned toward Marey for the last time; I could no longer make out his face clearly, but I felt that he was still smiling kindly at me and nodding. I waved to him, and he returned my wave and urged on his little filly.

"Gee-up," came his distant shout once more, and his little filly once more started drawing the wooden plow.

This memory came to me all at once—I don't know why—but with amazing clarity of detail. Suddenly I roused myself and sat on the bunk; I recall that a quiet smile of reminiscence still played on my face. I kept on recollecting for yet another minute.

I remembered that when I had come home from Marey I told no one about my "adventure." And what kind of adventure was it anyway? I forgot about Marey very quickly as well. On the rare occasions when I met him later, I never struck up a conversation with him, either about the wolf or anything else, and now, suddenly, twenty years later, in Siberia, I remembered that encounter so vividly, right down to the last detail. That means it had settled unnoticed in my heart, all by itself with no will of mine, and had suddenly come back to me at a time when it was needed; I recalled the tender, maternal smile of a poor serf, the way he crossed me and shook his head: "Well you did take a fright now, didn't you, lad!" And I especially remember his thick finger, soiled with dirt, that he touched quietly and with shy tenderness to my trembling lips. Of course, anyone would try to reassure a child, but here in this solitary encounter something quite different had happened, and had I been his very own son he could not have looked at me with a glance that radiated more pure love, and who had prompted him to do that? He was our own serf, and I was his master's little boy; no one would learn of his kindness to me and reward him for it. Was he, maybe, especially fond of small children? There are such people. Our encounter was solitary, in an open field, and only God, perhaps, looking down saw what deep and enlightened human feeling and what delicate, almost feminine tenderness could fill the heart of a coarse, bestially ignorant Russian serf who at the time did not expect or even dream of his freedom. Now tell me, is this not what Konstantin Aksakov had in mind when he spoke of the advanced level of development of our Russian People?

And so when I climbed down from my bunk and looked around, I remember I suddenly felt I could regard these unfortunates in an entirely different way and that suddenly, through some sort of miracle, the former hatred and anger in my heart had vanished. I went off, peering intently into the faces of those I met. This disgraced peasant, with shaven head and brands on his cheek, drunk and roaring out his hoarse, drunken song—why he might also be that very same Marey; I cannot peer into his heart, after all. That same evening I met M-cki once again. The unfortunate man! He had no recollections of any Mareys and no other view of these people but "Je hais ces brigands!" No, the Poles had to bear more than we did in those days!

2

1. Apropos of the Kroneberg Case

I think that everyone knows about the Kroneberg case, which was heard about a month ago in the St. Petersburg District Court, and that everyone has read the accounts and the comments about it in the newspapers. It is a most interesting case, and the accounts of it were remarkably passionate. Since I am writing a month after the fact, I do not intend to take up all the details of it, but I feel a need to say my word apropos as well. I am certainly not a lawyer, but there was so much falsehood here on all sides that even a non-lawyer can see it. Cases such as this spring up unexpectedly somehow and only confuse society and, it seems, even the judges. But since such cases also involve our common and most precious interest, one can see why they touch a nerve, and sometimes one cannot help but discuss them even though a month (i.e., a whole eternity) may have passed.

Let me refresh your memory about the case: a father had whipped his child, a girl of seven, with excessive cruelty; according to the charge, he had treated her cruelly before this as well. A stranger—a lower-class woman—could not stand the screams of the tortured girl who, for a quarter of an hour (according to the charge), had cried out, "Papa! Papa!" while being beaten with a switches. The switches, according to the testimony of an expert, turned out not to be switches but *Spitzruten*—that is, proper sticks—absolutely unthinkable to be applied to someone of seven. They were displayed in court, by the way, as material evidence, and everyone could see them, even Mr. Spasovich himself. Among other things, the charge noted that when someone told the father before he began beating his child that he ought at least to break off a branch from the stick, the father replied, "No, it's more effective this way." It was also disclosed that the father himself almost fell into a faint after beating her.

I recall the first impression produced on me by the issue of *The Voice* in which I read the beginning of the case, the first account of it. It happened sometime after nine in the evening, quite by chance. I had spent the whole day at the printer's and had had no chance to look through *The Voice* earlier, and knew nothing about this new case. When I had read the article I decided that in spite of the late hour I simply had to find out that same evening about the further course of the trial, supposing that it might have already ended that same day, a Saturday, and knowing that newspaper accounts are always delayed. I decided that I would at once go to see a certain man whom I knew very well by reputation but scarcely at all personally, counting on the fact that, for certain reasons, he would be more likely to know the outcome of the trial than any of my other acquaintances, and that he himself might well have been in the courtroom. I was not mistaken: he had been in court and had only just returned. I found him at home sometime after ten o'clock, and he told me of the acquittal of the defendant. I was angry at the court, at the jurors, and at the defense lawyer. This was three weeks ago now, and I have changed my opinion in many respects after reading the reports in the newspapers and hearing several reliable outside opinions. I am very pleased that I need no longer regard the defendant-father as a villain who enjoys torturing children (such types do exist), and that it was really only a matter of "nerves," and that he was only "unskilled at raising children," as his lawyer put it. The main thing I wish to do now is only to draw attention in some detail to the speech the defense lawyer made in court so as to show more clearly the kind of false and absurd position in which a prominent, talented, private individual may be put solely because of the false manner in which the case itself was originally built.

What is false here? First, take the girl, a child: he "tormented, tortured" her, and the judges want to protect her—now that seems to be something truly noble, but what happens? Why, they almost destroyed all her future happiness, and perhaps they have destroyed it! In fact, what if the father had been convicted? The prosecution put the case in such a way that in the event of a guilty verdict the father could have been sent to Siberia. What, we might well ask, would remain in the heart of that daughter, now a child who understands nothing, for the rest of her life, even in the event that for the rest of her life she were wealthy and "happy"? Would not the family have been destroyed by the court itself, an institution which, as we all know, is intended to preserve the sanctity of the family? Now consider yet another feature of the case: the girl is seven years old—what impression might she have at such an age? The father was acquitted and not exiled, and that is a good thing (although I think it was inappropriate for the spectators to applaud the jurors, and apparently there was loud applause); still, the girl was dragged into court; she made an appearance; she saw it all, heard it all, and herself admitted: "Je suis voleuse, menteuse." The secret vices of this little child (only seven years old!) were revealed by adult, serious, even humane people before all the spectators—how monstrous! *Mais il en reste toujours quelque chose*, for the rest of her life, don't you see that? And it will remain not only in her heart but, perhaps, be reflected in her fate as well. She has been touched by something in that courtroom, by something vile and pernicious, and it has left its mark on her forever. And, who knows, perhaps in twenty years someone will say to her, "You appeared in criminal court when you were only a child." However, once more I realize that I am not a lawyer and will not be able to express all this, so I'd better turn directly to the speech of the defense lawyer: all these erroneous premises reveal themselves there with striking clarity. Mr. Spasovich defended the accused; he is a man of talent. Wherever his name is mentioned, people always say, "He is a man of talent." I'm very pleased at that. I note that Mr. Spasovich was assigned to the defense by the court, and so one might say that he conducted his defense under a certain compulsion. . . . However, once again I find myself beyond my competence and I say no more. But before I turn to the aforementioned and remarkable speech, I would like to insert a few remarks about lawyers in general and about talented ones in particular; I want to convey to the reader some of my own impressions and my own perplexity, so to say, which of course may not be at all serious in the eyes of competent people; but then I am writing my *Diary* for myself, and these thoughts have settled solidly in my head. I admit, however, that they may not even be thoughts; yet they are feelings at any rate. . . .

2. Something on Lawyers in General. My Naive and Hasty Assumptions. Something on Talented People in General and in Particular

However, two points specifically about lawyers. I've only just picked up the pen and already I feel afraid. I blush in advance for the naiveté of my questions and assumptions. It would be far too naive and innocent on my part to expound, for instance, on what a useful and pleasant institution the bar is. Take a man who has committed a crime but who knows nothing of the law; he's ready to confess, but a lawyer comes along and proves to him not only that he has done nothing wrong, but that he's a regular saint. He cites the laws that apply to his case and digs out precedents of the Senate's Court of Appeal that suddenly put the case in a whole new light, and he ends by pulling the wretched fellow out of the hole. Now that's a most pleasant thing! Granted, some might disagree and object that this is just a bit immoral. But now take an innocent man, completely innocent, a simple fellow, yet there is a good deal of evidence that the prosecutor has assembled in such a way that it would seem the man will be condemned for someone else's crime. Besides, the man is ignorant; he hasn't a clue about the law and can only stand there mumbling, "I didn't know anything; I didn't do anything," and this finally gets on the nerves of both the jury and the judges. But a lawyer comes along who has cut his teeth on the law, he cites the applicable section and a precedent of the Senate's Court of Appeal, confuses the prosecutor, and, sure enough, the innocent man is acquitted. Say what you will, but this is useful. What could an innocent man in Russia do without a lawyer?

All these, I repeat, are naive remarks, and everyone has heard them before. But it's still an extraordinarily pleasant thing to have a lawyer. I myself experienced this once when I was editing a newspaper and, unintentionally, through an oversight (which could happen to anyone), passed for publication a news item that should have appeared only with the permission of the Minister of the Imperial Court. And all of a sudden I learned that I was to be brought to trial. I had no intention of conducting any defense; my "guilt" was obvious even to me. I had transgressed a clearly stated law, and there could be no *legal* dispute about it. But the court appointed a lawyer for me (a man I knew slightly and who had been a member of a certain society to which I once belonged). He

suddenly announced to me that not only was I not guilty but that
what I had done was absolutely right, and that he was fully determined to defend me with every means at his disposal. Of course,
I was pleased to hear that; but when it came to the trial, I confess
that the impression I got was not at all what I expected: I watched
and listened to my lawyer speak, and the thought that I, completely
guilty, might suddenly walk out as totally innocent was so amusing,
and also so appealing, that I must say this half-hour in court was
among the most entertaining I have ever spent; but then I wasn't
a man of the law and so I didn't realize that I was completely
innocent. I was convicted, of course: literary men are judged harshly; I paid a twenty-five-ruble fine and, in addition, spent two days
in the jail on Haymarket Square, where I passed the time most
pleasantly and, to some extent, even usefully, becoming acquainted
with certain people and certain things. However, I see that I have
gotten far off the topic; let me return to serious matters once more.

It is a highly moral and touching thing when a lawyer applies
his effort and talent in defense of the unfortunate; he is a friend
to humanity. But then the thought occurs to you that he is knowingly defending and justifying a guilty person and, besides that,
he can do nothing else, even if he wanted to. People will reply
that the court cannot deprive any criminal of legal assistance and
that an honest lawyer in such an event will always remain honest,
for he will always find and determine the true degree of his client's
guilt and will only prevent his client from being punished more
harshly than his crime warrants, etc., etc. All that is true, even
though the proposition also smacks of the most boundless idealism.
It seems to me that avoiding falsehood and preserving his integrity
and conscience is just as difficult for a lawyer, generally speaking,
as it is for any person to attain a state of bliss. We have already
heard, have we not, how lawyers addressing a jury in court do
everything but swear an oath that they undertook to defend a client
solely because they were totally convinced of his innocence. When
you hear an oath such as this, the meanest sort of suspicion inevitably creeps into your mind: "Suppose he's lying and is just
doing it for the money?" And in fact the result often has been that
a client defended with such ardor turned out to be completely,
undeniably guilty. I don't know—have we had cases where lawyers,
wishing to play to the end their role as people utterly convinced
of the innocence of their client, have fainted when the jurors
brought in a "guilty" verdict? But that they have shed tears, it

seems, is something that has already happened in our still-so-new courts. Say what you will, but here in this whole institution, beyond all those undeniably beautiful things, lies something rather sad. In truth, one can imagine the shouts of "Shyster!" and "Bloodsucker!"; one recalls the popular saying "A lawyer is a hired conscience"; but the main thing, aside from all this, is that one calls to mind a most absurd paradox: that a lawyer can never act according to his conscience, that he cannot help but toy with his conscience, even if he does not want to do so, that he is a man doomed to be dishonest, and that, finally, the most important and most serious thing in all this is that such a sad state of affairs has been, as it were, written into law by someone and something so that it is considered not an aberration but, on the contrary, even a most normal order of things.

Let's leave this topic, however; everything tells me that I have taken up a topic that is wrong for me. And I'm sure that jurisprudence has long ago resolved all these puzzling issues to everyone's complete satisfaction, and that I am the only one who is unaware of it. I will speak, rather, about talent; at least I am a little bit more competent here.

What is talent? Talent, first of all, is a most useful thing. Literary talent, for example, is the ability to say or express well what a mediocrity would say and express poorly. You will say that first of all one needs a set of views and only then the talent. All right, I agree: I didn't intend to speak about artistic value, but only about certain qualities of talent in general. The qualities of talent, in general, are remarkably varied and sometimes simply impossible to handle. In the first place, *talent oblige*, "talent has an obligation," but to do what? Sometimes to do the worst things. An insoluble question arises: does the talent possess the person or the person his talent? It seems to me, as far as I have followed and observed people of talent both alive and dead, that it is very rare to find a person capable of handling his gift and that, on the contrary, the talent almost always enslaves its possessor, taking him, as it were, by the scruff of the neck (indeed, it often happens in just such a degrading fashion) and carrying him off far, far away from his proper path. Somewhere in Gogol (I've forgotten where) a certain liar began to tell a story and might, perhaps, have told the truth, "but certain details popped up, all by themselves" in the story so that there was just no way he could tell the truth. I mention that, of course, only by way of comparison, although there really are those who have a specific talent for lying. The novelist Thackeray depicts one such socialite liar and wag who, however, moved in polite society and idled away his time in the company of one lord or another; Thackeray says that this man liked to leave a burst of laughter behind him whenever he went out the door of someone's house, and so he saved his best sally or witticism till the end. Do you know, I think it is very difficult to remain and to preserve yourself as an honest person when you have to be so concerned about saving your sharpest witticism till the end so as to leave a burst of laughter behind you. Such concern itself is so trivial that it must finally drive out everything serious from a person. And besides, if one has not saved a witticism for one's exit, then it has to be invented, and for the sake of a witty word, "one spares neither mother nor father."

People will say that if this is what has to be done then it's scarcely possible to go on living. That's true. Yet you must agree that every talent always has this almost ignoble, excessive sensitivity of response to one's audience which is always ready to lead even the soberest of persons astray; "Whether 'tis the beast that roars in the thick forest" or whatever else might happen, the fellow is at once ready to take flight; he's flushed with the emotions that well up within him and is utterly carried away. When I was speaking to Belinsky on one occasion, he compared this "responsiveness" with "depravity of talent" and had nothing but scorn for it, perceiving, of course, in its antithesis sufficient spiritual fortitude to keep the responsiveness under control, even in the most ardent poetic frame of mind. Belinsky was referring to poets, but almost all talented people have a bit of the poet in them, after all—even carpenters, if they are talented. Poetry is, so to say, the inner fire of every talent. And if even a carpenter can be a poet, then surely a lawyer can as well, in the event that he also has talent. I don't at all dispute the fact that, given rigidly honest principles and spiritual fortitude, even a lawyer can keep his "responsiveness" under control; but there are cases and circumstances when a person just cannot resist: "certain details will just pop up, all by themselves," and the person will get carried away. Gentlemen, all the things I am saying here about this sensitivity of response are not really trivialities; however simple they might seem, they are a matter of extraordinary importance in everyone's life, even in yours and mine: look into it more carefully and consider, and you will see that it is extremely difficult to remain an honest person precisely because of this excessive and pampered "responsiveness" that compels us to lie without ceasing. However, the words "honest person" I understand here only in the "higher sense," so that you may remain quite calm and not get upset. Anyway, I am sure no one will get upset at what I am saying. Let me go on. Does any one of you, gentlemen, recall Alphonse Lamartine, the former head of the Provisional Government during the February Revolution of 1848? People say that he found nothing more pleasant and delightful than to deliver endless speeches to the people and to the various deputations that were then coming from towns and villages all over France to introduce themselves to the Provisional Government in the two months following the proclamation of the Republic. He delivered, perhaps, several thousand such speeches at that time. He was a poet and a man of talent. His whole life was full of innocence, and that innocence was combined with a handsome and most imposing appearance created, so to say, to provide keepsakes. I am certainly not equating this historic figure with those types of poetically inclined responsive people who are born dewy-eyed, although he did write *Harmonies poètiques et religieuses,* an unusual volume of endlessly protracted verses in which three generations of young misses graduating from institutes became bogged down. On the other hand, he later wrote an extraordinarily talented book, *A History of the Girondists,* which won him popularity and ultimately the post, if one can call it that, of head of the Provisional Government—and that was when he delivered such a number of endless speeches, reveling in them and floating about in some sort of never-ending rapture. One talented wit pointed at him at the time and cried: "Ce n'est pas l'homme, c'est une lyre!" ("That's not a man, that's a lyre!").

That was a high compliment, but a very sly one, for what could be more ridiculous, tell me, than comparing a man with a lyre? It reverberates the moment you touch it! It goes without saying that one cannot compare Lamartine, that man endlessly speaking in verses, that orator-lyre, to any of our smart lawyers who are cunning even in their innocence, always in control of themselves, never at a loss, and always enriching themselves. Could they possibly not know how to play their lyres? Yet is this true? Is it really true, ladies and gentlemen? People have a weakness for praise and they are "responsive"; they are even cunning as well. Instead of the business with the sensitive lyre, some of our talented lawyers may be faced—in an allegorical sense—with the same sort of thing as happened to one of our Moscow merchants. His papa gave up the ghost, leaving him a certain capital (or, as he would say, "cap-'i-tal"). But his mamma was also carrying on some business in her own name and she got into difficulties. He had to help out his mamma, which meant paying out a lot of money. Our young merchant dearly loved his mamma, but he hesitated: "Still, we just can't get along without the money. We couldn't give up the money 'cause there's just no way folks like us can get by without money." So he didn't give her anything, and mamma was dragged off to jail. You may take this as an allegory and replace money with talent—the two are even similar—and the result is as follows: "Still, we can't get along without creating a flash and making a big impression; there's just no way we can get by unless we create a flash and make a big impression." And this can happen even to the most serious and honest lawyer of talent, even at the very moment he undertakes to defend a case that sickens his conscience. I read once that in France, many years ago now, a lawyer became convinced during the course of a trial that his client was guilty, and when it came time for his defense speech, he simply rose, bowed to the court, and silently took his seat again. I think that could not happen here: "How can I not win, if I am a talent; can I, myself, really destroy my reputation?" So it follows that a lawyer should fear *not only money* as a temptation (the more so that he never fears money in any case); he should fear the power of his own talent.

Still, I'm sorry I wrote all this: you know very well that Mr. Spasovich, too, is a remarkably talented lawyer. His speech in this case, I believe, is a masterpiece of art; but still, it left an almost foul taste in my mouth. You see: I begin by being completely sincere. But the whole fault here lies in the falsity of all the circumstances that arranged themselves around Mr. Spasovich in this case and from which he was prevented from extricating himself by the very force of things; that is my opinion, and so everything that was strained and forced in his position as a defense lawyer could not help but be reflected in his speech. The case was put so that in the event of a guilty verdict his client could have suffered an extreme and disproportionate punishment. The result would have been a disaster: a family destroyed, no one's interests upheld, and everyone unhappy. His client was accused of "torture"—that charge alone was dreadful. Mr. Spasovich began directly by rejecting any notion of torture. "There was no torture; the child was in no way abused!" He denied it all: the "spitzrutens," the bruises, the blows, the blood, the honesty of the prosecution's witnesses—absolutely everything—that's a remarkably bold tactic, an assault, if you will, on the conscience of the jury; but Mr. Spasovich is well aware of his own strength. He even repudiated the child and her tender years; he destroyed any pity for the child among his audience and tore it from their hearts by its very root. The cries of "Papa! Papa!" "that went on for a quarter of an hour" while the child was being beaten (and even if they only lasted five minutes)—all this disappeared, while in the foreground appeared "an active little girl with a rosy face, laughing, sly, perverse, with secret vices." His audience all but forgot that she was seven years old. Mr. Spasovich cleverly confiscated her age as the thing most dangerous for him. Having destroyed all this, he naturally obtained an acquittal; but what else could he have done? What if the jurors had found his client guilty? And so the force of things made it impossible for him to demur at the means and to handle the case with kid gloves. "Any means are good if they lead to a noble end." But let us take a detailed look at this remarkable speech; it's well worth a look, you will see.

3. Mr. Spasovich's Speech. Clever Tactics

From the very first words of his speech you sense that you are dealing with an exceptional talent, a real force. Mr. Spasovich at once reveals himself in full and is himself the first to point out to the jury the weak side of the case he has undertaken; he reveals its weakest point, the thing he fears most of all. (I am quoting this speech from *The Voice*, by the way. *The Voice* is a newspaper with such lavish means that it probably is able to keep a good stenographer at its disposal.)

> "Gentlemen of the jury," Mr. Spasovich says, "I am afraid not of the decision of the Appellate Court nor of the charges brought by the Prosecutor. . . . I am afraid of an abstract idea, a phantom; I am afraid that the crime—as it has been labeled—has a weak, defenseless creature as its object. The very words 'torture of a child' arouse in the first place a feeling of great compassion for the child, and in the second place, a feeling of extreme indignation against the one responsible for its torture."

Very clever. Remarkable sincerity. The listener, his hackles raised, already prepared to hear something very clever, tricky, deceptive, and who has only just said to himself, "Well now, mister, let's just see you try and put one over on me," is suddenly struck by the fact that this man barely has any defense. He who was supposed to be such a tricky fellow is looking for defense himself, and he's looking to find it in you, the very ones he was supposed to deceive! With such a tactic Mr. Spasovich at once breaks the ice of mistrust and already manages to insinuate himself just a tiny way into your heart. True enough, he talks about a *phantom*; he says that he is afraid only of this "phantom"; in other words, the thing he is afraid of is almost a prejudice; you haven't heard the rest of his speech, but you're already ashamed that you might be unfairly regarded as a man with prejudices, isn't that so? Very clever.

> "Gentlemen of the jury, I am not a proponent of the rod," continues Mr. Spasovich. "I am fully aware that *a system of education may be introduced*" (don't worry, these are all such new expressions and are borrowed wholesale from various pedagogical manuals) "in which corporal punishment will be eliminated. Nonetheless, I no more expect that corporal punishment be completely and unconditionally eliminated than I do your ceasing to function in court because criminal acts and violations of that truth which must prevail in both the family and the state should come to an end."

So the whole case, it seems, centers on the use of a switch, not a bundle of switches, and not the "spitzrutens." You look closely and you listen—but no, the man is speaking seriously; he isn't joking. All the fuss, it seems, began over a little switch applied to a child and over the question of whether or not the switch should be applied. Hardly worth getting together in court over something like that. It's true enough that he's not a proponent of the rod; he tells you that himself, but still:

> "In the normal state of affairs, normal measures are employed. In the present instance a clearly abnormal measure has been employed. But if you examine closely the circumstances that evoked that measure, if you take into consideration the nature of the child, the temperament of the father and the aims that led him to punish the child, then you will understand a great deal in this instance; and once you understand, you will pardon him, because with a *profound* understanding of the case much will inevitably become clear and seem natural and not in need of penal retribution. Such is my task—to clarify the case."

So, you can see, it's "punishment," not "torture"—he says so himself, and so it's only a case of a father being tried for beating his child a little too hard. What sort of times are we living in anyway? But if you go more deeply into the case . . . but that's just the point: neither the court nor the prosecutor knew how to go more deeply into the case. And once we, the jury, examine it, we simply acquit him because "a *profound* understanding leads to acquittal"—he says so himself—and so only we, sitting on the jurors' bench, have this *profound understanding*! "Dear Mr. Spasovich must have been so anxious to see us jurors; why he's worn himself out dealing with the courts and the prosecutors!" In short: "Flatter them, flatter them!"—it's an old technique, often used but still so reliable.

After this Mr. Spasovich turns directly to outlining the history of the case and begins *ab ovo*. Of course I won't quote him word for word. He relates the whole history of his client. Mr. Kroneberg, you see, is a man of learning: he studied first at university in Warsaw, then in Brussels where he took a liking to the French, then again in Warsaw where in 1867 he graduated from the Central School with a Master of Law degree. In Warsaw he made the acquaintance of a certain lady some years older than himself, had a liaison with her but parted because he could not marry her; but when he went away he did not know that he had left her pregnant. Mr. Kroneberg was distressed and sought some diversion. He entered the ranks of the French army during the Franco-Prussian War and took part in twenty-three battles; he was awarded the Legion of Honor and retired as a second lieutenant. At that time, of course, every last Russian was also hoping for a French victory; we seem to have little heartfelt love for the Germans, although we are prepared to respect them intellectually. When he returned to Warsaw, he again met that same lady whom he had so much loved; she was already married and told him for the first time that he had a child and that the child was now in Geneva. The mother had gone to Geneva at the time in order to have her child and had left it with some farmers, whom she paid to look after it. As soon as Mr. Kroneberg learned of his child, he wanted to provide for it. At this point Mr. Spasovich makes several stern and liberal remarks about the strictness of our legislation concerning illegitimate children, but at once consoles us with the fact that "within the boundaries of the empire there is a country, the Kingdom of Poland, that has its own special laws." In short, in that country one can adopt an illegitimate child more easily and conveniently. Mr. Kroneberg "wished to do the maximum the law allowed for the child, even though at that time he had no means of his own. But he was certain that in the event of his death his relatives would care for the little girl who bore the name Kroneberg, and that if worse came to worst she, as the daughter of a knight of the Legion of Honor, might be taken into one of the state institutions of France to be educated." Then Mr. Kroneberg took the girl from the Geneva farmers and placed her in the home of Pastor de Combe, also of Geneva, where she was to be educated; the pastor's wife was the girl's godmother. Thus passed the years from 1872 to 1874. At the beginning of 1875 Mr. Kroneberg's circumstances changed, and he traveled to Geneva once more and brought his daughter back to St. Petersburg.

Mr. Spasovich tells us, by the way, that his client is a man with a keen desire to have a family. Once he almost married, but the wedding was called off; one of the biggest obstacles was precisely his refusal to hide the fact that he had a "natural daughter." This is only the first "little drop"; Mr. Spasovich adds nothing more, yet you already understand that Mr. Kroneberg has paid a price for his good deed of recognizing as his own a daughter whom he did not have to recognize and whom he could have abandoned to the farmer's family forever. So it follows that he had some cause for complaint, so to speak, against this innocent creature; at least, that is the way it appears. But Mr. Spasovich is most accomplished at making such slight, subtle, seemingly fleeting but unremitting insinuations; he is unrivaled in this, as you shall see when we proceed further.

Further, Mr. Spasovich suddenly begins to speak of Miss Jessing. Mr. Kroneberg met Miss Jessing in Paris, you see, and in 1874 he brought her back to St. Petersburg with him. "'You can judge,' Mr. Spasovich announces suddenly, 'the extent to which Miss Jessing does or does not resemble those women of the *demimonde* with whom gentlemen form only short-lived liaisons. She is not Kroneberg's wife, of course, but their relationship excludes neither love nor respect.'"

Well, that is a matter of opinion, I suppose, and it is their business and none of ours. But Mr. Spasovich is absolutely determined to get us to respect her. "'Have you seen an instance when this woman treated the child cruelly? Did the child not love her? She wanted to do all she could for the child....'"

The whole point is that the child called this lady *maman*, and it

was from the lady's trunk that the child took the prune for which
she was beaten so. So you mustn't think that Jessing hates the
child and that she made false accusations so as to turn Kroneberg
against her. Of course we don't think that; we think even that this
lady has no cause to hate the child: the child has been taught to
kiss the lady's hand and to call her *maman*. It emerges that this
lady was frightened by the "spitzrutens" and even implored Kroneberg (unsuccessfully) to break off one dangerous twig before the
beating. Mr. Spasovich states that it was even Jessing who gave
Kroneberg the idea to take the child from de Combe in Geneva:
"'Kroneberg at that time still had no definite notion of taking the
child, but decided to go to Geneva to have a look at her. . . .'"
    This piece of information reveals a great deal, and we must keep
it in mind. It turns out that at that time the child was not very
much on Mr. Kroneberg's mind and that he had no heartfelt need
whatever to keep her with him. "'In Geneva he was astounded:
the child, whom he visited unexpectedly and unannounced, was
found to be sullen and unsociable and *did not recognize her father.*'"
    Take special note of the phrase "did not recognize her father."
I have already said that Mr. Spasovich is most accomplished at
tossing off such little phrases; it would seem that he simply let
this phrase slip out, yet at the end of his speech it shows its real
purpose and bears its fruit. If she "did not recognize her father,"
it means that the child was not only sullen but also perverse. All
this will be needed later on; we shall see eventually that Mr. Spasovich, who tosses off these little phrases here and there, will at
last utterly destroy your illusions about this child. Instead of a little
creature of seven, instead of an angel, you will see before you an
"active" girl, sly, a cry-baby, hard to manage, a girl who cries as
soon as she is made to stand in the corner, who is "a great one
for bawling" (such language!), who lies, who steals, who is untidy,
and who has a nasty, secret vice. The whole tactic is to destroy
somehow your sympathy for her. It's human nature, after all: you
have no pity for one whom you dislike, for whom you feel an
aversion; and Mr. Spasovich fears your compassion more than anything; otherwise, when you take pity on her you might put the
blame on her father. This is the essential falsehood on which the
case rests. Of course, all the arrangement of these remarks, all
these facts he collects to hold over the child's head are, when taken
individually, of no consequence at all, and you will undoubtedly
see that for yourselves in time. There is no person, for example,

who could not know that a three- or even four-year-old child abandoned by someone for three years would certainly forget that person's face, forget every last detail about that person and that time;
everyone knows that a child's memory at that age extends no further
than a year, or even nine months. Any father and any doctor will
confirm this. The blame here rests rather with the ones who abandoned the child for so many years, and not with the child's perverse
nature, and, of course, a juror will also understand that, should
he find the time and the inclination to think and consider carefully;
but he has no time to consider carefully, he is impressed by the
irresistible pressure of talent; Mr. Spasovich's carefully arranged
remarks hover over him: the point is not in each fact taken separately, but in the whole, in the conglomeration of facts, so to
speak—and say what you will, but all these trivial facts, taken
together, at last do produce a hostile feeling toward the child. *Il
en reste toujours quelque chose*—an old and well-known technique,
especially when the facts are arranged with skill and studied
purpose.

I shall jump ahead and present yet another such example of Mr.
Spasovich's art. For instance, using the same technique at the end
of his speech, he absolutely destroys at a stroke the most telling
witness against his client, Agrafena Titova. Here it's not even a
matter of the arrangement of facts; here he merely seized upon one
short phrase and exploited it. Agrafena Titova is Mr. Kroneberg's
former maid. It was she, together with Uliana Bibina, the porter's
wife at the dacha in Lesnoe that Mr. Kroneberg was renting, who
first instituted the charge of torturing the child. I might say, by
the way, that in my view this Titova, and particularly Bibina, are
almost the most sympathetic people in the whole case. They both
love the child. The child was bored. She had only just been brought
here from Switzerland, and she scarcely saw her father. The father
was busy looking after the affairs of a railway company and would
leave the house in the morning and return late in the evening.
Returning home in the evening and learning of some childish prank
the girl had committed, he would whip her and slap her face (these
facts were established and were not denied by Mr. Spasovich); as
a result of this cheerless life, the poor girl grew withdrawn and
became more and more dejected. "The girl just sits by herself now
and will speak to no one"—these are the very words spoken by
Titova when she brought her complaint. One hears not only a deep
sympathy in these words but also perceives the discerning view of

a good observer, a view that expresses her own private torment over the sufferings of this tiny, abused creature of God. After that it is only natural that the girl should come to love the servants, the only ones who showed her love and tenderness, and that she should sometimes run downstairs to visit the porter's wife. Mr. Spasovich blames the child for this and attributes her vices to the "corrupting influence of the servants." Note that the girl spoke only French, and that Uliana Bibina, the porter's wife, could not understand her well, and so she grew to love her simply out of pity and sympathy for the little child, a trait so characteristic of our common People.

> "One evening in July" (the indictment states), "Kroneberg again began to beat the girl, and on this occasion he whipped her for so long and she cried so dreadfully that Bibina was alarmed, fearing that the child might be beaten to death. Therefore she jumped from her bed dressed only in her nightgown, ran to Kroneberg's window, and shouted that he stop beating the child or she would send for the police; *at this point the beating and the crying ceased....*"

Can you picture this mother hen standing before her chicks and spreading her wings to defend them? These poor hens who defend their chicks sometimes become almost frightening. When I was a child in the country I knew a little peasant lad, the son of the servants, who was terribly fond of tormenting animals and particularly liked to slaughter chickens whenever some were needed for our dinner. I remember he used to climb on the straw roof of the barn to look for sparrows' nests: when he found a nest he would at once begin wringing off their heads. But can you imagine—this torturer had a dreadful fear of a mother hen, and when she, furious, would stand in front of him with outspread wings, defending her chicks, then he would always hide behind me. And so it was that three days later this poor mother hen once more could not restrain herself and went off to complain to the authorities, taking along a bundle of the switches used to beat the girl and some bloodstained linen. Here you must keep in mind how averse our common people are to law courts and how afraid they are of becoming involved with them, hoping only that they themselves will not be dragged into court. But she did go, and went to lodge a complaint on behalf of a stranger, a child, knowing that in any case she would earn no personal benefit but only unpleasantness and bother. And so it is these two women to whom Mr. Spasovich refers when he speaks

of the "corrupting influence of the servants on the child." Moreover,
he seizes upon the following little fact: the child, as you will see
further, had been accused of theft. (You will see later how skillfully
Mr. Spasovich transformed the one prune the child took without
permission into the theft of banknotes.) But the girl did not confess
to *theft* at first and even stated that "she had taken nothing from
them."

> "The girl responded with stubborn silence" (says Mr. Spasovich);
> "then, several months later, she told of how she *wanted to take some
> money for Agrafena*. Had he (i.e., the girl's father) investigated the
> circumstances of the theft more carefully, he would, perhaps, have
> come to the conclusion that the bad habits the girl had developed
> must be attributed to the influence of the people around her. The
> girl's refusal to answer in itself testifies to the fact that she did not
> want to betray those with whom she was on good terms."

"She wanted to take some money for Agrafena"—that's the
phrase! "A few months later" the girl, of course, *invented* a story
that she wanted to take some money for Agrafena. This was either
a total fabrication or was done at someone else's prompting. After
all, she stated in court: "Je suis voleuse, menteuse," when she had
never stolen anything except a single prune; and for those several
months the irresponsible child was made to believe that she had
stolen; they made her believe this without even trying to do so
deliberately, simply because she continually heard everyone around
her saying every day that she was a thief. But even if it were true
that the child wanted to take some money for Agrafena Titova,
then it by no means follows that Titova herself taught her and
influenced her to steal money. Mr. Spasovich is artful; under no
circumstances will he say this directly; he could not slander Titova
in this way unless he had direct and solid evidence; yet immediately
after the girl's remark that she "wanted to take some money for
Agrafena," he slips in his own suggestion that "the bad habits the
girl had developed must be attributed to the influence of the people
around her." And, of course, that's sufficient. Into the heart of the
juror creeps the notion: "So we know the character of both principal
witnesses; it was for them that she stole, then, and it was they who
taught her to steal. What is their testimony worth after that?" No
one could possibly avoid thinking such a thought once it had been
expressed in such circumstances. And so the dangerous testimony
has been crushed and destroyed precisely when Mr. Spasovich

needs it to be destroyed—right at the end of his speech where it can have decisive influence and effect. Say what you like, but this is artfully done. Indeed, the lawyer placed in such a tight situation has a difficult job; what else could he do? He must save his client. Still, as we say, these are only the flowers; the berries are yet to come.

4. The Berries

I have already said that Mr. Spasovich denies that the girl was treated cruelly in any way or that she was tortured; he will not even take such suggestions seriously. Moving on to the "catastrophe of July 25," he begins directly to count the welts and bruises, every little scar and scab and every piece of flayed skin; then he places them all on the balance: "so many ounces—there was no torture!"—such is his view and his method. The press has already pointed out to Mr. Spasovich that such counting of welts and scars is irrelevant and even absurd. But in my view all of this book-keeping must definitely have made a deep impression on the jury and on the public: "What precision," they think. "How thorough the man is!" I am convinced that some of those who listened to him must have been particularly pleased to learn that information about a certain welt was requested specially from de Combe in Geneva. Mr. Spasovich triumphantly points out that there was no broken skin: "'Despite the wholly unfavorable opinion of Mr. Lansberg' (the doctor who examined the girl on July 29 and whose opinions Mr. Spasovich treats with extreme sarcasm) 'toward Kroneberg, I am borrowing many facts from his statement of July 29 for my defense. Mr. Lansberg certified that there was no broken skin on the posterior of the girl's body but *only* some dark-purple subcutaneous spots and red streaks. . . .'"

Only! Note that little word. And, most importantly, five days after her ordeal! I could testify to Mr. Spasovich that these dark-purple subcutaneous spots disappear very quickly and pose not the least threat to life; nonetheless, does that mean they do not constitute cruelty, suffering, torture?

> "The spots were found most prominently on the left ischial region, spreading also to the left hip. Finding no signs of trauma nor even any scratches, Mr. Lansberg testified that the streaks and spots represented *no danger* to life. Six days later, on August 5, the girl was

A Writer's Diary

examined by Professor Florinsky, who found no spots but only streaks, some short and others longer; but he maintained that these streaks represented no serious injury, although he admitted that the punishment had been harsh, especially in view of the instrument used to punish the child."

I will inform Mr. Spasovich that in the prisoners' wards of the hospital in Siberia I happened to see the backs of prisoners who had just been administered five hundred, a thousand, and even two thousand blows with "spitzrutens" (the prisoners had been forced to pass through ranks of soldiers armed with the sticks). I saw this several dozen times. Believe me, Mr. Spasovich, some backs had swollen up nearly two inches (literally), and imagine how little flesh there is on the back. They were precisely this dark-purple color with a few scratches that seeped blood. You may be sure that not one of our expert medical men nowadays has seen anything of this sort (and where could we see it in our time?). These convicts, if they had received no more than a thousand blows, would arrive always maintaining a most sanguine air, although they were apparently in a highly agitated state; but even that lasted only for the first two hours. None of them, as far as I can remember, lay or sat down during those first two hours but would only pace about the ward with a wet sheet over their shoulders, sometimes heaving a shudder of their whole body. The only treatment they received was a bucket of water, in which the punished man would dip the sheet when it dried out on his back. As I recall, they all wanted to be discharged from the ward as soon as possible (because they had been locked up for a long time preliminary to their trial, while others simply wanted to arrange an escape at the first opportunity). And here is a fact for you: such men were almost always discharged on the sixth, at most on the seventh day after their punishment, because during that time the back *had almost always completely healed*, aside from a few comparatively minor traces. But in ten days, for example, everything had always disappeared entirely. Punishment with the "spitzrutens" (i.e., in fact always with sticks), if not inflicted excessively—i.e., no more than two thousand blows at a time—never presented the slightest threat to life. To the contrary, I heard all the prisoners at hard labor and the military prisoners (and they had seen a thing or two!) say regularly that switches are more painful ("they have more of a bite") and are incomparably more dangerous, because one could bear even more than two thousand blows of the "spitzrutens," but one might die after only four hundred blows of a switch; five or six hundred *at a time* meant almost certain death—no one could endure it. And so now I ask you, Mr. Defense Attorney: even though these sticks did not pose a threat to life and did not cause even the slightest injury, do you really believe that such a punishment was not cruel? Do you really believe that this was not a case of torture? Did this little girl not suffer and cry, "Papa! Papa!" for a quarter of an hour under the dreadful sticks that lay on a table in the court? Why do you deny her suffering and her torture?

But I have already said why there is such a tangle here; I'll repeat it again: the fact is that in our *Code of Punishments,* as Mr. Spasovich states, there is "ambiguity, deficiency, omissions" in the way "torture" is understood and defined.

> "... Therefore the Governing Senate has determined, in those same decisions cited by the prosecution, that, on the other hand, torture and torment are to be understood as those infringements upon the person or upon the sanctity of the individual that are accompanied by cruel treatment. In the opinion of the Senate, a case of torture or torment must necessarily involve an extreme and more protracted degree of suffering than an ordinary beating, even a severe beating. If the beating cannot be called severe (and a case of torture must be more severe than a severe beating), and if not a single expert—apart from Mr. Lansberg, who repudiated his own conclusion—could call this a severe beating, then the question is *how can the concepts of torture and cruelty be applied to the actions of my client? I submit that this is impossible.*"

And so we see the point. There is ambiguity in the *Code of Punishments,* and Mr. Spasovich's client could, if convicted of torture, fall under one of the most severe articles of the law, an article which in any case is inapplicable given the measure of his crime, an article which brings with it a punishment utterly incommensurate with his "action." Well, it would seem that our confusion could be cleared up quite simply: "The child was tortured, but not in such a manner as defined by law, i.e., *not more severely than a severe beating,* and therefore my client cannot be convicted of torture." But no, Mr. Spasovich is prepared to yield nothing; he wants to prove that there was no torture at all, neither legal nor illegal, and no suffering, none at all! But tell me, please, what is it to us that the torture and cruel treatment of this child do not conform to the exact legal definition of torture? The law is incomplete; you said so yourself. The child still suffered, after all: did she not suffer? Was she not, in fact, tortured in the true sense of the word? Have we been so distracted from the essence of the case? Indeed, Mr. Spasovich undertook to do just that; he is determined to distract us: the child, he says, on the very next day was "playing," she "attended a lesson." I don't think she was playing. Bibina, to the contrary, testifies that when she examined the girl before going to lay a complaint, "the girl was weeping bitterly and kept saying, 'Papa! Papa!'" Heavens! Such small children are so impressionable and so pliant! And so what if she did, perhaps, go out and play the next day, still with the bluish-purple spots on her body? I have seen a five-year-old boy, almost dying from scarlet fever, utterly weakened and exhausted, yet still lisping that he had been promised a doggie and asking that all his toys be placed on his bed—"Just so I can have a look at them." But Mr. Spasovich attains the summit of his art when he "appropriates" entirely the child's age! He keeps telling us about some girl, perverse and corrupt, caught stealing more than once, with a secret vice in her soul, and he seems to forget entirely (and we do as well) that the case concerns an infant who is only seven, and that same *flogging* that lasted a quarter of an hour with those nine "spitzrutens" of rowan wood would probably have been ten times easier for an adult and even for a fourteen-year-old than it was for this poor, tiny creature! You cannot help but ask why Mr. Spasovich is doing all this? Why must he so stubbornly deny the girl's suffering? Why must he lavish almost all his art on this and contort himself so as to distract us? Can it really all be only because of a lawyer's vanity? "Not only will I save my client's neck, I'll prove that the whole case is utterly ridiculous and nonsensical and that a father is being tried only because he once administered a beating to a nasty little girl." But I have already said that he needs to destroy any sympathy you might have for her. And even though he has reserved a good many resources to do that, he still fears that the child's sufferings will evoke in you—who knows?—humane feelings. And these same humane feelings are a threat to him: what if you get angry at his client? He needs to crush your humane feelings in advance, to distort them and ridicule them; in a word, he has to undertake what might seem an impossible task, impossible because of the very fact that you have before you the utterly clear, precise, completely frank testimony of the father, who makes a firm and truthful admission that he tortured the child:

"'On July 25, irritated by my daughter,' the father testified, 'I beat her with this bundle of sticks; I beat her severely and, this time, *I beat her for a long time, beside myself, unaware of what I was doing, with whatever was at hand.'* Whether the sticks broke during this last beating he does not know, but he remembers that they were longer when he began beating the girl."

It's true that in spite of this testimony the father still did not admit at the trial that he was guilty of torturing his daughter, and he declared that until July 25 he had always administered light punishments. I note in passing that the notion of lightness and severity here is a subjective one: blows to the face of a seven-year-old infant that cause a bloody nose—something that is denied neither by Kroneberg nor by his defense attorney—evidently are considered light punishment by both. Mr. Spasovich has some other priceless tricks to perform in this line, a good many of them. For example: "You have heard that the marks on the girl's elbows were almost certainly caused only by her *being held down by the arms* while the punishment was administered."

Listen to that: *only* by her being held down. They must have held her down well to cause bruises! Oh, of course Mr. Spasovich does not come right out and say that all this is beautiful and smelling of roses; here, for example, is another nice little argument:

"They say that this punishment goes beyond the bounds of what is normal. Such a definition would do very well if we could define what a normal punishment is. *But since there is no such definition,* anyone would find it difficult to say whether it exceeded the bounds of normality" (and this after the father's testimony that he beat her *for a long time, unaware of what he was doing and beside himself!!!*). "Let us grant that this is so. But what does this mean? That this punishment is one that, in the majority of cases, should not be administered to children. But there can be exceptional cases with children. Do you not admit that a father's authority, in exceptional cases, may be so disposed that the father must use a more severe measure than is normal, one unlike those normal measures that are applied daily?"

And that is all that Mr. Spasovich agrees to give up. This whole case of torture he reduces only to "a more severe measure than is normal"—but he repents even of this concession: at the end of his speech he takes it all back and says: "A father is being tried, but for what? For abuse of his authority; but where, I ask you, is the limit to that authority? Who can determine how many blows a father may administer, and in what cases he may administer them, so long as he causes no injury to the child's organism?"

Meaning without breaking the child's leg, is that it? And so long as he doesn't break the child's leg he can do anything he likes? Are you serious, Mr. Spasovich? Are you serious in saying you do not know where the limit of this power lies and "how many blows a father can administer and in what circumstances he can administer them"? If you don't know, I'll tell you where that limit lies! The limit of his authority is that he must not take a tiny, seven-year-old creature who cannot be held responsible for all her "vices" (vices which ought to be corrected in a different manner entirely)— one must not, I say, take a creature who has the countenance of an angel, who is incomparably purer and less sinful than you and I, Mr. Spasovich, less sinful than all those who were present in the courtroom and who judged and condemned this girl—he must not, I say, *flog* her with nine "spitzrutens" of rowan wood, flog her for a quarter of an hour without heeding her cries of "Papa! Papa!" cries that almost drove a simple peasant woman, the porter's wife, into a frenzy of madness; he must not, at last, frankly confess that "I beat her for a long time, beside myself, unaware of what I was doing, with whatever was at hand!"—he must not be *beside himself*, because there is a limit to all rage, and even rage at a seven-year-old irresponsible infant for a single prune and a broken crochet hook!

Yes, indeed, you are a skilled attorney; but there is a limit to everything, and if I weren't aware that you are saying all this by design and only shamming for all you are worth in order to save your client, I would add one more thing specifically for your benefit: there is a limit even to every "lyre" and to a lawyer's "responsiveness." That limit is not letting your own eloquence carry you up to the Pillars of Hercules as your eloquence has carried you, Mr. Defense Attorney! But alas, you were only sacrificing yourself for the sake of your client, and it's not my right to talk to you about limits; I am only amazed at the magnitude of your sacrifice!

5. The Pillars of Hercules

But we see the real Pillars of Hercules when Mr. Spasovich reaches the "just wrath of the father."

"When this bad habit" (i.e., the habit of lying) "became evident in the girl," Mr. Spasovich continues, "coupled with all her other flaws, and when the father learned that she was *stealing*, he was truly enraged. I think that *every one of you would have been just as enraged*, and I think that to victimize a father for punishing his child severely, but *with good reason*, does a disservice to the family and a disservice to the state, because the state is only strong so long as it rests on the strong family.... If the father became incensed, he was entirely within his rights...."

Wait now, Mr. Defense Attorney, for the moment I won't raise any objections to the word "stealing" you used, but let us talk a little bit about this "just wrath of the father." What about her upbringing from the age of three in Switzerland by the de Combes, where you yourself testify the girl was corrupted and acquired some bad habits? At her age how could she be held to blame for her bad habits? If such is the case, then where is the justness in the father's wrath? I maintain that the girl is not in the least responsible in this case, even if we admit that she had some bad habits, and whatever you say, you cannot dispute the fact that a seven-year-old child cannot be held responsible for her actions. She still does not have and cannot have enough intelligence to perceive her own wrong. Why none of us—perhaps not even you, Mr. Spasovich— are saints, despite the fact that we have more intelligence than a seven-year-old child. How can you, then, impose this burden of responsibility on such a tiny creature, a burden that you yourself are unable to bear? Remember the words "for they bind heavy burdens and grievous to be borne." You will say that it is our duty to correct children. But listen: we ought not to exalt ourselves above children; we are worse than they. And if we teach them something to make them better, then they also teach us much and also make us better by our very contact with them. They humanize our souls by their mere presence in our midst. And so we ought to treat them and their angelic images with respect (assuming that we have anything to teach them). We must respect their innocence, even when they have some perverse habit; we must respect their lack of responsibility, their touching defenselessness. You argue, to the contrary, that blows on the face until the blood flows, when dealt by a father, are just and cause no offense. This child had some sort of scab in her nose, and you say: "Perhaps the blows on the face accelerated the discharge of blood from the scrofulous scabs in her nostril; but this does not mean the child was harmed: *there would have been bleeding a little later even if there had been no injury.*

This bleeding, therefore, can in no way be prejudicial to Kroneberg. At the moment he hit her *he might not have remembered nor even known that the child had frequent nosebleeds.*"

"Might not have remembered; might not have known!" Do you really suppose Mr. Kroneberg might deliberately have struck her in a sore spot? Of course he didn't know. And so your own testimony tells us that the father did not know of his child's illness, yet you support his right to beat the child. You claim that the father's striking the child on the face caused no harm. Well, perhaps this did cause no harm to a tiny seven-year-old, but what of the emotional damage to that child? You, Sir, in your entire speech never mentioned the moral and emotional damage done to the child, but spoke the whole time only of the physical pain. Why was she struck across the face, after all? What are the causes for such terrible anger? Is she really a hardened criminal? This little girl, this criminal, will now run off to play at "robbers" with the boys. You are dealing here with a child who is only seven years old, and you should never lose sight of that fact in this case; why it's all a mirage, the things you are saying! Do you know what it means to abuse a child? Their hearts are full of innocent, almost unconscious love, and blows such as these cause a grievous shock and tears that God sees and will count. For their reason is never capable of grasping their full guilt. Have you seen or heard of little children who were tormented, or of orphans, say, who were raised among wicked strangers? Have you seen a child cowering in a corner, trying to hide, and weeping there, wringing his hands (yes, wringing his hands—I've seen it myself) and *beating his chest with his tiny fist,* not knowing himself what he is doing, not clearly understanding his own guilt or why he is being tormented but sensing all too well that he is not loved? I know nothing about Mr. Kroneberg personally; I cannot and do not wish to enter into his soul and his heart, nor those of his family, because, not knowing him at all, I might do him a great injustice, and so I base my judgment solely on your words and statements, Mr. Advocate. You said in your speech that Mr. Kroneberg was "not good at raising children"; I think that is the same as saying he is an inexperienced father or, to put it better, he is unaccustomed to fatherhood. Let me explain: these little creatures only enter into our souls and attach themselves to our hearts when we, having begotten them, watch over them from childhood without leaving them from the time of their first smile; and then we continue to grow into one another's souls every day, every hour, all through our lives. Now that is the family; that is something sacred! A family, after all, is also *created*, not provided ready-made, and there are no rights and no obligations that are provided ready-made here; they all derive one from the other. Only then is it solid, and only then is it sacred. The family is created by a ceaseless labor of love. However, you, Sir, admit that your client made two *logical* errors (only logical ones?), and that one of them, incidentally, was that he "'... acted overzealously. He supposed that one could eradicate at once, with one stroke, all the evil that had been sown and had taken root in the heart of the child over the years. But that cannot be done; one must act slowly and have patience.'"

I swear that not much of that patience would have been needed because this tiny creature is only seven years old! Once again we find these seven years, the seven years that disappear entirely from your speech and from your considerations, Sir! "She was stealing," you exclaim. "She was a thief!"

> "On July 25 the father arrives at the dacha and for the first time learns to his surprise that the child has been rummaging in Jessing's trunk, that the child has broken a hook" (a crochet hook, that is— not a lock of some kind) "and was *trying to get at* the money. I wonder, gentlemen, if you could react with indifference to such behavior by your daughter? 'But why was she punished?' you ask. 'Can one really inflict such strict punishment for a few prunes and some sugar?' I submit that from prunes to sugar, from sugar to loose change, from loose change to banknotes is a straight path and an open road!"

Let me tell you a little story, Sir. A father who earns his money through hard work is sitting at his desk. He is a writer, just as I am, and he is writing. After a while he puts down his pen and his daughter, a girl of six, comes up to him; she begins telling him that he must buy her a new doll and then a carriage, a real carriage with horses; she and her doll and her nurse would get in the carriage and go to visit Dasha, her nurse's granddaughter. "And then, papa, you should buy me . . ." etc., etc. There's no end to the things she wants. She's only just invented and imagined all these things while playing with her doll in the corner. These six-year-old infants have an amazing imagination, and that is a fine thing: it helps them develop. The father listens with a smile.

"Ah, Sonia dear," he says suddenly, half in jest, half in sorrow, "I would buy you all these things, but where would I get the money? You don't know how difficult it is to get money!"

"This is what you do, papa," exclaims Sonia, with a very serious, confidential air. "You take a pot and a shovel and you go into the woods and dig under a bush; you'll find some money; put it into the pot and bring it home."

I assure you that this little girl is certainly not stupid, but that is her concept of how one gets money. Do you really think that our seven-year-old has gone much beyond this six-year-old in her concept of money? Of course, she perhaps has already learned that one cannot dig up money from under a bush; but where money in fact comes from, what laws it follows, what banknotes are, and stock shares, and concession rights—this she scarcely knows. Come now, Mr. Spasovich: can you really say that the girl was *trying to get at* the money? That expression and the meaning attached to it are applicable only to an adult thief who understands what money is and how it is used. And even if a little girl like this had taken some money, it would certainly not be a case of theft but only a bit of childish mischief like taking the prune, because she has no idea of what money is. Yet you try to tell us that it won't be long before she's taking banknotes and shout that "this is a threat to the state!" Is it permissible, after this, to consider the flogging this girl was subjected to as *just* and *justifiable*? But she wasn't even touching the money and never took a penny of it. She was only rummaging in the trunk where the money was; she broke a crochet hook but took nothing else. What good was the money to her? Was she planning to run off to America with it, or maybe get a railway concession? You were the one who mentioned banknotes, after all: "It's not far from sugar to banknotes." So why should she shrink at the thought of a railway concession?

Haven't you reached the Pillars of Hercules, Sir?

"She has a vice, a nasty, secret vice...."

Now just wait a moment, you who would prosecute her! Was there no one among you who sensed how monstrous, how inconceivable this scene was? A tiny little girl is brought out before people—serious, humane people; the child is humiliated; her "secret vices" are spoken of aloud! And what does it matter that she does not yet understand her own disgrace and admits: "Je suis voleuse, menteuse"? Say what you like—this is inconceivable and intolerable; this is falsehood that cannot be endured. And who could be so bold as to say that she "stole," that she "was trying to get at" the money? Can such words be uttered about an infant like this? Why is she besmirched by people discussing aloud her "secret vices" for the whole court to hear? Why was she splashed with so much filth and left with a stain that will never disappear? Oh, acquit your client, Sir, as quickly as you can, if only to lower the curtain as soon as possible and preserve us from this spectacle. But leave us, at least, our pity for this infant; do not judge her with such a serious air, as if you yourself believed in her guilt. This pity is our treasure, and it is a terrible thing to tear it out of our society. When a society ceases to pity its weak and oppressed, it will itself be afflicted; it will grow callous and wither; it will become depraved and sterile. . . .

"But if I leave you your pity, your great pity may convict my client."

And that, indeed, is the situation.

6. The Family and Our Sacred Ideals. A Concluding Note about a Certain Modern School

Mr. Spasovich makes a pointed remark in conclusion: "'In concluding I will permit myself to say that in my opinion the whole case against Kroneberg has been put quite incorrectly so that the questions that will be put to you are utterly impossible to answer.'"

Now that's clever: the whole essence of the case is here, and this is the cause of all its falsity. But Mr. Spasovich adds still a few more rather solemn words on the subject: "I submit that you all acknowledge the fact of the family and the fact of paternal authority. . . ." Earlier he was shouting that "the state can only be strong when it rests on the strong family."

Here I, too, will permit myself to insert just a few words, and those just in passing.

We Russians are a young people; we are only just beginning to live, although we have existed for a thousand years; but a big ship is meant to sail on a long journey. We are a fresh people, and we do not hold sacred ideals *quand même*. We love our sacred ideals, but only because they are, in fact, sacred. We do not uphold them simply as a means of supporting *l'Ordre*. Our sacred ideals persist not because of their utility but because of our faith in them. We will even refuse to defend any sacred ideals in which we no longer believe, unlike the ancient priests who, in the twilight of paganism, defended the idols which they had long since ceased to consider as gods. Not a single one of our sacred ideals is threatened by free inquiry, but this is precisely because they are strong in reality. We love the sacred ideal of the family when it is sacred in reality, and not only because the state rests firmly upon it. And when we believe in the strength of the family, we will have nothing to fear if occasionally some bad examples of the family come to light, and we will not be frightened even if cases of abuse of parental authority are publicized and prosecuted. We will not defend this authority *quand même*. The sacred ideal of a genuinely sacred family is so solid that it will never be shaken by this but will grow even more sacred. But in every instance there is a limit and a measure, and this we are also prepared to accept. I am not a lawyer, but in the case of Kroneberg I cannot help but see something deeply false. Something is wrong here; something else must have happened here, despite the very real guilt. Mr. Spasovich is certainly correct when he speaks about the way the question was put; but this does not settle anything. Perhaps we need a profound and *independent* examination of our laws on this point so as to fill in the gaps and make the laws conform to the nature of our society. I can't decide what we need here; I'm not a lawyer. . . .

Still, I cannot help but cry out: indeed, establishing the legal profession was an excellent thing but somehow also a sad one. I said that at the beginning and I repeat it. This is how it seems to me, and only because I am not a lawyer; that is my whole trouble. I keep imagining some sort of modern school in which people are trained to have agile minds and arid hearts, a school in which every healthy feeling is distorted when the occasion demands distortion; a school that teaches every possible method of personal attack, made without fear or punishment, continually and unrelentingly, based on need and demand, whose techniques have been elevated to the level of a principle and (because we have so little experience here) have acquired a luster of heroism that is universally applauded. So tell me, am I trying to discredit the legal profession and the new courts? God forbid: I would only like us all to become a little better than we are. This is a most modest wish, but, alas, a most idealistic one. I am an incorrigible idealist; I am seeking sacred ideals; I love them, and my heart thirsts after them because I have been so created that I cannot live without sacred ideals; still, I would like our ideals to be a bit more sacred—otherwise, is there any point in worshipping them? One way or another I've managed to spoil my February *Diary* by dwelling excessively in it on a sad topic, simply because it made such an impression on me. But, *il faut avoir le courage de son opinion*, and I think that this wise French saying could serve as a guide to many who are seeking answers to their questions is this confused time of ours.

March

1

1. How True Is the Notion That "The Ideals May Be Base So Long as the Reality Is Good"?

I read the following comment in Mr. Gamma's "Leaflet" (*The Voice*, no. 67) on my remarks about the People in my February *Diary*:

> Nevertheless, we find in the space of one month two sharply opposed views about the People from the same writer. And this is not some farcical little play but a painting at a traveling exhibition: this is a verdict on a living organism; this amounts to twisting the knife in a man's body. Mr. Dostoevsky tries to excuse his real or imagined contradictions by inviting us to judge the People "not by what they are but by what they would like to become." The People, you see, are the vilest sort of rabble in actuality; however, their ideals are good. These ideals are "powerful and sacred," and have "saved the People through centuries of suffering." Excuses of that sort don't make one feel very good! Hell itself is paved with good intentions, after all, and Mr. Dostoevsky knows that "faith without works is dead." How have these ideals become public knowledge, in any case? Who has the gift of prophecy or the knowledge of the human heart to penetrate and decipher them if the reality contradicts and is unworthy of these ideals? Mr. Dostoevsky justifies our People in the sense that "they may take the odd bribe, but at least they don't imbibe." One need not take this much further to arrive at the moral: "Better let our ideals be base, so long as our reality is good."

The most important thing in this excerpt is Mr. Gamma's question "How have these ideals (the People's, that is) become public knowledge?". I categorically refuse to answer such a question, for no matter how much Mr. Gamma and I were to discuss the topic

we would never come to an agreement. This is a long-standing
dispute and a most important one for us. Do the People have ideals
or do they not?—this is a question of life and death for us. This
argument has been going on far too long already and is now at the
point where these ideals have become as bright and as obvious as
the sun for some people, while others do not see them at all and
have, in fact, refused to see them. Which side is right will not be
decided by us, but it will be decided, perhaps, rather soon. Recently
a number of voices were raised saying that there can be nothing
conservative in Russia because we have "nothing worth conserving." Indeed, if we have no ideals of our own, is it worth concerning
ourselves with this matter and trying to conserve anything? Well,
if people are pacified by this thought, good luck to them.

"The People, you see, are the vilest sort of rabble, but their
ideals are good." I did not make that statement or express that
thought. I am replying to Mr. Gamma solely in order to make my
position clear. In fact, I said just the opposite: "there are true
saints among the People, and what saints they are: they give off
light and illuminate the way for us all." They do exist, my respected
commentator friend, they truly do exist, and blessed is he who is
able to discern them. I think that here, that is to say in these
particular words, there isn't the least bit of ambiguity. Besides,
ambiguity does not always come from the fact that a writer is unclear
but sometimes from quite opposite reasons. . . .

As far as the moral with which you conclude your remarks is
concerned—"Let our ideals be base so long as our reality is good"—
let me point out to you that this is a hope that can never be realized:
without ideals—that is, without at least some partially defined hopes
for something better—our reality will never become better. One
can even state positively that there will be nothing but even worse
abominations. In my way of seeing things, at least, there is a chance
left: if things are not attractive now, then with a clear and conscious
desire to become better (i.e., with ideals of something better), we
may indeed one day collect ourselves and become better. At least
this is not so impossible as your proposal to become better with
"base" ideals, that is to say, having base aspirations.

I hope that these few words of mine do not make you angry, Mr.
Gamma. Let us remain, the both of us, with our own opinions
and await the denouement; I assure you that that denouement,
perhaps, is not far off at all.

2. A Hundred-Year-Old Woman

"I was really very late that morning," a lady told me the other day, "and it was almost noon when I left home; to make matters worse, there were so many things to be done. I had to stop in at two places on Nikolaevsky Street, one not far from the other. At the first place, going into an office, I met this really old woman near the gate, and she looked so old and bent as she walked along with her cane; but I just couldn't tell how old she was. She went as far as the gate and sat down on the porter's bench at the corner to rest. I walked past and only caught a glimpse of her.

"Ten minutes later I come out of the office; two doors down the street is the store where I ordered some shoes for Sonia last week, and since I was passing I went to pick them up; but I look and see that same old woman now sitting by that building, sitting on another bench and looking at me; I smiled at her, went into the store, and got the shoes. Well, three or four minutes passed, I went on along to the Nevsky, and—who do I see but my little old lady, now at another building, sitting by the gate again, but now she's not on a bench—she's managed to find a cosy spot on a projecting bit of the foundation, since there was no bench by this gate. I couldn't help but pause in front of her, wondering why it was that she stopped and sat down in front of every building.

"'Are you tired, my good woman?' I asked.

"'I do get tired, my dear; I'm always getting tired. It's a warm day, I'm thinking, and the sun's shining; so why don't I go and have dinner at my granddaughters'.'

"'So you're on your way to have dinner?'

"'Indeed I am, my dear.'

"'But you'll scarcely make it at the pace you're going.'

"'Oh, I'll make it. I'll go on a bit and then take a rest, and then get up and walk a bit more.'

"Looking at her I got terribly curious. She was a tiny little thing, neat but dressed in old clothes, a townswoman probably, with a cane and a pale, yellow face, colorless lips, and her skin stretched dryly over her bones like a mummy. But she sits there smiling, the sun shining right on her.

"'You must be pretty well on in years, Granny,' I ask, trying to make a little joke.

"'A hundred and four, my dear, one hundred and four years old, *that's all*' (she was joking now).... 'And where might you be going?'

"She looks at me, laughing, pleased, I imagine, to have someone to talk to; only it seemed odd to me that this hundred-year-old would be concerned to know where I was going.

"'Look at this, Granny,' said I, laughing as well. 'I picked up some shoes for my little girl in the store and I'm taking them home.'

"'What tiny wee shoes they are. She's a little one, your girl? Now that's good. And do you have other wee ones?'

"And again she's all smiles as she looks at me. Her eyes are dim with scarcely any life left in them, and yet they seem to radiate warmth.

"'Granny, please take five kopecks from me and buy yourself a roll,' and I give her the coin.

"'Now why should I need five kopecks? Never mind, I'll take it with thanks.'

"'There you are, Granny. Take it with my good wishes.'

"She took the coin. It was clear she'd not been reduced to begging, but she took the coin with such dignity, not at all like charity but as if from politeness or the goodness of her heart. And, who knows, maybe she was very pleased that someone should strike up a conversation with her, an old woman, and not only talk to her but even show some loving concern for her.

"'Well, good-bye, Granny,' I say. 'I hope you reach your grand-daughters' without trouble.'

"'I'll manage it, my dear, don't worry. And you get back to your granddaughter,' the old woman said (in error), forgetting that I had a daughter, not a granddaughter, and thinking, evidently, that everyone had granddaughters. I went on and turned to look at her for the last time; I see that she's risen and is slowly, painfully tapping her cane as she makes her way down the street. Perhaps she'll stop to rest ten more times along the way before she reaches her granddaughters' place to have dinner. And where might that place be? Such a strange old woman."

I had listened to the story that morning—indeed, it wasn't even a story but only some sort of impression of a meeting with a hundred-year-old woman (and in fact how often do you meet a hundred-year-old woman, let alone one so full of inner life?)—and had forgotten it entirely, but then, late at night, I was reading an article in a magazine and when I set the magazine aside I suddenly recalled that old woman, and for some reason I at once I sketched in an ending to the story of how she reached her own folks to have dinner: there emerged another, perhaps quite plausible little scene.

Her granddaughters, and perhaps her great-granddaughters (still, she calls them all granddaughters) are probably tradespeople of some sort, married women, of course, or else she would not be going to have dinner with them. They live in a basement and maybe they rent a barber's shop as well; they are poor people, of course, yet they eat well and observe the proprieties. It was probably past one o'clock when the old woman managed to get there. They weren't expecting her, yet they probably greeted her quite warmly.

"Well, and here's Maria Maximovna! Come in, come in, and welcome to you, servant of God!"

The old woman comes in, laughing a bit, while the little bell at the door goes on ringing sharply and shrilly for a long time. Her granddaughter is probably the barber's wife; he, the barber, is not yet an old man—about thirty-five, perhaps—and has the dignity of his trade, even though the trade may be a frivolous one; and of course he's wearing a frock coat as greasy as a pancake; that's caused by the pomade, I suppose, but I never saw a barber dressed any other way. And the collars on their coats always look as if they had been rolled in flour. Instantly three little children—a boy and two girls—run in to their great-grandmother. Such very aged women almost always have some very close kinship with children: they themselves become very much like children in their hearts, and sometimes exactly the same. The old woman sat down; someone else, perhaps a guest or someone on business—a man of forty or so and acquainted with the barber—was just getting ready to leave. In addition they have a nephew staying with them, the son of his sister, a lad of about seventeen who wants to find work in a printer's shop. The old woman crosses herself and sits down, looking at the guest.

"Oh, but I'm tired out! Now who's this you have here?"

"Do you mean me?" asks the guest, laughing. "Don't tell me you didn't recognize me, Maria Maximovna! Why, a couple of years ago you and I were planning to go out into the woods to look for mushrooms."

"Oh, now I know who you are. What a tease! I know who you are, only I just can't place your name, but I remember. Oh, I'm just worn out."

"Well now, Maria Maximovna, I've been wanting to ask you

why it is that a venerable old lady like yourself just doesn't seem
to grow at all?" the guest teases.

"Go on with you," laughs the grandmother, evidently pleased.

"I'm a good man, Maria Maximovna."

"And it's worthwhile to talk to a good man. Ah, Heavens, I
can't seem to catch my breath. I see you've already had an overcoat
made for little Seriozha."

She points at the nephew.

The nephew, a chubby, healthy little fellow, gives a broad smile
and moves closer. He is wearing a new gray coat that still gives
him a thrill to put on. He will only be able to wear it with equanimity in a week or so, but now he is constantly examining the
cuffs and the lapels and checking himself in the mirror; he feels
particularly proud of himself.

"Come on, now, turn around and show us," chatters the barber's
wife. "Look at that, Granny, what a job we did; six rubles exactly.
They were telling us over at Prokhorych's that it's not worth starting
the job for less; you'd regret it afterward, they said; but there's no
end of wear in this one. Just feel that material! Turn around now!
Look at that lining—feel the strength of it! Turn around, you! And
so the money goes, Granny. Our last kopeck's drained away."

"Oh, Heavens, everything's so dear these days there's just no
way of making ends meet. You'd better not talk to me about things
like that, it just upsets me," Maria Maximovna remarks fervently,
still out of breath.

"Yes, enough of that," says the husband. "We ought to have a
bite to eat. Maria Maximovna, I can see that you've really got
yourself tired out."

"Oh, I certainly have, my dear. It's a warm day, and the sun's
shining, so I think why not pay them a visit ... what's the point
of lying around? Ah! And I met a nice lady on the way, a young
woman, who'd bought some shoes for her wee children. 'Now why
are you so tired, Granny?' she asks me. 'Here's five kopecks for
you, buy yourself a roll....' And you know, I took the five
kopecks...."

"Come on, Granny, you'd better have a little rest before we do
anything else. Why is it you're so short of breath today?" the
husband says suddenly, with particular concern.

Everyone is looking at her; she has suddenly become very pale,
and her lips have gone quite white. She also looks around at everyone, but her gaze seems somehow dull.

"So, I think . . . some gingerbread for the children . . . that five kopecks. . . ."

Once more she stops, trying to catch her breath. Everyone suddenly falls silent for about five seconds.

"What is it, Granny?" says the husband, bending over her.

But the grandmother gives no reply; there is silence for another five seconds. The old woman seems to grow even more pale and her face suddenly seems to shrink. Her eyes stop moving and the smile freezes on her lips; she looks straight ahead but apparently sees nothing.

"We ought to get a priest!" the guest says suddenly in a quiet voice behind them.

"Yes . . . but . . . I think it may be too late," murmurs the husband.

"Grandmother! Listen, Grandmother!" the barber's wife, suddenly alarmed, calls out to the old woman; but the grandmother is motionless, her head leaning to one side. Her right hand, which rests on the table, holds the five kopecks, while her left hand has remained on the shoulder of her eldest great-grandson Misha, a boy of about six. He stands stock still, staring at his great-grandmother with huge, astonished eyes.

"She has passed on!" says the husband, slowly and with dignity, stooping and crossing himself unobtrusively.

"She has indeed! I could just see her fading away," the guest says tenderly, with a catch in his voice. He is quite shaken and looks around at everybody.

"My Lord, such a thing! What are we to do now, Makarych? Should we have her taken away?" the wife says excitedly, deeply upset.

"What do you mean, away?" her husband solemnly replies. "We'll look after everything ourselves; she's part of your family, is she not? But we'll have to go off and report it."

"A hundred and four years, think of that!" says the guest, squirming in his chair and growing more and more moved. He even blushes furiously.

"Yes, these last years she even began forgetting life itself," remarks the husband even more solemnly and soberly as he looks for his cap and puts on his coat.

"And only a minute ago she was laughing and so cheerful! Look at the coin in her hand! 'Gingerbread,' she said. What a life we have!"

"Well, shall we go, then, Petr Stepanych?" the host interrupts, and they both leave. There is no mourning, of course, for a woman such as this. One hundred and four years old and "she passed on without pain or regrets." The barber's wife sends to the neighbor women for help. They rush over at once, almost pleased to hear the news, sighing and exclaiming. First of all, of course, the samovar is put on. The children crowd into a corner, looking at the dead grandmother with astonished faces. No matter how long Misha lives he will always remember the old woman and how she died, forgetting her hand on his shoulder. And when he dies not a single person on the whole earth will remember or will realize that once upon a time there was such an old woman who lived out her hundred and four years, how and why no one knows. Why remember anyway? It doesn't matter. Millions of people pass away like this: they live unnoticed and they die unnoticed. But maybe only at the very moment of the deaths of these hundred-year-old men and women there is something that seems touching and peaceful, something that seems even solemn and calming: even these days, a hundred years can have a strange effect on people. May God bless the lives and deaths of simple, good people!

Well, still, this is just an inconsequential little scene without a story. True enough, one sets out to recount something with a bit of interest in it from the things heard in the course of a month, but when you sit down to write it turns out to be quite impossible to retell or is irrelevant, or it's simply a case of "not telling everything you know," and so in the end you're left with only little things such as this with no story to them....

3. Dissociation

But still, I'm supposed to be writing about "the things I have seen, heard, and read." At least it's a good thing that I didn't limit myself with a promise to write about *everything* I have "seen, heard, and read." And I keep hearing things that are stranger and stranger. How can I convey them, when they all go off on their separate ways and simply refuse to arrange themselves into one neat bundle! Indeed, I keep thinking that we have begun the epoch of universal "dissociation." All are dissociating themselves, isolating themselves from everyone else, everyone wants to invent something of his own, something new and unheard of. Everybody sets aside all those things that used to be common to our thoughts and feelings and begins with his own thoughts and feelings. Everybody wants to begin from the beginning. The links that once united us are broken without regret, and everyone acts on his own accord and finds his only consolation in that. If he doesn't act, then he would like to. Granted, a great many people don't undertake anything and never will, yet they still have torn themselves away and stand apart, looking at the torn place and waiting idly for something to happen. Everyone in Russia is waiting for something to happen. Meanwhile, there is scarcely anything about which we can agree morally; everything has been or is being broken up, not even into clusters but into single fragments. And the main thing is that sometimes this is done with the simplest and most satisfied manner. Take, for instance, our contemporary man of letters—one of the "new people," I mean. He begins his career and will have nothing to do with anything that came before; what he has comes from himself, and he acts by himself. He preaches new things and flatly sets as his ideal a new word and a new man. He knows neither European literature nor his own; he has read nothing, nor will he take up reading. Not only has he not read Pushkin and Turgenev, he has scarcely even read his own people, that is Belinsky and Dobroliubov. He depicts new heroes and new women, and their whole novelty consists in the fact that they confidently take their tenth step having forgotten about the nine preceding ones, and so they suddenly find themselves in the most false situation one can conceive; and they perish so that the reader may be edified and enticed. The falseness of the situation comprises the entire edification. There is very little new in all this; to the contrary, there is an extraordinary lot of worn-out old castoffs. But that's not the point at all; the point is that the author is completely convinced that he has spoken his new word, that he is acting independently, that he has dissociated himself; and, of course, this pleases him a good deal. This little example, however, is old and trivial; but the other day I heard a story about one of these "new words." There was a certain "nihilist" who did his denying and his suffering and, after getting into many scrapes and even spending time in prison, he suddenly found religious feeling in his heart. And what do you think he immediately did? He instantly "isolated and dissociated himself"; promptly and gingerly he steered clear of our Christian faith, disposed of all our legacy from the past, and quickly invented his own faith, also Christian, yet "his very own." He has a wife and children. He does not live with his wife, and his children are looked after by others. Recently he ran off to America, very likely to preach his new faith there. In a word, everyone is on his own, doing things his own way. Can they all only be trying to appear original or be pretending to be so? By no means. We are now living in a period that is more concerned with truth than reflection. Many, and perhaps very many, are truly sorrowing and suffering; they have indeed, and in the most serious fashion, broken all their former links and they are *compelled* to begin from the beginning, for no one gives them light. And our wise men and intellectual leaders only nod in agreement, some of them out of Judaical fear ("Why not let him go to America?" they say; "running off to America is something liberal, after all"), while others are simply making money off them. And so our fresh energies perish. You might say that these are still only two or three facts that don't mean anything; that, on the contrary, everything is undoubtedly more solidly integrated and united than before; that banks, societies, and associations are coming onto the scene. But can you really and truly hold up as an example this crowd of triumphant Jews and kikes that has thrown itself on Russia? Triumphant and full of enthusiasm, because nowadays there have appeared even kikes full of enthusiasm, both of the Hebraic and the Orthodox persuasions. Just think: our newspapers write that even they are isolating themselves and that, for instance, the foreign press will make even more fun of the congresses of representatives of our Russian land banks because of "the secret sessions of the first two congresses, asking, not without irony: in what manner and by what right have the Russian land-credit institutions the boldness to make a claim on the public's trust when their secret sessions, held behind carefully guarded Chinese walls, hide everything from the public, thereby making it obvious that something unsavory is being cooked up. . . ."

So it seems that even these gentlemen are isolating themselves, shutting themselves up, and devising something of their own to be done their way, not the way it is done in the rest of the world. The business about the banks I slipped in as a joke, however: that's not my topic at the moment. I'm speaking only about "dissociation." How can I better explain my thought? By the way, I'll mention a few ideas about our corporations and associations that come from a certain manuscript. It's not one of mine but was sent to me and has never been published. The author addresses his opponents in the provinces:

You say that the artels, associations, corporations, cooperatives, trading companies and all these other associations are based on man's inborn sense of sociability. Defending the Russian artel, which has still been researched far too little to be spoken of positively, we believe that all these associations, corporations, etc., are only unions of some against others, unions founded on the sense of self-preservation evoked by the struggle for survival. Our opinion is supported by the history of the origin of these unions, which were first formed by the poor and weak against the wealthy and strong. Subsequently, the latter began to employ the same weapon against their opponents. History indeed testifies that all these unions originated out of fraternal enmity and were based not on the need for social intercourse, as you suppose, but on the feeling of fear for one's survival or on the wish for gain, profit, or benefit, even at the expense of one's neighbor. When we examine the structure of all these progeny of utilitarianism, we see that their main concern is to organize firm control of everyone over all and of all over everyone—to put it simply, wholesale espionage arising from the fear that one person may cheat another. All these associations, with their internal controls and their external activity that envies everything outside them, present a striking parallel with what is happening in the world of politics, where the mutual relations of nations are characterized by an armed peace, broken by occasional bloody clashes, while their internal life is one of endless factional strife. How can one speak of communion or love in such a case? Is that not why such institutions take root so poorly in Russia? We still live too expansively, so that we still have insufficient basis to take up arms against one another; we still have too much affection for and faith in one another, and these feelings hinder us from setting up the control and mutual espionage that is required when all of these associations, cooperatives, trading, and other companies are established. With insufficient control they cannot work and inevitably go bankrupt.

So should we lament these defects of ours as compared with our better-educated Western neighbors? No: for we, at least, can perceive in these defects our wealth; we can see that the feeling of unity, without which human societies cannot exist, is still effective among us, even though it acts unconsciously on people and leads them not only to do great deeds, but also, very often, to do great wrong. Yet one in whom this feeling is not yet dead is capable of everything, provided that the feeling can be transformed from something unconscious and instinctual into a conscious force, one that would not toss him this way and that by the blind caprice of chance but would direct him toward the realization of rational aims. Without this feeling of unity and mutual love, of communion among people, nothing great is conceivable because society itself is inconceivable.

So the author, you see, perhaps is not entirely condemning these associations and corporations; he is simply stating that their *present* governing principle consists only in utilitarianism, and in espionage as well, and that this is certainly not a *unity of people.* This is all something youthful, fresh, theoretical, and impractical, yet in principle it is absolutely correct and is written not only with sincerity but with suffering and distress. Note the common trait: the whole issue in Russia now depends on the first step, on the practice, but everyone to the last man is shouting and worrying only about principles, so that the practice has, willy-nilly, fallen into the hands of the Israelites alone. The history of the manuscript from which I took the above excerpt is as follows. The worthy author (I don't know if he is a young man or one of those young old men) published one small item in a certain provincial publication, while next to it the editor printed his own note of qualification, which partly disagreed with the author. Then, when the author of the item wrote a whole article (not a very long one, however) to refute the editor's note, the latter refused to print it under the pretext that it was "more of a sermon than an article." Then the author wrote to me, forwarding the rejected article and asking that I read it, think about it, and express my opinion in my *Diary.* First, I thank him for his confidence in my opinion; and second; I thank him for the article, because it has given me a great deal of satisfaction: rarely have I read anything more *logical,* and although I am unable to include the whole article, I used the preceding excerpt with an intention I do not hide: the fact is that in its author, who pleads for a genuine unity of humans, I also noted a certain "dissociationist" flourish, specifically in those parts of the manuscript which I will not venture to quote but which are so "dissociated" that one rarely meets the like. And so it is not only the article but also the author himself who bears out my thought of the "dissociation" of individuals and the remarkable, virtually chemical decomposition of our society into its constituent elements, a process that has begun suddenly in our time.

I might add, however, that if nowadays everybody is "on his own and by himself," then there still is some link with what has gone before. Indeed, this link absolutely must exist, even if all might seem to be uncoordinated and full of mutual misunderstanding, and it is most interesting to follow this link. To put it briefly (although the comparison is an old one), our educated Russian society reminds me most of all of that ancient bundle of twigs which is strong only so long as the twigs are bound together; but as soon as the bonds are broken, the whole bundle flies apart into many weak stalks that the first wind will carry off. And so it is just this kind of bundle that has come apart and been scattered in our Russia. Isn't it true that our government, all through the twenty-year period of its reforms, never enjoyed the *full* support of its intelligentsia? On the contrary, did not the vast majority of young, fresh, precious talents go off on some tangent, toward a dissociation full of scorn and threats? And this happened precisely because, instead of taking the first nine steps, they immediately took the tenth one, forgetting that the tenth step without the preceding nine will *in any case* certainly become only an illusory one, even if it meant anything on its own. What is most painful is that only one in a thousand of these "solitudinarians," perhaps, understands anything about the meaning of this tenth step, while the others have only been listening to common rumors and gossip. The result is a farce: the egg the hen laid was sterile. Have you ever seen a forest fire during a hot summer? What a pitiful, sad sight it is! How much valuable material perishes in vain, how much energy, fire, and heat are used up for nothing and disappear without a trace, having accomplished no useful purpose.

4. Musings about Europe

"But in Europe, in fact everywhere, isn't it just the same? Haven't the forces that should unite people over there and on which we so relied—haven't they turned into a pathetic mirage? Isn't the disintegration and dissociation over there even worse than our own?" These are questions that a Russian cannot help but confront. Indeed, what real Russian doesn't think about Europe first of all?

Yes, at first glance the situation there probably seems even worse than ours; but the historical causes for the dissociations are more evident; yet that probably makes the picture there all the more doleful. But the fact that in Russia it is so difficult to uncover any sort of logical reason for our dilemma and to pick up all the loose ends of our torn threads—precisely that fact contains a certain consolation for us: people will finally fathom that our loss of energy is premature and not something conforming to historical law, that it is half-artificial and induced; and, in the end, perhaps, people

400 A Writer's Diary

will want to come to an accord. So there is still hope that the bundle of twigs can be bound together once more. But over there in Europe they are beyond any tying together of the twigs. Everything there has become dissociated, not in our way but maturely, clearly, and distinctly; there the groups and units are living out their last days and they know it; no one wants to give anything up to anyone else and would rather die than yield.

By the way, everyone in Russia is talking about peace now. Everyone predicts a lasting peace; everyone sees a clear horizon all around, with new alliances and new forces. Even the establishment of a republic in Paris is seen as a sign of peace; even the fact that this republic was established by Bismarck is seen as a sign of peace. People see great promises of peace in the accord between the great powers of the Orient, while some of our newspapers have suddenly begun to regard the present turmoil in Herzegovina, about which they were only recently expressing apprehension, as a definite indicator of the stability of European peace. (Is that not, I wonder, also because the key to the Herzegovinian question also turned up in Berlin and turned up in Prince Bismarck's own key case?) But the French Republic brings us the most joy. By the way, why is it that France still continues to stand in the foreground in Europe, despite Berlin's victory over her? The most trivial event in France still arouses more sympathy and attention in Europe than sometimes even a major event in Berlin. There is no question that this country has always been the one to take the first step, make the first experiment, be the first to initiate an idea. And that is why everyone surely expects the "beginning of the end" to come from here as well: who can take this fatal and final step if not France?

And that is why, perhaps, more irreconcilable "dissociations" have taken shape in this "advanced" country than anywhere else. Peace is utterly impossible there until the very "end." When they greeted the Republic, everyone in Europe said that it was essential for France and for Europe because only a republic could rule out a war of revenge with Germany; only a republic, among all the governments that had recently been making claims to govern France, would neither risk nor desire to undertake such a war. Yet this is only a mirage, and the Republic was proclaimed precisely to make war, if not with Germany then with an even more dangerous rival, a rival and enemy for all Europe: communism. And now, with the Republic, this rival will rise up much sooner than under any other form of government! Any other government would have reached an agreement with it and thus postponed the denouement; but a republic will yield nothing to it and will itself be the first to challenge and compel its rival to do battle. And so let no one state that "the Republic means peace." In fact, who was it who proclaimed the Republic this time? All the bourgeoisie and small-property owners. How long have they been such solid republicans? Was it not they who until now were most afraid of a republic, seeing in it only disorder and a single step toward the communism they so dread? During the first revolution the Convention broke up the large land holdings of the French emigrés and the church into small allotments and began selling them off because of the continual financial crisis of the time. This measure enriched a vast number of Frenchmen and allowed them, eighty years later, to pay a five-billion contribution without scarcely even a frown. But while it fostered a temporary prosperity, this measure paralyzed democratic aspirations for years and years by enormously increasing the army of landowners and by passing France over into the boundless power of the bourgeoisie, the prime enemy of the demos. Had they not taken this measure, the bourgeoisie would never have been able to maintain their power in France for so long once they had replaced the former rulers, the nobility. But the result was to provoke the implacable hatred of the demos; the bourgeoisie itself diverted the natural course of democratic aspirations and transformed them into hatred and a thirst for revenge. The dissociation of political parties has reached the point where the entire organism of the state has been utterly ruined, so that there is no longer even the possibility of restoring it. If France still hangs on as some apparent whole, it is only due to that law of nature which states that even a handful of snow cannot melt before its appointed time. It is this illusion of wholeness that the unhappy bourgeois (and many naive people in Europe as well) continue to accept as the living force of an organism, deceiving themselves with hope and at the same time trembling with fear and hatred. But in essence the integrity of the society has disappeared once and for all. The oligarchs are only concerned with the interests of the wealthy; democracy, only with the interests of the poor; but the interests of society, the interests of all and the future of France as a whole—no one there bothers about those things except the dreamer-socialists and the dreamer-positivists who extol science and expect it to solve everything—that is, to provide a new sense of unity and a new set of founding principles for the social organism, ones that are mathematically solid and unshakeable. But science, in which people have so much faith, is scarcely capable of tackling this matter right now. It's difficult to conceive that it already has sufficient knowledge of human nature to institute new laws for the social organism without making an error; and since this problem must be solved without hesitation or delay, the question arises of itself: is science prepared to undertake such a task *at once*, supposing that it is within its means as it develops in the future? (I will not, at the moment, state flatly that this task really is beyond the powers of human science no matter how advanced it becomes.) Since science itself will probably not respond to such an appeal, it follows that at present the whole movement of the demos is being governed in France (and everywhere else in the world) only by the dreamers, and the dreamers are governed by all sorts of speculators. Besides, aren't there dreamers in science as well? It is true that the dreamers took over the movement by right, for they were the only ones anywhere in France who were concerned about the unity of all and about the future; and so the succession in France passes on moral grounds, so to say, to them, despite all their evident weakness and fantastical notions, and everyone senses this. But the most terrible thing here is that, apart from all these fantastic notions, there has appeared a most cruel and inhuman tendency, not a fantastic one but something quite real and historically inevitable. It's all expressed in the saying: "ôte toi de là, que je m'y mette" ("step aside so that I can take your place!"). Millions of the demos (apart from far too few exceptions) have as their primary aim and principal aspiration the plunder of property owners. But one cannot blame the impoverished: the oligarchs themselves have kept them in darkness to such an extent that, apart from the most insignificant exceptions, all these millions of unhappy and blind people doubtless do have a most naive belief that they will enrich themselves precisely through such plunder and that this is the whole content of the social idea which their leaders preach to them. In any case, how can they understand their dreamer-leaders or the prognostications about science? Nevertheless, they will certainly win, and if the wealthy do not yield in time, then terrible things will ensue. But no one will yield in time, perhaps because the time for concessions has already passed. And indeed, the impoverished themselves don't even want concessions and are not willing to come to any accord now, even if they were given everything; they will continue to think that they are being deceived and cheated. They want to settle scores themselves.

The Bonapartes kept themselves in power by promising the possibility of reconciliation with the impoverished, and they even made some microscopic movements in that direction; but their efforts were always underhanded and insincere. The oligarchs lost faith in them, however, and the demos doesn't trust them a bit. As far as government by kings is concerned (the senior line), it can essentially offer the proletariat only the Roman Catholic religion as a means of salvation, and this is something that not only the demos but also the vast majority in France have long ignored and do not wish to know. I have even heard that spiritualism has lately been spreading among the proletariat with extraordinary power, at least in Paris. The junior line of kings (the Orleans line) has become the object of hatred by even the bourgeoisie, although at one time this dynasty was considered the natural leader of French property owners. But their incompetence became evident to everyone. Nevertheless, the property owners had to save themselves; they had, urgently and without fail, to find themselves leadership for the great and final battle with the terrible foe of the future. Consciousness and instinct whispered the real secret to them, and they chose a republic.

There is a political and maybe even a natural law that states that two powerful and near neighbors, however friendly they may be, always end by wanting to destroy one another and that sooner or later they bring this desire into action. (We Russians as well ought to think a bit more about this law of powerful neighbors.) "From a red republic runs a straight line to communism"—that's the notion that has struck fear into the French property owners until now. And so much time had to pass before suddenly, in a huge majority, they at last realized that the nearest of neighbors will be the bitterest of enemies simply through the principle of self-preservation. In fact, even though a red republic is such a close neighbor to communism, what, indeed, can be more hostile and more radically opposed to communism than a republic, even the bloody republic of 1793? In a republic, the republican form stands above all else— "La république avant tout, avant la France." In a republic, all hopes are in form alone: let there be "MacMahonia" instead of France, but let it at least be called a republic: that is the characteristic of the present "victory" of the republicans in France. And so they seek salvation in form. On the other hand, what business does communism have with the republican form when its very basis denies not only every form of government but even the state itself, even all contemporary society? It took the mass of Frenchmen eighty years to conceive of this direct opposition, this mutual antithesis of two forces; but at last they did conceive of it and—they gave their approval to the republic: against their enemy they finally set its most dangerous and most natural rival. When the republic makes its transition to communism it will certainly not want to destroy itself. In its essence the republic is the most natural expression and form of the bourgeois idea, and the whole of the French bourgeoisie is the child of the republic; it was created and organized by the republic alone during the first revolution. So, in that fashion, dissociation has been accomplished once and for all. People might say that war is still a long way off. It is hardly that far away. Perhaps it's even better not to want the denouement postponed. Socialism has corroded Europe even now, but by then it will have undermined it completely. Prince Bismarck knows this, but in far too German a fashion he puts his trust in blood and iron. But what can you do here with blood and iron?

5. An Expired Force and the Forces of the Future

People will say: but still, there's not the least cause for alarm at present; everything is clear; everything looks bright; we have "MacMahonia" in France; we have the great accord of powers in the Orient; military budgets everywhere are swelling enormously—isn't that peace?

What about the pope? He'll die one of these days, and then what? Do you think that Roman Catholicism will consent to die along with him to keep him company? Oh, never has Catholicism longed so intensely to live as now! However, can our prophets do other than laugh at the pope? We haven't even bothered to raise the question of the pope and have reduced it to insignificance. And meanwhile this is a "dissociation" too enormous and too full of boundless and incompatible aspirations to permit their renunciation for the sake of world peace. And for what, and for whose benefit should they be renounced? For humanity's sake? Catholicism has considered itself to be above all of humanity for a long time now. Until now it has been consorting only with the powerful of the earth and has been counting on them until the last moment. But

that moment has now come, it seems, for certain, and Roman
Catholicism will surely abandon those who have dominion over the
earth, who, however, have themselves betrayed Catholicism and
who undertook to persecute it throughout Europe a long time ago;
that persecution has now, in our time, been at last fully organized.
There's nothing surprising here: Roman Catholicism itself has made
turnabouts that were even sharper: once, when it was necessary,
it sold Christ without hesitation in exchange for earthly power.
Having proclaimed as dogma that "Christianity cannot survive on
the earth without the earthly power of the pope," it thereby proclaimed a new Christ, unlike the former one, one who has yielded
to the third temptation of the Devil—the temptation of the kingdoms of the world: "All these things will I give Thee if Thou wilt
but fall down and worship me!" Oh, I have heard strong objections
to this idea; people have argued that faith and the image of Christ
even now continue to live in all their former truth and purity in
the hearts of many Catholics. No doubt this is true, but the largest
wellspring has been muddied and poisoned beyond restoration.
Besides, it is only very recently that Rome proclaimed its assent
to the third temptation of the Devil in the form of a firm dogma,
and therefore we have not been able to see all the direct consequences of this enormous decision. It is worth noting that the
proclamation of this dogma, this revelation of "the whole secret"
happened precisely at the moment when united Italy was already
knocking at the gates of Rome. Many in Russia found that amusing,
saying that "there was a lot of anger but not much force. . . ." Only
one can hardly say there wasn't much force. No, people like that,
capable of such decisions and such turnabouts, cannot die without
a struggle. People may object that this has always been the way in
Catholicism—by implication, at least—and that accordingly there
has been no revolution at all. Indeed; yet there always was the
secret: for many centuries the papacy pretended to be satisfied with
its tiny dominion, the Papal States, but this was done just for the
sake of allegory. What is most significant is that the seed of the
principal ideal was concealed within the allegory under the papacy's
certain and constant hope that this seed would eventually grow in
the future into a luxuriant tree that would spread its branches over
the whole earth. And so, at the very last moment, when the last
acre of his worldly dominion was being taken away, the lord of
Catholicism, seeing his death coming, suddenly arises and proclaims to the world the whole truth about himself: "Did you think

I was content with only the title of the Sovereign of the Papal
States? But know that I always considered myself lord over all the
earth and over all earthly kings, and not only their spiritual ruler
but their earthly ruler as well, their true lord, sovereign, and emperor. This is I—the king of kings and the lord of lords, and to
me alone on earth belong the destinies, the ages, and it is for me
to determine the time; and this I now proclaim to all in the dogma
of my infallibility." Say what you like, but there is a force here; it
is majestic and not absurd; it is the resurrection of the ancient
Roman idea of world domination and unity, which never died in
Roman Catholicism; it is the Rome of Julian the Apostate, not of
a conquered Christ but of one who conquers in a new and final
battle. In such manner the sale of the true Christ in exchange for
worldly kingdoms was completed.

And in Roman Catholicism it will be completed and finalized in
fact. I repeat, this awesome army has eyes too sharp not to discern
at last where real force now exists, a force on which it can base
itself. Having lost the kings as its allies, Catholicism will surely
rush to the demos. It has tens of thousands of tempters, wise and
clever psychologists and seers of the human heart, dialecticians and
confessors, while the people everywhere are simple and kind. Besides, in France, and now even in many other places in Europe,
although the people may hate religion and scorn it, they still have
not the slightest knowledge of the Gospels—not in France, at least.
All of these psychologists and seers of the human heart will rush
to the people and bring them their new Christ, one who consents
to everything, the Christ who was proclaimed at the last impious
conclave in Rome. "Yes, friends and brethren," they will say, "all
your concerns have already long been met in our book, and your
leaders have stolen it all from us. If previously we spoke to you a
little differently, it was only because until now you were like little
children, and it was too soon for you to know the truth; but now
the time has come for your truth as well. You must know that the
pope has the keys of Saint Peter and that faith in God is only faith
in the pope who has been placed for you on the earth by God
himself in His stead. The pope is infallible, and divine power has
been given to him; and he is the lord of ages and it is to him to
determine the time. He has decided that your time has come as
well. Formerly the main force of religion lay in humility, but now
the time of humility has passed; and the pope has the power to
cancel it, for all power has been granted to him. Yes, you are all

brothers, and Christ himself commanded you all to be brothers; if your elder brothers do not want to accept you, then take up sticks and go into their houses and compel them by force to be your brothers. Christ has long awaited the repentance of these sinful elder brothers of yours, and now He grants you permission to proclaim: "Fraternité ou la mort" ("Be my brother, or off with your head!"). If your brother does not want to give you half his possessions, then take them all, for Christ has long awaited his repentance, and now the time has come for anger and vengeance. Know also that you are innocent of all your past and future sins, for all your sins have arisen only because of your poverty. And if your former leaders and teachers have already made this known to you, then know that although they spoke the truth, they had no authority to tell you this before the appointed time, for that authority is possessed by the pope alone, and it comes from God himself. The proof is that these teachers of yours led you nowhere but to punishments and still worse miseries, and everything they undertook failed of itself. Besides, they have all been cheating you so that with your help they might appear strong and then sell themselves even more dearly to your enemies. But the pope will not sell you because there is no one more powerful than he, and he is the first among the first. Only believe: not in God, but in the pope alone and in the fact that only he is the earthly king, while the others will disappear because their time has come. Rejoice now, and be glad, for the earthly paradise has come; you will all be rich and, through your riches, you will be righteous, because all your desires will be satisfied and you will have no more reason to do evil." These are flattering words, but no doubt the demos will accept the offer: they will see a great unifying force in this unexpected ally, a force that agrees to everything and hinders nothing, a real and historical force instead of leaders, dreamers, and speculators, in whose practical abilities—indeed, sometimes in whose honesty—even now they have not the least confidence. Suddenly, here, there is both a ready point where the force can be applied and a lever put into their hands; the whole mass need only lean on it and move it. Will the people not move it? Are they not a mass? To crown the whole matter, they are once more given a faith, and thereby the hearts of many are set at rest, for too many of them have long been heartsick without God. . . .

I have spoken about all this once already, but I spoke only in passing in a novel. I hope my presumption will be forgiven, but

I am certain that all this will surely come to pass in western Europe
in one form or another; that is to say, Catholicism, will fling itself
into democracy, into the people, and will abandon the earthly kings
because they have already abandoned Catholicism. All those in
power in Europe already despise it because it appears to be too
impoverished and defeated, but they still do not regard it in such
a comic aspect and situation as do our political journalists, in all
their naiveté. Yet Bismarck, for example, would not have oppressed
Catholicism so had he not sensed in it a terrible, approaching enemy
of the immediate future. Prince Bismarck is a man who is too proud
to waste so much force against a comically weak enemy. But the
pope is stronger than he. I repeat: now the papacy is, perhaps,
the most terrible of all the "dissociations" that threaten the peace
of the whole world. And there are many things that threaten the
peace. Never before has Europe been so filled with so many elements of enmity as in our time. It is just as if everything has been
undermined and stuffed with gunpowder and is only awaiting the
first spark. . . .

"So of what concern is this to us? That's all over in Europe, not
in Russia." The concern for us is that Europe will start knocking
at our door, crying for us to come and save her when the final
hour of her "present order of things" strikes. And she will demand
our help as if by right, demand it with a challenge and a command;
she will tell us that we, too, are Europe; that we, accordingly, have
just the same "order of things" as she has; that it was not in vain
that we copied her for two hundred years and boasted of being
Europeans; that in saving her we thereby will save ourselves as
well. Of course, we might not be disposed to settle the matter
exclusively in favor of one side; but are we capable of such a task,
and have we not forgotten long ago every notion of what constitutes
our true "dissociation" as a nation and what comprises our true
role in Europe? Not only do we not understand such things now,
we do not even entertain such questions, and even to listen to them
we consider a sign of stupidity and backwardness. And if Europe
really does come knocking at our door for us to rise up and go
save her *Ordre*, then, perhaps, and only then, will we understand
for the first time—all of us suddenly at once—to what degree we
have always been unlike Europe, despite our two hundred years
of wishing and dreaming of becoming Europe, wishing and dreaming that sometimes found such passionate expression. Perhaps even
then we won't understand, for it will be too late. And if such is

the case, then of course we shall be unable to understand what Europe needs from us, what she asks from us, and how, in fact, we could help her. Should we not, on the contrary, set off to pacify the enemy of Europe and the European order with that same blood and iron as Prince Bismarck? Oh, then, in the event of such a victory, we could boldly congratulate ourselves on being *completely European*.

But all this lies ahead of us, all this is just a collection of fantasies, while the present day is all so, so bright!

2

1. Don Carlos and Sir Watkin. More Signs of "The Beginning of the End"

I was most interested to read of the arrival of Don Carlos in England. People always say that real life is dull and monotonous; they turn to art and fantasy for diversion; they read novels. For me the opposite is true: what could be more fantastic and surprising than real life? What can be even more improbable than real life sometimes is? A novelist could never imagine possibilities such as real life offers every day by the thousand in the guise of the most ordinary things. There are times when no fantasizing could come up with the like. And what an advantage over the novel! Just try to *invent* an episode in a novel such as happened to, say, the lawyer Kupernik; concoct it yourself, and the following Sunday a critic in his column would prove to you clearly and beyond dispute that you are talking nonsense and that things like that never happen in real life and, most important, that they never can happen due to this reason and that reason. And, in the end, embarrassed, you would agree with him. But then someone gives you an issue of *The Voice* and suddenly you read in it the whole episode of our marksman—and what happens? At first you read in amazement—in terrible amazement, such that you cannot believe what you are reading; but as soon as you have read through to the final period, you put down the newspaper, and suddenly, not knowing why yourself, you say at once, "Yes, it all absolutely must have happened this way." And some people might even add, "I had a feeling something like that would happen." Why a newspaper produces such a different impression from a novel I don't know, but such is the privilege of real life.

Don Carlos makes his calm and majestic entry into England as

410

a guest after all the blood and butchery "in the name of the King, the Faith, and the Madonna." Now here's a figure, here's another example of "dissociation!" Could anyone invent something like that? By the way, do you remember what happened to Count Chambord (Henry V) two years ago? He's another king, a legitimist, who was making his claim to the French throne at the same time that Don Carlos was making his claim in Spain. They can consider each other relatives, being of the same lineage and the same ancestry, but what a difference between them! One is firmly bound up in his own convictions, a melancholy, elegant, humane figure. Count Chambord, at that fatal moment when he really could have become king (only for an instant, of course) was never tempted by anything; he never gave up his "white banner," and thereby proved that he was a true and magnanimous knight, almost a Don Quixote, an ancient knight with a vow of chastity and poverty, a figure worthy of bringing his ancient and royal lineage to a majestic end (majestic and just a touch absurd, for life does not exist without absurdity). He rejected power and the throne simply because he wanted to become the king of France not merely for himself but for the salvation of his country; and since in his view that salvation could not be reconciled with the concessions demanded of him (the concessions were quite within his means), he did not want to rule. How different from the recent Napoleon, a wily old fox and a proletarian, a man who promised everything, gave away everything, and cheated everyone just to attain power. I made a comparison between Count Chambord and Don Quixote just now, but this is the highest praise I know. It was Heine, wasn't it, who told of how, when reading *Don Quixote* as a child, he burst into tears on reaching the place where the hero was overcome by the wretched and commonsensical barber Samson Carrasco. There is nothing deeper and more powerful in the whole world than this piece of *fiction*. It is still the final and the greatest expression of human thought, the most bitter irony that a human is capable of expressing, and if the world came to an end and people were asked somewhere *there*: "Well, did you understand anything from your life on earth and draw any conclusion from it?" a person could silently hand over *Don Quixote*: "Here is my conclusion about life; can you condemn me for it?" I don't claim that the person would be right in saying that, but. . . .

Don Carlos, a relative of Count Chambord, is also a knight, but in this knight one can see the Grand Inquisitor. He has spilled

rivers of blood *ad majorem gloriam Dei* and in the name of the
Madonna, that meek supplicant for humanity, the "swift intercessor
and helper," as our People call her. Proposals were made to him,
just as they were to Count Chambord, and he also rejected them.
This happened soon after Bilbao, it seems, and immediately after
his great victory when the commander of the Madrid army perished
in battle. Then Madrid sent emissaries to him: "What would he
say if they allowed him to enter Madrid? Would he not offer some
little program for the possible opening of negotiations?" But he
haughtily declined any notion of negotiations and did so, of course,
not only from pride, but also from the principle that was so deeply
entrenched in his soul: he could not accept emissaries from the
belligerents and he, a "King," could not enter into any sort of
agreements with the "revolution"! In a few concise words—almost
hints, but clear hints—he made it known that "a king himself
knows what he must do when he arrives in his capital," and he
added nothing more. Naturally they quickly turned away from him
and soon summoned King Alfonso. The favorable moment was
lost, but he continued to wage war; he wrote manifestos in an
elevated and majestic style, and he himself was the first to believe
in them totally; haughtily and majestically, he shot a number of
his generals "for treason" and put down rebellions of his exhausted
troops; and—one must do him justice as a warrior—he battled to
the last inch of territory. Now, as he left France for England, he
stated in a gloomy and haughty letter to his French friends that
he was "satisfied with their service and support, and that serving
him they served themselves, and that he was always ready to bare
his sword once more at the summons of his unfortunate country."
Don't worry, we haven't seen the last of him. By the way, this
letter to his "friends" casts a little glimmer of light on the riddle
of who supplied the means and the money for this dreadful man
(young and handsome, they say) to wage war so stubbornly and
for such a long time. These friends, it would seem, are powerful
and numerous. Who might they be? It's most likely that his biggest
supporter was the Catholic church, since he was its last hope among
the kings. Otherwise, no friends could have collected so many
millions for him.

Note that this man who haughtily and flatly rejected any compromise with "revolution" went to England knowing full well that
he would seek hospitality in that free and freethinking country, a

revolutionary country by his definition. What a peculiar combination of ideas! And so when he arrived in England he was involved in a trivial but characteristic incident. He boarded the boat in Boulogne, intending to land at Folkestone; but that same boat was also taking to England certain guests, members of the Boulogne municipal government, whom the English had invited to the peaceful celebration of the opening of a new railway station in Folkestone. A crowd of Englishmen—notables, elegantly dressed ladies, guilds, and deputations of various societies with banners and bands—was waiting on the shore to greet the French visitors, among whom was also the deputy from the Department of Pas-de-Calais. A member of parliament, Sir Edward Watkin, happened to be there, and he was accompanied by two other members of parliament. When he learned that Don Carlos was among the passengers who had arrived, he approached him at once to introduce himself and pay his respects; he accompanied him to the station with the greatest courtesy and found a place for him in a private compartment. But the rest of the crowd was not so courteous: whistling and hissing were heard when Don Carlos passed by to board the train. Sir Edward was deeply offended by such behavior on the part of his compatriots. He himself wrote about it in a newspaper, toning down his account of the "guest's" rude reception as best he could. He tells of how it was only one chance happening that was to blame for it all; had it not been for that, everything would have turned out differently:

> ...At the moment (he writes) we came onto the platform and Don Carlos raised his hat in reply to the cries of several persons who greeted him, the wind unfurled the banner of the Odd Fellows Association; on the banner appeared a picture of Charity protecting children and the device: "Remember the Widows and Orphans!" The effect was sudden and striking: a murmur came from the crowd, but it expressed sorrow rather than outbursts of anger. Although I regret the incident, I must say that no crowd, having assembled for a happy celebration and suddenly encountering, face to face, the chief actor in a bloody, fratricidal war, could have displayed such courtesy as was exhibited by the vast majority of the people of Folkestone.

What a strange outlook; what solid faith in one's own opinion; what jealous pride in one's own people! Many of our liberals might regard Sir Edward's behavior as almost base—a low attempt to

ingratiate himself with a famous person or an effort to advance his
own interests in some petty way. But Sir Edward does not think
as we do: oh, he knows very well that the newly arrived guest was
the main actor in a bloody and fratricidal war; but meeting him
is a means of satisfying his patriotic pride and serving England to
the best of his ability. When he, in the name of England and in
his capacity as a member of parliament, extends his hand to a
tyrant stained scarlet with blood, he thereby says to him in effect:
"You are a despot, a tyrant, yet you have come to seek refuge in
a land of freedom; that was what could be expected; England
accepts all and is not afraid to give refuge to anyone: *entrée et sortie
libres*; welcome." And it was not only the rudeness of "a small
section of the crowd that had gathered" that offended him, but
also the fact that, in the unrestrained feeling, in the whistles and
hisses, he saw a lapse in that sense of personal dignity which ought
to be the inalienable possession of every true Englishman. Over
there on the Continent, or among humans generally, it may be
considered an excellent thing when people do not restrain their
offended feelings and publicly brand a villain with scorn and whistles, even if he is their guest. That's all very well for some Parisian
or German, but an Englishman is obliged to behave differently. At
moments like that he ought to be calm and collected, a gentleman,
and not express his own opinion. It would be much better if the
guest never found out what those who greeted him were thinking;
and it would be best of all if every one were to stand still with his
hands behind his back, as befits an Englishman, casting a glance
full of chilly dignity at the new arrival. A few polite exclamations,
but done quietly and in moderation, would not have hurt, either:
the guest would at once have realized that this was only custom
and etiquette and that even if he were as wise as Solomon he could
not arouse any particular excitement among us. But now, with all
the shouts and whistles, the guest will think that this is only a
mindless street mob such as one finds on the Continent. This
reminds me, by the way, of a lovely little story I read not long
ago—where and by whom I don't recall—of Marshal Sébastiani and
a certain Englishman. It happened at the beginning of the century
during the reign of Napoleon I. Marshal Sébastiani, an important
figure of the time, wanted to show some kindness to an Englishman
(the English at that time were held in disdain because of their
continual and stubborn war with Napoleon). After heaping praise

upon the English, the marshal said very graciously, "If I were not a Frenchman, I would like to become an Englishman."

The Englishman listened but, not the least bit touched by this gracious remark, replied, "And if I were not an Englishman, I would still like to become an Englishman."

So in England all Englishmen respect themselves in this same way, perhaps only because they are Englishmen. This in itself, it would seem, should be enough to provide a solid bond to unite people in that country: the bundle of twigs is strong. In actuality, however, things are the same there as everywhere else in Europe: there is a passionate desire to live and a loss of a higher purpose for living. I will cite here, as another example of originality, the view of a certain Englishman on his own religion, Protestantism. Remember that the English, in the overwhelming majority, are a highly religious nation: they crave a faith and seek it continuously, but instead of a religion, and despite their official Anglican faith, they are divided into hundreds of sects. This is what Sydney Dobell says in his recent article "Thoughts on Art, Philosophy and Religion":

> Catholicism is (potentially) great, beautiful, wise, powerful, one of the most consistent and congruous constructions man has made; but it is not *educational* and will, therefore, die; nay, must be killed as pernicious in proportion to its excellence.
>
> Protestantism is narrow, ugly, impudent, unreasonable, inconsistent, incompatible: a Babel of logomacy and literalism: a wrangling club of half-thinking pedants, half-taught geniuses, and untaught egotists of every type: the nursery of conceit and fanaticism: the holiday ground of all the "fools rush in."
>
> But it is *educational* and therefore it will live; nay, must be fed and housed, cared for and fought for, as the *sine qua non* of the spiritual life of Man.

What absolutely impossible ideas! But meanwhile thousands of Europeans seek their salvation in statements such as these. In fact, can a society which, seriously and fervently, arrives at such conclusions about human spiritual needs be truly healthy? "Protestantism, don't you see, is primitive, ugly, shameless, narrow, and stupid; but it is *educational* and so it must be preserved and defended!" In the first place, what a utilitarian outlook on a question such as this! A matter to which everything else should take second

place (if, indeed, Sydney Dobell is concerned about *religion* at all)
is, on the contrary, examined here only from the point of view of
its benefit to an Englishman. And, of course, such a utilitarian
outlook is equal to the noneducational narrowness and restriction
of Catholicism, which this Protestant so vigorously condemns. And
aren't these words similar to other remarks of those "profound
thinkers in matters of state and politics" of all countries and peoples, thinkers who sometimes utter exceedingly wise statements
like the following: "There is no God, of course, and religion is
nonsense, but religion is needed for the masses because this is the
only way to restrain them." The one difference, really, is that at
the basis of this wise statesman's view is only cold, hard-hearted
depravity, while Sydney Dobell is a friend of humanity and is
concerned only for its immediate benefit. Still, his view on that
benefit is valuable: the entire benefit, you see, lies in the fact that
the doors are left wide open to all sorts of opinions and conclusions;
there is *entrée et sortie libres* to both mind and heart; nothing is
locked away, nothing is kept protected, nothing is finished: you
must swim in the boundless sea and save yourself as you please.
This opinion is a broad one, however, as broad as this boundless
sea, and, of course, "nothing's to be seen amid the waves"; yet
this is a national point of view. Oh, there is deep sincerity here,
but isn't it true that this sincerity seems to border on despair? His
method of reasoning is also characteristic; the things people over
there are thinking, writing, and worrying about are characteristic,
too: do you think those Russians who write on current topics, for
instance, would take up their pens on such fantastic subjects and
give them such prominence? One could even say that we Russians
are people with much greater realism, with a deeper and more
sensible view of things than any of these Englishmen. But the
English are ashamed neither of their own convictions nor of our
opinion of them; one sometimes finds something even deeply touching in their extraordinary sincerity. Here, for example, is what one
observer, who pays close attention to these things in Europe, told
me about the nature of certain totally atheistic doctrines and sects
in England:

> You enter a church and see the magnificent service, the expensive
> vestments, censers, solemnity, silence, and reverence of those praying.
> The Bible is read, and everyone approaches and kisses the sacred
> book with tears and with love. But what is this, in fact? This is the

church of the atheists. All those praying do not believe in God; their absolute dogma and absolute condition for joining this church is atheism. Why do they kiss the Bible, listen reverently to readings from it, and weep over it? Because once they have rejected God they have begun to worship "Humanity." Now they believe in Humanity; they have deified Humanity and they worship it. And what was more precious to humanity through the course of so many centuries than this sacred book? They bow down before it because of its love for humanity and because of humanity's love for it. It has worked on behalf of mankind for so many centuries; it has enlightened humanity like the sun and poured out power and life upon it. And even though "its sense has now been lost," those who love and worship mankind cannot be ungrateful and forget those good things the Bible has done for them. . . .

There is much here that is touching, and there is much enthusiasm. It really is a matter of deification of humanity and the passionate need to manifest love for it; but yet, what an urge there is for prayer and worship; what a longing for God and faith these atheists have; what despair, what sorrow is here; what a funeral ceremony instead of a living, radiant life overflowing with the fresh spring of youth, strength, and hope! But whether this is a funeral or a new, emerging force is still a question for many. I'll permit myself to make an excerpt from my recent novel, *A Raw Youth.* I only learned about this "Church of the Atheists" in the last few days, long after I had finished and published my novel. I also wrote about atheism, but this was only the dream of a Russian of our times, one of the men of the forties—those former landowner-progressives, noble and passionate dreamers who, at the same time, had that most Russian breadth of outlook on life in actual practice. This landowner himself also has utterly lost his faith and also worships humanity "as befits a Russian progressive person." He tells of his dream of humanity in the future, when every notion of God will have vanished, something that, in his view, will certainly happen all over the world.

"I imagine, my dear," he began with a pensive smile, "that the battle is already over and that the struggle is abating. After the cursing, the mud slinging, and the jeering, a lull has descended and people have found themselves *alone* as they wished: the former grand idea has abandoned them; the great source of strength which has nourished them until now has been receding like a majestic, inviting sun; but this was, as it were, humanity's last day. And people suddenly realized that they had been left quite alone, and at once they felt a great sense of being orphaned. My dear boy, I never could imagine people as ungrateful and stupid. The people, having become orphaned, at once would begin to draw closer and more lovingly toward one another; they would grasp each other's hands, understanding that now they and they alone constituted everything for one another. The grand notion of immortality would disappear and it would have to be replaced. And in each person that whole grand superabundance of love for the One who was Immortality would now be directed toward nature, toward the world, toward people, toward every blade of grass. They would come irresistibly to love the earth and life in proportion to their gradual realization of their own transience and mortality, and now with a special love, unlike their former one. They would begin to perceive and discover in nature such phenomena and such mysteries as they had not dreamed of formerly, for they would look at nature through new eyes, with the look of a lover gazing at his beloved. They would awaken and hasten to kiss one another, eager to love, knowing that their days were short and that this was all that was left to them. They would work for one another, and each would give away all he had to the others and only in so doing would he be happy. Every child would know and feel that everyone on earth was his father and mother. "Tomorrow may be my last day," each one would think as he watched the setting sun; "I may die, but still, they will all remain and their children after them." And the thought that they would remain, loving one another and trembling for one another, would take the place of the notion of meeting them beyond the grave. Oh, they would make haste to love so as to quell the great sorrow in their hearts. They would be bold and proud of themselves, but would become meek before one another; each would tremble for the life and happiness of every other. They would become tender to one another and would not be ashamed of it, as they are now; they would be kind to each other, as children are. When they met they would gaze on one another with a profound and meaningful look, and in that look there would be love and sorrow. . . ."

Isn't it true that this fantasy contains something similar to what already exists in the "Church of the Atheists?"

2. Lord Radstock

A few words apropos of these sects. I have heard that Lord Radstock is here in St. Petersburg at this very moment, the same Lord

Radstock who spent a whole winter preaching among us three years ago and who also created something in the nature of a new sect. At that time I happened to hear him preaching in a certain "hall" and, I recall, I didn't find anything special in him: he did not speak particularly well, nor particularly badly. Yet he works miracles over human hearts; people flock to hear him; many are deeply moved: they seek out the poor so as to do good deeds for them and almost reach the point of giving away their possessions. However, this may be happening only among us in Russia; it seems he is not so prominent abroad. However, it would be unfair to say that the whole force of his charm lies only in the fact that he is a lord and an independent person preaching what we might call a "pure, gentleman's" religion. True enough, all these sectarian preachers always destroy, even if they did not set out to, the image of faith provided by the church and supply their very own. Lord Radstock's real success is based exclusively on our "dissociation," on our detachment from the soil and from our nation. It turns out that we, that is, the intelligentsia of our society, now comprise some sort of little foreign nation of our own—a very small, insignificant one, but still having its own customs and its own prejudices that are taken for originality; and so it turns out that we now even have a longing for our own religion as well. It's difficult to say what Lord Radstock's teaching is really about. He is an Englishman, but people say that he is not a member of the Anglican church and has broken with it; he preaches something of his own. Such a thing is so easy in England: there, just as in America, there are more sects, perhaps, than among our own "dark people." There are sects such as the Jumpers, the Shakers, the Convulsionaries, the Quakers awaiting the millennium, and, finally, the Flagellants (a universal and very ancient sect)—there are simply too many to list. Of course, I'm not making fun when I speak of these sects together with Lord Radstock, but he who has departed from the true church and thought up his own, no matter how respectable it may appear, will undoubtedly end the same way these sects do. Lord Radstock's admirers should not frown at this: the philosophical basis of these same sects, these Shakers and Flagellants, sometimes contains remarkably profound and powerful ideas. Tradition has it that in her home in the Mikhailovsky Castle in the 1820s, Mme. Tatarinova and her guests, such as one government minister of the day, used to twirl and speak prophecies along with the enserfed servants. So there must have been some power of thought

and feeling if such an "unnatural" union of believers could be
created; and Tatarinova's sect was, evidently, also part of the Flagellants or of one of its innumerable branches. I have never heard
any accounts of people twirling and speaking prophecies with Lord
Radstock. (Twirling and speaking prophecies is a most indispensable and ancient attribute of almost all these Western and Russian
sects, at least of an overwhelming majority of them. And the Templars, too, whirled and spoke prophecies and also had their element
of flagellation and were burned at the stake for it, although later
they were lauded and glorified by French thinkers and poets before
the first Revolution.) I have heard only that Lord Radstock preaches
particularly about "the descent of grace" and that, in the words
of one informant, Lord Radstock has "Christ in his pocket"; that
is, he treats Christ and His grace with extraordinary levity. I must
confess that I didn't understand the reports of people throwing
themselves down on cushions and awaiting some sort of inspiration
from on high. Is it true that Lord Radstock wants to go to Moscow?
It would be a good thing if this time none of our clergy expressed
their approval of his sermons. Nevertheless, he produces remarkable conversions and arouses magnanimous feelings in the hearts
of his followers. However, that is as it should be: if he is indeed
sincere and is preaching a new faith, then, of course, he is possessed
by all the spirit and fervor of the founder of a sect. I repeat, here
we have our lamentable dissociation from one another, our ignorance of our own People, our rupture with nationality, and, above
all, our weak, barely perceptible knowledge of Orthodoxy. It is
remarkable that, with only a few exceptions, there is scarcely a
word about Lord Radstock in our press.

3. A Word or Two about the Report of the Scholarly
Commission on Spiritualistic Phenomena

Are the spiritualists another "dissociation?" I think they are. The
spiritualism that we see developing among us threatens to become
a most dangerous and despicable "dissociation," in my view. Indeed, "dissociation" is disunity; it is in this sense I say that our
nascent spiritualism contains powerful elements that can only contribute to the already growing and progressive disunity of the Russian people. How absurd and annoying I find it to read some of
our thinkers who write that our society is asleep or is lazily and
indifferently drowsing. To the contrary: we have never seen such

unrest, such rushing this way and that, such questing for something to rely on morally, as we do these days. Every little idea, no matter how absurd, can count on certain success so long as it suggests even the slightest hope of solving something. And this success is always confined to the "dissociation" of some other new handful of people. So it is with spiritualism. And imagine my disappointment when I finally read in *The Voice* the report of the well-known commission, about which there has been such a hue and cry, on the spiritualistic phenomena that were observed all through the winter in the home of Mr. Aksakov. You see, I was just waiting and hoping that this report would crush and destroy this indecent (in its mystical sense) new doctrine. It is true that we still, apparently, have not seen any new *doctrines*, and we are still only "making observations." But is that really the case? It's a pity that at the moment I have neither the time nor the space to expound my idea in detail; but in the following, April, number of my *Diary* perhaps I will venture to take up the topic of spiritualism once more. However, I may be condemning the commission's report unfairly: the report is not to blame, of course, for the fact that I had built such high hopes on it and was expecting from it something quite impossible which it could never provide. But in any case, the report fails in its exposition and in its form. The report is framed in such a manner that its opponents will undoubtedly seize upon its "biased" (and so a very unscientific) attitude to its subject, even though the commission may not have had such bias as to justify the charge. (There was a certain amount of bias, but we really can't avoid that). But the text is certainly poorly framed. For example, the commission permits itself to draw conclusions about certain spiritualistic phenomena (the materialization of spirits, for instance), which, by its own admission, it had never witnessed. We may suppose that it did this with an edifying purpose, to draw a moral, so to say, by jumping the gun in the interests of society so as to save frivolous people from going astray. It is a worthy idea, but scarcely an appropriate one in the given instance. Still, what of it? Could the commission itself, composed of so many learned people, have seriously hoped in its very first effort to suppress such a silly idea? Alas, if the commission had produced even the most obvious and direct proofs of trickery, even if it had caught and exposed people in the act of producing fakeries, seizing them by the arms, as it were (which, of course, never happened)—even then, no one who is now an enthusiast for spiritualism would have believed it, nor would those who only want to take a mild interest in it, because there is a primordial law of nature stating that, where mystical notions are concerned, even strictly mathematical proofs carry no weight whatsoever. And here, in our nascent spiritualism, the mystical idea alone is foremost, believe me—and what can you do about that? Faith and mathematical proof are two irreconcilable things. There's no stopping someone who makes up his mind to believe. Besides, the proofs in this case are far from mathematical.

Nevertheless, the report might still have been useful. It might certainly have been useful for all those who had not yet been led astray and who were still indifferent to spiritualism. But now, given this "urge to believe," the urge is supplied with a new weapon. The overly scornful and haughty tone of the report could have been toned down as well; indeed, when reading it one might think that both esteemed parties had a personal quarrel for some reason during the course of their observations. This will not influence the masses favorably toward the report.

4. Isolated Phenomena

But there is also another category of phenomena, a rather curious one, especially when it appears among young people. It's true that as yet these are isolated phenomena. Along with stories of a few unfortunate young people who "go to the People," we begin to hear stories of another type of young person altogether. These new young people are also restless; they write you letters or come in person with their problems, their articles, and their unexpected ideas, but they are not at all like those young people whom we have grown accustomed to meeting. Thus, there are some grounds for supposing that among our young people a certain movement is beginning that is quite the reverse of the former one. Well, perhaps we should have expected it. In fact, whose children are they? They are the very children of those "liberal" fathers who, at the beginning of Russia's renaissance during the present reign, seemed to tear themselves away en masse from the common cause, imagining that in so doing they were serving Progress and Liberalism. And yet—since all this is largely a thing of the past—were there many genuine liberals then? Were there many truly suffering, pure, and sincere people such as Belinsky, for example (his intellect aside), who was then not long deceased? To the contrary, in the majority they were still only a coarse mass who were petty in their atheism and serious in their turpitude; in essence, they were the same greedy and petty tyrants who boasted of their liberalism, in which they contrived to find only the right to be dishonest. And just remember the things that were said and the beliefs that were expressed then; recall the abominations that were often held up as examples of honor and valor. It was, in essence, only a filthy alleyway into which an honest idea had strayed. And it was just at this point that the liberation of the peasants came along, and with it the disintegration and "dissociation" of our educated society in every possible sense. People did not recognize one another, and the liberals did not recognize their own liberalism. And how many melancholy misunderstandings followed, and how many grievous disillusionments! The most shameless reactionaries sometimes suddenly pushed their way forward as progressives and leaders, and they were successful. What could many of the children of that time see in their fathers? What memories of childhood and youth could they have? Cynicism, mockery, and merciless attacks on the first tender, sacred manifestations of belief in the children; and then the often open debauchery of their fathers and mothers, done confidently and from the *doctrine* that this is how it should be, that such are genuine, "sane" relationships. Add to this a great number of families that suffered financial ruin, and the result is impatient dissatisfaction and impressive words that hide only egotistical, petty spite over material reverses. Oh, our young people eventually were able to puzzle all this out and make sense of it! And since our young people are pure, serene, and magnanimous, then naturally it could happen that some of them did not want to follow in the footsteps of fathers such as these, and they rejected their "sane" admonitions. So it was that such "liberal" education was able to produce results that were not at all liberal, in some instances at least. So perhaps it is these very young people, these "raw youths," who are now seeking new paths in life and who are beginning by flatly rejecting that cycle of ideas they find so hateful and which they first encountered in childhood, in the wretched nests of their own parents.

5. On Yury Samarin

And the steadfast men of conviction are passing away. Yury Samarin, a man of immense talent and unshakeable convictions, a man who did most useful work, has died. There are people who command the respect of everyone, even of those who do not agree with their convictions. *The New Times* printed a very characteristic story about him. Not that long ago, at the end of February, while passing through St. Petersburg, Samarin read the article by Prince Vasilchikov, "The Black Soil Lands and Their Future," in the February issue of *Notes of the Fatherland*. This article made such an impression on him that he did not sleep the whole night: "It's a very fine and true article," Samarin said to a friend the next morning. "I read it yesterday evening, and it made such an impression on me that I could not get to sleep. All night long I kept seeing a terrible picture of the arid, treeless wasteland into which our central black soil region is being transformed because of continuous and unhindered deforestation."

"Are there many among us who lose sleep worrying about their motherland?" *New Times* adds. I think that we still will find some, and, who knows, perhaps now, judging by our alarming situation, there will be even more of them than before. We have always had enough worriers, in every sense imaginable, and we are certainly not asleep, as some would have it. The point, however, is not that we have worriers; it lies in the manner in which they think, and in Yury Samarin we lost a steadfast and deep thinker; that is a loss indeed. The old forces are departing, and we are still too bedazzled by the new ones, the people of the future, to make out what they are. . . .

April

1

1. The Ideals of a Stagnant, Vegetative Life. Kulaks and Bloodsuckers. Superior People Who Drive Russia Forward

The March issue of *The Russian Messenger* of this year contains a "criticism" of me by Mr. A., i.e., Mr. Avseenko. There's no use in my answering Mr. Avseenko: it's difficult to conceive of a writer who has a poorer grasp of his subject. However, if he had grasped his subject, the result would be the same. Everything in the article that touches on me revolves around the theme that it is not we, the people of culture, who ought to bow down before the People—for "the ideals of the People are predominantly the ideals of stagnant, vegetative life"—but, on the contrary, it is the People who ought to receive enlightenment from us, the cultured, and adopt our way of thinking and our likeness. In short, Mr. Avseenko was very displeased with what I said about the People in the February *Diary*. I suppose that there is only one misunderstanding here, for which I am to blame. This misunderstanding ought to be cleared up, but answering Mr. Avseenko is literally impossible. What, for example, can one have in common with a man who suddenly says the following things about the People:

> It was on their shoulders [i.e., on the People's shoulders], on their endurance and self-sacrifice, on their vital strength, ardent faith, and magnanimous disregard for their own interests that Russia's independence, strength, and capacity for a historic mission were founded. They have preserved the purity of the Christian ideal for us, displaying heroism that is both lofty and humble in its grandeur, and have perpetuated those beautiful traits of the Slavic nature which, when reflected in the hearty sounds of Pushkin's poetry, *continually thereafter nourished the living stream of our literature....*"

427

And so, no sooner had he written that (or copied from the Slavophiles, rather) than on the very next page Mr. Avseenko states just the reverse about that same Russian People:

> The fact is that our People have not provided us with any ideal of a dynamic personality. All those beautiful things we perceive in them and which our literature, to its great credit, has taught us to love in them, are only on the level of elemental being—a self-contained, idyllic [?] way of life or passive existence. No sooner does an *active, energetic* personality emerge from the People than its charm usually vanishes, and most often this manifestation of individuality assumes the unattractive form of the bloodsucker, the kulak, the stupid and petty tyrant. The People still do not have active ideals, and to place one's hopes in them means to begin from an unknown and perhaps imaginary quantity.

And to say all that immediately after stating on the preceding page that Russia's independence was founded "on the shoulders of the People, on their endurance and self-sacrifice, on their vital strength, ardent faith, and magnanimous disregard for their own interests!" But really, in order to display this vital strength they could not be *merely* passive! And to create Russia they could not help but use their strength! To show their *magnanimous* disregard for their own interests, they certainly had to *work* magnanimously and actively in the interests of others, that is, in the common, brotherly interest. In order "to bear on their shoulders" Russia's independence, they could certainly not sit *passively* on the spot; they surely had to get up and move, even a little, and at least take a step; they had to do some little thing, at least. Yet Mr. Avseenko at once adds that no sooner do the People begin to do something then they at once assume "the unattractive features of the bloodsucker, the kulak, or the stupid and petty tyrant." So it turns out that it is the kulaks, the bloodsuckers, and the petty tyrants who have borne Russia on their shoulders. Thus all these saintly metropolitans of ours (who defended the People and who built the Russian land), all our pious princes, all our boyars, our men of state who toiled and who served Russia to the point of sacrificing their lives and whose names history has reverently preserved—all of them were only bloodsuckers, kulaks, and petty tyrants! I may be told, perhaps, that Mr. Avseenko was not talking about people of years gone by, but about people now; that it is a matter of history, and all happened long ago, in some Stone Age or other.

But if that's the case, then have our People undergone some total transformation? What kind of contemporary people is Mr. Avseenko talking about, anyway? When did they have their beginning? From the time of Peter the Great's reforms? From the period of culture? From the final establishment of serfdom? But if that's the case, then the cultured Mr. Avseenko is betraying himself; then everybody will tell him: "What was the use of bringing you culture, so that in return you could corrupt the People and transform them merely into kulaks and cheats?" Do you really possess this "gift of seeing only the dark side" to that degree, Mr. Avseenko? Can it really be that our People, who were enserfed specifically for the sake of your culture (at least according to General Fadeev), now, after their two hundred years of slavery, deserve from you, a man who has been able to acquire culture, only this coarse insult about kulaks and cheats instead of gratitude or even compassion? (I set no store by the fact that you praised them on one page, because you canceled it all on the next page.) It was for you that for two hundred years they were bound hand and foot, so that Europe's intellectual tradition might be delivered to you, and so now that you have acquired this European intellect (?), you stand, hands on hips, before those who are bound hand and foot, looking down on them from the height of your culture, and suddenly come to the conclusion that they are "bad and passive and have shown little ability to act (these, the bound ones), but have displayed only certain passive virtues which, though they have nourished our literature with living juices, are not worth a penny in essence because as soon as the People do begin to act, they at once turn out to be kulaks and swindlers." No, I should not have replied to Mr. Avseenko, and if I did so it was only as an admission of my own mistake, about which I will explain below. Nevertheless, since I have taken up the subject I feel it is relevant to provide the reader with some idea about Mr. Avseenko. As a writer he represents a minor cultural type which is most interesting to observe and which has a certain wider meaning; and that is not a good thing at all.

2. Minor Cultural Types. Damaged People

Mr. Avseenko has been writing criticism for a long time, for some years now, and I confess that I still had some hopes for him: "If he writes long enough," I thought, "he'll finally say something." But I did not know him very well. My error continued right up to the October 1874 issue of *The Russian Messenger* where, in his article on Pisemsky's comedies and dramas, he suddenly came out with the following: "... Gogol caused our writers to pay too little attention to the inner content of their works and to rely too heavily on the artistic element alone. Such an attitude toward the task of literature was very common in our literature of the 1840s; and that is partly the reason why *this literature was lacking in inner content*[!]."

So the literature of the 1840s was lacking in inner content! Never in my whole life did I expect to hear such news. This is the same literature that gave us Gogol's complete works, his comedy *The Marriage* (lacking in inner content—hah!), that later gave us his *Dead Souls* (lacking in inner content—why the man could have said anything else, even the first thing that came into his head, and it would still have made more sense than this). Then the 1840s produced Turgenev with his *Hunter's Sketches* (and are these lacking in inner content?), and then Goncharov who, in the forties, wrote his *Oblomov* and published its best episode, "Oblomov's Dream," which all Russia read with delight! This is the same literature that gave us, finally, Ostrovsky; but it is specifically Ostrovsky's types that provoke Mr. Avseenko, in this same article, to his coarsest insults:

> Due to external reasons, the world of government officials was not entirely available as a subject of theatrical satire; and so our comedy rushed off all the more eagerly to the world of the merchants of Zamoskvorechie and the Apraksin Court, to the world of pilgrims and matchmakers, drunken clerks, bailiffs, psalm singers, and citified peasants. The range of comedy became incredibly narrowed to mere imitation of drunken or illiterate jargon and the reproduction of the savage manners of coarse, offensive characters and types. Genre works were enthroned on stage, but not the warm, happy bourgeois [?] genre which is sometimes so appealing on the French stage [Does he mean those little farces where one character crawls under a table and another tries to drag him out by the leg?]; what we have is coarse genre, unclean, and repulsive. Some writers, such as Mr. Ostrovsky, for example, brought much talent, emotion, and humor into this literature, but in general our theater reached a low point in terms of content, and it quickly became obvious that it *had nothing to say* to the educated portion of society and nothing in common with them.

And so Ostrovsky lowered the level of the stage; Ostrovsky had nothing to say to the "educated" elements of society! It follows that the society that delighted in Ostrovsky on the stage and devoured his writings was an uneducated one. Oh, yes, you see educated society used to go to the Mikhailovsky Theater to see that "warm, happy, bourgeois genre which sometimes is so appealing on the French stage." But Liubim Tortsov is "coarse, unclean." It would be interesting to know which educated society Mr. Avseenko is talking about. There is nothing dirty about Liubim Tortsov: he is "pure in spirit"; but what is dirty, perhaps, is the place where this "warm bourgeois genre that sometimes is so appealing on the French stage" holds sway. And what does he mean by saying that the artistic element excludes *inner content?* On the contrary: artistry promotes content to the highest degree. Gogol may be weak in his *Selected Correspondence,* yet he is characteristic; but Gogol, in those passages in *Dead Souls* where he ceases to be an artist and begins to convey his own views directly, is simply weak and not even characteristic. But his *Marriage* and his *Dead Souls* are his most profound works, the richest in inner content, precisely because of the artistically rendered characters who appear in them. These portrayals, so to say, almost overburden the mind with the most profound and agonizing problems; they evoke the most disturbing thoughts in the Russian mind, and one feels it will be a long time before we will be able to cope with them; indeed, will we ever be able to cope with such thoughts? And Mr. Avseenko shouts that *Dead Souls* has no inner content! But take *Woe from Wit:* it achieves its power only from its brilliant, artistically rendered types and characters, and it is the labor of artistry alone that provides the whole inner content of this work; just as soon as Griboedov abandons his role as an artist and begins to convey his own ideas from his own intellect (through the mouth of Chatsky, the weakest character in the play), he at once sinks to a most unenviable level, far lower than even the representatives of the intelligentsia of the day. The level of Chatsky's moralizing is far lower than the comedy itself, and it consists in part of the most errant nonsense. All the profundity, all the content of a work of art thus resides only in its types and its characters. And this is almost always the case.

So the reader can see the sort of critic he is dealing with. And I can already hear you asking: why do you bother with him, then? I repeat: I want only to correct my own negligence, and I am dealing with Mr. Avseenko now, as I said above, not as a critic but as a distinct and curious literary phenomenon. We have here didn't understand Mr. Avseenko. I don't mean his articles—these I never could understand and, in any case, there is nothing in them to understand or not understand. I gave up on him altogether after that same article in the October 1874 issue of *The Russian Messenger,* wondering all the while, however, how pieces by such a confused writer could appear in a journal as serious as *The Russian Messenger.* But then suddenly something quite amusing happened, and I suddenly understood Mr. Avseenko at once: at the beginning of the winter he suddenly began publishing his novel *The Milky Way.* (And why did the publication of the novel stop?) This novel suddenly clarified for me the whole nature of Avseenko as a writer-type. It's not fitting that I speak specifically about the novel: I myself am a novelist and I shouldn't criticize a colleague. And so I won't criticize the novel at all, the more so that it provided me with a few genuinely happy moments. For example, the young hero, a prince, is sitting in a box at the opera and is sniveling for all to hear because the music has touched his tender feelings; a lady from the beau monde, deeply moved by his sobs, keeps pestering him: "You're crying? You're crying?" But that's really not the point; the point is that I grasped the essence of this writer. Mr. Avseenko as a writer represents a figure who has lost his presence of mind in his worship of high society. To put it briefly, he has prostrated himself and is worshiping the gloves, carriages, perfumes, pomades, silk dresses (especially the moment when a lady takes her seat in an armchair and her dress rustles around her feet and her body), and finally, the servants who greet their mistress when she returns from the Italian opera. He writes about all this constantly, reverently, piously, and devoutly; in short, it is as if he were celebrating some kind of Mass. I heard (perhaps it was said in fun) that he began this novel with the aim of correcting Leo Tolstoy, who depicted high society too objectively in his *Anna Karenina;* one ought to have depicted it more devoutly, on one's knees, as it were. And of course it would not be worth mentioning this at all unless, I repeat, it had not brought to light a completely new cultural type. It turns out that the critic Avseenko sees the whole point of our culture—its whole achievement, the whole culmination of the two-hundred-year period of our debauchery and our suffering—in carriages, in pomade, and particularly in the manner in which servants go out to greet their mistress; and he admires these things, without a hint of mockery. The seriousness

and sincerity of his admiration constitute a most curious phenomenon. The most important thing is that Mr. Avseenko, as a writer,
is not alone; even before him we had the "merciless Juvenals in
calico dickeys," but never with such a degree of reverence. Granted,
they are not all like that, but my problem is that, little by little,
I have at last become convinced that there are even an extraordinary
number of such representatives of culture in literature and in life,
although not in such a rigid and pure type. I admit, it was as if
the light had finally dawned on me. And then, of course, I could
understand the disparaging remarks about Ostrovsky and about
the "warm, happy, bourgeois genre which is sometimes so appealing on the French stage." Well—it's really not Ostrovsky and
not Gogol and not the 1840s that are at issue here (who needs
them, anyway?); what's at issue is simply the Mikhailovsky Theater
in St. Petersburg that is patronized by the people of high society
who come driving up to it in their carriages. That's all it is; that's
what has seized his imagination with such merciless force; it has
seduced him and sent his mind into a whirl from which it will
never recover. I repeat once more: one mustn't regard this from
only a comic point of view; it's much more interesting than that.
In short, there is much here that is caused by a particular mania,
an almost pathological weakness, one might say, for which one
must make allowances. Let's take an example: a high-society carriage is going to the theater; just look how it rolls along and how
the light from the lanterns shines through the carriage window,
casting a romantic glow over the lady sitting within. This is no
longer the subject for a pen, it is a prayer, and one must have a
deep feeling for it! Of course, many of them are showing off before
the People with something apparently much loftier than gloves;
among them are even many ultraliberals, almost republicans, and
yet, once in a while, you'll see the glove-worshiper emerge. This
debility, this mania for the charms of high society with its oysters
and hundred-ruble watermelons served at balls, this mania, no
matter how innocent it may seem, has even given rise to a special
sort of confirmed advocate of serfdom among those who never
owned serfs in their lives. But once they have accepted carriages
and the Mikhailovsky Theater as the culmination of the cultured
period of Russian history, they suddenly became advocates of serfdom by conviction; and although they haven't the least intention
of restoring it, they at least can spit upon the People quite openly

and with the air of the fullest cultural right. These are the very ones who shower the most astonishing accusations on the People: he who has been in bondage for two hundred years is taunted for his passivity; the poor man who has been squeezed for his quit-rent is accused of slovenliness; he who has never been taught is accused of lacking education; he who has been beaten with a stick is blamed for having coarse manners; and sometimes they are ready to blame him for not having his hair pomaded and trimmed by a barber on Bolshoi Morskoi Street. This is by no means an exaggeration; it is literally so, and the whole point is that it is not an exaggeration. Their disgust for the People is utterly furious, and if they sometimes do praise the People—well, then it is done as a matter of politics; simply for the sake of decency they pick out a few resounding phrases in which they understand nothing, because they contradict themselves a few lines later. By the way, I remember an incident now that happened to me two and a half years ago. I was taking the train to Moscow and struck up a conversation at night with a landowner who was sitting next to me. As far as I could tell in the darkness, he was a wizened little man of about fifty with a red and rather swollen nose; I think he also had something wrong with his feet. He was a very respectable type—in manners, in conversation, in his opinions—and he even spoke quite sensibly. He spoke of the difficult and uncertain situation of the nobility, of the remarkable economic disorganization all over Russia, and he spoke almost without malice but held a stern view of the subject; and he interested me intensely. And what do you think? Suddenly, in passing and quite unawares, he announced that he considered himself incomparably superior to the peasant in a physical sense and that this, of course, was a fact beyond dispute.

"You mean to say, in other words, as an example of a cultivated and educated person?" I said, trying to make clear his meaning.

"No, not at all. Not only my moral nature but my physical nature as well is superior to the peasant's; my *body* is better and finer than a peasant's, and this is the result of our many generations of development into a superior type."

There was no point in arguing with him: this weak little man with a red, scrofulous nose and ailing feet (perhaps he had gout, the nobleman's ailment) considered himself in good conscience to be physically, *in body*, superior to and more attractive than a peas-ant! I repeat, he bore no malice whatsoever. But you must agree that this amiable man, even in his amiability, might, were he given an opportunity, commit some terrible injustice to the People, quite innocently, calmly, and in good conscience, precisely as a result of his contemptuous view of the People, a view that was almost unconscious and existed almost independently of him.

Nonetheless, it is essential that I set right my own negligence. I was writing at that time about the People's ideals and about the fact that we, "like prodigal children returning home, ought to bow down before the People's truth and await from it alone our ideas and the form of those ideas. But, on the other hand, the People should take from us something of what we have brought with us; that this *something* truly does exist; that it is not a mirage, but has an image and a form and a weight; and that, should the reverse hold true, should we not come to an agreement, then it is better that we part and perish separately." And it was all that, I now see, that seemed unclear. First, people began asking: what ideals do the People have to which we should bow down? Second, what do I have in mind when I speak of the precious thing we brought with us and which the People must accept from us sine qua non? And would it not be easier, finally, if the People were to bow down to us, and not vice versa, solely because we are Europe and we are cultured, and they are only Russian and *passive?* Mr. Avseenko answers this question affirmatively; however I am replying now not only to Mr. Avseenko, but to all those "cultured" people who did not understand me, beginning with the "merciless Juvenals in calico dickeys" right up to the gentlemen who recently announced that we have *nothing at all worth preserving.* And so, to business. If I had not tried to express myself succinctly at that time and had gone into more detail, then, of course, you could still have disagreed with me, but my ideas would not have been distorted and called unclear.

3. Confusion and Inaccuracy in the Points at Issue

It is plainly stated that the People possess no Truth whatsoever, but that Truth exists only in culture and is preserved by the highest levels of cultured people. To be quite honest, I accept this dear European culture of ours in its highest sense, but not in the sense of carriages and servants only; I accept it specifically in the sense that we, compared to the People, have developed morally and spiritually, have become humanized and humane, and in so doing, to our credit, we have become quite distinct from the People. Having made such a dispassionate declaration, I at once pose myself the question: "Are we indeed so good and so faultlessly cultured that we can toss aside our People's culture and worship our own? And, finally, just what did we bring from Europe for the People?"

Before answering such questions, let us, in the interests of orderly discussion, exclude any mention of science, industry, and other such things in which Europe justly can take pride over our country. Excluding these things is quite just, for this is not the question at the *present* time; moreover, this science is over there, in Europe, while we ourselves, i.e., the upper levels of cultured people in Russia, are still not much noted for our science, despite our two hundred years of schooling; and so it is still too early to bow down to us cultured people on account of our science. So science certainly does not constitute any essential and irreconcilable difference between both classes of Russian people, i.e., between the common people and the upper cultured strata, and to say that science is the principal, fundamental difference between us and the People is, I repeat, quite untrue and would be a mistake; we must seek the difference in something else entirely. Besides, science is a matter of common concern, and is the invention of no single nation in Europe; all peoples, beginning from the ancient world, played their part and shared the legacy. For its part, the Russian People were never the enemy of science; indeed, it began penetrating Russia even before Peter the Great. Tsar Ivan IV did everything he could to conquer the Baltic coast thirty years before Peter. Had he conquered it and taken possession of its harbors and ports, then he would inevitably have had to begin building his own ships just as Peter did; and since one cannot build ships without science, then science from Europe would have inevitably appeared then, just as it did under Peter. Our Potugins may try to dishonor the People by sneering that the Russians have invented nothing but the samovar, but Europeans will not likely join the chorus. It is all too clear and comprehensible that everything happens according to well-known laws of nature and of history and that it is not intellectual weakness or the limited capacities of the Russian People or shameful laziness that have been the cause of our scant contribution to science and industry. One type of tree may mature in so many years, while another type takes twice as long. Everything here depends on how nature and circumstances have placed a people,

and what it had to accomplish first. There are geographical, ethnographical, political, and a thousand other reasons, all of them
clear and precise. No one of good sense would reproach and shame
a thirteen-year-old because he isn't twenty-five. "Europe," people
claim, "is more active and clever than the passive Russians, and
therefore she has acquired science while the Russians haven't." But
while Europe was acquiring her science, the passive Russians were
giving evidence of an activity that was no less striking: they were
founding a kingdom and *consciously* unifying it. For a whole thousand years they fought off cruel enemies who would have fallen
upon Europe had it not been for the Russians. The Russians were
colonizing the farthest corners of their boundless motherland; the
Russians were defending and strengthening their borders, and did
so in ways that we cultured people could not now match; to the
contrary, we may yet weaken our borders. At last, after a thousand
years, there emerged there a kingdom and a political entity without
parallel in the world, so much so that England and the United
States, the only other states which still have a strong and original
form of political unity, may be far behind us. Well, in Europe,
under different political and geographical circumstances, there arose
science instead. But at the same time as science developed, the
moral and political health of Europe weakened almost everywhere.
Thus everyone has his own accomplishments, and we still cannot
say who should be envious of whom. We'll acquire science in any
case, but can we tell what will happen to Europe's political unity?
The Germans, perhaps, only fifteen years ago might have agreed
to trade half their scientific renown for that strength of political
unity which we had long possessed. The Germans have now
achieved a strong political union, at least as they define it, but at
that time the German Empire did not yet exist and they envied
us—without showing it, of course—despite their scorn for us. And
so there is no point in posing the question about science and
industry; the question is, specifically: in what way have we, the
cultured people, become *morally and essentially* superior to the
People when we returned from Europe? What priceless treasure
did we bring them in the guise of our European culture? Why are
we *clean*, while the People are still dirty? Why are we all, while
the People are nothing? I propose that there is an enormous lack
of clarity among us cultured people on these questions, and that
very few of the "cultured" could answer them correctly. On the

contrary, there is a total muddle here, with people asking with a sneer why a pine tree does not mature in seven years but requires seven times that long to grow to full height. Such questions are so common and so usual that one often hears them not only from the Potugins but even from those who have progressed much further. I won't even mention Mr. Avseenko. And now it's time to address directly the question posed at the beginning of the chapter: are we indeed so fine and so faultlessly cultured that we can cast aside the People's culture and bow down to our own? And if we bear something with us, then what is it, exactly? I shall state plainly in reply that we are much worse than the People, and worse in almost all respects.

We hear that as soon as an active man appears from among the People he becomes a kulak and a swindler. (It's not only Mr. Avseenko who says that; in general, Mr. Avseenko never has anything new to say.) In the first place, this isn't true; and in the second place, do we not find the same kulaks and swindlers all the time among cultured Russians? And there probably are even greater numbers of them here, and it is all the more shameful because they have acquired culture while the People have not. But what's most important is that one simply cannot argue that whenever an active person does appear among the People he usually becomes a kulak and a cheat. I do not know where those who maintain this grew up, but since childhood and all through my life I have seen something quite different. I was only nine years old when once, I recall, on the third day of Easter week, sometime after five in the afternoon, our whole family—father, mother, brothers, and sisters—were sitting at our round table having tea; we happened to be talking about the country and how we would all go there for the summer. Suddenly the door opened and on the threshold appeared our house serf, Grigory Vasilev, who had only just arrived from the country. In the absence of the masters he had even been charged with the management of the estate; and now, instead of an imposing "foreman," always dressed in a German frock coat, there appeared a man in an old peasant coat and bast shoes. He had come on foot from the estate and he said not a word when he entered the room.

"What's wrong?" cried my father in alarm. "What is it?"

"The estate has burned down," Grigory Vasilev announced in his deep voice.

I shall not describe what ensued; my father and mother were

working people and not wealthy, and this was the present they received for Easter! It turned out that everything had burned to the ground: the peasants' huts, the granary, the barn—even the seeds for spring sowing perished, with some of the cattle and one peasant, Arkhip. In our initial fright we imagined that this meant total ruin. We fell on our knees and began to pray; my mother wept. And then suddenly up stepped our nurse, Alena Frolovna, who worked for us on salary (she was not a serf but a Moscow townswoman). She had raised and cared for all us children. At that time she was a woman of about forty-five with a serene, happy disposition; and she always told us such marvelous fairy tales! She had not drawn her salary from us for many years: "I don't need it," she would say. A sum of about five hundred rubles had accumulated and had been invested at a pawnbroker's: "It might come in handy in my old age." And suddenly she whispered to Mama: "If you need some money, take what I have; I've got no use for it. . . . "

We didn't take her money and managed without it. But let me ask you: to which type did this humble woman belong, a woman who passed on long ago in a home for the aged where her money was very useful? I don't suppose that people like her can be included among the kulaks and swindlers; and if they cannot, then how is one to explain what she did: was it only something "on the level of elemental being—a self-contained, idyllic way of life and passive existence," or did she display something rather more energetic than mere passivity? It would be most interesting to hear how Mr. Avseenko would answer that. People will scornfully reply that this is an isolated case; but in the course of my life I myself have managed to remark many hundreds of such instances among our common people; and I know full well that there are also other observers who can regard the People without spitting on them. Do you not recall how, in Aksakov's *Family Chronicle*, the mother with tears in her eyes implored the peasants to take her to her sick child over the thin, spring ice on the broad Volga at Kazan, when for some days already none of them had dared set foot on the ice, which was breaking up and which was carried downstream only a few hours after they did cross it? Do you remember the charming description of this crossing and how later, when it was over, the peasants did not even want to accept any money, realizing that they had done it all for the sake of a mother's tears and for Christ our God. And this happened during the very darkest period of serfdom!

Tell me, are these still isolated instances? And if they are worthy
of praise, then is it only "on the level of elemental being—a self-
contained, idyllic way of life and passive existence?" Is that really
true? Are these only isolated, random facts? This active risking of
one's own life out of compassion for a mother's grief—can that be
considered mere passivity? Was it not, on the contrary, due to
Truth, the People's Truth; did it not happen *because of compassion
and all-forgivingness and the breadth of vision of the People;* and this
in the most barbaric period of serfdom? But the People don't even
know religion, you will say; they can't even say a prayer; they
worship a wooden plank and mumble some nonsense about Holy
Friday and Florus and Laurus. To this I reply that you have got
such notions simply because you continue to hold the Russian
People in contempt, a habit that stubbornly persists in the typical
cultured Russian. We have some two dozen liberal and salacious
anecdotes about the People's religion and about their Orthodoxy,
and we relish the mocking stories of how the priest hears an old
woman's confession or how a peasant says his prayers to Friday.
If Mr. Avseenko truly understood what he wrote about the People's
religion that saved Russia and had not simply copied it from the
Slavophiles, then he would not have insulted the People this way
by calling virtually all of them "kulaks and bloodsuckers." That,
of course, is just the point: these men haven't the slightest understanding of Orthodoxy, and therefore they will never have the
slightest understanding of our People. The People know Christ,
their God, even better than they know ours, perhaps, although
they never attended school. They know because for many centuries
they endured much suffering, and always in their grief, from the
beginning until this day, they would hear of this God-Christ of
theirs from their saints who worked for the People and who defended the Russian land to the point of laying down their lives—
from these same saints whom the People still revere, keeping their
names fresh in their memories and praying over their graves. Believe me, in this sense even the darkest strata of our People are
much better educated than you, in your cultured ignorance of them,
suppose; perhaps they are more educated than you are yourself,
even though you may have mastered the catechism.

4. The Beneficent Swiss Who Liberates a Russian Peasant

Here is what Mr. Avseenko writes in his March article. I want to
be completely dispassionate, and therefore I'll permit myself to

include this very long quotation so that you won't accuse me of picking out only a few isolated sentences. Besides, I believe that these same words of Mr. Avseenko express the common opinion Westernizers now hold of the Russian People, so I am very pleased to have an opportunity to respond.

> ... It is important for us to know the conditions under which our educated minority first looked closely over that wall that separated it from the People. No doubt the things that were revealed to its eyes made a striking impression and in many respects met the inner needs that were evident in the minority. People who were not satisfied with being the foster children of Western civilization found there ideals that were totally different from European ones but that were still beautiful. People who were disenchanted and, as the expression of the time had it, were torn in two by this borrowed culture found there simple, integral characters, a strength of faith that recalled the early years of Christianity, the austere vigor of patriarchal life. As we said earlier, the contrast between the two ways of life must have produced a remarkable effect that was hard to resist. People wanted to refresh themselves in the untroubled waves of this elemental existence, to breathe the pure air of the fields and forests. The best people were struck by the fact that in this stagnant life, to which not only the notion of education but even of simple literacy was foreign, could be found traits of such spiritual grandeur that the enlightened minority had to bow down before them. All these impressions created an enormous need for closer contact with the People.
>
> But what exactly did they mean by this contact with the People? The ideals of the People were only clear because the life of the People flowed its course at an infinitely remote distance from the life of the educated; because the conditions and the content of the two ways of life were utterly different. Just recall that those of little education who have lived very close to the People have long since met this need for contact practically and materially; they have found no sign of these beautiful Popular ideals and are firmly convinced that the peasant is a dog and a scoundrel. This is very important because it shows to what extent, in practice, the educational impact of the People's ideas is weak and how vain it is to expect salvation from them. To understand these ideals and elevate them to the level of the pearl of creation demands a certain high level of culture. Therefore we consider ourselves fully justified in saying that this bowing down to popular ideals was a product of the European culture we assimilated and that without it the peasant would have remained to this day a dog and a scoundrel in our eyes. It follows that the primary evil, a common evil for us

and the People, was not a matter of "culture," but of the weakness
of cultural principles, of the insufficiency of our "culture."

What a surprising and unexpected conclusion! Here, in this clever
selection of words, the most important conclusion is that the principles of the People (and Orthodoxy with them, because in essence
all the principles of the People have emerged entirely from Orthodoxy) have no cultural efficacy and not the slightest educative
significance, so that in order to get all these things we had to go
off to Europe. You see, it was not because "those of little education
who have lived very close to the People" still never saw any of the
"beautiful Popular ideals" and continued to be firmly convinced
that the peasant was a "dog and a scoundrel"; it was not because
they had already been corrupted to the tips of their fingers by
culture, despite their own lack of education and despite the fact
that they had already broken free from the People, although they
lived in close proximity to them—it was because there was still not
enough culture, you see. The main thing here is the malicious
insinuation that the principles of the People have little educational
significance and the conclusion that, accordingly, they can take us
nowhere, while culture leads us everywhere. As far as I am concerned, I stated a long time ago that we began our European culture
with debauchery. But in saying that I must stress specifically the
following: these same people of little education who have still managed to acquire some culture, even if only poorly and superficially,
even if only in a few aspects of their behavior, in a new set of
prejudices, or in a new set of clothes—these same people, without
exception, begin precisely by expressing scorn for their former
milieu, their People, and even their religion, sometimes even to
the point of hatred. Such is the case with certain superior "counts'
lackeys," wretched little clerks who have pushed themselves into
the ranks of the nobility, and so on. They have even more scorn
for the People than do the bigwigs, who are much more thoroughly
cultured; and there is certainly no need to be surprised by that,
as Mr. Avseenko is. In the first issue of my *Diary* in January, I
recalled one of my impressions from childhood: the picture of the
courier who was beating a peasant. This courier, no doubt, was
close to the People; he spent his whole life on the highway, yet he
scorned and beat the peasants. Why? Because he was already far,
far removed from the People, even though he may have lived close
to them. There is no doubt whatsoever that he had not a shred of

higher culture; yet he did get a courier's uniform with a tailcoat that gave him the right to beat people without restraint, "as much as he felt like." And he was proud of his uniform and considered himself immeasurably superior to a peasant. The landowner, whose estate was some hundred paces from the peasants' huts, was placed in almost the same position; it was not a matter of a hundred paces, however, but of the fact that this man had already tasted of the corruption of civilization. He was close to the People—a mere hundred paces away—but a huge gulf lay in these hundred paces. This landowner might never have acquired more than a drop of culture, but this drop was enough to corrupt him thoroughly. This must have been true of the majority of cases at the beginning of the reform period. But I can state very definitely that, here as well, Mr. Avseenko has little more idea than an infant: not all, certainly not all people of little education were corrupted, nor did they despise the People even in those days; to the contrary, there were others on whom the People's principles never ceased to have a remarkable educational influence. Such a group survived from the reforms of Peter the Great and has continued to flourish right up to our time. There were many, even a very great many, who tasted of this culture and who returned again to the People and the People's ideals without losing their culture. Later on, the stratum of the Slavophiles, people who were already fully at home in European civilization, emerged from this group of "faithful." But it was not the high European civilization of the Slavophiles that led them to remain faithful to the People and the People's principles, not at all; on the contrary, it was the inexhaustible, ceaseless educative work of the People's principles on the minds and development of this stratum of genuinely Russian people, who by virtue of their innate qualities were capable of resisting the force of civilization without being personally annihilated. This was a stratum that goes back, I repeat, to the very beginning of the reforms. I dare say that many of our Slavophiles appeared as if they had fallen straight from the sky; and they cannot trace their origins to the protest against everything that was wrong and fanatically exclusive in Peter's reforms. But once more I repeat that there were also people of little culture who never thought of the People as dogs and scoundrels. They never lost their Christianity and looked on the People as a younger brother, not as a dog. But our cultured people scarcely know about this, and if they do know then they scorn these facts and do not take them into account, and they never will, because these people of little culture who clung to their Christianity would flatly contradict the basic and prevailing thesis that the People's principles fail as a means of education. They would then have to agree that it was not the People's principles that were so weak and powerless to educate but, on the contrary, that culture was already entirely corrupted even though it was only in its early stage, and therefore it succeeded in ruining a multitude of *infirm* people. (Infirm people are always in the majority.) Mr. Avseenko therefore directly concludes that "the evil, the primary evil, a common evil for us and the People, was not a matter of 'culture,' but of the weakness of cultural principles," and therefore we had to run quickly to Europe to put the finishing touches to our culture so that we should no longer regard the peasant as a dog and a scoundrel.

And that was what we did: we went to Europe ourselves and brought back teachers. Before the French Revolution, in the days of Rousseau and of Catherine the Great's correspondence with Voltaire, having Swiss teachers was much in fashion. "... And the Swiss who brings culture to us all."[1]

"Come, take the money, but enlighten us and make us humane"—there truly was such a fashion at that time. Turgenev, in his *Nest of Gentlefolk*, has a superb little description of a nobleman's son who returns to his father's estate after acquiring his culture in Europe. He boasted of his humaneness and his education. His father began reproaching him for seducing and dishonoring an innocent servant girl, and the son said to him, "Never mind, I'll marry her." Do you remember the picture of the father picking up his stick and setting after the son who, in his blue English tailcoat, tasseled boots, and tight elkskin trousers, scampered away through the garden and the threshing barn as fast as his legs would carry him? Although he escaped, he did marry the girl a few days later, partly in the name of Rousseau's ideas, which were floating about in the air at that time, but mainly because of a whim, because of an infirmity of convictions, will, and feelings, and because of a bruised ego: "Just look at me," he says, "see what a sort I am!"

---

[1]I think the verse is by Count Khvostov. I even remember the quatrain in which the poet enumerates all the peoples of Europe:

Turk, Persian, Prussian, Frank, and vengeful Spaniard,
The son of Italy, the German, son of science,
The son of commerce, watching o'er his goods [i.e., the English],
And the Swiss who brings culture to us all.

[Dostoevsky's note]

Later on he lost respect for his wife; he tormented her by going away; he treated her with the greatest contempt, and abandoned her. He lived to an old age and died a completely cynical, malicious, petty, useless old fellow who spent his last moments cursing and shouting to his sister, "Glashka, you fool, bring me some broth!" How charming this story of Turgenev's is, and how true! And yet this was a man of some real culture. But this is not what Mr. Avseenko means: he demands genuine culture, i.e., the culture of our own time, the kind that finally acculturated our Petersburg landowners to the point where they could sob over *Anton Goremyka* and then go off and liberate the peasants with land and decide to address these erstwhile dogs and scoundrels with the formal *you*. Such progress! Later on, after closer study, it was determined that these landowners who sobbed over Anton Goremyka had not the slightest comprehension of the People, their way of life, or their principles; that they regarded the Russian peasants almost as some French villagers or shepherdesses on porcelain teacups. When the government began its long and arduous labor to liberate the peasants, some of the opinions of these highly placed landowners were striking in their almost anecdotal ignorance of the subject, the countryside, the life of the People, and everything else that was connected with the People's principles. Meanwhile, Mr. Avseenko specifically states that it was European culture that enabled us to comprehend the People's ideals, while the ideals themselves are without any educative significance. Supposedly, one had to go to Paris to comprehend the ideals of our People, or at least go to some second-rate little farce at the Mikhailovsky Theater, one to which carriages keep driving up. Still, let us grant that progress and an understanding of Russian principles came to us only from Europe; let it be so. Praise be to culture! "There it is—genuine culture—see what it does to people," exclaims the crowd of Avseenkos! "And what can any of your wretched 'Popular principles,' with Orthodoxy at their head, mean before that? They have no educative significance. Down with them!"

Let's assume this is so. But then, gentlemen, please give me an answer to just this one question: why didn't these teachers of ours—the Europeans, all these beneficent Swiss, who taught us to liberate the peasants with land—why didn't they liberate anyone over there in Europe, even without land, even as naked as their mothers bore them, and do so everywhere? Why was it that liberation in Europe came not from the owners, the barons, and the landlords, but from uprising and rebellion, fire and sword, and rivers of blood? And if anyone in Europe was liberated without rivers of blood, then it was always done on proletarian principles, so that the newly liberated became absolute slaves. And we shout that we learned about liberation from the Europeans! "We acquired culture," people say, "and so we stopped treating the peasant like a dog and a scoundrel." But why is it, then, that in France and everywhere else in Europe any proletarian, any worker who owns nothing, is still treated like a dog and a scoundrel? And this, of course, you cannot dispute. Of course, the law says that you can't call him a dog and a scoundrel; but still you can do whatever you like to him just as if he were a dog and a scoundrel; the cleverly written law only demands that the appropriate measure of civility be observed. "I'll be civil, but I won't give you any bread, even though you may starve like a dog"—this is how things are in Europe now. How can it be? What sort of contradiction is this? How is it that they taught us the very opposite notion? No, gentlemen, it is obvious that something quite different happened here, and not at all the way you say it did. Judge for yourselves: if it was only the effect of culture that led us to stop treating the peasant like a dog and a scoundrel, then we certainly would have liberated him on the basis of culture as well, i.e., on proletarian principles, just as our teachers in Europe did. "Be off now, dear brother," we would have said. "Enjoy your freedom in the nakedness in which you were born, and think it an honor." That's precisely how the People were liberated in the Baltic provinces. And why? Because the Balts are Europeans, while we are only Russians. It thus turns out that we accomplished this task like Russians and not at all like cultured Europeans; and we liberated the People with land only to the amazement and horror of our European teachers and all the beneficent Swiss. Indeed, they were horrified: voices in Europe were raised in alarm, don't you remember? They even started shouting something about communism. Do you remember what the late Guizot said about the liberation of our People? He told one Russian: "After what you have done, how can you expect us not to be afraid of you?" No, gentlemen, we liberated the People with land not because we had become cultured Europeans, but because we saw ourselves as Russians with the tsar at our head, exactly as the landowner Pushkin dreamed forty years ago when, at that very time, he cursed his European upbringing and turned to the principles of the People. *It was in the name of these same principles of the People* that the

Russian People were liberated with land, not because Europe taught us to do it; on the contrary, it was precisely because we suddenly, for the first time, resolved to bow down before the People's truth. This was not only a great moment in Russian life, in which cultured Russian people for the first time resolved to do something original, but it was also a prophetic moment in Russian life. And, perhaps, that prophecy will come to pass very soon. . . .

But . . . I must break off here for the moment. I see that this article is going to take up all the space in the *Diary.* And so, until the following, May, issue. And of course I'll leave the most important part of my explanation for the May issue. Let me list for the record the things that will go into it. I want to point out the total bankruptcy and even the insignificance of precisely *this aspect* of our culture, an aspect which some people regard, to the contrary, as our light, our sole salvation and our crowning glory before the People, and from whose height they spit upon the People and consider themselves fully justified in doing so. For to heap praise on these "principles of the People," to delight in them and in the same breath to say that they have no power, no educative significance, and that they are all only "passivity," means to spit on these principles. To assert, as does Mr. Avseenko, that the People are no more than "wanderers who have still not chosen which road to travel" and that "to expect thought and form from this riddle, from this sphinx which has not yet found either thought or form for itself, is an irony"—to assert that, I say, means only that one knows nothing about one's subject, i.e., knows nothing about the People. I want specifically to point out that the People are by no means as hopeless, by no means as easily swayed and lacking in form as is our cultured stratum, in which all these gentlemen take pride as Russia's most precious two-hundred-year-old acquisition. Finally, I would like to point out that a solid core has been preserved within our People, a core that will save them from the excesses and aberrations of our culture and will persist even through the process of education which will soon occur, so that the image and form of the Russian People will survive undamaged. And if, indeed, I did say that "the People are an enigma," then it was not at all in the sense in which these gentlemen took my meaning. Ultimately, I wish to explain fully my view of that confusing question which emerges of itself out of this little war of words. As I put it in my February *Diary*: "If we, the cultured Russian strata, are so weak and easily swayed as compared to the People, then what can we bring them that is so precious that they should bow down before it and accept this treasure from us sine qua non?" It is this aspect of our culture—which we must regard as a treasure but which all these gentlemen *until now* have totally ignored—that I wish to point out and explain. And so, until the May issue. As far as I am concerned, I can imagine nothing more absorbing and more *urgent* than these questions; I don't know how you, the reader, feel. But I promise to do my very best to be concise, and I shall even try to make no more references to Mr. Avseenko.

2

1. Something on Political Questions

Everyone is talking about current political questions and taking a great interest in them; indeed, how can one help but be interested? One very serious man whom I ran into by chance asked me suddenly, in dreadful earnest, "Well, is there going to be a war?" I was quite astonished: although I follow current affairs very closely, as we all do now, I had never heard the question of the inevitability of war raised. And it seems that I was correct: the newspapers announce the coming imminent meeting of the three chancellors in Berlin, and, of course, that endless question of Herzegovina will then be settled, most likely in a manner most acceptable to Russian sentiment. I admit I was not particularly troubled by the statement of this Baron Rodich a month ago; indeed, I was somewhat amused when I first read it. His remarks did cause a bit of a row later. Yet I think that Baron Rodich had no intention of provoking anyone; there wasn't even any "politics" in what he said; he simply made a slip of the tongue when he came out with this nonsense about Russian impotence. I even believe that before he spoke of our impotence he thought to himself: "If we are stronger than Russia then Russia must be totally impotent. And we really are stronger, because Berlin will never surrender us to Russia. Oh, Berlin may let us get into a scrap with Russia, but only for her own enjoyment and to see who gains the upper hand and what sort of resources each of us has. But if Russia wins and pins us to the wall, Berlin will tell her 'Stop!' And Berlin would never permit any real injury— at least no truly serious injury—to be inflicted on us, although some small damage might be done. And since Russia will not resolve to go against both us and Berlin, the matter will be settled without doing us any great harm; yet we have a chance to win a great deal if we beat Russia. And so on the one hand we have a chance of winning a great deal, and on the other hand we have little to lose if Russia defeats us. This is very good, very politic. And Berlin is our friend; she loves us deeply because she wants to take our German possessions from us; and she certainly will take them, and perhaps quite soon. But since this is the cause of her great love for us, she will certainly compensate us for the German possessions she seizes and in their place will give us the right to rule over the Turkish Slavs. Berlin will certainly do that, because it will be much to her advantage: if we gain the Slavs as compensation, we will still be nowhere near to rivaling Berlin in strength; but if Russia gains the Slavs, Russia will be superior to Berlin. That is why we, not Russia, will get the Slavs; that is why I could not resist and said it in my speech to the Slavic leaders. We must prepare them bit by bit for the proper ideas...."

It's quite possible that these are not only Rodich's ideas and that they are shared by the Austrians generally. And, of course, there is such a chaotic situation there. Just imagine the Slavs coming under Austrian rule and Austria at once trying to Germanify them, even after having lost her own German possessions! It's true enough, however, that in Europe it is not only Austria who is inclined to believe, first, in Russia's impotence and, second, in Russia's avidity to bring the Slavs under her rule as soon as possible. The most complete revolution in Russia's political life will come precisely when Europe becomes convinced that Russia has no desire to bring anything under her rule. Then a new era will begin, both for us and for the whole of Europe. This conviction of Russia's disinterest, should it come, will at once renew and change the whole face of Europe. Ultimately this conviction will come about, but not as the result of any assurance from us: until the very end, Europe will not believe any of our assurances and will keep on looking at us with hostility. It is difficult to imagine the depth of their fear of us. And if they fear us, then they must also hate us. Europe dislikes us immensely, and has never liked us; she has never considered us as one of her own, a fellow European, but always only as an annoying newcomer. That is why she is sometimes so fond of consoling herself with the thought that Russia supposedly is "still impotent."

And it is a good thing that she is inclined to think that way. I am convinced that the most terrible disaster would have befallen

Russia had we been victorious in the Crimean campaign, for example, and gained the upper hand over the allies! Once they saw how strong we are, everyone in Europe would have at once risen up against us with a fanatical hatred. Of course, had they been beaten, they would have signed a peace treaty that was unfavorable to them, but no peace could ever have been achieved in actual fact. They would immediately have begun preparing for a new war with the aim of annihilating Russia; most important, the whole world would have been behind them. The year 1863 would then have cost us more than an exchange of caustic diplomatic notes: on the contrary, a general crusade against Russia would have begun. Moreover, some European governments would certainly have used this crusade to settle their internal affairs, so that it would have been advantageous to them in all respects. The revolutionary parties and all those who were dissatisfied with the French government of the day, for example, would have quickly come to the side of the government in view of its "most sacred ideal"—the expulsion of Russia from Europe—and the war would have been a popular one. But Fate was looking out for us in tipping the scales in favor of the allies while preserving and even magnifying all our military honor so that we were able to bear this defeat. In a word, we endured the defeat, but the burden of victory over Europe we would never have been able to endure, despite all our vitality and strength. In just the same way Fate saved us once before, at the beginning of the century, when we threw off Napoleon's yoke from Europe; Fate saved us specifically by giving us Prussia and Austria as allies. Had we then been victorious alone, Europe would no sooner have recovered from Napoleon than—without Napoleon—she would immediately have thrown herself on us once more. But things happened differently, thank God: Prussia and Austria, whom we liberated, quickly took all the honor of victory for themselves, and later on—nowadays, that is—they flatly claim that they were victorious by themselves, while Russia only hindered them.

And in general our European fate has so placed us that we simply cannot make conquests in Europe even if we had the ability to do so: this would be something highly dangerous and not at all in our best interest. They might "forgive" us some of our private, domestic victories—the conquest of the Caucasus, for example. But the first war with Turkey, under the late emperor, and our settling affairs in Poland, which followed shortly thereafter, came very close to causing an explosion all over Europe. They have evidently now "forgiven" us our recent acquisitions in central Asia, but the frogs are still croaking over there, and they won't settle down.

Nonetheless, the course of events will probably very soon change the way in which the European nations regard Russia. In my last *Diary* in March, I set forth a few of my musings about Europe's immediate future. But I can say (and this is not musing but almost a certainty) that even in the immediate and, perhaps, the very near future Russia will prove to be stronger than anyone else in Europe. This will happen because the great powers in Europe will be destroyed for one very simple reason: they will all be rendered impotent and undermined by the unsatisfied democratic aspirations of an immense part of their own lower-class subjects—their proletariat and their paupers. This simply cannot happen in Russia: our demos is content, and the farther we go, the more satisfied it will become, for everything is moving toward that end via the common mood or, to put it better, the general consensus. And therefore there will remain but one colossus on the continent of Europe—Russia. This will happen, perhaps, even much sooner than people think. The future of Europe belongs to Russia. But the question is: what will Russia do in Europe then? What role will she play in it? Is she prepared for this role?

2. A Paradoxicalist

By the way, a word or two about war and rumors of war. I know a man who is a paradoxicalist. I have known him for a long time. He is an obscure person with an odd character: he is a *dreamer.* I shall certainly talk about him in more detail sometime. But now I recall how once, some years ago, he got into an argument with me about war. He defended war in general and did so, perhaps, solely out of his love of paradox. I can tell you that he is a civilian and the most peaceable, affable person you could find on earth and here in Petersburg.

"It is an outrageous notion," he said, in passing, "that war is the scourge of mankind. On the contrary, it is a most useful thing. There is only one form of war that is hateful and truly pernicious: that is a civil, fratricidal war. It paralyzes and shatters the state; it always goes on too long; and it brutalizes the people for centuries on end. But a political, international war brings only benefit in every respect, and thus it is absolutely essential."

"Wait now—a nation goes against another nation, and people set out to kill one another—what is essential in that?"

"Everything is, and to the highest degree. But in the first place, it's a lie that people set forth to kill one another; this is never uppermost in their minds. On the contrary, they set out to sacrifice their own lives; that must be uppermost in their minds. And that is something altogether different. There is no idea more elevated than sacrificing one's own life while defending one's brothers and one's fatherland or even simply defending the interests of one's fatherland. Humanity cannot live without noble ideas, and I even suspect that humanity loves war precisely in order to be a part of some noble idea. It is a human need."

"But does humanity really love war?"

"Of course it does. Who is in low spirits in time of war? Quite the contrary: everyone is full of cheer, their spirits rise, and there is no mention of the usual apathy or boredom you hear of in peacetime. And then, when the war ends, how people love to reminisce about it, even if they were defeated! And don't believe those who, when they meet during time of war, shake their heads and say to each other: 'Such a calamity. We've come to this!' They're only being polite. In reality, everyone is a festive mood. Do you know, there are some ideas one finds terribly difficult to admit having. People will call you a beast and a reactionary and condemn you; they fear these ideas. No one dares to praise war."

"But you're talking about noble ideas and about humanizing. Can't there be noble ideas without war? On the contrary, in peacetime there is even more scope for such ideas to flourish."

"No, it's quite the reverse. Nobility perishes during periods of prolonged peace, and in its place appear cynicism, indifference, boredom, and, most of all, an attitude of malicious mockery—and that almost as an idle pastime, not for any serious purpose. I can say positively that a prolonged peace hardens people's hearts. During such a prolonged peace the social balance always shifts to the side of all that is stupid and coarse in humanity, principally toward wealth and capital. Immediately after a war honor, philanthropy, and self-sacrifice are respected, valued, and highly regarded; but the longer the peace lasts, the more these beautiful, noble things grow pale, wither, and die off, while everyone is in the grip of wealth and the spirit of acquisition. In the end, the only thing left is hypocrisy—hypocrisy of honor, self-sacrifice, and duty; these things may continue to be respected despite all the cynicism, but only formally, in fine words. There will be no genuine honor, but the formulas will remain. When honor becomes a formula, it dies. A prolonged peace produces apathy, mean-spirited ideas, depravity, a dulling of the feelings. Pleasures do not grow refined but coarsen. Crude wealth cannot take delight in nobility but demands less elevated and more immediate pleasures, i.e., the most direct satisfaction of the urges of the flesh. Pleasures become carnivorous. Sensuality evokes lechery, and lechery is always cruel. You cannot deny all this, because you cannot deny the main fact: that the social balance during a prolonged peace in the end always shifts toward crude wealth."

"But science, the arts—can they truly flourish in wartime? And these are great and noble ideas."

"Ah, but this is where I catch you. Science and the arts flourish particularly in the immediate postwar period. War renews and refreshes them; it stimulates and strengthens thought and gives it some impetus. But a long peace, on the other hand, will stifle even science. There's no doubt that the pursuit of science demands a certain nobility, even self-denial. But can many of these scientists survive the pestilence of peace? False honor, self-love, and sensuality will catch them up as well. Just try to cope with a passion like envy, for example: it is crude and vulgar, but it also will find its way into the noblest heart of a scientist. He, too, will want to participate in the general prosperity and glamour. Compared to the triumph of wealth, what can the triumph of some scientific discovery mean, unless it is something as sensational as the discovery of the planet Neptune, for example? Now what do you think: will there be many left who are truly devoted to humble toil? On the contrary, there will be a desire for fame, and so charlatanism will invade science; there will be the pursuit of the sensational; and there will be utilitarianism above all, because there will be a desire for wealth as well. The same will be true of art: the same pursuit of the sensational, the ultrarefined. Simple, clear, noble, and healthy ideas will no longer be in fashion: something much meatier will be in demand; simulated passions will be in demand. Little by little the sense of measure and harmony will be lost; distorted feelings and passions will appear—the so-called ultrarefinement of the feelings which in essence is only their vulgarization. Art inevitably falls victim to this at the end of a prolonged peace. Had war never existed on this earth, art would have completely died. All the best ideas of art are provided by war and by struggle. Think of tragedy, look at statues: here is Corneille's *Horace*; here is the Apollo Belvedere overpowering a monster...."

"And what about the Madonnas; what about Christianity?"

"Christianity itself recognizes the fact of war and prophesies that the sword shall not pass until the end of the world: this is quite remarkable and striking. Oh, there's no doubt that in the highest sense, in the moral sense, it rejects war and demands brotherly love. I myself shall be the first to rejoice when the swords are beaten into plowshares. But the question is: when is this going to happen? And is it worth beating the swords into plowshares at present? The peace of today is always and everywhere worse than war, so much worse that it even becomes immoral in the end to support the peace. It is nothing to value, nothing worth preserving; it is shameful and vulgar to preserve it. Wealth and vulgarity give birth to indolence, and indolence gives birth to slaves. In order to keep slaves in their servile state, one must take away their free will and their opportunity to better themselves. For can you not help but feel the need to have a slave, even though you may be the most humane sort of person? I note as well that during a period of peace cowardice and dishonesty take root. Man by nature is terribly inclined to cowardice and shameless acts, and he himself knows this very well. And that, perhaps, is why he is so fond of war: he senses a medicine in it. War fosters brotherly love and unites nations."

"How does it unite nations?"

"By forcing them to respect one another. War refreshes people. Love for one's fellow human beings develops best on the field of battle. It's a strange fact, indeed, that war does less to rouse people's anger than peace. In fact, something that could be considered a political outrage in time of peace, some treaty that demanded too much, some political pressure, some demand couched in arrogant language—of the sort that Europe made of us in 1863—all these things rouse people's anger much more than open warfare. Think back: did we hate the French and the English during the Crimean campaign? Not in the least; in fact we seemed to grow closer to them, almost as if they had become our kin. We were interested to hear their views on our courage in battle; we treated their prisoners with great kindness; during times of truce our soldiers and our officers left their forward positions and almost embraced the enemy; they even drank vodka together. Russia was delighted to read about this in the newspapers, yet it did not prevent us from putting up a magnificent fight. A spirit of chivalry was fostered. And I won't even bring up the material losses of war: everyone knows the law by which things seem to come to life with renewed vigor in the postwar period. The economic forces of the country are stimulated ten times more than before, just as if a storm cloud had poured down an abundant rain on the parched earth. Everyone at once lends a hand to those who have suffered during the war, while in peacetime whole provinces can die of hunger before we get around to doing anything or donating a few rubles."

"But don't the People suffer more than anyone else in wartime? Don't they suffer the ruination and bear burdens that are inevitable and incomparably greater than those borne by the upper levels of society?"

"Perhaps, but only temporarily. Yet they do gain much more than they lose. It is specifically for the People that war has the finest and the most sublime consequences. Say what you like: you may be the most humane person, yet you still consider yourself above the common folk. These days who measures soul against soul by a Christian standard? The standard is money, power, and strength, and the common folk as a mass know this very well. This isn't exactly envy; there is some oppressive feeling of moral inequality here that is extremely painful for the common person to live with. You can liberate them however you like and write any sort of laws you choose, but inequality cannot be ended in today's society. The only medicine is war. It is only a palliative, and it is instantaneous, but it brings comfort to the People. War raises the spirits of the People and their awareness of their own dignity. War makes everyone equal in time of battle and reconciles the master and the slave in the most sublime manifestation of human dignity—the sacrifice of life for the common cause, for everyone, and for the fatherland. Do you really think that the masses, even the most benighted masses of peasants and beggars, do not feel this urge for an *active* display of noble feelings? And how can the mass show its nobility and its human dignity in time of peace? We look at isolated noble acts among the common People, barely condescending to take notice of them, sometimes with a skeptical smile, sometimes simply not believing what we've seen. And when we do acknowledge the heroism of some isolated individual, we at once make a fuss as if it were something utterly unusual; the result is that our astonishment and our praise amount to contempt. All this disappears of its own accord in time of war and there ensues the complete equality of heroism. Blood that has been shed is an important thing. A noble exploit that is shared creates the most solid bond between unequal classes. The landowner and the peasant were closer to each other on the battlefield in 1812 than they were while living on some peaceful estate in the country. War gives the masses a reason to respect themselves, and therefore the People love war: they compose songs about it, and for many years thereafter they are eager to hear stories and legends about it.... Blood that has been shed is an important thing! Say what you like, but war *in our time* is necessary; without it the world would have collapsed or, at least, would have been transformed into some sort of slime, some squalid muck full of putrefaction...."

I gave up the argument, of course. There is no point in arguing with dreamers. There is, however, one very strange fact: people are now beginning to argue and raise issues that, it would seem, were long ago resolved and consigned to the archives. These things are all being dug up once more. And what's most important is that this is happening everywhere.

3. Just a Bit More about Spiritualism

Once again I don't have enough space left for a proper article about spiritualism, and once again I must postpone it to another issue. However, back in February I attended a spiritualists' seance conducted by a "genuine" medium, and this seance impressed me rather strongly. Others who were present have already commented on it in the press, so that it seems I have nothing left to pass on beyond my own personal impressions. But I didn't want to write anything about it until now, and I have *concealed* my impressions from the reader these two whole months. I will say in advance that my impression was of a most peculiar sort and scarcely had anything to do with spiritualism. My impression arose from something else that only came to light apropos of spiritualism. I am very sorry to have to postpone it again, all the more because now I have the urge to talk about it, whereas previously I found it rather distasteful. This distaste arose from an almost morbid sense of doubt. I did tell some of my friends about the seance at the time; one person, whose opinions I value greatly, heard me out and then asked if I intended to describe it in the *Diary*. I replied that I still did not know. And suddenly he remarked, "Don't write about it." He added nothing more, and I did not press him but I caught his

drift: he would have been displeased, apparently, if I should somehow have promoted the spread of spiritualism. At the time I was
particularly struck by this, because in my remarks about the February seance I had, to the contrary, dismissed spiritualism with
sincere conviction. Yet this person, who hates spiritualism, must
have discerned in my account *something* that seemed to place it in
a favorable light despite all my attempts to dismiss it. That is why
I refrained from discussing it in print until now—precisely out of
my sense of doubt and lack of self-confidence. But now, I think,
I have complete confidence in myself and have cleared my doubts.
Besides, I am convinced that no article of mine could work either
to support or destroy spiritualism. Mr. Mendeleev, who is delivering
his lecture in Solianoi Gorodok at the very moment I am writing
these lines, probably looks at the matter differently and is lecturing
with the noble intent of "crushing spiritualism." It's always pleasant to listen to lectures with such admirable tendencies; yet I think
that whoever *wants* to put his faith in spiritualism will not be
stopped by lectures or even by entire commissions, while those
who do not believe, at least if they truly *do not want* to believe,
will not be swayed by anything. That was precisely the conviction
I took away from the February seance at A. N. Aksakov's; it was,
at least, my first strong impression then. Up to that time I had
simply rejected spiritualism, i.e., in essence I was perturbed only
by the mystical sense of its doctrine. (I was never able *completely*
to reject spiritualistic phenomena, with which I had had some
acquaintance even before the seance with the medium, nor can I
now—especially now—after having read the report of the Scholarly
Commission on Spiritualism.) But after that remarkable seance I
suddenly surmised—or rather, I suddenly discovered—not only that
I do not believe in spiritualism but that I haven't the least *wish* to
believe in it, so that there is no evidence that will *ever* cause me
to change my views. That is what I took away from the seance and
later came to understand. And, I confess, this impression was
almost gratifying because I had been a little apprehensive on my
way to the seance. I might add that this is not merely a personal
matter: I think there is something that applies to us all in this
observation of mine. I have a sense of some special law of human
nature, common to all and pertaining specifically to faith and disbelief in general. I somehow came to understand then—specifically
through experience, specifically through this seance—what power
disbelief can uncover and develop within you at a given moment,

absolutely despite your own will, although it may be in accordance with your secret desire. . . . The same thing is probably true of faith. That's what I wanted to talk about.

And so, until the next issue. But now, let me add a few more words to supplement what I have already said in the March issue regarding that same Report of the Commission that is now well known to us all.

I said a few words then about the unsatisfactory nature of the report and about how it might even be damaging to its own cause. But I did not say the most important thing. I shall now try to amplify this briefly, the more so that this is a very simple matter. The commission did not want to concede the most important need in this affair, the need of the society that was awaiting its decision. The commission, it seems, had so little concern for society's need (otherwise one would have to suppose that it was simply unable to understand that need) that it even failed to understand that "some little crinoline springs flashing in the darkness" are not enough to dissuade anyone and will not establish anything after people have already been harmed. When one reads the report it certainly begins to appear that these scholars of ours assumed a spiritualism that existed in Petersburg only in A. N. Aksakov's apartment and seemed to know nothing at all of that avid interest in spiritualism which has sprung up in our society and of the grounds on which spiritualism has begun to spread specifically among us Russians. In fact they did know all this; they just ignored it. Everything indicates that they regarded all this in the same way as those private individuals who, when hearing about the our society's fatal mania for spiritualism, can only sneer and giggle, and that only in passing, believing it scarcely worth serious thought. But once they were organized into a commission, these scholars became public figures and not private individuals. They were given a mission, and that fact, it seems, they did not take into account; they took their seats at the spiritualist's table while continuing as private individuals just as before, that is to say, laughing, sneering, and giggling, and also, perhaps, a little angry at having to concern themselves seriously with such a ridiculous thing.

Well, let us grant that this whole house, this whole apartment of A. N. Aksakov was strung out with springs and wires, while the medium had some sort of little machine between her feet to make clicking noises (this clever little theory was later advanced in print by N. P. Wagner). But every "serious" spiritualist (oh, don't laugh at that word; it's true—this is quite serious) will ask as he reads the report: "How is it that in my own house, where I know everyone—children, wife, family, acquaintances—perfectly well, how is it that these same things can happen in my house? The table rocks and rises up; we hear sounds; we get intelligent answers to our questions. I know very well and am completely convinced that there aren't any little machines or wires in my house and that my wife and children will not try to deceive me." The main point is that there are already quite a number of people—all too many of them, even—in Petersburg, Moscow, and Russia generally who will say or think this. And the commission should have thought about that, even if it meant descending from its scholarly heights; we have something like an epidemic, after all, and these people need to be helped. But the commission's haughtiness will permit no such thoughts: "It's simply a matter of frivolous and poorly educated people, and that's why they believe in it." "Very well," a serious and alarmingly convinced spiritualist continues to insist (for they are now still in their initial period of wonder and anxiety—it's such a new and unusual matter), "let's suppose that I am frivolous and poorly educated. Still, I have no such little machine making clicking noises anywhere in my house, and that I know very well; I don't even have the means to buy such amusing instruments; where to get them and who sells them and such like is, God knows, a total mystery to me. So what makes these clicking noises in my house and where do these sounds come from? You say that we ourselves are pressing on the table unconsciously. I assure you that we are not so childish as that; we watch one another carefully, very carefully, to see that we are not pushing the table ourselves. We are conducting experiments, with curiosity and objectivity. . . ."

"We have no answer for you," concludes the commission, now somewhat peeved. "You are being deceived just as all the others are; everyone is being deceived, and you are all fools. So it must be; so speaks Science; we are Science."

Well, that's not an explanation. "No, obviously something else is going on here," the convinced spiritualist will conclude "seriously." "It can't be all trickery. That may be true of Madame Claire, but I know my own family: there is no one in my house who would play such tricks." And spiritualism carries on.

Just now I read in *New Times* the account of Mr. Mendeleev's first lecture at Solianoi Gorodok. Mr. Mendeleev solidly affirms, as an established fact, that: "tables move and emit tapping sounds at spiritualist seances, both when hands are placed on the tables and when they are not. One can, with the help of a special alphabet, create from these sounds whole words, sentences and utterances that always bear the stamp of the mentality of that medium who is conducting the seance. This is a fact. Now we must explain who is doing the knocking and how. The following six hypotheses are set forth in explanation."

This is the most important point: "Who is doing the knocking and how?" And then six hypotheses which have already been made in Europe are set forth. It would seem that all six of these would be enough to dissuade even the most "serious" spiritualist. But for the honest spiritualist who *wants* to explain the matter, what is most interesting is not the fact that there are six hypotheses, but which of them Mr. Mendeleev himself believes. What does he say, and what was our commission's conclusion? Our own views are closer and more authoritative for us, while who knows what is going on over there in Europe or in the American States! It is evident from the rest of the account of the lecture that the commission has nevertheless accepted the hypothesis of conjuring tricks; and not just simple conjury, in fact, but preconceived deception with little machines held between the feet that make clicking noises (this, I repeat, according to the evidence of N. P. Wagner). But this is not enough; this scientific "haughtiness" is not enough for our spiritualists, not enough even in the event *that the commission was correct*. And this is the whole problem. Besides, who knows? Perhaps a "seriously" convinced spiritualist is right when he concludes that if spiritualism really is nonsense, then there still is something else at work here apart from gross deception, something that should be treated more gently, more delicately, so to say, because, after all, "his wife, his children, his friends would not deceive him," and so on and so on. Believe me, he has his own views on the matter, and you are not going to change his mind. He knows very well that not everything here is "deliberate deception." He has already convinced himself of that.

In fact, everything else that the commission has to say is almost as presumptuous as this: "They are frivolous people," the commission says, "and they themselves are unconsciously pushing the table, and that is what makes it rock; they want to deceive themselves, and so the table makes tapping sounds; their nerves are

frayed; they sit there in the dark; it's an accordion playing; little
hooks have been placed in their shirtsleeves" (this, at least, is what
Mr. Rachinsky supposes); "they lift the table with the tips of their
feet," etc., etc. And still this will convince none of those *who want
to be led astray.* "Come now, for Heaven's sake, my table must
weigh seventy pounds; I can't even move it with the tip of my foot
and there is no way I could raise it up into the air. Anyway, that
sort of thing just can't be done, unless by some sort of fakir or
magician or your Mrs. Claire with her little crinoline machine. But
I don't have any of those magicians or equilibrists in my family."
To put it briefly, spiritualism is, without a doubt, a great, extraordinary fallacy of the stupidest kind, an aberrant doctrine and a
form of ignorance; but the problem is that not everything around
the spiritualists' table happens as simply, perhaps, as the commission would have us believe, and one cannot call every single
spiritualist a fraud and a fool. This will only insult them all personally and so will achieve nothing. One should regard this fallacy,
I think, within the context of our current social conditions, and
therefore find a different tone and technique. We must give particular consideration to the mystical significance of spiritualism,
which is the most harmful thing that can be; but the commission
gave no thought at all to this facet of spiritualism. Of course, the
commission would not have had the ability to stamp out this evil
in any case; but at least it could—using other less naive and presumptuous methods—have instilled some respect for its conclusions
in spiritualists as well, and it could have had a powerful influence
on those followers who are still wavering. But the commission
evidently considered any approach to the matter other than as a
form of legerdemain (and not simple legerdemain but deliberate
deception) to be an insult to its scientific dignity. Every assumption
that spiritualism is *something* and not merely gross deceit and trickery the commission found unthinkable. Indeed, what would people
in Europe say about our scientists then? And so, by flatly assuming
that all that had to be done here was to expose the fraud and no
more, the scientists have thereby given their conclusions the appearance of being predetermined. Believe me, some clever spiritualist (I assure you that there are also clever people who think
deeply about spiritualism—they are not all stupid)—some clever
spiritualist will read the newspaper account of Mr. Mendeleev's
public lecture and see the following: "One can, with the help of
a special alphabet, create from these sounds whole words, sentences

and utterances *that always bear the stamp of the mentality of that medium who is conducting the seance.* This is a fact." And when he reads that, he will most likely think to himself: "This inevitable 'stamp of the mentality of the medium,' now, is very likely the most important point in the whole investigation, and the conclusion should have been made on the basis of the most careful experiments; but here is our commission, which only just sat down to do its task (and how long did they spend on it?), when they at once determined that *this is a fact.* A fact, indeed! Perhaps it relied in this instance on some German or French opinion, but in that case where is the commission's own experience? This is only an opinion, not a conclusion drawn from its own experience. They could not reach a conclusion about the answers given by tables 'corresponding to the mentality of the medium' on the basis of Mrs. Claire alone and make it a general fact. Indeed, they have scarcely examined the higher, intellectual, cerebral aspect of Mrs. Claire, but have only found a little machine that emits clicks; and even that was located in an altogether different place from her brain. Mr. Mendeleev was a member of the commission, and when he delivered his lecture he spoke, as it were, representing the commission. No, such a quick and hasty conclusion by the commission *on such an important point of inquiry* and using such trivial experiments—this is too presumptuous and is, as well, scarcely scientific. . . ."

Indeed, people may think that. So such haughty superficiality in *certain* conclusions will give society and, most of all, those spiritualists who are already convinced a reason to hold even more strongly to their fallacies: "Presumption," they will say, "pride, prejudice, preconceived ideas. They're much too grumpy! . . ." And spiritualism will carry on.

P.S. I have just read the account of Mr. Mendeleev's second lecture on spiritualism. Mr. Mendeleev is already saying the commission's report has had a salutary influence on writers: "Suvorin no longer is such a believer in spiritualism as before; Boborykin, too, has evidently been cured, or at least is on the road to recovery. Finally, Dostoevsky in his *Diary* has made a recovery as well: in January he was inclined toward spiritualism, but in March he attacks it. It seems that the 'Report' has had something to do with this." So, it seems the esteemed Mr. Mendeleev thought that I was praising spiritualism in January. I wonder if that was because of the devils?

Mr. Mendeleev must be an unusually kindly man. Just imagine: after having crushed spiritualism in two lectures, he sets to praising it in the conclusion of his second lecture. And what do you think he praises it for? "Honor and glory to spiritualists." (Well now! We've gotten to the point of honor and glory, but why so suddenly?) "Honor and glory to the spiritualists," he said, "for emerging as honorable and bold fighters for what they consider the truth, without fear of prejudices!" It's evident that this was said out of pity and, so to say, from a sense of tact caused by a surfeit of his own success; but I don't know whether it came out tactfully. This is just the way in which the proprietors of boarding schools sometimes attest to the qualities of their pupils before their parents: "Now while this young man cannot boast of the same intellectual capacities as his elder brother, and even though he won't go far, still he is pure in heart and is always very reliable." Imagine what the younger brother thinks when he hears this! Mr. Mendeleev also praised the spiritualists (and once more with "honor and glory") for taking an interest in the soul in this materialistic age of ours. They may be a bit shaky in the sciences, he says, but they are firm in the faith, they believe in God. The esteemed professor, it seems, is a great one for a joke. But if he has said this out of naiveté and not as a joke, then he must be quite the opposite: he must have no sense of humor at all. . . .

4. On Behalf of One Deceased

I read with a heavy heart the story appearing in *New Times* and reprinted from *The Cause*, a story that casts shame on the memory of my brother Mikhail Mikhailovich, the founder and publisher of the journals *Time* and *The Epoch*, who died twelve years ago. I quote the story in full:

> In 1862, when Shchapov no longer wanted to deal with the *Notes of the Fatherland* of the time and the other journals had been temporarily suspended, he sent his article "The Runners" to *Time*. That autumn he was in great financial need, but the late editor of *Time*, Mikhail Dostoevsky, held up the payment due to Shchapov for a long time. The cold weather set in, and Shchapov did not even have warm clothes. Finally he lost his temper and summoned Dostoevsky, whereupon the following scene took place: "Please try to be patient, dear Afanasy Prokopevich; I'll bring you all your money in a week," said Dostoevsky. "But can't you understand, I need the money now!"

"Why must you have it now?" "I don't have a warm overcoat; I don't even have any warm clothes." "I'll tell you what: I know a tailor who'll give you what you need on credit. I'll pay him later out of your money." And Dostoevsky took Shchapov to a Jewish tailor who supplied the historian with an overcoat of sorts and a waistcoat and trousers of most dubious quality and for which he was billed very dearly, something which later caused even the impractical Shchapov to complain.

This is from Shchapov's obituary in *The Cause*. I don't know who wrote it; I haven't yet asked the people there and haven't read the obituary itself. As I said above, I am taking it from *New Times*.

My brother died a long time ago: the matter thus is an old, obscure one; it is difficult to defend him, and there are no witnesses to the incident described. The accusation, thus, is unsubstantiated. But I state flatly that this whole story is ridiculous, and if there are some things in it that have not been invented, then at least all the facts are distorted and the truth has been very badly mangled. I shall demonstrate this as best I can.

First of all, I declare that I took no part in my brother's financial affairs concerning the journal or in his previous business dealings. Although I worked with my brother in editing *Time*, I had no connection with any monetary matters. Still, I know very well that the journal *Time* had a brilliant success by the standards of the day. I also know that not only did the journal not incur debts to writers but that, to the contrary, it constantly advanced large payments to contributors. This I certainly do know and witnessed many times. And the journal was not short of contributors: they came of their own accord and sent in great numbers of articles, beginning even from the first year we published. One need only look through the issues of *Time* over the whole two and one-half years of its life to see that a huge majority of the literary figures of the day took part in it. That would not have been the case had my brother not paid contributors or, more precisely, had he treated them dishonorably. However, many people even now can testify to the advance payment of substantial sums of money. This did not happen in some dark corner. Many of those who once worked, and worked quite closely, with the journal and who are still living will, of course, not refuse to attest to how, in their view and to their recollection, my brother managed the journal's affairs. Briefly, then, my brother could not have "held back payment to Shchapov," particularly if Shchapov were without proper clothes. If Shchapov had summoned my brother, it was not because he "lost his temper" over nonpayment, but specifically because he was *asking for money in advance* like many others. Many letters and notes from contributors to the editor have been preserved, and I do not lose hope that Shchapov's notes will be found among them. Then the nature of their relationship will be clarified. Aside from this, however, the fact that Shchapov was then most likely asking for money in advance is doubtless more in accord with the truth and with all the recollections and accounts of how *Time* was managed and published; and, I repeat, one could collect many such accounts even now, fourteen years later. Despite his good business sense, my brother was rather vulnerable to requests and did not know how to say no: he would advance money, sometimes without even the hope of receiving in return an article for the journal. I witnessed this and could mention certain names. But my brother had other experiences as well. One of our *regular* contributors asked him for a six-hundred-ruble advance, and the very next morning went off to serve in the Western Provinces where government officials were then being recruited; and there he stayed, sending neither articles nor money. But what is most remarkable is that my brother did not take a single step to recover the money, despite the fact that he had a document in his hands. Only many years later, after his death, did my brother's family manage to recover the money from this person (a man of means) through a lawsuit. This was a publicly tried case, and the precise details of it are available. I wanted only to show how easily and readily my brother sometimes advanced money and that a man such as he would not have held back payment to a writer in need. The person who wrote Shchapov's obituary, when listening to my brother's conversation with Shchapov, might simply not have known specifically which money was at issue: money owed by my brother or money which he had advanced. It is also quite possible that my brother suggested that Shchapov order clothes on credit from a tailor he knew. This is a very simple matter: not wanting to refuse Shchapov help, he might, for his own reasons, have preferred this means rather than giving Shchapov a direct monetary advance. . . .

Finally, I don't recognize my brother's manner of speaking in the story quoted: he would never have spoken in *such a tone*. This is not him at all. My brother never tried to ingratiate himself with anyone. He could not hover over another person, dripping honeyed phrases and sweet words. And of course he would never have permitted anyone to say to him: "Can't you understand, I need the money now!" The author of this anecdote has, in the course of fourteen years, somehow transformed and rewritten these words into full-scale reminiscences in accordance with a point of view we all know very well. Let everyone who remembers my brother (and there are many) recall whether he ever spoke in such a fashion. My brother was an exceptionally decent man and he conducted himself like the gentleman he truly was. He was highly educated, a gifted writer, an expert on European literatures, a poet, and a well-known translator of Schiller and Goethe. I cannot conceive how such a man could grovel before Shchapov as this "anecdote" suggests.

Let me cite one more fact about my late brother, one that is little known, I think. In 1849 he was arrested over the Petrashevsky affair and spent two months imprisoned in the fortress. When two months had passed, several persons (quite a number, in fact) were freed as innocent and uninvolved in the case. And this truly was so: my brother had taken no part either in the secret society of Petrashevsky or of Durov. Nevertheless, he attended Petrashevsky's "evenings" and borrowed books from the society's secret library, which was located in Petrashevsky's house. At that time he was a Fourierist and was studying Fourier with a passion. So it was that during these two months in the fortress he could in no way consider himself out of danger and count on being let off. The facts that he was a Fourierist and that he used the library were discovered, and of course he could expect a term of exile—if not in Siberia then in some remote area—as a suspicious person. And many of those freed after two months surely would have been exiled (and this I can state for certain) had they not been let off by command of the late emperor. I learned of this at the time from Prince Gagarin, who was conducting the whole investigation into the Petrashevsky case. At least I learned then of the facts of my brother's release; Prince Gagarin told me of it in order to raise my spirits, having had me brought specially from the casemate to the commandant's house where the case was being heard. I was alone, a bachelor and childless; but when my brother went to the fortress he left a frightened wife and three children in his apartment; his eldest child was then only seven, and the family were left penniless as well. My brother loved his children tenderly and ardently, and I can imagine what he went through during those two months! Yet he gave *no testimony* that might have compromised others in order to ease his own lot, even though he could have said things; although he took no part in anything, he still *knew a great deal.* Are there many who would act that way in his place, I ask you? I ask the question frankly because I know what I am talking about. I know and have seen how people react to such adversities, so I am not looking at this merely from a theoretical point of view. People may judge this act of my brother as they like, yet he refused to do anything contrary to his convictions even to save himself. This is no mere unsubstantiated statement: I can support everything that I say with the most accurate evidence. Meanwhile, every day and every hour for two months my brother was tormented by the thought that he was destroying his family, and he suffered in thinking of those three dear little creatures and what awaited them. . . . And now people want to show such a man in collusion with some Jew tailor to cheat Shchapov so that he and the tailor might share the profit and put a few rubles in their pockets! What utter rubbish!

May

1

1. From a Private Letter

People ask if I am planning to write about the Kairova case. I have already had several letters asking this question. One letter is especially characteristic and was not, apparently, written for publication; still, I'll venture to quote a few lines of it while preserving strict anonymity, of course. I hope that my worthy correspondent will not complain; I'm quoting him only because I am convinced of his complete sincerity, which I can fully respect.

> . . . It was with a feeling of the deepest repugnance that we read about the Kairova case. This case reveals, as in the focus of a lens, a picture of the carnal instincts which the leading personage of the case (Kairova) developed under the influence of her milieu: her mother, during pregnancy, abandoned herself to drink; her father was a drunkard; her brother lost his mind because of drink and shot himself; a cousin murdered his wife; her father's mother was insane. And this was the milieu that gave birth to a despotic person with unbridled carnal urges. Even those who prosecuted the case were baffled by her and had to ask themselves whether she was insane. Some of the experts positively denied this, while others admitted the possibility of insanity, not in her personally, but in her actions. Yet it is not insanity that one sees through this whole trial; it is a woman who has reached the extreme limits of rejection of everything sacred: for her there exists neither the family nor the rights of another woman—not only that woman's right to a husband but to her very life: all these things exist for herself and her carnal lusts alone.
>
> She was acquitted, perhaps, on grounds of insanity, and we must thank God for that! At least moral depravity was attributed not to intellectual progress but to the category of mental illnesses.
>
> However, in the "lower section of the courtroom, filled *exclusively with ladies*, applause broke out" (*Stock Exchange News*).

471

What was the applause for? Was it for the acquittal of an insane
woman, or was it for the triumph of an uncontrolled, passionate nature,
for the cynicism the woman personifies?

Ladies applaud! Wives and mothers applaud! They ought to weep
and not applaud the spectacle of such desecration of the feminine
ideal. . . .

[N.B. I omit several very harsh lines here.]

Will you really pass over this case in silence?

2. A New Regional Voice

It is too late to bring up the story of Kairova (which, I think,
everyone already knows), and in any case I can give no special
significance to my remarks on such typical phenomena of today's
life, and amid such typical public feeling. But it still would be
worth saying a few words apropos of this "case," late though they
may be. For nothing ever comes to an end, and so nothing can
ever be too late; every event continues and takes on new forms,
even though it may have finished its initial stage of development.
But the main thing, again, is that I hope my correspondent forgives
me for quoting parts of his letter. Judging only by the letters I
receive personally, I could draw a conclusion about one extremely
important fact of our Russian life which I have already hinted at
indirectly not long ago: namely, that everyone is restless, everyone
wants to participate in everything, everyone wants to express an
opinion and state his views; the one thing that I cannot make up
my mind about is whether each person wants to dissociate himself
through his opinions or join his voice in one common, harmonious
choir. This letter from the provinces is a private one, but I remark
here in this connection that our provinces truly want to live their
own kinds of lives and almost emancipate themselves altogether
from the capitals. I am not the only one who has remarked on this,
and it was stated in the press long before I said it. For two whole
months now I have had lying on my desk a literary anthology, *The
First Step*, published in Kazan; and some comment really ought
to be made about it, precisely because it comes with the specific
intention of stating a new point of view, not a view from the capital
city, but a regional and "urgently necessary" view. Well, these are
all only new voices in the old Russian choir; therefore they are
useful and, at least, interesting. This new tendency must stem from
something, after all. It is true of all these proposed "new voices"

that none, in essence, has yet spoken up; yet perhaps we really may hear something from our regions and border areas that we have never heard before. Judging theoretically and in the abstract, it should happen this way: from the time of Peter the Great to the present, Petersburg and Moscow have been leading Russia; but now, when the role of Petersburg and the cultural period of "the window cut through to Europe" have come to an end—now. . . . But that's just the question: have the roles of Petersburg and Moscow really been played out? As I see it, if these roles have changed, they have changed very little; and even formerly, all through those one hundred and fifty years, were Petersburg and Moscow really leading Russia? Was that how things were in actual fact? Was it not, to the contrary, the whole of Russia that flowed and crowded into Petersburg and Moscow for the entire century and a half so that, in essence, the country has been leading itself, constantly renewing itself with this fresh flow of new forces from her regions and fringes, in which, I might note in passing, the problems were exactly the same as those of all the Russians in Moscow or Petersburg, in Riga or in the Caucasus, or anywhere else. If one judges by theory and by principle, after all, what two things could be more opposed to one another than Petersburg and Moscow? Petersburg in fact was founded in opposition to Moscow and *her whole idea*, as it were. And yet these *two centers* of Russian life in essence have comprised but one center; and this was true immediately, from the very beginning, from the very time of Peter's reforms, despite certain traits that set the two cities apart. Exactly in the same way, those things that originated and developed in Petersburg quickly and *exactly as independently* originated, were consolidated and developed in Moscow, and vice versa. There was one soul, and not only in these two cities, but in any two cities anywhere in Russia *so that all over Russia and in every place there existed the whole of Russia.* Oh, we realize that each corner of Russia can and should have its local peculiarities and the complete right to foster them; but are these peculiarities such as to threaten spiritual dissolution or even simply confusion of some sort? On the whole, what lie ahead of us are "unknown waters," but this point I think is clearer than anything else. In any case, God grant that everything that can develop does develop—at least every good thing; this is the first point. The second and main point is: God grant we do not lose our sense of unity, no matter what blessings, promises, and treasures are given in exchange; it is better that we are together than apart, and this is the main thing. We will hear a new voice, of this I have no doubt; yet I do not think that anything very new and distinctive will be said by our regions and fringe areas, not at the moment at least, and nothing unprecedented or hard to tolerate. The Great Russian is only now beginning to live, only now rising up to utter his word, perhaps to the whole world. And therefore I think that Moscow, this center for the Great Russian, will live for a long time yet, and God grant it be so. Moscow has still not been the third Rome, yet the prophecy must be fulfilled because "there will be no fourth Rome." The world cannot get by without its Rome. And Petersburg is now more than ever at one with Moscow. I admit that, when I say "Moscow" here, I mean not so much the city itself as I do a kind of allegory, as it were, so that there is no cause for any Kazan or Astrakhan to feel offended. But we are happy to see their anthologies, and if a *Second Step* should make its appearance, then so much the better, so much the better.

3. The Court and Mrs. Kairova

However, we've strayed far from the Kairova case. I wanted only to draw my correspondent's attention to the fact that, although I agree with his view on the "depraved instincts and despotic lack of restraint of her urges," I still find the opinions of my worthy correspondent to be overly harsh; there is not even any point to his harshness (for he all but admits that the woman is insane); he also exaggerates unduly, the more so that he finishes by acknowledging *the influence of the environment* almost to the point of admitting the futility of struggling against it. As for me, I am just happy that Kairova was released; I am only unhappy that she was acquitted. I am happy she was released, even though I don't for a moment believe she is insane, despite the views of some experts: accept this as my personal opinion, which I will not force on anyone else. Besides, if this poor woman is not insane, one feels even more pity for her. If she is insane, then "she knew not what she did"; but if she is not, how will she be able to go off bearing such a burden of torment! A murder, at least when it is not committed by some "Jack of Hearts," is a difficult and a complex thing. These several days of her indecision after the lawful wife of Kairova's lover returned to him; her sense of insult that kept seething away day after day; her resentment that grew stronger every hour (oh, Kairova is the offender here—I still haven't lost my senses—but what is all the more pitiable is that in her fall she could not even understand that it was she who was the offender and kept seeing and feeling exactly the opposite!); and finally, this last hour before the "deed," at night, on the stairs, holding the razor that she had bought the day before—say what you will, but this is all rather difficult to bear, especially for such a disorderly and unstable soul as Kairova! The burden is too much for her; one seems to hear her groans as she is crushed by it. And then, ten months of tribulations, madhouses, experts. How they dragged her about here and there and everywhere, and all the while this wretched, heinous criminal, completely guilty, represents in essence something so lacking in seriousness, so careless, so totally uncomprehending and unaccomplished, trivial, licentious, incapable of self-control, and mediocre—and so she was to the very last moment of the verdict, so that it somehow was a relief when she was let off. It's a pity only that this could not have been done without acquitting her because—say what you like—it caused a scandal. I think that Mr. Utin, her attorney, should certainly have sensed an acquittal coming and so could have limited himself simply to setting forth the facts rather than starting in to sing praises to the crime, because he *almost sang praises to the crime*, after all. . . . That's just the point: we have no sense of measure in anything. In the West, Darwin's theory is a brilliant hypothesis; in Russia it has long become an axiom. In the West the notion that crime is very often only an illness makes a good deal of sense because people there *discriminate* carefully among crimes; but in Russia this same notion makes no sense at all because we do not discriminate at all, and everything, every sort of nasty villainy committed even by a Jack of Hearts we also accept almost as an illness and—alas!—people even see something liberal in this! Of course, I'm not talking about serious people (although do we have many serious people in that sense?). I'm talking about the man in the street, about the untalented mediocrities, on the one hand, and about the scoundrels who trade in liberalism on the other, and these latter people are ones who couldn't care a fig for anything, so long as it is or seems to be liberal. As far as the attorney Utin is concerned, he "sang praises to crime" probably imagining that as an attorney he could do nothing else—and this is just how undeniably clever people get carried away and achieve results that aren't clever at all. Had the jurors been in different circumstances, i.e., had they had the opportunity of pronouncing a different verdict, then I think they probably would have taken exception to Mr. Utin's exaggerations, so that he would have weakened his client's case. But the fact was that they literally were unable to bring in a different verdict. Some newspapers commended them for it, while others, I've heard, censure them. I think there is no place here either for praise or for blame: they simply brought in the verdict they did because they were utterly unable to bring in any other. Judge for yourselves; this is what we read in the newspaper account:

> In accordance with the request of the prosecution, the following question was put by the court: "Did Kairova, *having premeditated her act*, inflict on Alexandra Velikanova, *with intent to take her life*, several wounds with a razor on her neck, head and chest, *but was prevented from the ultimate consummation of her intent* of murdering Velikanova by Velikanova herself and her husband?" The jury answered this question in the negative.

Let us pause here. This is the answer to the first question. But really, can one give an answer to a question posed *that way?* Who, and whose conscience, will undertake to answer such a question in the affirmative? (It's true that it's equally impossible to answer in the negative, but we are discussing only the jury's affirmative decision). One can only give an affirmative answer to a question posed that way if one has supernatural, divine omniscience. Indeed, even Kairova herself might have no idea of whether she would slash her rival to death or not, and yet the jury was asked positively: "Would she have murdered her had they not stopped her?" When she bought the razor the day before, she might well have known why she bought it but still might not have known whether she would attack her with it, never mind whether she would slash her to death. Most likely she hadn't the slightest idea of this even when sitting on the steps with the razor in her hand, while just behind her, on her own bed, lay her lover and her rival. No one, no one in the world could have had the slightest idea of this. Moreover, even though it may seem absurd, I can state that even when she had begun slashing her rival she might *still not have known* whether she wanted to kill her or not and whether *this was her purpose* in slashing her. Note, please, that I certainly am not arguing here that she was acting unconsciously; I don't even admit the slightest element of insanity. To the contrary: it is very likely that at the moment when she was slashing her rival *she knew what she was doing*, but whether she consciously, *having made it her purpose*, wanted to take her rival's life—of this she may well have not had the least idea. For Heaven's sake, don't think this is absurd: she could be slashing with the razor, in anger and hatred, with not the slightest thought of the consequences. Judging by the character of this disorderly and tormented woman, it likely happened exactly that way. And note that the whole fate of this unfortunate woman hung on the jury's answer (an affirmative one, say) to the question of whether she would have gone through with the murder and, most important, whether she attacked her rival with the deliberate intent to kill her. She would be ruined, condemned to forced labor. How can a jury take such a burden on their conscience? And so they answered in the negative because they had no alternative answer to give. You might say that Kairova's crime was not something premeditated, not a rational or bookish one, but simply "women's business," very uncomplicated, very simple; her rival was lying on Kairova's own bed as well. But is it that way and that simple? What if she had passed the razor across Velikanova's throat once and then cried out, shuddered, and ran off as fast as she could? How do you know that this might not have happened? And if it had happened, it's very likely that the affair would never have come to court. But now you've been pinned to the wall and are being forced to make a definite answer: "Would she have murdered Velikanova or not?" And of course this is done so that your answer will determine whether or not she is exiled. And the slightest variation in your answer corresponds to whole years of imprisonment or forced labor! And what if she made one slash and then took fright and turned the razor on herself and, indeed, perhaps even killed herself right there? And what, finally, if she not only had not taken fright but had flown into a frenzy when she felt the first spurts of hot blood and not only murdered Velikanova but even begun to abuse the body, cutting off the head, the nose, the lips; and only later, suddenly, when someone took that head away from her, had realized what she had done? I am asking this because it all could have happened and could have been done by this very same woman and sprung from the very same soul, in the very same mood and under the very same circumstances; I say this because I somehow sense that I am not mistaken. And so how could one answer such a tricky question from the court? This isn't a family conversation around the tea table, after all: someone's fate is being decided here. Posing questions in this way runs the strong risk of getting no answer at all.

Yet you may respond that if such were the case, we would never be able to charge or try anyone for murder or attempted murder so long as the crime was not brought to completion or the victim survived. No, I think that there is no cause for alarm here because there are very obvious cases of murder where, though the crime was never completed (even because of the criminal's own will), it is still quite evident that they were undertaken solely *with the intent to murder* and could have had no other purpose. But I repeat the most important thing: for this we have the conscience of the jury, and that is something great and important; that is the good service rendered by the new courts, and that conscience truly will prompt the jury to a new decision. If a person feels within himself, at such an important moment, the resolve to answer firmly, "Yes, guilty," then in all likelihood he will not be mistaken about the criminal's guilt. At least mistakes have happened so rarely as to be anecdotal. Only one thing is desirable: that the conscience of the jury be truly enlightened, truly firm, and strengthened by a civic sense of duty; that it should avoid being diverted toward one side or the other, i.e., toward harshness or pernicious sentimentality. It's also true that this second hope, i.e, the avoidance of sentimentality, is rather difficult to achieve. Everyone is capable of sentimentality; it's such an easy thing and requires no effort; sentimentality is so profitable these days; sentimentality with the right tendency will make even an ass look like a refined man. . . .

The second question posed to the jury—"Did she inflict these wounds with *the same intent*, in a state of frenzy and passion?"— could likewise be answered only negatively, i.e., "No, she did not"; for here again the phrase "with the same intent" signifies "with the premeditated intention of taking Velikanova's life." It became especially difficult to answer this because "frenzy and passion" in the vast majority of cases exclude "premeditated intention." And so this second question of the court seems even to contain an element of the absurd.

However in the court's *third* question—"Did Kairova act in a clearly established state of mental derangement?"—there is a rather larger element of the absurd, for the first two questions and the third are mutually exclusive. If the jury had answered the first two questions in the negative, or even if they had simply left them unanswered, it would then have been unclear what was being asked and even what the word "act" meant, i.e., what sort of act are they asking about and how do they define it? The jury had no room at all to modify their answer because of their duty to answer only *yes* or *no* and nothing in between.

Finally, the *fourth* question of the court—"If she was not acting under the influence of mental derangement, is she guilty of the aforesaid crime?"—was naturally also left unanswered by the jury in view of the fact that it only repeated the first two questions.

So it was that the court *let Kairova off*. The jury's answer, "No, she did not inflict..." also contains an absurdity, of course, for it is repudiated by the very fact that wounds were inflicted, a fact which no one disputes and which is obvious to all. But the jury found it difficult to give any other answer because of the way the question was put. But at least one could not say that in letting Kairova off, or at least in "pardoning" her, the court vindicated the defendant; but Mr. Utin certainly does justify the act of this criminal, and he almost finds it right and good. This is hard to believe, but this is what happened.

4. The Defense Attorney and Kairova

I am not going to analyze Mr. Utin's speech; it was not even a very good one. There was a terrific lot of high-flown language, various "feelings," and that conventionally liberal humaneness to which almost everybody resorts nowadays in "speeches" and in literature and which sometimes even the most complete nonentity (so that Mr. Utin is not at all apropos here) uses in order to give his writing an air of decency to ensure it "passes." The more that time goes by, the more this conventionally-liberal humaneness betrays itself in Russia. And everybody knows now that it is all no more than a handy crutch to lean on. I should have thought that this would scarcely even be popular nowadays—unlike the situation ten years ago—yet just look at how naive people are, especially here in Petersburg! And our naiveté is just what the aspiring careerist wants. The careerist doesn't have the time to study the "case," for example, and think carefully about it. Besides, almost all of them have grown callous over the years as their successes have piled up; they have already paid their dues to the humanitarian cause and have earned their humanitarian's badge, so to say, so they feel no need to spend still more time fussing over the misfortunes of some suffering and muddled little soul of a silly client who has thrust herself upon them. In many of their breasts there has long ceased to beat a real heart; there is only a little scrap of something official and bureaucratic. And so such a person hires a little stock of conventional words and phrases, trivial thoughts and feelings, gestures and opinions suitable for all future emergencies; all of them, of course, are in the latest liberal fashion. And then, for a long time, for the rest of his life, he can sink into a state of blissful repose. And he almost always gets away with it. I repeat, this definition of the most current kind of careerist is certainly not meant to be applied to Mr. Utin: he is talented, and his feelings, most likely, are natural ones. Yet he did insert an excessive number of ringing phrases into his speech, something that compels one to suspect not exactly a lack of taste but certainly a careless and, perhaps, not even an entirely humane attitude to the case in question. It must be admitted that the more talented our attorneys are, the busier they are; accordingly, the less time they have. Had Mr. Utin had more time, he would, in my view, have treated this case with more heartfelt feeling; and had he had more feeling, he would have been more circumspect and would not have burst forth with dithyrambs for what in essence is a most vulgar intrigue; he would not have indulged in high-flown phrases about "aroused lionesses whose cubs are being taken away"; he would not have attacked the victim of the crime, Mrs. Velikanova, with such naive fury; he would not have reproached her for not being slashed to death (he almost did that!); and he would not, at last, have uttered his most unexpected pun on Christ's words from the Gospels about the woman taken in adultery. However, it's possible that in reality all this did not happen this way, and Mr. Utin delivered his speech with a completely serious air. I was not in the courtroom; but judging by newspaper accounts, there seems to have been a certain lack of orderliness. . . . In short, there was a very serious absence of deliberation and, beyond that, much that was comical.

From virtually the beginning of the speech I was baffled and unable to understand whether Mr. Utin was serious in thanking the prosecutor for a summation that was not only "brilliant and talented, eloquent and humane," but at the same time was more a speech for the defense than for the prosecution. There is no doubt that the prosecutor's speech was eloquent and humane, just as it was liberal to the highest degree; on the whole, these gentlemen spend a terrific lot of time heaping praise on each other while the jury listens. But having praised the *prosecutor* for his *defense*, Mr. Utin failed to carry his original approach to its logical conclusion by launching into an accusation of his client, Mrs. Kairova, instead of defending her. That's a pity, because it would have been very amusing and perhaps would have suited the case. I even think that the jury would not have been overly surprised, because it's difficult to surprise our jurors. This innocent observation of mine, of course, is only a joke: Mr. Utin did not prosecute, he defended, and if his speech had its faults, then they were, to the contrary, specifically that his defense was too passionate; in fact, he overdid things, something which, as mentioned above, I attribute to a certain preliminary carelessness in his attitude to the case. "Never mind, when the time comes I'll be able to get away with it by throwing around a few fine words; that's enough for this . . . 'gallery.'" That, no doubt, is how some of our busiest attorneys are thinking more and more often these days. Mr. Utin, for instance, goes well out of his way to present his client in as ideal, romantic, and fantastic a light as possible, though there was no need whatever to do that: Mrs. Kairova is even easier to understand without these extra touches; but the defense lawyer played to the jurors' bad taste, of course. Everything about her is ideal; her every step is extraordinary, noble, gracious, while her love is something burning, a poem of epic proportions! To take one example: Kairova, who had never been on the stage, suddenly signs a contract as an actress and goes off to a distant corner of Russia, Orenburg. Mr. Utin does not maintain or insist that this action "revealed her usual placid temper and self-sacrifice"; but "here we see," Mr. Utin continues, "a kind of idealism, an eccentricity of a sort, and chiefly a renunciation of her self. She needed this work in order to help her mother, and so she accepts a position for which she is not at all suited, leaves Petersburg, and sets off on her own to Orenburg," etc., etc. Well, what are we to make of this? It would seem that nothing very special or amazing has happened; many a person travels here or there, and many a poor young girl who is pretty, unfortunate, and talented accepts a position away from her home that is far worse than the one Mrs. Kairova obtained. But the defense attorney, as you can see, turns this into some sort of sacrifice of self-renunciation, and an acting contract is virtually transformed into a feat of heroism. His speech continues in the same fashion. Kairova very soon "becomes intimate" with Velikanov, the manager of the troupe. His business was in a bad state: "she works to obtain a subsidy for him and manages to get him released." Once again, what's special about that? There's many a woman, especially one with as lively and active a nature as Kairova has, who would start a campaign in such a case for the sake of a man who was dear to her after she had become romantically involved with him. Then there began scenes with Velikanov's wife. Having described one such scene, Mr. Utin remarks that from that moment his client considered Velikanov "her own," and saw him as her creation, her "beloved child." I have heard, by the way, that this "beloved child" is tall, stout, and built like a grenadier, with hair curling down the back of his neck. In his speech Mr. Utin maintains that she regarded him as "her child," as her "creation"; that she wanted "to raise him up and ennoble him." Mr. Utin, evidently, rejects the notion that Mrs. Kairova could attach herself to Velikanov without this special aim in mind; in the meantime, however, this "beloved child," this "creation" was not ennobled in the least but, on the contrary, sank lower and lower as time went by.

To put it briefly, Mr. Utin's voice is always pitched far too high to be appropriate to these people and these events, so that one sometimes simply has to marvel. The adventures begin; the "beloved child" and Kairova come to Petersburg; then he goes to Moscow to look for work. Kairova writes him sincere, heartfelt letters; she is filled with passion and feelings, while he is simply unable to write a good letter and from this point of view is terribly "ignoble." "These letters," Mr. Utin observes, "contain the first appearance of that little cloud that later covered the whole sky and produced the storm." But Mr. Utin cannot express himself in terms any simpler; this is his style throughout. Finally Velikanov returns once more, and once more they are living in Petersburg (*martialement*, of course)—and then suddenly comes the most important episode of the romance: Velikanov's wife arrives, and Kairova "roused herself like a lioness whose cub is being taken away." We really have a lot of eloquence at this point. Were it not for this eloquence, of course, we would have even more pity for this poor, foolish woman who is trapped between a husband and wife and who does not know what to do. Velikanov turns out to be "treacherous," simply a weak man. At one point he is deceiving his wife by assuring her of his love; then he leaves the dacha to go to

Petersburg to see Kairova and mollify her with the news that his
wife will soon be going abroad. Mr. Utin depicts the love of his
client not only as something appealing but even edifying and, one
might say, highly moral. Kairova, you see, even intended to approach Mrs. Velikanova with a proposal to give her back her own
husband altogether (and so, obviously, she thought she had full
rights to him). "If you want him, take him; if you want to live
with him, then do so; but either you must leave here or I will.
Decide one way or the other." That's what she intended to say,
but I don't know whether she actually said it. But no one made
any decision, and instead of leaving herself (if she really wanted
so badly to somehow end the affair), Kairova only seethed and
rushed frantically about, asking no questions and awaiting no improbable solutions. "To give him up without a struggle would not
be the act of a woman," Mr. Utin suddenly observes. Well, then,
why all the talk about these various intentions, questions, and
"proposals?" "She was dominated by passion," Mr. Utin explains
to the court, "her mind was consumed and destroyed by jealousy,
which drove her to play this dreadful game." And then: "jealousy
turned her reason to dust and nothing of it remained. How could
she have kept herself under control?" Things continued this way
for ten days. "She languished; she had fits of fever and could not
eat or sleep; she rushed to Petersburg and to Oranienbaum, and
thus, when she was in such a state of torment, the ill-starred
Monday of the 7th of July arrived." On that ill-starred Monday
the woman, worn out by her torments, arrived at her dacha and
was told that Velikanov's wife was there; she comes to the bedroom
and. . . .

> Gentlemen of the jury, is it possible for the woman to remain calm?
> One would have to be made of stone; one would have to be without
> a heart. The man she passionately loves is in her bedroom, in her
> bed, with another woman! This was too much for her to bear. Her
> emotions burst forth like a raging torrent that destroys everything in
> its path; she rushed about, enraged; she was capable of *destroying
> everything around her* (!!!). If we try to ask this torrent what it was
> doing and why it was causing such damage, could it answer us? No,
> it would give no answer.

Just listen to all those fine phrases and all those "emotions"!
"As long as it's hot they'll surely find some flavor in it." But let
us pause at these words: they are deplorable; and even worse, they
are the very foundation of Mr. Utin's defense.

I am only too ready to agree with you, Mr. Utin, that Kairova
could not have remained calm during the scene you described; but
this is simply because she is Kairova—i.e, a weak woman, perhaps;
a very good-hearted woman, perhaps; maybe even a likable and
affectionate woman (however, at this point I know about these
qualities of hers only from your speech); yet at the same time she
is a loose woman, is she not? I don't mean that she is loose in the
sense of being depraved: she is an unfortunate woman, and I will
not insult her, all the more that I cannot undertake to judge her
on this point. I mean only the looseness of her mind and her heart,
which I think is undeniable. And so it was because of this looseness
that at the fatal moment she could not settle the matter any differently than the way she did; it was not because "one would have
to be made of stone; one would have to be without a heart" to do
anything else, as you said, Mr. Utin. Just think, sir, that when
you say that, you are, as it were, refusing altogether to admit any
other clearer, more noble and magnanimous outcome. And if there
had been a woman who at such a moment were capable of throwing
away the razor and finding another solution to the problem, then
it follows that you would have called her not a woman but a stone,
a woman without a heart. And so you did "almost sing praises to
the crime," as I said before. Of course, you were carried away,
and this was certainly noble of you; but it is a pity that such rash
words are uttered from the still new tribunes of our society. You
must pardon me, sir, for taking your words so seriously. But then,
stop and think: there are superior types and superior *ideals* among
women. There is no disputing the fact that these ideals have existed
and do exist in reality. And what if even Mrs. Kairova herself at
the last moment, with the razor in her hand, had suddenly looked
clearly at her own fate (don't worry, this sometimes is quite possible,
and precisely at the last moment), recognized her own misfortune
(for loving such a man is a misfortune), recognized all her shame
and disgrace, all her degradation (for in fact it is not only "nobility
and self-denial" that one finds in such "women taken in adultery,"
Mr. Utin, but much falsehood, shame, vice, and degradation as
well)? What if she had suddenly sensed within her a woman resurrected into a new life who at the same time recognized that she,
after all, was the offender, and even more, that by leaving this man
she might truly ennoble him? And, having felt all this, she had
gotten up and left, tears pouring from her eyes, saying, "What
have I come to?" Well, what if this really had happened even to

Mrs. Kairova? Would you really not have taken pity on her? Would
your undeniably good heart not have responded to her? Would you
have called this woman, who suddenly was resurrected in heart
and in spirit, a stone, a creature without a heart? Would you have
used our new tribune, to which we all still listen so eagerly, publicly
to place your stigma upon her?

I hear voices, however: "You must not demand this from every
woman; this is inhuman!" I know, and I make no such demand.
I shuddered when I read the part where she sat hidden, listening
by the bed; only too well can I imagine what she underwent in
this final hour, her razor in hand. I was very, very happy when
Mrs. Kairova was let off. I whisper to myself the majestic words,
"For they bind heavy burdens, and grievous to be borne." But He
who said those words also added, when He forgave the guilty
woman, "Go forth and sin no more." That means that He still
called the sin a sin; He forgave it, but He did not justify it. But
Mr. Utin says, "She would not have been a woman but a stone,
a creature without a heart," so that he does not even understand
how she could have acted differently. I merely timidly venture to
observe that evil must still be called evil, despite any humane
feelings, and must not be raised almost to the level of a heroic
deed.

5. The Defense Attorney and Velikanova

And if you are going to proclaim your humanitarian principles,
then you might spare a little pity for Mrs. Velikanova. He who
has too much pity for the offender probably has no pity left for
the offended. Meanwhile, Mr. Utin would deny Mrs. Velikanova
even her status as victim of a crime. I think I am certainly not
wrong in concluding that throughout his speech Mr. Utin was
constantly on the verge of saying something bad about Mrs. Velikanova. I admit that this technique is a most naive and, I think,
a most awkward one; it is too primitive and hasty. People will
probably say, Mr. Utin, that you are humane only toward your own
clients, i.e., as a function of your job; but is that really so? For
instance, you certainly fastened upon and used that "savage, terrible" scene when an angry Mrs. Velikanova said aloud that she
would "kiss the dear hands and feet of anyone who would rid her
of such a husband"; and when Kairova, who was there, replied at
once, "I'll take him," Mrs. Velikanova's response was, "Go right

ahead." After you told us this *fact,* you even observed that it was
from this very moment that Kairova began to regard this gentleman
as *her own* and began seeing him as her creation and "her beloved
child." That's all very naive. In the first place, what is "savage
and terrible" here? The scene itself and the words spoken are
nasty, to be sure, but if you allow the possibility of overlooking
even the razor in Kairova's hands and acknowledging that she could
not have remained calm—and I believe you completely here—then
how can you not overlook the impatient, albeit foolish, outburst of
an unhappy wife! You yourself acknowledge that Mr. Velikanov is
an intolerable man, so much so that the very fact of Kairova's love
for him is itself sufficient demonstration of her insanity. So then
why are you surprised when Mrs. Velikanova talks about kissing
"the dear hands and feet"? With an intolerable person the relationship itself often becomes intolerable, and intolerable statements
sometimes slip out. Yet that is only *sometimes* and only just a phrase.
And I must admit that if Mrs. Kairova seriously believed that the
wife was indeed giving up her husband and that she henceforth
had the right to regard him as her own, she must have had an
exceptionally fine sense of humor. It probably all happened somehow differently. And you needn't look down your nose so at a few
words of some poor, depressed person. In families like this (and
not only in ones like this—you wouldn't believe where these things
go on) even worse things are said. Sometimes there is poverty, a
heavy burden of life, and under their weight family relationships
inevitably grow coarse so that things are said which Lord Byron,
for example, would never have said to his Lady Byron, even at the
moment of their final rupture, or, say, as Arbenin to Nina in
Lermontov's *Masquerade.* Of course there is no excuse for this sort
of shoddy behavior, even though it is only shoddiness, *mauvais ton,*
impatience, while the *heart* remains, perhaps, even better than
before; so that if one regards such matters from a more commonplace point of view, the result will truly be more humane. Mrs.
Kairova's response—"I'll take him"—is much worse, in my view:
there is a terrible insult to the wife here; there is torment, the
direct mockery from a triumphant mistress who has stolen a husband away from his wife. You, Mr. Utin, make some truly ven-
omous remarks about this wife. For example, in expressing your
regret that she did not appear in court but sent a doctor's certificate
saying she was unwell, you remark to the jury that if she had
appeared, her testimony would have lost all its significance because

the jury would have seen a healthy, strong, attractive woman. But in the case at hand what concern of yours are her beauty, her strength, and her good health? You go on to state: "Gentlemen of the jury! What sort of a woman is this who comes to her husband, who is living with another woman, who comes to the home of her husband's mistress knowing that Mrs. Kairova is living there? She decides to spend the night and retires to Kairova's bedroom, to Kairova's bed.... This is beyond my comprehension." It may be beyond your comprehension, but you are still being too aristocratic and—unjust. And do you realize, Mr. Utin, that your client may have gained a good deal when Mrs. Velikanova did not appear in court? Many bad things were said about Mrs. Velikanova in court— about her character, for instance. I don't know anything about her character, but for some reason the fact that she did not testify even appeals to me. She did not testify, perhaps, out of the pride of an offended woman, or perhaps even because she wanted to spare her husband. For no one can say why she did not testify.... But in any case it is obvious that she is not one of those individuals who love to tell publicly of their passions and describe their feminine feelings to all and sundry. And who knows, perhaps if she had testified she would have had no trouble at all in explaining why she spent the night in the apartment of her husband's mistress, an act which you find so amazing and which you say casts particular shame on her. I think that she spent the night not at Kairova's but at the apartment of her repentant husband who had invited her there. And there are no grounds whatsoever to conclude that Mrs. Velikanova counted on Kairova's continuing to pay for this apartment. She perhaps even found it difficult to determine, immediately after her arrival, who was paying for the apartment and who was its owner. The husband asked her to come to him, so it would seem that the apartment was the husband's. And it is highly probable that this is just what he told her; he was deceiving both of them at the time, after all. The very same thing applies to your fine points about the bedroom and the bed. Here some tiny thread, some apparently utterly insignificant detail could perhaps have explained it all at once. In general, it seems to me that everyone was unjust toward this poor woman, and I'm given to think that had Velikanova caught Kairova in the bedroom with her husband and killed her with a razor, then she would have gained nothing in her dreadful status as legal wife apart from squalor and a term of forced labor. Can you really say, as you did, Mr. Utin, that

Velikanova lost nothing in this case because a only few days after
the incident she appeared on the stage and then performed all
winter long, while Kairova was incarcerated for ten months? We
have no less pity for your poor client than you do, but you must
agree that Mrs. Velikanova has endured more than a little. Never
mind what she lost as a wife and a self-respecting woman (the latter
is something I have no right to take away from her); but just
imagine, Mr. Utin—you, the subtle jurist who so clearly revealed
himself as a humane person in his speech—just imagine how much
she must have endured that terrible night! She endured several
minutes (far too many minutes) of *mortal fear.* Do you know what
mortal fear is? One who has not had a close confrontation with
death has difficulty in understanding it. She was awakened at night
by the razor of the woman who wanted to murder her as the razor
passed across her throat; she saw the infuriated face bending over
her; she fought off her attacker, while Kairova continued slashing
at her; naturally, she must have been convinced in these first savage,
impossible moments that she had been fatally slashed and that
death was inevitable. That's unbearable, after all; it's a delirious
nightmare, but a nightmare while awake and so a hundred times
more painful. It's almost the same as a death sentence being read
to one tied to the stake for execution while they pull the hood over
his head. . . . Merciful Heavens, Mr. Utin—you regard even torment
like that as insignificant! Can it be that not one of the jurors smiled
when he listened to that? And what of the fact that Mrs. Velikanova
was performing onstage two weeks later? Does that make the horror
that she had to endure two weeks earlier any less, or does it lessen
the guilt of your client? We had a case not long ago of a stepmother
who threw her six-year-old stepdaughter out of a fourth-floor window, but the child got up quite unharmed. Does that in any way
alter the cruelty of the crime, and did this little girl truly not suffer
at all? By the way, I can't help but imagine how a defense attorney
would defend this stepmother: he could cite her hopeless situation,
the fact that she was recently married against her will or by mistake
to a widower. We would have pictures of the impoverished lives of
impoverished people, their endless labor. She, a simple, innocent
woman who, like an inexperienced girl (especially given our manner
of child rearing!), married thinking that there were only joys awaiting her thereafter; but instead of joys she has the washing of dirty
linen, cooking, bathing the child—"Gentlemen of the jury, it is
only natural that she should conceive a hatred for this child"—

(who knows, we might even find such a "defense attorney" who would begin to blacken the child's character and seek out some nasty, hateful qualities in this six-year-old!)—"in a moment of despair, in a passing fit of madness, scarcely knowing what she was doing, she seizes the girl and. . . . Gentlemen of the jury, who among you would not do the same? Which one of you would not have thrown the girl out the window?"

What I'm saying, of course, is only a caricature, but if one should undertake to *compose* such a speech, then one really might say something rather similar, precisely in this manner, i.e., precisely in the manner of this caricature. And what is truly shocking is that it really does resemble a caricature, whereas the act of this monster-stepmother is truly bizarre; perhaps it really should be given a detailed and deep analysis that might even serve to lighten the case against this criminal woman. And so one sometimes gets annoyed at the naive and worn-out techniques that are coming into use for various reasons among our most talented lawyers. On the other hand, one thinks as follows: the tribunes of our new courts are truly a school of ethics for our society and our People. This is the school in which our People learn truth and morality; how, then, can one listen indifferently to the things one hears from these tribunes? But sometimes one hears most innocent and amusing jokes. Mr. Utin cited the following words from the Gospels as applying to his client: "She loved much, and much is forgiven her." That's very nice, of course, the more so as Mr. Utin knows very well that Christ did not at all have *that kind of love* in mind when he forgave the woman taken in adultery. I think it a sacrilege to refer here to this great and touching place in the Gospels. Yet I cannot refrain from referring to a very minor yet rather characteristic observation I made not long ago. This observation, of course, has nothing to do with Mr. Utin. Ever since my childhood, when I was a military cadet, I have noticed that many "raw youths"—high-school pupils (some), military school cadets (more), former cadets (most of all)—have truly been instilled with the notion from their school days that Christ forgave the woman for that sort of love, that is, precisely for her amorousness or, to be more precise, for her excess of amorousness; that he forgave her what we might call this attractive debility. Even now one encounters this conviction among very many people. I recall that a few times I even seriously asked myself the question: why is it that these boys are so inclined to interpret this part of the Gospels in this way? Is their religious

instruction really so careless? Yet they have a rather good understanding of the other parts of the Gospels. I concluded, finally,
that the reasons were probably more physiological, so to say: given
the undeniably good nature of Russian boys, they probably also
have that particular excess of youthful energy which comes to the
fore whenever they look at a woman. Yet I feel that this is nonsense
and should not have been mentioned at all. I repeat, Mr. Utin of
course knows very well how this text should be interpreted, and
I have no doubt that he was only making a joke at the end of his
speech; but what his point was I don't know.

2

1. Something about a Certain Building. Some Appropriate Thoughts

Lies and falsehood, that's what we have on all sides, and that's what is sometimes so hard to bear!

And just at the very time the case of Mrs. Kairova was being tried, I happened to visit the Foundling Home, a place I had never before visited and one I had long wanted to see. Thanks to a doctor I know, we were able to look at everything. However, I will give you my impressions in detail later on; I did not even take any notes and record any facts or figures; from the first step it became clear that it was impossible to examine everything on a single occasion and that it was well worth returning here again and again. This is what my most worthy guide, the doctor, and I resolved to do. I even intend to take a trip to the villages to see the Finnish women who have been given care of the infants. Accordingly, my description is still to come, but for now there are only flashes of my recollections: the monument to Betskoi; a series of splendid wards in which the infants are kept; the remarkable cleanliness (which hinders nothing); the kitchens; the barn where the calves are prepared for vaccination; the dining rooms; the groups of little children around the table; groups of five- and six-year-old girls playing at horses; a group of adolescent girls of perhaps sixteen and seventeen, former pupils of the home, who are preparing to be children's nurses and who are trying to complete their education. The latter already have some knowledge and have read Turgenev; they have a clear view of things and speak very nicely with you. But it was the supervisors who made the best impression on me: they have such a kindly air (and they weren't putting it on just for our visit), and had such calm, good-natured, and intelligent faces. Some of them, evidently, are educated. I was also very interested to hear that the mortality rate among the infants brought up in the home (in this building, that is) is incomparably lower than that of infants outside who are raised in families; the same cannot be said of infants placed in villages, however. I saw, finally, a room downstairs where mothers bring their infants to leave them here forever.... But this is all for later. I remember only that I gazed at these nursing infants with a particular and, probably, rather strange look. As absurd as it may be, they seemed to me to be terribly bold, so that, I recall, I even smiled inwardly at my thought. In fact, here you have a child who was born somewhere and brought to this place—yet just look at him crying, squalling, and declaring that his little chest is healthy and that he wants to live; his little red arms and legs thrash about and he keeps crying as if he had the right to disturb you this way; he seeks the breast as if he had a right to it and a right to be cared for; he demands care as if he had exactly the same right as those other children with families. So people drop everything and run to him: what an arrogant fellow he is! And to be sure, I say this in all seriousness; you look around and right away, like it or not, the thought comes that what if he really does offend someone? And what if someone should suddenly decide to take him in hand and say, "Look here, you little tyke, do you think you're the son of a prince or something?" And surely they must have to take them in hand. This isn't some idle fancy of mine. Children are even thrown out of windows, and once some ten years ago another stepmother, I think (I've forgotten, but it would be better if she were a stepmother), got tired of dragging around a child, born of the former wife, that was continually crying from some sort of pain; she went up to the boiling, bubbling samovar, held the child's little hand right under the tap . . . and opened it. It was in all the newspapers at the time. She certainly knew how to take the child in hand, the dear woman! I don't know what kind of a sentence she got, or, indeed, if she was even tried. Don't you think she "deserves every sort of clemency"? Sometimes these little brats can make a dreadful fuss, after all, and get on your nerves; and then there's the whole business of poverty and doing the washing, and so on. On the other hand, there are some mothers who may still "take in hand" a squalling child but do it much more humanely: an "interesting" and attractive young girl will creep into some dark corner; and suddenly she has a fainting spell and can remember nothing more; suddenly—just how, no one can tell—her little child, an arrogant, squalling little fellow, just accidentally gets into the water and chokes. Choking, still, is more pleasant than the samovar tap, isn't that so? You can't even pass judgment on one like that; she's a poor, deceived, sympathetic girl; she ought to be eating candies, but suddenly she has a fainting fit, and besides, if you think of Marguerite in *Faust* (some of these jurors are uncommonly well educated), then there is simply no way one can pass judgment on her; one even ought to take up a subscription for her. Thus one even rejoices over all these babies for managing to find their way here, to this building. And I admit that at the time some very idle thoughts and ridiculous questions kept coming into my mind. For example, I would ask myself—and I truly wanted to find out—precisely when these children begin to learn that they are worse than everyone else, that is, that they are not the same children as "those others" but are much worse and are alive not by any right but only, so to say, out of a sense of humanity? It's impossible to determine that without a great deal of experience, a great deal of observation of the babies, but a priori I still decided and am convinced that they find out about this "sense of humanity" very early, so early one can scarcely believe it. In fact, if the child were to develop only by means of scientific aids and scientific games and to get its knowledge of the world from such "scientific" questions as "Why does the duck have feathers?" then, I think, it would never reach the depth of understanding—so terrifying that one can scarcely believe it—through which by quite unknown means it manages to understand certain ideas that would seem to be quite beyond it. A five- or six-year-old child sometimes knows things about God or about good and evil that are so amazing and are of such surprising profundity that one can't help but conclude that Nature has given this child some other means of acquiring knowledge, one that not only is unknown to us but which, on a pedagogical basis, we even ought to reject. Oh, of course the child doesn't know the facts about God, and if a clever jurist were to examine the six-year-old on his notions of good and evil, the result would be merely laughable. But you need only be a little more patient and attentive (for it's worth being so), overlook the child's ignorance of certain facts, admit certain absurdities, try to get at *the essence of his understanding,* and you will at once see that he knows as much about God, perhaps, as you, a clever lawyer who sometimes is carried away by haste; perhaps he knows much more than you do about good and evil and about what

is shameful and what is laudable. To those terrible, difficult ideas
which are acquired so unexpectedly and in such a mysterious manner I would add, for the children here, this initial but utterly
unshakeable conviction that stays with them for their whole lives:
that they are "worse than all the others." And I am certain that
the child learns this not from his nurses and guardians; moreover,
it lives without seeing these "other children" and is thus unable
to make comparisons. Yet when you look closely you will see that
it already knows a terrific amount, that it has already figured out
a great deal with a most unnecessary precocity. Of course, I've
launched into speculations, but at the time I simply was unable to
manage the rush of my thoughts. For example, the following aph-
orism suddenly popped into my head: if fate has deprived these
children of a family and of the joy of growing up with parents
(because not all parents throw their children out the window, after
all, or scald them with boiling water)—then does it not reward
them in some other way? They are raised in this magnificent building, for instance; they are given a name, then an education, and
even the highest education possible; they are seen through university, and then found a position and set on a life's path; and this
is done by the whole state, so to say, taking them in as children
of the community or the state. True enough, if we are going to
forgive, then we should forgive completely. And then I thought to
myself: some people will probably say that this means encouraging
vice, and will take offense. But what a silly idea: to think that
these lovely girls will deliberately start bearing one child after
another just as soon as they hear that their children will be sent
to university.

"No," I thought, "we must forgive them and forgive them completely. If we are going to do it, then we must go all the way!" It
is true that many—very many—of our most honest and industrious
people will be envious and that some will think: "How is it that
I have worked like an ox all my life and have never done a single
wrong thing; I loved my children and struggled all my life to give
them an education and make them good citizens, but I have failed.
I haven't even been able to put them all the way through high
school. And now I've got a cough and am short of breath, and if
I die next week then it's good-bye to my dear children, all eight
of them! They'll all leave school at once and take to wandering
the streets or go to work in a cigarette factory; and that's the best

they can expect out of life.... But these little outcasts will finish university and find good positions. And to top it all off, I'm the one who, directly or indirectly, has been contributing each year to support them!"

There is no doubt that someone will deliver this monologue; but in fact what contradictions does it contain? In fact, how did everything get arranged so as to eliminate all accord? Just think: what could be more legitimate and fair than this monologue? And yet, at the same time, it is highly illegitimate and unfair. Thus it's legitimate and illegitimate at the same time—what a muddle!

I can't resist telling you some of the other things that I was thinking about at the time. For example: "We may forgive them, but will they forgive us?" Now that's also something to think about. There are some creatures of a superior type, and they will forgive; others, perhaps, will want revenge—on whom and for what they will never figure out and will never understand, yet they will take revenge. But let me say the following about "vengeance on society" on the part of these "outcasts," should such occur: I am convinced that this vengeance will always be something negative rather than direct and positive. No one will take revenge directly and consciously, and he himself will not even guess that he craves revenge; to the contrary, if they are only given an education, a great many of those who emerge from this building will emerge ardently seeking to be respectable, to be parents with their own families. Their ideal will be to build a nest of their own and to make a name for themselves, to gain some prestige, to bring up children, love them, and, in bringing them up, to do so without resorting to this building or to help from the state. And in general their first rule will be to forget even the way back to this building and to forget its very name. On the contrary, this new head of a family will be happy and will see his own babies through university at his own expense. Well—this is a longing for a bourgeois, *established* order that will stay with him all his life; and what will this be: servility or the highest form of independence? I think it will more likely be the latter; yet all through his life his soul will still remain not entirely independent; it will not quite be the soul of a *master,* and therefore there will be much in it that is not entirely attractive, although it may be totally honest. Complete spiritual independence is achieved through quite different means.... But we'll discuss that later; it's also a long story.

2. One Inappropriate Thought

I said "independence" just now. But do we love independence?—
that's the question. And what do we mean by independence? Could
we find two people who would understand it in the same way—in
fact, I'm not sure if we have even one such idea in which anyone
seriously believes. Our average, unexceptional person, rich or poor,
doesn't like to think about anything and so, without paying much
mind to it, simply indulges in a little vice while he has the strength
and the interest. People who are better than the average "dissociate" themselves in little groups and give the appearance of believing in something; yet it seems they force themselves to do it
and do so only as an amusement. There are also particular people
who have seized upon the formula "The worse, the better," and
are working out its implications. There are, finally, paradoxicalists,
who are occasionally very honest but on the whole rather untalented; these, especially if they are honest, most often end by suicide.
And, in truth, suicides lately have become so common that people
don't even talk about them any more. The Russian land seems to
have lost the capacity to hold people on it. And how many truly
honest people—and honest women in particular—there are among
them! Our women are beginning to make their presence felt and,
perhaps, will save a great deal; I'll say more about that later. Women
are perhaps our great hope and will serve the whole of Russia in
her fateful moment. But this is the problem: we have a lot of honest
people, a terrific lot of them; I mean to say that they are good
rather than honest, but none of them knows the meaning of honesty
and hasn't the least shred of belief in any expression of honesty;
they even reject its clearest expressions from the past, and that is
the case almost everywhere and with everyone. Should that surprise
us? But the so-called living force, the vital sense of existence,
without which no society can live and no land endure, is vanishing
away, God knows where. So why was it that in this building I set
to thinking about suicides, looking at this nursery and at these
infants? Now that really is an inappropriate thought.

We have many inappropriate thoughts, and it is they that crush
us. Here in Russia an idea falls on a person like a huge boulder
and half crushes him; there he is, squirming under it, unable to
get free. Some people accept living crushed, while others do not,
and they kill themselves. Extremely characteristic is the long letter,
published in *New Times*, of a girl who committed suicide. She was

twenty-five, and her name was Pisareva. She was the daughter of landowners who had once been prosperous; but she came to Petersburg and paid her dues to progress by becoming a midwife. She got through the course, passed the examination, and found a position as a zemstvo midwife. She herself states that she was never in need and was able to earn a rather good living. But she got *tired*, very tired, so tired that she wanted to rest. "Where better to rest than in the grave?" She had really become terribly tired! This poor girl's whole letter simply exudes fatigue. The letter is even cranky and impatient: just leave me alone, I'm tired. "Don't forget to have them pull off my new blouse and stockings; I have some old ones on my night table. Have them dress me in those." She doesn't write *take off* but *pull off*, and it's all like that—in terrible impatience. All these sharp words come from being impatient, and the impatience from fatigue; she even uses some abusive language: "Did you really think that I would come home? Why the hell would I go there?" Or: "Now, Lipareva, forgive me and may Petrova forgive me as well" (it was in her apartment the girl took poison) "especially Petrova. I'm doing a filthy, swinish thing...." She evidently loves her family, but she writes: "Don't let Lizanka know, or else she'll tell her sister and they'll come here and start sniveling. I don't want anyone sniveling over me, but a family never fails to do that when one of them dies." *Snivel*, she writes, and not *weep*—all that obviously comes from impatient fatigue: hurry up and get it over with as quickly you can, and let me rest! There is a terrible, agonizing amount of disgusted and cynical unbelief in her: she has no faith in Lipareva or Petrova, whom she loves so. This is how the letter begins: "Don't lose your heads, don't start moaning. Get a grip on yourselves and read this to the end. And then decide what's the best thing to do. Don't frighten Petrova. Maybe nothing will come of it but a good laugh. My residence permit is on top of the trunk."

Only a good laugh! The thought that they would laugh at her, at her wretched body—and who else but Lipareva and Petrova! And that thought flashed through her mind at such a moment! That's dreadful!

It is truly strange how concerned she is with the arrangements for disposing of that little sum of money she left: "This bit of money must not be taken by my relatives; this bit is to go to Petrova; the twenty-five rubles that the Chechetkins gave me for my trip should be returned to them." This importance she attributes to money is, perhaps, the last echo of the main prejudice of her life—"that these stones be made bread." In sum, one sees here the conviction that guided her whole life, i.e., "if everyone were provided for, everyone would be happy; there would be no poor people and no crimes. There would be no crimes whatsoever. Crime is a pathological condition resulting from poverty and from an unhappy environment," etc., etc. This is the entire petty, well-worn, and very typical, self-enclosed catechism of convictions to which such people so faithfully devote themselves in life (despite the fact that they so quickly grow bored with their convictions, as well as their lives). For them, such convictions take the place of everything: a living life, the link with the earth, belief in truth—simply everything. Evidently, having lost all belief in the truth and all faith in duty, the tedium of life tired her. In short, there was a complete loss of any higher ideal of existence.

And the poor girl died. I'm not going to snivel over you, you poor thing, but let me at least have pity for you; allow me that, please. Let me wish that your soul be resurrected into a life where you will not be bored. You people who are kind and good and honest (and you have all of these qualities!)—where are you going, and why has the dark, solitary grave become so attractive to you? Just look: there is a bright spring sun in the sky, the buds are forming on the trees, and you have grown tired before you have lived. How can your mothers, who raised you and who looked at you so fondly when you were still tiny children, help but *snivel* over you? Think how much hope is invested in a tiny child! I've just been seeing how these "outcast" children in the Foundling Home want so much to live; how they declare their right to live! You were also such an infant and you wanted to live; and your mother remembers that; and when she now compares your dead face with that laughter and joy she saw and remembers on your tiny infant's face, how can she help but break out "sniveling," and how can you reproach her for doing so? Just now I was shown a little girl, Dunia; she was born with a crippled leg, or rather with no leg at all; instead of a leg she had something that looked like a cord dangling down. She is only a year and a half old, healthy, and very pretty; everyone cuddles her, and she nods and smiles to everyone and babbles to anyone who comes near. She still is not aware of the problem with her leg; she doesn't know that she is a freak and a cripple. But is she also destined to develop a hatred for life? "We'll make her an artificial leg and give her a crutch, and when she learns to walk she won't notice the difference," said a doctor as he cuddled her. May God grant she doesn't *notice the difference.* No, to grow tired, to come to hate life and thus to hate everyone—oh, no, that cannot be. This pitiful, monstrous, prematurely born generation squirming under the boulders that have fallen on them will disappear; a new and great idea will start to shine like the sun; erratic minds will grow firm, and everyone will say, "Life is good; it is we who have been bad." I'm not accusing anyone when I say that we have been bad. I see that peasant woman over there, that rough wet-nurse who is only "hired milk," suddenly kiss a child, one of those very "outcast" children! I never thought that the wet-nurses here would kiss these children; why, to see this alone would have made the trip here worthwhile! And she kissed the child and didn't notice that I was watching her. Do you think they are paid to love these children? They are hired to feed the children, but they're not required to kiss them. Children who are raised by Finnish women in villages have it worse, so I'm told, but some of the women become so attached to their nurslings that they are in tears when they have to return them to the home; and then come especially from far away to look at them, bringing them little presents from the village and "sniveling over them." No, this isn't a matter of money: "the family, after all, always wants to snivel," as Pisareva concluded in her suicide note, and so these women come to snivel and bring their poor presents from the village. These are not merely hired breasts, taking the place of the breasts of the mother, this is *motherhood*; this is that "living life" of which Pisareva had grown so tired. But is it true that the Russian land no longer holds Russian people on it? Why, then, do we see right at hand a life that is in the full flower of health?

And of course there are many babies here also born of that interesting sort of mother who will sit on the steps of a dacha, honing a razor for her rival. In conclusion I will say: these razors may be nice things in their way, but I was very sorry that I came here, to this building, at a time when I was following the trial of Mrs. Kairova. I know nothing at all of Mrs. Kairova's life story and I certainly cannot, nor have I the right, to connect her in any way to this building. But this whole romance of hers and this whole eloquent analysis of her passions at the trial somehow lost any power they had for me and destroyed any of my sympathy for her once I left this building. I admit this quite frankly, because perhaps that was the reason I wrote so unsympathetically about Mrs. Kairova's "case."

3. A Democratic Spirit, for Certain. Women

I feel I have to answer yet another letter from a reader. In the last (April) issue of the *Diary*, when I spoke of political matters, I mentioned in passing something we might call a fantasy:

> . . . Russia will prove to be stronger than anyone else in Europe. This will happen because the great powers in Europe will be destroyed for one very simple reason: they will all be rendered impotent and undermined by the unsatisfied democratic aspirations of an immense part of their own lower-class subjects—their proletariat and their paupers. This simply cannot happen in Russia: our demos is content, and the further we go the more satisfied it will become, for everything is moving toward that end via the common mood or, to put it better, the general consensus. And therefore there will remain but one colossus on the continent of Europe—Russia.

In reply to this view, my correspondent cites one most curious and instructive fact and provides it as his reason for doubting that "our demos is satisfied and content." My worthy correspondent will understand all too well (should he chance to read these lines) why I cannot now discuss this fact that he has passed on and reply to him, although I do not lose hope in the possibility of discussing this same fact in the very near future. But now I wish to give only a word of explanation about the demos, the more so that I have been informed of other opinions that likewise do not agree with my conviction that our "demos" is content. I want merely to direct my opponents' attention to one line in the passage from the April issue quoted above: " . . . because everything moves toward that end via the common mood or, to put it better, the general consensus." In fact, had my opponents not shared in this common *mood* or, rather, *consensus*, then they would have let my words slip past without objecting to them. And therefore this mood certainly must exist; it certainly is democratic and certainly is disinterested; moreover, it is universal. It's true that one cannot believe everything in the democratic declarations one hears these days and that they contain a good deal of journalistic double-dealing. People get carried away, for example, in making exaggerated attacks on opponents of democracy, of whom, by the way, we now have very few. Still, the honest, disinterested, forthright, and frank democratic feelings of the majority of Russian society cannot be doubted at all. In that respect, we, perhaps, have displayed or are beginning to display something that has not yet been displayed in Europe, where democratic feelings have so far generally been evidenced only from below; in Europe democracy is still struggling, while the (supposedly) vanquished upper classes are still stubbornly resisting. Our upper classes were not vanquished; our upper classes themselves became democratic or, rather, became allied with the People; who can deny that? And if that is so, then you yourselves will agree that our demos can expect a happy future. And if our present contains much that is unattractive, then at least it is permissible to cherish great hopes that the temporary ills of the demos will certainly be healed under the steady and continuing influence of such enormous *principles* (for I cannot call them otherwise) *as the general democratic mood and general consensus* for such healing among all Russians, beginning from the very top. That was the sense in which I meant that our demos is content and "the further we go, the more content it will be." Say what you like, but it's hard not to believe that.

And in conclusion I want to add one more word about the Russian woman. I have already said that she contains one of our great hopes, one of the pledges of our renewal. The renaissance of the Russian woman in the last twenty years is undeniable. The upsurge in her strivings has been lofty, frank, and fearless. This upsurge has inspired respect from the very first; it has at least caused people to think, despite several superfluous irregularities that have turned up in this movement. Now, however, one can already make an accounting and not fear to reach a conclusion. The Russian woman has chastely ignored obstacles and mockery. She has firmly declared her wish to participate in the common cause and has applied herself to it not only disinterestedly but even self-denyingly. The Russian man, in these last decades, has become terribly prone to the vices of acquisition, cynicism, and materialism; woman has remained much more purely devoted than he to the idea and to serving the idea. In her eagerness for higher education she has displayed seriousness and patience and showed an example of the greatest courage. *A Writer's Diary* has given me the means to see the Russian woman at closer hand; I have received some remarkable letters; they ask me, who knows so little, "What is to be done?" I value these questions, and by being frank I try to compensate for my lack of knowledge in answers. I regret that there is so much that I cannot and have not the right to say here. I see, however, some flaws as well in today's woman, and the principal flaw is her extraordinary dependence on certain specifically masculine notions, her capacity to accept these as given and to believe in them without question. I am speaking by no means of all women; but this flaw also testifies to the good qualities of her heart: she values above all spontaneity of feeling and a living word, but principally and above all she values sincerity; and having put her faith in sincerity, sometimes sincerity that is not genuine, she is carried away by certain opinions, and sometimes carried away too far. In the future, higher education could do a great deal to help this. By permitting, sincerely and completely, higher education for women along with all the rights that this bestows, Russia would once more take an enormous and original step ahead of all Europe in the great cause of the regeneration of humanity. God grant that the Russian woman might also grow less tired and become less disillusioned than the tired Miss Pisareva, for example. Let her, rather, assuage her own grief like Shchapov's wife, through self-sacrifice and love. But both Mrs. Shchapova and Miss Pisareva are painful and memorable phenomena—the former because of her high level of feminine energy that reaped such a poor reward, the latter as a poor, tired, withdrawing, succumbing, and vanquished woman. . . .

June

1

1. The Death of George Sand

The type for the May issue of the *Diary* had already been set, and it was being printed when I read in the newspapers of the death of George Sand. She died on May 27 (June 8 by the European calendar), and so I was not able to say a word about her passing. And yet merely reading about her made me realize what her name had meant in my life, how enraptured I had been with this poet at one time, how devoted I was to her, and how much delight and happiness she once gave me! I write each of these words without hesitation because they express quite literally the way things were. She was entirely one of our (I mean *our*) contemporaries—an idealist of the 1830s and 1840s. In our mighty, self-important, yet unhealthy century, filled with foggy ideals and impossible hopes, hers is one of those names that emerged in Europe, "the land of sacred miracles," and drew from us, from our Russia which is forever creating itself, so many of our thoughts, so much of our love, so much of the sacred and noble force of our aspirations, our "living life," and our cherished convictions. But we must not complain about that: in exalting such names and paying them homage, we Russians served and now serve our proper mission. Do not be surprised at these words of mine, particularly when said about George Sand, who is still, perhaps, a controversial figure and whom half, if not nine-tenths of us, have already managed to forget; yet she still accomplished her task among us in days gone by. Who, then, should assemble around her grave to say a word in remembrance if not we, her contemporaries from all over the world? We Russians have two homelands: our own Russia and Europe, even if we call ourselves Slavophiles (and I hope the Slavophiles won't be angry at me for saying so). We need not dispute this point. The greatest of all the great missions that the Russians realize lies ahead of them is the common human mission; it is service to humanity as a whole, not merely to Russia, not merely to the Slavs, but to humanity as a whole. Think about it and you will agree that the Slavophiles recognized that very thing, and that is why they called on us to be more rigorous, more firm, and more responsible as Russians: they clearly understood that universality is the most important personal characteristic and purpose of the Russian. However, all this needs to be explained much more clearly: the fact is that service to the idea of universality is one thing, while traipsing frivolously around Europe after voluntarily and peevishly forsaking one's native land is something utterly opposed to it, yet people continue to confuse the two. No, this is not the case at all: many, very many of the things we took from Europe and transplanted in our own soil were not simply copied like slaves from their masters as the Potugins always insist we should; they were inoculated into our organism, into our very flesh and blood. There are some things, indeed, that we lived through and survived *independently*, just as they did there in the West, where such things were indigenous. The Europeans absolutely refuse to believe this: they do not know us, and for the moment this is all to the better. The essential process—which eventually will astonish the whole world—will take place all the more imperceptibly and peacefully. Part of that very process shows clearly and tangibly in our attitude toward the literatures of other peoples. For us—at least for the majority of our educated people—their poets are just as much ours as they are for the Europeans in the West. I maintain and I repeat: every European poet, thinker, and humanitarian is more clearly and more intimately understood and received in Russia than he is in any other country in the world save his own. Shakespeare, Byron, Walter Scott, and Dickens are more akin to the Russians and better understood by them than they are by the Germans, for example, despite the fact that we have not a tenth of the translations of these writers that Germany, with its abundance of books, has. When the French Convention of 1793 bestowed honorary citizenship *au poète allemand Schiller, l'ami de l'humanité*, it did something admirable, grand, and prophetic; yet it did not even suspect that at the other end of Europe, in barbaric Russia, that same Schiller was far more "national" and far more familiar to the Russian barbarians than he was to France, not only the France of the time but subsequently as well, all through our century. This was an age in which Schiller, the citizen of France and *l'ami de l'humanité*, was known in France only by professors of literature, and not even known by all of them, and not known well. But he, along with Zhukovsky, was absorbed into the Russian soul; he left his mark on it and all but gave his name to a period in the history of our development. This Russian attitude to world literature is a phenomenon whose extent is scarcely found among other peoples anywhere in world history. And if this quality is truly our distinctively Russian national trait, then surely no oversensitive patriotism or chauvinism could have the right to object to it and not desire, on the contrary, to regard it primarily as a most promising and prophetic fact to be kept in mind as we speculate about our future. Oh, of course many of you may smile when you read of the significance I attribute to George Sand; but those who find it amusing will be wrong: a good deal of time separates us from those events, and George Sand herself has died as an old woman of seventy having, perhaps, long outlived her fame. But everything in the life of this poet that constituted the "new word" she uttered, everything that was "universally human" in her—all of this at once created a deep and powerful impression among us, in our Russia at the time. It touched us, and thus it proved that any poet and innovator from Europe, anyone who appears there with new ideas and new force, cannot help but become at once a Russian poet, cannot but influence Russian thought, cannot but become almost a Russian force. However, I do not mean to write a whole critical article about George Sand; I intended only to say a few words of farewell to the deceased by the side of her fresh grave.

2. A Few Words about George Sand

George Sand appeared in literature when I was in my early youth, and I am very pleased that it was so long ago because now, more than thirty years later, I can speak almost with complete frankness. I should note that at the time her sort of thing—novels, I mean— was all that was permitted; all the rest, including virtually every new idea, and those coming from France in particular, was strictly suppressed. Oh, of course it often happened that they weren't able to pick out such "ideas," and indeed, where could they learn such a skill? Even Metternich lacked it, never mind those here who tried to imitate him. And so some "shocking things" would slip through (the whole of Belinsky slipped through, for instance). And then, as if to make up for Belinsky (near the end of the period, in particular) and be on the safe side, they began to forbid almost everything so that, as we know, we were left with little more than pages with blank lines on them. But novels were still permitted at the beginning, the middle, and even at the very end of the period. It was here, and specifically with George Sand, that the public's guardians made a very large blunder. Do you remember the verse:

> The tomes of Thiers and of Rabaut
> He knows, each line by line;
> And he, like furious Mirabeau
> Hails Liberty divine.

These are very fine verses, exceptionally so, and they will last forever because they have historic significance; but they are all the more precious because they were written by Denis Davydov, the poet, literary figure, and most honorable Russian. But even if in those days Denis Davydov considered Thiers, of all people (on account of his history of the revolution, of course) as dangerous and put him in a verse along with some Rabaut fellow (such a man also existed, it seems, but I don't know him), then there surely could not have been much that was permitted officially then. And what was the result? The whole rush of new ideas that came through the novels of the time served exactly the same ends, and perhaps by the standards of the day in an even more "dangerous" form, since there probably were not too many lovers of Rabaut, but there were thousands who loved George Sand. It should also be noted here that, despite all the Magnitskys and the Liprandis, ever since the eighteenth century people in Russia have at once learned about every intellectual movement in Europe, and these ideas have been at once passed down from the higher levels of our intellectuals to the mass of those taking even a slight interest in things and making some effort to think. This was precisely what happened with the European movement of the 1830s. Very quickly, right from the beginning of the thirties, we learned of this immense movement of European literatures. The names of the many newly fledged orators, historians, publicists, and professors became known. We even knew, though incompletely and superficially, the direction in which this movement was heading. And this movement manifested itself with particular passion in art—in the novel and above all in George Sand. It is true that Senkovsky and Bulgarin had warned the public about George Sand even before her novels appeared in

Russian. They tried to frighten Russian ladies, in particular, by telling them that she wore trousers; they tried to frighten people by saying she was depraved; they wanted to ridicule her. Senkovsky, who himself had been planning to translate George Sand in his magazine *Reader's Library*, began calling her Mrs. Yegor Sand in print and, it seems, was truly pleased with his witticism. Later on, in 1848, Bulgarin wrote in *The Northern Bee* that she indulged in daily drinking bouts with Pierre Leroux somewhere near the city gates and participated in "Athenian evenings" at the Ministry of the Interior; these evenings were supposedly hosted by the Minister himself, the bandit Ledru-Rollin. I read this myself and remember it very clearly. But at that time, in 1848, nearly the whole of our reading public knew George Sand, and no one believed Bulgarin. She appeared in Russian translation for the first time around the middle of the thirties. It's a pity that I don't recall when her first work was translated into Russian and which it was; but the impression it made must have been all the more startling. I think that the chaste, sublime purity of her characters and ideals and the modest charm of the severe, restrained tone of her narrative must have struck everyone then as it did me, still a youth—and this was the woman who went about in trousers engaging in debauchery! I was sixteen, I think, when I read her tale *L'Uscoque* for the first time; it is one of the most charming among her early works. Afterward, I recall, I had a fever all night long. I think I am right in saying, by my recollection at least, that George Sand for some years held almost the first place in Russia among the whole Pleiad of new writers who had suddenly become famous and created such a stir all over Europe. Even Dickens, who appeared in Russia at virtually the same time, was perhaps not as popular among our readers as she. I am not including Balzac, who arrived before her but who produced works such as *Eugénie Grandet* and *Père Goriot* in the thirties (and to whom Belinsky was so unfair when he completely overlooked Balzac's significance in French literature). However, I say all this not to make any sort of critical evaluation but purely and simply to recall the tastes of the mass of Russian readers at that time and the direct impression these readers received. What mattered most was that the reader was able to derive, even from her novels, all the things the guardians were trying so hard to keep from them. At least in the mid-forties the ordinary Russian reader knew, if only incompletely, that George Sand was one of the brightest, most consistent, and most upright representatives of the group of Western "new people" of the time, who, with their arrival on the scene, began to refute directly those "positive" achievements which marked the end of the bloody French (or rather, European) revolution of the preceding century. With the end of the revolution (after Napoleon I) there were fresh attempts to express new aspirations and new ideals. The most advanced minds understood all too well that this had only been despotism in a new form and that all that had happened was "ôte toi de là que je m'y mette"; that the new conquerors of the world, the bourgeoisie, turned out to be perhaps even worse than the previous despots, the nobility; that *Liberté, Égalité, Fraternité* proved to be only a ringing slogan and nothing more. Moreover, certain doctrines appeared which transformed such ringing slogans into utterly impossible ones. The conquerors now pronounced or recalled these three sacramental words in a tone of mockery; even science, through its brilliant representatives (economists) came with what seemed to be its new word to support this mocking attitude and to condemn the utopian significance of these three words for which so much blood had been shed. So it was that alongside the triumphant conquerors there began to appear despondent and mournful faces that frightened the victors. At this very same time a truly new word was pronounced and hope was reborn: people appeared who proclaimed directly that it had been vain and wrong to stop the advancement of the cause; that nothing had been achieved by the change of political conquerors; that the cause must be taken up again; that the renewal of humanity must be radical and social. Oh, of course, along with these solemn exclamations there came a host of views that were most pernicious and distorted, but the most important thing was that hope began to shine forth once more and faith again began to be regenerated. The history of this movement is well known; it continues even now and, it seems, has no intention of coming to a halt. I have no intention whatever of speaking either for or against it here, but I wanted only to define George Sand's real place within that movement. We must look for her place at the very beginning of the movement. People who met her in Europe then said that she was propounding a new status for women and foreseeing the "rights of the free wife" (this is what Senkovsky said about her). But that was not quite correct, because she was by no means preaching only about women and never invented any notion of a "free wife." George Sand belonged to the whole movement and was not merely sermonizing on women's rights. It is true that as a woman she naturally preferred portraying *heroines* to *heroes;* and of course women all over the world should put on mourning in her memory, because one of the most elevated and beautiful of their representatives has died. She was, besides, a woman of almost unprecedented intelligence and talent—a name that has gone down in history, a name that is destined not to be forgotten and not to disappear from European humanity.

As far as her heroines are concerned, I repeat that from my very first reading at the age of sixteen I was amazed by the strangeness of the contradiction between what was written and said about her and what I myself could see in fact. In actual fact, many, or at least some, of her heroines represented a type of such sublime moral purity as could not be imagined without a most thorough moral scrutiny within the poet's own soul; without the acceptance of one's full responsibility; without an understanding and a recognition of the most sublime beauty and mercy, patience, and justice. It is true that along with mercy, patience, and the recognition of one's obligations there was also an extraordinary pride in this scrutiny and in protest, but this pride was precious because it stemmed from that higher truth without which humanity could never maintain its high moral ideals. This pride is not a feeling of hostility *quand même,* based on the fact that I am supposedly better than you and you are worse than I; it is only a sense of the most chaste impossibility of compromise with falsity and vice, although, I repeat, this feeling excludes neither universal forgiveness nor mercy. Moreover, along with the pride came an enormous responsibility, voluntarily assumed. These heroines of hers sought to make sacrifices and do noble deeds. Several of the girls in her early works particularly appealed to me; these were the ones depicted, for example, in what were called at the time her Venetian tales (including *L'Uscoque* and *Aldini*). These were of the type that culminated in her novel *Jeanne,* a brilliant work which presents a serene and, perhaps, a final solution to the historical question of Joan of Arc. In a contemporary peasant girl she suddenly resurrects before us the image of the historical Joan of Arc and graphically makes a case for the actual possibility of this majestic and marvelous historical phenomenon, a task quite characteristic of George Sand, for no one but she among contemporary poets, perhaps, bore within her soul such a pure ideal of an innocent girl, an ideal that derives its power from its innocence. In several works in succession we find all these girl characters engaged in the same task and exemplifying the same theme (however, not only girls: this same theme is repeated later in her magnificent novel *La Marquise,* also one of her early works). We see depicted the upright, honest, but inexperienced character of a young female having that proud chastity, a girl who is unafraid and who cannot be stained by contact with vice, even if she were suddenly to find herself in some den of iniquity. The need for some magnanimous sacrifice (which supposedly she alone must make) strikes the heart of the young girl, and, without pausing to think or to spare herself, she selflessly, self-sacrificingly, and fearlessly takes a most perilous and fateful step. The things she sees and encounters subsequently do not trouble or frighten her in the least; to the contrary, courage at once rises up in her young heart, which only now becomes fully aware of its power—the power of innocence, honesty, purity. Courage doubles her energy and shows new paths and new horizons to a mind that had not fully known itself but was vigorous and fresh and not yet stained by life's compromises. In addition to this, there was the irreproachable and charming form of her poem-novels. At that time George Sand was particularly fond of ending her poems *happily,* with the triumph of innocence, sincerity, and young, fearless simplicity. Are these images that could trouble society and arouse doubts and fears? To the contrary, the strictest fathers and mothers began permitting their families to read George Sand and could only wonder, "Why is everyone saying these things about her?" But then voices of warning began to be heard: "In this very pride of a woman's quest, in this irreconcilability of chastity with vice, in this refusal to make any concessions to vice, in this fearlessness with which innocence rises up to struggle and to look straight into the eyes of the offender—in all this there is a poison, the future poison of women's protest, of women's emancipation." And what of it? Perhaps they were right about the poison; a poison really was being brewed, but what it sought to destroy, what had to perish from that poison and what was to be saved—these were the questions, and they were not answered for a long time.

Now these questions have long been resolved (or so it seems). It should be noted, by the way, that by the middle of the forties the fame of George Sand and the faith in the force of her genius stood so high that we, her contemporaries, all expected something incomparably greater from her in the future, some unprecedented of the most sincere forgiveness and love. They write that she died as an admirable mother who worked to the end of her life, a friend to the local peasants, deeply beloved by her friends. It seems she was somewhat inclined to set great store by her aristocratic origins (she was descended on her mother's side from the royal house of Saxony), but, of course, one can state firmly that if she saw aristocracy as something to be valued in people, it was an aristocracy based only on the level of perfection of the human soul: she could not help but love the great, she could not reconcile herself with the base and compromise her ideas; and here, perhaps, she may have shown an excess of pride. It is true that she also did not like to portray humble people in her novels, to depict the just but pliant, the eccentric and the downtrodden, such as we meet in almost every novel of the great Christian Dickens. On the contrary, she proudly elevated her heroines and placed them as high as queens. This she loved to do, and this trait we should note; it is rather characteristic.

new word, even something final and decisive. These
not realized: it turned out that at that same time, tha
end of the forties, she had already said everything t
destined to say, and now the final word about her can
her fresh grave.

George Sand was not a thinker, but she had the
clearly intuiting (if I may be permitted such a fancy wor
future awaiting humanity. All her life she believed
magnanimously in the realization of those ideals prec
she had the capacity to raise up the ideal in her ow
preservation of this faith to the end is usually the lot o
souls, all true lovers of humanity. George Sand died a
believing in God and her own immortal life, but it i
to say only that of her: beyond that she was, perha
Christian of all her contemporaries, the French writ
she did not formally (as a Catholic) confess Christ.
a Frenchwoman George Sand, like her compatriots,
confess consciously the idea that "in all Creation the
other than His by which one may be saved"—the
of Orthodoxy. Still, despite this apparent and formal
George Sand was, I repeat, perhaps one of the most
confessors of Christ even while unaware of being
her socialism, her convictions, her hopes, and her
human moral sense, on humanity's spiritual thirst,
toward perfection and purity, and not on the "ne
ant heap. She believed unconditionally in the hum
(even to the point of its immortality), and she el
panded the conception of it throughout her life,
works. Thus her thoughts and feelings coincided
most basic ideas of Christianity, that is, the ackn
the human personality and its freedom (and acc
sponsibility). From here arise her acknowledgme
rigorous moral scrutiny to that end, along with a con
of human responsibility. And there was not a thin
the France of her time, perhaps, who understoo
"man does not live by bread alone." As far as
scrutiny and her protest are concerned, I repea
never excluded mercy, the forgiveness of an offen
itless patience based on compassion toward the
fense. On the contrary, in her works George
attracted by the beauty of these truths and often cre

2

1. My Paradox

Again a tussle with Europe (oh, it's not a war yet: they say that we—Russia, that is—are still a long way from war). Again the endless Eastern Question is in the news; and again in Europe they are looking mistrustfully at Russia. . . . Yet why should we go running to seek Europe's trust? Did Europe ever trust the Russians? Can she ever trust us and stop seeing us as her enemy? Oh, of course this view will change *someday;* someday Europe will better be able to make us out and realize what we are like; and it is certainly worth discussing this *someday;* but meanwhile a somewhat irrelevant question or side issue has occurred to me and I have recently been busy trying to solve it. No one may agree with me, yet I think that I am right—in part, maybe, but right.

I said that Europe doesn't like Russians. No one, I think, will dispute the fact that they don't like us. They accuse us, among other things, of being terrible liberals: we Russians, almost to a man, are seen as not only liberals but revolutionaries; we are supposedly always inclined, almost lovingly, to join forces with the destructive elements of Europe rather than the conserving ones. Many Europeans look at us mockingly and haughtily for this—they are hateful: they cannot understand why we should be the ones to take the negative side *in someone else's affair;* they positively deny us the right of being negative as Europeans on the grounds that they do not recognize us as a part of "civilization." They see us rather as barbarians, reeling around Europe gloating that we have found something somewhere to destroy—to destroy purely for the sake of destruction, for the mere pleasure of watching it fall to pieces, just as if we were a horde of savages, a band of Huns, ready to fall upon ancient Rome and destroy its sacred shrines

515

without the least notion of the value of the things we are demolishing. That the majority of Russians have really proclaimed themselves liberals in Europe is true, and it is even a strange fact. Has anyone ever asked himself why this is so? Why was it that in the course of our century, virtually nine-tenths of the Russians who acquired their culture in Europe always associated themselves with the stratum of Europeans who were liberal, with the left—i.e., always with the side that rejected its own culture and its own civilization? (I mean to a greater or a lesser degree, of course: what Thiers rejects in civilization and what the Paris Commune of 1871 rejected are very different things). And like these European liberals, Russians in Europe are liberals "to a greater or lesser degree" and in many different shades; but nonetheless, I repeat, they are more inclined than the Europeans to join directly with the extreme left at once rather than to begin by dwelling among the lesser ranks of liberalism. In short, you'll find far fewer Thierses than you will Communards among the Russians. And note that these are not some crowd of ragamuffins—not all of them, at least—but people with a very solid, civilized look about them, some of them almost like cabinet ministers. But Europeans do not trust appearances: "Grattez le russe et vous verrez le tartare," they say (scratch a Russian and you'll find a Tatar). That may be true, but this is what occurred to me: do the majority of Russians, in their dealings with Europe, join the extreme left because they are Tatars and have the savage's love of destruction, or are they, perhaps, moved by other reasons? That is the question, and you'll agree that it is a rather interesting one. The time of our tussles with Europe is coming to an end; the role of the window cut through to Europe is over, and something else is beginning, or ought to begin at least, and everyone who has the least capacity to think now realizes this. In short, we are more and more beginning to feel that we ought to be ready for something, for some new and far more original encounter with Europe than we have had hitherto. Whether that encounter will be over the Eastern Question or over something else no one can tell! And so it is that all such questions, analyses, and even surmises and paradoxes can be of interest simply through the fact that they can teach us something. And isn't it a curious thing that it is precisely those Russians who are most given to considering themselves Europeans, and whom we call "Westernizers," who exult and take pride in this appellation and who still taunt the

other half of the Russians with the names "kvasnik" and "zipunnik?" Is it not curious, I say, that these very people are the quickest
to join the extreme left—those who deny civilization and who would
destroy it—and that this surprises absolutely no one in Russia, and
that the question has never even been posed? Now isn't that truly
a curious thing?

I'll tell you frankly that I have framed an answer to this question,
but I don't intend to try to prove my idea. I shall merely explain
it briefly in an effort to bring forth the facts. In any case, it cannot
be proven, because there are some things which are incapable of
proof.

This is what I think: does not this fact (i.e., the fact that even
our most ardent Westernizers side with the extreme left—those who
in essence reject Europe) reveal the protesting Russian soul which
always, from the very time of Peter the Great, found many, all too
many, aspects of European culture hateful and always alien? That
is what I think. Oh, of course this protest was almost always an
unconscious one; but what truly matters here is that the Russian
instinct has not died: the Russian soul, albeit unconsciously, has
protested precisely in the name of its Russianness, in the name of
its downtrodden and Russian principle. People will say, of course,
that if this really were so there would be no cause for rejoicing:
"the one who rejects, be he Hun, barbarian, or Tatar, has rejected
not in the name of something higher but because he himself was
so lowly that even over two centuries he could not manage to make
out the lofty heights of Europe."

People will certainly say that. I agree that this is a legitimate
question, but I do not intend to answer it; I will only say, without
providing any substantiation, that I utterly and totally reject this
Tatar hypothesis. Oh, of course, who now among all us Russians,
especially when this is all in the past (because this period certainly
has ended)—who, among all us Russians can argue against the
things that Peter did, against the window he cut through to Europe?
Who can rise up against him with visions of the ancient Muscovy
of the tsars? This is not the point at all, and this is not why I
began my discussion; the point is that, no matter how many fine
and useful things we saw through Peter's window, there still were
so many bad and harmful things there that always troubled the
Russian instinct. That instinct never ceased to protest (although it
lost its way so badly that in most cases it did not realize what it

was doing), and it protested not because of its Tatar essence but, perhaps, precisely because it had preserved something within itself that was higher and better than anything it saw through the window.... (Well, of course it didn't protest against everything: we received a great many fine things from Europe and we don't want to be ungrateful; still, our instinct was right in protesting against at least half of the things.)

I repeat that all this happened in a most original fashion: it was precisely our most ardent Westernizers, precisely those who struggled for reform, who at the same time were rejecting Europe and joining the ranks of the extreme left.... And the result: in so doing they defined themselves as the most fervent Russians of all, the champions of old Russia and the Russian spirit. And, of course, if anyone had tried to point that out to them at the time, they would either have burst out laughing or been struck with horror. There is no doubt that they were unaware of any higher purpose to their protest. On the contrary, all the while, for two whole centuries, they denied their own high-mindedness, and not merely their high-mindedness but their very self-respect (there were, after all, some such ardent souls!), and to a degree that amazed even Europe; yet it turns out that they were the very ones who proved to be genuine Russians. It is this theory of mine that I call my paradox.

Take Belinsky, for example. A passionate enthusiast by nature, he was almost the first Russian to take sides directly with the European socialists who had already rejected the whole order of European civilization; meanwhile, at home, in Russian literature, he waged a war to the end against the Slavophiles, apparently for quite the opposite cause. How astonished he would have been had those same Slavophiles told him that he was the most ardent defender of the Russian truth, the distinctly Russian individual, the Russian principle, and the champion of all those things which he specifically rejected in Russia for the sake of Europe, things he considered only a fantasy. Moreover, what if they had proved to him that in a certain sense he was the one who was the real conservative, precisely because in Europe he was a socialist and a revolutionary? And in fact that is almost the way it was. There was one huge mistake made here by both sides, and it was made first and foremost in that all the Westernizers of that time confused Russia with Europe. They took Russia for Europe, and by rejecting Europe and her order they thought to apply that same rejection to

Russia. But Russia was not Europe at all; she may have worn a
European coat, but beneath that coat was a different creature altogether. It was the Slavophiles who tried to make people see that
Russia was not Europe but a different creature altogether when
they pointed out that the Westernizers were equating things that
were dissimilar and incompatible and when they argued that something true for Europe was entirely inapplicable to Russia, in part
because all the things the Westernizers wanted in Europe had
already long existed in Russia, in embryo or potentiality at least.
Such things even comprise Russia's essence, not in any revolutionary sense but in the sense in which the notions of universal
human renewal should appear: in the sense of divine Truth, the
Truth of Christ, which, God grant, will someday be realized on
earth and which is preserved in its entirety in Orthodoxy. The
Slavophiles urged people to study Russia first and then draw conclusions. But it was not possible to study Russia then and, in truth,
the means to do so were not available. In any case, at that time
who could know anything about Russia? The Slavophiles, of course,
knew a hundred times more than the Westernizers (and that was
a minimum), but even they almost had to feel their way, engaging
in abstract speculation and relying mainly on their remarkable
instincts. Learning something became possible only in the last
twenty years: but who, even now, knows anything about Russia?
At most, the basis for study has been set down, but as soon as an
important question arises we at once hear a clamor of discordant
voices. Here we have the Eastern Question coming up again: well,
admit it, are there many among us—and who are they?—who can
agree on this question and agree on its solution? And this in such
an important, momentous, and fateful national question! But never
mind the Eastern Question! Why take up such big questions? Just
look at the hundreds, the thousands of our internal and everyday,
current questions: how uncertain everyone is; how poorly our views
are established; how little accustomed we are to work! Here we see
Russia's forests being destroyed; both landowners and peasants are
cutting down trees in a kind of frenzy. One can state positively
that timber is being sold for a tenth of its value: can the supply
last for long? Before our children grow up there will be only a
tenth of today's timber on the market. What will happen then?
Ruination, perhaps. And meanwhile, try to say a word about cur-
tailing the right to destroy our forests and what do you hear? On
the one hand, that it is a state and a national necessity, and, on

the other, that it is a violation of the rights of private property—
two opposite notions. Two camps will at once form, and one still
doesn't know where liberal opinion, which resolves everything, will
side. Indeed, will there be only two camps? The matter will drag
on for a long time. Someone made a witty remark in the current
liberal spirit to the effect that there is no cloud without a silver
lining, since cutting down all the Russian forests would at least
have the positive value of eliminating corporal punishment: the
district courts would have no switches to beat errant peasants. This
is some consolation, of course, yet somehow it is hard to believe:
even if the forests should disappear altogether, there would always
be something to flog people with; they'd start importing it, I
suppose. Now the Yids are becoming landowners, and people shout
and write everywhere that they are destroying the soil of Russia.
A Yid, they say, having spent capital to buy an estate, at once
exhausts all the fertility of the land he has purchased in order to
restore his capital with interest. But just try and say anything against
this and the hue and cry will be at once raised: you are violating
the principles of economic freedom and equal rights for all citizens.
But what sort of equal rights are there here if it is a case of a clear
and Talmudic *status in statu* above all and in the first place? What
if it is a case not only of exhausting the soil but also of the future
exhaustion of our peasant who, having been freed from the landowner will, with his whole commune, undoubtedly and very quickly
now fall into a far worse form of slavery under far worse landowners—those same new landowners who have already sucked the
juices from the peasants of western Russia, those same landowners
who are now buying up not only estates and peasants but who have
also begun to buy up liberal opinion and continue doing so with
great success? Why do we have all these things? Why is there such
indecisiveness and discord over each and every decision we make?
(And please note that: it is true, is it not?) In my opinion, it is
not because of our lack of talent and not because of our incapacity
for work; it is because of our continuing ignorance of Russia, of
its essence and its individuality, its meaning and its spirit, despite
the fact that, compared with the time of Belinsky and the Slavophiles, we have had twenty years of schooling. Even more: in these
twenty years of schooling the study of Russia has in fact been
greatly advanced, while Russian instinct has, it seems, declined in
comparison with the past. What is the reason for this? But if their
Russian instinct saved the Slavophiles at that time, then that same

instinct was present in Belinsky as well, and sufficiently present so that the Slavophiles might have considered him their best friend. I repeat, there was an enormous misunderstanding on both sides here. Not in vain did Apollon Grigorev, who also sometimes had rather acute insights, say that "had Belinsky lived longer he would certainly have joined the Slavophiles." He had a real idea there.

2. Deduction from My Paradox

And so, people will ask me: "Do you mean that when any Russian turns into a European Communard he thereby at once becomes a Russian conservative?" No, it would be too risky to come to a conclusion like that. I wanted only to observe that this idea, even if taken literally, contains a drop of the truth. So much of this has happened with no conscious awareness, while on my part I may be placing too much faith in the continuity of Russian instinct and in the living power of the Russian spirit. But let that be; I know myself that this is a paradox. Here is what I would like to place before you by way of conclusion: it is also a fact and a deduction from that fact. I said above that Russians are noted in Europe for their liberalism and that at least nine-tenths of them side with the left, the extreme left, just as soon as they come into contact with Europe. . . . I don't insist on that figure—perhaps it isn't a matter of nine-tenths of them; I insist only on the fact that there are incomparably more liberal Russians than illiberal ones. But there are also illiberal Russians. Yes, indeed, there are and there always have been such Russians (you know the names of many of them), who not only did not reject European civilization but, to the contrary, paid such homage to it that they lost their last scrap of Russian instinct; they lost their Russian personality and their Russian language; they changed homelands, and if they didn't take on foreign citizenship, then at least they went on living in Europe for whole generations. But it is a fact that all such people (in contrast to the liberal Russians, in contrast to their atheism and Communardism) sided with the right, the extreme right, and became terrible, European conservatives.

Many of them changed their religion and went over to Catholicism. Aren't they conservatives? Aren't they the extreme right? Yet note, please: they are conservatives in Europe, but, contrary to what we might expect, they reject Russia entirely. They became Russia's enemies and would annihilate her! And so this is what it

meant for a Russian to be refashioned into a genuine European
and to become a genuine child of civilization. This is a remarkable
fact that has been derived from two hundred years of experience.
The deduction is that a Russian who has become a real European
cannot help but become at the same time a natural enemy of Russia.
Is that what was wanted by the people who opened up the window
to the West? Is that what they had in mind? And so we found two
types of civilized Russians: the European Belinsky who, while
denying Europe, turned out to be Russian to the highest degree
despite all the mistaken views he expressed about Russia; and the
fundamentally native, ancient Russian Prince Gagarin who, on
becoming European, found it necessary not only to embrace Catholicism but to skip directly into the ranks of the Jesuits. Now
which one of them, tell me, is the greater friend of Russia? Which
one of them remained the more Russian? And does not this second
example (from the extreme right) support my original paradox that
the Russian European socialists and Communards are above all
non-European and will end by becoming fundamental, good Russians again once the misunderstanding has been cleared up and
once they have learned something of Russia? Second, it is utterly
impossible to turn a Russian into a genuine European and have
him remain even a little bit Russian. And if such is the case, then
it follows that Russia, too, is something independent and distinctive,
utterly unlike Europe and important in its own right. Europe itself,
perhaps, is not at all unjust in condemning the Russians and mocking their revolutionary tendencies. It means that we are revolutionaries not merely for the sake of destroying things we have not
built, like the Huns and the Tatars, but for some other purpose
of which we still, to be sure, are unaware (and those who do know
keep it to themselves). In short, we are revolutionaries, so to say,
out of some internal necessity, even out of conservatism. . . . But
this is all something transitory, some irrelevant side issue, as I have
already said. At the moment the stage is occupied by the eternally
insoluble Eastern Question.

3. The Eastern Question

The Eastern Question! Which of us did not experience some rather
unusual feelings this month? What a lot of different views there
were in the newspapers! And what confusion in some heads, and
what cynicism in some judgments, and what good, honest alarm

in some hearts, and what an uproar among some Yids! One thing
is certain: there is nothing to fear, although there were many who
were trying to frighten us. Indeed, it was hard to imagine so many
cowards in Russia. Russia has *intentional* cowards, to be sure, but
they, it seems, erred in the date and now even for them it is too
late to show cowardice and there is little benefit in it: they will
have no success. But even the intentional cowards know their limitations and will not demand dishonor from Russia as they did in
times gone by, when Ivan the Terrible sent ambassadors to King
Stefan Batory and demanded that they submit even to beatings so
long as they were able to plead successfully for peace. In short,
public opinion has, it seems, declared itself and will not agree to
beatings for the sake of peace of any sort.

Prince Milan of Serbia and Prince Nicholas of Montenegro, trusting in God and in their own just cause, have come out against the
Sultan. When you read these lines there already may be news of
some significant encounter, or even of a decisive battle. The matter
will proceed quickly now. The indecisiveness and delay of the major
powers, England's diplomatic eccentricity in refusing to agree to
the conclusions of the Berlin conferences, the revolution in Constantinople and outburst of Moslem fanaticism that followed suddenly thereafter, and, finally, the terrible massacre by bashibazouks
and Circassians of sixty thousand peaceful Bulgarians, including
old men, women, and children—all this at once set things ablaze
and led to war. The Slavs have many hopes. If one considers all
their forces, they have as many as one hundred and fifty thousand
fighting men of whom more than three-quarters are capable troops
of the regular army. But the main thing is their spirit: they march
with faith in their own just cause and in their victory, whereas the
Turks, despite their fanaticism, are sorely lacking leaders and in
a great state of confusion; it will be no great surprise if this confusion turns into panic after the first encounters. I think that one
can already predict that if there is no interference from Europe,
the Slavs will surely be victorious. Evidently, Europe has decided
not to interfere, but it is difficult to say that there is anything firm
and decided in European politics at the present moment. In view
of the immense question that has suddenly arisen, they all seem
to have quietly resolved to wait and postpone their final decision.
We hear, however, that the alliance of the three great Eastern powers
is continuing; personal meetings of the three monarchs are continuing as well, so that noninterference in the struggle of the Slavs

from this side is, *for the moment,* certain. England, which has isolated herself, is looking for allies: the question is, will she find them? If she does find an ally, then it seems it will not be in France. In short, all of Europe will be watching the struggle of Christians with the Sultan without interfering in it, but . . . only for the moment, until the time when . . . the legacy is divided. But is this legacy a possibility? Will there still be any legacy? If God grants success to the Slavs, then what limit will Europe set on their success? Will she permit the sick man to be dragged completely off his bed? The latter is very difficult to imagine. To the contrary, after a new and solemn concilium will Europe not decide on some new means of curing his ailments? . . . Thus the efforts of the Slavs, even in the event of a very major success, may be rewarded only by rather weak palliatives. Serbia has entered the field relying on her own strength, but of course she realizes that her ultimate fate depends entirely on Russia. She knows that only Russia will preserve her from ruin in the event of a great disaster and that Russia herself, by means of her strong influence, will help her preserve the maximum benefit possible in the event of success. She knows this and relies on Russia, but she also knows that the whole of Europe is now watching Russia with concealed mistrust and that Russia's situation is a difficult one. In short, everything remains in the future; but how will Russia act?

Is this a question? This cannot help but be a question for every Russian. Russia will act *honorably*—that is the entire answer to this question. Let England's prime minister distort the truth before Parliament for political reasons and tell it officially that the massacre of sixty thousand Bulgarians came at the hands, not of the Turks, nor of the bashibazouks, but at the hands of Slavic emigrants. And let the entire Parliament, for political reasons, believe him and tacitly give approval to his lie. Nothing of the sort can or should happen in Russia. Some will say that Russia cannot, in any event, act directly against her own best interest. But where is Russia's interest here? Russia's best interest is precisely to act even against her best interest if necessary; to make a sacrifice, so as not to violate justice. Russia cannot betray a great idea which has been her legacy from past centuries and which she has followed unswervingly until now. This idea is, among other things, one of the unity of all the Slavs; but such unity is based not upon seizure of territory or on violence; it is done as service to the whole of mankind. Indeed, when and how often did Russia act out of a policy of direct benefit to herself? To the contrary, through the whole Petersburg period of her history did she not more often unselfishly serve the interests of others? This is something that would astonish Europe if Europe were able to see clearly and did not always look at us mistrustfully, suspiciously, and hatefully. On the whole, no one in Europe has any belief in unselfishness at all, never mind Russian unselfishness—they will sooner believe in dishonesty or stupidity. But we have nothing to fear from their opinions: Russia's whole power, her whole personality, so to say, and her whole future mission lie in her self-denying unselfishness. It is only a pity that this power has sometimes been rather misdirected.

4. The Utopian Conception of History

The whole century and a half that followed Peter's reforms was nothing more than a period of living in contact with all the human civilizations and of making their history and their ideals our own. We studied and learned to love the French, the Germans, and all the rest as if they were our brothers, despite the fact that they never loved us and had made up their minds that they never would. But that was the essence of our reform and of everything that Peter did: in the course of a century and a half we derived from it a *broadening* of our outlook that perhaps has no precedent in any other nation in either the ancient or the modern world. Pre-Petrine Russia was active and strong, although she developed slowly in a political sense. She worked out her own form of unity and set about consolidating her border regions. She understood implicitly that she bore within her a precious thing—Orthodoxy—that no longer existed anywhere else and that she was charged with preserving the truth of Christ, the real truth, the genuine image of Christ which had been obscured in all the other religions and in all the other nations. The best Russians of the time believed that this precious gift, this truth—eternal, inherent in Russia, and given to her to preserve—could somehow relieve their consciences of the obligation to acquire any other form of enlightenment. Moreover, Moscow came to believe that any closer contact with Europe could even have a harmful, corrupting influence on the Russian mind and on the Russian *idea;* that it could distort Orthodoxy itself and lead Russia on to the road to perdition, "in the manner of all other nations." So it was that ancient Russia, isolated within herself, was *prepared to be unjust:* unjust to humanity in her decision passively to keep her treasure, her Orthodoxy, to herself and to isolate herself from Europe—from humanity, that is—in the manner of certain religious sectarians who will not eat from the same dish as you and consider it a sacred duty for each to keep his own cup and spoon. This is a fair comparison, because prior to Peter we had evolved almost this very sort of political and spiritual relationship to Europe. With Peter's reforms came an enormous broadening of our outlook and this, I repeat, constitutes Peter's whole great achievement. This also constitutes that same precious gift of which I have already spoken in one of the preceding issues of my *Diary*. It is a precious gift which we, the higher cultured level of Russia, are bringing to the People after our century-and-a-half absence from Russia and which the People, once we ourselves have acknowledged their truth, should accept from us as a sine qua non, "without which it will be impossible to unite the People and the cultured classes and everything will come to ruin." What is this "broadening of outlook," what does it consist of, and what does it signify? It is not a matter of enlightenment in the strict sense of the word, and it is not science; neither is it a betrayal of the moral principles of the Russian People in the name of European civilization. No, it is specifically something characteristic of the Russian People alone, for a reform such as Peter's has never taken place anywhere else. It is really and truly our almost brotherly love for other nations, which derived from our century and a half of contact with them; it is our need to serve humanity in every way, even if sometimes at the expense of our own best and major immediate interests; it is our reconciliation with their civilizations, our comprehension and our *excusing* of their ideals when these ideals were not in harmony with our own; it is our acquired capacity to discover the truth contained in each of the civilizations of Europe or, more correctly, in each of the personalities of Europe, despite the fact that they contain much with which we cannot agree. It is, finally, our need to be just above all and to seek only the truth. In short, it perhaps is the beginning, the first step toward that active application of our gift, our Orthodoxy, to the universal service of humanity for which it was intended and which, in fact, constitutes its very essence. So it was that from Peter's reform there came a broadening of our *former* idea, the Russian Muscovite idea; there came an expanded and strengthened conception of that idea: through the reform we became aware of our universal mission, our personality, and our role in humanity, and we could not help but become aware that this mission and this role were unlike those of other nations, for among them each individual nationality lives only for itself and in itself, while we, now that the time has come, will begin directly by becoming the servant of all for the sake of universal reconciliation. And there is no shame in this whatsoever; to the contrary, it is what makes us great, because it all leads to the ultimate unifying of humanity. He who would be first in the Kingdom of God must become the servant of all. This is how I understand Russia's destiny *in its ideal form*. The first step of our new policy appeared of itself after Peter's reform: this first step had to consist in the uniting of all of Slavdom, so to say, under the wing of Russia. And this process of unification is not for seizing territory, nor for committing violence, nor for crushing the other Slavic personalities beneath the Russian colossus; it is for restoring them and placing them in their proper relationship to Europe and to humanity; it is for giving them, at last, the opportunity for relief and rest after their innumerable and centuries-long sufferings; it is for renewing their spirits and, once they have found new strength, for enabling them to contribute their own mite to the treasury of the human spirit so that they can utter their own word to civilization. Oh, of course you may laugh at all these "daydreams" about Russia's destiny, but still, tell me: is this not precisely the basis on which all Russians want the Slavs to be resurrected, precisely for their complete personal freedom and for the restoration of their spirit? But it is certainly not so that Russia may acquire them politically and use them to enhance her own political might (although Europe suspects the latter). This is so, is it not? And accordingly, this lends weight to at least some of my "daydreams," does it not? It follows that for this same purpose Constantinople must, sooner or later, be ours. . . .

Heavens, what a mocking smile would appear on the face of some Austrian or Englishman if he had the opportunity to read all these *daydreams* I have just written down and if he were to read as far as such a *positive* conclusion: "Constantinople, the Golden Horn, the most critical political area in the world—is this not a seizure of territory?"

Yes, I answer, the Golden Horn and Constantinople—all that will be ours, but not for the sake of merely annexing territory and not for the sake of violence. And in the first place it will happen of its own accord precisely because the time has come, and if the time has not yet arrived just now, then it is truly at hand, as all the signs indicate. This is a natural result; this is something decreed by Nature herself, as it were. If this has not happened before, it is simply because the time was not yet ripe. People in Europe believe in some sort of "Testament of Peter the Great." This is no more than a forged document concocted by the Poles. But had Peter then hit upon the notion of seizing Constantinople rather than founding Petersburg, then it seems to me that he would have abandoned the idea after some thought, even if he had had sufficient strength to crush the Sultan, precisely because the matter was still inopportune and might even have led to Russia's ruination.

If in Finnish Petersburg we couldn't avoid the influence of neighboring Germans (who, despite their usefulness, paralyzed Russian development before its true path had been clearly revealed), then how, in the huge and distinctive city of Constantinople with its remnants of a mighty and ancient civilization—how could we have avoided the influence of the Greeks, a nation far more subtle than the coarse Germans, a nation with whom we have much more in common than the Germans, who are utterly unlike us? The throne would have at once been surrounded by throngs of courtiers; they would have become educated and learned sooner than the Russians; they would have enchanted Peter himself, not to mention his immediate successors, exploiting his weak point by demonstrating their knowledge and skill in seamanship. In short, they would have gained political power in Russia; they would have at once dragged her off on some new Asiatic road, into another sort of seclusion, and of course the Russia of that time would not have survived it. The development of Russia's strength and her sense of nationhood would have been halted in their course. The mighty Great Russian would have remained in isolation in his gloomy and snowy North, serving as no more than raw material for the renewal of Tsargrad, and ultimately, perhaps, the Russian would have found it unnecessary even to follow Constantinople. The South of Russia would have fallen entirely into the clutches of the Greeks. Orthodoxy itself might even have divided into two entirely separate worlds: one in a renewed Tsargrad, the other in old Russia.... In short, the matter would have been most untimely. Now, however, things are quite different.

Now Russia has already spent time in Europe and is herself educated. The principal thing is that she has become aware of all her power and has in truth become powerful; she also has become aware of where her real strength lies. Now she understands that

Tsargrad can certainly not be ours as Russia's capital, but two centuries ago, had Peter seized Tsargrad, he could not have done other than transfer his capital there, and this would have been a fatal move since Tsargrad is not in Russia and *could not* have become Russia. Had Peter been able to resist making this error, then his immediate successors would not have been able to resist. And if Tsargrad can now be ours not as Russia's capital, then neither can it be ours as the capital of Slavdom as a whole, as some people imagine. Slavdom as a whole, without Russia, would exhaust itself there in struggling with the Greeks, even if it could manage to create some sort of political unity from its various entities. But to leave Constantinople as a legacy to the Greeks alone is now utterly impossible: we must not give them such a critical point on the globe; this would be altogether too generous a gift to them. But the whole of Slavdom with Russia at its head—oh, of course, that is a different matter entirely. Whether it is a proper matter is another question. Would this not look like a Russian political annexation of the Slavs, something we surely have no need of? And so in the name of what, in the name of what *moral* right could Russia make a claim on Constantinople? What lofty purpose could we use as a basis to demand it from Europe? On just this lofty purpose: as leader of Orthodoxy, as its protector and guardian, a role set out for Russia since Ivan III, who placed as an emblem the double-headed eagle of Tsargrad above the ancient coat of arms of Russia, but a role revealed clearly only after Peter the Great, when Russia realized that she had the power to fulfill this mission and in fact became the actual and sole guardian both of Orthodoxy and of the nations who profess it. This is the reason and the *right* to ancient Tsargrad, one that would be clear and inoffensive even to the Slavs who guard their independence most jealously, or even to the Greeks themselves. This would be the means to reveal the essence of the political relationships that must inevitably ensue in Russia toward all the other Orthodox nationalities, Slavic and Greek alike: Russia is their protector and even, perhaps, their leader, but not their ruler; she is their mother, but not their mistress. And if she should become their sovereign at some time, then it would be only be because they would have proclaimed her so, allowing themselves to keep all those things by which they would define their own independence and individuality. And so, sometime, even the non-Orthodox European Slavs might join such a union, for they themselves would see that such a unity under Russia's protection means only the consolidation of the independent individuality of each, while without this immense unifying force they, perhaps, would again exhaust themselves in mutual strife and discord, even if they should one day achieve political independence from the Moslems and the Europeans to whom they now belong.

"What's the point of playing with words?" people will say. "What is this 'Orthodoxy?'" Where can one find here any such idea, any such right to unify the nations? And is this not a purely political union like all the others, even though it may be based on the broadest foundations, like those of the United American States or perhaps broader still?" That is a question which may be put, and I will answer it. No, it will not be like that, and this is not playing with words; there *truly* will be something special and unprecedented here; it will be not merely a political union, and certainly not a matter of political annexation and violence (the only way in which Europe can conceive of something like this). And it will not be done merely in the name of some merchants' wheeling and dealing, personal gain, and all those eternal, unchanging, and idolized vices cloaked in an official Christianity in which no one aside from the *mob* can truly believe. No, it will be a true exaltation of the truth of Christ, which has been preserved in the East, a true, new exaltation of the cross of Christ and the ultimate word of Orthodoxy, at whose head Russia has long been standing. It will be a temptation for all the mighty of this world who have been triumphant until now and who have always regarded all such "expectations" with scorn and derision and who do not even comprehend that one can seriously believe in human brotherhood, in the universal reconciliation of nations, in a union founded on principles of universal service to humanity and regeneration of people through the true principles of Christ. And if believing in this "new word," which Russia at the head of a united Orthodoxy can utter to the world—if believing in this is a "utopia" worthy only of derision, then you may number me among these utopians, and leave the ridicule to me.

"But," people may still object, "it is utopian indeed to imagine that Russia will ever be *permitted* to stand at the head of the Slavs and enter Constantinople. You can dream about it, but these are still only dreams!"

Is that really so? Russia is powerful, and perhaps much more powerful than she herself may suppose. Aside from that, have we not seen, even in recent decades, mighty empires rise to power in

Europe, one of which has disappeared like dust and ashes, swept
away in a day by the winds of God, while in its place arose a new
empire whose might, it seemed, had never been equaled on earth?
Who could have predicted this? If such revolutionary changes are
possible, and if they happen in our time and before our very eyes,
then can the human mind predict without error the outcome of the
Eastern Question? What real basis is there to despair of the resurrection and the unity of the Slavs? Who can know the ways of
the Lord?

5. About Women Again

Almost all the newspapers have changed to sympathizing with the
Serbs and Montenegrins who have risen up for the liberation of
their brothers, while educated society, and now even the People,
avidly follow the successes of the insurgent troops. But the Slavs
need help. Apparently reliable news has come that the Turks are
being very actively, though anonymously, aided by the Austrians
and the English. In fact the aid is scarcely even anonymous. The
Turks are being provided with money, weapons, shells, and—men.
There are many foreign officers in the Turkish army. A mighty
English fleet stands at Constantinople ... out of political considerations, but more likely—just in case. Austria already has assembled an enormous army—also just in case. The Austrian press reacts
angrily toward the rebelling Serbs and—toward Russia. It should
be noted that if Europe presently regards the Slavs so *unfeelingly,*
then naturally it is because the Russians are also Slavs. Otherwise
the Austrian newspapers would not be so afraid of the Serbs, who
in military terms count for next to nothing before Austrian might,
and would not be comparing Serbia with Piedmont. . . .

And therefore Russian society must again help the Slavs, though
only with money and some supplies, of course. General Cherniaev
has already sent word to Petersburg that the medical services in
the whole of the Serbian army are extremely poor: there are no
doctors or medicines and little treatment available for the wounded.
In Moscow the Slavic Committee has launched an energetic appeal
to the whole of Russia for aid to our insurrectionary brothers, and
all the committee's members, together with an immense crowd of
people, went to the church of the Serbian community for a solemn
service of prayer for victory of the Serbian and Montenegrin forces.
Petersburg newspapers are beginning to publish declarations of

support from private citizens and are receiving their donations. The movement is evidently growing, despite the so-called dead season of summer. But it is dead only in Petersburg.

I was about to conclude my *Diary* and was already checking the proofs when a young girl unexpectedly called on me. I had met her in the winter after I had begun publishing my *Diary*. She wants to take a rather difficult examination and is energetically preparing for it; she'll pass it, of course. She's from a wealthy family and doesn't lack means, but is very concerned about her education. She would come to ask my advice on what to read and what to pay particular attention to. She has been visiting me about once a month, staying no more than ten minutes; she would speak only of her own affairs, but briefly, modestly, almost shyly, showing remarkable trust in me. Yet I could also see she had a very resolute nature, and it seems I was not mistaken. This time she came to me and said directly: "People are needed to tend the sick in Serbia. I have decided to postpone my examination for the time being so I can go look after the wounded. What do you think?"

And she looked at me almost timidly, yet her look told me clearly that she had already made her decision and that it was an absolutely firm one. She wanted some parting words of approval from me, however. I cannot convey all the details of our conversation lest I might in some small way violate her anonymity; I am passing on only its general content.

I suddenly felt very sorry for her—she is so young. It would have been quite pointless to frighten her with the difficulties, the war, the typhus in the field hospitals; this would mean only pouring oil on the flames. Here was a pure case of longing for sacrifice, for some noble feat, for some good deed; most significant and most precious was her total lack of conceit and self-infatuation; she wanted only to "look after the wounded" and to be of help.

"But do you know anything about treating wounded soldiers?"

"No, but I've been collecting information and have been to the Committee. Those who enlist are given two weeks to prepare, and of course I'll manage."

And she will, of course; here the word is equal to the deed.

"Listen," I told her, "I don't want to frighten you or dissuade you, but consider my words well and try to weigh them in your conscience. You have grown up in surroundings quite different from those you'll encounter there; you've seen only good society and have met people only in that calm state of mind where they remain within the bounds of etiquette. But the same people at war, in crowded conditions, in hardship and labor, may change utterly. Suppose you spend a whole night tending the sick; you've worn yourself out and are so exhausted that you can barely stand, when a doctor—a very good man at heart, perhaps, but tired and over-strained after just amputating a number of arms and legs—turns to you in irritation and says: 'All you do is make a mess of things; you can't do anything! If you've taken on this job, then do it properly!' and so on. Won't you find that hard to bear? Yet you certainly have to expect that sort of thing, and what I'm suggesting is only a tiny part of what's ahead of you. Real life often surprises us. And finally, are you certain that, even with all your resolve, you'll be able to cope with looking after the wounded? Might you not faint at the sight of some death, some wound or operation? This happens despite one's will, unconsciously. . . . ' "

"If I'm told that I'm doing things wrong and not working properly, then I'll certainly understand that this doctor is himself ir-ritable and tired; it's enough to know in my own heart that I'm not to blame and have done everything properly."

"But you're still so young; how can you be certain what you'll do?"

"What makes you think I'm young? *I'm already eighteen;* I'm not so young at all. . . . "

In short, it was impossible to dissuade her: she was ready to go off the very next day, in any case, regretting only that I did not approve of what she was doing.

"Well, God be with you," I said. "Go on; but come back just as soon as the thing is finished."

"Of course. I have to take my examination. But you'll never believe how happy you've made me."

She went away radiant and, of course, she will be *there* in a week.

At the beginning of this *Diary,* in the article about George Sand, I wrote a few words about the young female characters I had found particularly appealing in the stories of her earliest period. Well, this girl was just like one of them. She had just the same sort of direct, honest, but inexperienced young feminine character, along with that proud chastity which is unafraid and which cannot be stained even by contact with vice. This girl felt the need for sac-rifice, for undertaking a task that seemed to be asked of her spe-cifically; she had the conviction that she must first begin herself, with no excuses, to do all those fine things that we expect and demand from others. This is a conviction which is genuine and moral to the highest degree, but which, alas, is most often characteristic only of youthful purity and innocence. But the main thing, I repeat, is that here there is only a cause and not the slightest element of vanity, conceit, or infatuation with one's own heroism, something that we very often see among today's young people, even among mere adolescents.

After she had left I could not help but think once more about the need for higher education for women in Russia, a need that is most urgent at this moment in particular, in view of the serious pressure among today's women to be active, to be educated, and to participate in the common cause. I think that the fathers and mothers of these daughters ought themselves to insist on it for their own sake, if they love their children. In fact, it is only higher learning that is serious, attractive, and powerful enough to settle what is almost an agitation that has begun among our women. Only science can provide answers to their questions, strengthen their intellects, and take their heterogeneous thoughts under its wing, as it were. As far as this girl was concerned, though I had pity for her youth (and even though I was unable to stop her in any case), I rather think that this journey might even be of some value to her in a sense: this is not the world of books or abstract convictions after all; it is an immense experience that awaits her, an experience that perhaps God Himself, in His immeasurable goodness, fated for her in order to save her. Here a lesson in the living life is being prepared for her; before her stands the possibility of expanding her ideas and her views; she will have something to remember all her life, something precious and beautiful in which she participated, something that will compel her to value life and not weary of it before she has lived, as did the unfortunate suicide Pisareva of whom I spoke in my last, May, *Diary*.

*July
August*

1

1. Going Abroad. Something about Russians in Railway Carriages

I haven't chatted with the reader for two months now. Once I had brought out the June issue (marking six months of my publication), I immediately boarded a train and set off for Ems—oh, not to have a rest but for the reasons people usually go to Ems. And of course all this is extremely personal and private; but the fact is that I sometimes write my *Diary* not only for the public but for myself (that's probably why it occasionally contains some rough spots and surprising ideas—I mean ideas quite familiar to me and which I've been inwardly elaborating for a long time but which seem to the reader to have sprung up unexpectedly and unconnected to what has preceded them); and so how can I fail to include my trip abroad as well? Oh, of course, had it been up to me, I would have set off for somewhere in the south of Russia,

> Where bounteous meadows, fertile soil
> Demand but trifling, easy toil,
> Reward the plowman and restore
> His seed a hundred-fold or more;
> Where herds of mares run proud and free
> O'er boundless plain and verdant lea;
> Heard only is the muted roar
> Of breakers crashing on the shore.

But, alas, it seems that things are quite different there now from the time when the poet dreamed of that area. The plowman's easy toil, or even his hard labor, is rewarded by a good deal less than a hundredfold yield. Even the mares, apparently, should now be spoken of in a much less extravagant tone. Incidentally, not long ago I found an article in the *Moscow News* about the Crimea, the expulsion of the Tatars, and the general "desolation" of the region. The *Moscow News* advances the bold notion that it is pointless to grieve over the Tatars: let them be expelled and set up colonies of Russians in their place. I call this a bold notion indeed: it is one of those ideas or issues I spoke about in my June *Diary*, where I said that as soon as something like this comes up "we at once hear a chorus of discordant voices." It's difficult to decide whether everyone in Russia will agree with this view of the *Moscow News*, a view with which I agree wholeheartedly because I myself have long held just that view on the "Crimean question." There are certainly some *risks* attached to such a view, and we still do not know whether liberal opinion, which decides everything, will fall into line with it. It is true that the *Moscow News* expresses the wish "not to shed tears over the Tatars," etc., not only because of the political aspect of the matter and not only to strengthen our border areas, but also because of the economic needs of the region. The newspaper states as facts that the Crimean Tatars have demonstrated their inability to work the soil of the Crimea properly and that the Russians, specifically the South Russians, would be much better at this, pointing to the Caucasus as proof. On the whole, if the resettlement of Russians in the Crimea (gradually, of course) should require large expenditures by the state, then I think this would be a very possible and very profitable course of action. In any case, if Russians do not occupy these areas, the Yids will certainly fall upon the Crimea and ruin the soil of the region....

It is a long trip from Petersburg to Berlin—almost two days—and so I took along two pamphlets and a few newspapers just in case. And I truly meant "just in case," because I have always been afraid of being left in a crowd of strange Russians of our educated class, wherever it may be—in a railway carriage, a steamship, or in any kind of public gathering. I admit this is a weakness and blame it, above all, on my own suspicious nature. When I am abroad among foreigners I always feel more at ease: there, when some foreigner wants to get somewhere he heads straight to his destination, but our Russian goes on looking around the whole time, thinking, "What will people say about me?" He may look decisive and unshakeable, but in actual fact there is no one more uncertain and lacking in self-confidence. If a Russian stranger

begins a conversation with you, it is always in an extremely confidential and friendly manner; but from the first word he utters
you can see his deep mistrust and even his underlying suspicious
irritation, which will burst out in the form of some biting or even
downright rude remark the moment he finds something not to his
liking, and this despite all his "good upbringing." What's significant is that this can happen for the very slightest of reasons. Every
one of these people seems to want to avenge himself on someone
else for his own insignificance, yet he may not be an insignificant
person at all—sometimes just the reverse. There is no person who
will say oftener than a Russian: "What do I care what people say
about me?" or "I don't worry a bit about public opinion." And
there is no person who is more afraid than a Russian (again, I
mean a civilized Russian), who has more fear and trepidation of
public opinion and of what people will say or think of him. This
comes precisely from his deep-seated lack of self-respect, which,
of course, is concealed behind his boundless egotism and vanity.
These two opposing factors are always present in *almost* every
educated Russian, and he is also the first to find them intolerable,
so that each one of them bears his own "hell" in his soul, as it
were. It is especially awkward to meet a Russian stranger abroad
somewhere, face to face (shut up with him in a railway car, for
instance), so that there is no possibility of running away should
something disastrous happen. And yet, it would seem, "it's so nice
to meet a fellow countryman on foreign shores." And the conversation almost always begins with that very phrase. Once he's found
out that you're a Russian, your fellow countryman will be certain
to begin: "So you're a Russian? How nice to meet a fellow countryman on foreign shores. I'm here as well...." And then at once
come some candid remarks in a most cordial and, so to say, brotherly manner appropriate to two compatriots who have embraced
each other on some foreign shore. But don't be misled by the
manner: although your compatriot may be smiling, he already has
his suspicions of you, and that's obvious from his eyes, from the
little lisp he has when he speaks, and from the careful way he
stresses his words. He's sizing you up; he's certainly afraid of you
already; he already wants to tell you some lies. And, indeed, he
can't help but regard you suspiciously and tell lies simply because
you are also a Russian and he, willy-nilly, is measuring himself
against you; and also, perhaps, because you really deserve such
treatment. It's worth noting as well that a Russian stranger abroad

(more often when abroad, and indeed almost always when abroad) will always, or at least frequently, hasten to put in after the first three sentences he utters that he has only just met so-and-so or has only just heard something from so-and-so, i.e., from some prominent or famous Russian personage. But he brings up this person in the nicest and most familiar manner, as if he were one of his friends and one of yours as well: "You know him, of course. The poor fellow has been making pilgrimages from one local medical luminary to another. They send him off to watering places, and the fellow is absolutely worn out. You know him, do you not?" If you reply that you don't know him at all, the stranger will at once find something personally offensive in this circumstance: "Surely you didn't think that I wanted to boast of my acquaintance with a prominent person?" You can already read that question in his eyes, and yet that may be precisely what he wanted to imply. And if you reply that you do know the person, he will take even more offense; but just why that is I truly don't know. In short, insincerity and animosity grow on both sides; the conversation suddenly breaks off, and you fall silent. Your compatriot suddenly turns away from you. He is prepared to go on chatting the whole while with some German baker sitting opposite, as long as he doesn't speak to you, and he does this specifically so that you will notice it. Having begun in such a friendly fashion, he now will have nothing more to do with you and rudely ignores you altogether. When night comes he stretches out on the cushions if there is room enough, almost putting his feet on you or perhaps even deliberately putting his feet on you; and when the journey is over he leaves the carriage without even nodding good-bye. "Why did he take such offense?" you think to yourself, saddened and greatly confused. Best of all is an encounter with a Russian general. The Russian general abroad is most concerned with ensuring that none of the Russians he meets ventures to address him in a manner inappropriate to his rank, trying to take advantage by assuming that "we're abroad, and so we're all equal." And so, for instance, when he's traveling he sinks into a stern, marmorial silence from the very beginning. So much the better: he doesn't disturb anyone. By the way, a Russian general setting off for foreign parts is sometimes very fond of putting on a civilian suit he's ordered from the best tailor in Petersburg. And when he arrives at the spa, where there are always so many pretty ladies from all over Europe, he is very fond of making a show. When the season is over he takes particular

pleasure in being photographed in civilian clothes so that he can
give out pictures to his friends in Petersburg or use one to gladden
the heart of a devoted subordinate. But in any case, keeping a book
or a newspaper on a journey is a great help, particularly to ward
off Russians: it tells them, "I'm reading; leave me alone."

2. Something on Petersburg Baden-Badenism

I began reading and immediately came upon an article in *The Stock-
Exchange News* that takes me to task for my July *Diary*. However,
despite the tongue-lashing, the article is written in a rather kindly—
but not too kindly—manner. The columnist, Mr. B., makes a terrific
lot of jokes at my expense, politely but condescendingly, because
I filled the article with paradoxes and "took Constantinople." "And
so Constantinople has already been taken," he says, "mysteriously,
magically, but taken nonetheless. We were never involved in a war
of conquest, yet the city belongs to us for the simple reason that
it ought to belong to us." Come now, my dear Mr. B., you've made
that up: I certainly didn't take Constantinople in the current war
"in which we were never involved"; I said that this would happen
in time and added only that it might be within a very short time.
And who knows: perhaps I wasn't mistaken after all. And it's not
my fault if the Russia and her mission that you see from Petersburg
has now shrunk to the dimensions of some Baden-Baden or even
the Fürstentum of Nassau where I now sit and write these lines.
You seem to think that it's only Petersburg that will go on and on.
But even now there are the beginnings of a protest against Petersburg in certain elements of the provincial press (and in fact the
protest is not even against Petersburg but against people like you
who have settled in there and "dissociated" yourselves from the
rest of the country). The provinces have their own new ideas to
express. And perhaps they will express something, particularly
when they get over their anger; at the moment, though, their anger
hinders them from saying very much. The idea of Constantinople
and of the future of the Eastern Question as I set it forth is an old
one and by no means some Slavophile concoction. In fact, the idea
is not an old but an *ancient* one, a Russian historical idea, and
therefore something real, not fantastic; it began with Ivan III.
Whose fault is it that you now see Baden-Baden everywhere and
in everything? I'm not talking about you alone, after all. If it were
a matter of just you, I would never have opened my mouth. But

a lot of Baden-Badenism has set in generally in Petersburg, not just in you. I understand what it was that so shocked you: it is Russia's future destiny among the family of nations, about which I concluded: "this is how I understand Russia's destiny *in its ideal form.*" This irritated you. The future, the near future of humanity, is full of dreadful problems. The leading intellects, both our own and Europe's, have long agreed that we stand on the eve of the "final dénouement." And here you are, *ashamed* that Russia, too, might have a role to play in this dénouement, ashamed even at the proposition that Russia might venture to utter its own new word in the general cause of humanity. For you this is something shameful, but for us it is an article of faith. And it is even the faith that Russia will utter, not only its own, but perhaps the final word as well. This is something that every Russian should and, indeed, must believe if he is a member of a great nation and a great union of people; if, finally, he is a member of the great family of man. Do you think it bizarre that I ventured to propose that the principles of the People of Russia and her Orthodoxy (by which I mean the *idea* of Orthodoxy, which is not compromised in any way) contain pledges that Russia can utter her new word of the living life in the future of humanity? As far as your remarks on the Slavophiles are concerned, one must know something about them in order to discuss them. And who knows anything about them now? Everyone relies mainly on hearsay and faulty memory. People in Russia now have forgotten a good deal; they have long lost much of the learning they had, but they haven't acquired any new learning. I made a grave error in beginning directly from the end and stating the result, the final word of my faith. It's a mistake to express your views to the end. And so you jeer, "Oh, everyone's ashamed to talk about that, but he does; so let's ridicule him!" Leaving some things unsaid is better and more advantageous. One can write and write, throwing out hints but never expressing oneself fully: in this way one can gain great respect; one can even win renown as a thinker without ever having an idea. But I don't want to do that. My readers will reproach me—and I know it—for "responding to criticism," as they have already reproached me more than once. This is not a reply to one person, however, but to many. There is a fact here. If I do not respond, then at least I have to point out that fact.

3. On the Pugnacity of the Germans

Just as soon as we entered German territory and were locked into our compartment, all the six Germans with us immediately began talking among themselves about the war and about Russia. I found that curious, for although I knew there was widespread discussion of Russia in the German press at that very moment, I still didn't think that it was being discussed on the street as well. These were by no means "upper" Germans; I don't think there was a single baron there, and not even one German army officer. And they weren't discussing "higher" politics but only the current strength of Russia, predominantly her military strength, and her strength only at the given, present moment. With solemn and even rather haughty equanimity, they told one another that never before had Russia's armaments been in such a weak state, and so on. One pompous and strapping German traveling from Petersburg declared with the tone of a genuine expert that we had no more than two hundred and seventy thousand barely decent repeating rifles; our others were only some sort of adaptations of older models, so that the total sum of our repeating rifles would be no more than a half-million. He claimed that we still had supplies of no more than sixty million metal cartridges, i.e., only enough for sixty shots per soldier if one considers the whole wartime army to be a million strong; apart from that, he claimed that these cartridges were poorly made. Their discussion was rather jolly, however. I should note that they knew that I was a Russian, but judging from my few words with the conductor, they apparently concluded that I knew no German. But although I speak German badly, I do understand it. After a certain time I considered it my "patriotic duty" to object. As calmly as possible, so as to fit into their mood, I noted that all their facts and figures were exaggerated for the worse; that even four years ago the armaments of our military forces had reached a highly satisfactory level, and that since then they had been even further expanded, since the build-up of armaments had continued uninterrupted; that we now took second place to no one. They heard me out attentively, despite my poor German, and they even prompted me whenever I couldn't think of a German word or stumbled over one, nodding to show they understood. (N.B. If you speak German badly, then the better educated your listener is, the more easily he will understand you. It's quite another matter with people on the street or servants, for example: they are slow to understand, even though you may have missed only one word in a whole sentence and especially if, instead of some commonly used word, you use another, less common one. In this case they sometimes won't understand you at all. I don't know if that's the case with Frenchmen and Italians, but there are accounts of the Russian soldiers at Sevastopol who spoke with French prisoners in the Crimea [also using gestures, of course] and were able to understand them. It follows that, had they known even only half the words the Frenchmen used, they would have understood them completely.) The Germans did not disagree with anything I said; they only smiled at my words, not haughtily but even with approval, completely assured that I, as a Russian, spoke only in defense of Russian honor. But it was obvious from their eyes that they didn't believe a word I was saying and that their opinions were unchanged. Five years ago, in 1871, they were not nearly so polite, however. I was living in Dresden then and I recall seeing the Saxon troops return after the war. The city arranged for them to make a triumphal entry and gave them an ovation. I recall, however, these same troops a year earlier when they were only just marching off to war: suddenly, on all the street corners and in all the public places of Dresden appeared a poster that stated in huge letters: *Der Krieg is erklärt!* (War is declared!). I saw these troops then and could not help but admire them: what vigor in their faces, what serene, happy, and at the same time solemn, expressions they wore! They were all young men, and looking at some company that marched past, one could not help admiring their remarkable military bearing, their orderly step, their straight, exact ranks, yet at the same time the unusual sort of freedom with which they marched; this was something I had not seen before in soldiers; it was a conscious sense of purpose that was expressed in every gesture, in every step of these fine young men. It was obvious that no one was driving them off to war, but that they were going of their own accord. There was nothing mechanical here, nothing of the corporal and his stick; and these were Germans, those same Germans from whom we, beginning with Peter the Great, had borrowed the corporal and his stick as we developed our own military. No, these Germans marched along without any stick, as one man, with a total sense of purpose and with complete confidence in their victory. The war was a popular one: the citizen radiated from the soldier and, I confess, I felt very uneasy for the French even though I was still firmly convinced that they would give the Germans a thrashing. You can imagine how these same soldiers entered Dresden a year later, after finally gaining victories over the French who had humiliated them so many times for a whole century. Then add to that the usual German boastfulness—their national propensity to boast without measure when they have some sort of success, a boastfulness which even in trivial things reaches the point of childishness and which in the German always is transformed into arrogance—a rather unattractive national trait that is almost astonishing among them. Compared with any other nation, this one has too much to boast about to display such pettiness. As it turned out, the honor of this victory was such a novelty that they themselves didn't expect it. And in fact they were so caught up in their own triumph then, that they even began insulting the Russians. There were many Russians in Dresden at that time, and many of them reported later that as soon as anyone, even a shopkeeper, struck up a conversation with a Russian—even if the Russian had only come into the shop to buy something—he would at once try to insert some remark into the conversation such as, "Now that we've settled scores with the French, it's time to take on you Russians." This anger at the Russians welled up of itself among the people then, despite everything being said in the newspapers, which understood Russia's policy during the war—a policy without which the victor's laurels might have slipped from their grasp. It is true that this was the first glow of an unexpected military success, but the fact is that in the glow of this success they at once thought of the Russians. This animosity toward the Russians, which appeared almost involuntarily, astonished even me at the time, although I have known all my life that, always and everywhere, since the very time of the German Suburb in Moscow, the German has had little love to spare for the Russian. A certain Russian lady, Countess K., who lived in Dresden at the time, was sitting at one of the seats designated for spectators during this triumphal ovation for the troops entering the city; behind her a few gloating Germans began to abuse Russia in the worst sort of way. "I turned to them and said a few salty peasant words of my own," she told me later. They fell silent: the Germans are very polite to ladies, but had it been a Russian man they would not have let him get away with it. I myself read in our newspapers at the time that drunken bands of our own Petersburg Germans provoked quarrels and fights while off drinking somewhere with our soldiers, and that they did this specifically out of "patriotism." Incidentally, the majority of German newspapers now are filled with the most furious outbursts against Russia. *The Voice*, referring to the fury of the German press, which would have its readers believe that Russia wants to seize the East and the Slavs so that, strengthened, she could launch an attack on European civilization, remarked not long ago in one of its editorials that this whole furious chorus is all the more astonishing in that it was raised as if deliberately, immediately after the amiable congresses and meetings of the three emperors, and that this, to say the least, is strange. A very subtle remark.

4. The Very Last Word of Civilization

Indeed, something is gathering in Europe that seems unavoidable. The Eastern Question is growing and swelling like waves of the tide and may, in fact, end by carrying off *everything* so that no spirit of peace, no good judgment, no firm resolve not to ignite a war will withstand this pressure of circumstances. But most important is that even now a terrible fact has come to light and that this fact is the *last word* of civilization. This last word has been uttered and has become clear; it is now known and it is the result of eighteen whole centuries of development, of the entire humanization of mankind. All of Europe, at least all of its foremost representatives, are these very same peoples and nations who cried out against slavery; who ended the trade in Negro slaves; who ended their own despotic systems; who proclaimed the rights of man; who created science and astounded the world with its power; who brought life and delight to the human soul with art and its sacred ideals; who kindled rapture and faith in people's hearts, promising them justice and truth in the near future. Yet these same peoples and nations suddenly all (almost all) at this moment turn their backs on the millions of unfortunate creatures—Christians, human beings, their own brothers who are living in dishonor and perishing—and who go on waiting, waiting with hope and impatience till they are all crushed like reptiles, like insects; till at last all these desperate appeals for help which so annoy and disturb Europe fall silent. The victims are regarded precisely like reptiles, insects, or even worse: tens, hundreds of thousands of Christians are being wiped away like pernicious scabs; they are being torn from the face of the earth, roots and all. Sisters are being violated before the eyes of their dying brothers; infant children are being tossed in the air and caught on the point of a bayonet before the eyes of their mothers; villages are being annihilated, churches smashed to splinters; there is a wholesale *obliteration* of everything, and by a savage, repulsive Moslem horde, the sworn enemy of civilization. This is a systematic extermination; this is not some band of robbers that has sprung up by chance during the confusion and disorder of war but still fears the law. No, here there is a system at work, a method of war undertaken by a vast empire. The robbers are acting by decree, by orders of ministers and rulers of the state, by orders of the Sultan himself. And Europe, Christian Europe, a great civilization, looks on impatiently ... "until these insects are exterminated!" Moreover, in Europe these facts are disputed and denied in national parliaments; people do not believe them, or pretend not to believe them. Every one of these national leaders knows (in his heart) that all this is true, and they are all vying to divert one another's attention: "This is not true; it never happened; it's an exaggeration; they themselves have slaughtered sixty thousand of their own Bulgarians to blame it on the Turks." "Your Excellency, she flogged herself!" The Khlestakovs and Skvoznik-Dmukhanovskys are in real trouble! But why is all this happening? What are these people afraid of? Why do they refuse to see and hear, but only lie to themselves and disgrace themselves? Well, you see, it's because Russia is involved here: "Russia will be strengthened, gain control of the East, Constantinople, the Mediterranean, seaports, trade. Russia will fling herself upon Europe like a barbarian horde and 'destroy civilization'" (that same civilization which tolerates such barbarities!). That is what people are now shouting in England and in Germany, and once again every last one of them is lying; they themselves do not believe a single word of these accusations and apprehensions. These are all only words designed to rouse hatred among the masses. In Europe at present there is not a single person with any education and capacity for thought who could believe that Russia wants to destroy civilization and is capable of doing so. They may not believe in our disinterestedness; they may attribute all sorts of bad intentions to us: that is understandable; but what is difficult to believe is that they, after so many indications and experiences, could still believe that we are more powerful than all united Europe together. It is difficult to believe that they would not know that Europe is twice as powerful as Russia, even if we held Constantinople in our grasp.

They ought to know that Russia's strength is exceptional only at home when she is defending her land from an invader, but she is four times weaker when she attacks. Oh, they know all this very well, but they make believe and keep fooling everyone and themselves as well, simply because in England they have some merchants and manufacturers who are morbidly suspicious and morbidly greedy when defending their own interests. But even these people know very well that Russia, even under the most favorable conditions, would still not be able to surpass their industry and commerce and that this is still a matter that will not be decided for centuries. But even the slightest expansion of someone else's trade, the slightest development of someone else's sea power, and at once they are full of alarm, panic, and worry about their profits; and it is because of this that their whole "civilization" suddenly turns out to be no more than a soap bubble. Well, and what of the Germans? Why has their press suddenly taken alarm? For the Germans, it is because Russia stands at their backs and binds their hands; it was because of Russia that they missed the *opportune* moment to wipe France from the face of the earth once and for all so as never to have to worry about her again. "Russia is hindering us; Russia must be driven back behind her boundaries, and how can we do that when, on our other side, France is still *sound?*" Indeed, Russia is at fault simply for being Russia, and the Russians simply for being Russians, i.e., Slavs. Europe hates the Slavic tribe, *les esclaves,* or slaves, as they say, and the Germans have so many of these slaves: they might rebel, who can tell? And so eighteen centuries of Christianity, humanization, science, and progress suddenly turn out to be rubbish, a schoolchild's fable, a copybook maxim, the moment the weak spot is touched. But the problem, the horror is that this is "the last word of civilization," and that this word has been uttered, and uttered without shame. Oh, don't bother pointing out that in Europe, indeed, in England herself, voices were raised in protest and appeals were made to collect money for the people who were being slaughtered. But that's all the sadder; these are individual instances that only prove their impotence against their general, state, national tendency. The person who seeks answers is left in confusion: where is the truth? Is the world really so far away from it? When will the strife cease? Will humans ever join together, and what is preventing them from doing so? Will Truth ever be strong enough to overcome the corruption, cynicism, and egotism of people? Where are the truths that have been elaborated and acquired with such painful effort? Where is the love of humanity? And are these, indeed, truths? Are they not, perhaps, only exercises for "higher" feelings, for oratory and for keeping schoolchildren in hand? But once there is a deed to be done, a *real* deed, a *practical* deed, everything is pushed aside and the ideals are sent to the Devil! Ideals are nonsense, poetry, pretty verses! And is it not true that the Yid has again enthroned himself everywhere; indeed, that he has not only "enthroned himself again," but has never ever ceased to reign?*

*This article was written in July. [Dostoevsky's note.]

2

1. Idealist-Cynics

I wonder if anyone remembers the article on the Eastern Question by the unforgettable professor and unforgettable Russian, Timofei Nikolaevich Granovsky, an article he wrote, apparently, in 1855, right in the midst of our war with Europe when the siege of Sevastopol had already begun? I took it with me on the train and reread it specifically with a view to the Eastern Question, which has now come up once more. This old, respectable article struck me as unusually interesting, much more so than the first time I read it, when I agreed with it totally. What I particularly noted this time was, first, the view of the People held by a Westernizer of that time; second, and most important, what I might call the psychological content of the article. I cannot resist sharing my impression with the reader.

Granovsky was the very purest of the people of that time; he was something irreproachable and truly fine. He was an idealist of the 1840s in the highest sense, and he certainly had his own particular, highly original, and subtle shading among our "advanced" people of a certain stripe. He was one of our most honorable Stepan Trofimovichs (the idealist of the forties whom I portrayed in my novel *The Devils* and whom our critics found to ring true. I love my Stepan Trofimovich, after all, and deeply respect him); and he perhaps lacked any of the comic traits that are rather characteristic of this type. But I said that I was struck by the *psychological* significance of the article and found that notion very amusing. I don't know if you'll agree, but when our Russian idealist, a renowned idealist who knows that everyone thinks of him only as an idealist, a "patented" proponent, so to speak, of "the sublime and the beautiful"—when such a person suddenly finds it necessary to offer or announce his opinion on some matter (I mean on some "real," practical, current matter—not on poetry of some sort, but on an important and *serious* matter, almost a civic one); and when he must not merely make a statement in passing, but express a decisive, conclusive judgment that will have some influence, then through some miracle he is abruptly and totally transformed into a confirmed, prosaic realist; even more, he becomes a cynic. Moreover, it is the absence of poetry, the very cynicism of the thing, in which he takes most pride. He offers his opinion and almost clucks his tongue in doing so. Ideals are shoved aside; ideals are nonsense, poetry, pretty verses; in their place is only "the hard truth of life." But instead of telling this hard truth, he always overdoes things to the point of cynicism. He seeks the hard truth in cynicism and presumes to find it there. The coarser, the drier, the crueler—the more real he thinks it is. Why is that so? Because in such a case our idealist is always ashamed of his idealism. He's ashamed and afraid that he'll be told: "Well, you're an idealist; what do you understand of practical matters? Go ahead and preach about *the beautiful*, but let us settle these practical matters." Even Pushkin had this trait: more than once the great poet was ashamed that he was *only* a poet. Perhaps this trait can be found among other nationalities as well, but I doubt it. I doubt, at least, that it's found to the same degree as among us. In other countries, everyone has long been used to working, and they have managed to sort themselves out through centuries of having people with professions and significance of their own, and almost everyone over there knows, understands, and respects himself, in terms of both his profession and his significance. In Russia, on the other hand, owing to our two-hundred-year lack of habit of any practical activity, things are somewhat different. Even people such as Pushkin and Granovsky cannot escape a deeply concealed lack of self-respect. And, in fact, when he found it necessary suddenly to transform himself from a professor of history into a diplomat, this most innocent and upright of men went to amazing lengths in his pronouncements. For example, he utterly denies even the possibility that Austria might be grateful to us for helping her in her dispute with the Hungarians and literally saving her from collapse. And he denies this not because Austria is "crafty" and we should have been able to see this in advance; no, he sees no craftiness whatsoever and flatly concludes that Austria could have done nothing else. But that's not enough for him: he concludes flatly that she *should have* done nothing else and she should have acted just as she did; accordingly, our hopes for her gratitude are nothing more than an unforgivable and ridiculous lapse in our foreign policy. A private person, apparently, is one thing, and a state something else. A state has its higher, immediate aims and its own advantages to consider; to expect gratitude to the point of a state's sacrificing its own interests is simply ridiculous. "Austrian craftiness and ingratitude," he says, "have become a truism for us. But to speak of gratitude or ingratitude in political matters shows only that one does not understand them. The state is not a private individual; it cannot sacrifice its own interests out of gratitude, the more so that in political matters magnanimity itself *is never disinterested*" (i.e., it shouldn't be disinterested, is that what he means? That's exactly the notion). In short, the respectable idealist said a lot of terribly clever things, but what's most important about them is that they are *realistic*: we can do more than write pretty little verses, you see! . . . That's clever, to be sure, even though it's not new but has been with us as long as there have been diplomats on the earth; yet to justify Austria's action with such fervor, and not only to justify it, but to prove plainly that she *should* have acted in no other way—well, say what you like, but this is like cutting your mind in two. There is something here that one simply cannot agree with, something that prohibits agreement, despite this unusual, practical, and political faculty which our historian, poet, and high priest of the beautiful has so suddenly and unexpectedly displayed. With this admission of the sanctity of proximate advantage, of direct and quick profit, of the justice of spitting upon honor and conscience so long as one can tear off a chunk of wool, one can truly go a long way. Why, if you like you can use this to justify Metternich's policy: it's a matter of the higher and *real* aims of state. But, indeed, do only practical advantages and immediate profit make up a nation's genuine interests and therefore also its "higher" policy, as opposed to all these "Schilleresque" sentiments, ideals, and what not? This is the question. On the contrary, isn't the best policy for a *great* nation precisely one based on honor, magnanimity, and justice, even if it may seem to go against the interests of the state (but in practice it never does)? Did our historian really not know that great and honorable ideas (not only profit and a handful of wool) ultimately triumph among peoples and nations despite all the apparent absurd impracticality of these ideas and despite all their idealism, which is so humiliating in the eyes of the diplomats and the Metternichs? That a policy of honor and disinterestedness is not only higher but, perhaps, the most *advantageous* policy for a great nation, precisely because it is great? The policy of immediate practicality and endless rushing about to seek greater profit and achieve more practical aims exposes the triviality, the inner weakness, and the unhappy condition of the state. The diplomatic mind, the practical mind, and the *pragmatic* benefit are always inferior to truth and honor, while truth and honor always end triumphant. And if they have not ended triumphant, then they will, for this is what people have eternally and inevitably desired and continue to desire. When the slave trade was abolished, were there not profound and highly intelligent objections that this "abolition" was impractical, that it would harm the most vital and essential interests of peoples and states? Things reached the point where trade in Negroes was held up even as something morally essential; it was justified by natural racial differences, and people concluded that the Negro was scarcely a human.... When England's North American colonies revolted against her, did not people in practical England cry out for years on end that the liberation of these colonies from England's control would mean the ruin of England's interests; that it would be a dreadful setback, a calamity? When our own peasants were liberated, did we not hear those same cries in many places? Did not the "profound and practical minds" say that the state was setting off on the wrong path, an unknown and terrible path; that this would shake the very foundations of the state: that our higher policy that looks after realistic interests should not be based only on fashionable economic considerations and theories unproven by experience and, indeed, on "sentimentality"? But why look so far away? We have the Slavic Question before us: why not abandon the Slavs altogether? Although Granovsky insists that we want the Slavs only to increase our power and that we act only for our practical advantage, I think that here he made a slip. What sort of practical advantage will we have with them, even in the future, and how will they help us expand our power? Through the Mediterranean, some time in the future? Or through Constantinople, "which they will never give us?" Why this is nothing more than a crane flying across the sky; even if we did manage to catch it, we would only earn ourselves more trouble, a thousand years of trouble. Is this prosperity? Is this the view of a wise man? Is this genuine, practical interest? We shall have only fuss and trouble with the Slavs, especially now when they are still not ours. Because of them, Europe has been looking askance at us for a hundred years, and now she is not only looking askance but—at the least sign of movement from us—will at once draw her sword and aim her cannon at us. Let us simply abandon them once and for all so as to reassure Europe for good. But we should not abandon them pure and simple: Europe may, even then, not believe that we have abandoned them. Accordingly, we must do it with some proof: we ourselves must fall upon them and crush them in brotherly fashion so as to support Turkey. "So, dear brother Slavs, the state is not a private individual; it cannot sacrifice its own interests out of magnanimity; didn't you know that?" And how many advantages, practical, genuine, and immediate—not some rosy dreams of the future—would Russia at once derive from this! The Eastern Question would at once be solved; Europe would regain her trust in us, at least for the moment; and as a result our military budget would be reduced, our credit restored, our ruble would rise to its real value. And that's not all: why this crane of ours would not fly away anywhere; it would just go on hovering over us! Now we'll have to stifle a few twinges of conscience and bide our time; after all, "the state is not a private individual; it cannot sacrifice its own interests," but eventually.... Well, if the Slavs are destined not to manage without us, then they themselves will join us when the time comes; then we will again cling to them with love and brotherhood. However, Granovsky finds that very thing as well in our policy. He assures us specifically that our policy has done nothing but oppress the Slavs through the last hundred years, "denouncing them and betraying them to the Turks," so that our Slavic policy was always one of annexation and violence; indeed, it could be nothing else. (Does he mean that that was how it should have been? He justifies others for such a policy, after all, so he should justify us as well.) But was this really always our policy on the Slavic Question? Has it really not been clarified even now? Those are the questions!

2. Should One Be Ashamed of Being an Idealist?

Granovsky, of course, was a proud man, but I think that a sense of pride—even injured pride—must have been a common feature of all able people at the time; this was precisely because they had no work to do and no possibility of finding some occupation. They were longing for work, one might say. Things reached the point where those who seemed to have some occupation (a professor, for instance, or a man of letters, a poet, even a great poet) set little store by it, not merely because of the constraints in which they found themselves and their professions, but also because almost every one of them tended to see within himself the rudiments of some other occupation that he felt was higher, more useful, more "civic" than the one he was pursuing. The injured pride of our finest progressive and capable people (of some of them, at least) strikes one even now, and it stems from these same reasons. (However, I am speaking only of certain capable and talented people; I will pass over for the moment the unbecoming, insufferably irritated conceit and vanity of so many of today's untalented and trivial "activists" who imagine themselves geniuses, even though this phenomenon is particularly striking at the present time.) This longing for activity, this eternal quest for activity, which stems exclusively from our two centuries of inactivity—an inactivity that has reached the point where now we do not even know what approach to take to work (indeed, we do not even know where to find an occupation and what it consists of)—is a terrible irritant for us. We see conceit—sometimes even indecent conceit, judging by the man's moral level—which makes him almost ridiculous. But all this arises specifically because this high-minded, moral person himself is often incapable of defining himself and determining his strong points and his significance; of discovering his own specific gravity, so to say, and finding his own real value through practical work. Had he been able to discover this, he, as one filled with the loftiest of sentiments, would naturally not consider it degrading to admit that he had no capacity for certain things. At the present time he is quick to take offense, and in his touchiness he often undertakes work for which he is unsuited. Granovsky's article, I repeat, is written very cleverly, although it contains some political errors that were later confirmed by facts in Europe. I could point them out, of course, but that's not what I want to talk about; in any case, I'm not setting out to pronounce judgment on Granovsky for these things. What struck me this time was just the remarkable irritability of the article. Oh, I don't attribute its irritability to his pride, and I am not *attacking* the well-known tendentiousness of the article. I understand only too well the "topicality" that is reflected in this piece, the feeling and the sorrow of a citizen. There are, at last, moments when even the most just person cannot be dispassionate . . . (alas, Granovsky did not live to see the liberation of the peasants and never conceived of it even in his fondest dreams!). No, I am not attacking that; but why did he look so scornfully on the People in this "Eastern Question" of his and refuse to give them their due? He refuses altogether to recognize the People's participation and their thought in this matter. He states positively that the People had no opinion whatsoever in the Slavic Question and in the war at the time but only felt the burden of levies and providing recruits. Evidently the People were not even supposed to have an opinion. Granovsky writes:

> First it is necessary to dismiss the notion that this war (i.e., from 1853 to 1855) is a holy war. The government attempted to convince the People that it was marching in defense of the rights of the Christian church and their fellow believers. The defenders of Orthodoxy and the Slavic nationalities *joyfully raised this banner* and preached a crusade against the Moslems. *But the age of crusades had passed; in our time no one will make a move to defend the Holy Sepulchre* [or to defend the Slavs either?]; *no one regards the Mohammedans as eternal foes of Christianity;* the keys to the temple of Bethlehem serve only as a pretext for achieving political aims. [In another place, he says this directly about the Slavs.]

Of course, we too are prepared to agree that Russian policy in regard to the Slavic Question in this last century was perhaps sometimes not beyond reproach; at some moments it may have been much too restrained and cautious, and therefore certain impatient people found it insincere. Perhaps there was excessive concern for immediate interests, ambiguity caused by certain external diplomatic pressures, half-measures, and hesitations; but, in essence and on the whole, Russia's policy was scarcely concerned *only* with bringing the Slavs under her control and so increasing her own strength and political significance. No, of course, this is not how it was, and *in essence* our policy, even through the whole Petersburg period of our history, was hardly ever at odds with the Slavic, i.e., Eastern Question and with our most ancient historical covenants and traditions and the views of the People. And our government always knew very well that as soon as our People heard its summons in this cause, the People would answer it wholeheartedly; and therefore the Eastern Question, in its true essence, was always a question for the People. But Granovsky does not admit this at all. Oh, Granovsky had a deep love for the People! In his article he grieves and laments over their sufferings in the war and the burdens

they had to carry. Indeed, can people such as Granovsky feel other
than love for the People? This compassion and this love reveal all
his beautiful soul; but at the same time they inadvertently reveal
the view of the People of this confirmed Westernizer, a man always
prepared to see the embryo of something beautiful in the People,
but only "passively" and on the level of a "self-contained, idyllic
way of life." But as far as the People's real and possible activity
is concerned—"of that it is best not to speak." For him, our People
in any circumstances are only an inert, mute mass. And this is
hardly surprising: almost all of us at that time believed him. That
is why I simply do not dare to "attack" Granovsky and wish only
to point my finger at his time, not at him. This article made the
rounds then and it had an influence. And that's just the point: I
was struck most of all by the parallel between the remarkable point
of view of this remarkable article and the present moment today.
No, today even the Westernizer Granovsky might be astonished
and, perhaps, might even *believe*. The People's voluntary sacrifices
and contributions for the Orthodox Slavs; the donations by Old
Believers who send medical detachments from their communities;
the donations of artel workers who send their last pennies; the
donations sent by community decision from entire villages; the
donations made by soldiers and sailors from their salaries; and
finally, the Russian people of all classes who go to fight for their
oppressed Slavic brethren and to shed their blood—no, this is
something that is evident and that cannot be called passive, something that one has to take into account. The movement has been
made manifest and one can no longer dispute it. Women—prominent ladies—are on the streets collecting for the Slavic brethren.
The People solemnly and tenderly look at this phenomenon that
is utterly new to them: "So, they're all gathering together again;
that means we're not always going our separate ways; it means
we're all the same Christians." That is certainly what the People
feel and perhaps what they already think. And, of course, news
reaches them as well; they listen to newspapers being read to them
and are themselves already beginning to read them. And of course
they have heard and have prayed in church for the repose of the
soul of Nikolai Alexeevich Kireev, who gave his life for the cause
of the People; and, who knows, perhaps they will compose their
own folk song about this death and sacrifice:

And though he fell, yet will he live,

In hearts and minds throughout our land;
No end more glorious than this,
A sacrifice both bold and grand
That he, a brave and noble soul
Made for the People, one and all.

Yes, "he died for the People," and not for the Slavic People alone but for the common, Orthodox, Russian cause as well, and the People will always understand that. No, our People are not materialists nor yet so corrupt in spirit as to think only of their day-to-day advantages and positive interests. They are joyous in spirit when a great purpose is set before them, and they will accept it as their spiritual bread. And do the People now, at the present moment, not know and understand that the ultimate development of this Slavic cause may threaten even us with war or ignite some conflict? Then, of course, requisitions and burdens will be their lot just as in the Eastern war of twenty years ago. But look at them now: are they afraid of anything? No; one sees among our People a good deal more spiritual and practical strength than various "experts" suggest. Granovsky would have done better to leave this opinion to others—to that horde of "experts on the People" and, perhaps, to some of our literary men who wrote about the People but remained all their lives only foreigners who have made a study of the Russian peasant.

In conclusion, I repeat: the idealist in Russia often forgets that idealism is by no means a shameful thing. Both the idealist and the realist, as long as they are honest and magnanimous, have the same essence—love for humanity—and the same object—the human being; it is only that the *forms* of representation of that object are different. There is no need to be ashamed of one's idealism: it is the same path to the same goal. Thus idealism, in essence, is just as practical as realism and can never disappear from the earth. The Granovskys should not be ashamed that they exist specifically to preach "the beautiful and the sublime." And if even the Granovskys should feel ashamed and, dreading the mocking and haughty wise men of the Areopagus, become virtual allies of the Metternichs, then who will be our prophets? And the *historian Granovsky* should not be ignorant of the fact that the most precious thing of all is for peoples to have and preserve ideals, and that some sacred idea, no matter how unsubstantial, impractical, ideal, and absurd it might first appear in the eyes of the wise men, will

always find some Areopagite and some "woman called Damaris"
who from the very beginning will place her faith in who propounds
it and will join this glorious cause without fear of breaking with
her wise men. And so a small, untimely, and impractical "absurd
little notion" will grow and multiply and ultimately conquer the
world, while the wise men of the Areopagus keep silent.

3. The Germans and Labor. Inexplicable Tricks. On Wit

Ems is a bedazzling and fashionable place. Sick people, mainly
those with chest ailments ("catarrh of the pulmonary tract") come
here from all over the world and are treated with great success at
the mineral springs. As many as fourteen or fifteen thousand visit
Ems in summer, mainly wealthy people, or at least those with
sufficient means not to stint themselves over their own health. But
there are poor people as well who come here *on foot* to be treated.
There are about a hundred of these, and perhaps they do not really
come on foot but use some other means of transportation. I was
very interested in the *fourth*-class cars that have been set up on the
German railways, although I don't know if they are a feature of
all the railways. During a stop on the way, I asked the conductor
(almost all the conductors on the German railways are not only
very capable but are attentive and kind to the passengers as well)
to explain to me what this fourth class was. He showed me an
empty car—I mean one without any seats, only walls and a floor.
It turned out that the passengers had to stand up.

"Perhaps they sit on the floor?"

"Oh yes, of course, they do as they like."

"And how many places are there in a car?"

"Twenty-five."

Making a rough estimate of the dimensions of the empty car for
twenty-five people, I concluded that they must certainly have to
stand up, and shoulder to shoulder as well. Thus, if twenty-five
people—that is, the full capacity—were crowded into the car, not
a single one of them would be able to sit down, even if he wanted
"to do as he liked." Of course, they would have to carry their
baggage with them; however, they would probably have only some
small bundles.

"On the other hand, you know, the fares are only half as much
as third class, and that is a great boon to a poor man."

Well, that truly does mean something. And so these poor people

who come to Ems not only take the cure but are maintained at the
expense of . . . well now, at whose expense I don't know. As soon
as you arrive at Ems and take rooms at a hotel (and in Ems all
the buildings are hotels) you will certainly be called upon on your
second or third day by two people, one after the other, collecting
donations and carrying little books. These are people of humble,
patient appearance but having their own sense of personal dignity.
One of them collects for the maintenance of these same impoverished sick people. Attached to his book is a printed proclamation
from the doctors of Ems to their patients that urges them not to
forget about the poor. You make a contribution that is within your
means and write your name down in the book. I looked through
the book and was struck by how small the contributions were: one
mark, half a mark, rarely three marks, and very rarely five marks.
Yet it would seem that people in Ems are not overly pestered by
appeals for contributions: aside from these two collectors, there
were no others. While you are making your contribution and writing
down your name, the official (I'll call him an official) meekly stands
in the middle of your room.

"Do you collect a lot over the season?" I asked.

"About a thousand talers, *mein Herr,* but that's far too little when
you look at what's needed. There are a lot of them—as many as a
hundred people—and we provide for them completely, with treatment, food, drink, and accommodation."

That truly is a small sum: a thousand talers is three thousand
marks; if there are as many as fourteen thousand visitors, then how
much does each one donate? There must be some who give nothing
at all, who refuse and have the collector thrown out (and there are
such, and they do literally *throw out* the collector, as I learned later).
Yet the visitors form a dazzling society, remarkably dazzling. Just
go out for a walk while they are drinking their mineral water or
listening to the band and take a look at them.

By the way, as early as last spring I read in our newspapers that
we Russians had donated very little for the Slavic rebels (of course,
these statements were made before the most recent donations).
Compared with us, the Europeans had contributed much more.
These figures did not even include Austria, which alone has contributed many (?) millions of guldens to support the unfortunate
families of the insurgents, tens of thousands of whom have made
their way into Austrian territory. The accounts say that in England,
for instance, people have contributed much more than we have,

and the same is true even of France and Italy. But say what you will, I do not believe in the enormity of these European contributions for the Slavs. A lot has been said about England, but I would be interested to know the real sum of her contributions, a figure which, it seems, no one can yet state accurately. As far as Austria is concerned, from the very beginning of the rebellion she had in mind the acquisition of a part of Bosnia (discussions have already begun about this in the diplomatic world), and so contributed not entirely disinterestedly but with an eye to her future interests; and her contribution came not from the people but from the state treasury pure and simple. Even the "many" millions of guldens mentioned are subject to some doubt, I think. There were contributions or, to put it better, appropriations, but whether they were in fact of any great help will be determined only sometime in the future.

The second official—I mean the collector of donations in Ems—who always calls after the first one, is collecting for "blödige Kinder," i.e., for retarded children. There is an institution for them here. And of course the idiot-children in the institution come not only from Ems; indeed, it would be indecent for such a small town to give birth to so many idiots. A sum from public funds is appropriated for the institution, but evidently it is necessary to resort to voluntary donations as well. Some luminary or magnificent lady is cured and restored thanks to the local mineral springs and, if not exactly out of gratitude to the place then at least as a token of remembrance, she leaves two or three marks for the poor, abandoned, unfortunate little creatures. In this second book the contributions are also one or two marks; sometimes, but very rarely, the sum of ten marks stands out. This second official collects up to fifteen hundred talers in a season: "But it used to be better; they used to give more," he added sadly. One donation in this book stood out in particular; it was, so to say, a donation made with some purpose in mind: 5 pfennigs (1½ silver kopecks). This reminded me of the donation for a monument to Lermontov that was entered in a book in Piatigorsk by a certain Russian State Councilor: he had donated *one kopeck, silver* and signed his name. This was mentioned in the newspapers about a year ago, although the donor's name wasn't published. But I think it should have been published: he had signed his name, after all, and perhaps he did so thinking specifically of becoming famous. But the State Councilor evidently intended to display his intellectual strength, his point of view and tendency; he was protesting against art, against the insignificance of poetry in our age of "realism," steamships, and railways, i.e., against all the things that every ragtag, third-rate liberal shouts about (he doesn't shout so much as simply parrot someone else's liberal ideas, in fact). But this one, the first, local *blödige*, what did he want to express with his five pfennigs? I really don't know which tendency this should be ascribed to. *Blödige Kinder* are little unfortunate creatures, the castoffs of the poorest families: are they really a subject for witticisms? "And if you give a poor man but one glass of water, even this will be credited to you in the Kingdom of Heaven." And yet, what am I saying? A glass of water in Ems, of course, costs no more than five pfennigs to be sure, and so even for five pfennigs one can get into Paradise. He was just figuring out the minimum price of admission: "Why pay any more?" He's only a child of the times; these days, as they say, you can't put anything over on people.

Since my first visit to Ems three years ago, and from my very first day, I was interested in one thing, and it continues to interest me every time I come. The two most popular mineral springs in Ems, despite the fact that there are several others, are the Krenchen and the Kesselbrunen. A building has been erected over the springs; a balustrade divides them from the public. Several girls stand behind this balustrade—three for each spring—and they are pleasant, young, and neatly dressed. You hand them your glass, and they at once fill it with water. In the two morning hours set aside for drinking, thousands of patients come to these balustrades; during these two hours each patient drinks several glasses of water— two, three, four, or however many have been prescribed for him. The same thing happens during the evening drinking hours. And so each of these three girls fills and hands out an enormous number of glasses of water during a two-hour period. Yet this is done with total order—calmly, methodically, and without haste, so that you are never delayed; and what I find most amazing is that each of these girls possesses an all but supernatural ability to keep track of things. When you first arrive you need only say to her once: "Here is my glass; I need so many ounces of the Krenchen and so many ounces of milk," and she will not make a single mistake during your whole month of treatment. Aside from that, she knows you by sight and can pick you out in the crowd. People crowd in tightly, several rows deep, and everyone is holding out a glass; the girl will take six or seven glasses at once, fill all of them in some fifteen seconds, and without spilling a drop or breaking them, will return each one without a mistake. She holds out the glass to you and knows that out of a thousand glasses, this one is yours and that one is someone else's; she remembers how many ounces of water you need, how many ounces of milk, and how many glasses you are supposed to drink. There is never the least error; I kept a close watch and made enquiries. And this is most surprising when you consider that there are several thousand patients here. It may very well be that this is a most ordinary thing and no cause for astonishment, but for me, now in my third year here, it is something almost inexplicable; I still regard it as some inexplicable feat of magic. Although it is ridiculous to be amazed at everything, this is one problem I am absolutely unable to solve. Evidently, one can only conclude that these German girls have exceptional memories and the ability to keep track of things very quickly; and yet, perhaps, it may only be that they are accustomed to work, a job that they have been learning since early childhood, and so, one can say, they have *triumphed over work*. As far as work itself is concerned, the Russian who studies the matter here also finds himself much perplexed. Living a month in the hotel (although, strictly speaking, it's not a hotel—every house here is a hotel, and the majority of them, aside from a few large ones, are simply apartments with maid service and meals by arrangement), I was simply amazed at the servants. In the hotel where I lived there were twelve apartments, all occupied, and some holding entire families. Each one of them is ringing for the maid, demanding something, and everyone must be looked after or served something; the maid must run up the stairs many times a day. And for all that, the hotel's entire staff of servants consisted of one girl of about nineteen. In addition, the proprietress has this same girl run errands and do various tasks: she must go buy wine for someone's dinner; run to the pharmacy for someone else; go to the laundry for a third; and to the shop for the proprietress herself. The proprietress, a widow, had three small children, and they also had to be looked after and dressed for school in the mornings. Every Sunday all the floors in the hotel had to be washed; each room had to be cleaned daily, including a change of bed and table linen; and whenever a guest left, his whole apartment had to be washed and cleaned at once without waiting until Sunday. This girl went to bed at half-past eleven, and in the morning the proprietress rang

a bell to wake her up at exactly five o'clock. I am telling you quite
literally how it all happened and am not exaggerating in the least.
Add the fact that she works for a most modest wage, inconceivable
to us in Petersburg, and is required to be neatly dressed as well.
Note that she seems in no way to feel humiliated or downtrodden:
she is cheerful, bold, and healthy, with a remarkably contented air
and an imperturbable calm. No, people in Russia do not work like
that. No servant girl would undertake such a regime of hard labor,
however high the wage. Moreover, she would not work as the
German girl did: a hundred times she would forget something, spill
something, fail to bring something, break something, make mistakes, get angry, and talk back to her employer. During a whole
month in Ems, however, there was absolutely nothing to complain
about. I find that astonishing, and I, as a Russian, really don't
know whether this is cause for praise or blame. However, I'll take
a chance and praise it, although there is something here to think
about. Here in Germany everyone has accepted his status as it is
and has come to terms with it, neither envying nor supposing that
things could be otherwise, apparently—at least in the vast majority
of cases. But work is still attractive: established work that has been
structured over the course of centuries; work with designated methods and techniques; work that is given to everyone almost from
the day of his birth. And therefore everyone knows how to approach
his job and *master* it completely. Everyone knows his job here,
although everyone knows only his job. I say that because everyone
works here—not only maidservants but their employers as well.

Look at a German civil servant, one who works in a post office,
say. Everyone knows what the Russian civil servant is like, particularly the one who deals with the public every day: he is angry
and irritable, and if his irritation isn't always displayed obviously,
then it is concealed and you can tell that by looking at his face.
He has a face as haughty and proud as Jupiter. This is particularly
evident in the pettiest little fellows among them, such as those who
sit and issue various documents to the public, who take your money
and give you a ticket, etc. Just look at him when he's busy, "on
the job": a crowd gathers, a line forms, everyone is eager to get
his document, his answer, his receipt, his ticket. But this fellow
just doesn't pay the least attention to you. At last your turn comes;
you stand there, talking to him, but he isn't listening; he isn't
looking at you; he's turned around and is talking to the civil servant
sitting behind him; he's taken a piece of paper and is checking

something, although you are quite ready to suspect that this is only for show and he has no need whatsoever to check anything. But you're prepared to wait and ... he gets up and goes away. And suddenly the clock strikes and the office hours are over—clear off, people! Compared with the German, our civil servant spends far fewer hours per day at his job. Boorishness, inattentiveness, carelessness, *hostility* to the public only because it is the public and, above all, the attitude of the petty Jupiter. He absolutely has to show you that you are dependent on him: "Just look at me, now; you can't do anything to me standing there behind the balustrade, but I can do anything I like to you. And if you get angry, I'll call the guard and have you thrown out." He has to take revenge for an insult of some sort, to take revenge on you for his own insignificance. Here in Ems there are usually two or at most three people working in the post office. There are months during the height of the season (in June and July, for example) when there are thousands of visitors here, and you can imagine how much mail there is and how much work the post office has to do. Aside from some two hours for lunch and so on, they are busy the whole day through. They have to collect mail and send it off; a thousand people come to ask for general delivery letters or to inquire about something. To serve each person he must look through whole heaps of letters; he listens to each, provides each with information or an explanation, and does all this patiently, kindly, politely, while still preserving his personal dignity. From some insignificant little creature he becomes a real person and not vice versa. ... When I arrived in Ems I spent a long time impatiently waiting for a letter and inquired every day at General Delivery. One morning, as I was coming back from drinking my daily dose of mineral water, I found this letter on the table in my room. It had only just arrived and the postal worker, remembering my name but not knowing where I lived, made a special check in the printed listing of the names and addresses of all who arrive here; then he sent me the letter by special messenger, despite the fact that it was addressed "General Delivery." And he did all this only because when I inquired the day before he had noticed that I was extremely anxious. Now would any of our postal workers do that?

As far as German sharp-wittedness and calculation are concerned (topics that came to mind apropos of what I said about German work just now), several different opinions exist. The French, who even formerly had no love for the Germans, always found and still find the German mind to be rather slow but not, of course, dull. They perceive in the German mind a kind of tendency, always and in everything, to avoid the direct approach and, on the contrary, a constant wish to resort to something intermediary, to make of a single thing something containing two distinct parts. As far as we Russians are concerned, we have always had a lot of anecdotes about the slowness and dullness of the Germans, despite our sincere admiration of their learning. But it seems to me that the Germans have only too much distinctiveness, a national character that is too stubborn, even to the point of haughtiness, a character that sometimes can make one indignant and therefore often lead one to wrong conclusions about them. However, living with them, particularly as a foreigner newly arrived in Germany, can produce some truly strange first impressions.

On the way from Berlin to Ems, the train stopped for four minutes at one station. It was nighttime; I had grown weary of sitting in the carriage and wanted to take a walk, if only a short one, and to smoke a cigarette in the fresh air. Everyone in the carriages was asleep, and no one got out of the whole long train but me. But the bell rang and suddenly I realized that in my usual absent-minded way I had forgotten the number of my carriage, whose door I had closed when I got out. There were, perhaps, only a few seconds remaining, and I was about to go to the conductor, who was at the other end of the train, when suddenly I heard someone calling "Psst, psst!" from the window of a carriage. Well, I thought, that must be my carriage. It is true that the Germans, in their small compartments holding a maximum of eight persons, do look out for one another during a journey. If there is a stop at a large station where dinner or supper is available, the German will certainly make sure to awaken his sleeping neighbor so that he won't have cause to regret sleeping through his supper, etc. And so I thought that this was one of my companions who had awakened and was calling me after noticing that I had lost my place. I went up to the window where a concerned German face was thrust out.

"*Was suchen Sie?*" (What are you looking for?)

"My carriage. Wasn't I with you? Is this my carriage?"

"No, this isn't your carriage and you weren't sitting here. But where is your carriage?"

"That's just the problem; I've lost it!"

"I don't know where it is either."

And it was only at the very last second that the conductor appeared and showed me my carriage. One might ask why this German called me and asked me questions. But once you've lived in Germany for a while, you soon realize that any German would act in just the same way.

About ten years ago I arrived in Dresden, and on the very next day as I came out of the hotel I set off directly for the picture gallery. I did not ask the way: the Dresden picture gallery is one of the most remarkable places in the world, and I thought that any passing citizen of the educated class would certainly be able to point out the way for me. And so when I passed one certain street I stopped a German who had a most serious and educated appearance.

"Could you tell me, please, where the picture gallery is?"

"The picture gallery?" The German stopped and considered my question.

"Yes."

"The Ro-yal Picture Gallery?" (He put particular emphasis on the word *Royal*.)

"Yes."

"I don't know where that gallery is."

"But . . . is there any other gallery here?"

"No, none whatsoever."

3

1. Russian or French?

What a lot of Russians there are at these German spas, particularly the fashionable ones such as Ems! On the whole, the Russians are terribly fond of taking cures. Even the main contingent of patients coming to the "Wunderfrau," who has a sanatorium near Munich (without waters, however), is from Russia, so they say. For the most part, though, this Frau is frequented by solid citizens—the generals of society, so to say—who have sent their urine specimens ahead of them from Petersburg and who have had places reserved in her institution ever since the winter. This Frau is formidable and obstinate. But in Ems the Russians can be most easily distinguished by their manner of speaking, that is, by that Russo-French dialect which is characteristic only of Russia and has begun to astonish even foreigners. I say that it "has begun," yet until now we have heard it only praised. I know, people will tell me that it's terribly passé to attack Russians for their French and that both the topic and its moral lesson are far too outworn. What surprises me, though, is not that the Russians do not speak Russian among themselves (and it would even be strange if they did); what surprises me is that they imagine they speak good French. Who put that silly notion into our heads? There's no doubt at all that it persists only because of our ignorance. Russians who speak French (that is, the overwhelming majority of educated Russians) are divided into two general categories: those who speak undeniably bad French, and those who imagine that they speak like true Parisians (our whole higher society), but who in fact speak just as badly as those of the first category. Russians of the first category can go to absurd lengths. I myself, for instance, while on a lonely evening walk on the banks of the Lahn, met two Russians, a man and a

568

lady; they were elderly people who were conversing with a most preoccupied air about some family matter that evidently was very important to them and that deeply absorbed and even disturbed them. They spoke in an agitated way, but in French and very badly, bookishly, using dead, awkward phrases; they were sometimes terribly hard-pressed to express an idea or some nuance of an idea, so that the one would often prompt the other impatiently. They went on prompting one another, but it never occurred to them to begin expressing themselves in Russian; on the contrary, they preferred to express themselves badly and even risk being misunderstood, just as long as they could do it in French. I was struck by this; it seemed to me to be patently absurd, yet I've encountered the same thing a hundred times in my life. The main thing here is that it is probably not a matter of preference—even though I said just now that they "preferred to speak French"—or of choice of language: they simply speak abominable French by custom and habit, never even posing the question of which language is the more convenient to speak. What is also disgusting about this awkward, artificial language they speak is their coarse, awkward, equally artificial pronunciation. The French spoken by Russians of my second category—the language of higher society, that is—is likewise distinguished above all by its pronunciation: it seems as if it really is a Parisian speaking, yet there's something quite wrong. The falsity is evident from the very first sound, particularly in the exaggerated, strained manner of pronunciation, in the crude manner of imitation, in the exaggerated gutturals and *grasseyement*—in the indecent pronunciation of the "r," in fact—and finally, in the moral aspect: the haughty self-satisfaction with which they make these guttural sounds, the childish boastfulness—which they don't even bother to conceal—with which they parade before one another their imitation of the language of the *garçon* of a Petersburg hairdresser. All this self-satisfied servility is repulsive. You may well say that this is all old hat, but it continues to astonish simply because living people, in the flower of their health and strength, decide to speak in an emaciated, colorless, sickly language. Of course, they themselves do not realize how worthless and impoverished that language is (not French, I mean, but the language they speak) and, because their thoughts are not fully developed but sketchy and impoverished, they are still quite happy with the medium they've chosen for expressing these sketchy little thoughts. They haven't the capacity to comprehend that once they have been born and raised in

Russia they will never degenerate entirely into Frenchmen, despite
the fact that under the influence of their French nurses they lisped
their very first words in French, subsequently practiced it with
tutors, and used it in society; they do not realize that this is why
this language of theirs must always sound dead and not alive; that
it is not a natural but an artificial, fantastic, and preposterous
language precisely because they so stubbornly accept it as a genuine
one. In short, it is not French at all, because the Russians, like
anyone else, have never been able to master all the fundamental,
inherent elements of living French because they were not born as
Frenchmen; they master only the alien jargon they have been given
and, at most, some hairdresser's insolent phrases and subsequently,
perhaps, some insolent ideas as well. This is like a stolen language,
and therefore not one of these Russian Parisians is, even once in
his life, able to generate in this stolen language a single expression
of his own or a single new, original word that might be taken up
and come into currency on the street—something which any hairdresser's *garçon* is able to do, however. In one of his novels Turgenev
tells the story of one such Russian in Paris; the fellow enters the
Café de Paris and shouts: "Garçon, bifteck aux pommes de terre!"
Another Russian, who had already managed to imitate the new
manner of ordering a steak, arrives and shouts: "Garçon, bifteck-
pommes!" The Russian who had shouted his order the old-fashioned way, "aux pommes de terre," is in despair over his ignorance
and his missing this new expression "bifteck-pommes," and is
afraid that now, perhaps, the *garçons* may look at him scornfully.
The author, evidently, took this story from an actual event. The
Russian Parisians, groveling slavishly before the forms of the language and the opinion of the *garçons*, are naturally just as enslaved
to French ideas. So it is that they themselves condemn their poor
heads to the pathetic fate of never ever containing a single idea of
their own.

Yes, to discuss the harm of assimilating from earliest childhood
a foreign language in place of one's own native one is certainly a
ludicrous and old-fashioned topic, and naive to the point of indecency; but it seems to me that it has by no means become so
outworn that one should not attempt to express one's own opinion
about it. Indeed, there is no such old topic on which one could
not say something new. I, of course, make no claim to anything
new (how could I!), but I take the risk if only to clear my conscience;

still, I will say something. I also would like to set down my arguments in a rather more accessible manner, in the hope that some dear mamma from higher society might read me.

2. What Language Should a Future Person of Consequence Speak?

I would ask the dear mamma whether she knows what language is and what the purpose of the word is. There is no doubt that language is the form, the body, the outer casing of thought (of course, this doesn't explain what thought is); it is, so to say, the ultimate and concluding word of organic evolution. It follows that the richer the material and the forms I acquire to express thought, the more fortunate I will be in life; the more distinctly and comprehensibly I will express myself—both to myself and to others; the more powerful and successful I will be; the more quickly I will be able to tell myself what I want to say; the more profoundly I will be able to express my thought and the more profoundly I will be able understand what I wanted to say; the stronger and calmer I will be in spirit; and, of course, the wiser I will be. And again, does dear mamma know that even though a person's thoughts are capable of moving at the speed of electricity, he will never actually think at such speed but much, much more slowly—although it will be much more quickly than he speaks. Why is this? It is because he has no choice but to think in some language. And in truth, we may not be aware that we are thinking in a language, but this is so; and if we do not think in words, i.e., by pronouncing words mentally, at least, then we still think using the "elemental, fundamental power of that language" in which we prefer to think, if I may express it that way. It is understood that the more flexibly, the more richly, the more diversely we master the language in which we choose to think, the more easily, diversely, and richly we will express our ideas in it. In essence, why is it that we study European languages—French, for instance? In the first place, it is simply to read French, and in the second place, it is to be able to speak to Frenchmen when we meet them; but it is certainly not to speak to other Russians or to ourselves. For any higher life, for any true depth of thought, a foreign, borrowed language will not be enough precisely because it will always remain foreign to us; for this one needs the native language into which one has been born. But it is right here that we run into an obstacle: Russians, at least Russians of the highest classes, have for the most part long since ceased to be born into a living language but only later acquire some sort of artificial one; they are almost in school before they learn Russian, and then only through the grammar. Oh, of course if one has enough desire and diligence one can finally reeducate oneself and even learn, to some extent, the living Russian language after having been born into a dead one. I knew a certain Russian writer who made a name for himself and who had not only mastered the Russian language, after having no knowledge of it, but had also mastered the Russian peasant—and then he wrote novels of peasant life. Such comic cases have occurred more than once in Russia, sometimes even on a very serious level: the great Pushkin, by his own admission, was also compelled to reeducate himself and study both the language and the spirit of the People; he learned, by the way, from his old nurse, Arina Rodionovna. The expression "to learn the language" is particularly appropriate for us Russians because we, the upper class, are to such an extent cut off from the People, i.e., from the living language ("language" and "people" are synonyms in Russian, and what a rich, profound thought lies therein!). But people may say that if you have to study a living language, then is it not all the same whether it is Russian or French? But the point is that the Russian language is still easier for a Russian, despite the presence of the French governess and the other circumstances, and we must take advantage of that fact while there is time. To master this Russian language in a more natural manner, without particular strain, and not only theoretically (when I say theoretically here I mean, of course, not only schoolroom grammar), one must absolutely acquire it from a Russian nurse in childhood, following the example of Arina Rodionovna, without fear that the nurse will pass on various prejudices to the child such as the "three whales." (Heavens above, what if those whales should stay with the child all life long!) Moreover, we must not be afraid of the common people and even servants, against whom some "experts" warn parents. And then, in school the child must absolutely memorize some classics of our literature, beginning from its earliest period—the chronicles, the epic legends, and even some works from Church Slavonic. And he must particularly commit these to memory, despite the fact that learning things by heart is considered to be so old-fashioned. By mastering in this way our native language—

the language in which we think—as well as possible, that is, sufficiently well so that it resembles something living, and by accustoming ourselves to thinking in this language, we shall derive the benefit of our particular Russian capacity to learn European languages and be multilingual. In fact, it is only by mastering fully the original material—one's native language, that is—that we shall have the capacity to master fully the foreign language as well, but not before. Then, unbeknownst to ourselves, we shall borrow certain alien forms from the foreign language and, again without our even being aware of it, we shall harmonize them with the forms of our own thought, and thereby expand it. We should be aware of one significant fact: we, in our still unorganized and youthful language, are able to convey the most profound forms of the spirit and the thought of the European languages: the European poets and thinkers can all be translated into and conveyed in Russian, and some of them have already been translated to perfection. At the same time, there is a mass of material in the Russian folk language and many works of our literature that are still utterly impossible to translate and to convey in the European languages, and especially in French. I cannot help laughing when I recall one translation (now a great rarity) of Gogol into French. It was done in the mid-1840s in Petersburg by M. Viardot, the husband of the well-known singer, in collaboration with a Russian who is now rightly famous but who then was still only a young novice writer. What resulted was not Gogol but only a jumble of nonsense. Pushkin in many ways is also untranslatable. I think that if one were to translate something like the *Narrative* of Archpriest Avvakum, the result would also be nonsense or, to put it better, nothing would come of it. Why is that so? It's a terrible thing to say, after all, that the European spirit is, perhaps, not as versatile as ours but is more self-enclosed and particular, despite the fact that that spirit has certainly been elaborated with more detail and clarity than ours. But if that is a terrible thing to say, then at least one cannot but admit with hope and a joyous spirit that the spirit of our language is certainly a versatile one, rich, universal, and all-encompassing, for in its still disorganized forms it can already convey the gems and treasures of European thought; and we sense that they are conveyed faithfully and precisely. It is of such "material" that we deprive our children—and for what? Certainly it is to make them unhappy. We scorn such material; we consider it the coarse language of the street in which it is indecent to express the feelings or thoughts of polite society.

By the way, it is exactly five years ago that we had our so-called classical reform of education. Mathematics and the two ancient languages, Latin and Greek, were acknowledged as the best means to mental and even spiritual development. This is not something that we alone acknowledged or invented: it is a fact, and an incontestable fact, derived from the experience of the whole of Europe over the course of centuries, and we merely adopted it. But the point here is this: along with the much intensified teaching of these two ancient languages and mathematics, the teaching of Russian has been all but suppressed. The question arises as to how, by what means, and through what material will our children master the forms of these two ancient languages if Russian is neglected? Can it be that the very mechanics of teaching these two languages (and by teachers who are Czechs as well) will provide the force to develop our children? In any case, one cannot cope with the mechanics without a parallel, extremely intense, and thorough teaching of the *living* language. The whole power for moral development of these two languages—these two most elaborated forms of human thought which over centuries have raised the entire barbaric West to the summit of development and civilization—this whole power, naturally, is not being used by our new schools precisely because of their neglect of Russian. Or is it the case, perhaps, that our reformers considered that we do not need to study Russian at all, except to learn where to write the letter "yat," because we are born into it? But that's just the point: we, the upper classes of Russian society, are no longer born into the living Russian language and have long since ceased to be. We will not have our living language until we merge completely with the People. But I've gotten carried away: I meant to begin speaking with our dear mammas, and I've gotten onto the classical reform in education and merging with the People.

Our dear mammas, of course, are bored listening to all this; mamma waves her little hand in indignation and turns away with a mocking smile. Mamma really doesn't care in which language her little boy thinks; if it's Parisian, then so much the better: "It's more elegant, more clever, and more tasteful." But she doesn't even realize that to do this one must be entirely reborn as a Frenchman, and with the French governesses and tutors one still can't achieve this great boon but will only reach the first station along this road, that is, to cease being a Russian. Oh, dear mamma doesn't know the poison with which she infects her child from the age of two when she hires a French governess for him. Every mother and father knows, for example, about one terrible childish physical habit that begins in some unfortunate children almost as early as the age of ten and that, if left unchecked, can sometimes transform them into idiots, into enervated, decrepit old men while still in their youth. I will venture to say flatly that the governess—meaning the French language from early childhood, from the first childish babblings—is in the moral sense just the same as is this terrible habit in the physical sense. It's all very well if the child is naturally dull or disinclined to go beyond the bounds of mediocrity: then he will live out his life in French, taking nothing seriously, with only cramped little thoughts, and with the mentality of a hairdresser; and he will die without even being aware that he lived his life a fool. But if he is a person of ability, a person with ideas in his head and magnanimous impulses in his heart, can he be happy? Without mastering the material to organize all the profundity of his thought and the questings of his spirit, having all his life a dead, sickly, stolen language with timid forms learned by rote, forms which are coarse and which do not expand for him, he will constantly agonize because of the unceasing effort and strain—both intellectual and moral—of expressing himself and his soul. (Heavens above! is it so difficult to understand that this is not a living, natural language?) He himself will be pained to realize that his thoughts are incomplete, frivolous, and cynical—cynical precisely because they are incomplete, the result of the insignificant, trivial forms in which they have been encapsulated all his life; he will become aware, at last, that even his heart has been corrupted. Corruption comes from anguish as well. Oh, of course his career will not suffer: all his sort who are born with French governesses have been unalterably designated by their mammas as future persons of consequence and live with the pretension that they are absolutely indispensable. He will make his mark, issue his directives, and urge others on to do great deeds; he will introduce new procedures and will know how to get things done. In short, he will very often be pleased with himself, especially when he gives long speeches composed of other people's thoughts and other people's phrases and which will have *plus de noblesse, que de sincerité*. But still, if he is any kind of a man at all, he will not be happy on the whole. He will forever be suffering as if from some sort of impotence, just

like those prematurely aged young men whose nasty habits have
sapped their strength before its time. But, alas, will any mamma
believe me when I say that all these misfortunes can arise from the
French language and the French governess! I can anticipate that
more than just one mamma will tell me that I have exaggerated;
and yet, strictly speaking, I have told the truth without exaggeration. They will object that, to the contrary, it is all the better that
one lives in a foreign language; that one can get by more easily,
more pleasantly, more smoothly that way; that it is precisely these
questions and questings that one must avoid; and that is the French
language specifically that promotes all this, not because it is French,
but because it is foreign and assimilated in place of one's native
language. "What do you mean? This brilliant young man, a salon
charmer and wit—will he be unhappy? He's so well-dressed, so
well-groomed, so healthy, with such an aristocratic complexion and
such a charming rose in his buttonhole?" Mamma smiles haughtily.
And yet, even without that (I mean without an upbringing in
French), the vast majority of educated Russians are even today
nothing other than intellectual proletarians, creatures with no
ground beneath their feet, no native soil or principles; they are
cosmopolitans whose minds are neither here nor there, borne about
by all the winds of Europe. And yet this fellow who has been
worked over by French governesses and tutors is, even in the best
cases and even if he does have thoughts about something and can
feel something, in essence still nothing more than a young man
wearing exquisite gloves who perhaps has already swallowed a few
fashionable *ouvrages* but whose mind wanders in eternal shadow
and whose heart longs for nothing more than *argent*. I repeat: of
course he will become a person of consequence in his country;
he'll attain the rank (in Russia the designation of a person of
consequence begins with the rank of Privy Councilor); in any case,
who should be a person of consequence if not he? Well, I've said
enough to mamma for the moment; but only to mamma. . . .

4

1. What Effects the Cure When Taking the Waters: 1 Water or the *Bon Ton?*

I do not intend to describe Ems; besides, there are already
very detailed descriptions of Ems in Russian, such as 1
Hirschorn's little book *Ems and Its Healing Springs*, publisl
St. Petersburg. You can get all the information you need
beginning with medical facts about the springs right down
tiniest details of life in the hotels, hygiene, walks, the town
and even the people who come here. As for me, I'm incapa
describing these things, and if I were compelled to do so
that I have returned home, I would recall first of all the
sun, the truly picturesque gorge of the Taunus in which E
situated, the immense and well-dressed crowd of people fro
over the world, and my own deep, deep sense of isolation i
crowd. And yet, despite the isolation, I even love such a c
but in a special way, of course. I even found an acquaintance a
that crowd, a Russian, that very same *paradoxicalist* who
some time ago, defended war in an argument with me and
in war all the truth and justice that one cannot find in contemp
society (see the April issue of my *Diary*). I have already sai
he is most humble and civilian in appearance. Everyone k
that we Russians or, to be more precise, we who live in Peters
have arranged our lives so that we visit and do business some
with God knows what sorts of people, and although we d
forget our friends (can a resident of Petersburg ever forget an
or anything?), we can go quite calmly for years on end wit
ever seeing them. My friend was also taking the waters in 1
He is about forty-five years old, or perhaps younger.

"You're right, you know," he told me. "You develop a ce

fondness for this crowd here and can't even tell why. In fact, one likes a crowd anywhere—a fashionable crowd, of course, the cream of society. You needn't hobnob with anyone from this society, but on the whole there's still nothing on earth that's better."

"Oh, come now. . . ."

"I'm not going to argue with you, not at all," he agreed hastily. "When a better society comes into being and people consent to live more sensibly, we'll have no regard at all for today's society and won't even give it a thought; it will only be a couple of words in the history of the world. But now—today—can you conceive of anything better to take its place?"

"Can we really conceive of nothing better than this idle crowd of well-off people, people who, if they weren't now jostling one another at the mineral springs, probably would have no idea of what to do with themselves and how to waste another day? There are some fine individual personalities, that's true; you can still find them even in this crowd. But as a whole—as a whole, this crowd doesn't deserve particular praise, let alone particular attention! . . ."

"You're speaking like a confirmed misanthrope or simply following the fashion. You say: 'They wouldn't know what to do with themselves and how to waste their day!' Believe me, every one of them has his things to do, even things on which he's wasted his whole life, not just one day. Each one of them can't be blamed because he's unable to make a paradise of his life and suffers in consequence. I enjoy watching all these suffering people laugh."

"Aren't they laughing out of politeness?"

"They're laughing because of the habit that crushes them all and compels them to participate in playing at paradise, if you want to call it that. They don't believe in paradise; they have to force themselves to play the game, but they still play it and so find diversion. The habit has already become too ingrained. There are some here who have taken this habit as a very serious thing, and so much the better for them, of course: they are already living in a real paradise. If you love them all (and you ought to), then you ought to rejoice that they have the opportunity to rest and forget themselves, if only in a mirage."

"But you're making fun of them. And why should I love them?"

"Why, they are humanity, and there is no other; how can you not love humanity? Over the past decade it's been impossible not to love humanity. There is one Russian lady here who is a great lover of humanity. And I'm not making fun at all. To put an end

to this topic, I'll conclude by telling you frankly that every society
of *bon ton*—this one, this fashionable crowd—has a number of
positive qualities. For example: every fashionable society is good
in that, even though it may look like a caricature, it is in closer
touch with nature than any other society, even agricultural ones,
which mostly all still live in a quite unnatural fashion. Now I'm
not talking about factories, armies, schools, universities: all those
are the ultimate in unnaturalness. The people here are the freest
of all because they are the richest of all, and therefore they can at
least live as they choose. Oh, of course they are in touch with
nature only insofar as decorum and *bon ton* permit. To open oneself,
to dissolve oneself, to reveal oneself totally to nature, to this golden
ray of sun, for example, that shines down from the blue sky on us
sinners without discriminating between those who are worthy of it
and those who are not—that would doubtless be indecorous, at least
in the degree which the two of us or some poet might want at this
moment; the little steel lock of *bon ton* is set over every heart and
every mind, as it was before. Still, one cannot but agree that *bon
ton* has taken just a tiny step on the road to contact with nature,
not only in our century but even in our generation. I have observed
this and I can conclude that the further we go into our century,
the more we realize and agree that contact with nature is the very
latest word in progress of every sort, be it science, reason, common
sense, good taste, or exquisite manners. Go into that crowd and
lose yourself in it: you see joy and good cheer on their faces. They
all speak to one another in a gentle manner; they are unusually
polite, kind, and unusually cheerful. Just think, the entire happiness of that young man with a rose in his buttonhole lies in
raising the spirits of that stout lady of fifty. In fact, what is it that
compels him to try so hard to please her? Can he really want her
to be happy and cheerful? Of course not; and he probably has
some particular and very private reasons for making such efforts,
reasons that are none of our business. But the most important thing
is this: it is probably only *bon ton* that can compel him to do this,
without any special, private reasons, and that is an extremely important fact; it shows the degree to which *bon ton* in our age can
overcome even the wild nature of some young fellow. Poetry produces Byrons, and they produce the Corsairs, the Childe Harolds,
the Laras; but just look how little time has gone by since they
appeared, and already all these characters have been cast aside by
bon ton, recognized as the very worst kind of society. And that's

even more true of our own Pechorin or the Captive of the Caucasus: they have turned out to be altogether *mauvais ton*; they're only Petersburg officials who had a brief moment of social success. And why have they been cast aside? Because these characters truly are evil, impatient, and quite openly concerned only with themselves, so that they disrupt the harmony of *bon ton*, which, above all, has to maintain the appearance that each is living for everyone else and everyone for each. Look at them over there, bringing flowers. There are bouquets for the ladies and single roses for the buttonholes of the gentlemen; and just look at how beautifully tended those roses are, how well chosen, sprayed with water! No young maid of the fields will ever choose or cut anything more elegant for the young lad she loves. But these roses are brought here for sale at five and ten German groschen apiece, and the maid of the fields has had nothing to do with them at all. The golden age is still to come, while now we have the age of enterprise. But what concern is it of yours? Does it matter at all? They are beautiful and finely dressed, and the scene looks truly like paradise. Does it make any difference whether it is 'real paradise' or 'just like paradise'? Now think about what is happening here: what good taste we see; what a fine idea this is! What is better suited to taking the waters, that is, to a hope of regaining one's health, than flowers? Flowers are hopes. How much taste there is in that notion. Remember the verses: 'And why take ye thought for raiment? Consider the lilies of the field, how they grow ... and Solomon in all his glory was not arrayed like one of these. Wherefore ... shall God not more clothe you?' I don't remember it exactly, but what wonderful words! All the poetry of life is there, all the truth of nature. But until the truth of nature is made manifest and people in their simplicity and joy of heart adorn one another with the flowers of genuine human love—all this can be bought and sold for five groschen without any love. And again I say: does it make any difference to you? I think it's even better this way because, in truth, there are some kinds of love that make you take to your heels, for they demand too much nobility; but here you pull out five groschen and you're done with it. And still, in reality, we have something very like the golden age; and if you're a man with imagination, then you're satisfied. No, the wealth of the present day ought to be encouraged, even though at other people's expense. It provides luxury and *bon ton*, things the rest of humanity can never give me. I can look at a beautiful picture here that brings me joy, and joy always costs money. Gladness and joy have always been the most expensive things; yet I, a poor man, paying nothing, can also participate in the general joy, at least vicariously. Look: the band is playing, people are laughing, the ladies are dressed like no one ever dressed in the days of Solomon—and although this is all a mirage, you and I are still happy. Finally—and quite honestly—aren't I a decent man? (I am speaking only about myself.) But thanks to the mineral waters, here am I rubbing shoulders with the very *crème de la crème*. And what an appetite you'll have now to go and drink your wretched German coffee! That's what I call the positive aspect of good society."

"Well, you're just making fun; and what you say isn't even new."

"I *am* making fun, but tell me: has your appetite improved since you came here to take the waters?"

"Of course it has, remarkably."

"That means the positive aspect of *bon ton* is so powerful that it acts even on your stomach."

"Oh, come now. That's the effect of the mineral water, not the *bon ton*."

"And of the *bon ton* as well, unquestionably. And so we still do not know what has the most effect at the mineral springs: the waters or the *bon ton*. Even the local doctors are not sure which factor should be given more weight. And on the whole it's difficult to express the immense step medicine has taken in our age: it now can even produce ideas, while in the past it had only drugs."

2. One on Whom Modern Woman Has Shown Favor

Naturally I won't describe all my conversations with this man of the old school. I knew, however, that for him the most ticklish topic was women. And yet he and I once did get into a conversation about women. He remarked that I was staring very fixedly at something.

"I'm staring at those Englishwomen, and there's a good reason for it. I took along two pamphlets for the journey here: one by Granovsky on the Eastern Question, and the other on women. There are some very fine, well-considered ideas in the pamphlet on women. But, just imagine, one sentence confused me utterly. The author writes: 'However, all the world knows what an English-woman is. The Englishwoman typifies exalted feminine beauty and feminine spiritual qualities, and our Russian women cannot equal this type. . . . ' Indeed? I cannot agree with that. Does the Englishwoman really represent such an exalted type in comparison with our Russian women? I disagree with that profoundly."

"Who wrote the pamphlet?"

"Since I did not praise those things in the pamphlet that deserve praise, and since I quoted only this one sentence, with which I cannot agree, I will not mention his name."

"The author must be a bachelor who has not yet managed to discover all the qualities of the Russian woman."

"You may have meant that sarcastically, but you were right about the 'qualities' of the Russian woman. Indeed, it's not for a Russian man to repudiate his women. How are our women inferior to others? I won't mention the ideals our poets have held up—beginning with Tatiana—or the women of Turgenev or Tolstoy, even though those things themselves form a major piece of evidence: if our writers were able to incarnate ideals of such beauty in art, they must have taken them from somewhere; they weren't created out of nothing. Therefore, such women must exist in reality as well. I won't mention the wives of the Decembrists, for instance, or a thousand other examples that are well known. And how can we, who know Russian reality, not know of thousands of such women; how can we be unaware of the thousands of their unpublicized, unseen achievements, which sometimes take place in the worst of circumstances—in such dark and terrible corners and slums, amid vices and horrors! In short, I don't intend to defend the right of the Russian woman to a lofty place among the women of Europe, but I will say only this: I think it's true, is it not, that there must exist some sort of natural law among nations and nationalities whereby every man must first seek out and love women in his own nation and in his own nationality. And if a man begins placing the women of other nations above his own and becomes attracted primarily to them, then the time will soon come for that nation to disintegrate and the identity of that nationality to be weakened. Really and truly, something like that has already been happening among us over the last hundred years, in direct proportion to our alienation from the People. We have been fascinated by Polish, French, and even German women; and now there are those who place Englishwomen above our own. I think that is a symptom which can offer us very little comfort. There are two possibilities here: either it is because of our spiritual divorce from our own nationality, or it is simply a propensity for the seraglio. We must return to our woman; we must study her if we have lost our understanding of her. . . . "

"I would be happy to agree with you on all points, although I don't know if there exists such a law of nature or nationality. But let me ask you: why did you think I was being sarcastic when I remarked that the author of the pamphlet, as a bachelor, must not have had the opportunity to acquaint himself with all the lofty qualities of the Russian woman? There can't be the slightest element of sarcasm on my part because of the very fact that I myself, I may say, have been favored by a Russian woman. Yes, whatever I am and whatever you might think I am, I myself was at one time in my life the fiancé of a Russian woman. This young lady had a station in life even higher than my own, so to say; she was surrounded by admirers; she could take her pick, and she. . . . "

"She chose you? Excuse me, I didn't know. . . . "

"No, she made her choice, and I was the one rejected; but that was the whole point! I'll tell you frankly, until I was engaged, everything was fine, and I was happy merely in being able to see her most every day. Incidentally, I might say that the impression I produced was not, perhaps, completely unfavorable. I should also add that this young lady had a good deal of freedom in her own home. And so once, at an extraordinarily strange moment unlike any other I have known, I daresay, she suddenly gave me her word she would marry me. You wouldn't believe what I felt at that moment. . . . It was all kept a secret between us, of course, but when I returned to my apartment, barely in my senses, the thought that I would be the possessor and the mate of such a dazzling creature simply crushed me like a weight. I cast my gaze over my furniture—all my wretched bachelor's belongings and what-nots that were, nonetheless, so necessary to me—and I grew so ashamed of myself, my position in society, my figure, my hair, my shabby things, and the limitations of my mind and my heart, that I was even prepared to curse my lot in life a thousand times at the thought that I, the most insignificant of men, should possess such treasures that suited me so little. I am mentioning all this so as to express a rather obscure aspect of the truth about marriage or, rather, a feeling that unfortunately is all too rarely experienced by fiancés: in order to marry, one must have an extraordinary stock of the most stupid pride in oneself. You know what I mean: this foolish, trivial pride, and all of it expressed in that utterly absurd tone to which a man of delicate feelings can never get accustomed. How can you compare yourself even for a moment with a creature like a young society lady? How can you compare with the refined perfection that reveals itself through her education, her curls, the ethereal fabric of her dresses, her dancing, her innocence, her artless yet charmingly sophisticated remarks and feelings? Just imagine: all this would be coming into my apartment, and there I'd be in my dressing gown—you're laughing? And yet, that's a terrible thought! Here's another problem: people will say that if you're afraid of such perfection and don't feel a worthy match for her, then you should choose some blowzy girl (as long as she's not morally blowzy). But of course there's no doing that: you refuse, even indignantly, and have no intention of lowering your sights. So I'll spare you the details; they were all in the same spirit. For example, when I lay down on my couch, helpless and in despair (and I must tell you that it was the most wretched couch in the whole world; I'd bought it at the flea market, and it had a broken spring), I had one trivial thought: 'So when I'm married I'll at last have some little bits of rags—from dressmaking or whatever— I can use to wipe my pens.' Now what could be more ordinary than a thought like that, and what is so terrible about it? This idea flashed through my mind by chance, no doubt, just in passing— this you can understand, because God knows what sorts of ideas can sometimes flash through the human soul, even at the moment when that soul is being dragged off to the guillotine. The thought probably came to me because I have an almost hysterical hatred of leaving my steel pens unwiped—something that no one else in the world bothers about. And what of it? I reproached myself bitterly for thinking such a thought at a moment like that: in view of the enormity of the event and the object, to dream of rags for pens, to find the time and the place for such a low, common idea— 'well, what can you be worth after something like that?' In short, I felt that my whole life would now be spent in self-reproach for my every thought and my every deed. And so when she suddenly told me, a few days later with a laughing face, that she had been joking and was in fact going to marry a certain man of high rank, I——I. . . . However, at this point instead of joy I betrayed such alarm, such an air of defeat, that she herself took fright and ran off to get me a glass of water. I set myself right, but my alarm served to help me: she realized how I loved her and . . . how I regarded her, how very highly I regarded her. . . . 'And I thought,'

she told me later, after she was married, 'that you were so proud
and educated and that you would only despise me terribly.' Since
then I have had her as a friend, and I repeat: if anyone was ever
favored by a woman, or more precisely, by a Russian woman, that
man of course was I, and I will never forget it."

"And so you became her friend?"

"As dear a friend as anyone can be. But we see one another
rarely—once a year, or even more seldom. Russian friends usually
see one another once in five years; and many of them could not
tolerate it more often than that. At first I did not call on them
because her husband's position in society was higher than mine,
but now—now she is so unhappy that I find it painful to look at
her. In the first place, her husband is an old man of sixty-two,
and a year after the wedding he was taken to court on some charge.
He had to give up almost everything he owned in order to make
good some deficiency in government funds. During the trial he
lost the use of his legs, and now he's being wheeled about in a
chair at Kreuznach, where I saw them both ten days ago. He is
pushed about in the chair, while she is constantly at his right side
fulfilling the lofty duty of the contemporary woman, all the while
listening to his sarcastic reproaches, mind you. I found it so painful
to look at her, or both of them, rather, because even now I don't
know which of them to pity more. And so I promptly left them
and came here. I'm very glad that I didn't tell you her name. To
make matters worse, I had the misfortune even in that brief time
to make her angry at me, perhaps forever, when I told her quite
frankly my view of happiness and the duty of the Russian woman."

"You couldn't have found a more opportune moment to do that,
of course."

"Are you criticizing me? But who else would have told her? I've
always thought, rather, that the greatest happiness consists in knowing why one is unhappy. And, if you like, since we've come to the
topic, I'll give you my views on happiness and on the duty of a
Russian woman. I didn't manage to say all I wanted to in
Kreuznach."

3. Children's Secrets

But I shall stop here for the moment. I wanted only to portray
this person and to give the reader some preliminary acquaintance
with him. I felt that I should portray him only as a narrator; I'm

not fully in agreement with his views. I have already explained
that he is a "paradoxicalist." His views on "happiness and the
duty of today's woman" are not even strikingly original, although
he sets forth his views almost angrily; one would think that this
is a very sore point with him. To put it simply, in his view a
woman absolutely must marry and have as many children as possible if she is to be happy and fulfill all her obligations; she must
have "not just two or three children, but six or ten, until she is
worn out, utterly exhausted." "Only then will she attain a living
life and come to know life in all its many manifestations."

"Come now," I said. "She'd never get out of the bedroom!"

"No, quite to the contrary! I can anticipate all your objections
and know them all before you make them. I have weighed everything: 'university, higher education, etc., etc.' Leaving aside the
fact that among men, only one in ten thousand acquires any real
learning, I ask you in all seriousness: in what way does university
stand in the way of marriage and child-bearing? On the contrary,
university absolutely must be available for all women, both for
future scholars and for those who simply want an education; but
later, after university, 'marry and bear children.' We still have not
thought of anything in this world cleverer than bearing children,
and so the more brains one can collect to do this, the better things
will be. It was Chatsky, wasn't it, who said: 'Whoever lacked the
wit/To bear children . . . ?' And he said that simply because he
himself was only a most uneducated Muscovite who spent his whole
life proclaiming other people's ideas on European education, so
that he wasn't even able to write a proper will, as it later turned
out, and left all his estate to some unknown person, 'my friend,
Sonechka.' This witticism about 'whoever lacked the wit' lasted
for fifty years simply because for fifty years thereafter we had no
educated people. Now, thank God, some educated people are beginning to appear in Russia, and believe me, they will at once
understand that having children and raising them is the principal
and most serious job in the world; it always has been and has never
ceased to be. 'Whoever lacked the wit . . . ?' Just imagine! Well,
it seems that it is lacking: women in Europe today are ceasing to
bear children. I won't mention our own women, for the moment."

"What do you mean, ceasing to bear children?"

I ought to mention in passing that this man has one most unexpected peculiarity: he loves children. He is, if you like, an *amateur*
of children, small children specifically, tiny ones "who still dwell

in angels' ranks." He loves them so much that he will run after them. In Ems he even became quite notorious for this. He was most fond of taking walks along the avenues where children are taken out for walks. He would get acquainted with them, even with one-year-olds, and managed to have many of them recognize him; they would wait for him, laughing and stretching out their tiny hands. He would always question a German nurse about the age of the child, heap compliments on it and thus indirectly on the nurse as well, which she would find flattering. In short, this is a kind of passion with him. He was always in particular rapture when every morning on the avenues at the mineral springs there would suddenly appear among the people whole crowds of children going to school, nicely dressed, sandwiches in hand, with little knapsacks on their backs. I must admit that these crowds of children were lovely, especially the youngest ones, the four-, five-, and six-year-olds.

"*Tel que vous me voyez*, I bought two penny-whistles today," he told me one morning with a very pleased air. "But they're not for these schoolchildren; they're too grown-up. Only yesterday, however, I had the pleasure of meeting their teacher, the worthiest man you can imagine. No, I bought the whistles for two chubby little fellows, brothers, one three years old, the other two. The three-year-old was taking his brother for a walk; they're both very clever. And they both stopped in front of a toy booth, their mouths wide open in that silly and sweet childish delight which is more charming than anything on earth. The shopkeeper, a sly German woman, at once understood why I was watching and immediately thrust a penny whistle at each of them. It cost me two marks. I can't describe how delighted the boys were, walking along and blowing on their whistles. That was an hour ago, but I just went back to check and they're still blowing their whistles. I told you once when referring to local society that it is still the best the world has to offer. I wasn't telling the truth, but you believed me, don't deny it. No, this is the best; this is perfection: these crowds of children of Ems with their sandwiches in hand, knapsacks on their backs, going off to school. . . . The sun, the Taunus, the children, their laughter, their sandwiches, and the elegant crowd of all the milords and marquises in the world admiring the children—all of it together is charming. Have you noticed how the crowd admires them each time? That shows their good taste and their impulse for something serious. But Ems is stupid, Ems cannot help being stupid, and so it still continues to bear children; Paris, on the other hand—Paris has already stopped."

"What do you mean, stopped?"

"In Paris there is an immense industry called *Articles de Paris* which, with silk, French wine, and fruits, has helped pay the five-billion reparation. Paris holds that industry in such reverence and is so concerned with it that it forgets to produce children. And the rest of France follows Paris. Every year the minister solemnly reports to the Chambers that *la population reste stationnaire*. Little ones aren't being born, you see, and if they are born, they don't survive long. On the other hand, the minister adds approvingly, 'old people thrive and live long in France.' But in my view, these old —— that fill the Chambers ought to pay their debt to nature. As if their longevity were anything to rejoice over, the doddering old fools."

"I still don't understand. What's your point about the *Articles de Paris*?"

"It's very simple. However, you are a novelist and so perhaps you know a certain quite brainless and very talented French writer and idealist of the old school, Alexandre Dumas-fils? Several quite fine 'movements' have risen up in his wake. He demands that the French woman bear children. More than that: he has quite plainly announced to everyone the secret, which everyone already knows, that women in France of the prosperous bourgeoisie all bear two children apiece. They somehow contrive with their husbands to bear only two—no more, no less. Two children and then they go on strike. They all do that, and won't bear any more; this secret spreads with amazing speed. Two offspring means that the family line is continued, and besides, two children will inherit larger estates than six will—that's the first point. And the second point is that the woman preserves herself longer: her beauty is maintained, her health as well; she gains more time for socializing, dancing, buying dresses. And as far as parental love is concerned— I mean, the moral aspect of the question—they say that one can love two children more than six, while six of them will misbehave, annoy their parents, and break things. Think of all the fuss with them! Just counting the cost of their shoes alone will make you exasperated! But the point is not that Dumas is angry; the point is that he has ventured frankly to announce the existence of the secret: two children, he says, no more, no less, and you can go on living in wedded bliss; in short, that's the whole salvation. Malthus, who was so afraid of the world's growing population, would not have proposed such measures even in his wildest dreams. And what can you say: it's such an attractive solution. As you know, France has a terrific number of property owners, with both an urban and a rural bourgeoisie. This is a godsend for them. It's their own invention. But this godsend is spreading beyond the borders of France as well. In another quarter-century or so you'll see even stupid Ems get wiser. I've heard that Berlin has grown very much wiser in this sense. But even though the number of children is decreasing, the French minister would not have noticed the difference if it had been limited only to the bourgeoisie, i.e., the prosperous class. But there was another aspect to the matter. The other aspect is the proletariat—eight, ten, maybe all twelve million of them—unbaptized and unwed people who live in 'rational relationships' instead of marriage so as to 'escape tyranny.' They throw their children right out onto the street. These Gavroches are born and die off; if they do survive, they fill the foundling homes and the prisons for under-aged criminals. In his novel *Le Ventre de Paris*, Zola, whom we call a realist, made a very apt portrayal of contemporary marriage—or rather, cohabitation—among the working class in France. And note that the Gavroches are no longer French; but most remarkable of all is that the upper class as well—those who are born as property owners, two apiece and in secret—aren't French either. At least I venture to argue that; so that both aspects and both poles converge. The first result is this: France is beginning to cease to be France. (Is it really possible to say that these ten million consider France their fatherland?) I know that there will be people who say: 'So much the better: the French will disappear and human beings will remain.' But are they really human beings? Let's suppose they are, but they are the savages of the future who will swallow up Europe. It is from them that the senseless rabble of the future—little by little, but certainly and surely—is being produced. I think there's not the least doubt that a whole generation is physically degenerating, growing impotent and base. And the physical aspect drags morality behind it. These are the fruits of the reign of the bourgeoisie. I think that the whole reason behind it is the land, or rather the soil, the native soil and the way it is now divided into private property. So I'll explain that to you."

4. The Land and Children

"The land is everything," my paradoxicalist continued. "I make no distinction between the land and children, and this point will

emerge of itself from what I say. However, I am not going to develop
the point for you: you will realize it if you think about it carefully.
The point is that it all comes from a mistake in our management
of the land. It may even be that all the rest, and all of humanity's
other misfortunes as well, perhaps, come from that same mistake.
Millions of paupers have no land, particularly in France, where
there is little enough land to begin with; and so they have no place
where they can give birth to children and are compelled to give
birth in some cellar, and not to children but Gavroches, half of
whom cannot name their own fathers, and the other half, perhaps,
their own mothers. That's one side of the problem, and on the
other side—the higher side if you like—there is also the error in
land use; but it's quite different. It's an error of the opposite extreme
that may even stem from the time of Clovis, the conqueror of the
Gauls. The people on this side all have too much land; they have
seized far more than they need and keep too strong a hold on it,
giving up nothing. And so in both cases you have abnormality.
Something must happen to change this; I know only that everyone
should have land, and that children ought to be born on the land
and not on the street. I truly don't know how this will be set right,
but I know that at present there is nowhere there to give birth to
children. I think that it's fine to work in a factory: a factory is
also a legitimate business, and it is always set up alongside land
that is already being worked: that's the way it's done. But every
factory worker should know that he has his own Garden somewhere,
with golden sun and vineyards, a place of his own or, rather, a
communal Garden; and he should know that living there is his
wife—a fine woman, not one from the street—who loves him and
waits for him; and along with his wife are his children, who play
at horsies and who all know their own father. *Que diable*, every
decent and healthy little child is born with his own 'horsie,' and
every decent father ought to know that, if he wants to be happy.
This is where he'll bring the money he's earned; he won't drink
it up in the tavern with some female of the species he's found on
the street. In the worst cases (in France, for instance, where there
is so little land), the Garden may not feed him and his family, so
that he won't be able to manage without the factory; but he should
know, at least, that his children will grow up there with the land,
the trees, the quail they catch; they will go to school, and the school
will be in a field; and he himself, when he has ended his working
life, will still go there to take his rest and at last to die. And yet,

who knows? Perhaps the Garden will be able to feed him; in any case, there's no cause to fear the factories—perhaps the factory will be built in the middle of the Garden. In short, I'm not sure how all this will happen, but it will happen; there will be a Garden. Mark my words: though it be a hundred years from now, remember that I explained it to you in Ems, in the middle of an artificial garden among artificial people. Humanity will be renewed in the Garden, and the Garden will restore it—that is the formula. Do you see how it happened? First there were castles and around them only mud huts; the barons lived in the castles and the vassals in the huts. Then the bourgeoisie began to arise in walled cities, slowly, microscopically. Meanwhile the castles came to an end and the capital cities of kings arose, large cities with royal palaces and halls for the courtiers; and so it was until our age. In our age came the terrible revolution, and the bourgeoisie prevailed. With it appeared the terrible cities, which no one had even dreamt of. Humanity had never seen cities of the sort that appeared in the nineteenth century. These are cities with crystal palaces, international expositions, international hotels, banks, budgets, polluted rivers, railway platforms, and all that goes with them. Around them stand factories and mills. And now we await the third phase: the bourgeoisie will depart the scene and Regenerated Humanity will come to the fore. This new humanity will divide the land into communes and will begin to live in the Garden. 'It will be regenerated in the Garden, and the Garden will restore it.' And so it proceeds, from castles to cities to the Garden. If you want to hear all of my idea, then I think that children—I mean real children, I mean children of human beings—should be born on the land and not on the street. One may live on the street later, but a nation— in its vast majority—should be born and *arise* on the land, on the native soil in which its grain and its trees grow. But now the entire proletariat of Europe is a creature of the street. But in the Garden the little children will be springing directly up from the earth, like Adams, and not going to work at the factories at the age of nine when they still want to play; they won't be breaking their backs over some lathe, deadening their minds before some common machine to which the bourgeois says his prayers; they will not exhaust and ruin their imaginations before endless rows of gas lamps, and ruin their morals through the depravity of the factory, which is such as was never seen in Sodom. And these are boys and girls of ten. That's terrible enough here; but it's happening in Russia, where there is so much land and where factories are still only a joke, but wretched little towns exist wherever there are three petty bureaucrats. And yet if there is any place where I can see the seed or the idea of the future, it is in Russia. Why is that? It's because we have had and still preserve among the People one principle: that the land for them is *everything*, and that they derive everything from the land; this is still what the huge majority of them believe. But the main thing is that this principle is the normal law of humanity. There is something sacramental in the land, in one's native soil. If you want humanity to be reborn into something better, if you want to make human beings out of creatures that are almost beasts, then give them land and you will achieve your aim. At least in Russia the land and the commune exist—in a most wretched state, I agree; but still they are an immense seed for the future idea, and that is my point. I think that order arises in the land and from the land, and this happens everywhere, throughout humanity. The whole order in every country, be it political, civil, or whatever, is always linked with the soil and with the character of agriculture in that country. The character in which agriculture has developed has determined the way everything else developed. If there is anywhere in Russia now where maximum disorder prevails, it is in the area of land tenure, in the relationship between landowner and worker and among landowners themselves; it is in the very way the land is worked. And until all that is set right, do not expect anything else to be set right. I do not assign blame to anyone or anything: this is a matter of world history, and we realize it. I think that we have still paid very cheaply to end serfdom, thanks to the *consent* of the whole country. And it is on this consent that I stake everything else. This consent is, after all, one more principle of the People, another one of those same principles which the Potugins still deny. Well, all these railways of ours, all our new banks and associations and credit institutions—all these things, in my opinion, are still only dust and ashes; as far as the railways are concerned, I recognize only the strategic ones. All these things should have come about only after the land question had been properly settled; then they would have appeared naturally, but now it is only a matter of a game on the stock exchange, the stirrings of the Jew. You're laughing; you don't agree. Well, so be it. But just lately I was reading the memoirs of a certain Russian landowner written in the middle of this century; as far back as the 1820s he wanted to set his peasants free. That was a rare novelty in those days. By the way, when he went to the country, he set up a school and began teaching the peasant children choral church music. When a neighboring landowner called on him and heard the choir, he said: 'That's a clever thing you've thought up; train them well and you'll surely find a buyer for the whole choir. People like that sort of thing and will pay good money for a choir.' So at a time when one could still sell choirs of young children 'for export' away from their mothers and fathers, freeing peasants was still cause for bafflement and amazement in our Russian land. And so he began telling the peasants about this new and curious thing; they heard him out and were amazed and frightened; they spent a long time talking it over among themselves, and then they came to him: 'Well, and what about the land?' 'The land is mine; you can have the huts and your farm buildings, but you will work the land for me each year and we'll share the harvest equally.' The peasants scratched their heads: 'No, it's better the old way; we belong to you, and the land belongs to us.' Of course this surprised the landowner: these, he thought, are a savage people, on such a lowly moral plane that they don't even want their own freedom—freedom, this first blessing of a human being, and so on. Subsequently this saying or, rather, formula—'We are yours, but the land is ours'—became known to everyone and no longer caused any surprise. However, the most important thing is this: where could such an 'unnatural and utterly unique' notion of world history have come from, at least if one compares it to Europe? And bear in mind that it was just at this time that the war was raging most furiously among all our learned compatriots on the question: 'Do our People, in fact, have any principles that might be worthy of the attention of our educated classes?' No, indeed, sir: this means that the Russian from the very beginning could never imagine himself without land. But what is most surprising here is that even after serfdom the People kept the essence of that same formula, and the overwhelming majority of them still cannot conceive of themselves without land. Since they didn't want to accept freedom without land, it means that the land came first for them; it was the basis for everything else. The land is everything, and everything else derives from it—freedom, life, honor, family, children, order, the church—in short, everything that has any value. It's because of that same formula that the People have maintained such a thing as the commune. And what is the commune? Sometimes a much heavier burden than serfdom! Everyone has his opinion about communal land tenure; everyone knows what a hindrance it is to economic progress alone. But at the same time, does it not contain the seed of something new and better, a future ideal that awaits us all? No one knows how it will come to pass, but we alone have it in embryo, and it will only happen among us because it will be realized not through war and rebellion but, once more, through a grand and universal consent. It will be through consent because even now great sacrifices are being made for it. And so children will be born in the Garden and they will be set right; no longer will ten-year-old girls drink cheap vodka in taverns with factory hands. It's a hard thing for children to grow up in our age, sir! I intended, after all, to talk to you only about children, and that's why I took up your time. Little children are the future, you see, and one only loves the future. Who worries about the present? Not I, of course, and probably not you either. And that's why one loves children more than anything else."

5. An Odd Summer for Russia

The other day I told this peculiar fellow of mine: "You keep talking about children, but just now in the *Kursaal* I read in the Russian papers (and I might say that all the Russians here are crowding around the newspapers now) a story about a Bulgarian mother. Entire districts have been massacred over there in Bulgaria. An old woman who survived in one village was found wandering through the ashes of her home, out of her mind. When they began questioning her, she did not reply in ordinary words but at once put her right hand to her cheek and began to sing. She sang improvised verses of how she once had had a home and family, a husband, children—six of them—and how her eldest children had children of their own, her little grandchildren. But cruel people came and by the wall they burned her old man to death, butchered her fine children, raped a young girl, and carried off another one, a beauty; they tore out the bellies of the infants with their sabers; then they set fire to the house and threw them all into the raging flames; and she had seen it all and heard the shrieks of the children."

"Yes, I also read it," replied my peculiar friend. "It's truly remarkable. And in verse, that's the main thing. But in Russia, although our critics have sometimes had praise for poetry, they are generally inclined to the view that poetry is created more as a form of indulgence. It's interesting to be able to follow a spontaneous epic in its elemental conception. It's really a question of art."

"Stop it; you're not being serious. However, I've noticed that you're not overly fond of discussing the Eastern Question."

"No, I've also made a donation to the cause. But since you mention it, there is something about the Eastern Question that I don't care for."

"What, specifically?"

"Well, the great outpouring of love, for instance."

"Come now; I'm sure. . . . "

"I know; I know; you needn't finish; and you're quite right. Besides, I sent in my contribution at the very beginning. You see, the Eastern Question up to now has been only a question of love, so to say, and it came from the Slavophiles. In fact, a lot of people have done very well from this outpouring of love, especially last winter with the Herzegovinians; there were even some careers made on it. Mind you, I'm not making accusations; besides, an outpouring of love in itself is an excellent thing, but a jaded old nag can be ridden to death, after all. That's just what I've been afraid of ever since spring, and so I was skeptical. Later in the summer I was still concerned that this whole feeling of brotherhood might somehow wear off. But now—now I'm not afraid any more; Russian blood has been shed, and shed blood is an important thing, a unifying thing!"

"But did you really think that our feeling of brotherhood would wear off?"

"I did, indeed, sinner that I am. And how could one help it? But I don't believe that any longer. You see, even here in Ems, some six miles from the Rhine, we have news straight from Belgrade, in effect. Travelers have arrived who have heard Russia being accused in Belgrade. On the other hand, I myself have read in *Temps* and *Débats* that after the Turks invaded Serbia people in Belgrade shouted, 'Down with Cherniaev!' Other correspondents and eye-witnesses claim, to the contrary, that this is all nonsense and that the Serbs simply worship Russia and expect everything from Cherniaev. You know, I believe both versions of the news. No doubt there were shouts of both kinds, and it could be no other way: Serbia is a young nation; it has no soldiers, and they do not know how to wage war; there is an unlimited amount of magnanimity, but no practicality at all. Cherniaev had to create an army there, but I'm sure that the overwhelming majority of the Serbs cannot conceive of the immensity of the task of creating an army in such a short time and under such conditions. They will understand later, but by then it will be a matter of world history. Besides, I'm certain that even among some of the soundest and, so to say, most ministerial minds there are those who are convinced that Russia is holding back and looking for ways to seize them and so increase her own political power immensely. And so I was afraid that all this might pour cold water on our Russian sense of brotherly love. But it turned out to be the contrary, so much so that it was a surprise even to many Russians. The whole of the Russian land suddenly spoke up and suddenly said what was foremost in its mind. The soldier, the merchant, the professor, the saintly old woman—they all spoke with one voice. And there was not a single word, mind you, about seizing Serbia; as they said, it was all 'for the Orthodox cause.' It's not the few pennies for the Orthodox cause that matter, it's the fact that they themselves are willing to lay down their lives. And again, mind, these words 'for the Orthodox cause' are a truly extraordinary political slogan both for the present and for the future. One can even say that this is the slogan of our future. And the fact that there is not a sound from anywhere about 'annexation' is something most peculiar. Europe could never ever believe that, because she would have acted with no other aim than to seize Serbia; and so, strictly speaking, we mustn't even blame Europe for crying out against us, don't you think? In short, this time our final conflict with Europe has begun, and ... could it begin any other way than through a misunderstanding? For Europe, Russia is a puzzle, and Russia's every action is a puzzle; and so it will be until the very end. Yes, it has been a long time since the Russian land has so declared itself, so consciously and in agreement; and besides, we have truly found our kinsmen and brethren, and these are no longer merely fine words. And we found them not through the Slavic Committee but directly, through our whole land. And that is what surprises me; I never would have believed it. This accord of ours, universal and so *sudden*, would be difficult to believe had anyone even foretold it. And yet what happened did happen. You were just talking about that unfortunate Bulgarian mother, but I know that another mother has come on the scene this summer: Mother Russia has found her own new children, and we hear her great, plaintive voice crying out for them. And they truly are her children, and it truly is a great maternal lament for them. Once more there is a great political sign of things to come; mark it well: 'she is their mother, not their ruler!' And should it happen that some new children who do not understand the matter grumble against her—for however brief a time—she should pay them no heed but continue to do her good work with endless and patient maternal love, as every genuine mother would do. This summer, you know—this summer will be inscribed in our history. How many Russian misunderstandings were cleared up at once! How many Russian questions were answered at once! This summer was almost an epoch in the consciousness of Russians.

6. Postscript

"The Russian People are sometimes terribly terribly *implausible.*" I happened to hear this little phrase this summer as well, and of course it was because the person who said it found so many of the things that happened over the summer unexpected and, perhaps, even "implausible." However, what happened that was so new? To the contrary, had not all these things that had come to light lain long, even always, in the hearts of the Russian People?

In the first place, the People's idea emerged and the People's feeling was expressed. The feeling was one of selfless love for their unfortunate and oppressed brethren, and the idea was "the Orthodox cause." And truly, in this alone something rather unexpected was expressed. Unexpected (although not for everyone, by any means) was the fact that the People had not forgotten their great idea, their "Orthodox cause"; they had not forgotten it over the course of two centuries of slavery, dismal ignorance, and—of late—repulsive corruption, materialism, vile Jewry, and cheap vodka. In the second place, unexpected was the fact that the People's idea, the "Orthodox cause," found allies in almost all shades of opinion among the most educated levels of Russian society, from that same group which we had regarded as utterly alienated from the People. And note here as well the unusual enthusiasm and unanimity of almost all our press. . . . The saintly old woman offers her few kopecks and adds, "for the Orthodox cause." The journalist picks up this expression and sets it down in his newspaper with genuine reverence, and you can see that he himself supports this "Orthodox cause" with all his heart; you sense this when you read his article. Perhaps even those among us who do not believe in anything have at last understood what in essence Orthodoxy and "the Orthodox

cause" mean to the Russian People. They have understood that
this is by no means a religion based merely on ritual, and on the
other hand it is by no means some *fanatisme religieux* (as people
in Europe are already beginning to call the present general movement in Russia); they realize that it is precisely a matter of human
progress and the humanization of all humanity, as understood by
the Russian People. The People derive everything from Christ;
they incarnate their whole future in Christ and Christ's truth and
cannot even conceive of themselves without Christ. The liberals,
the doubting Thomases, the skeptics, as well as the proponents of
social ideas, have all—or at least the majority of them—suddenly
become ardent Russian patriots. That means, then, that they were
patriots all along. But can we positively state that we did not know
this until now? Have we not heard, to the contrary, so many bitter
mutual reproaches that now have turned out to be futile in so many
ways? We have found so many more Russians—genuine Russians—
than many of us who are also genuine Russians ever supposed.
What is it that united these people or, more accurately, what is it
that showed them that in the principal and essential things they
had not even formerly been disunited? But this is just the point:
the Slavic idea, in its highest sense, has ceased to be only a matter
of Slavophilism and has suddenly, as a result of the pressure of
circumstances, entered the very heart of Russian society, made itself
distinctly known in the general consciousness, while in its *living*
feeling it has coincided with the movement of the People. But what,
then, is this "Slavic idea in its higher sense"? It has become obvious
to all what it is: it is, first of all (that is, before any historical,
political, or other interpretations), the notion of sacrifice, the need
to sacrifice even oneself for one's brethren, and a feeling of voluntary
duty by the strongest of the Slavic tribes to intercede on behalf of
a weaker one with the aim of making it equal to him in liberty
and political independence, and thereby to found the great pan-
Slavic unity in the name of Christ's truth, that is, for the benefit,
love, and service of all humanity and the defense of all the world's
weak and oppressed. And this is by no means just a theory; to
the contrary, the current Russian movement, fraternal and selfless,
goes as far as conscious willingness to sacrifice even one's own vital
interests, even peace with Europe if need be. This has been shown
as a fact; and can the uniting of the Slavs in the future occur with
any other purpose than the defense of the weak and the service of
humanity? This must happen, because the majority of the Slavic

tribes have themselves been schooled and have developed only
through suffering. We wrote above that we are amazed that the
Russian People, in their slavery of serfdom, in their ignorance and
oppression, never forgot their Orthodox duty, never sank irretrievably into bestiality or became gloomy, self-absorbed egotists concerned only for their own advantage. But probably this is just their
nature as Slavs; that is, to ascend spiritually in their suffering, to
strengthen themselves politically in their oppression; amid slavery
and humiliation, to join together in love and in the truth of Christ.

> Emburdened by the weighty cross,
> Christ our Lord, in slavish dress
> Traversed thee all, my native soil;
> And everywhere the land did bless.

And so it is because the Russian People themselves were oppressed and bore the burden of the cross for so many years that
they did not forget their "Orthodox cause" and their suffering
brethren; and they ascended in spirit and in heart, totally prepared
to help the oppressed in every way possible. And this is what our
higher intelligentsia understood in supporting the wishes of the
People with all their hearts. And when they had expressed support,
they suddenly and entirely felt themselves united with the People.
The movement that caught up everyone was magnanimous and
humane. The greatest happiness in the life of a nation is found in
every higher and unifying idea, every true feeling that unites all.
This happiness was bestowed upon us. We could not help but fully
sense our increased accord, the clarification of many former misunderstandings, our strengthened self-consciousness. A political
idea, plainly perceived by society and by the People, was revealed.
Perceptive Europe at once saw this and now follows the Russian
movement with the greatest attention. Conscious political thought
in our People is something totally unexpected for Europe. Europe
senses something new with which she must reckon; we rose in her
estimation. The talk and rumors that have long been growing in
Europe of the political and social disintegration of Russian society
as a national entity must certainly now be refuted in her eyes: it
turned out that the Russians have the capacity for unity when
needed. And the forces of disintegration themselves, should Europe
continue to believe in them, must naturally now, in her view, move
in another direction and assume another outcome. Yes, from this
epoch henceforth there are many views that will have to change.

In short, this general Russian movement that expresses accord also testifies in a large way to our national maturity and cannot but evoke respect.

Russian officers are going to Serbia and giving up their lives there. The movement of Russian officers and retired Russian soldiers into Cherniaev's army has grown steadily and continues to grow progressively. People may say: "These are lost souls who had nothing to do at home and who went off simply in order to go somewhere; they are careerists and adventurers." But aside from the fact that (according to many accurate reports) these "adventurers" have received no monetary gain and that the majority of them have barely even managed to make their way to Serbia, some of them who had still been on active service must unquestionably have suffered a loss through retirement, temporary though it may be. But whoever they may be, what do we hear and read about them? They are dying by the dozens in battles and are carrying out their duty heroically; the young army of insurgent Slavs created by Cherniaev is already beginning to rely heavily on them. They are bringing glory to the Russian name in Europe, and through their blood they are uniting us with our brethren. This blood of theirs, heroically spilled, will not be forgotten and will be taken into account. No, they are not adventurers: they are consciously beginning a new era. They are the pioneers of the Russian political idea, Russian desires, and Russian will, which they have made known to Europe.

One more Russian personality has made itself known, calmly and even majestically: this is General Cherniaev. His military actions have to date proceeded with mixed success, but on the whole he still holds the evident advantage. He has created an army in Serbia; he has displayed a severe, firm, unshakeable character. Aside from that, when he went off to Serbia he risked all the military fame he had acquired in Russia and, accordingly, risked his future as well. In Serbia, as was shown only recently, he agreed to accept command only over a separate detachment and only recently was confirmed in the post of commander-in-chief. The army with which he marched into battle consisted of militia men, new recruits who had never seen a rifle and peaceful citizens who had come straight from the plow. The risk was extraordinary, the chances of success doubtful: it was in truth a sacrifice for a great purpose. Having created the army, trained it, and organized it as best he could, General Cherniaev began to act more decisively and boldly.

He succeeded in gaining a highly significant victory. Just recently he has been compelled to withdraw under pressure of an enemy three times stronger than himself. But he withdrew in time, keeping the army intact, not beaten but strong; and he has occupied a strong position that the "victor" did not dare attack. If one makes a proper assessment of the facts, it is obvious that General Cherniaev is only just beginning his main actions. His army, however, can no longer expect support from anywhere, whereas the enemy can increase its forces immensely. Besides, the political considerations of the Serbian government may do much to prevent him from taking his cause to its completion. Nonetheless, his character has shown itself firmly and clearly: his military talent is indisputable, while his character and lofty ideals have placed him at the summit of Russian aspirations and aims. But the full story of General Cherniaev remains to be told in the future. It is noteworthy that since his departure for Serbia he has acquired remarkable popularity in Russia; his name is on everyone's lips. And this is not difficult to understand: Russia realizes that he has begun and continues a task which coincides with its very best and most heartfelt desires; by his action he made those desires known to Europe. Whatever might subsequently happen, he can already take pride in his activity, while Russia will not forget him and will love him.

September

1

1. *Piccola Bestia*

About seven years ago I happened to spend a whole summer, right until September, in Florence. The Italians think that Florence has the hottest summer and the coldest winter of any city in Italy. The summer in Naples is considered far more tolerable than the one in Florence. And so once, in the month of July, a great commotion broke out in the apartment I was renting: two maidservants, with the landlady in the lead, rushed into the room shouting that they had just seen a *piccola bestia* scurrying into my room from the corridor and they absolutely had to find and kill it. The *piccola bestia* is a tarantula. So they set to searching under the chairs and tables, in all the corners, and in the furniture; they began sweeping under the cupboards and stamping their feet to frighten it, and so lure it into the open. At last they rushed into the bedroom and began hunting under the bed, in the bed, through the linen and . . . they never found it. They found it only the next morning when they were sweeping out the room and, of course, executed it at once; still, I had had to spend the preceding night in my bed with the most unpleasant awareness that the *piccola bestia* was spending the night along with me. People say that a tarantula bite is rarely fatal, although I did know of one instance during my time in Semipalatinsk, exactly fifteen years before Florence, when a Cossack of the line died from a tarantula bite despite medical treatment. For the most part, though, the victims escape with only a high fever or feverish attacks; in Italy, where there are so many doctors, the matter is perhaps even less serious. I don't know about these things, not being a doctor; but still I had a very anxious night. At first I tried to drive the thought from my mind; I even laughed, recalling and reciting aloud Kuzma Prutkov's didactic fable "The

Conductor and the Tarantula" (an absolute masterpiece of its kind);
then I fell asleep. But my dreams were truly unpleasant ones. I
didn't have a single dream of a tarantula, but there were other
things—most unpleasant, painful, and nightmarish; I awoke frequently, and only toward morning, when the sun had come up,
did I sleep more soundly. Do you know why I remembered this
little old story just now? It's because of the Eastern Question! . . .
Yet I'm scarcely surprised: people are writing and saying the wildest sorts of things about the Eastern Question these days!

I think this is what has happened: along with the Eastern Question some sort of *piccola bestia* has scurried into Europe's bedrooms
and is keeping all the good people from settling down quietly—all
those people who love peace, who love humanity and hope that it
will flourish, all those who long for that bright moment when *at
least this* elementary, crude strife among nations will come to an
end at last. In fact, if you think carefully about it, it sometimes
seems that with the final solution of the Eastern Question every
other kind of political strife in Europe will be solved as well; that
the phrase "Eastern Question" contains, perhaps unknown to itself, all of Europe's other political questions, misunderstandings,
and prejudices. In short, something quite new would begin, and
for Russia a whole new phase of development; for it is all too clear
now that only with the final solution of this question could Russia—
for the first time in her history—at last come to an understanding
with Europe and be understood by her. But some sort of *piccola
bestia* is preventing all this happiness from being realized. The
piccola bestia was always there, but now, with the Eastern Question,
it scurries right into the bedrooms. Everyone is expectant and
uneasy; some sort of nightmare hangs over everyone's head; everyone has bad dreams. Who or what this *piccola bestia* is that produces
such commotion—that no one can explain, because some kind of
general madness has set in. Every person imagines it in his own
way, and no one understands anyone else. And yet it seems that
everyone has been bitten already. The bite of the *piccola bestia*
quickly brings on the most extraordinary fits: people in Europe,
it seems, now no longer understand one another, as in the days of
the Tower of Babel; each one no longer even understands what he
wants himself. There is only one thing that unites them all: they
all immediately point to Russia; each one is certain that the malicious vermin always emanate from there. Meanwhile, only in
Russia is everything bright and clear—except, of course, for the

deep sorrow over her Eastern Slavic brethren—a sorrow which, however, illuminates the soul and elevates the heart. In Russia the Eastern Question always produces something quite the opposite of what it does in Europe: everyone here at once begins to understand everyone else more clearly; each one truly realizes what he wants; and everyone senses that he agrees with everyone else; the very last peasant knows what he should yearn for, just as the most educated person does. We are all quickly united by the beautiful and noble feeling of selfless and noble aid to the brethren who have been nailed to the cross. But Europe does not believe this; Europe believes neither in Russia's nobility nor in her selflessness. It is this "selflessness" in particular that causes all the ignorance, all the temptation; it is the principal thing that causes the confusion— the condition which everyone loathes and despises; and so no one wants to believe in Russia's selflessness; everyone is somehow drawn away from believing in it. Were it not for this "selflessness," the matter would in an instant be simplified tenfold and Europe would be able to understand it; but selflessness is a blank spot, an unknown, a riddle, a mystery! Oh, people in Europe have been bitten! And, of course, those who have been bitten believe that the whole mystery lies in Russia alone which, they feel, wants to reveal nothing but is proceeding steadily and persistently toward some goal of her own, moving slyly and quietly and deceiving everyone. For two hundred years now Europe has lived with Russia, which compelled Europe to accept her into the European union of nations and into civilization; but Europe always looked askance at Russia, sensing something improper; it is as if Russia were a fateful riddle that appeared from God knows where but which must be solved at all costs. And so each time the Eastern Question, in particular, arises, Europe's ignorance and misunderstanding of Russia develops into something pathological, and nothing is solved: "Who is it and what is it, and when will we finally learn the answer? Who are they, these Russians? Are they Asiatics? Are they Tatars? It would be good if they were, for then the matter would be clear; but it seems that they are not. The point is that they are not Asiatics; the point is that we must admit to ourselves that they are not. And yet they are so unlike us. . . . And what about this union of the Slavs? What's that for? What's its purpose? What will it tell us— what new thing can this dangerous union tell us?" They end, as before and as always, by answering these questions according to their very own measure: "They want to appropriate new territory," they say, "and that means conquest, treachery, deceit, the future extinction of civilization, a united Mongol horde, the Tatars!..."

And yet, even this very hatred of Russia is insufficient to unite completely those who have been bitten: every time the Eastern Question comes up, the ostensible unity of Europe at once and all too obviously begins to collapse into its personal, distinctly national egoisms. All this comes from the mistaken notion that someone wants to seize and plunder something: "I should have some of this, too; otherwise they'll grab it all and I won't get a thing!" And so every time this fateful question appears on the scene, all the old political conflicts and ailments of Europe become inflamed and come to a head. Therefore everyone naturally wants to suppress the matter, at least temporarily. The main thing is to suppress it in Russia, to find some way of diverting her from it, to exorcise, bewitch, and frighten her.

And so Viscount Beaconsfield, an Israelite by birth (né d'Israeli), in his speech at one banquet, suddenly reveals a great secret to Europe: all these Russians who, with Cherniaev at their head, have rushed to Turkey to save the Slavs, are only a lot of socialists, communists, and communards. In short, they represent all the destructive elements with which Russia is supposedly so well stocked. "You may trust me, for I am Beaconsfield, after all, the Premier, as the Russian newspapers call me to give their articles added weight: I am the Prime Minister; I have secret documents, and so I know better than you; I know a great deal, in fact." That is what shines through every phrase of this Beaconsfield. I am certain that he thought up this name, worthy of a family album and reminiscent of our own Lenskys and Gremins, when he was soliciting the queen for his nobility; he's a novelist, after all. By the way, when I was writing about the mysterious *piccola bestia* a few lines above, a thought suddenly occurred to me: what if the reader imagines that I am trying to depict Viscount Beaconsfield in this allegory? But I assure you this is not the case: the *piccola bestia* is only an idea, not a person, and it would do too much credit to Mr. Beaconsfield, even though one has to admit that he is very similar to a *piccola bestia*. When he proclaimed in his speech that Serbia, having declared war on Turkey, took a dishonorable step and that the war Serbia is now waging is a dishonorable one— so having spit in the face of the whole Russian movement and the whole upsurge of Russian spirit, having spit in the face of our sacrifices, our wishes, our earnest prayers (and he could not help crosses . . . hmm . . . well, of course. . . . However, 'the state is not a private individual; it cannot sacrifice its own interests out of sensitivity, the more so that in political affairs magnanimity itself is never disinterested.' It's wonderful what beautiful sayings there are," Beaconsfield muses; "they even refresh the mind and, most important, they sound so elegant. Indeed, isn't the state. . . . But I'd best go to bed. . . . Hmm. Well, and what of those two priests? 'Popes,' they call them, *les popes.* It's their own fault for turning up there, in any case. They ought to have hidden somewhere . . . under a sofa. . . . *Mais, avec votre permission, messieurs les deux cru- cifiés,* I am terribly fed up with your stupid little adventure, *et je vous souhaite la bonne nuit à tous les deux.*"

And Beaconsfield falls asleep, sweetly, tenderly. He dreams all the while that he is a viscount, while around him are roses and lilies of the valley and the most charming ladies. Now he delivers a most charming speech: what *bon mots!* Everyone applauds. He has just destroyed the coalition. . . .

And all these captains and majors of ours, old veterans of Sevastopol and the Caucasus, in their rumpled, worn, old frock coats with white crosses in their buttonholes (many of them were so described)—all these are socialists! There are some among them who will take a drink, of course; we've heard about that. The serviceman has a weakness for that, but it's certainly not socialism. On the other hand, look at how he dies in battle; what a fine figure he cuts, what a hero he is at the head of his battalion, bringing glory to the Russian name and through his example transforming cowardly recruits into heroes! Is this your idea of a socialist? Well, and what of these two young fellows whose mother led them by the hands (there was such a case, indeed)—are they communards? And this old warrior with a family of sons—does he really want to burn down the Tuileries? These old soldiers, these Cossacks from the Don, these parties of Russians who come with medical detachments and field chapels—do they really sleep, dreaming only of shooting an archbishop? These Kireevs, these Raevskys—are they all our destructive elements that are to make Europe shake in her boots? And Cherniaev, this most naive of heroes and our former publisher of the *Russian World*—is he the leading representative of Russian socialism? Phoo—this is beyond belief! If Beaconsfield only knew how silly this sounds in Russian and . . . how shameful, then, perhaps, he would not have ventured to insert such a ridiculous passage in his speech.

but know our feelings)—this Israelite, this new ajudicato
in England, continues as follows (I am not quoting
"Russia, of course, was pleased to rid herself of all her
elements by sending them off to Serbia, although she
realize that they would join forces there, merge, cons
acquire an organization; they will grow into a real force. .
rope must take note of this new, menacing force," Be
stresses, threatening English farmers with the future so
Russia and the East. "In Russia they will take notice
sinuation about socialism," he also thinks to himself. "V
give Russia a scare."

A spider, to be sure, a *piccola bestia;* indeed, he is av
a spider, a shaggy little *bestia!* And how nimbly he can
around! This massacre of the Bulgarians was somethin
mitted, after all—and not just permitted—he plotted it h
is a novelist, and this is his *chef-d'oeuvre.* But he's seve
old and the grave is not far off—he knows it himself.
overjoyed he must have been at becoming a viscount; he
must have dreamt about this all his life, when he was st
novels. What do these people believe in? How do they ge
at night? What dreams to they dream? What do they do
are alone with their souls? Oh, their souls are no doubt
most refined things! . . . Every day they eat such elegant
the company of such refined and witty people; evenings
the favorites of such charming ladies from the highest, mo
elements of society. Oh, their lives are beyond reproa
digestion is excellent; their dreams are as light as infants'.
ago I read that the bashibazouks crucified two priests; th
died after twenty-four hours of torment that exceeds all im
Although Beaconsfield at first denied in Parliament that
any kind of torture at all—not even the slightest—he,
knows very well about all of this himself, even about
crosses; "he has documents, after all." Doubtless he banis
trivial, worthless, and even filthy, indecent pictures from
but those two blackened corpses hanging twisted on the
can pop into one's head at the most unexpected times-
example, when Beaconsfield is preparing for slumber in
appointed bedroom, smiling brightly as he recalls the
evening he has just spent, the ball and all the charmi
things he said to this gentleman and that lady.

"Well," Beaconsfield will think, "the blackened corpses

2. Words, Words, Words!

There are certain opinions on solving the Eastern Question, expressed both here and in Europe, which are truly astounding. By the way, there are people in our own world of journalism who seem to have been bitten by the *piccola bestia* as well. Oh, I'm not planning to run through all my impressions—I don't have the stamina for that. "Administrative autonomy" alone is enough to give you paralysis of the brain. You see, if we could manage to give Bulgaria, Herzegovina, and Bosnia equal rights with the Moslem population and also find the means to guarantee those rights, "then we certainly can see no reason why the Eastern Question cannot be solved," etc., etc. This opinion, as we know, enjoys particular influence in Europe. In short, they conceive a plan so complex that its realization would be more difficult than recreating the whole of Europe anew or separating water from earth or whatever you like; and yet they think that the matter is solved, and they are tranquil and satisfied. No, gentlemen, Russia agreed to this only *in principle*, but wanted to supervise the execution of such a plan herself, *in her own way*, and of course would not allow you phrasemongers to profit from it. "To grant autonomy?" "To find the right combination?" But how can this be done? Who is going to carry it out? Who is going to obey, and who is going to make them obey? Finally, who is ruling Turkey? Which parties and which forces? Is there, even in Constantinople (which is still *more advanced* than the rest of Turkey), even one Turk who in fact, by virtue of his inner conviction, could finally recognize a Christian subject with rights sufficiently equal to his own that something genuine could come from such an "autonomy?" I say, "is there even one person...." But if there is not even a single one, then how can anyone conduct talks and make agreements with such a people? The experts object: "We must establish some supervision and find the right combination." Well, just you try and find the combination! There are problems whose nature is such that they simply defy solution in the manner in which people at a given moment want to solve them. The Gordian knot could not be untied with fingers, yet people kept wracking their brains to try to untie it that way; but Alexander came and cut through the knot with a sword and so solved the riddle.

Here's another example, a view expressed by a newspaper; this is not only the view of a newspaper, however, but is an old, diplomatic view shared by a host of scholars, professors, newspaper

columnists, journalists, novelists, Westernizers, Slavophiles, etc.,
etc. It is this: Constantinople ultimately will belong to no one; it
will be something in the order of a free, international city—a kind
of "common place" in short. Its existence will be guaranteed by
the European balance of power, and so on. In short, instead of a
simple, direct, and clear solution—the only one possible—there
appears some complex and unnatural scholarly amalgam. But one
need only ask: what is the European balance of power? This balance
of power was supposed to exist until now among several of the
strongest European powers—the five, say, of equal strength (i.e.,
there was a tactful assumption that they were of equal strength).
And so the five wolves lie down in a circle, and in the middle sits
the tasty morsel, Constantinople; and all five of them do nothing
more than keep the others from seizing the prey. And this is what
people call the *chef d'oeuvre*, the *Meisterstück* that solves the problem! But does this solve anything at all? The point is that it is all
based on a fundamental absurdity, on some fantastic fact that never
existed, even on an unnatural fact: the balance of power. Did a
political balance of power ever exist on earth, in fact? Absolutely
not! This is only a cunning formula once invented by cunning
people to fool simpletons. And although Russia is not a simpleton,
she is an honest person; and therefore, it seems, she was more
prone than anyone else to believe in the indestructibility of the
truths and the laws of this balance of power; many times she herself
sincerely complied with them and served as their guarantor. In that
sense, Europe has exploited Russia in a remarkably brazen manner.
Yet it seems that none of the other "equal powers" took these laws
of power balance seriously, although they observed the formalities
up to a point—but only up to a point. When their calculations
showed that some gain might be made, each one disrupted this
balance with little concern for the consequences. What is most
amusing is that these actions were always successful, and that a
new "balance of power" immediately ensued. But when Russia,
too, without disrupting anything, only took a little thought for her
own interests, all the other members of the balance of power at
once joined forces and moved on Russia, saying, "You are upsetting
the balance." Well, the same thing will happen with an international
Constantinople: the five wolves will be lying there, baring their
teeth at one another, each one trying to come up with the proper
combination: how to ally with its neighbors and, having killed off
the other wolves, to divide the spoils in the most profitable manner.

Is that really any solution? Meanwhile, certain new schemes are arising among the guardian-wolves: suddenly one of these five wolves, the grayest of the lot, suffers some sort of accident, and in a single day, in a single hour, is transformed from a wolf into the tiniest of lapdogs which can't even bark. And now you have the equilibrium utterly shaken! Besides, at some time in Europe's future the five equal powers might simply be reduced to two; and then—then where would your complex plan be, O Wise Men? . . . By the way, I would venture to express one axiom: "In Europe there will never be a moment and a political situation when Constantinople *is not someone's*, i.e., when it does not belong to someone." That is the axiom, and it seems to me impossible that it could be otherwise. If you will permit me a little joke, I would say that it is most likely that at the final and decisive moment the English will suddenly seize Constantinople as they seized Gibraltar, Malta, and so on. And it will be precisely at a time when the great powers will still be thinking about their balance. It is these same Englishmen now watching with such maternal concern over Turkey's inviolability who see the possibility of a great future and civilization for her; it is they who believe in her vital principles; and it is precisely they who, when they see that the matter has come to a head, will gobble up the Sultan and Constantinople. This is so much in character for them, so much in their disposition; it is so in keeping with their eternal brazen arrogance, with their policy of oppression, with their malice! Whether they will be able to hold on to Constantinople as they have Gibraltar is another question! Of course, at the moment this is all only a little joke, and I pass it on as such; still, it would not be a bad idea if we were to remember this little joke: it has a ring of truth about it. . . .

3. Schemes and More Schemes

And so all schemes are admitted for solving the Eastern Question except the clearest, soundest, simplest, and most natural one. One might even say that the more unnatural the solution suggested, the more quickly public and common opinion grasps at it. Here, for example, is yet another "unnatural thing": it is proposed that "if Russia were to declare publicly her disinterest to the whole of Europe, the matter would at once be solved and done with." Well, happy is he who believes this! Indeed, if Russia not only stated but even proved as well, de facto, her disinterest, then Europe would probably be even more confused. Well, suppose we take nothing for ourselves but simply do our good deeds and return home having taken advantage of nothing, but only showing Europe that we are disinterested. Europe will find that still worse: "The more selflessly you have aided them, the more convincingly you have proved to them that you are making no encroachments on their independence; they will become all the more trusting and devoted to you—henceforth they will regard you as a sun, a summit, a zenith, an empire. And what does it matter that they are autonomous and not your subjects? Still in their hearts they will consider themselves your subjects; unconsciously, involuntarily they will think this way." The very inevitability—sooner or later—of the Slavs' moral affiliation with Russia, the naturalness and legitimacy of this fact—this is what Europe finds so frightening; this is what constitutes her nightmare and her main dread for the future. On her part there are only forces and schemes, while on ours there is the law of nature, normality, kinship, truth; with whom, then, lies the future of the Slavic lands?

And yet there is in Europe itself one scheme, based on a completely opposite principle and so *probable* that, perhaps, it may even have a future. This new scheme is also of English workmanship; it is, one might say, a corrective to all the mistakes and miscalculations of the Tory party. It is based on England itself at once bestowing its blessings on the Slavs, but with the aim of making them eternal enemies and haters of Russia. The proposal is to renounce the Turks at last, to destroy them as a hopeless, good-for-nothing people, and to form a union of all the Christian peoples of the Balkan peninsula with its center in Constantinople. The liberated and grateful Slavs would naturally be drawn to England as their savior and liberator, while she would "open their eyes to Russia." "There," England would say, "is your most bitter enemy; she, behind a mask of concern for you, dreams of swallowing you up and depriving you of your inevitable and glorious political future." Thus, when the Slavs come to believe in Russia's duplicity, they will at once form a new and powerful bulwark against her, and then, "Russia will never even catch a glimpse of Constantinople; they will never let her come here!"

It's difficult even to invent anything more clever and, at first glance, more apt. The main thing is that it is so simple and based on actual fact. I have already mentioned this fact in passing elsewhere. It consists of this: in parts of the Slavic intelligentsia and among certain of the highest representatives and leaders of the Slavs there truly exists a certain mistrust of Russia's motives, and therefore even an enmity toward Russia and the Russians. Oh, I am not talking about the masses of people. For the Slavic peoples, for the Serbs and for the Montenegrins, Russia still remains their sun, their hope, their friend, their mother and protectress, their future liberator! But the Slavic intelligentsia is another matter. Of course I am not talking about the whole of the intelligentsia; I will not venture or permit myself to speak of them all. But *"even though it is by no means all of them,* still among some of their most ministerial minds" (as I expressed it in my August *Diary)* "one can find those who imagine that Russia is duplicitous, is holding back and looking for ways of seizing them and swallowing them up." We should not conceal from ourselves the fact that even many educated Slavs, perhaps, do not love us at all. For example, they still consider us to be undeveloped in comparison with themselves— all but barbarians. They are even not interested in the achievements of our civic life, the organization of our society, our reforms, our literature. There may be a few very educated ones among them who know about Pushkin, but few of those who do know him there would be likely to accept him as a great Slavic genius. Very many of the educated Czechs, for example, are certain that they have already had forty poets like Pushkin. Aside from that, all these separate Slavic entities in their present condition are politically proud and ultrasensitive, like inexperienced nations who know little of life. Among such people the English scheme could have success if it could be set in motion. And it is hard to imagine that it would not be set in motion if, with a victory of the Whigs in England, the plan were to be placed on the agenda. And still, how artificial, unnatural, impossible, and full of lies this is!

In the first place, how can such dissimilar, separate peoples as live in the Balkan peninsula be united, and with a center in Constantinople? There are Greeks, Slavs, and Romanians here. To whom will Constantinople belong? A city for all. And then dissension and strife, at least between the Greeks and the Slavs, to begin with (even assuming that the Slavs could be in agreement). People will say that a ruler can be appointed and an empire founded; such, it seems, is proposed in this scheme. But who will be the emperor: a Slav, a Greek—surely not one of the Hapsburgs? In any case, dualisms and splits would at once begin. The main thing is that the Greek and Slavic elements cannot be united: both these elements have immense, utterly exaggerated, and false dreams about the glorious political future that awaits them. No, if England really resolves to abandon the Turks, then she will arrange things in a much more solid fashion. And I think this is the point when that scheme I mentioned earlier, as a joke, might occur, i.e., England herself will swallow up Constantinople "for the good of the Slavs." "I will create from you Slavs," England will say, "a union and a bulwark in the north against the northern colossus to keep him out of Constantinople, because once he seizes Constantinople he will seize you all. Then you will have no glorious political future. And you Greeks need not be alarmed either. Constantinople is yours; I specifically want it to be yours, and it is for that reason that I am occupying it. I am doing it only so as not to give it to Russia. The Slavs will defend it from the north, and I will defend it from the sea; and we will not let anyone in. I will only stay in Constantinople temporarily, until you become stronger and until you can form a solid and mature federated empire. But until that time, I am your leader and defender. I have occupied a good many places; I have Gibraltar and Malta; and I gave back the Ionian islands, didn't I . . . ?"

In short, if this piece of Whiggish workmanship could even gain currency it would be difficult, I repeat, to doubt its success; but success only temporarily, of course. Never mind that this temporary period might stretch on for many years, but . . . it is all the more certain that the whole thing would collapse when it attained that natural limit; and then its collapse would be final, because this whole scheme is founded only on slander and unnaturalness.

It's falsity lies in its slander of Russia. There is no fog that can withstand the rays of truth. A time will come when even the Slavic peoples will comprehend the whole truth of Russian disinterestedness, and at that time their spiritual unity with us will come to pass. Our active unity with the Slavs began a very short time ago, after all; but now—now it will never cease and will continue to grow and grow. The Slavs will at last be convinced, despite all the slander, of Russia's kindred love for them. The irresistible charm of the great and powerful Russian spirit, as something akin, will work its way on them. They will realize that they cannot develop spiritually in petty unions amid dissension and envy but only on a larger, all-Slavic scale. The enormity and might of the Russian union will no longer trouble and frighten them; on the contrary, they will be irresistibly attracted to it as to a center or a basic principle. Unity of faith will also serve as an extremely strong bond. Russian faith, Russian Orthodoxy, is everything that the Russian People consider most sacred; it contains their ideals and all the truth and justice of life. And what united the Slavic peoples, what did they live by, if not by their faith during their suffering under four hundred years of the Moslem yoke? They bore so many sufferings for the sake of their faith that this alone must have made it dear to them. Finally, Russian blood has already been shed for the Slavs, and blood is never forgotten. The crafty people have overlooked all this. The opportunity to slander Russia before the Slavs encourages their success and their faith in the solidity of that success. But such success is never eternal. Temporarily though, I repeat, it can be attained. This particular scheme may be put into effect if the Whigs win, and that should be kept in mind. The English will resolve to do it simply to warn Russia when the final deadline comes, as if to say: "We ourselves shall be able to do a few good deeds."

A few words about the blood that has been shed, by the way. What if our volunteers at last smash the Turks and liberate the Slavs, without even a declaration of war? As we hear, so many Russian volunteers are arriving from Russia and donations are coming so steadily, that, if this continues, Cherniaev may at last form a whole army of Russians. In any case, Europe and her diplomats would be quite astonished at such an outcome: "If they were able to overcome the Turks with only volunteers, then what would happen if the whole of Russia took up arms?" People in Europe would not overlook an argument like that.

May God grant success to our Russian volunteers. We hear that dozens of Russian officers are again being killed in battles. The dear lads!

It's not out of place to make one more little observation, a rather urgent one, in my opinion. Our newspapers, in keeping with the flow of Russian volunteers to Serbia and the many heroic deaths in battle, have recently begun collecting donations under a new category: "*In aid of the families of Russians who have fallen in the war with the Turks for the liberation of the Balkan Slavs.*" Donations have begun to come in. *The Voice* has already collected some three thousand rubles in this category, and the more donations the better, of course. The only thing that isn't quite right, in my opinion, is that this formula for contributions is not quite stated in sufficient detail. Contributions are collected only for the families of Russians who have *fallen* in the war, etc. But what of the families of those wounded? Will these really get nothing? And these families, after all, may have a more difficult time than those of the fallen. The one who has fallen has fallen, and he is mourned; but the other comes back a cripple, armless, legless, or so seriously wounded that his health will constantly require intensive care and medical assistance. Aside from that, even though he may be crippled, he will still eat and drink; consequently, he is an extra mouth to feed in a poor family. Aside from that, it seems to me that this heading contains one serious error through lack of definition: "*In aid of the families of Russians who have fallen,*" etc. But there are families of means or at least ones in little need, and there are quite poor families who are in great need. If money is given to them all, then little will be left for those who are truly poor. And therefore it seems to me that this whole heading should be recast thus: "*In aid of needy families of Russians who fell or were disabled in the war with the Turks for the liberation of the Balkan Slavs.*" However, I am only setting forth my idea; and if someone else manages to formulate it even more precisely, then, of course, so much the better. It would only be desirable that this category of donations should be filled as quickly and generously as possible. It is extremely helpful and absolutely essential; it can have a great moral influence on our noble volunteers who are fighting for the Russian idea.

4. Dressing Gowns and Soap

Among the various opinions on the Eastern Question I encountered one that was utterly queer. Not long ago a strange thing appeared in the foreign press: in heated, almost preposterous terms, the writer began to speculate about the effect on the rest of the world if Turkey were to be utterly crushed and pushed back into Asia. It turned out that this would be a disaster and a terrible trauma. There were even predictions of the rise of a new caliphate in Asia— in Arabia somewhere; there would be a renewed surge of fanaticism, and the Moslem world would again fall upon Europe. More profound thinkers limited themselves only to the opinion that seizing and expelling a whole nation from Europe into Asia in this way was something impossible and even unthinkable. When I read all this I was, for some reason, quite astonished, but I still had not divined what the real issue was. And suddenly I realized that all these diplomat-thinkers were in fact posing the question literally, i.e., that once the Turkish empire is politically crushed, the issue really seems to be one of the actual, literal physical removal of all these Turks and their transportation into Asia somewhere. I truly do not understand how such a notion could arise; but they certainly must have used it to frighten people at various banquets and meetings: "There will be terrible repercussions from all this," they would say, "a real disaster." It seems to me, however, that absolutely nothing of this sort could happen, and not a single Turk would need to be resettled in Asia. Something like this has already happened to us in Russia. When the Tatar Horde came to an end, the Duchy of Kazan suddenly grew in strength to the point that there was a time when it was even difficult to predict whether the Russian land would belong to the Christian or the Moslem world. This duchy ruled over what was then the Russian East; it had relations with Astrakhan and controlled the Volga, while on Russia's flank there appeared a superb ally for the duchy in the person of the Khan of the Crimean Horde, the dreadful bandit and despoiler from whom Moscow had suffered so much. It was a most critical situation, and the young tsar Ivan Vasilevich—not yet called Ivan the Terrible—decided to settle the Eastern Question of his day and seize Kazan.

The siege was a terrible one, and Karamzin later described it with remarkable eloquence. The inhabitants of Kazan put up a desperate, magnificent, stubborn, tenacious, and persistent defense. But then the saps were blown, allowing crowds of Russians to storm the city, and Kazan was taken! And what do you think Tsar Ivan did when he entered Kazan? Did he annihilate every single inhabitant, as he did later in Novgorod the Great, to prevent them from ever bothering him again? Did he deport them all to the steppes of Asia? Certainly not. Not even one little Tatar urchin was exiled; everything stayed as it was, and the heroic inhabitants of Kazan, who had formerly been so dangerous, were pacified forever. And this happened in the simplest and most appropriate manner: no sooner had the Russians taken the city than they at once carried in the icon of the Virgin and held the first Orthodox service in Kazan since the city's founding. Then they laid the foundation for an Orthodox church, carefully collected the armaments from the inhabitants, installed a Russian government, and sent the ruler of Kazan where he belonged. That's all that happened, and it all happened in a single day. A little while thereafter, the people of Kazan began selling us oriental dressing gowns, and a little while after that—soap as well. (I think that it happened just in that order—first the dressing gowns and then the soap.) And so the matter ended. The case of Turkey could be settled in exactly the same way should the happy thought of ending this caliphate politically only occur to someone.

First of all, a mass would at once be sung in Saint Sophia; then the Patriarch would consecrate the cathedral once again; a bell would arrive from Moscow that very day, I think, and the Sultan would be sent to an appropriate place—and thus the matter would be ended. It's true that the Turks have a law—almost a Koranic dogma—that only Moslems and not Christian subjects can and should bear arms. Lately they have begun permitting Christians as well to own arms, but only after paying a high tax, thus even creating a new source of income for the state; those who do have arms are a comparatively very small number. Well, perhaps this one law could be reversed on the very first day, that is, the day of the first service in Saint Sophia, so that only the Infidels could and should bear arms, while the Moslems could not, even on payment of a tax. So that's all that's needed to ensure peace; and I assure you that absolutely no more is necessary. A little time would pass and the Turks would also start selling us oriental dressing gowns; and in a little more time—soap as well, perhaps even better than Kazan soap. As far as agriculture (the tobacco and wine industries) is concerned, under new arrangements and new laws these areas would, I think, develop with such speed and such success that they could finally manage to pay off little by little even the former Turkish government's unpaid debts to Europe. In short, nothing would happen but the very best and most appropriate things; there would not be the least repercussions and, I repeat, not even a single Turkish urchin would have to be exiled from Europe.

Nothing would happen in the East either. As far as a caliphate is concerned, one might be established somewhere in the steppes of Asia or in the desert. But to launch an attack on Europe in our time requires so much money, so many modern armaments, so many repeating rifles, so many supply trains, and so many factories and plants set up in advance, that not only Moslem fanaticism but even English fanaticism itself would be incapable of aiding the new caliphate in any way. In short, nothing would come to pass apart from the very best things. And may God grant that these best things to come to pass as quickly as possible; otherwise so many of the worst things could happen!

2

1. Outmoded People

"The greatest happiness in the life of a nation is found in every higher and unifying idea, every true feeling that unites all. This happiness was bestowed upon us. We could not help but fully sense our increased accord, the clarification of many former misunderstandings, our strengthened self-consciousness."

That is what I said in the concluding article in my *Diary* of last August, and I believe that I was not mistaken. A genuine unifying feeling in the life of a nation is happiness indeed. If I was mistaken in anything, then it is only, perhaps, in that I exaggerated somewhat the level of our "increased accord and self-consciousness." But I am still not ready to take back even that. Anyone who loves Russia has long been sick at heart over the alienation of the upper levels of Russians from the lower ones—from the People and the lives of the People—which as an actual fact is now doubted by no one. It is this very alienation which has partially given way and weakened, in my view, under the impact of this year's genuine all-Russian movement on the Slavic question. Of course, one simply cannot conceive that our split from the People could be completely ended and healed over. It continues and will long continue, but historical moments such as those we have experienced this year doubtless promote "increased accord and clarification of misunderstandings." In short, they promote our clearer understanding of the People and of Russian life, on the one hand, and, on the other—the closer acquaintance of the People themselves with the strange folk they apparently regard as foreigners and not Russians—with the "masters," as they still call us.

It must be admitted that the People even now, in all this general Russian movement of this year, have revealed in themselves a sounder, more precise and clear aspect of character than many of the intellectuals of our class. The People have expressed a direct, simple, and powerful feeling, a firm outlook, and—most important—have done this with amazing communality and accord. No dispute ever arose among them about "Why, specifically, to help the Slavs. Must we help them? Who should be helped most, and who not at all? Will we not somehow compromise our moral standards and hinder our civic development by helping too much? With whom, at last, should we go to war? In fact, is it necessary to go to war?" Etc., etc. In short, our intelligentsia was beset by a thousand misunderstandings. This happened in particular in certain sections of our higher intelligentsia, specifically among those who still regard the People from the (sometimes quite imaginary) heights of European education; there, in these higher "isolated groupings" we saw some rather remarkable dissonances, uncertainty, a strange lack of understanding of sometimes the simplest things, an almost ridiculous hesitation about what to do and what not to do, and so on. "Should we help the Slavs or not? And if we do help them, why should we do it? And what cause would be most moral and most attractive: this one or that one?" All these things, which sometimes were strikingly bizarre, really did come to the surface, were heard in conversation, were evidenced in actual events, and were reflected in literature. But nothing of this sort was stranger than the article I read in *The European Messenger* of September of this year, in the "Survey of Domestic Life" section. The article deals specifically with the current Russian movement and is written apropos of the fraternal aid to the oppressed Slavs; it endeavors to make a truly profound statement on this matter. The portion of the article that touches on the Russian People and society is not extensive—four or five pages—and so I will permit myself to make my way through these pages in sequence but without quoting everything, of course. In my opinion these little pages are remarkably interesting, and one might say they constitute a kind of document. My purpose will make itself evident at the end this undertaking, so that I think it will not even be necessary to draw any particular moral.

However, by way of a brief forewarning I shall note only that the author of the article quite obviously subscribes to that outmoded theoretical Westernism which, a quarter-century ago, constituted in our society the very zenith of our intellectual forces. Now, however, it has become so outmoded that to encounter it in its pure, pristine state is a rare event indeed. We might call these the left-overs, the last Mohicans of theoretical Europeanizing that tore itself away from the People and from life. Although this Europeanizing in its time was the inevitable result of historical conditions, its legacy was, apart from a certain amount of benefit, an extraordinary amount of the most harmful, prejudicial nonsense, which continues its baleful influence even to this day. The principal historical contribution of these people was negative: it lay in the extremity of their opinions, in the finality of their judgments (for they were so arrogant that the only judgments they pronounced were final ones), and in those ultimate limits to which they took their frenzied theories. This extremism unintentionally promoted a sobering of minds and a turning to the People, toward unity with the People. Now, after that whole quarter-century and after a host of new, unprecedented facts since derived from a practical study of Russian life, these "last Mohicans" of the old theories unintentionally reveal their comic aspect, even despite their exaggeratedly dignified deportment. Their chief comic trait is their persistence in seeing themselves as youthful, as the sole guardians and, so to say, the trailblazers of the paths they believe Russian life ought to follow. But they have lagged so far behind that life that they can no longer recognize it at all; therefore they are living in a complete world of fantasy. That is why it is so interesting and edifying, at a moment of great excitement in society, to observe the degree to which this theoretical Europeanism has unnaturally split itself off from the People and society, to see the degree to which its views and its conclusions, at certain extraordinary moments of public life, while still remaining arrogant and haughty, are in essence weak, irresolute, obscure, and erroneous when compared with the clear, simple, firm, and unshakeable convictions of the People's mind and sentiments. However, let us turn to the article.

One must, however, give due credit to the author of the article; he acknowledges, or rather, consents to acknowledge, the Popular and the public movement to help the Slavs; he acknowledges that it is even quite a sincere movement. Of course, how could he fail to acknowledge that! . . . Still, for such an outmoded "European" as our author, this is no small achievement. Yet he still seems dissatisfied with something; for some reason he is displeased that this movement has begun. True, he doesn't in so many words state that he is displeased the movement has begun, but he grumbles and picks at details. It seems to me that Granovsky, one of the purest and earliest representatives of our Westernism, a man who in his time also wrote about the Eastern Question and about the Popular movement during the Crimean War of 1854-56—a movement, however, that had only a few things in common with the present movement (see my article about Granovsky in my August Diary)—Granovsky, I say, would also have been dissatisfied at our current Popular movement, and of course he would have preferred to see our People as the immobile, inert mass of former years rather than manifesting themselves in forms that are not yet fully developed and "primitive," inappropriate for our European age. On the whole, even though all these old theorists of the past loved the People (although I must say we don't know much about that), they loved them only to a certain extent—in theory, i.e., in those imaginative images and forms in which they would have liked to see them, which means, in essence, that they did not love them at all. However, in their defense it must be admitted that they never knew the People at all; indeed, they never found it necessary to know them or have anything to do with them. It was not that they *distorted the facts*, it was simply that they had no understanding of them whatever, so that many—all too many—times they attributed the purest gold of the People's spirit, thought, and profound, pure feeling directly to common vulgarity, ignorance, and obtuse Russian national idiocy. Had the People appeared before them even slightly other than in those aspects and images which they found appealing (for the most part, this was the aspect of a French mob in Paris), they might well have renounced them altogether. "First of all one must abandon any notion that this is a holy war," Granovsky exclaims in his brochure on the Eastern Question. "These days no one is going to be roused to set off on a crusade; such is not our age; no one will make a move to liberate the tomb of our Lord," etc., etc. The theoretician of *The European Messenger* says exactly the same thing: he doesn't like these categories either; he finds fault with them. He is very displeased, for instance, that our People and society are making contributions under a category which seems not to be of his choosing. He prefers a view more appropriate, so to say, to our age, a more enlightened view. But we have digressed once again.

Let us omit the beginning of that portion of the article dealing with the Russian movement to aid the Slavs; it is a very characteristic beginning, but we cannot pause at every line. This is what the author says further on.

2. Kifomokievism

> However, one cannot deny that among the many statements on this matter that have appeared in our newspapers, there were some that were rather peculiar and tactless. Omitting those which showed only the desire to exhibit the writer's own personality, since that is not important, we must note those which questioned the feelings of citizens of Russia who are not of Russian nationality. This bad habit, unfortunately, has still not left us, but the very essence of the point at issue demanded particular caution in respect to all nationalities forming part of the general population of Russia. We also note that, on the whole, an excessively religious character should not be attributed to the movement to aid the Slavs, with constant mentions of "our fellow Orthodox believers." Those motives which can unite all Russian citizens are quite sufficient to rouse Russian society to aid the Slavs; those motives which could drive them apart are unnecessary. If we are to explain our compassion for the Slavs principally by the fact that they are our fellow Orthodox believers, then how shall we regard those of our Moslem population who might begin collecting contributions to aid the Turks or who declared their desire to serve in the Turkish army? ... The disturbances that have broken out in certain regions of the Caucasus should remind us that the Orthodox Great Russian lives in a family; that although he may be the eldest son of Russia, he is not the only son.

This passage alone ought to be enough to show the extent to which the theoretical Europeanism of certain "trailblazers," outmoded but stubbornly persistent, is alienated from the public sense of things and the level of idle "Kifo-Mokievism" which that Europeanism can reach in our time. The author poses to us—and is himself perplexed by—questions which, in their artificiality and affectation, in their fantastically theoretical nature, and, principally, in their utter pointlessness, are quite astonishing. "If we are going to contribute because of our common religion," he says, "then how shall we regard those among our Moslem population who might begin collecting contributions for the Turks or who express the wish to serve in the Turkish army?" Well, can one ask such a question in this case, and can one hesitate in the least in answering it? Every simple, uncorrupted Russian person will at once give you a most precise answer. Indeed, not only a Russian person, but any European as well, and any North American, will give you the clearest answer; only a European, before answering, would probably look at you with extreme astonishment. I will note, in passing, that on the whole our Russian Westernism (meaning our copying of Europe), in taking root on Russian soil, very often gradually takes on nuances that are not European at all; thus a certain European idea that has been borne to us by certain "trailblazers" sometimes cannot even be recognized, so much has it altered in being ground up with Russian theories and in being applied to Russian life—a life which, in the bargain, the theoretician does not know nor even finds it necessary to know. So, you see, "how shall we regard those among our Moslem population who . . ." etc., etc. Well, it's very simple: in the first place, if we go to war with the Turks, and our Tatars, for example, begin sending the Turks money or enlisting in their army, then even before society responds I think the government itself will treat them as traitors to their country and, of course, will stop them in time. In the second place, suppose no war is declared but the Turks begin slaughtering the Slavs, with whom all Russians are equally in sympathy; in that case, if donations were collected or volunteers for the Turks were found among Moslems, do you really think that any Russians could react without feeling insulted and angry? . . . You seem to think that the whole problem lies in the religious nature of the contributions—that is, if the Russian began to help the Slav as a fellow *Orthodox believer,* then how could he, without violating civic equality and justice, forbid similar contributions by a Russian Tatar to help his fellow believer, the Turk? On the contrary, he may very well have the full right to do this even if he has no thought of becoming an enemy of the Tatar and going to war with him, while the Tatar, in helping the Turk, tears himself away from Russia; he becomes a traitor, and in entering the ranks of the Turks he goes directly to war with his country. Aside from that, if I, a Russian, contribute to a Slav who is waging war with a Turk, even though it may be out of common religious feelings, I am certainly not wishing for his victory over the Turk because the latter is a Moslem but only because he is slaughtering the Slav; whereas the Tatar who goes over to the Turkish side can do so only because I am a Christian and supposedly want to destroy Islam, whereas I have no wish whatsoever to destroy Islam but only want to defend my fellow believer. . . . In helping the Slav I not only am not attacking the Tatar's faith, I am not even concerned about the Mohammedanism of the Turk himself: he can be as Moslem as he likes so long as he leaves the Slav alone. People may say at this point: "If you help your fellow believer against the Turk, then in so doing you are going against the Russian Tatar and his faith because they have the *shariah* and the Sultan is the Caliph of all the Moslems. Christian subjects, according the Koran itself, cannot be free and cannot have rights equal to a Moslem; when the Russian helps him acquire equal rights, every Moslem sees him as opposing not just the Turk but the whole of Mohammedanism." But in such a case the instigator of the religious war is the Tatar and not I; you must agree that this is an objection of a quite different kind and no tricky moves or categories will settle it.... You seem to think that the whole problem stems from common religion and that if I concealed from the Tatar the fact that I was helping the Slav as my fellow believer and pretended, to the contrary, that I was helping the Slav under some other pretext—because he was oppressed by the Turk, let's say, and being denied his freedom, "this first blessing of man"—then the Tatar would believe me. But it's quite the contrary: I venture to assure you that in the eyes of any Moslem, helping the Christians against the Moslems under any pretext whatever is absolutely the same as if I helped the Christians because of their religion. Did you really not know that? Yet this is just what you say: "Those motives which can unite all Russian citizens are quite sufficient to rouse Russian society to aid the Slavs; those motives which could drive them apart are unnecessary...." That's just what you wrote about a common religion as a motive that drives people apart and about the Russian Moslems—and at once you explained it. You propose the "struggle for freedom" as the best and highest pretext or "motive," as you say, for Russian contributions to the Slavs, and evidently you are quite convinced that "the struggle of the Slavs for freedom" will have much appeal to the Tatar and reassure him to the highest degree. But again, I assure you, the Russian Moslem who decides to go and help the Turks—if such a one exists—finds all motives the same, and no matter under which category the war began, in his eyes it will still be a religious war. But the Russian is not to blame, after all, if the Tatar sees things this way....

3. Continuation of the Preceding

It bothers me a good deal that I had to go on at such length. If there had ever been a possibility of war between France and Turkey, and the Moslems who belonged to France—the Arabs of Algiers—had become disturbed at the prospect, do you really think that the

French would not have pacified them at once in a most energetic manner? Would they have worried about the Moslems' tender feelings and shamefully hidden their best and most noble "motives" out of apprehension that their Moslems might somehow feel insulted and take offense? You write a moral injunction to the whole of Russia using words of such majesty: "The disturbances that have broken out in various regions of the Caucasus" (N.B.: you yourself thus admit that there have been some disturbances) "ought to remind us that the Orthodox Great Russian lives in a family, and that though he may be the eldest son of Russia, he is not the only son." I grant that this is stated majestically, but what is the Great Russian to do if the Caucasian peoples really do rise up? How is the eldest son in the family to blame if the Caucasian Moslem, the youngest son, is so sensitive about his faith and has such conceptions that when the eldest son opposes the Turk, the youngest son feels himself and the whole of Mohammedanism threatened? You are concerned lest the "eldest son in the family" (the Great Russian) somehow wound the feelings of his younger brother (the Tatar or the Caucasian). What humane and highly enlightened concern! You press the point that although the Orthodox Great Russian may be the eldest son, he is not the only son of Russia. May I ask, please, what you mean? The Russian land belongs to the Russians, to the Russians *alone;* it is a Russian land, and *there is not a bit of Tatar land in it.* The Tatars, the former oppressors of the Russian land, are outsiders here. But the Russians, having pacified them, having won back their land from them, having conquered the Tatars themselves, did not take vengeance on the Tatars for two centuries of torment; they did not humiliate them like the Moslem Turks have tormented and humiliated the Christians who had never done them any harm; on the contrary, the Russians gave the Tatars civil rights equal to their own, rights such as, perhaps, you will not encounter in the most civilized lands of the West, which you find so enlightened. It may even be that the Russian Moslem sometimes enjoyed privileges even greater than the Russian, the owner and master of the Russian land. . . . Neither did the Russian abuse the faith of the Tatar; he did not persecute or oppress him. Believe me, nowhere in the West, nor anywhere in the world, will you find such a broad, humane tolerance of the religions of others as in the heart of the real Russian. Believe me as well that it is rather the Tatar who prefers to keep apart from the Russian (this is precisely a result of the Tatar's Mohammedanism), and not the Russian who shuns the Tatar. Anyone who has lived near the Tatars will confirm this. Nonetheless, the master of the Russian land is the Russian alone (the Great Russian, the Little Russian, the White Russian—they are all one), and so it will be for all time; and if the Orthodox Russian finds it necessary to go to war with the Moslem Turk, then believe me that the Russian will never permit anyone to veto this on his own land! To treat the Tatars with such delicacy that we fear to show them our most noble and spontaneous feelings that cause no offense to anyone—feelings of compassion for the tormented Slav who happens to share our faith; and moreover, to take pains to hide from the Tatar everything that comprises our mission, our future and—principally—our responsibility—why this is a demand that is ridiculous and humiliating for the Russian. . . . How am I offending the Tatar by having compassion for my own faith and my own fellow believers? How am I oppressing his religion? And how am I guilty if, in his perception, any war of ours with the Turks must be a religious war? The Russian, after all, cannot change the fundamental concepts of the whole of Mohammedanism. "Well, then," you say, "handle the matter delicately; keep it quiet and try not to offend him." But tell me, please, if he is that sensitive then may he not, perhaps, suddenly take offense at the fact that on the same street where his mosque stands there also stands our Orthodox church? Should we not tear it down so he won't be offended? Should the Russian flee from his own country? Should he not crawl under some table so he won't be seen or heard because his younger brother, the Tatar, lives in the Russian land?

You said something about *"questioning feelings."* "We must note those [articles in Russian newspapers] which questioned the feelings of citizens of Russia who are not of Russian nationality. This bad habit, unfortunately, has still not left us, but the very essence of the point at issue demanded particular caution in respect to all nationalities forming part of the general population of Russia." What habit of ours is that? I venture to assure you that this is only a false note of the old theoretical liberalizing tendency which is incapable even of sensibly applying a liberal idea imported from Europe. No, indeed, sir, it is not for you and me to teach religious tolerance to the People or to give them lectures about freedom of conscience. In that respect they have something to teach you and the whole of Europe as well. You speak, however, about the newspapers and Russian journalism. So what kind of questioning do you have in mind? And what deeply ingrained *habit of ours* are you lamenting so? The habit of our literature to "question" things? But that is also a fantasy of theoretical liberalism which is not justified by actual fact. I assure you that we have never denounced anyone in literature for his faith, nor even for any sort of local patriotic feelings. If in fact there were some separate instances of this at some time, then they are so isolated and exclusive that it is shameful and wrong to hold them up as general practice: "This habit has still not left us," you say. What is meant by denunciation or "questioning" anyway? There are facts which one cannot avoid mentioning. I don't know which articles you have in mind and what you are suggesting. I recall reading something about disturbances caused by incipient fanaticism in the Caucasus; but you yourself have just written about these disturbances as *a factual event that has already occurred*. I have heard that proponents of fanaticism have made their way from Turkey into the Crimea as well. Whether these disturbances in fact happened or did not happen is something I will not discuss at the moment; in truth, I myself do not know for certain. I will only ask you: if some newspaper did report such a rumor or even a such a fact, could this be called "questioning the feelings of our non-Orthodox population"? Well, let us suppose that these facts of disturbances really had happened; how can they be passed over in silence, and indeed, by a newspaper, which exists in order to inform us of the facts? This is how a newspaper can prevent a dangerous situation from arising. If it keeps silent and lets the matter develop—fanaticism, I mean—then both the fanatics and those Russians who live in proximity to them will suffer. Now if a newspaper *deliberately* publishes false information in order to make an *accusation* to the government and provoke persecution, then that, of course, would amount to "questioning" and denunciation; but if the facts are accurate, is the newspaper to keep silent about them? In any case, who in Russia has ever oppressed outlanders for their faith or even for their "religious sentiments," or even simply for their sentiments in the widest sense of the term? To the contrary: on that account we have almost always been very permissive, not at all like certain highly enlightened states in Europe. As far as religious sentiments are concerned, scarcely anyone persecutes our own sectarians nowadays, never mind those from other countries. And if there have been lately some few, quite singular instances of persecution of Stundists, then these instances were at once severely condemned by the whole of our press. By the way, maybe you think we should agree with certain German newspapers that have accused us and continue to accuse us even now of tormenting and oppressing our Baltic Germans for their faith and their *sentiments?* It is truly a great pity that you did not specify the articles and provide some real evidence so that it would be completely clear which "questioning" you had in mind. You should be aware of and understand the usage of words and not play with terms such as "questioning."

The main thing is that you dislike the category of "a common religion." "Help them from other motives," you say, "but not on account of a common religion." But, in the first place, this "motive" has not been made up and has not been deliberately chosen; it appeared and declared itself of its own accord; it was expressed by everyone at once. It is a historical motive, and this *history* continues to the present. You say: "*We must not* attribute a religious character to the movement to aid the Slavs with constant mentions of 'our fellow believers.'" But what is one to do with history and with a genuine living life? Whether we should or should not attribute religious significance, it comes of its own accord in any case. Consider this: the Turk slaughters the Slav because the latter, being a Christian, an infidel, dares to look for rights equal to the Turk's. Should a Bulgarian be converted to Islam, the Turk would at once cease tormenting him; on the contrary, he would at once recognize him as his own—so it is written in the Koran. It follows that if the Bulgarians are being subjected to such cruel torment it is obviously because they are Christians; that is as clear as day. So how is the Russian going to avoid the "religious question" when he contributes to the Slav? Besides, a Russian would never think of avoiding it! In any case, apart from historical and current necessity, the Russian knows nothing higher than Christianity and cannot even conceive of anything higher. His whole land, all the commonality, the whole of Russia he has called Christianity, or Krestianstvo. Take a closer look at Orthodoxy: it is by no means only clericalism and ritual; it is a living feeling that our People have transformed into one of those basic living forces without which nations cannot survive. In Russian Christianity—real Russian Christianity—there is not even a trace of mysticism; there is only love for humanity and the image of Christ; those are the essentials, at least. In Europe people have long and quite rightly regarded clericalism with apprehension; particularly in some places where clericalism hinders the flow and flourishing of the living life and, of course, hinders religion itself. But is our quiet, meek Orthodoxy akin to the prejudiced, gloomy, conspiratorial, aggressive, and cruel clericalism of Europe? How can it not be something close to the hearts of the People? The aspirations of the People are created by the whole of the People; they are not composed in the editorial offices of the press. "Should one or shouldn't one?"—but it will happen as it actually is happening. Further on you write: "The noble cause of freedom has seen the Russians among the ranks of its defenders. From this point of view alone, which is even more exalted than compassion for fellow believers and for those of common ancestry, the cause of the Slavs is a sacred one." You are correct, this is a very lofty motive, yet what does the motive of "common religion" express? Common religion here signifies the unfortunate, tormented person nailed to a cross, and it is because of his oppression that I rise up in anger. This means "lay down your life for the oppressed, for one dear to you; there is no deed more noble." This is what the motive of common religion expresses! Aside from that, I venture to observe—only in general, however— that seeking out "categories" for good deeds is a dangerous thing. If I help a Slav as a fellow believer, for example, then this is not a category at all; it is only a designation of his historical situation at the given moment: "He is a fellow believer and so a Christian, and for that he is being oppressed and tormented." But if I say that I am helping him because of the "noble cause of freedom," in so doing I am exhibiting, as it were, the reasons for my help. And if one is to look for reasons for help, then the Montenegrins, for instance, and the Herzegovinians, who have displayed a nobler quest for freedom than the others, turn out to be more worthy of help than the rest. The Serbs are then somewhat less worthy, while the Bulgarians did not rise up for their freedom at all except in the beginning, in some insignificant little groups at a few places in the mountains. They could only howl when the tormenters would take little children and, in the presence of their fathers and mothers, would cut a child's finger off every five minutes to prolong the agony; but they did not defend themselves; they could only wail in agony, as if demented, and kiss the feet of the torturers so that they would stop the torture and give them back their poor little children. Well, perhaps we shouldn't give these people much help because all they did was suffer; they did not elevate themselves to the noble cause of freedom, "this first blessing of man." But let's suppose that you do not think in such a base way; still you must admit that once you introduce reasons and "motives" for love of your fellow man, you almost always arrive at rather similar opinions and conclusions. The best thing of all is to help simply because another person is unfortunate. Helping one's fellow believer means just that; I repeat: the phrase "fellow believer" for us is by no means some clerical rubric but only a historical designator. Believe me, our "common religion" also greatly loves and cherishes the noble cause of freedom; moreover, it is and will be prepared to die for that cause when necessary. But at the moment I am only speaking out against the incorrect application of European ideas to Russian reality. . . .

4. Fears and Apprehensions

What is most amusing here is that our honorable theoretician discerns in the contemporary enthusiasm to help the Slavs a serious danger for us, and he does his best to warn us of it. He thinks that at a moment of self-delusion we are going to issue ourselves with a diploma to prove our maturity and then fall into peaceful slumber. This is what he writes:

> In this sense there is a danger in all those arguments, which we read so often, about aiding the Slavs—arguments such as the following: "these facts show a gratifying awakening of Russian society; they prove that Russian society has matured to the point of . . ." etc. The tendency to admire ourselves in the mirror over international questions and declare sympathy for various nationalities, and then to sink into the slumber of a workman who has done his job, is so strong in us that all such arguments, even though they may contain a measure of truth, are positively dangerous. We did, after all, acclaim our readiness to make sacrifices at the beginning of the Crimean War; we celebrated our social maturity in the matter of our Chancelor's communiqués in 1863; and in the matter of the heartfelt reception we gave to the officers of the North American battleship; and in collecting aid for the Candiots; and over the ovation given to Slavic writers in Petersburg and Moscow. Read what the newspapers said at the time and you will be convinced that certain phrases are being repeated literally to-day. . . . We ask ourselves what was the result of all these "maturities" that we celebrated one after the other and whether those moments we celebrated did, in fact, move us forward? . . . But we should remember that in following our inclinations we do not have the right to claim our "certificate of graduation. . . ."

In the first place, nothing here, from the first word to the last, corresponds to actual reality. "The tendency to sink into the slumber of a workman who has done his job is so great in us," etc. This "tendency to fall into slumber" is one of the most prejudiced and incorrect accusations of this outmoded theorizing that has such a great fondness for pontificating but little fondness for doing anything; it is the theorists who enjoy their slumber and enjoy moralizing; it is they who, in rapture over their own eloquence, are continually admiring themselves in the mirror. This prejudiced accusation, which now has become incredibly clichéd, arose precisely at the time when the Russian, if he was slumbering by the stove or doing little else but playing cards, did so only because he was never given anything to do or allowed to do anything; he was prohibited from doing anything. But the moment some gaps appeared in the fences that surrounded us, the Russian at once in fact displayed a feverish restlessness and impatience to get down to work; rather than any propensity for slumber, he even showed perseverance in his work. And if our work is still not proceeding with total success, then it's certainly not because it's not being done; it's because after the two-hundred-year period in which we lost the habit of working, we cannot so immediately acquire the capacity to understand what work means, to approach it properly, and to be able to undertake it. You merely continue to moralize and to rebuke the Russians because of past sins. I say this to the older theoreticians, who never deigned to come down from the heights of their grandeur, enter into Russian life and learn something from it, even, say, to check and correct their prejudiced views from days long past.

But the apprehension fully worthy of Kifa Mokievich is the one about the "graduation diploma." We'll give ourselves a diploma, he says, and then settle down and fall asleep. On the contrary: it's only the old theorizing that so long ago issued itself a diploma, the theorizing that is inclined to be enraptured with itself, to moralizing, and to sweet semislumber; but such young, fine, unifying movements of the whole of society such as occurred this year can only rouse us to further development and accomplishment. Moments such as these leave only positive results. And where could you have gotten the notion that Russian society is so inclined toward self-praise and self-admiration in the mirror? All the facts contradict that. To the contrary: ours is the least self-assured and most inclined to self-criticism of any society in the world!... Not only did we sympathize with the Slavs, we liberated the peasants. And just look: has there ever in the history of the Russian people been a more skeptical moment, a moment of greater self-analysis, than these last twenty years of Russian life? In these years our lack of trust in ourselves went to pathological extremes, to impermissible self-mockery, to undeserved self-scorn; but we were far, far removed from rapture over our own accomplishments. You say that we also took pity on the people of Crete and welcomed a battleship; and each time we wrote about our own maturity and nothing came of that maturity. But after that you even cease to understand the commonest facts of life, not only of Russian life but of life everywhere. If we exaggerated a little then in our rejoicing over ourselves and our success, then surely that is quite a natural thing in a young society eager to live, a society that believes so strongly in life and takes its own mission seriously! This happens everywhere, always, and with every nation. Take any very ancient book and you will see that just such *initial*, youthful delight with one's success was a quality of even the most ancient peoples of the world and so has existed from the beginning of the world—given, of course, that these peoples were young and full of life and future promise. We might have had an excess of premature joy at our success and the fact that now we, at last, have given up card playing and that we, too, have begun working at something. But is that in any way dangerous, as our Jeremiah proclaims with alarm? To the contrary: these are the very people who take the real living life seriously and joyfully, with such feeling and such heart; these are the people who will not let themselves fall asleep from self-praise. Believe me, the life that has once been roused to action and has welled up like a fountain will not stop; rapture with oneself will pass away in an instant, and the stronger it was, the more surely there will ensue a salutary sobering, together with movement ever farther forward. But even though we will grow sober, we will still go on respecting our salutary, youthful, noble, and innocent rapture of recent days. You ask: "What was the result of these 'maturities'?" What do you mean? Perhaps the present moment is the result. Had there not been the excitement over the Cretans and the reception of the Slavic visitors, nothing might have happened now. Society has become more serious and acquainted with a certain cycle of ideas and views. For Heaven's sake, everything happens gradually on earth; indeed, nations are formed gradually, not born as sober-minded young pedants. And what are you angry about? "We become too carried away by this movement," you say; but premature prudence, the pedantry of youths playing the role of elders, is more dangerous. You do not like any sort of lively movement and prefer something more academic; well, what can I say? Such is your taste. Oh, of course, you at once cite the example of Europe: "France," you say, "did not do for Italy what we are now doing for the Slavs; but did French society, after the liberation of Italy, begin to consider itself more mature than before?" That's what you write. But really, that's ridiculous! You find us a model of modesty in—France? When, tell me, did not the Frenchman look at himself in the mirror and admire himself? During the time of Napoleon, for example, they roused the hatred of the whole of Europe toward them for their intolerably proud ways, their boundless self-satisfaction and sanctimoniousness. In fact, that is how they always were, right up until 1871. But France is now a nation too disunited internally, and therefore it is rather difficult to examine her in that respect. But what would you say, for instance, about the English or, especially, the Germans? Do you mean to say that these don't like looking at themselves in the mirror? Don't they like boasting— especially the Germans? And how accurate are your conclusions from history? "France," you say, "has not done for Italy what we are now doing for the Slavs...." I assure you that France herself has done absolutely nothing for Italy. Napoleon III liberated northern Italy for his own political considerations, and we have absolutely no way of knowing whether the French people would have liberated Italy themselves without Napoleon III and without his political considerations. At least it is very difficult to decide whether this liberation of the Italians would have occurred solely for their liberation and not for some sort of political annexation.... It still seems to me that both Napoleon III and France herself have since been gazing upon the exploits of Cavour, who deceived them somewhat, without a lot of enthusiasm; and when the French government's loud *"Jamais!"* was heard toward any further Italian claims on Rome, then the French people, perhaps, listened to this *jamais* with some sympathy. Oh, of course, it's true that France has still done more for Italy than the Russians have yet done for the Slavs; this matter is still not completed, and its further consequences are known only to God. But it is still difficult to admit that such a sincere movement of Russians for the Slavs, full of love and already bolstered by feats of the greatest self-sacrifice, is in need of such supremely edifying examples of valor as the liberation of northern Italy by Napoleon III.... However, you even set the Hungarians as an example of magnanimity for the Russian People. The Hungarians are particularly fine and noble at the moment, are they not? What a narrow-minded hatred they display toward any thought of lightening the lot of the Slavs! What hatred for Russia! How did you ever think of such an example and such a people?...

5. Postscript

Once again I must express my apologies for going on at such length, but in these words—quite innocent in themselves—of an author who is unquestionably intelligent and well-meaning, although somewhat outmoded, and in the tone in which these words are expressed, I once more seemed to hear voices from what may be the very near and perturbing future. For that reason I could not resist.... Oh, of course these possible voices of the future have nothing in common with the voice from *The European Messenger*, but still I seemed to catch their sound. In fact, should it happen that this whole generous and noble Russian movement to aid the Slavs comes, through force of circumstances, to naught; should the cause not succeed; should everyone turn back and fall silent—oh, what new shouts would we hear then, and in what a triumphant, victorious tone. They would no longer be innocent but mocking, sarcastic, and celebrating their victory! Then voices, which at present seem temporarily silenced or are even singing in unison to the "noble impulse," would cry out unconstrainedly. They would laugh in the face of this noble impulse, and the people of the noble impulse would again be embarrassed and diffident, while many of the poor things would even believe and think, "Yes, we should have foreseen it." "Well, you true believers, did you achieve anything?" the victors would shout. "What came from your unity and from your 'unifying idea'? You valiant heroes were left with nothing! Intelligent people knew beforehand how this would end. Did you really think anything could come of it? The cause itself, in fact, isn't worth a candle. And you've given yourself a graduate's diploma. Well, gentlemen, are you more mature now? No, my friend, go off into your corner and snicker into your hand as you did before—that's an undertaking that will turn out better!" That's what will be heard, along with much, much more that can't be written down. And how much cynicism we would at once see again; how much mistrust in our own strength, mistrust in Russia herself. Once more they would begin singing a requiem over her! And how many gangs like the

Jack of Hearts would appear! And how many young people of the purest heart would again flee from society! Once again, disunity! Once again, uncertainty! Incidentally, Viscount Beaconsfield, of course, knew very well that he was lying when he spoke about our destructive elements. Perhaps he even sensed that if we did have any destructive elements, then at present, with Russia's new upsurge of enthusiasm, these would shift to a new course; and, of course, Viscount Tarantula would find such a thought most annoying. But now—should the the upsurge fail, I mean—the tarantula would rejoice; he would have good cause! But . . . is this really near to the truth? Will this in fact come to pass? What a bad dream! A dream and nothing more. . . .

October

1

1. A Case That Is Not as Simple as It Seems

On October 15 the court reached its decision on the case of the stepmother who, some six months ago, in May, you may recall, threw her little six-year-old stepdaughter from a fourth-story window; the little girl, through some miracle, survived in good health. The stepmother, a peasant woman of twenty named Ekaterina Kornilova, was married to a widower who, she testified, regularly quarreled with her; he did not allow her to visit her relatives or allow relatives to visit her; he criticized her by comparing her to his late wife, claiming that the latter was a better housekeeper, and so on. In short, he "drove her to the point where she could no longer love him," and to get even with him she conceived the notion of throwing the daughter of his former wife out the window; this, in fact, she did. In sum, it would seem—apart from the miraculous survival of the child—to be a rather simple and clear-cut story. The court regarded the case from this same "clear-cut" point of view and itself, in the simplest fashion, sentenced Ekaterina Kornilova, "being more than seventeen and less than twenty years of age when she committed the crime, to be exiled to hard labor for a term of two years and eight months and on completion of this sentence to be exiled permanently to Siberia."

However, despite all its simplicity and clarity, there remains something in this case that seems not entirely clarified. The defendant (a rather pretty young woman) went to trial in the late stages of pregnancy, so that a midwife had been summoned to the courtroom for any eventuality. Back in May, when the crime was committed (and when, accordingly, the accused was in her fourth month of pregnancy), I wrote in my May *Diary* (briefly and just in passing, however, while looking at the predictable and bureaucratic ways of our legal profession) the following words: "And what is truly shock-ing ... is that the act of this monster-stepmother is *truly bizarre;* perhaps it really should be given a detailed and deep analysis that might even serve to lighten the case against this criminal woman." That is what I wrote then. Now please look at the facts. In the first place, the defendant herself admitted her guilt, and did so immediately after committing the crime; she reported it herself. Right at the police station she told of how, on the night before the crime, she had decided to kill her stepdaughter, whom she had come to hate out of resentment of her husband; but her husband's presence that evening prevented her from doing anything. The next day, however, when he had gone to work, she opened the window and moved all the flowerpots to one side of the windowsill; then she told the girl to climb onto the sill and look down through the open window. The girl did this, perhaps even eagerly; goodness knows what she expected to see below the window. When she had climbed up and knelt, looking out and clinging to the sides of the window, the stepmother lifted the girl's legs from behind and sent her tumbling out into space. After looking down on the fallen child, the woman (as she recounts it herself) closed the window, got dressed, locked the room, and went off to the police station to report what had happened. Those are the facts, and it would seem that nothing could be more straightforward; and yet, how fantastic, is it not? Our juries are still frequently accused of bringing in some truly fantastic acquittals. Sometimes even the moral feelings of people utterly unconnected with the case have been aroused. We realized that one could have mercy on the criminal, but that good could not be called evil in such an important and great matter as criminal justice; and yet there were acquittals of almost this kind, i.e., evil was *almost* acknowledged as good, or at least it almost reached that point. Either there was pseudosentimentality or a lack of understanding of the very principle of justice, a misunderstand-ing of the fact that in court the first thing, the very first principle, is to define and specify, as far as possible, what is evil, and to proclaim it publicly as evil. And only then come the issues of easing the criminal's lot, concern for his rehabilitation, and so on. The latter are different problems, very profound and immense, but totally distinct from the business of the court; they belong to other areas of social life entirely, areas which, we must admit, have still not been properly defined and not even formulated in Russia, so that we perhaps have not yet pronounced our first word in these areas of our public life. And, in the meantime, our courts confuse both these *different ideas;* the results, Heaven knows, are bizarre. Crime seems not to be acknowledged as crime at all; to the contrary: it seems that a public proclamation is made—and by the court, indeed—that there is no crime and that crime, don't you see, is only an illness caused by the abnormal state of society, a notion that *in some* specific instances and *in some* certain categories is dazzling in its truth, but which is absolutely mistaken when applied as a whole and in general; for here there is a certain line that cannot be crossed without altogether depriving people of their human image, without removing their very selfhood and life and reducing them to the level of a tiny bit of fluff whose fate hangs on the first breath of wind. In short, this amounts to announcing that some new kind of science has just discovered some new kind of human nature. However, this new science does not yet exist and has not yet even begun. And so all these compassionate verdicts by juries—verdicts in cases where a crime clearly proved and supported by the criminal's full confession, was sometimes flatly denied: "He's not guilty; he didn't do it; he committed no murder"—all these compassionate verdicts (aside from some rare instances when they were really appropriate and correct) have caused astonishment among the People and aroused mockery and perplexity in society. And so now, just having read of the verdict on the fate of the peasant woman Kornilova (two years and eight months at hard labor), the thought suddenly occurred to me: "This is a time when they should have let her off; this time they should have said: 'There was no crime; she committed no murder; she did not throw the girl out the window.'" I will not, however, develop my ideas on the basis of abstractions or emotions. It *simply* seems to me that in this case there was a most legitimate legal ground for acquitting the accused: this is the fact that she was pregnant.

Everyone knows that a pregnant woman (particularly when she is carrying her first child) is very often subject to certain strange influences and impressions that take a strange and fantastic hold on her psyche. These influences sometimes—in rare instances, however—assume extraordinary, abnormal, almost bizarre forms. But despite the fact that they happen rarely (I mean the truly extraordinary manifestations), in the present case the fact that they do happen, or even that they can happen, is more than enough for those who must decide the fate of a human being. Doctor Nikitin, who examined the woman (after the crime), stated that in his opinion Kornilova committed her crime *consciously*, although her angry state of mind and the possibility of a fit of passion could be taken into account. But in the first place, what could the word *consciously* mean here? People rarely do anything unconsciously, apart from those who are insane or delirious or suffering from delirium. Even medicine surely recognizes that someone can commit an act quite consciously but yet not be fully responsible for committing it. Take insane people, for instance: the majority of their insane acts are committed quite consciously, and those who commit them remember doing so. Moreover, they can give an account of what they have done, defend their actions, argue with you about them, and sometimes argue so logically that you may well be at a loss for an answer. I'm not a doctor, of course, but I can remember being told as a child about a certain Moscow lady who, whenever she was pregnant and during specific periods of her pregnancy, would acquire an unusual and irresistible passion for stealing things. She would steal things and money from friends she visited, from her own visitors, and even from the shops and stores where she made her purchases. Afterward, her family would return the stolen things to their owners. Yet she was a lady who was well-educated, from respectable society, and by no means poor; after these few days of strange passion had passed, the thought of stealing would never enter her head. At that time everyone, including medical people, realized that this was only a temporary affect of her pregnancy. Still, of course, she stole consciously and with full awareness of what she was doing. She was completely conscious but simply was unable to resist this impulse when it came upon her. I must suppose that even now medical science can say little with certainty about such cases—I mean about their psychological aspect: which laws produce such crises, manias, and influences in the human psyche; what causes such fits of madness in a sane person; what precisely does consciousness mean here and what role does it play? There seems no doubt of the possibility of these influences and extraordinary manias during pregnancy, and that is sufficient. . . . And what, I repeat, of the fact that these very extraordinary influences occur so rarely? For the conscience of one sitting in judgment in such cases it is enough to consider that they still may occur. Suppose, though, that people argue as follows: she did not go off to steal things like that lady or think up something very unusual to do; on the contrary, she did precisely the thing that was *relevant to the case*, i.e., she simply took revenge on her hated husband by trying to murder his daughter by his former wife, whose example the husband was always citing. Well, say what you like, but even though this may be comprehensible, it is still *not simple;* it may be logical, but you must agree that, had she not been pregnant, perhaps this logical thing would never have happened. It might have happened like this, for instance: left alone with her stepdaughter, abused by her husband and angry at him, she might have thought to herself in her fury, "What if I throw this wretched little girl out the window just to spite him?" She might have thought it, *but she would not have done it.* She would have sinned in mind but not in deed. But now, pregnant, *she carried it out.* The logic is the same in both cases, but the difference is immense.

At least if the jury had acquitted the defendant they would have had something on which to base their verdict: "Although such pathological affects occur but rarely, they do occur. What if there was an affect of pregnancy in this case as well?" That is something to consider. At least in this case everyone would have understood the grounds for mercy and no doubts would have been aroused. And what of the possibility of an error? Surely an error on the side of mercy is better than an error on the side of punishment, the more so as there is no way of verifying anything in this case. The woman is the first to consider herself guilty; she confessed immediately after committing the crime, and she confessed again in court six months later. So she will go to Siberia, perhaps, in conscience and in the depths of her soul considering herself guilty; so she will die, perhaps, repenting in her final hour and considering herself a murderer. And never will it occur to her, nor to anyone else on earth, that there is a pathological affect that can arise during pregnancy and that it, perhaps, was the cause of it all, and that, had she not been pregnant, nothing would have happened. . . . No, of two errors here, it is better to choose the error of mercy. One would sleep better afterward. . . . And yet, what am I saying? A busy man cannot be thinking of sleep; a busy man has a hundred such cases, and he sleeps soundly when he crawls into bed, exhausted. It's the idle man who encounters one or two such cases a year who has a lot of time to think. He's the one who might have such thoughts, from lack of anything better to do. In short, idleness is the mother of all vices.

By the way, there was a midwife present in court, and just imagine: when they convicted the woman, they convicted along with her an infant not yet born. Don't you find that strange? But let's suppose that's not entirely true: still, you must agree that it seems very close to the truth, and indeed, the whole truth. In fact, here he is, condemned to Siberia before he's even born, along with his mother who has to look after him. If he goes with his mother, he loses his father; if the outcome of the case should be such that his father keeps him (I don't know whether the father can do that now), then the child loses his mother. . . . In short, in the first place the child loses his family even before he's born, and in the second place, when he eventually grows up, he'll learn everything about his mother and he'll. . . . However, who knows what he'll do? It's best to take a *simplified* view of the case. Looking at it from such a point of view, all the phantasmagoria disappear. So it should be in life. I even think that all such things that seem so unusual are in actuality arranged in a most ordinary fashion, prosaic to the point of indecency. Just look, in fact: this Kornilov is now a widower again; he's also free once more, since his marriage has been annulled by his wife's exile to Siberia; his wife, or non-wife, will shortly bear him a son (because they will surely allow her to bear the child before she sets off), and while she is recuperating in the prison hospital or wherever they place her, Kornilov—and I'll stake a bet on this—will visit her in a most prosaic manner and—who knows—perhaps he will bring along this same little girl who flew out the window. And they will get together and talk about the simplest, most everyday things—about some wretched canvas cloth, about warm shoes or felt boots for the journey. Who knows, they may strike up a very close relationship now that they have been divorced, whereas formerly they used to quarrel. And they may never utter a word of reproach to one another but only sigh over their fate with compassion for one another. And that same little girl who flew out the window, I repeat, will likely run errands every day from her father to her "sweet mummy," taking her fancy loaves of bread: "Here, Mummy," she'll say, "Daddy's sent you some tea and sugar as well, and tomorrow he'll come himself." The most tragic thing may be that when they bid one another farewell at the railway station they will break into wailing, just at the last minute, between the second and the third bell. The little girl will also begin to wail, her mouth gaping, as she looks at them; and each, one after the other, will probably fall down at the other's feet. "Forgive me, Katerina Prokofievna, my dearest," he'll say. "Don't think badly of me." And she will say to him: "And you forgive me, Vasily Ivanovich (or whatever his name is), my dear; I'm guilty before you, and there's much to blame me for. . . ." And now the infant, still being nursed—he will certainly be there as well—will raise his voice, whether she takes him along or leaves him with his father. In short, with our People the result will never be an epic poem, will it? They are the most prosaic people in the world, so that one is almost ashamed of them in that respect. Now just compare this with how it would happen in Europe: what passions, what vengeance, and what dignity there would be! Just try to describe this case in a story, event by event, beginning with a young wife of a widower, going on to throwing the girl out the window, up to the minute when she looked out to see whether the child had been hurt and at once went off to the police; then to the moment when she sat in court with the midwife, and right to those last words of farewell and bows and . . . and imagine, I almost wrote, "And of course nothing would come of it," yet it might well turn out better than any of our poems and novels with heroes "with deep insight and lives torn asunder." Do you know, I simply don't understand why our novelists have to go off looking for material; here would be a subject for them. Why not just describe the whole truth, step by step? And yet, it seems, I forgot the old rule: what matters is not the subject but the eye. If there is an eye, a subject will be found; if there is no eye, if you are blind, you won't find anything in any subject. Oh, the eye is an important thing; what one eye sees as an epic poem, another sees as only a heap of. . . .

Is it really not possible now to reduce this sentence on Kornilova somehow? Is there no way this could be done? Truly, there might be an error here. . . . I just keep thinking that there was an error!

2. A Few Remarks about Simplicity and Simplification

Now, another topic. Now I would like to state something about simplicity in general. I recall a little thing that happened to me a long time ago. Some thirteen years ago, during what to some people was the height of our "time of troubles" and to others was most "straight and direct," one winter evening I dropped into a library on Meshchansky Street (as it was then called), not far from my home. I had decided to write a critical article and I needed to make some excerpts from a Thackeray novel. In the library I was served by a certain young lady (she was then a young lady). I asked for the novel; she listened with a stern expression.

"We don't keep such rubbish," she said before I had even finished, with inexpressible scorn, which, God knows, I didn't deserve.

Of course, I wasn't surprised and realized what was the matter. Many things of the sort happened at that time, and they seemed to happen in a rush of rapture. An idea dropped onto the street and took on a most common, street-corner appearance. Pushkin was given a terrible going-over at that time, while "boots" were praised to the skies. Nevertheless, I still attempted to talk it over with the girl.

"Do you really consider Thackeray to be rubbish?" I asked, assuming a most humble air.

"You ought to be ashamed for asking. The olden days are past; now there is rational demand. . . ."

With that I departed, leaving the young lady remarkably pleased with the lesson she had given me. But I was powerfully struck by the simplicity of her view, and it was just at that time that I began to ponder *simplicity* in general and our Russian haste for generalization in particular. Our capacity for being satisfied with the simple, small, and insignificant is striking, to say the least. People may object that this incident was trivial and insignificant; that the young lady was an uninformed and, more important, uneducated fool; that it was not worth recalling the incident; and that it was all too easy for the young lady to imagine that until she arrived the whole of Russia had been populated only by fools, but that now, suddenly, a lot of wise people had materialized and that she was one of them. I know all that myself; I also know that this young lady was straining her abilities in saying what she did—that is, about the "rational demand" and about Thackeray—and even then she had to use someone else's words—one could tell that from her face. But still this incident has stayed in my mind until now as a metaphor, as an kind of fable, almost even as an emblem. Think carefully about today's common opinions, about today's "rational demand," about today's flat judgments—not only upon Thackeray but upon the whole Russian People: what *simplicity* there is at times! What a straight-line approach; what quick satisfaction with the petty and insignificant as means of expression; what a general rush to set one's mind at rest as quickly as possible, to pronounce judgment so as not to have to trouble oneself any longer.

Believe me, this tendency will remain with us for a long time. Just look: everyone now believes in the sincerity and actuality of the People's movement of this year, and yet even this belief does not satisfy; something even more simple is demanded. One of the members of a certain committee related in my presence that he had received rather a lot of letters with questions such as the following: "Why are the Slavs so important now? Why are we helping the Slavs as Slavs? If the Scandinavians were in a similar position, would we be helping them as we are the Slavs?" In short, why this category "Slavs" (recall the concerns over the rubric "common faith" in *The European Messenger* that I spoke about in the last issue of my *Diary*). It would seem at first glance that this is not a case of simplicity at all, and not an urge for simplification; to the contrary, one can sense disquiet in these questions. But the simplicity in this case consists precisely in the effort to achieve *nihil* and a *tabula rasa* and so, in a way, to set one's mind at rest. For what is simpler and more restful than a zero? Note as well that in these questions one can catch the sound of "rational demand" and "you ought to be ashamed of yourself."

There is no doubt that very many of our most intelligent and, so to say, our "highest" people were not at all pleased to hear this quiet and humble, yet firm and powerful, voice of our People. This was not because they failed to understand it; on the contrary, it was because they understood it all too well, to the point where it even caused them some perplexity. At least there are certain signs now that a strong reaction is beginning. I'm not talking about those innocent voices we heard even earlier, voices that could not help but grumble and disagree on old questions because of their beloved old principles. We hear, for example, that "we mustn't hurry so and get carried away with as crude and unenlightened a cause as helping the Slavs simply because they are supposed to be brothers of ours." No, I am not talking about these rationally liberal old men who chew over old phrases, but about the real reaction to the Popular movement, a reaction that, by all signs, will soon rear its head. It is this reaction which naturally and despite itself will ally with those gentlemen who, having long ago simplified their view of Russia to the ultimate degree of clarity, are prepared to say, "We really ought to stop this whole movement so that everything can rest in the state of inertia it did before." And just imagine: it is not at all the fantastical nature of this "phenomenon" that causes the simplifiers to dislike it; I mean, it is not because something

they had considered inert, senseless, and utterly simple suddenly
ventured to speak out as though it really had consciousness and
life. Such dislike we could understand: they simply felt offended
and nothing more. But it's quite the contrary: they didn't like this
whole phenomenon because from something fantastical it suddenly
became comprehensible to everyone. "How did it dare become
comprehensible to everyone so suddenly," they ask. "How did it
dare take on such a simplified and sensible appearance?" It was
this sort of indignation, as I said earlier, that met with support
both among our intellectual old men, who strive with all their
might to "simplify" and bring this "phenomenon" down from the
rational level to something elemental and primitive, which, though
it may be good-hearted, is still ignorant and potentially harmful.
In short, the reaction is attempting with all its might and with all
its means to simplify above all.... Meanwhile, because of this
excessive simplification of views on certain things, the cause itself
is sometimes lost. In some instances simplicity harms the simplifiers
themselves. Simplicity does not change; simplicity moves in a
straight line and is arrogant above all. Simplicity is the enemy of
analysis. The end result, very often, is that in your simplicity you
begin to lose your grasp of the subject and lose sight of it altogether,
so that the reverse happens; that is, your own view involuntarily
changes from something simple into something fantastic. This happens precisely because of the mutual, lengthy, and ever-growing
alienation of one Russia from the other. Our alienation began precisely from *one Russia's simplified view of the other*. It began a very
long time ago, as we know, still in the time of Peter the Great,
when there first developed the unusual simplification of views of
"upper" Russia on the People's Russia. Since then, from generation
unto generation, this view has done nothing more than grow ever
more simple.

3. Two Suicides

Not long ago I happened to be speaking to one of our writers (a
great artist) about the comical aspects of life and the difficulty of
defining a thing and giving it its proper name. Just prior to that
I had remarked to him that I, who have known *Woe from Wit* for
almost forty years, had only this year properly understood one of
the most vivid characters of this comedy, Molchalin, and had come
to this sudden understanding of him only when he (the writer with

whom I was speaking) had portrayed him in one of his satirical sketches. (I shall have something to say about Molchalin some time in the future; he's an important topic.)

"But do you know," the writer said to me suddenly, apparently deeply struck by his long-held idea, "do you know, whatever you write or portray, whatever you set down in a work of art, you can never match real life. It doesn't matter what you depict—it will always come out weaker than real life. You might think you've found the most comical aspect of some certain thing in life and captured its most grotesque aspect—but not at all! Real life will at once present you with something of this same sort that you never even suspected and that goes far beyond anything your own observation and imagination were able to create! . . ."

I had known this ever since 1846, when I began writing, and perhaps even earlier, and this fact has struck me more than once and has caused me no small bewilderment: what is the use of art when we can see it so lacking in power? In truth, if you investigate some fact of real life—even one that at first glance is not so vivid—you'll find in it, if you have the capacity and the vision, a depth that you won't find even in Shakespeare. But here, you see, is the whole point: *whose vision and whose capacity*? Not only to create and to write a work of literature, but merely even to pick out the fact requires something of the artist. For some observers all the facts of life pass by in the most touchingly simple manner and are so plain that it's not worthwhile to think about them or even to look at them. Those same facts of life will sometimes perplex another observer to the extent that he (and this happens not infrequently) is at last incapable of simplifying and making a general conclusion about them, of drawing them out into a straight line and so setting his mind at rest. He resorts to simplification of another sort and *very simply* plants a bullet in his head so as to quench at one stroke his tormented mind and all its questions. These are only the two extremes, but between them lies the entire range of the human intellect. But of course we can never exhaust a whole phenomenon and never reach its end, or its beginning. We know only the daily flow of the things we see, and this only on the surface; but the ends and the beginnings are things that, for human beings, still lie in the realm of the fantastic.

By the way, one of my respected readers wrote last summer to tell me of a strange and unexplained suicide, and I have been wanting to talk about it. Everything about this suicide, both its

external and its internal aspects, is a riddle. I, of course, following
the dictates of human nature, have tried to come up with some
solution to this riddle so as to be able "to pause and rest my mind."
The victim is a young girl of no more than twenty-three or twenty-
four, the daughter of one very well-known Russian emigré; she was
born abroad, Russian by origin but scarcely Russian at all by
education. The newspapers made some vague mention of her at
the time, but the details of the case are very curious: "She soaked
a piece of cotton wool in chloroform, bound this to her face and
lay down on the bed...." And so she died. She wrote the following
note before her death:

> Je m'en vais entreprendre un long voyage. Si cela ne réussit pas
> qu'on se rassemble pour fêter ma résurrection avec du Cliquot. *Si
> cela réussit*, je prie qu'on ne me laisse enterrer que tout à fait morte,
> puisqu'il est très désagréable de se réveiller dans un cercueil sous
> terre. *Ce n'est pas chic!*

Which, translated, is:

> I am setting off on a long journey. If the suicide should not succeed,
> then let everyone gather to celebrate my resurrection with glasses of
> Cliquot. *If I do succeed*, I ask only that you not bury me until you
> have determined that I am completely dead, because it is most un-
> pleasant to awaken in a coffin underground. *That would not be* chic
> *at all!*

In this nasty, vulgar *chic* I think I hear a challenge—indignation,
perhaps, or anger—but about what? Persons who are simply vulgar
end their lives by suicide only for material, obvious, external reasons; but it is apparent from the tone of this note that she could
not have such reasons. What could she be angry about? About the
simplicity of the things she saw around her? About the lack of any
meaningful content in life? Was she one of those very well-known
judges and negators of life who are angry at the "stupidity" of
man's presence on earth, at the senseless unintentionality of his
appearance here, at the tyranny of brute causality with which they
cannot reconcile themselves? Here we have a soul of one who has
rebelled against the "linearity" of things, of one who could not
tolerate this linearity, which was passed on to her from childhood
in her father's house. The most hideous thing of all is that she
died, of course, without any apparent doubt. Most probably, there
was no conscious doubt in her soul, no "questions." It is most

likely of all that she believed everything she had been taught since childhood, without question. And so she simply died from "chilly gloom and tedium," in animal, so to say, and unaccountable suffering; it was as if she could not get enough air and she began to suffocate. Her soul instinctively could not tolerate linearity and instinctively demanded something more complex....

About a month ago all the Petersburg newspapers carried several short lines in fine print concerning a suicide in the city. A poor young girl, a seamstress, threw herself out of a fourth-floor window "because she was absolutely unable to find enough work to make a living." These accounts added that she leapt and fell to the ground *holding an icon in her hands*. This icon in the hands is a strange and unprecedented feature in suicides! This, now, is a meek and a humble suicide. Here, apparently, there was no grumbling or reproach: it was simply a matter of being unable to live any longer—"God did not wish it"—and so she died having said her prayers. There are some things which, no matter how simple they seem on the surface, one still goes on thinking about for a long time; they recur in one's dreams, and it even seems as if one is somehow to blame for them. This meek soul who destroyed herself torments one's mind despite oneself. It was this latter death that reminded me of the suicide of the emigré's daughter I had heard about last summer. But how different these two creatures are—just as if they had come from two different planets! And how different the two deaths are! And which, I ask, of these two souls bore more torment on this earth—if such an idle question is proper and permissible?

4. The Sentence

By the way, here are the thoughts of one person—a materialist, of course—who committed suicide *out of boredom*.

> ...In fact, what right did this Nature have to bring me into the world as a result of some eternal law of hers? I was created with consciousness, and I was *conscious* of this Nature: what right did she have to produce me, a conscious being, without my willing it? A conscious being, and thus a suffering one; but I do not want to suffer, for why would I have agreed to that? Nature, through my consciousness, proclaims to me some sort of harmony of the whole. From this message human consciousness has created religions. Nature tells me—even though I know full well that I cannot participate in the "harmony of the whole" and never will be able to and haven't the least idea

what this means in any case—that I still ought to submit to this message, to humble myself, to accept suffering in view of the harmony of the whole and agree to live. However, if I am to make a conscious choice, then naturally I would prefer to be happy only during the moment while *I* exist; but as regards the whole and its harmony, once *I* have been annihilated, I haven't the least concern if this whole with its harmony remains after I am gone or is annihilated at the same instant as I am. And why should I have to worry so whether it is preserved after I am gone? That is the question. It would have been better had I been created like all animals, that is, as a living being, but without a rational conception of myself. My consciousness is certainly not a harmony but just the opposite, a disharmony, because I am unhappy with it. Just look at those who are happy on earth, look at the sort of people who *consent* to go on living. It is precisely those people who are like animals and who are most closely akin to those species because of the limited development of their consciousness. They willingly consent to live, but on condition that they live like animals; that is, they eat, drink, sleep, build their nests, and raise their offspring. To eat, drink, and sleep in human fashion means to grow rich and to steal; building a nest above all means to steal. You may object, perhaps, that one can arrange one's life and build one's nest on a rational foundation, on scientifically proven social principles and not by stealing, as was the case heretofore. Granted; but I ask you: what for? What is the point of arranging one's life and expending so much effort to arrange social life correctly, rationally, and in a morally righteous manner? No one, of course, can give me an answer to that. All that anyone could reply is: "In order to derive pleasure." Indeed, if I were a flower or a cow I would derive some pleasure. But continually posing questions to myself, as I do now, I cannot be happy, even with the supreme and *direct* happiness of love for my neighbor and the love of humanity for me, since I know that tomorrow it will all be annihilated. I, and all this happiness, and all the love, and all of humanity will be transformed into nothing, into the original chaos. And under such a condition I simply cannot accept any happiness—not from my refusal to agree to accept it, not from stubbornness based on some principle, but simply because I will not and cannot be happy under the condition of the nothingness that threatens tomorrow. This is a feeling, a direct feeling, and I cannot overcome it. Well, suppose I were to die but humanity were to remain eternal in my place; then, perhaps, I might still find some comfort in it. But our planet, after all, is not eternal, and humanity's allotted span is just such a moment as has been allotted to me. And no matter how rationally, joyously, righteously, and blessedly humanity might organize itself on earth, it will all be equated tomorrow to that same empty zero. Though there may be some reason why this is essential, in accordance with some almighty, eternal, and dead laws of Nature, believe me, this idea shows the most profound disrespect to humanity; it is profoundly insulting to me, and all the more unbearable because there is no one here who is to blame.

And finally, even if one were to admit the possibility of this fairy tale of a human society at long last organized on earth on rational and scientific bases; if one were to believe in this, to believe in the future happiness of people at long last, then the mere thought that some implacable laws of Nature made it essential to torment the human race for a thousand years before allowing it to attain that happiness—that thought alone is unbearably loathsome. Now add the fact that this very same Nature, which has permitted humanity at last to attain happiness, tomorrow will find it necessary for some reason to reduce it all to zero, despite the suffering with which humanity has paid for this happiness; and, more important, that Nature does all this without concealing anything from me and my consciousness as she hid things from the cow. In such a case one cannot help but come to the very amusing yet unbearably sad thought: "What if the human race has been placed on the earth as some sort of brazen experiment, simply in order to find out whether such creatures are going to survive here or not?" The sad part of this thought lies mainly in the fact that once again no one is to blame; no one conducted the experiment; there is no one we can curse; it all happened simply due to the dead laws of Nature, which I absolutely cannot comprehend and with which my consciousness is utterly unable to agree. *Ergo*:

Whereas Nature replies through my consciousness to my questions about happiness only by telling me that I can be happy in no other way than through harmony with the whole, which I do not understand and, evidently, never will be capable of understanding;

And whereas Nature not only refuses to recognize my right to receive an account from her and indeed refuses to answer me at all, and not because she does not want to answer, but because she cannot answer;

And whereas I have become convinced that Nature, in order to answer my questions, has assigned to me (unconsciously) *my own self* and she answers me through my own consciousness (because I am saying all this to myself);

And whereas, finally, under such circumstances I must assume simultaneously the roles of plaintiff and defendant, accused and judge, and find this comedy utterly absurd on Nature's part and even humiliating on my part;

Therefore, in my incontrovertible capacity as plaintiff and defendant, judge and accused, I condemn this Nature, which has so brazenly and unceremoniously inflicted this suffering, to annihilation along with me.... Since I am unable to destroy Nature, I am destroying only myself, solely out of the weariness of enduring a tyranny in which there is no guilty party.

N.N.

2

1. A New Phase in the Eastern Question

The Eastern Question has entered its second period, while its first has come to an end, but not because of the supposed defeat of Cherniaev. Suvorov suffered the same sort of defeat in Switzerland in that he had to retreat; but can we say that Suvorov was defeated? It was not his fault that he led the Russian People into France under impossible conditions. We are not comparing Cherniaev with Suvorov, but wish only to say that there are such circumstances under which even the Suvorovs must retreat. It's true that in St. Petersburg at present certain of our future military leaders are loudly criticizing Cherniaev's maneuvers, while politicians have taken up the cry that he has led the Slavs and the Russians into battle "under impossible conditions." But none of these future military leaders of ours have ever found themselves in the tight spots in which Cherniaev has been. All these soldiers are really still civilians trying to invent gunpowder without ever having smelled it themselves. As far as the politicians are concerned, they ought to recall the legend of Suvorov's pit in Switzerland: he ordered a pit to be dug, then jumped into it, ordering the soldiers to fill it in with earth if they did not want to obey and follow him. The soldiers burst into tears, pulled him out of the pit, and followed him. Well, it looks as if the entire Russian People will pull Cherniaev out of the pit that all the plotters and schemers have dug for him in Serbia. You have forgotten, gentlemen, that Cherniaev is a national hero, and it is not for you to bury him in a pit.

The Eastern Question has entered its second period because the resounding words of the tsar have produced echoes of endorsement in the hearts of all Russian people and echoes of trepidation in the hearts of all Russia's enemies. The Porte kept silent and accepted the ultimatum; but what will happen now is more than ever a mystery. There is talk of a conference in Constantinople (or in some other place—does it really matter where?) or of a congress of diplomats. So it is to be diplomacy again, to the joy of those who worship diplomacy!

And now, after Russia's word has been ringingly pronounced, the European press once more presumes to give us lessons. Why even the Hungarians, almost on the very eve of the ultimatum, wrote that we are afraid of them and therefore were equivocating and would not dare to declare our intentions. Once more the English will be intriguing and giving us advice, imagining once more that we are so afraid of them. Even the French, of all people, will pronounce their word at the conference with a scornful and pompous air, telling us what they want and what they don't want; but what do we care about France, and why should we be interested in what she wants or doesn't want? It's no longer 1853, and never, perhaps, has there been a moment for Russia in which her enemies were less able to harm her. But still, let diplomacy reign, to the consolation of its Petersburg admirers. But what of Bulgaria and the Slavs? What will happen to them in these two months? This is the question. This is an urgent matter, after all, and one that cannot be put off for a moment. What will happen to them in these two months? Bulgarian blood will flow once more, perhaps! The Porte, after all, has to show its zealots that it did not accept the ultimatum out of cowardice; and so Bulgaria will pay: "You see; we're not afraid of the Russians when we can slaughter Bulgarians during the very conference." Well, and what shall we do if that happens (and it well may happen)? Shall we express our indignation right there at the conference? But the Porte will at once deny any massacre and blame everything on the Bulgarians themselves; she might even assume a nobly offended air and quickly set up a commission of inquiry: "Now, gentlemen, representatives of Europe, you can see for yourselves how Russia offends me and how she won't leave me alone!" Meanwhile, more and more Bulgarians will be slaughtered, while the press of Europe will, perhaps, again support the bashibuzouks and say that Russia is pressing the issue because of her own conceit, that she is deliberately laying plots against the conference and wants war and.... And it is very possible that Europe will again propose a peace that is even worse than war—a peace that is heavily armed; a peace in which nations are agitated and restless, with gloomy expectations. And this may

well last for a whole year! Another whole year of uncertainty! . . .
And after that year, of course, and after such a peace, the war will
begin once more. The Slavs need peace, but not that kind of peace.
It's not peace at all that's needed now, but simply an end.

Yet people have been speaking out against Cherniaev, and these
are only the first to take potshots at him. Just wait a bit—the chorus
will grow larger and stronger. The main thing here is not Cherniaev:
what we have is a reaction against the whole movement of this year.
The *Petersburg Gazette*, in its excellent article replying to the attacks
on Cherniaev, warned the *Stock Exchange News* that it would lose
subscribers and that readers would turn away from it; but this is
scarcely to happen now: there are many, many people now who
find the *Stock Exchange News* entirely in tune with their views.
These are the same people who stored up so much spleen over the
past year; they are angry and exasperated people who see themselves as lovers of order above all. For them the entire movement
of this past year was nothing but disorder, while Cherniaev is only
a shameless rogue. "A Lieutenant-General," they say, "yet he flew
off to look for adventure like some condottiere." But these are
people who love bureaucratic order, so to say. There is yet another
type of lover of order, however: these are the upper intelligentsia
who look on with bleeding hearts at "the waste of so much force
on such a medieval, so to say, cause when the schools, for example . . ." etc., etc. Those who attack Cherniaev shout that Russian
blood was shed in vain *with no advantage for Russia. New Times*
gave a fine reply about advantage and about what advantage means;
it answered directly in frank words, unashamed at the *idealism* of
its words—something of which everyone else is so ashamed. As
early as June, at the very beginning of the movement, I happened
to write in my *Diary* of where Russia's advantage lay in this situation. Such a lofty organism as Russia ought also to project a
powerful spiritual significance. Russia's advantage lies not in seizing
the Slavic provinces but in a sincere and deep concern for them,
in protecting them, in fraternal union with them, in conveying to
them our spirit and our view on the union of the entire Slavic
world. An organism as exalted as Russia cannot be satisfied with
material advantage alone, cannot be satisfied with "bread" alone.
This is neither an ideal nor a set of empty phrases: as proof, we
have the whole Russian People and the whole movement of this
past year. This is a movement which, in its self-sacrificing nature
and disinterestedness, in its pious religious thirst *to suffer for a*

righteous cause, is almost without precedent among other nations. Such a People can cause no concern for order; this is not a People of disorder, but a People of firm views and unshakeable principles, a People devoted to sacrifice, seeking truth and knowing where truth can be found, a humble but strong People, as honest and pure in heart as one of their high ideals, the epic hero Ilya Muromets, whom they cherish as a saint. The heart of the One who preserves this People must rejoice over them; and it does rejoice, and the People know it! No, this was not a matter of disorder. . . .

2. Cherniaev

Even those who defend Cherniaev now no longer consider him a *genius*, but only a valiant and brave general. But the mere fact that he headed the whole movement in the Slavic cause already showed the foresight of genius; such tasks are undertaken only by those having the power of genius. The Slavic cause, of necessity, had at last *to begin*, that is, to move into its active phase; and without Cherniaev it would not have done this. People will say that this was the whole problem: that Cherniaev gave it its initial nudge and inflated it to the dimensions it has; that this was his fault and that he began it prematurely. But the great Slavic question could not but be raised, and, in truth, I don't know if we can still argue about its timeliness. But once the Slavic cause has been taken up, then who but Russia should stand at its head? This is Russia's mission, and Cherniaev understood that and raised Russia's banner. To resolve to do this, to take this step—no, this could not be done by a man without some special power.

People will say that this was all done out of vanity and that he is an adventurer who only wanted to make a name for himself. But vain, ambitious people in such instances seek first to stake their bet on a sure thing, and if they do take a risk, then it is only up to a certain limit: when conditions threaten certain failure they quickly abandon the cause. Cherniaev, of course, had long foreseen the impossibility of *immediate* military victory with only the Serbs and without Russian help: we now know too much and have too many details about this affair to have any doubts about that. But he could not abandon the cause, for the cause is not limited to *immediate* military victory alone: it involves the future of both Russia and the Slavic lands. In any case, his hope for immediate Russian military assistance was not a vain one, for Russia has at last pronounced her great and decisive word. Had this word been uttered even a little earlier, Cherniaev would not have erred in anything. Oh, there are many who, in Cherniaev's place, would have refused to wait so long: these are the vain ones and the careerists. I am certain that many of his critics would not have held up under half of what he has borne. But Cherniaev was serving this mighty cause and not merely his vanity, and he preferred rather to sacrifice all—his fate, his fame, his career, and perhaps even his life—than to abandon the cause. This was precisely because he was working for Russia's honor and *advantage* and he knew it. For the Slavic cause is a Russian cause and should be resolved *ultimately* only by Russia alone and through the Russian idea. Cherniaev persisted also for the sake of the Russian volunteers who all rallied around his banner, rallied both for an idea as well as for the one who represented that idea. He simply could not abandon them, and here again, of course, we see an example of his magnanimity. How many of his critics in his place would have abandoned all and everything—the idea, Russia, the volunteers, no matter how many of them there were! One has to speak the truth, after all. . . .

Cherniaev is criticized from the military side as well. But in the first place, and once again, these military men were not in the tight spots in which Cherniaev found himself; and in the second place, everything that Cherniaev has already done "under impossible conditions" could not have been done by any of his critics. These "impossible conditions," which had so much influence on military developments, also belong to history; but their main features are already known even now and are so characteristic that one cannot overlook them even from a strategic viewpoint. If it is true that the intrigues against Cherniaev reached the point that at the most critical moments the highest bureaucrats of the country, in their suspicious hatred of a Russian general, left his most important requests and demands for the army *unanswered* and even on the eve of the final and decisive battles left him without artillery shells, then can we make a just criticism of military actions without clarification of this point? All these intrigues and all this aggravation are unprecedented: this "untrustworthy" general was still the commander of their armies and was defending the approach to Serbia; and they, out of vexation and malice, sacrificed everything—the army, even their fatherland—simply in order to destroy a man they disliked. At least that is how it was according to very reliable sources. All the correspondents and all the newspapers in Europe testify that these intrigues certainly went on; they began and continued in Belgrade the whole time, from the moment of Cherniaev's arrival in Serbia. The English, as a matter of policy, had a strong hand in these intrigues, as did certain Russians as well—for what reason we do not know. It is very likely that Cherniaev somehow offended the vanity of Serbian officials when he began his work. Nonetheless, the main reason for their suspicious and perpetual anger at him was doubtless the one I spoke of earlier, that is, the preconceived notion of a great many Serbs that if the Slavs are to be liberated by the Russians, then it would be for Russia's benefit alone; Russia would annex them and deprive them of their "so glorious and certain political future." As we know, they decided to declare war on Turkey even before Cherniaev's arrival, hoping precisely that after they assumed leadership of the Slavic movement and vanquished the Sultan, they could form a united Slavic Serbian kingdom of several million people "with so glorious a future." The large Serbian party, which is influential in its own lands, dreamed only of this. In short, they were dreamers, very like small seven-year-old children who put on toy epaulets and imagine themselves generals. Cherniaev and the volunteers, of course, must naturally have alarmed the *party* "by the future annexation by Russia which was to come in their wake." And now, no doubt, after the recent military misfortunes, there will begin (and already has begun) even more bitter wrangling. All of these dreamers will begin privately, and perhaps publicly as well, to disparage the Russians and to affirm that the whole misfortune arose because of the Russians. . . . But a little time will pass and a reaction will ensue to set things right; for all these Serbs who are now so suspicious are ardent patriots just the same. They will recall the Russian dead who gave their lives for Serbia. The Russians will leave, but the great idea will remain. The great Russian spirit will leave its traces in their souls, and their own Serbian valor will spring up from the Russian blood that was shed for them. Someday, after all, they will satisfy themselves that the Russian help was selfless and that none of the Russians who died for them was thinking of annexation!

But still, this should not cause a rift between us and the Slavs. There are two Serbias: the upper Serbia, proud and inexperienced, which still has not lived and acted, but which has passionate dreams about the future, beset with parties and intrigues which (again, as a result of rash inexperience) can go to lengths one will not find among long-lived, far larger, and more independent nations than Serbia. But along with this upper Serbia, which is so eager to live politically, there is the Serbia of the people, which considers the Russians alone as their saviors and brethren and the Russian tsar as their sun; this is the Serbia that loves and trusts the Russians. It is impossible to express a view on this subject better than did the *Moscow News*, which is unquestionably our finest political newspaper. Its words are as follows:

> We are certain that the feelings of the Russian People toward Serbia will not be altered by the success of the intrigues which were harmful to both sides. . . . The Serbs of the Duchy are a peaceful, agricultural people who, in the course of a long peace, have managed to forget their military traditions and have not managed to elaborate in their place the firm national consciousness that binds every historical nation. Finally, the Serbs of the Duchy cannot be called a nation: they are only the fragment of a nation that has no organic significance. But we cannot forget that the Serbs rose up with enthusiasm and unanimity to help their blood brethren who were being villainously tortured. . . . The Russian People will not abandon the Serbs at this terrible moment; the blood of Russian People has shown how pure was their sympathy, how heroically selfless was their sacrifice, and how senseless were the hostile calumnies of Russia's supposed desire to derive some benefit for herself out of Serbia's dilemma. May the memory of the valorous Russians who fell for Serbia serve as a link of brotherly love between two nations, so similar in blood and in faith.

I will say in conclusion: granted that this summer we Russians have suffered, apart from all the *disorders* (?), even material losses and have already expended, perhaps, some tens of millions (which, however, went to organize and improve our army—also a good thing, of course), still, the fact alone that this year's movement has shown us who our *best people* are—that alone is an achievement beyond compare. Oh, if only all nations, even the most advanced and intelligent in Europe, could know certainly and agree unanimously on whom to consider their truly best people—would Europe and European humanity appear as they do today?

3. The Best People

The best people—this is a topic that merits a few words of comment. These are people without whom no society and no nation can live

or endure, even given the broadest equality of rights. *The best people*
are, naturally, of two kinds: (1) those to whom the people themselves and the nation itself pay reverence voluntarily, recognizing
their genuine valor; and (2) those to whom all or very many of the
people or the nation pay reverence through a certain compulsion,
one might say, and even if they do consider them their "best
people," they do so rather as a matter of convention and not completely and genuinely. One can't complain about the existence of
this "conventional" category of best people who are, so to say,
"officially" recognized as the best because of the higher considerations of order and administrative stability: the "best people" of
this sort arise through a historical law, and they have always existed,
in all nations and states, from the beginning of the world, so that
no society could organize and bind itself into a whole without a
certain amount of such voluntary compulsion. In order to maintain
itself and live, every society must necessarily respect someone and
something and—most important—this must be done by society as
a whole, not by each individual choosing for himself. The best
people of the first category—the truly valorous, to whom everyone
or the vast majority of the nation pays sincere and genuine reverence—are sometimes rather elusive, because even the ideal people
are often difficult to define and have peculiarities and odd habits,
while outwardly they very often have even a somewhat disreputable
air. Because of that, a group of "best people" are *conventionally*
set up in their place, forming, so to say, a caste of best people
having official support: "These," the nation is told, "are the people
you must respect." And if, when this occurs, these "conventional"
ones actually coincide with the best people of the first category
(because not all of those in the first category have a disreputable
air) and are also truly valorous, then the aim is not only fully but
doubly achieved. In Russia in the earliest times such best people
were the prince's bodyguard; later there were the boyars, the clergy
(but only the highest of them), and even certain well-known merchants; although there were very few of the latter. I should note
that these best people, in Russia and elsewhere (I mean in Europe)
eventually always elaborated a rather formalized code of valor and
honor; and although this code as a whole was, of course, always
rather arbitrary and sometimes differed sharply from popular ideals,
some aspects of it were quite high-minded. The "best" person was
always obliged to die for his country, for example, if such a sacrifice

were demanded of him; and he indeed would die as bound by honor, "lest great injury be done to the good name of my family." And of course this was far better than the right to dishonor, by which a person abandons everything and everyone in a moment of danger and runs off and hides, saying "let the whole world perish so long as my life is secure." This was how it was in Russia for a very long time; and I should point out once more that in Russia these "official" best people very, very often shared very many of the ideals of the unofficial or popular best people. Of course, this was certainly not true in all respects, but at least one can confidently say that at that time the Russian boyars and the Russian People had much more in common morally than the conqueror tyrants in most of Europe—the knights—had with their conquered slaves— the people.

But suddenly there appeared a radical change in the organization of our best people as well: by decree of the state, all the best people were sorted out into fourteen categories called classes, one higher than the other in a kind of staircase, so that we had precisely fourteen categories of human valor, each with a German name. This change, as it developed further, did not fully manage to achieve the purpose for which it was originally set up, for the former "best people" themselves at once filled all these fourteen new categories; they simply began to be called aristocracy instead of boyars. But this change did achieve its aim in part because it considerably expanded the limits of the old barriers. There came an influx of fresh forces from the depths of society—democratic forces, by our terminology—and from the ranks of the seminarians in particular. This influx brought much that was vivifying and productive into the group of best people, for there appeared people with talents, with new outlooks, and with education that was unprecedented at the time; but at the same time they had tremendous scorn for their own origins and avidly hastened to transform themselves, by means of the table of ranks, as quickly as possible into pure-blooded aristocrats. I should point out that, aside from the seminarians, only a very few from the People and the merchants, for instance, managed to make their way into the category of "the best people"; the aristocracy continued to stand at the head of the nation. This category was always strongly organized; and whereas money, property, the sack of gold already held sway all over Europe and were considered quite sincerely as all that was valorous and all that was

best in people and among people, in Russia—and this is still in
living memory—a general, for instance, was so highly regarded
that even the richest merchant considered it a great honor to lure
one into his home for dinner. Only recently I read an anecdote—
which I would not have believed had I not known that it was
absolutely true—about a certain Petersburg lady from a circle of
the very highest class who publicly forced a merchant-lady worth
ten million to give up her seat at a concert, took her place, and
gave her a proper scolding in the bargain; and this was only some
thirty years ago! One must also point out, however, that these
"best" people who settled themselves in place so solidly also set
up some very fine rules to live by—the virtual *obligation* to acquire
some education, for example—so that this whole caste of best people
at the same time made up the bulk of Russia's educated class, the
guardian and the bearer of Russian enlightenment, such as it was
then. It goes without saying that this class was also the only guardian and bearer of the code of honor, but entirely on the European
model, so that the letter and the form of the code at last entirely
overcame any genuine feeling in its content: there was a lot of
honor, but ultimately there were not such a lot of honorable people.
During this period, and particularly at its end, the class of "best
people" had already grown far away from the People and their
ideals of what was "best"; in fact, there was open mockery of
almost everything the People considered "best." But suddenly there
occurred one of the most colossal revolutions Russia had ever experienced: serfdom was abolished and everything changed profoundly. It is true that all fourteen classes remained as they were,
but the "best people" seemed to falter. Their former influence over
the mass of society seemed to disappear; the views on what was
"best" seemed somehow to change. It's true that they did not
change for the better in entirety; moreover, something extremely
confusing and ambiguous began to happen to the conception of
"best." Nevertheless, the old view was no longer satisfactory, giving
rise to most serious questions in the minds of very many: "Whom
can we now consider our *best* people? Most important, where shall
we find them? Who will take the responsibility for proclaiming
them the best, and on what basis? Does someone need to take this
responsibility? And finally, do we know what this new basis is?
Will anyone accept that this is the proper basis on which we must
build so much anew?" Truly, these questions arose in the minds
of very many people....

4. On the Same Topic

The whole point was that the shield of authority, as it were, was removed from the former "best people"; their official status was somehow canceled. And so, in the first instance, there was some comfort in the fact that the former caste pattern of "best people," although not utterly destroyed, at least was forced to yield considerably and broaden itself so that each one of them, if he wished to maintain his former significance, was forced willy-nilly to move from the category of "conventionally best people" into the category of "naturally best people." There dawned the beautiful hope that, little by little, the latter would occupy all the places of the former "best people." How all this was to take place remained a mystery, of course. But for many people—very honorable, but hot-blooded and liberal—there was no mystery at all. For them everything was already resolved as though by decree; some among them even thought that everything had already been achieved and that if the "natural" man had still not taken first place today, then tomorrow, just as soon as it brightened a bit, he certainly would take his place. . . . Meanwhile, more thoughtful people had not stopped raising questions on the old topic: "Just who are they, these natural people? Does anyone know what they're called these days? Haven't they, perhaps, lost their ideals altogether? Where do we find this commonly acknowledged 'best person?' To what and whom should our whole society pay honor and whom should we choose as a model?"

All these things, perhaps, were not repeated literally in these terms, nor exactly in the form of these questions; however, there is no doubt that our society experienced all this tumult in one form or another. Fiery people, full of rapture, cried out to the skeptics that the "new man" exists, has been discovered, defined, and given. They decided, at last, that this new, "best" man is simply the enlightened man, the man of science *without the old prejudices*. There were many, though, who could not accept this view for one very simple reason: the educated man is not always the honest man, and knowledge still does not ensure valor in a man. At that moment of general indecision and uncertainty, some were ready to suggest that perhaps it was time to turn to the People and their principles. But there were so many who had long found the expression "the People's principles" repellent and hateful; besides, the People themselves, after their liberation, seemed in no particular hurry to display their valor, so that it seemed a dubious proposition to go off seeking answers to such questions among them. The contrary seemed to be the case: there were reports of disorder, depravity, rotgut vodka, unsuccessful attempts at self-government; about kulaks and exploiters who had taken the place of the former landowners; finally, there were reports of the Yids. Even the most artful writers proclaimed that the kulak and the exploiter held sway over the People, and the People, in the bargain, were accepting them as their genuine "best" people. There appeared, finally, even one view, absolutely liberal in the highest sense, that our People now *cannot be* competent to create the ideal of the best person; in fact, they are not only incompetent, they are even incapable of taking part in this glorious affair; they must first be taught to read and write, to be educated and developed; schools must be built, etc., etc. We have to admit that very many of the skeptics found themselves at a loss and had no answer to this. . . .

And meanwhile a new storm was brewing and a new disaster was looming—"the money bag!" In the place of the former "conventional" best people there appeared a new *convention* that almost immediately assumed a most terrible significance among us. Oh, of course we had had the money bag earlier as well; it always existed in the person of the former merchant-millionaire; but never was it elevated to such a status and given such significance as in our recent history. Our old-style merchant, despite the role that a million in capital played everywhere in Europe, had a relatively modest place in the social hierarchy. Truth to tell, he did not deserve any better. Let me stipulate beforehand: I am speaking only of the truly wealthy merchants; most of them, who had not yet been corrupted by wealth, lived in the same fashion as Ostrovsky's characters. These, perhaps, were no worse than many others, at least if one speaks in relative terms, while the lowest and most numerous merchants were almost on the same level as the People. But the more wealth our old-style merchant acquired, the worse he became. In essence, he was just as much a peasant as before, only a depraved peasant. The old-style millionaire merchants were divided into two categories: those who continued to wear beards, despite their millions, and who, despite the mirrors and parquet floors in their enormous houses, lived rather swinishly, in both a moral and a physical sense. The best thing about them was their love for church bells and powerfully voiced deacons. Despite this love, they had already split away entirely from the People in a moral sense. It is difficult to imagine anything less compatible morally than the People and some millionaire factory owner. I have heard that when Ovsiannikov was recently transported to Siberia by way of Kazan, he kicked aside the kopecks which the People naively tossed into his carriage: that in itself is the ultimate degree of moral alienation from the People, the loss of even the slightest comprehension of the People's thought and spirit. And the People have never endured such servitude as they do in the factories of some of these gentlemen! The other category of millionaire merchants was marked by their dress coats and shaven chins, by the splendid European furnishings of their houses, by the education of their daughters in French and English and music, often by the orders they were awarded for large donations, by their insufferable scorn for everyone a bit lower than themselves, by their contempt for the ordinary "dinnertime" general and at the same time by the most abjectly servile attitude toward any important dignitary, especially if the merchant managed—through God knows what sort of scheming and striving—to entice such a dignitary to his house for a ball or a dinner arranged, of course, especially for that dignitary. These attempts to give a dinner for some personage became a whole program of life. This was something avidly sought after; the millionaire spent his time on earth almost for that alone. It goes without saying that this old-style wealthy merchant prayed to his million as to a god: the million was everything in his eyes; the million pulled him up from insignificance and gave him his entire meaning. In the coarse soul of this "corrupted peasant" (since that was what he continued to be, despite all his dress coats), there could never arise a single thought or a single feeling which even for a moment could raise his consciousness above that million of his. It goes without saying that, despite their superficial polish, the whole family of such a merchant was raised without any education. The million not only did not promote education, it had the contrary effect and served as the principal cause of ignorance: what point was there for the son of a millionaire to go to university when he could get everything without studying at all, the more so that when all these millionairelings got their million they very often acquired the rights of noblemen. Wealth brought nothing into the soul of such a carnivorous and arrogant youth except for a life of dissipation from his tenderest youth and the most distorted notions of his world, his native land, his honor, and his duty. And the distortion of his notion of the world was monstrous, for over everything loomed the conviction, which had been transformed into an axiom, that "I can get anything for money—any distinction, any valor; I can buy anyone and buy my way out of anything." It is difficult to imagine the barrenness of the heart of a youth brought up in such a wealthy home. From conceit, and so as to be no worse than others, such a millionaire might, perhaps, sometimes donate immense sums for the good of his country—in times when it was in danger, for example (although the only time this happened was in 1812); but he made his donation with some reward in mind and was prepared at every moment of his existence to join forces with the first Yid who came along in order to betray everyone and everything so long as he could make a profit from doing so; patriotism and civic feeling are all but absent from these hearts.

Oh, of course I'm speaking about our Russian commercial millionaire only as a caste. There are exceptions everywhere and always. One can also point out merchants here in Russia who were noted for their European education and valiant public accomplishments; still, there were very few of them among our millionaires, and they are well known; the caste doesn't lose its character because of a few exceptions.

And now the former limits of the old-style merchant have suddenly expanded enormously. He has been joined by the European-style speculator, previously unknown in Russia, and the stock-exchange gambler. The contemporary merchant no longer needs to lure a "personage" to his house for dinner or give a ball for him; he already has become his kinsman and rubs elbows with him at the stock exchange or a shareholders' meeting or at a bank which he and the personage establish; he himself is now a somebody, a personage. The main thing is that he has suddenly found himself in one of the highest places in society, the very place which the whole of Europe—officially and quite genuinely—has assigned to the millionaire. He, of course, never doubted for a moment that he was truly worthy of such a place. In short, he is now becoming more and more convinced, from the bottom of his heart, that it is now he who is the "best" person on earth and that he has taken the place of all who preceded him. The calamity that threatens lies not in the fact that he believes such nonsense but that others as well (and many of them), it seems, are beginning to believe just the same thing. The money bag is seen now by a *terrible* majority to be the best thing of all. Of course, there will be those who try to dismiss such fears. Yet the actual worship of the money bag today is not merely indisputable; the sudden expansion of that worship is unprecedented. I repeat: we understood the power of the money bag before as well, but never in Russia until now was the money bag regarded as the worthiest thing on earth. In the official classification of Russians the old-style merchant's money bag could not displace even a bureaucrat in the social hierarchy. But now, even the former hierarchy seems ready, without even any outside compulsion, to take second place to such a gracious and fine new "conventional" best person who "so long and so unjustly did not assume his proper rights." Today's stock-exchange gambler hires literary men to serve him; lawyers hover around him: "this young school of agile minds and arid hearts; a school in which every healthy feeling is distorted when the occasion demands distortion; a school that teaches every possible method of personal attack, done without fear of punishment, continually and unrelentingly, based on need and demand"—this young school has fallen into complete harmony with today's stock-exchange gambler and has begun to sing his praises. Oh, please don't think that I'm hinting at the Strusberg affair. The lawyers who proclaimed their clients who "happened" to get involved in the case to be ideal people, and who sang them a hymn as "the best people in Moscow" (exactly in this line), have only missed their mark. They have demonstrated that it is they who lack not only the slightest serious conviction but are even lacking restraint or sense of measure; and if it is they who are playing the role of the "European talents" in our midst, then it is only because we have nothing better. In actual fact they, like diplomats, have demanded as high a price as possible so as to obtain the best possible minimum: "Not only are they innocent, they are holy!" Word has it that on one occasion the spectators in court even hissed them. But a lawyer is certainly not a diplomat; this comparison is false in its very essence. It would be more correct, far more correct, to point to the client and ask the question of the Gospel: "Gentlemen of the jury, which of you is without sin?" Oh, I am not speaking out against the verdict: the verdict is just, and I accept it fully; it should have been pronounced, if only on the bank. The case was of just such a nature that to convict by "the public conscience" this unfortunate Moscow Loan Bank, which just "happened" to become involved, meant at the same time to convict all our banks, and the whole stock exchange, and all the gamblers on the exchange, even though they have not yet been caught—does it really make any difference? Which one of them is without sin, without that very same sin—tell me truly, which one? Someone has already written that the punishment was mild. I must make it plain that I am not referring to Landau; he is truly guilty of an unusual crime, and I don't wish to go into that. But Danila Shumakher, convicted of petty swindling, received a terrible punishment. Let us look into our own hearts: are there many among us who would not have done the same as he did? You needn't confess out loud, but simply think about it privately. But long live Justice! Didn't we pack them off to jail, though! "Take that," we say, "for our depraved and plutocratic age; take that for our own egotism; take that for our base, materialistic views of the joys and delights of life, for our barren and treacherous feeling of self-preservation!" Say what you will, it's useful to convict even one bank for our own sins. . . .

My Lord, haven't I wandered off the topic! Can I, too, be writing about the Strusberg case? Enough! I'll hurry and finish. I was speaking about "the best person" and wanted only to make the point that the ideal of the genuine best person, even one of the "natural" type, stands in real danger of being obscured in our society. The old has been shattered or has worn out, the new is still soaring in the heights of fantasy, while in actuality and before our very eyes there has appeared something repulsive, an unprecedented development in Holy Russia. The fascination that people have ascribed to this new force—the bag of gold—begins to inspire in some hearts (hearts that are all too suspicious) even fear for the People, for instance. We, the upper levels of society, let's say, though we might be seduced by this new idol, still have not been utterly lost: it was not in vain that the torch of education shone over us for two hundred years. We have the mighty weapon of enlightenment; we can repel this monster. At a moment of the filthiest financial debauchery did we not send the Moscow Loan Bank off to jail? But the People, all hundred million of our People, this "sluggish, depraved, insensate mass" into which the Yid has already penetrated—what will they use to withstand the monster of materialism, in the form of the bag of gold, that is moving upon them? Will they use their poverty? Their rags? Their taxes and their failed harvests? Their vices, their rotgut vodka, their flogging? We feared that the People would at once collapse before the growing power of the bag of gold and that a generation would not pass before they would become enslaved to it far worse than they were enslaved before. We feared that their submission would not only of cases like his! Well, had anyone told us before—in the winter, for example—that such a thing would happen here, we would never have believed him; we would never have believed in this "crusade," whose beginning is plain to see (but whose end is far from visible). Even now, though we can plainly see what is happening, we cannot help but ask ourselves at times: "How on earth could this happen? How could such an unforeseen thing as this occur?" The Russian land has proclaimed for all to hear everything that it reveres and in which it believes; it has shown what it considers "best" and which people it regards as "the best." And it is the question of the kind of people these are and the kind of ideals that have been revealed which I am postponing until my next *Diary*. In essence, these ideals and these "best people" are clear and evident from the first glance: "the best person" in the conception of the People is the one who does not give in to material temptation; he is the one who continually seeks to work for God's cause, who loves the truth, and who, when it is necessary, rises up to serve that truth, leaving his home and his family and sacrificing his life. I wanted to state specifically why we, the educated classes, may trust boldly and firmly that not only is the image of the "best man" not lost in our Russia but, on the contrary, this image has shone forth more brightly than ever before; that those who provide it, guard it, and bear it are now those same simple Russian People whom we, in our enlightened pride and, at the same time, our naive ignorance, were wont to consider "incompetent." I particularly wanted to take up the question of how the requirements and demands of our enlightenment could even now be brought fully into accord with the People's notion of "the best person," despite the obviously simple and naive forms in which that notion is expressed. It is not the form that is important, but its content (even though the form is beautiful). The content, though, is beyond dispute. And that is why we can joyously allow ourselves to hope anew: our horizon has cleared, and our new sun rises with dazzling brilliance. . . . And if it were only possible that we could all agree and join the People in their understanding of whom we henceforth must consider our "best" person, then, perhaps, this past summer could mark the beginning of a new era in Russian history.

be from compulsion but would be moral as well, with their e
will. We feared that it would be precisely the People, before an
else, who would say: "This is the most important thing; th
where power, peace, and happiness are to be found! This is
we shall worship and follow." That's what was to be truly dre
at least for a long time. Many of us fell to thinking
suddenly. . . .

But what it was that *suddenly* happened last summer I sh
about in the next issue of my *Diary*. I'd like to talk about
no "humor," straight from my heart and *in plain fashion*
happened this past summer was so touching and hearten
it is even difficult to believe. It is difficult to believe bec
had already lost faith in these People of ours and consider
grossly incompetent to express their own opinion on the
of who ought to be the Russian "best man." We had tho
the entire organism of this People was already infected by
and spiritual corruption; we had thought that the People ha
forgotten their spiritual principles and were no longer p
them in their hearts; that in their destitution and depr
had lost or distorted their ideals. And suddenly, this e
mogeneous and torpid mass" (this, of course, being t
some of our clever thinkers), whose hundred millior
sprawled, silent and unbreathing, over thousands of n
land in a state of eternal genesis and apparently eterna
to say or do anything, appearing as something eternall
and submissive—suddenly this entire Russia awakens
humbly but firmly expresses its splendid opinion t
nation. . . . Moreover, Russian people take up their s
off in crowds a hundred strong, accompanied by
people, on some sort of new crusade (and that is p
this movement is being called; it was the English w
pared this Russian movement of ours to a crusade)
the sake of some of their brethren, because they ha
their brethren were being tortured and oppressed. A
soldier—instead of living at his ease, suddenly take
sets off on foot for thousands of miles, asking direc
way, to go fight the Turks and support his brethre
his nine-year-old daughter along with him (this is a
be good Christians to be found who'll look after my
I'm off wandering." And off he goes. . . . And the

November

1

The Meek One: A Fantastic Story

Author's Foreword

I apologize to my readers for providing, in place of my *Diary* in its usual form, merely a story this time. However, I truly have been working on this story for the better part of a month. In any case, I beg the indulgence of my readers.

Now, a few words about the story itself. I called it "fantastic," even though I consider it to be realistic to the highest degree. But it truly does contain something fantastic, which is the form of the story itself, and it is this which I find necessary to explain beforehand.

The fact is, this is neither a story nor a memoir. Imagine a husband whose wife only a few hours earlier has killed herself by jumping out a window; her body now lies on the table before him. He is in a state of bewilderment and still has not managed to collect his thoughts. He paces through the apartment, trying to make sense of what has happened, to "focus his thoughts." He is, as well, an out-an-out hypochondriac, the sort who talks to himself. And so he is talking to himself, telling the story, and trying to *make it clear* to himself. Despite the apparent coherence of his speech, he contradicts himself several times, both logically and emotionally. At times he justifies himself and blames her, then he launches into explanations of things which have little to do with the case: we see here the crudity of his thoughts and spirit, and we see deep feeling as well. Little by little he really does *make it clear* and "focus his thoughts." The series of memories he has evoked irresistibly leads him at last to *truth*; and truth irresistibly elevates his mind and his spirit. By the end, even the tone of the story changes as compared with its confused beginning. The truth is revealed quite clearly and distinctly to the unhappy man—at least as far as he is concerned.

That is the subject. Of course, the process of the narrative goes on for a few hours, with breaks and interludes and in a confused and inconsistent form: at one point he talks to himself; then he seems to be addressing an invisible listener, a judge of some sort. But so it always happens in real life. If a stenographer had been able to eavesdrop and write down everything he said, it would be somewhat rougher and less finished than I have it here; still, it seems to me that the psychological structure would perhaps be just the same. And so it is this assumption of a stenographer recording everything (and whose account I simply polished) that I call the fantastic element of my story. Yet something quite similar to this has already been employed more than once in art: Victor Hugo, for example, in his masterpiece *The Last Day of a Man Condemned to Death*, employed virtually this same device, and even though he did not depict any stenographer, he allowed an even greater breach of verisimilitude when he presumed that a man condemned to execution could (and would have time to) keep a diary, not only on his last day, but even in his last hour and literally in his last moment of life. But had he not allowed this fantastical element, the work itself—among the most real and most truthful of all his writings—would not have existed.

1. Who Was I and Who Was She?

. . . So as long as she's still here everything's all right: every minute I go up to have a look at her; but they'll take her away tomorrow, and how will I ever stay here by myself? She's on the table in the anteroom now, they put two card tables together, but tomorrow there'll be a coffin, a white one—white *gros de Naples*. That's not the point, though. . . . I just keep walking, trying to find some explanation for this. It's been six hours now, and I still can't focus my thoughts. The fact is that I just keep on walking, back and forth, back and forth. . . . This is how it happened. I'll just tell it in order. (Order!) Gentlemen, I'm certainly not a literary man, and you'll see that for yourselves; but never mind: I'll tell you what happened as I understand it myself. That's what I find so horrible: I understand it all!

If you really want to know—I mean, if I'm going to start from the very beginning—then it was she who just started coming to me then to pawn some things in order to pay for an advertisement in *The Voice*: "So-and-so, a governess, willing to travel, give lessons in private homes, etc., etc." That was at the very beginning, and I, of course, didn't see her as any different from the others. She came like all the rest, and so on. And then I did begin to see something different about her. She was so delicate and blonde, a little taller than average; she was always a little awkward with me, as if she were embarrassed (I suppose she was the same with all strangers, and of course to her I was no different from anyone else, I mean if you take me as a man and not as a pawnbroker). As soon as she got her money she would turn around and leave at once. And never a word. The others would argue, plead, try to haggle. Not this one, she'd just take what I offered. . . . Wait now, I think I'm getting confused. . . . Yes. What struck me first were the things she brought: cheap silver-plated earrings, a trashy little locket—twenty kopecks was all she'd get. And she herself knew they were worth next to nothing, but I could tell by her face that to her they were treasures. And sure enough, as I learned later, these were the only things she had left from mommy and daddy. Only once I allowed myself a little smirk at her things. You see, I never allow myself to do anything like that. I maintain a gentlemanly tone with my clients: keep it short, keep it polite, and be strict. "Strict, strict, strict." But one day, to my surprise, she actually brought in the remnants (I mean, literally) of an old hareskin jacket. I couldn't help myself and made a joke of sorts about it. Heavens, how she flushed! She had big, blue, wistful eyes, but there was fire in them then! She didn't say a word, though. Just took up her "remnants" and left. It was then that I *particularly* noticed her for the first time and thought something of this sort about her—I mean something quite particular. Oh yes, and I also recall an impression. What I mean is the main impression, the synthesis of everything: she seemed terribly young, so young she might have been fourteen. Whereas in actual fact she was only a few months short of sixteen. But that's not what I meant; that certainly wasn't the synthesis. She came back again the next day. I found out later that she had gone to gone to Dobronravov's and to Moser's with this jacket, but neither of them takes anything but gold, so they wouldn't even talk to her. I, on the other hand, had once taken a cameo from her (a cheap little thing), but later, when

I had thought about it for a while, I was surprised. You see, I don't accept anything but gold and silver either, yet I allowed her to pawn a cameo. And that was my second thought about her at the time; that I remember.

This time—I mean after she had come from Moser—she brought an amber cigar-holder. It wasn't much of a thing, amateurish workmanship, and again, worthless to me because I only accept gold. Since this was right after her little *rebellion* of the previous day, I was strict with her. With me, being strict means being curt. However, as I was handing her the two rubles, I couldn't resist and said, as if somewhat irritated: "You know I'm only doing this *for you*; Moser wouldn't take a thing like this." I particularly stressed the words "for you," and did so deliberately, to give them *a certain implication*. I was angry. She flushed again when she heard the "for you," but she didn't say a word, didn't throw down the money; she took it. Well, that's what poverty is! How she flushed, though! I realized that I had stung her. And when she had gone I suddenly asked myself: "Is this victory over her really worth two rubles? Hee-hee-hee!" I recall that I asked myself that very question twice: "Is it worth it? Is it worth it?" And with a laugh I answered the question in the affirmative. I had tremendous fun at the time. But it wasn't a bad feeling on my part: I had something in mind; there was a purpose to what I was doing. I wanted to test her, because certain ideas about her suddenly began floating around in my mind. This was my third *particular* thought about her.

. . . Well, it all began from that time. Of course, I immediately tried to find out everything about her indirectly, and I waited with particular impatience for her to come again. You see, I had a feeling she would come soon. When she did come, I began a friendly conversation, was as polite as could be. I've not been badly brought up, after all, and have good manners. Hmm. It was just then that I realized she was kind and meek. Kind, meek people don't resist for long, and though they don't open themselves very easily, they still just don't know how to duck out of a conversation: they may not give you much of an answer, but they do answer, and the further you go, the more you get out of them. Only you mustn't let up if there's something you want. Of course, she didn't explain anything at that time. It was only later that I found out about *The Voice* and all the rest. At that time she was using her last resources on advertisements, and of course these were a bit presumptuous, at least at first: "Governess, willing to travel. Submit offers by

return mail." But later: "Willing to accept any work: teach, serve
as companion, manage household, nurse an invalid lady; have sewing skills" and so on—you know what it is! Of course, all these
latter things were added to the advertisements bit by bit, while at
last, when she had reached the point of despair, they would read:
"Willing to work without salary, for board alone." No, she couldn't
find a position! I decided then to give her a final test: I suddenly
picked up the latest issue of *The Voice* and showed her an ad:
"Young lady, orphaned, seeks position as governess to young children, preferably with elderly widower. Can provide comforts in the
home."

"There, you see, this girl's placed her ad this morning, and by
evening she'll surely have found a position. That's how to write
an ad!"

She flushed again, and again her eyes flashed; she turned and
walked out at once. I was very pleased. However, at that time I
was already certain of everything and wasn't the least bit concerned:
no one else was going to take her cigar-holders. But she had used
up even her cigar-holders. And so it was that she came in two days
later, so pale and upset—I realized that something must have happened at home, and something really had happened. I'll explain
in a minute what it was, but now I only want to recall how I
managed to show her a bit of style and raise myself in her esteem.
Suddenly this plan popped into my head. The fact was that she
had brought this icon (she had at last made up her mind to bring
it).... Oh, but listen to me! It had already begun then, and I'm
getting things mixed up.... The point is that now I want to bring
it all back in my mind, every little thing about it, every tiny detail.
I just want to focus my thoughts and I can't, and all these tiny
details....

It was an image of the Virgin Mary. The Virgin with the Infant
Jesus—an ancient, family household icon in a silver, gilded frame,
worth, maybe, six rubles. I could see that the icon meant a lot to
her, and she was pawning it all, frame included.

"Wouldn't it be better to remove the frame and take back the
icon?" I said. "It's an icon, after all, and somehow it seems not
quite the thing to do...."

"Is it against the rules to take an icon?"

"No, it's not against the rules, but still, you yourself,
perhaps...."

"Well, take off the frame."

"I'll tell you what," I said, after a little thought, "We'll keep it in the frame; I'll put it over there in the icon case with my others, under the lamp" (ever since I opened my pawnshop I've kept an icon lamp burning), "and I'll just give you ten rubles for it."

"I don't need ten. Just give me five, and I'll certainly redeem it."

"You don't want ten? The icon's worth that much," I added, noticing that her eyes again were flashing. She said nothing. I brought her the five rubles.

"Don't despise me," I said. "I've been in a similar bind myself, and even worse. And if you see me now, working at a profession like this . . . it's just the result of all that I've been through. . . ."

"You're taking revenge on society? Is that it?" she interrupted suddenly, with a rather sarcastic smile which, however, contained a good deal of innocence (I mean her sarcasm was general and not directed at me personally, because at that time she did not see me as any different from the others, so she said it almost without malice). "Aha!" —I thought to myself. "That tells me something about you! You're showing your character. One of the new generation."

"You see," I remarked, half in jest, half mysteriously, "'I am a part of that whole that wills forever evil but does forever good. . . .'"

She cast a quick glance at me, showing great interest (and also a good deal of childish curiosity).

"Wait. . . . What does that mean? Where does it come from? I've heard it somewhere. . . ."

"You needn't rack your brain; Mephistopheles introduces himself to Faust with those words. Have you read *Faust*?"

"Not . . . not very carefully."

"In other words, you haven't read it at all. You must read it. But I can see that sarcastic smile again. Please, don't assume I have so little taste as to embellish my role as a pawnbroker by passing myself off as Mephistopheles. A pawnbroker is a pawnbroker, and so he shall remain. We all know that."

"You are a strange sort of person. . . . I didn't mean to imply anything of the kind. . . ."

She meant to say, "I never expected you to be a man of education," but she didn't say it, although I knew that she thought it. I had pleased her immensely.

"You see," I remarked, "one can do good in any field of endeavor.

I'm not speaking of myself, of course. Quite possibly I do nothing but evil, but. . . ."

"Of course one can do good in any place in life," she said, casting a swift and penetrating glance at me. "In any place, to be sure," she added suddenly.

Oh, I recall it; I recall all those moments! And I want also to add that when young people, those dear young people, want to say something very clever and profound they suddenly, with excessive sincerity and naiveté, put on a face that says: "There! Now I'm telling you something very clever and profound." And they do it not from vanity, as people like myself might. But you can see that they themselves put great store in all that; they believe in it and respect it, and think that you have the same respect as they do. Oh, the candor of youth! That is how they conquer. And in her it was so charming!

I remember it, I've forgotten nothing! When she left I at once made my decision. That same day I went off on my final investigation and learned the remaining facts about her, right down to the most intimate details of her current life. I had learned her earlier history from Lukeria, who was then their servant and whom I had bribed several days before. These details were so terrible that I simply cannot understand how she was able to laugh, as she had just now, and to take any interest in the words of Mephistopheles when she herself had to face such horrors. But such is youth! That was just how I thought of her then, proudly and joyfully, because here I could also see the signs of a great soul. It was as if she were saying: "Even on the very edge of perdition, the great words of Goethe shine out for me." Young people always have some greatness of soul—to a tiny degree, at least and perhaps in the wrong direction. I am speaking of her, I mean, of her alone. And the main thing was that I regarded her then as *my own* and had no doubt about my power over her. Do you know, that is a terribly voluptuous thought—when one no longer has any doubts.

But what's wrong with me? If I go on this way, when will I ever focus my thoughts? I must get on with it! Lord, this isn't the point at all!

2. A Proposal of Marriage

"The intimate details" I discovered about her I can explain in a few words: her father and mother had died some time ago, three

years before I met her, and she had been left in the charge of some
aunts whose way of life was rather improper; in fact, "improper"
is not a strong enough word to describe them. One aunt was a
widow with a large family—six little children, all close in age; the
other aunt, a spinster, was a nasty old piece of work. They were
both nasty, in fact. Her father had been a minor civil servant, a
copying clerk who had only personal, but not hereditary, nobility.
In short, the whole situation suited me to a tee. I appeared as if
from another, higher world: I was still a retired junior captain from
a renowned regiment, a nobleman by birth, of independent means,
and so on, and as far as the pawnshop was concerned, the aunts
could only look upon that with respect. She had been enslaved to
the aunts for three years, but still had managed to qualify at some
sort of examination; she had managed to qualify, snatching moments from her merciless daily labor, and that signified something
of her striving for what was sublime and noble! And why did I
want to marry her? However, let's forget about me for the moment;
that will come later. . . . As if that mattered, in any case! She gave
lessons to her aunt's children, sewed their underclothes, and, in
the end, not only washed clothes but, with her weak chest, scrubbed
floors as well. To put it plainly, they even beat her and reproached
her for every crust of bread. It ended by their planning to sell her.
Foo! I'm omitting the sordid details. Later she told me the whole
story. A fat shopkeeper in the neighborhood had watched the whole
thing for a year (he was not simply a shopkeeper, in fact, but owned
two grocery stores). He had already driven two wives to their graves
with his beatings, and now he was looking for a third. His eye fell
on her. "She's a quiet one," he thinks, "raised in poverty, and I'll
marry her for the sake of my motherless children." He had children,
to be sure. He started courting her and negotiating with the aunts.
On top of everything else, he was a man of fifty; she was horrified.
It was at this point that she started coming to me to get money
for the advertisements in *The Voice*. At last she began pleading
with the aunts to give her just a tiny bit of time to think the matter
over. They allowed her a little time, but only a little, and kept
nagging at her: "We don't know where our next meal is coming
from ourselves, never mind having an extra mouth to feed." I
already knew all about this, and during the day that followed our
morning encounter I made my decision. The shopkeeper called on
her in the evening, bringing a pound of sweets worth half a ruble
from his store. She was sitting with him, while I called Lukeria

from the kitchen and told her to go back and whisper that I was at the gate with something urgent to tell her. I was pleased with myself. On the whole, I was terribly pleased that whole day.

Right there at the gate, with Lukeria standing by, I explained to her (and she was still amazed at my sending for her) that I would be happy and honored if. . . . In the second place, so that she shouldn't be surprised at the way I proposed to her right on the street, I told her, "I'm a straightforward man, and I know the circumstances of your case." And I wasn't lying when I said I was straightforward. Well, to hell with it; it doesn't matter. I spoke not only politely, that is, showing myself as a man with good manners, but also with originality, and that was the most important thing. Well, and what of it? Is it a sin to admit that? I want to judge myself and I am judging myself. I'm supposed to speak both *pro* and *contra*, and that's what I'm doing. Even afterward I would recall those moments with pleasure, as silly as it might have been. I told her plainly then, without any embarrassment, that in the first place I was not particularly talented or particularly clever, and, perhaps, not even particularly kind. I said I was a rather cheap egotist (I remember that expression; I made it up on the way to her house and was pleased with it) and that it was very likely that I had many other disagreeable qualities as well. All this was spoken with a particular kind of pride—you know how it is done. I had enough taste, of course, not to launch into listing all my virtues after having so nobly declared my shortcomings to her. I didn't say, "On the other hand, I am such-and-such." I could see that she was still terribly frightened, but I didn't tone down anything; in fact, seeing that she was frightened, I deliberately laid it on: I told her plainly that she would have enough food to eat, but there would be no fine dresses, theater, or balls. These might come at some future time when my goal had been achieved. I was quite carried away with this severe tone of mine. I added—doing my best to make it seem like a passing thought—that if I had taken up such an occupation (meaning the pawnshop), it was only because I had a certain goal, that there was one particular circumstance. . . . But I had the right to speak that way, after all: I really did have such a goal, and there really was such a circumstance. Wait a moment, ladies and gentlemen: I was the first to hate that pawnshop, and I hated it all my life. But you see, in essence (and even though it's ridiculous to talk to oneself in mysterious phrases), I was "taking my revenge on society," I really and truly was! So her little joke that morning about my "taking revenge" was unfair. You see, if I had told her directly: "Yes, I'm taking my revenge on society," she would have laughed as she did in the morning and it really would have turned out to seem amusing. But by making an indirect hint and slipping in a mysterious phrase, I was able to capture her imagination. Besides, at that time I wasn't afraid of anything: I knew that the fat shopkeeper was more repulsive to her than I in any case, and that I, standing by her gate, would appear as her liberator. That I certainly did understand. Oh, human beings understand nasty tricks very well! But was that a nasty trick? How can one pass judgment on a man in a case like this? Did I not love her already, even then?

Wait a moment: of course, I didn't say a single word to her then about my doing her a good deed. On the contrary, quite on the contrary: "It is *I*," I said, "who is the beneficiary here, and not you." So I even expressed this in words, unable to restrain myself, and perhaps it came out stupidly, because I noticed a wrinkle pass over her brow. But on the whole I won a decisive victory. Wait now, if I'm going to recall this whole sordid thing, then I'll recall it down to the last bit of nastiness: I stood there and a thought stirred in my mind: "You are tall, well-built, well-mannered, and finally—speaking without any boasting—you're not bad-looking either." That was what was running through my mind. I scarcely need to tell you that she said yes right there by the gate. But . . . but I ought to tell you as well that she stood there by the gate and thought for a long time before she said, "Yes." She thought so long and hard that I was about to ask her, "Well, what is your answer?" And indeed, I couldn't restrain myself and asked, with a little flourish but very politely, "Well, what is your answer, Miss?"

"Wait a moment, let me think."

And her little face was so serious, so serious that even then I might have read it! But I was mortified. "Can she really be choosing between me and the shopkeeper?" I thought. Oh, but I still didn't understand it then. I didn't understand anything then, not a thing. I didn't understand until today! I remember Lukeria running out after me as I was leaving, stopping me on the road and saying, all in a rush: "God will reward you, sir, for taking our dear miss! Only don't tell her that; she's such a proud one."

A proud one, indeed! "I like those proud ones," I thought. Proud women are especially beautiful when . . . well, when you have no more doubts about your power over them, isn't it so? Oh, you mean, clumsy man! Oh, how pleased I was! You know, when she was standing there by the gate, deep in thought about whether to answer yes, I was amazed, you know, that she could even be thinking such a thing as this: "If there's misery in store both here and there, then wouldn't it be better just to choose the worse—the fat shopkeeper—straightaway? Then he can beat me to death in a drunken fit." Eh! So what do you think, could she have had such a thought?

But even now I don't understand; I don't understand a thing! I just said that she might have had such a thought: to choose the worse of two evils, meaning the shopkeeper. But who was the worse for her then: the shopkeeper or I? A shopkeeper or a pawnbroker who quotes Goethe? That's still a question! What question? And you don't understand even that: the answer is lying on the table, and you're talking about a "question"! Well, to hell with me! I'm not the issue here at all.... And what do I care now, anyway, whether I'm the issue or not? That's something I certainly can't solve. I'd better go to bed. My head aches....

3. The Noblest of Men, but I Don't Believe It Myself

I couldn't get to sleep. Anyhow, how could I sleep with this throbbing in my head? I want to come to terms with all this, all this filth. Oh, the filth! Oh, the filth I rescued her from then! Why, she must have understood that and appreciated what I did! There were other ideas I savored as well. For example: I'm forty-one, and she's only sixteen. That was alluring, that feeling of inequality; a thing like that is delectable, very delectable.

I wanted to arrange our wedding *à l'anglaise*, meaning just the two of us with only two witnesses, one of whom would be Lukeria, and then straight off to the train, to Moscow, say (it happened that I had some business to do there), to a hotel for a couple of weeks. She was very much against that and wouldn't hear of it, and I had to go pay my respects to the aunts as her nearest relatives from whom I was taking her. I gave in, and the aunts were paid appropriate respect. I even presented the creatures with a hundred rubles each and promised them still more—not saying anything to her, of course, so as not to grieve her with sordid dealings like this. The aunts at once became as cordial as could be. There was also an argument about her trousseau: she had—almost literally—nothing, but she didn't want anything. However, I managed to show her that it simply wouldn't do to have nothing at all, and so it was I who collected her trousseau, for if I hadn't, then who would have? But never mind about me; that's not important. I did manage to pass on some of my ideas to her then, so that at least she knew. Perhaps I was even hasty. What mattered was that, right from the very start, despite some attempt at restraint, she rushed to meet me with love, she would greet me with delight when I visited her in the evening, she would babble on (that charming, innocent babble of hers) about her childhood, her earliest years, her parents' home, her father and mother. But I at once threw cold water on all this rapture of hers. That was just my plan, you see. When she was elated, I would respond with silence—a benevolent silence, of course ... but still she would quickly see that we were two very different people and that I was an enigma. And my main point was to keep working at that enigma! Maybe it was just for the sake of solving an enigma that I did this whole stupid thing! Strictness, in the first place. It was strictness when I brought her into my house. In short, while I went on with my daily round, quite satisfied, I created a whole system. Oh, it happened without any effort and just sprang up on its own. And it couldn't have happened any other way: the course of events compelled me to create this system—why on earth should I slander myself! It was a genuine system. Wait a moment, now, and listen: if you are going to judge a man, then you have to know the facts of his case. . . . So listen.

I'm not sure how to begin this, because it's very difficult. When you begin to justify yourself—that's when it becomes difficult. You see, young people generally are scornful of money, for instance. So I at once set to work on the issue of money. I stressed the money question. And I stressed it so much that she began more and more to keep silent. She would open her big eyes, listen to me, look and me, and not say a word. Young people are noble, you see—the best young people, I mean; they are noble and impulsive, but have little tolerance; just as soon as something doesn't go quite their way, they show their contempt. But I wanted her to have a broad, tolerant outlook; I wanted to instill this breadth right into her heart, to make it a part of her. Don't you see what I had in mind? Let me take a trivial example: how could I explain my pawnshop to a person like her, for instance? Of course, I didn't start to talk of it immediately, or else it would have seemed as if I were apologizing for keeping a pawnshop; but I acted with pride, and barely said a word of it. I am an expert at speaking while barely saying a word; I've been speaking without saying a word all my life, and have endured whole inner tragedies without saying a word. Oh, of course I myself was unhappy! Everyone had cast me off, cast me off and forgotten me, and not a single soul knows it! And suddenly this sixteen-year-old got hold of a few details about me from some contemptible people and thought she knew everything; but the real secret still lay in the bosom of this man alone! I just kept silent, and especially with her I kept silent, right until yesterday. Why did I do that? Because I'm a proud man. I wanted her to find out herself, with no help from me, and this time not from tales told by scoundrels. No, she should come to a conclusion *herself* about this man and discover what he is! When I took her into my home I wanted complete respect. I wanted her to stand before me in ardent homage because of my sufferings, and I deserved that. Oh, I was always proud; I always wanted all or nothing! And that's just why I'm not content with halfway measures where happiness is concerned; I wanted it all. That's just why I had to act as I did then, as if to say to her: "You draw your own conclusion and appreciate my worth!" Because you have to agree that if I began explaining things to her myself and dropping hints, ingratiating myself and asking her to respect me, it would be no better than begging for charity. . . . But yet . . . yet why am I talking about this!

Stupid, stupid, stupid, and stupid again! Frankly and mercilessly (and I stress the fact that it was merciless), I explained to her then, in a few words, that "the nobility of youth is very charming but isn't worth a penny. And why not? Because it is acquired cheaply and is not obtained through experience. It's all 'the first impressions of existence.' But let's have a look at you when you have to earn your daily bread! Cheap nobility is always easy; even sacrificing your life—even that is cheap, because it's just a matter of a stirring of the blood and an excess of energy, a passionate longing for beauty! No, take on some noble deed that is difficult, unobtrusive, unsung, one with no glamour, but which involves criticism, a great deal of sacrifice, and not a drop of glory, one where you, the radiant youth, are held up as a scoundrel by everyone when you are more honorable than any of them. Well, now, try taking on a deed like that! No, ma'am, you'll turn it down! And I—I have done nothing but bear the weight of such a deed my whole life long." At first she would argue. And how she argued! But then she began to keep quiet,

and at last she wouldn't say a word; only she would open her eyes
as wide as could be while she listened, such big, big eyes, full of
attention. And . . . and apart from that I suddenly noticed a smile,
a skeptical, silent, unpleasant smile. And so it was with this smile
that I brought her into my house. It's true, of course, that she had
nowhere else to go. . . .

4. Plans and More Plans

Which one of us first began it? Neither of us. It began by itself
right from the very start. I said that I was going to be strict when
I brought her into the house, but from the first step I softened.
Even before we married I explained to her that she would take
charge of accepting the articles for pawn and paying out the money,
and she didn't say a word at the time (I draw your attention to
that). Moreover, she set about the job even with some enthusiasm.
Of course, the apartment and the furniture all remained as they
had been. It's a two-room apartment: the large anteroom has the
pawnshop and is divided by a counter; the other room, also large,
is our parlor and serves as a bedroom as well. I only have a little
furniture; even her aunts had better. The icon case and lamp are
in the anteroom with the pawnshop; the other room has my book-
case, with a few books in it, and a chest the key for which I keep;
and then there's the bed, a couple of tables, and some chairs.
Before we married I told her that I set aside a ruble a day and no
more for our subsistence—I mean for food for me, her, and Lukeria
(whom I'd managed to lure away). "I need thirty thousand in three
years," I told her, "and there's no other way to raise it." She didn't
object, but I raised our subsistence allowance by thirty kopecks.
The same with the theater. I had told my fiancée that there wouldn't
be any theater, but all the same I decided that once a month I
would take her to a play, and do it in proper fashion, too, with
orchestra seats. We went together, three times, and saw *The Pursuit
of Happiness* and *The Singing Birds*, I think. (Oh, to hell with it;
what difference does it make!) We went in silence, and we came
back in silence. Why was it that we started by keeping silent right
from the very beginning? Why? We didn't quarrel at first, you see,
but still we kept silent. I remember how she would always steal
furtive glances at me; as soon as I noticed that, I kept an even
more determined silence. True enough, it was I who insisted on
the silence, not she. Once or twice she had fits of affection when

she rushed to embrace me; but since these outbursts of hers were unhealthy and hysterical, while I needed happiness that was solid, with respect from her, I reacted coldly. And I was right: the day after every outburst we would have a quarrel.

They weren't really quarrels, I mean, but there was silence, and it took on a more and more insolent manner on her part. "Rebellion and independence"—that's what she had in mind, only she didn't know how to manage it. Yes, that gentle face of hers grew more and more insolent. Believe it or not, she began to find me obnoxious; I could tell that. And it was obvious enough that she was having fits of temper. Now tell me, how could she, coming from such squalor and poverty—after scrubbing floors, in fact—how could she suddenly start fuming because we lived poorly! But you see, ladies and gentlemen, it was not poverty, it was frugality, and in the things that mattered—even luxury: in our linen, for instance, or in cleanliness. I had always imagined before that a wife finds cleanliness attractive in her husband. However, it wasn't poverty that bothered her, it was my supposed stinginess in housekeeping: "He has a goal," she would probably say to herself, "and is showing off his strong character." She herself suddenly refused to go to the theater. And that mocking look of hers became more and more obvious . . . while I made my silence more and more intense.

Should I have tried to justify myself? The pawnshop caused the most trouble. Let me explain: I knew that a female, and especially a girl of sixteen, could do nothing other than submit completely to her husband. Women have no originality: why, that's an axiom, and even now, even now I consider that an axiom! What does it prove that she's lying out there in the anteroom: truth is truth, and even John Stuart Mill himself can do nothing about it! But a loving woman—oh, a loving woman will worship even the flaws, even the vices of her beloved. He himself can't find such ways to excuse his vices as she can. This is noble, but it's not original. It is lack of originality, and only that, that has been the ruin of women. And so, I repeat: what if you do point to that table out there? Is it something original that's lying on the table? Oh-h-h!

Listen to me: I was confident she loved me then. Why, she used to rush over to embrace me. So she loved me, or rather she wanted to love me. Yes, that's how it was: she wanted to love me; she was trying to love me. And the main thing was that I didn't have any vices that she'd have to try to excuse. "Pawnbroker," you say; everybody says it. And what if I am a pawnbroker? It means there must be reasons for the noblest of men to become pawnbrokers. You see, ladies and gentlemen, there are certain ideas...I mean, there are some ideas which, when you try to put them into words, sound very silly. They simply make one ashamed. Why is that? No reason at all. Because we are all worthless, and none of us can bear the truth. That's the only reason I can think of. I said "the noblest of men" just now. That may sound ridiculous, yet that's just how it was. It's the truth; it's the truest truth of all! Yes, at the time I *had the right* to try to secure my future and to open this pawnshop: "You have rejected me (you people, I mean); you have cast me out with your scornful silence. You answered my passionate longing to love you with an insult I will feel all my life. So now I am quite justified in walling myself off from you, collecting my thirty thousand rubles, and living the rest of my life somewhere in the Crimea, on the Southern Shore, amid mountains and vineyards, on my own estate, purchased with that thirty thousand. What matters most is to live faraway from all of you, bearing no malice, but with an ideal in my soul, with the woman I love next to me, with a family, if God blesses me with one, spending my days helping the neighboring settlers." It's all very well, of course, to say this to myself now, but what could have been stupider than to try painting her a picture of all that back then? That explains my proud silence; that explains why we sat without exchanging a word. Because what could she have understood? Sixteen years old, barely into her youth! Could she have accepted my justifications? Could she have understood my sufferings? She has a simple, "straight-line" way of thinking; she knows little of life, is full of young, cheap convictions, suffers from the blindness of "the beautiful soul"; and above all, there's the pawnshop—that was enough! (But was I some criminal in the pawnshop? Didn't she see how I acted? Did I ever charge more than my due?) Oh, what a dreadful thing is truth in the world! This charming girl, this meek one, this heavenly creature—she was a tyrant, an insufferable tyrant over my soul, a tormenter! I am defaming myself unless I say that! You think I didn't love her? Who can say that I didn't love her? Don't you see the irony here, the wicked irony of fate and nature? We are damned; human life in general (and mine, in particular) is damned! Of course, I understand now that I made some mistake! Something went wrong back then. Everything was clear; my plan was as clear as the air: "Severe, proud, needing no one's moral consolation, suffering in silence." That is how it was; I didn't lie, really I didn't! "One day she will see for herself that it was a matter of my nobility"—only she wasn't able to see it then—"and when she eventually realizes it, she will have ten times more esteem for me and will fall to her knees, her hands folded in ardent prayer." That was the plan. But at this point I forgot something; or there was something I didn't take into consideration. There was something I couldn't manage to do properly. But, never mind, that's enough. Whose forgiveness is there to ask now? What's done is done. Take courage, man, and be proud! It's not your fault! . . .

And so, I'll tell the truth; I'm not afraid to face the truth head on: it was *her* fault, *her* fault! . . .

5. The Meek One Rebels

The quarrels started because she suddenly took it into her head to loan money on her own terms and to appraise articles at higher than their real value. Twice she even presumed to quarrel with me on the topic. I wouldn't agree to what she was doing. It was at this point that the captain's widow turned up.

An old widow came in with a locket, a gift of her late husband, the captain, and a keepsake, of course. I gave her thirty rubles for it. She started whining and pleading for us not to sell the thing, and of course I said we wouldn't. Well, to cut the story short, she suddenly turned up five days later to exchange the locket for a bracelet that wasn't worth even eight rubles; I refused her, of course. I suppose she must have been able to read something in my wife's eyes; anyway, she came again when I wasn't there, and my wife exchanged the bracelet for the locket.

When I found out that same day what had happened, I spoke mildly but firmly and reasonably to her. She was sitting on the bed, looking at the floor, flicking her right toe against the carpet (a gesture of hers); a nasty smile played on her lips. Then, without raising my voice at all, I stated calmly that the money was *mine*, that I had the right to regard life through *my* eyes, and that when I brought her into my house I had hidden nothing from her.

Suddenly she jumped to her feet, all a-tremble, and—can you believe it?—suddenly started stamping her feet at me. She was a wild beast; she was having a fit; she was a wild beast having a fit. I was numb with amazement: I had never expected antics like this. But I kept my head and didn't even make a move; once more, in the same calm voice as before, I told her plainly that henceforth

I would let her have no more part in my business affairs. She laughed in my face and walked out of the apartment.

The fact is, she did not have the right to walk out of the apartment. Nowhere without me: such was the agreement made before we married. She came back toward evening; I didn't say a word.

The next day she went out in the morning, and did the same the day after that. I closed up the shop and went off to see her aunts. I had had no dealings with them since the wedding: I would not have them call on me or call on them. But it turned out that she had not been visiting them. They listened to my story with interest and then laughed in my face: "That's just what you deserve." Yet I had expected them to laugh. Right then I offered the younger aunt, the old maid, a hundred-ruble bribe, giving her twenty-five in advance. Two days later she came to see me, saying: "There's an officer, a Lieutenant Efimovich, one of your army friends, who's involved in the affair." I was astonished. This Efimovich had done me more harm than anyone in the regiment, and about a month before, being the shameless creature he is, he had come into the pawnshop twice, pretending he wanted to pawn something, and I recall he began laughing with my wife. I approached him right then and told him that in view of our former relations he should not dare to call on me again, but I hadn't the least notion of anything like this; I simply thought he was being impudent. And now, suddenly, the aunt tells me that she already has a rendezvous arranged with him and the whole affair is being managed by a former acquaintance of the aunts, a certain Julia Samsonovna, and a colonel's wife to boot. "She's the one your wife visits now," the aunt tells me.

Let me summarize this episode. The whole affair cost me nearly three hundred rubles, but within two days I had arranged things so that I could stand in an adjoining room behind a door and listen to my wife's first rendezvous alone with Efimovich. In anticipation of this, I had a brief but—for me—very significant encounter with her on the eve of the event.

She had returned home toward evening and sat on the bed looking mockingly at me, tapping her little foot against the rug. Looking at her, the thought suddenly flew into my head that for this whole past month or, rather, for the previous two weeks, she had absolutely not been herself; one could even say that she had become the antithesis of herself: here was a violent, aggressive creature—I couldn't call her shameless, but she was agitated and looking to cause a commotion. She was deliberately seeking out ways to cause a commotion. Her gentle spirit held her back, however. When a woman like that begins to revolt, even if she may have stepped over the limit, you can still always tell that she is only forcing herself, pushing herself further, and that she herself cannot overcome her own sense of morality and shame. And that is the reason such women sometimes go to such lengths that you can scarcely believe your eyes. The woman used to debauchery will, on the contrary, always tone things down; such a one will do something far worse, but will do it with an air of decorum and respectability that attempts to claim superiority over you.

"Tell me, is it true they kicked you out of the regiment because you were afraid to fight a duel?" she asked me suddenly, right out of the blue, her eyes flashing.

"It's true. By decision of the officers I was asked to leave the regiment, though I had sent in my resignation even before that."

"They kicked you out as a coward?"

"Yes, the verdict was that I was a coward. But I refused the duel not as a coward but because I didn't want to submit to their tyrannical decree and challenge a man who, in my view, had caused me no offense. You must realize," I couldn't resist adding, "that standing up to that sort of tyranny and accepting all the consequences meant showing far more courage than fighting in any duel."

I couldn't resist; I said it as if to justify myself. But this was all she needed, this new humiliation for me. She laughed spitefully.

"And is it true that for three years afterward you wandered the streets of Petersburg like a tramp, begging for small change and spending the nights under billiard tables?"

"I even used to sleep in the Haymarket, at the Viazemsky house. Yes, that's true. After leaving the regiment there were a good many shameful things in my life, and much degradation. But it wasn't moral degradation, because I was the first to despise my own actions even then. It was only a degradation of my will and my mind, and it was caused only by despair at my situation. But that's all past. . . ."

"Oh, and now you are an important figure—a financier!"

That was a dig at the pawnshop. But by then I had managed to gain my self-restraint. I could see that she was eager to hear some humiliating explanations and—I didn't provide any. At that point a customer rang and I went to the anteroom to look after him. An hour later, when she had suddenly dressed to go out, she stopped

in front of me and said, "Still, you didn't tell me anything about
that before the wedding?"

I did not reply, and she left.

And so, on the next day, I stood behind the door in this room
listening to my fate being decided. I had a revolver in my pocket.
She was sitting at the table, nicely dressed, and Efimovich was
preening himself in front of her. And what do you think? What
happened (and it's to my credit that I say this) was exactly the
thing I had supposed and anticipated would happen, although I
was not conscious of supposing and anticipating it. I don't know
if that makes sense to you.

This is what happened. I listened for a whole hour, and for a
whole hour I was present at a duel between the noblest and most
elevated of women and a depraved, dull creature of society with a
groveling soul. And how, I thought in utter amazement, how could
this naive, this meek, this reticent girl possibly know all this? The
wittiest author of a high-society comedy could not have created this
scene of ridicule, naive laughter, and the saintly scorn of virtue for
vice. And what brilliance there was in her words and little turns
of phrase; how witty were her quick replies; what truth there was
in her condemnations! And, at the same time, how much almost
girlish naiveté. She laughed in his face at his declarations of love,
at his gestures, at his propositions. Having arrived with the notion
of storming the fortress head on and not anticipating any resistance,
he suddenly was disarmed. At first I was prepared to believe that
she was simply playing the flirt: "the coquetry of a creature who,
though depraved, is witty, and so works to increase her own value."
But no: truth radiated like the sun, and there was no possibility
of doubt. She, with her lack of experience, might have decided to
arrange this rendezvous out of hatred for me, a hatred that was
both insincere and impetuous, but when it came to the crux of the
matter her eyes were opened at once. It was simply a matter of a
woman who was trying desperately to injure me in any way she
could but who, once she had resolved to do such a dirty deed, was
unable to bear the messy consequences. And could Efimovich, or
any of those other society creatures, seduce a woman like her—
she, pure and sinless, with her ideals? On the contrary: he only
made her laugh. The whole truth rose up from her soul, and her
anger brought the sarcasm from her heart. I repeat: this buffoon
at last fell into a complete daze and sat frowning, scarcely answering
her, so that I even began to fear that he might go so far as to insult

her out of a mean wish for revenge. Again I repeat: it is to my credit that I listened to this whole scene with scarcely any surprise. It was as if I were encountering only things I already knew. It was as if I had gone there to have that encounter. I had come believing nothing, with no accusation against her—although I had taken a revolver in my pocket: that's the truth! And could I have imagined her in any other way? Why was it I loved her? Why was it I cherished her? Why was it I had married her? Oh, of course I was all too convinced of how much she hated me then, but I was also convinced of how pure she was. I put a sudden end to the scene when I opened the door. Efimovich leapt up; I took her hand and invited her to leave with me. Efimovich recovered and suddenly burst into a loud peal of laughter.

"Oh, there's nothing I can say against sacred conjugal rights! Take her away! And do you know," he shouted as I left, "even though a real gentleman wouldn't stoop to fight a duel with you, out of respect for your lady, I'm at your service . . . that's if you dare, of course. . . ."

"Do you hear that!" said I, stopping her for a moment on the threshold.

And then not a single word all the way home. I led her by the hand, and she offered no resistance. On the contrary: she seemed terribly shocked. But that lasted only until we reached the apartment. When we arrived she sat down on a chair and fixed her gaze on me. She was extraordinarily pale; even though her lips at once assumed their mocking expression, she looked at me with a solemn and stern challenge, and I think for the first few moments she seriously believed that I was going to shoot her. But I silently drew the revolver from my pocket and laid it on the table. She looked at me and at the revolver. (Note this: she was already familiar with this revolver. I had acquired it when I opened the pawnshop and had kept it loaded ever since. When I opened the shop, I decided not to keep huge dogs or a muscular manservant as Moser does, for example. The cook lets in my customers. But those who practice our trade cannot deprive themselves of the means of self-defense— one never knows what might happen. And so I kept a loaded revolver. During her first days in my house, she took a great interest in this revolver and had a lot of questions about it. I explained its mechanism and how it works and once even persuaded her to fire at a target. Keep all that in mind.) Paying no heed to her frightened glance, I lay down on the bed, half undressed. I felt quite exhausted;

it was around eleven o'clock. She went on sitting in the same spot, not stirring, for nearly an hour more and then put out the light and lay down, also dressed, on the sofa by the wall. This was the first time she did not lie down beside me. Bear that in mind as well. . . .

6. A Dreadful Recollection

Now, this dreadful recollection. . . .

I woke up the next morning about eight o'clock, I think, and the room was already quite light. I awakened at once, my mind fully clear, and opened my eyes. She was standing by the table, holding the revolver. She didn't notice that I was awake and was looking at her. And suddenly I saw her begin to move toward me, still holding the revolver. I quickly closed my eyes and pretended to be sound asleep.

She came up to the bed and stood over me. I could hear everything; even though a deathly silence had fallen on the room, I could hear that silence. Then a shudder passed through me and, unable to resist, I suddenly—I couldn't help it—I had to open my eyes. She was staring right into my face, holding the pistol to my temple. Our eyes met. But we looked at each other for no more than a moment. With an effort I closed my eyes again and at the same time resolved with all the strength I could muster that I would not move another muscle and would not open my eyes no matter what fate awaited me.

In actual fact it happens that a soundly sleeping person can suddenly open his eyes, and even raise his head for a second and look around the room; then, a moment later, he can lay his head on the pillow once more and fall asleep without remembering a thing. When I, having met her gaze and having felt the pistol at my temple, suddenly closed my eyes again and did not stir, as if I were sound asleep, she certainly might have assumed that I really was sleeping and had seen nothing, the more so that it would be quite improbable for one who had seen what I had to close his eyes again at *such* a moment.

Yes, quite improbable. But still, she might have guessed the truth as well: that thought also flashed in my mind at that same moment. Oh, what a whirlwind of thoughts and sensations rushed through my mind in less than an instant. Hurrah for the electricity of human thought! If that were the case (I felt)—if she had guessed the truth and knew I was not sleeping—then I had already crushed her by my readiness to accept death, and her hand might be trembling in hesitation at this moment. The resolve she had shown earlier might have been shattered by this amazing new realization. I've heard that people standing on a great height seem to be drawn downward, into the abyss, by their own accord. I think that many suicides and murders have been committed simply because the person had already taken the pistol into his hand. There's an abyss here as well, a forty-five-degree slope that you cannot help but slip down; there is an irresistible call for you to pull the trigger. But the awareness that I had seen it all, that I knew it all, and was silently awaiting death at her hand—that might keep her from sliding down the slope.

The silence continued, and suddenly I felt the cold touch of iron at the hair on my temple. You might ask: was I firmly convinced I would survive? I will answer, as before God: I counted on nothing, except perhaps one chance in a hundred. Why, then, could I accept death? But let me ask you: what was my life worth now, after the creature I loved had pointed a revolver at me? Besides, I knew with all the strength of my being that a struggle was going on between us at that very moment, a terrible duel of life and death, a duel fought by that very same coward of yesterday, the man whose comrades had thrown him out of his regiment for cowardice. I knew it, and she knew it—as long as she had guessed the truth that I was not asleep.

Perhaps this didn't happen, perhaps I didn't think anything of the sort at the time; yet it all must have happened—without my thinking anything, perhaps—because I have done nothing but think of it every hour of my life ever since.

But now you ask: why didn't I save her from this criminal act? Oh, I have asked myself that same question a thousand times since, every time when, a chill gripping my spine, I recall that second. But I was in such a state of black despair at the time: I myself was perishing, truly perishing, so how could I save anyone else? And what makes you think I even wanted to save anyone? Who knows what I was feeling at the time?

Still, my mind was seething with activity; seconds passed; the silence was deadly; she continued to stand over me, and suddenly I shuddered with hope! I opened my eyes at once. She was no longer in the room. I rose from the bed: I had conquered, and she had been vanquished forever!

I went out to get myself some tea. The samovar was always set up in our other room, and she was always the one to pour the tea. I took a seat at the table without saying a word and accepted a glass of tea from her. Five minutes later I glanced at her. She was dreadfully pale, even paler than yesterday, and she was looking at me. And suddenly—suddenly, noticing that I was looking at her, her pale lips broke into a pale smile; her eyes posed a timid question. "So, she still doesn't know for sure and is asking herself: does he know, or doesn't he? Did he see, or didn't he?" Indifferently, I looked away. After I had tea I closed the shop, went to the market, and bought an iron bedstead and a screen. On returning home, I had the bed set up in the anteroom with the screen around it. This was a bed for her, but I said not a word to her about it. She needed no words to understand. This bed told her that I "had seen it all and knew it all," and that there could be no more doubts. I left the revolver on the table for the night, as always. That night she lay down in silence on this new bed: the marriage was dissolved, she was "vanquished, but not forgiven." During the night she became delirious, and by morning had developed a high fever. She was in bed for six weeks.

2

1. A Dream of Pride

Lukeria has just announced that she will not go on living here and will leave as soon as the mistress has been buried. I spent five minutes on my knees in prayer. I wanted to pray for an hour, but I kept thinking and thinking, and all my thoughts were painful. My head aches—so how can I pray? It would only be a sin! It's strange as well that I don't feel sleepy: when there is an immense grief—one that can scarcely be borne—one always wants to sleep, at least after the first paroxysms. I've heard that those condemned to death sleep exceptionally soundly on the last night. And so it should be; this is nature's way; otherwise they wouldn't have the strength.... I lay down on the sofa, but I couldn't fall asleep....

...We looked after her day and night for the six weeks of her illness—I, Lukeria, and a trained nurse whom I hired from the hospital. I didn't begrudge the money and even wanted to spend it on her. I called in Dr. Schroeder and paid him ten rubles per visit. When she regained consciousness I spent less time around her. Still, why bother to describe all this? When she was completely on her feet again, she quietly and without a word sat herself down in my room at a special table which I had also bought for her at that time.... Yes, it's true: we said not a word to one another. Well, actually, we did begin speaking later on, but only about quite ordinary things. I made a point, of course, of not letting myself talk too much, but I could see very well that she, too, was happy not to say more than she had to. It seemed to me that this was absolutely natural on her part: "She's too distraught, and feels too crushed," I thought, "and naturally I have to give her time to forget and to come to terms." And so it was that we went on in silence, although privately I was constantly preparing myself for the future. I assumed that she was doing the same thing, and I found it awfully intriguing to speculate on just what was going on in her mind.

One more thing: no one knows, of course, how much I suffered while grieving over her during her illness. But I suffered in silence and stifled my groans even from Lukeria. I couldn't imagine, I couldn't even suppose, that she might die before learning everything. But when she was out of danger and her health began to return, I recall that I quickly recovered my composure. Besides, I had decided to *put off our future* as far as possible and keep things in their present form for the time being. Yes, something very odd and peculiar happened to me then—I don't know how else to describe it. I was triumphant, and the very awareness of that turned out to be quite sufficient for me. And so the whole winter passed this way. Oh, I was satisfied as I had never been before, and for the whole winter.

You see, there had been one terrible external event in my life which up to this point—that is, until the catastrophe with my wife—had oppressed me every day and every hour: this was my loss of reputation and my leaving the regiment. To put it briefly, there had been a tyrannical injustice committed against me. It is true that my fellow officers did not like me because I was not an easy person to get along with and, perhaps, because there was an element of the ridiculous about me, although it often happens that something which you revere and regard as sublime and sacred will at the same time be cause for the amusement of your whole crowd of friends. Oh, even in school people never liked me. No one anywhere ever liked me. Even Lukeria isn't able to like me. That same incident in the regiment, while a consequence of the general dislike for me, still was largely a matter of chance. I mention this because there is nothing more offensive and painful than to be ruined by a matter of chance, by something that might or might not have happened, by an unlucky conglomeration of circumstances that might have simply passed over like a cloud. For an intelligent creature this is humiliating. The incident happened as follows.

Once, in the theater, I went to the bar during the intermission. The hussar A——v came in suddenly and, in the presence of all the officers and general public who were standing there, began loudly telling two of his fellow hussars that Captain Bezumtsev of our regiment had only just caused a disgraceful row in the corridor and that "he was drunk, by the look of it." This conversation did not go any further, and it was a mistake in any case, since Captain Bezumtsev was not drunk and, strictly speaking, the row wasn't really a row. The hussars began speaking of something else, and there the matter ended. But the next day the story had reached our regiment and talk at once began to the effect that I had been the only officer of our regiment present in the bar, and that when the hussar A——v had made such an impertinent remark about Captain Bezumtsev, I had not gone up and rebuked him. But what would have been the point of that? If he had a grudge against Bezumtsev, then it was their personal affair; why should I get involved? Meanwhile, our officers began insisting that it was not a personal affair but concerned the regiment as a whole; and since I was the only officer of our regiment present, in failing to act I had proved to all the other officers and civilians in the bar that our regiment could have officers who were not particularly fussy about their own honor and the honor of their regiment. I could not agree with such a view. They let me know that I could correct the matter even now— although belatedly—by asking for a formal explanation from A——v. I did not want to do this, and in my exasperation I gave them a haughty refusal. Then I resigned at once. That's the whole story. I left the regiment proudly, yet crushed in spirit. My will and my mind had suffered a very severe blow. At the same time, as it happened, my sister's husband in Moscow had squandered our modest legacy, including my own tiny share in it, so I was left on the street without a penny. I could have taken some civilian job, but I didn't: after wearing a brilliant uniform I couldn't accept work for some railway. And so: if it's to be shame, let it be shame; if disgrace, then disgrace; if degradation, then degradation—the worse, the better. That is what I chose. Thereafter, three years of gloomy memories, and even the Viazemsky house. A year and a half ago a wealthy old woman, my godmother, died in Moscow, and to my surprise she left me (among her other bequests) three thousand rubles. I thought things over for a time and then chose my fate. I decided on a pawnshop, offering apologies to no one: money, then a cozy home and, at last, a new life far removed from my old memories—that was my plan. Nevertheless, my gloomy past and my once honorable reputation, now destroyed forever, haunted me every hour and every minute. But then I married. Whether that was chance or not I don't know. But when I brought her into my house I thought that I was bringing in a friend, and

I was so much in need of a friend. But I saw clearly that I had to train my friend, that I had to add the final touches to her, even conquer her. And could I have explained it all at once to this sixteen-year-old with her prejudices? For example, how could I, without the chance assistance of the terrible catastrophe with the revolver, have convinced her that I was not a coward and that my regiment had unjustly accused me of cowardice? But the catastrophe came along at the right moment. When I held up against the revolver, I avenged myself on all my gloomy past. And even though no one knew about it, *she* knew, and that meant everything to me, because she herself meant everything to me—all my hope for the future of my dreams! She was the only human being whom I was developing for myself, and I had no need of any other. And now she had discovered it all; she had discovered, at least, that she had been unjust in rushing off to ally herself with my enemies. I was delighted by this thought. I could no longer be a scoundrel in her eyes, merely an odd sort of fellow. But after everything that had happened, even this thought was not entirely displeasing to me. Oddness is not a vice; on the contrary, women sometimes find it attractive. In short, then, I was deliberately putting off the de-nouement: what had already happened was, for the moment, more than enough to ensure my peace of mind and contained abundant images and material for me to dream about. That's the trouble, you see: I am a dreamer. I had enough raw material for myself, and as for her, I thought that she could *wait*.

And so the whole winter passed in a kind of expectation of something. I loved to steal glances at her as she sat at her little table. She would work at her sewing, and sometimes in the evening would read books she took from my shelf. The selection of books on my shelf also should have testified on my behalf. She scarcely went out at all. Just before dusk every day, after dinner, I would take her out for a walk for the sake of some exercise, but not in complete silence as before. I tried to keep up the appearance that we were not keeping silent but talking cordially; but as I said, neither of us spoke too much. I did this deliberately; as for her, I thought it was essential to "give her some time." It's odd, of course, that it was almost the end of winter before it occurred to me that while I loved to steal glances at her, never once through the winter did I catch her looking at me! I thought this was simply a matter of her shyness. Besides, she had a look of such submissive

timidity, such weakness after her illness. No, better wait and "su
denly she will approach you herself...."

I was absolutely delighted by this thought. I'll add one thi
more: sometimes, as if deliberately, I would work myself up a
in fact push my emotions and my mind to the point where I actu
seemed to feel as if she had offended me. And so it continued
some time. But my hatred never managed to ripen and take
in my inner being. And I myself felt that this was really on
game of some sort. And even then, although I had dissolved
marriage when I bought the cot and the screen, I never eve
garded her as a guilty party. That was not because I judged
offense lightly, but because I had the sense to forgive her compl
from the very first day, even before I bought the cot. In sh
was an oddity on my part, for I am a morally strict perso
the contrary: I could see that she was so vanquished, so hun
so crushed, that there were times when I was in an agony o
for her, even while sometimes being absolutely pleased wi
notion of her humiliation. The idea of this inequality betw
appealed to me....

That winter I deliberately did several good deeds. I forga
loans; I loaned money to one poor woman without a paw
I said nothing to my wife about it, and did not do it in o
her to find out; but the old woman herself came to tha
almost on her knees. And so the deed became known. I th
my wife truly was pleased to learn about the old woman.

But spring was coming on. It was already the middle o
the storm windows had been taken down and the sun
bring bright patches of light into our silent rooms. But
hung before me and blinded my reason. That terribl
shroud! How did it happen that it all suddenly fell away
eyes and that suddenly my sight was restored and I und
all! Was it a matter of chance, or had the appointed d
arrived, or was it a ray of sunlight that kindled the th
the surmise in my benumbed mind? No, it was not a th
not a surmise; it was a little vein that suddenly began
little vein that had all but atrophied but which twitched
to life, bringing new feeling to my benumbed soul an
my diabolical pride. At the time it seemed as though I
my chair. And it happened suddenly, when I least exp
happened before evening, about five o'clock, after din

2. Suddenly the Shroud Fell Away

A word or two first. As long as a month before I had noticed a
peculiar sort of melancholy in her. It wasn't just her silence, it was
real melancholy. That also I noticed suddenly. She was sitting at
her work, her head bent over her sewing, and she didn't notice
that I was looking at her. And it suddenly struck me right then
how thin and gaunt she had become; her face was pale, her lips
white. All this, together with her melancholy, gave me a great
shock. Even before this I had heard her little dry cough, especially
at nights. I got up at once to call Doctor Schroeder, saying nothing
to her.

Schroeder came the next day. She was quite surprised and looked
first at Schroeder, then at me.

"But I'm quite well," she said, smiling uncertainly.

Schroeder did not give her a very careful examination (the haughty manner of these medical men sometimes doesn't permit them
to be careful) and told me only, in the next room, that this was a
result of her illness and that when spring came it would not be a
bad idea to go to the seaside or, if that were impossible, simply to
move to a country place. In short, he didn't tell me anything except
that she was sickly or something of the sort. When Schroeder left
she said once more, looking at me with terrible seriousness, "I am
quite, quite well."

But having said that she blushed at once, evidently from shame.
Evidently it was shame. Oh, now I understand: she felt ashamed
that I, who was still *her husband*, was looking after her just as if
I still were her real husband. But at that time I did not understand
and assumed she blushed out of modesty. (The shroud!)

And so it was, a month after this, some time after four o'clock
on a bright, sunny day in April, I was sitting in the shop checking
my accounts. Suddenly I heard her, sitting in our room and working
at her table, begin ever so softly... to sing. This new event surprised me enormously, and even now I do not understand it. Previously I had scarcely ever heard her sing—oh, perhaps in the very
first days after I brought her home, when we still could rollick
about, target shooting with the pistol. Then her voice was still
quite strong and clear, although not always true, but very pleasant
and sound. But now her little song was so weak. I don't mean to
say it was mournful (it was an old love song of some sort); but it
was as if something in her voice had cracked and broken, as if her

little voice could not cope any more, as if the song itself were ill. She was singing in a low voice which rose and then suddenly broke off—such a poor little voice, and it broke off so pitifully. She cleared her throat and once more began to sing ever so quietly. . . .

You may laugh at my getting upset, but no one will ever understand why I was so moved! No, I still wasn't sorry for her; this was something quite different. At first, at least in the first moments, I felt suddenly perplexed and greatly surprised, strangely and terribly, painfully and almost spitefully surprised: "She's singing, and in my presence! *Has she forgotten about me or what?*"

Completely shocked, I remained at my place for a time; then I suddenly rose, took my hat, and went out, scarcely knowing what I was doing. At least I didn't know where I was going and why. Lukeria came to help me with my overcoat.

"She's singing?" I couldn't help but ask Lukeria. She did not understand and looked at me, still uncomprehending; however, it's no surprise that she failed to understand me.

"Is that the first time she's been singing?"

"No, she sometimes sings when you're not home," Lukeria answered.

I recall it all. I went down the stairs, onto the street, and set off with no notion of where I was going. I reached the corner and stared off into the distance. People passed and jostled me, but I didn't feel anything. I hailed a cab and told the driver to take me to the Police Bridge—Lord knows why. Then, suddenly, I gave him twenty kopecks and dismissed him.

"That's for your trouble," I said, laughing senselessly; in my heart, however, a sort of ecstasy suddenly welled up.

I turned toward home, increasing my pace. The poor, cracked, broken note began to ring in my soul once more. I could scarcely catch my breath. The shroud was falling from my eyes! If she could start singing in my presence, it meant she had forgotten about me— that was clear and that was dreadful. My heart could sense that. But rapture radiated in my soul and overcame the dread.

Oh, the irony of fate! You see, there had been nothing and could not have been anything in my soul that whole winter apart from this rapturous feeling. But where had I been all winter? Was I aware of what was happening in my soul? I ran up the stairs in a great rush; I don't recall if I had any apprehension when I entered the room. I remember only that the whole floor seemed to undulate beneath my feet and I moved as if floating down a river. I came

into the room; she was sitting in her usual place sewing, her head
bent over her work, but wasn't singing any more. She cast a passing,
uncurious glance at me; in fact, it was not a glance but merely an
instinctive and indifferent gesture, the kind directed at anyone who
enters a room.

I made straight for her and took a chair close beside her, like
one scarcely in his right mind. She glanced quickly at me, as if
taking fright; I took her hand and don't recall what I said to her—
or rather, what I tried to say to her, because I couldn't even speak
properly. My voice had broken and would not obey me. And in
any case, I didn't know what to say; I was gasping for breath.

"Let's talk . . . you know . . . say something to me!" I babbled
something stupid. How could I collect my thoughts? She shuddered
and drew back in great fear, staring at my face. But suddenly I
could see *stern amazement* in her eyes. Amazement, yes, and it was
stern. She looked at me wide-eyed. This sternness, this stern amazement was like a blow that shattered my skull. "So is it still love
you want? Is it love?" This was what her amazed expression seemed
to be asking me, although she still didn't say a word. But I could
read everything, absolutely everything. I felt a tremor pass through
my whole being and I simply collapsed at her feet. Yes, I fell down
at her feet. She leapt up quickly, but with extraordinary strength
I grasped both her hands to hold her back.

And I understood the full depth of my despair, I understood it
completely! But—can you believe it?—my soul was so overflowing
with rapture that I thought I would die. I kissed her feet in happiness, in ecstasy. Yes, in immeasurable, boundless happiness—and
this with complete awareness of the hopelessness of my despair! I
wept, I tried to say something but could not. Her frightened and
amazed expression suddenly changed to one of concern, to a look of
profound questioning, and she gazed at me strangely, even wildly;
there was something she wanted to understand at once and she
smiled. She felt terribly ashamed that I was kissing her feet and
pulled them away, but I at once began kissing the spot on the floor
where her feet had been. She noticed that and laughed with embarrassment (you know how people laugh with embarrassment). She
was about to go into hysterics, I could see; her hands were trembling.
But I wasn't thinking about that and kept mumbling that I loved
her, that I would not get up: "Let me kiss the hem of your dress . . .
let me worship you this way for the rest of my life. . . ." I don't
know—I don't remember, but suddenly she broke into shudders and
sobs; a terrible fit of hysterics began. I had frightened her.

I carried her over to the bed. When her fit had passed, she sat up on the edge of the bed, and with a terribly distraught air she seized my hands and begged me to calm down: "Enough! Don't torment yourself, calm down!" And she began to cry again. I didn't leave her the whole evening. I kept telling her that I would take her to Boulogne to bathe in the sea—right away, this moment, in two weeks; that her poor voice was so weak, as I had heard the other day; that I would close the shop, sell it to Dobronravov; that everything would begin anew. Above all, Boulogne, Boulogne! She listened, growing more frightened all the while. But the most important thing for me was not that, it was my urge—which grew ever stronger—to lie down again at her feet, to kiss them, to kiss the ground on which her feet stood, to worship her. "There is nothing, nothing more that I ask of you," I kept repeating. "Don't say anything, don't pay any attention to me, just let me sit in the corner and look at you. Turn me into your thing, your lapdog. . . ." She wept.

"And I thought you would just let me go on like that." This burst forth from her involuntarily, so much so that perhaps she wasn't even aware of saying it. And meanwhile—oh, this was the most important thing, the most fateful thing she said, the thing I understood best during that whole evening, and it was like a knife slashing my heart! It made everything clear to me, everything! But as long as she was by my side, as long as I could look at her, hope was overpowering and I was terribly happy. Oh, I exhausted her terribly that evening and I knew it, but I kept thinking that I would at once be able to remake everything anew. At last, much later in the evening, she became completely exhausted; I persuaded her to go to sleep, and she at once fell into a sound sleep. I expected that she might become delirious, and she was delirious, but only very slightly. I kept getting up during the night and tiptoeing quietly in my slippers to have a look at her. I wrung my hands over her, looking at that frail creature on that poor little bed, that iron cot I had bought her for three rubles. I got down on my knees but did not dare kiss her feet while she slept (without her permission!). I knelt to pray to God, but jumped up again. Lukeria kept coming out of the kitchen to keep an eye on me. I went out and told her to go to bed and that tomorrow "something altogether different" would begin.

And I believed that, blindly, madly, terribly. Oh, I was drowning in ecstasy! I could barely wait for the next day. The main thing was that I couldn't believe any disaster would happen, despite all the symptoms. My good sense had still not entirely returned to me, despite the shroud that had fallen; it did not return for a very long time—oh, not until today, not until this very day!! But then how could my good sense have returned to me then: she was still alive, after all; she was right before me, and I before her. "She'll wake up tomorrow and I'll tell her all this, and she will see everything." That was how I thought at the time—simply and clearly—and that was why I was in ecstasy! The main thing was this trip to Boulogne. For some reason I kept thinking that Boulogne was everything, that something conclusive would happen in Boulogne. "To Boulogne, to Boulogne!..." And with that insane thought I awaited the morning.

3. I Understand All Too Well

Why this was only a few days ago, five days, just five days ago, last Tuesday! No, no, if there had been only a little more time, if only she had waited just a little and—and I would have cleared away all the fog that surrounded us! But she did calm down, didn't she? The next day she listened to me with a smile, despite her confused state of mind.... The main thing was that this whole time, all five days, she was in a state of confusion or shame. And she was afraid, too, very much afraid. I won't dispute it; I won't contradict you like some madman: she was frightened, but why shouldn't she be, after all? We had been like strangers to one another for such a long time, you see; we had grown so far apart from one another, and then suddenly all this.... But I paid no attention to her fear; our new life was shining before my eyes!... It's true, absolutely true, that I made a mistake. And perhaps there were even many mistakes. Just as soon as we woke the next day I made a mistake, right that same morning (this was on Wednesday): I suddenly made her my friend. I was in far too great a rush, of course, but I absolutely needed to confess—much more than confess, in fact! I didn't even hide the things that I had been hiding from myself my whole life. I declared frankly that all winter long I had thought of nothing but the certainty of her love for me. I explained to her that my pawnshop had only been the perversion of my mind and my will, my personal idea of both punishing and exalting myself. I explained that in the theater bar I truly had been a coward—it was a matter of my character and my overly self-conscious nature: I had been taken aback by the circumstances, by the bar itself; taken aback by the thought that if I did step forward I might make a fool of myself. It wasn't the duel that made me fearful, it was the possibility of making a fool of myself. . . . And later I didn't want to admit it and tormented everyone, and tormented her because of it; in fact, that was the reason I married her—to torment her for my past. I spoke for the most part as if in a delirious fever. She took my hands and begged me to stop: "You are exaggerating . . . you're tormenting yourself." And the tears began again, and again she was on the verge of hysterics! She kept pleading with me to say no more about it and to stop dredging up my past.

I paid no heed to her pleas, or scarcely any heed: Spring! Boulogne! The sun over there, our new sun—that was all I could talk about! I closed the pawnshop and transferred my business to Dobronravov. I suddenly suggested to her that we should give it all away to the poor, apart from the original three thousand which I had inherited from my godmother. That we would use to go to Boulogne, and then return and begin a new life of honest labor. And so it was decided, because she didn't say a word . . . she only smiled. And I think that she smiled more as a matter of tact, so as not to hurt my feelings. I could see, after all, that I was putting a great burden on her, don't think that I was so stupid and such an egotist that I didn't see that. I could see it all, right down to the last detail; I saw it and knew it better than anyone: all my despair stood out for all to see!

I told her everything about me and about her. And about Lukeria. I told her that I had wept. . . . Oh, of course I would talk on other subjects. I was also trying hard not to remind her of certain things. And she even showed some enthusiasm once or twice, I remember that! Why do you say that I looked and saw nothing? And if only *this* had not happened, then everything would have been restored to life again. Why, she was telling me just the other day, when we began talking about reading and what she had read that winter; she laughed when she recalled that scene between Gil Blas and the archbishop of Granada. And how she laughed: sweet, childish laughter, just as she used to, before we were married. (A moment! A moment!) How delighted I was! I was much struck, however, by her mention of the archbishop: so she had found enough happiness and peace of mind to be able to laugh at this masterpiece as she sat there in the winter. That meant she must have begun to recover her stability; she must have begun to believe that I would not leave her *like that*. "I thought you would just let me go on *like that*." That's what she told me that Tuesday! Oh, this was how a ten-year-old girl would think! And yet she believed, she truly did, that everything in fact would remain *like that*: she sitting at her table and I at mine, and so we would both go on until we were sixty. And suddenly I come up to her, the husband; and the husband needs love! Oh, what misunderstanding, what blindness on my part!

It was also a mistake for me to look at her with such rapture on my face: I should have kept a grip on myself so my rapture wouldn't frighten her. And in fact I did keep a grip on myself. I didn't kiss her feet any more. Never once did I let it show that . . . well, that I was her husband. Oh, that never entered my mind; I only wanted to worship her! But, you see, I couldn't keep altogether silent; I had to say something! I suddenly told her how much I enjoyed her conversation and that I considered her vastly, incomparably more educated than I, and better developed mentally. She blushed terribly and said, embarrassed, that I was exaggerating. And here, like a fool, I couldn't restrain myself and told her of the ecstasy I had felt that time when I stood outside the door listening to her duel—a duel of innocence with that creature—and how I delighted in her intelligence, her brilliant wit, both coupled with her childish naiveté. Her whole body seemed to shudder and she mumbled something about my exaggeration; but suddenly her whole face clouded over and she covered it with her hands and burst into sobs. . . . And here again I couldn't restrain myself: once more I knelt before her; once more I began kissing her feet; and once more it ended in her having a fit, as she had on Tuesday. That was yesterday evening, and the next morning. . . .

The next morning?! Madman, why that was this morning, just a little while ago!

Listen and try to comprehend: when we sat together by the samovar a few hours ago (this was after her fit of yesterday), she surprised me by her air of calm. That's how she was! But I spent the whole night trembling with terror over what had happened that day. But suddenly she came up to me, stood before me, folding her hands (only hours ago!), and began to tell me that she was the guilty party and she knew it, that her crime had tormented her all winter and was tormenting her even now . . . that she cherished my magnanimity. . . . "I will be your faithful wife; I will respect you...."At this point I jumped up and, like a madman, I embraced her! I kissed her; I kissed her face and her lips, and I kissed her like a husband for the first time after a long separation. And why did I ever leave her? Only for two hours ... our passports for abroad.... Oh, God! Just five minutes, if only I had come back just five minutes earlier!... And here was this crowd of people at our gate, people staring at me.... Oh, Lord!

Lukeria says—(oh, now I'll never let Lukeria go; she knows everything. She was here all winter; she'll be able to tell me)—she says that after I left the house, and only some twenty minutes before I came back, she suddenly went to the mistress in our room to ask something—I don't remember what—and noticed that her icon (that same icon of the Virgin Mary) had been removed from the icon case and was standing before her on the table; the mistress, it seemed, had just been praying before it.

"What is it, ma'am?"

"It's nothing, Lukeria, you may go.... Wait, Lukeria."

She came up to Lukeria and kissed her.

"Are you happy, ma'am?" Lukeria asked.

"Yes, Lukeria."

"The master should have come to ask your forgiveness a long time ago, ma'am. Thanks be to God you've made it up."

"That's fine, Lukeria," she said. "You may go now."

And she smiled, but oddly somehow. It was such an odd smile that ten minutes later Lukeria came in again to have a look at her: "She was standing by the wall, right near the window, her arm against the wall and her head against her arm, just standing there, thinking. And she was so deep in thought that she didn't even notice me standing there watching her from the other room. I could see she had a kind of smile on her face, standing there, thinking and smiling. I looked at her, turned and went out on tiptoe, wondering about her. But suddenly I heard the window open. Right away I went in to tell her that it was still cool outside and she might catch a cold if she wasn't careful. And I saw that she'd climbed up on the windowsill and was standing upright in the open window, her back to me, holding the icon. My heart just sank inside me, and I shouted 'Ma'am, ma'am!' She heard me and made a move as if to turn toward me, but didn't. She took a step, pressed the icon to her bosom, and leapt out the window!"

I remember only that when I came through the gate she was still warm. The worst thing was that they were all staring at me. They shouted at first, and then suddenly they all fell silent and made way before me, and . . . and she was lying there with the icon. I have a vague memory of coming up to her, silently, and looking for a long time. They all surrounded me and were saying something to me. Lukeria was there, but I didn't see her. She tells me she spoke to me. I only remember some fellow shouting to me that "there wasn't but a cupful of blood came out of her mouth, you could hold it in your hand!" And he showed me the blood there on the paving stone. I think I touched the blood and smeared the end of my finger with it; I recall looking at my finger while he kept on: "You could hold it in your hand!"

"What do you mean, in your hand?" I yelled at the top of my voice (so people say) and raised my arms to attack him. . . .

Oh, savage, how savage! A misunderstanding! It's unbelievable! Impossible!

4. I Was Only Five Minutes Late

And isn't it so? Can you believe this? Can you really say it was possible? For what, why did this woman die?

Oh, believe me, I understand; but why she died is still a question. She was frightened by my love, asked herself the solemn question whether to accept it or not, found the question too much for her to bear, and thought it better to die. I know—there's no point racking my brain about it: she had made too many promises and got frightened that she wouldn't be able to keep them; that much is clear. There are some facts about the case that are absolutely terrible.

Because why did she die? The question remains. The question keeps pounding in my brain. I would have left her *like that* if she had wanted to be left *like that*. She didn't believe it, that was the thing! But no, wait, I'm not telling the truth; it wasn't that way at all. It was simply because with me there had to be honesty: if she was going to love me, then she had to love me completely, not as she would have loved that shopkeeper. And since she was too chaste and too pure to compromise on the kind of love that would have satisfied the shopkeeper, she didn't want to deceive me. She didn't want to deceive me with a half-love or a quarter-love that masked itself as complete love. People like her are just too honest, that's the thing! And I wanted to instill some breadth of feeling into her then, you remember? A strange idea.

I'm awfully curious: did she respect me? I wonder, did she despise me or not? I don't think she did despise me. It's awfully queer: why didn't it even once, all winter long, enter my head that she despised me? I was as convinced as could be of the contrary, right until that moment when she looked at me with *stern amazement*. And it was specifically *stern*. At that point I realized at once that she despised me. I realized it unalterably and forever! Ah, let her despise me, even for the rest of her life, but let her go on living! Only hours ago she was still walking about, talking. I simply can't understand how she could have jumped out of the window! And how was I to have suspected it even five minutes before? I've called Lukeria in. I will never let Lukeria go now. Never!

Oh, we still could have come to terms. It was just that we had grown so terribly alienated from one another over the winter. But couldn't we have made that up? Why, oh why couldn't we have come together and begun a new life? I'm a noble, generous person, and so is she: and there's a point in common! Just a few more words, no more than a couple of days, and she would have understood everything.

What hurts me most is that the whole thing was a matter of chance—simple, barbaric, blind chance! That's what hurts! Five minutes, just five short minutes late! Had I arrived five minutes earlier, the moment would have passed over like a cloud and the notion would never have entered her head again. And the result would have been her understanding everything. And now the empty rooms again, and I'm alone again. There's the pendulum ticking; what does it care? It has pity for no one. I have no one now—that's the calamity.

I just keep pacing and pacing the floor. I know, I know—don't tell me: you think it's ridiculous for me to be complaining about a matter of chance and "five minutes." But it's obvious, surely. Just think of this one thing: she didn't even leave a note saying, "Don't blame anyone for my death," as all the others do. Couldn't she have realized that even Lukeria might get into some trouble: "You were alone with her," they could say, "and you pushed her out." They might have dragged Lukeria off to jail if it hadn't been for the four people looking out of the windows of the building in the courtyard. They saw her standing with the icon in her hands and saw her throw herself out. But the fact that there were people standing there looking on is also a matter of chance, you see. No, the whole thing was just a moment, only one unaccountable moment. An impulse, a passing fancy! And what of the fact that she prayed before the icon? That doesn't mean she was saying her prayers just before dying. The moment lasted no more than ten minutes, perhaps; the decision was made just while she was standing by the wall, her head resting against her arm, and smiling. The thought flew into her head, made her dizzy and—and she couldn't resist it.

Say what you like, but this is a clear case of misunderstanding. She could have gone on living with me. And what if anemia were the cause? Simply a case of anemia, of exhaustion of her vital energy? She was worn out from that winter, that's all....

I was too late!!!

How slender she looks in her coffin, and how sharp her little nose has become! Her eyelashes lie straight as arrows. And when she fell she didn't break anything, she wasn't disfigured! There was only this little bit of blood, "you could hold it in your hand." Not more than a spoonful. It was internal concussion. Here's a queer idea: what if I didn't have to bury her? Because if they take her away, then ... oh, no, it's hardly possible that they can take her away! Oh, of course I know that they should take her away; I'm not a madman and I'm not raving. On the contrary, my mind was never so clear. But how can it be? No one in the house again, these two rooms again, alone with my pawned goods again. I'm raving! Now I'm raving! I tormented her till she couldn't take it any more. That's it!

What do I care for your laws now? What do I care for your customs and your manners, your life, your state, your religion? Let your judge judge me, let them bring me to court, to your public court, and I will say that I don't acknowledge any of it. The judge will shout, "Be silent, sir!" And I will shout in reply: "What force do you have that can compel me now to obey? Why did this blind, immutable force destroy what was dearest to me? Why do I need your laws now? I will withdraw from your world." Oh, what do I care!

She cannot see! She's dead; she cannot hear! You don't know what a paradise I would have created for you. I had a paradise in my soul and I would have planted it all around you! So what if you wouldn't have loved me—what would that matter? Everything would have been *like that*, everything would have remained *like that.* You would only have talked to me as to a friend, and we would have been happy and laughed joyously as we looked into each other's eyes. And so we would have lived. And if you had come to love another, well so be it! You would have walked with him, laughing, and I would have watched you from the other side of the street. . . . I don't care what would have happened, if only she would open her eyes just once! Just for a moment, only one moment, if she would look at me just as she did a little while ago when she stood before me and vowed to be my faithful wife! Oh, in one glance she would understand everything!

Immutability! Oh, nature! People are alone on earth, that's the calamity! "Is there a man alive on the field?" cries the hero of the Russian epic. I cry the same, though not a hero, and no one responds. They say the sun gives life to the universe. The sun will rise and—look at it, is it not a corpse? Everything is dead, and everywhere there are corpses. There are only people alone, and around them is silence—that is the earth! "Love one another." Who said that? Whose commandment is that? The pendulum ticks, unfeelingly, disgustingly. It's two o'clock in the morning. Her little shoes stand by her cot, just as if they were waiting for her. . . . No, in all seriousness, when they take her away tomorrow, what will become of me?

December

1

1. More about a Case That Is Not as Simple as It Seems

Just two months ago, in my October *Diary*, I made some remarks about an unfortunate woman, Katerina Prokofievna Kornilova, who had run afoul of the law. This is that same stepmother who in May, during a fit of anger at her husband, had thrown her six-year-old stepdaughter out of a window. The case is particularly well known because of the fact that the little girl who was thrown from the fourth-story window suffered no injuries or harm and is now alive and well. I am not going to recall all the details of my October article; my readers have perhaps not forgotten it. I shall remind them only of the purpose of my article: this whole case at once seemed to me to be absolutely extraordinary, and I was immediately convinced that it must not be treated *too simply*. The unfortunate woman was pregnant; she was angry at her husband's reproaches; she was depressed. But it was not that—i.e., not the desire to take revenge on a husband who reproached and pained her—that was the cause of her crime; it was the "affect of pregnancy." In my view, she had at the time been suffering several days or weeks from that particular, uninvestigated but undeniably existing condition of certain pregnant women in which their personalities undergo strange and sudden changes and in which they are subject to strange influences; it is a kind of madness without madness that may some-times reach the point of truly abnormal behavior. I gave the ex-ample, known to me since childhood, of a certain Moscow lady who, during a specific period of her pregnancy, would fall victim to a strange compulsion to steal things. Yet this lady owned a carriage and was in absolutely no need of the things she would steal; still, she stole quite consciously and knew full well what she was doing. She was fully conscious all the while but was simply

unable to resist this strange compulsion. That is what I wrote two
months ago, and I confess that I wrote it with a very remote and
hopeless purpose of somehow helping and easing the lot of this
unfortunate woman, despite the terrible sentence that had already
been pronounced upon her. In my article I could not refrain from
saying that if, so many times already, our jurors have brought in
acquittals, mostly of women, despite a full confession to a crime
and obvious evidence determined by the court that that crime had
been committed, then it seemed to me that Kornilova could have
been acquitted as well. (Just a few days after the sentence on the
unfortunate, pregnant Kornilova, a most bizarre criminal and murderer, the woman Kirilova, was completely acquitted.) However,
let me quote what I wrote at the time:

> At least if the jury had acquitted the defendant they would have
> had something on which to base their verdict: "Although such path-
> ological affects occur but rarely, they do occur. What if there was an
> affect of pregnancy in this case as well?" That is something to consider.
> At least in this case everyone would have understood the grounds for
> mercy and no doubts would have been aroused. And what of the
> possibility of an error? Surely an error on the side of mercy is better
> than an error on the side of punishment, the more so as there is no
> way of verifying anything in this case. The woman is the first to
> consider herself guilty; she confessed immediately after committing
> the crime, and she confessed again in court six months later. So she
> will go to Siberia, perhaps, in conscience and in the depths of her
> soul considering herself guilty; so she will die, perhaps, repenting in
> her final hour and considering herself a murderer. And never will it
> occur to her, nor to anyone else on earth, that there is a pathological
> affect that can arise during pregnancy and that it, perhaps, was the
> cause of it all, and that, had she not been pregnant, nothing would
> have happened. . . . No, of two errors here, it is better to chose the
> error of mercy.

When I had written all that, caught up with my idea, I fell into
speculation and added that this poor twenty-year-old wrongdoer
who was about to give birth in prison had perhaps already made
up with her husband. Perhaps her husband (now free and having
the right to remarry) visits her in prison, waiting for her to be
sent off to forced labor, and they both weep and grieve. Her little
daughter, the victim, also visits her "mummy," having forgotten
everything, and cuddles her with all sincerity. I even sketched in

the scene of their farewell at the railway station. All these "speculations" of mine flowed from my pen at the time not merely to create some strong effect or to paint a picture; I simply had a feeling of the truth of life which then consisted in the fact that, even though each of them—the husband and the wife—might well have considered the other the guilty party, in fact they *could not help* but forgive one another and be reconciled once more. I felt that this was not only because of Christian feeling but precisely due to an involuntary, instinctive sense that the crime that had been committed (which in their simple view was so obvious and indisputable) in essence *was perhaps not a crime at all* but rather some sort of odd happening, committed in an odd way, as if not by their will but as a result of God's judgment for the sins of both of them. . . .

When I had finished that article and put out the issue of my *Diary*, still in the grip of my own speculations, I decided to try my very best to have a meeting with Kornilova while she was still in prison. I confess that I was very curious to test whether there was any truth in what I had written about Kornilova and speculated about her later. And, indeed, one very fortunate circumstance arose that soon allowed me to visit her and get to know her. And I myself was amazed: imagine, at least three-quarters of my speculations proved to be true. I had discerned what had happened nearly as well as if I had been present myself. Her husband really had visited her, and was continuing to do so; they both really do weep and grieve over one another; they say their farewells and forgive one another. "My little girl would have come," Mrs. Kornilova told me, "but she is in a kind of school now where the children are not allowed out." I regret that I cannot pass on everything that I learned about the life of this devastated family; there are some features of the case that are most curious, in their own way, of course. Oh, naturally I was mistaken in some things; but not in the essentials. For example, although the husband is a peasant, he wears German clothes; he is a good deal younger than I had supposed. He works as a "ladler," dealing with the dyes used for bank notes in the Government Printing Office, and he earns a rather substantial monthly salary for a peasant; thus he is considerably better off than I had supposed. She is a seamstress and works at sewing even now, in prison, where she gets orders and also earns good money. In short, it's not at all a matter of "coarse cloth and felt boots for her journey, tea, and sugar"; the tone of their conversations is rather higher than that. She had given birth a few days before my first visit, not to a son but a daughter, and so on. These are minor differences from my imaginings, but in the main and in the essence there was no mistake at all.

At that time, after giving birth, she was in a special area of the prison and was alone; she was sitting in a corner, and next to her on the bed lay her newborn daughter, who had just been christened the day before. When I came in the infant gave a weak cry with that particular little cracked voice all newborn infants have. This prison, by the way, is for some reason not even called a prison but rather "a house of preliminary detention of criminals." A good many criminals are held in it, however, especially ones charged with some very curious crimes, about which, perhaps, I will speak in due course. But I will add in passing that I came away much gladdened, at least by the women's section of the prison, where I saw the obviously humane attitude of the prison staff toward the inmates. Later I visited some other wards, such as the one holding inmates who were nursing infants. I saw the concern, attention, and care accorded these women by the prison staff immediately responsible for them. And even though I did not have a long time to observe conditions there, there are certain features, certain words, and certain actions and movements that at once indicate a great deal. I spent about twenty minutes with Mrs. Kornilova on the first occasion. She is a very young, attractive woman with an intelligent expression, but very naive indeed. For the first minute or two she was somewhat surprised by my visit, but she quickly realized that she was seeing next to her *a friendly person* who sympathized with her, which was how I had introduced myself when I came in. She became quite frank with me. She is not a particularly talkative person, nor is she very quick in conversation; but what she does say she states firmly and clearly, with evident honesty, and always in a kindly way but without being at all fulsome or ingratiating. She spoke to me not really as an equal but almost as a friend. At the time, probably under the influence of the very recent verdict in her case (which was pronounced in the very final days of her pregnancy), she was somewhat agitated and even began to weep when recalling one witness's testimony against her concerning certain things she is alleged to have said on the day of the crime and which she claims she never said. She was very much grieved by the injustice of this testimony; but what struck me was that she spoke with no bitterness at all and only exclaimed, "So it seems that was my fate!" When I turned the conversation to her newborn daughter, her face at once broke out in a smile: "Just yesterday," she said, "we christened her." "And what's her name?" "The same as mine, Katerina." That smile of a mother condemned to hard labor for her child born in prison right after the sentence, and condemned with her mother even before her birth—that smile produced a strange and painful impression on me. When I began to question her carefully about her crime, the tone of her answers at once made a very favorable impression on me. She answered all my questions directly and clearly, with no evasion at all, so that I saw at once that I need take no special precautions. She admitted frankly that she was guilty of everything she had been charged with. I was also at once struck by the fact that when she spoke of her husband (in a fit of anger at whom she had thrown her child out of the window) she not only had nothing malicious or even in the least way accusatory to say, but in fact it was quite the contrary. "So how did it all happen?" I asked. And she told me frankly how it happened. "I wanted to do something wicked, but it was as if it wasn't my own will but someone else's." I recall that she added (in answer to my question) that even though she at once went off to the police station to report what had happened, she "didn't want to go to the station at all, but somehow got there— not knowing how—and confessed the whole thing."

The day before my visit I learned that her attorney, Mr. L., had filed a motion to quash the verdict; thus there still remained some hope, faint though it might be. But aside from that, I had another possibility in mind. I will say nothing about it now, but I did pass it on to her at the end of my visit. She heard me out with no great faith in the success of my plans; she did believe fully in my sympathy for her, however, and thanked me for it. When I asked whether I might assist her in some other way, she at once realized what I meant and answered that she was not in any need and had both money and paid work. There was not the slightest bit of touchiness in what she said, so that had she been without money she perhaps would not have refused to accept a small contribution from me.

I visited her once or twice after that. As we spoke on one occasion, I made a point of bringing up the acquittal of the murderer Kirilova, which had occurred only a few days after the guilty verdict was pronounced on her, Kornilova. I did not notice the slightest trace of envy or protest in her, however. She is inclined to regard herself as a having committed a serious crime, in the full sense of the word. As I observed her more closely, I couldn't help but notice that this rather curious feminine character is grounded in a good deal of steadiness, orderliness, and (something that particularly caught my interest) cheerfulness. Nevertheless, she is obviously tormented by her reminiscences. She has deep and sincere grief over her past strictness toward the child. "I didn't take to her at all," she says. Her response to her husband's continual criticisms of her, in comparison to his first wife, was to beat the child; as I had surmised, she was jealous of this first wife. It is obvious that she is troubled by the thought that her husband is now free and even can marry. She was very pleased to tell me once, just as soon as I arrived, that her husband had visited not long before and had told her, "How can I think of marrying at a time like this!" And so, I thought, she must have been the one to raise the question with him. I repeat: she is fully aware that after her conviction her husband is no longer her husband and the marriage has been dissolved. It occurred to me then that their meetings and their conversations must thus be truly odd.

In the course of my visits I had occasion to discuss Kornilova with some of the prison staff and with Mrs. A. P. B, the assistant warden. I was surprised at the obvious sympathy that Kornilova had evoked in all of them. Among other things, Mrs. A. P. B. told me one curious thing she had noticed: when Kornilova had entered the prison (this was right after the crime), she seemed a different person altogether—coarse, rude, malicious, and quick to answer back. But no sooner had a few weeks passed than she suddenly and radically changed: there appeared a kind, meek, and simple-hearted creature—"and so she remains to this day." This piece of information seemed to me to be highly relevant to her *case*. But the trouble was that this *case* had already been heard and decided upon and the sentence pronounced. And then, just the other day, I learned that the court's verdict, which had been appealed, had been quashed (as a result of violation of Article 693 of the Criminal Code) and that the case will be reexamined by a jury in another division of the court. Thus, at the present moment, Kornilova is again a defendant and not a convict sentenced to hard labor, and is again the legal wife of her legal husband! And so hope shines before her once more. God grant that this young soul, which has already borne so much, not be crushed forever by a new verdict of guilty. Such shocks are hard for the human soul to bear. Her experience is like that of a man about to be executed by a firing squad; suddenly, he is untied from the post; his hopes are restored, the blindfold is removed from his eyes, he sees the sun once more. Then, five minutes later, he is taken and tied to the post again. In fact, can it be that no consideration at all will be given to the accused's pregnant condition at the time the crime was committed? The most important element of the prosecution's case, of course, is that she committed the crime *consciously.* But once more I ask: what role does consciousness play in a case like this? She might well have been fully conscious, but could she have resisted the wild and perverted fit of temporary insanity even with the clearest consciousness in the world? Does this really seem so impossible? Had she not been pregnant, at the moment of her outburst of anger she might have thought: "That wretched little brat ought to be thrown out of the window; at least that would stop him from nagging me about her mother all the time." She might have thought it, but she would not have done it. But in her pregnant condition *she could not resist* and she did it. Could it not have happened just this way? And what does it matter that she herself testified that even on the day before she had wanted to throw the girl out of the window but her husband had prevented her. This whole criminal intent, so logically and resolutely thought out (including moving the flowerpots from the windowsill, and so on) and carried out the following morning, cannot in any way be regarded as an ordinary crime with intent: something unnatural and abnormal occurred here. Consider one thing: after throwing the girl out of the window and looking out to see where she had fallen (the child was unconscious for the first minute and Kornilova, looking from the window, might have thought her dead), the murderer closes the window, gets dressed, and goes off to the police station where she confesses the whole thing. But why would she confess if she had planned the criminal deed calmly and resolutely, with cold-blooded deliberation? Who and where are the witnesses to testify that she did in fact throw the child out? Or did the girl simply fall out through carelessness? Indeed, she could have convinced her husband, when he returned, that the child had fallen out herself and that she, Kornilova, was not to blame for anything (thus getting her revenge on her husband and exonerating herself). Even if, when she looked out the window, she had determined that the child had not been hurt and was alive and so could later testify against her—even so, she would have had nothing to fear: for a judicial investigation, what significance could there be in a six-year-old child's testimony that she had been lifted up from behind and pushed from a window? Any medical expert could have confirmed that at the moment she lost her balance and fell (that is, even if she had fallen out by herself), the child might well have believed someone had seized her legs from behind and pushed her out. If that were so, then why did the guilty woman at once go off to the police station to confess? People of course will reply: "She was in despair and wanted to end her life in one way or another." In fact, no other explanation can be found. Yet this explanation itself shows the sort of emotional strain and upset this *pregnant woman* suffered from. Her own words are interesting: "I didn't want to go to the police station, and yet somehow I did." That means she was acting as if in a state of delirium, *"as if it wasn't my own will,"* despite being completely conscious of what she was doing.

On the other hand, the things that Mrs. A. P. B. says also explain a great deal: "She was a different person altogether—coarse, malicious—and suddenly, two or three weeks later, she changed entirely: she became meek, placid, and kind." Why was that? It was because the well-known pathological period of pregnancy had ended, the period of malignancy of will and "madness without madness." With it the period of temporary insanity came to an end and a new person appeared.

And now this is the situation: she will once more be sentenced to hard labor; once more she, who has already suffered such shocks and who has undergone so much, will be shocked and crushed by a *second* sentence. She, twenty years old and scarcely beginning to live, with a nursing infant in her arms, will be cast into a hard-labor prison. And what will be the result? Will she derive much from her hard labor? Will her soul not harden? Will she not sink into depravity? Will she not become embittered for the rest of her days? When did hard labor ever reform anyone? And what is most important, this all takes place against the background of this mysterious yet quite genuine state of temporary insanity resulting from her pregnancy at the time of the crime. I said two months ago, and I repeat: "It is better to err on the side of mercy than on the side of punishment." Acquit the unfortunate woman lest a young soul perish, a young soul that, perhaps, has so much life ahead of her and so much potential for good. All this will certainly perish in hard labor, for her soul will become depraved. Now, however, the terrible lesson she has endured may well keep her from evil for the rest of her life. Above all, it may be a powerful aid in developing and maturing that embryo and that potential for good which are obviously and certainly now present in that young soul. And even if her heart really were hardened and malicious, mercy would certainly soften it. But I assure you that her heart is far from being hardened and malicious, and I am not the only one to bear witness to that. Can we really not acquit her? Can we not *risk* acquitting her?

2. A Belated Moral

That October issue of my *Diary* caused me problems of a sort in other ways as well. It contains a short article, "The Sentence," which left me in a certain amount of doubt. This "Sentence" is the confession of a suicide, his last words written to justify himself and, perhaps, to provide a *moral lesson* before he put the gun to his head. Several of my friends, whose opinions I most value, praised my little article but also confirmed my doubts. They praised it for truly discovering what might be called the formula for suicides of this sort, a formula that clearly expresses their essence. But they too were skeptical: would the intent of the article be understood by each and every reader? Might it not, on the contrary, produce just the opposite impression on some? Moreover, might not some of them—those very ones who had already begun to have visions of a revolver or a noose—even be seduced on reading it and have their unfortunate intentions confirmed even more deeply? In short, my friends expressed those very same doubts which had begun to creep into my own mind. As a result, they concluded that the article should have been followed by a clear and simple explanation from the author of his intent in writing it, and even that a clear moral should be added.

I agreed with that. Indeed, I myself, even while writing the article, felt that a moral was essential, yet somehow I felt embarrassed to add one. I felt ashamed to assume that even the most naive of readers would be so simple-minded as to miss the *inner sense* of the article, its intent and its moral. Its intent was so clear to me that I could not help but assume that it was equally clear to everyone. It seems that I was mistaken.

Some years ago one writer observed, quite justly, that it used to be considered shameful for a person to admit he did not understand certain things because it gave direct evidence of his dullness and

ignorance, of the stunted development of his mind and heart and
the weakness of his mental faculties. But now, by contrast, the
phrase "I don't understand it" is very often uttered almost proudly
or at least with an air of importance. As far as his listeners are
concerned, this phrase at once seems to place the man on a pedestal;
what is even more absurd is that he shares his listeners' feelings
and isn't the least bit ashamed at the cheapness of the pedestal he
has mounted. Nowadays the words "I don't understand a thing
about Raphael" or "I made a point of reading the whole of Shakespeare and I confess that I found absolutely nothing special in
him"—these words nowadays might be taken not only as a sign
of profound intellect but even as something valorous, almost a great
moral accomplishment. And is it only Shakespeare or Raphael who
is subjected to such judgment and skepticism these days?

That comment which I paraphrased here regarding people who
take pride in their ignorance is quite true. Indeed, the pride of
the ignorant has become excessive. Dull or poorly educated people
aren't the least bit ashamed of their unfortunate qualities; on the
contrary, things seem to have reached the stage where these same
qualities even add some life to their characters. I have also often
noticed that a strong tendency toward specialization and dissociation
has developed in literature and in personal life, and that the poly-
math is becoming extinct. People who argue with their opponents
to the point of frothing at the mouth haven't read a line their
opponents have written for decades: "My convictions are different,"
they say, "and I do not intend to read nonsense like that." It's
truly a case of a kopeck's-worth of ammunition and a ruble's-worth
of ambition. Such extremes of one-sidedness and seclusion, dissociation and intolerance, have appeared only in our own time,
meaning the last twenty years in particular. Along with these things
many people display a bold audacity: those having scarcely any
learning laugh at those who know and understand ten times as
much, and even laugh in their faces. But worst of all is the fact
that the more time passes, the more firmly entrenched this
"straight-line" approach to things becomes. One can see, for example, a noticeable weakening of the feeling for language, for
metaphor and allegory. One can also see that people (generally
speaking) have begun to lose their sense of humor, and this itself,
according to one German thinker, is one of the surest signs of the
intellectual and moral decline of an epoch. What we have, rather,
are gloomy dullards with wrinkled brows and narrow minds who

can only move in one way, in a single direction along a single straight line. Do you imagine that I'm talking only about our young generation and about our liberals? I assure you that I have our elders and our conservatives in mind as well. As if in imitation of the young generation (who are now gray-haired, however), some twenty years ago there had already appeared strange, straight-line conservatives, irritated little old men, who understood absolutely nothing about current affairs or about the "new people" or the younger generation. Their "straight-linedness," if you can call it that, was sometimes even more severe, harsh, and obtuse than the straight-linedness of the new people. Oh, it's quite possible that all this came from an excess of good intentions and from noble feelings that had been offended by the follies of the time. But still, these people are sometimes more blind than even the latest straight-line individuals. However, I think that in denouncing straight-linedness I have strayed too far from my topic.

As soon as my article appeared I was overwhelmed by inquiries—by letter and in person—about what I meant in my "Sentence." "What are you trying to say here?" people asked; "Aren't you justifying suicide?" Others, so it seemed to me, had found something to be happy about. And so the other day a certain author, a Mr. N. P., sent me his little article, written in a politely abusive style, which he published in Moscow in the weekly *Recreation*. I don't subscribe to *Recreation* and don't believe that it was the editor who sent me this particular issue, so I attribute its receipt to the kindness of the author himself. He condemns and ridicules my article:

> I received the October issue of *A Writer's Diary*, read it, and fell to thinking. There are many good things in this issue, but many *strange* things as well. I will set forth my perplexity in the most concise manner I can. What was the point, for instance, of printing in this issue the "reflections" of one who killed himself out of boredom? I truly do not understand the point of this. These "reflections"—if one can so call the ravings of this semilunatic—have been known for a long time, in somewhat paraphrased form of course, *by all those whose business it is to know such things*, and thus their appearance *in our time*, in the diary of a writer such as F. M. Dostoevsky, serves only as an absurd and pitiful anachronism. Our age is one of *cast-iron conceptions*, an age of positive opinions, an age whose banner bears the motto: "To live by all means! ..." In everything and everywhere, of course, there are exceptions; there are suicides *with* and

without deliberation, but no one nowadays pays any attention to such cheap heroics. Heroism of that sort is only too ridiculous! There was a time when suicide, especially suicide *with deliberation*, was elevated to the level of the greatest "awareness" (but awareness *of what?*) and heroism (again, heroism of what kind?), but that *rotten* time has passed and has passed irretrievably. Thank heaven for that; there is nothing to be regretted in its loss.

Any suicide who dies with deliberation of the sort that was printed in Mr. Dostoevsky's diary deserves no sympathy at all. Such a person is no more than a coarse egotist and attention-seeker and a most harmful member of human society. He is even unable to complete his ridiculous deed without having people talk about it. Even here he is unable to sustain his role and his affectations; he has to write his "reflections," though he could die very well with no reflection at all.... Oh, the Falstaffs of life! These knights mounted on stilts! ...

I felt very depressed after reading this. Good Lord, do I have many readers like this? Did Mr. N.P., who states that my suicide doesn't deserve any compassion, seriously believe that I described his case in order to win him sympathy? Naturally, the single opinion of Mr. N.P. would not have been so important. But the fact is that in the present instance Mr. N.P. surely represents a type, a whole collection of people like himself, a type which is even somewhat similar to that brazen type I was speaking about just now, brazen and single-minded, a type holding those same "cast-iron conceptions" of which Mr. N.P. himself spoke in the excerpt I quoted from his article. The notion that there might be a whole collection of people like that truly scares me. Of course, I may be taking this too much to heart. Yet I'll tell you frankly: despite my sensitivity, I still would not consider writing a reply to this "collection" of people. This is certainly not because I am scornful of them— why not have a little chat with people, after all?—but simply because there is little space in this issue. And so, if I am replying now and sacrificing space, then I am, so to say, answering my own doubts and replying to myself, as it were. I can see that I have to add a moral to my October article, and do so without delay; I must explain its purpose and spell it out in plain words. At least my conscience will be at rest, that's the point.

3. Unsubstantiated Statements

My article "The Sentence" concerns the fundamental and the loftiest idea of human existence: the necessity and the inevitability of the conviction that the human soul is immortal. Underlying this confession of a man who is going to die "by logical suicide" is the necessity of the immediate conclusion, here and now, that without faith in one's soul and its immortality, human existence is unnatural, unthinkable, and unbearable. And it certainly seemed to me that I had clearly expressed the formula of the logical suicide, that I had found the formula. Faith in immortality does not exist for him; he explains that at the very beginning. Little by little the thought of his own aimless existence and his hatred for the unresponsiveness of the stagnant life around him leads to the inevitable conviction of the utter absurdity of human existence on earth. It becomes as clear as day to him that only those people can *consent* to live who are akin to the lower animals and who most closely resemble them through their weakly developed consciousness and their strongly developed and purely carnal needs. They consent to live precisely as animals do, that is, in order to "eat, drink, sleep, build their nests, and raise their young." Oh, yes, eating, sleeping, despoiling the earth, sitting on a soft chair—these things will long attract people to the earth, but cannot attract the higher types of people. Meanwhile, it is the higher types who rule over the earth and who have always ruled; and always the result has been that millions of people follow them when the times demand it. What is the most sublime of words and the most sublime of thoughts? This word, this thought (without which humanity cannot live) is very often first spoken by poor, unknown, and insignificant people who are very often oppressed and who die in oppression and obscurity. But the thought and the word they utter does not die and never disappears without leaving a mark; it can never disappear once it has been uttered—and that is a remarkable thing in human history. In the next generation, or two or three decades later, the thought of a genius already envelops everything and everyone and captures their imaginations—and it turns out that it is not the millions of people who are triumphant, and not the material powers that seem to be so awesome and unshakeable; it is not money, not the sword, not physical might, but the thought that was imperceptible at first— often the thought of one who seemed to be the least among men. Mr. N.P. writes that the appearance of such a confession in my *Diary* "serves" (serves whom and what?) "as an absurd and wretched anachronism," for now we have "an age of cast-iron convictions, an age of positive opinions, an age that holds up a banner with the slogan 'To live by all means!'..." (Indeed! That's probably

just why suicide has become so prevalent among our educated class.)
I can assure the respected Mr. N.P. and all those like him that
when the time comes, all this "cast iron" will be swept away like
down before some idea, no matter how insignificant that idea may
at first seem to these gentlemen of "cast-iron convictions." For me
personally, however, one of the most dreadful portents for our
future, and even for our very near future, lies in the very fact that,
in my view, in an all-too-large portion of educated Russians, by
some particular, strange . . . well, let me call it predestination—there
has taken root more and more, and with remarkable progressive
rapidity, an absolute lack of faith in one's soul and its immortality.
And this lack of faith takes root not only through a conviction (we
still have very few convictions about anything); it does so through
some strange, universal indifference to this most sublime idea of
human existence, an indifference at times even derisive. God only
knows what laws caused it to become established among us. It is
an indifference not only to this idea alone but toward everything
that is vital and expresses the truth of life, toward everything that
generates and nourishes life, gives it health, and does away with
corruption and putrefaction. In our time this indifference is even
almost a Russian peculiarity, at least in comparison with other
European nations. It has long since permeated the educated Russian
family and has all but destroyed it. Neither a person nor a nation
can exist without some higher idea. And there is *only one* higher
idea on earth, and it is the idea of the immortality of the human
soul, for all other "higher" ideas of life by which humans might
live *derive from that idea alone*. Others may dispute this point with
me (about the unity of the source of all higher things on earth, I
mean), but I am not going to get into an argument just yet and
simply set forth my idea in unsubstantiated form. It cannot be
explained all at once, and it will be better to do it little by little.
There will be time to do this in the future.

The man I told you about who committed suicide is indeed a
passionate exponent of his idea—that is, the necessity of suicide—
and not an indifferent or "cast-iron" sort of person. He is truly
tormented and suffering, and I think I conveyed that clearly
enough. It is all too clear to him that he cannot go on living, and
he is utterly convinced that he is correct and cannot be refuted.
He cannot escape confronting the highest and most fundamental
questions: "What is the point of living when he is already aware
that it is disgusting, abnormal, and inadequate for a human to live

have absolutely nowhere to get advice about the higher meaning of life. From our clever people, and generally from those who are to guide our youth, they can borrow at present, I repeat, little more than a satirical view; but there is nothing *positive*, in the sense of what to believe, what to respect and worship, what to strive for—and these things are so necessary, so essential to young people; young people everywhere and in every age have craved and sought after these things! And even if there were the capacity—within the family and in the schools—to pass on some sound advice, then again the family and the schools (not without some exceptions, of course) have lost all interest in doing so because of the multitude of other tasks and aims that are more practical and of more contemporary concern. The young people of December 6 on Kazan Square were doubtless nothing more than a "herd" driven on by the hands of some crafty scoundrels, at least judging *by the facts* set forth in *The Moscow News*. What will emerge from this affair and what will develop I cannot tell. Without a doubt there was a good deal of malicious and immoral tomfoolery here, a monkeylike aping of someone else's doings; nevertheless, it would have been possible to bring them together simply by assuring them that they were to gather in the name of something sublime and beautiful, in the name of some remarkable self-sacrifice for the greatest of purposes. Only a very few of them may have been concerned with this "quest for an ideal," but these few rule over the others and lead them—that much is already clear. And so now who is to blame that their ideal is such a grotesque one? Of course, they themselves are to blame, but not only themselves. Oh, doubtless even the reality that now surrounds them could have saved them from their grotesque alienation from all that is vital and real, from their crude incomprehension of the simplest things; but the point is that the times are such that our young generation's alienation from the soil and from the truth of the People must amaze and horrify even their own "fathers," who so long ago alienated themselves from everything Russian and who are living out their lives in the blissful tranquillity of higher critics of the Russian land. And so here is a lesson, a lesson to the family and to the school and to the blissfully convinced critics: they themselves cannot recognize *their own products* and they renounce them; but . . . but can they, these "fathers," be charged with *all* the blame? Are they themselves not the products and the consequences of some particular fateful laws and predeterminations that have stood over the whole educated stratum of

Russian society for nearly two centuries now, almost right up until the great reforms of the present reign? No, it is clear that two hundred years of alienation from the soil and *from any kind of activity* cannot simply be shrugged off without paying a price. It is not enough to accuse, one must seek remedies as well. I think that there are remedies: they are to be found among the People, in the things the People hold sacred, and in our joining with the People. But . . . but more about that later. I undertook my *Diary* in part for the purpose of speaking about these remedies, insofar as my abilities permit me.

5. On Suicide and Arrogance

But I have to finish with Mr. N.P. What happened to him happens to many people of his "type": for them, what is clear and too easily comprehended must be stupid. They are much more inclined to scorn clarity than to praise it. It is another matter with something covered with flourishes and fog: "Ah, this we don't understand; therefore it must be profound."

He says that the "discourse" of my suicide is only the "ravings of a semilunatic" and that it has "*long been well known*." I am very much inclined to think that the "discourse" became "known" to him only after his reading of my article. As far as the "ravings of a semilunatic" are concerned, these ravings (does Mr. N.P. and all those like him know this?), i.e., the conclusion of the necessity of suicide, are for many—and for far too many in Europe—something like the very latest word of science. I expressed this "latest word of science" very briefly, clearly, and in popular fashion, but with the single intention of refuting it—not by reasoning or logic, for it is logically irrefutable (and I challenge not only Mr. N.P. but anyone you please to refute logically these "ravings of a semilunatic")—but by faith, by deducing the necessity of faith in the immortality of the human soul, by deducing the conviction that this faith is the single source of a genuine life on earth—of life, health, healthy ideas, and healthy deductions and conclusions. . . .

And, in conclusion, something quite comical. In that same October issue I informed my readers about the suicide of the daughter of an emigrant: "She soaked a piece of cotton wool in chloroform, bound this to her face, and lay down on the bed. And so she died. Before her death she wrote a note: 'I am setting off on a long journey. If the suicide should not succeed, then let everyone gather to celebrate my resurrection with glasses of Cliquot. If I do succeed, I ask that you not bury me until you have determined that I am completely dead, because it is most unpleasant to awaken in a coffin underground. That would not be *chic* at all!'"

Mr. N.P. mounted his high horse after reading of this "frivolous" suicide and decided that her act "merits no attention at all." He was angry at me for my "exceedingly naive" question about which of the two suicides suffered more on earth. But then there was an absurd note. He unexpectedly added: "I daresay that a person who wants to *greet* her return to life with a glass of champagne in her hand" (where else?) "could not have *suffered* very much in this life if she chooses to enter it again with such ceremony and without altering her way of life one bit, in fact, not even considering any alterations. . . ."

What a funny thing to say! What beguiled him most of all was the champagne: "Anyone who drinks champagne cannot possibly suffer." But you see, if she had loved champagne so much, then she would have gone on living in order to drink it; but as it was, she wrote about the champagne just before her death—before the serious fact of death—knowing full well that she would certainly die. She could not have had much faith in her chances of recovery, and recovery, in any case, did not hold any attraction for her since it only meant a recovery for another attempt at suicide. So the champagne is of no real consequence here; she had no intention of drinking it. Does that really require explanation? She mentioned the champagne simply out of the desire to make an outlandish and cynical statement when dying. She settled on champagne because she could find no picture more vile and obscene than sipping champagne at her "resurrection from the dead." She had to write this obscenity as an insult to everything she was leaving on earth, to curse the earth and her earthly life, to spit on it and so make that spitting her final statement to those friends she was leaving behind. What was the cause of such malice in this seventeen-year-old girl? (N.B.: She was seventeen, and not twenty, as I wrote in my article. Several people who knew more about the case corrected me afterward.) And at whom was the malice directed? No one had offended her; she was not wanting for anything; she died, apparently, also for no reason whatsoever. But it was precisely that note, precisely the fact that at such a moment she was so *concerned* to make such an obscene and outlandish statement that (obviously) leads one to the thought that her life had been immeasurably purer than this grotesque obscenity would suggest, and that the malice, the boundless bitterness of this gesture testifies, rather, to the great suffering and pain she had borne and her despair at the final moment of her life. Had her death been caused by some apathetic boredom that she herself could not recognize, she would not have made this grotesque statement. One must take a more compassionate attitude toward such a spiritual condition as hers. Obviously she was suffering, and certainly she died from spiritual yearning, having undergone great inner torment. What was it that caused her so much torment in her seventeen years? But here we raise the terrible question of our age. I have suggested that she died from heartache (much too precocious a heartache) and from a sense of the pointlessness of life, solely the result of the warped theory of child-rearing in her parents' home, a theory with a mistaken concept of the higher meaning and purposes of life, a theory that deliberately destroyed in her soul any faith in its immortality. Let this be only my suggestion; but surely she did not die only in order to leave this mean little note behind her so as to astonish people, as Mr. N.P. supposes. "No man shall hate his flesh." Destroying one's self is a serious thing, despite any *chic* that may be involved, and an epidemic of self-destruction spreading among the educated classes is an extremely serious thing which warrants constant observation and examination. A year and a half ago one highly talented and competent member of our judicial system showed me a bundle of letters and notes he had collected that were written by suicides, in their own hand, immediately before they had taken their lives, i.e., five minutes before death. I can recall two lines written by a fifteen-year-old girl; I also recall a note scribbled in pencil, written in a moving carriage in which the man shot himself before reaching his destination. I think that if Mr. N.P. had even glanced through this most interesting bundle of letters, then even in his soul, perhaps, there might have been a certain change and his peaceful heart would have become troubled. But I don't know for certain. In any case, one must look at these facts with greater compassion, and certainly not with such arrogance. We ourselves, perhaps, are to blame for these facts, and there is no cast iron that will later save us from the disastrous consequences of our complacency and arrogance when, in the fullness of time, we suffer the consequences.

But that's enough. My reply has been made, not to Mr. N.P. alone, but to many Messrs. N.P.

2

1. A Story from the Lives of Children

Let me tell you about this so that I won't forget it.

On the outskirts of Petersburg—in fact, even beyond the outskirts—there live a mother and her twelve-year-old daughter. The family is not well-off, but the mother has a job and earns her own living. The daughter attends school in Petersburg and always travels by public coach, which makes several scheduled trips a day between the Gostiny Dvor and the place where they live.

And so, recently, a couple of months ago, just at the time when winter so quickly and unexpectedly set in with a week of calm, bright days and a few degrees of frost and it first became possible to travel by sled, the mother looked at her daughter one evening and said: "Sasha, I don't see you studying your lessons. I haven't seen you do anything for some days now. Do you know your lessons?"

"Oh, Mama, don't worry; everything's done. I've even prepared a whole week ahead."

"Well, then, I suppose it's all right."

Sasha went off to school the next day; sometime after five o'clock the conductor of the coach on which Sasha was to return home jumped off as he was passing their house and handed Mama a note from her which read as follows: "Dear Mama, I have been a very bad girl all week. I got three zeros and I've been lying to you all the time. I'm ashamed to come home, and I'm never coming back again. Good-bye, dear Mama, forgive me. Your Sasha."

You can well imagine how the mother felt. She naturally wanted to drop everything at once, rush off to the city, and somehow try to find her Sasha. But where should she look? How could she ever find her? A close friend of the family happened to be there; he

743

was deeply concerned about the matter and volunteered to go at once to Petersburg to make inquiries at the school and then to check at all the homes of her acquaintances; if need be, he would search all night long. The main consideration that led the mother to put her trust in the deep concern of this kind man and stay at home herself was that, should Sasha think better of her decision and come back, she might leave again if she did not find her mother there. They decided that if Sasha were not found by morning, they would notify the police at dawn. The mother spent some very difficult hours at home, which you can well understand without my description.

"And so," the mother relates, "about ten o'clock I suddenly heard the familiar, hurried little steps in the snow outside and then on the stairs. The door opened, and there was Sasha."

"Mama, dear Mama, I'm so glad I came back to you!"

She clasped her little hands together, then hid her face behind them and sat down on the bed. She was so tired and worn out. Well then, of course, came the first cries and the first questions. The mother proceeded very cautiously, still afraid to reproach her daughter.

"Oh, Mama, after I told you those lies yesterday about my lessons I made up my mind: I wasn't going to go to school anymore and I wasn't going to come back home; because once I stopped going to school, how could I lie to you every day and tell you that I was?"

"But what on earth were you going to do? If you weren't at school and you weren't living here, then where would you go?"

"I thought I'd live on the street. As soon as it was day, I'd just keep walking around the streets. I've got a warm coat, and if I got cold I could stop in at the Arcade. I could buy a roll for my dinner every day, and I'd manage to find something to drink— there's snow on the ground now. One roll would be enough. I've got fifteen kopecks, and a roll costs three, so that's five days."

"And then?"

"And then I don't know what. I hadn't thought about it."

"And at night? Where were you planning to spend your nights?"

"Oh, I've thought about that. When it got dark and late I was going to go to the railway, way past the station where there aren't any people around, but there're an awful lot of railway cars. I'd crawl into one of those cars that looked like it wouldn't be moved anywhere and spend the night. And I did go there. I walked a long way, well past the station, and there wasn't a soul around. Off to one side I saw some cars, but not at all like the ones everyone rides in. There, I thought, I'll crawl into one of those and nobody will see me. I was just starting to get in, and suddenly a watchman shouted at me: 'Where do you think you're going? Those cars are for hauling dead people.'

"As soon as I heard that I jumped down; but I could see he was already getting close."

"'What do you think you're doing here?'"

"I just ran away from him as fast as I could go. He shouted something, but I just ran off. I went along, scared out of my wits. I came back to the street and I'm walking around when suddenly I see a building, a big stone house that's being built—it's only just bare bricks, no glass in the windows and no doors—they're boarded up—and there's a fence around it. Well, I think, if I can somehow get into that house, no one will see me there 'cause it's dark. I went down a little alleyway and found a spot where the boards were open enough for me to squeeze through. So I squeezed through and came right into a pit, still full of earth; I felt my way along the wall to a corner where there were some boards and bricks. Well, I thought, I can spend the night here on these boards. And so I lay down. But all of I sudden I hear voices speaking ever so quietly. I raised my head and right in the corner I hear people talking in low voices and I see someone's eyes that seem to be staring right at me. I was scared out of my wits and right away I ran out through that same door and onto the street again. I can hear them calling after me. I managed to slip away. And here I had thought that there was no one in the house!

"When I got back on the street again I suddenly felt so tired. So very, very tired. I walk around the streets, there're people about; what time it is I don't know. I came out on Nevsky Prospect and I'm walking by the Gostiny Dvor, crying my eyes out. 'Now,' I think, 'if only some nice person would come along and take pity on a poor little girl who has nowhere to spend the night. I'd tell him everything, and he'd say: "Come and stay with us for the night."' I keep thinking about that as I walk along, and suddenly I look up and see our coach standing there, ready to start off for its last trip here. And I thought it had surely left a long time ago. 'Ah,' I think, 'I'll go back to Mama!' I got on the coach, and now I'm so glad that I came back, Mama. I'll never lie to you again, and I'll study hard! Oh, Mama, Mama!"

"And so I asked her," the mother went on, "Sasha, did you really think up this whole plan yourself—about not going to school and living on the streets?"

"Well, Mama, you see, quite a while ago I made friends with a girl my age, only she's at a different school. But can you believe she hardly ever goes to school—she just tells them at home every day that she goes. She told me that she's bored in school, but it's lots of fun on the street. 'Once I leave the house,' she says, 'I just keep walking around. I haven't showed up at school for two weeks now. I look in the windows of the shops; I go to the Arcade, I eat a roll. And when evening comes, I go home.' When I heard that I thought: 'That's what I'd like to do.' And school started to seem so dull. But I didn't have the least notion of actually doing it until yesterday. And yesterday, after I lied to you, I made up my mind. . . ."

This story is true. Now, of course, the mother has taken some precautions. When the story was told to me I thought that it might fit very well into my *Diary*. I was given permission to publish it, without revealing the real names of the participants, of course. Naturally I will at once hear objections: "This is only one isolated case, and it happened simply because the girl was very stupid." I know for certain that the girl is not at all stupid. I also know that in these young souls, already past early childhood but still far from attaining even the first stage of maturity, there sometimes arise amazing, fantastic notions, dreams, and intentions. This age (twelve or thirteen years) is an unusually interesting one, even more so in a girl than in a boy. Speaking of boys, by the way: do you recall an item that appeared in the newspapers some four years ago about three very young high-school students who decided to run off to America? They were caught quite a distance away from their city and had a pistol in their possession. On the whole, even formerly— a generation or two ago—the heads of these young folks were just as full of dreams and fantastic plans as are the heads of today's youth. But today's young people are somehow more decisive and much less prone to doubt and reflection. Young people of past days might think up some project (running off to Venice, say, after reading all about the city in the tales of Hoffmann and George Sand—I knew one such person), but they never went on to carry it out. At most they might tell a friend about it after making him take an oath of secrecy; but today's young people think up plans and then carry them out. In the past, however, young people felt bound by a sense of duty and an awareness of their responsibility to their fathers and mothers and to certain beliefs and principles. But nowadays this sense of obligation has undoubtedly grown weaker. They have fewer restraints on them, both outer and inner. That, perhaps, is why their minds work in a more one-sided manner; and of course there are reasons for all this.

The main thing is that these are not isolated instances caused by stupidity. I repeat: this remarkably interesting age of twelve or thirteen years truly needs special study by our educational experts, who are so much involved with pedagogy, and by parents, who are now so much involved with matters of "business" and nonbusiness. And how easily all this can happen—the most terrible thing, I mean—and to whom? To our very own children! Just think of the place in this mother's story when the girl *"suddenly felt tired*, was walking along and crying, dreaming of meeting some kind man who would feel sorry for a poor girl with nowhere to spend the night and invite her to come home with him." Just imagine how easily this wish of hers, which reveals her childish innocence and immaturity, might have been fulfilled, given the fact that everywhere on our streets and in our wealthiest homes there are swarms of "kind men" of just that sort! And what, then, the next morning? Either a hole in the ice, or *the shame of confessing*, and after the shame of confessing would develop the capacity to *come to terms with this memory*—keeping everything to oneself but now pondering over it from a different point of view, to keep thinking and thinking about it, but with all sorts of new imaginings. And all this would happen little by little and of its own accord; and then at last, perhaps, would come the desire to repeat the experience, and then all the rest. And this at the age of twelve! And everything kept well concealed. Concealed in the full meaning of the word! What about this other girl who spent her time looking in the shops and visiting the Arcade instead of going to school and who taught our Sasha to do the same? I have often heard things of this sort about boys who found school boring and *vagrancy* fun. (N.B.: Vagrancy is a habit, an unhealthy one, and, in part, our national one; it is one of the things that distinguishes us from Europe. It is a habit which then is transformed into an unhealthy obsession, and it very often originates in childhood. I will certainly say something later about this national obsession of ours.) And so now, it seems, it is possible to have *vagrant* girls as well. And such a girl, let's say, is still completely *innocent*; but even if she is as innocent as the very first creature in the Garden of Eden, she still can't avoid "the knowledge of Good and Evil," even if only a bit of it, even if only in her imagination and in her dreams. The street, after all, is such a quick and ready school. And the main thing, which I repeat again and again: this is such a curious age, an age that, on the one hand, still completely preserves the most childish, touching innocence and immaturity but, on the other hand, has already acquired an avidly quick capacity for the perception of and rapid familiarization with such ideas and conceptions of which, in the view of so many parents and pedagogues, this age supposedly hasn't the haziest idea. It is this division, it is this joining together of these two so dissimilar halves of the young person, which presents such a danger and such a critical point in the lives of these young creatures.

2. An Explanation Regarding My Participation in the Forthcoming Publication of the Magazine *Light*

In *A Writer's Diary* (and once more in that same October issue) I placed an announcement of Professor N. P. Vagner's plans to publish a new magazine, *Light*, next year. No sooner had this announcement appeared than people began asking me about this new magazine and about my possible participation in it. I replied to everyone to whom I could reply that on N. P. Vagner's invitation I had promised to publish only a story in the magazine, and that that would be the *entire* extent of my participation in it. But now I can see that it is essential to make this clear in print as well, for the inquiries continue to come in. I receive letters from my readers every day which clearly show that, for some reason, they believe my participation in the magazine *Light* will be much more extensive than was indicated in Professor Vagner's announcement, i.e., that I will all but *transfer my activities* to *Light*; that I will undertake some new activities and expand my former ones, and that, if I will not be a direct participant in the editorial or publishing aspects of the magazine, then I am certainly closely involved in the concept, the views, the plan of the magazine, etc.

In reply to all this I now state that in the coming year I will be publishing only *A Writer's Diary* and that, as in the past year, my *entire* work as an author will be devoted to the *Diary*. As far as the new magazine *Light* is concerned, I am participating neither in its concept nor in its plan or its editorship. I do not even have any notion of the views of the forthcoming magazine and await the appearance of its first issue so that I may acquaint myself with them for the first time. I suppose that people assumed my particular close relationship with the magazine *Light* only from the fact that the first announcement about it appeared in *A Writer's Diary*, and that it somehow happened that the announcement appeared in no other newspaper for a rather long time thereafter. In any case, to promise a story to another publication does not mean abandoning one's own and switching to the new one. My most sincere wish for the success of the esteemed Professor Vagner's undertaking is based only on my personal hope, and even my conviction, that we shall find something new, original, and useful in his magazine. But I know no further details about the magazine *Light*. I have nothing to do with its publication and at the moment know nothing more than anyone who has read the newspaper advertisement about it.

3. Where Does the Matter Stand at the Moment?

A year has passed, and with this twelfth issue the first year of publication of *A Writer's Diary* comes to an end. I have had a most gratifying response from my readers, and yet I have not managed to say a hundredth part of what I intended to say; many of the things I did say, I now can see, I did not manage to express clearly the first time, and my views were even frequently misinterpreted, something which is, of course, mainly my fault. Although I didn't manage to say very much, I still hope that, even from what was expressed this year, my readers will understand the nature and the tendency the *Diary* will have in the coming year. The principal aim of the *Diary* thus far has been to elucidate as best I can the idea of the uniqueness of our national spirit and to point out as best I can its manifestations in the facts that present themselves day by day. In this sense, for example, the *Diary* has said quite a lot about this year's sudden national and Popular movement in the so-called "Slavic cause." Let me say in advance: the *Diary* does not make any claim to present monthly articles on politics; but it will always attempt as best it can to find and to point out our national and Popular point of view in current political events. For example, from my articles on the "Slavic movement" of this year the readers perhaps have already realized that the *Diary* wanted only to clarify the essence and the significance of this movement as it concerns us Russians, first and foremost; it wanted to show that for us this cause is not only a matter of Slavism and is not limited to the political side of the question as it is posed today. Slavism—the unity of all the Slavic peoples with the Russian People and among themselves—and the political aspect of the question— matters of borders and frontier regions, seas and straits, Constantinople, etc.—are both questions which, though certainly of top priority for Russia and her future destiny, still do not exhaust the essence of the Eastern Question for us, i.e., in the sense that it can be solved in the spirit of our People. In that sense, these questions of top priority must take second place. For the essence of the whole matter, as the People understand it, consists entirely and without a doubt only in the fate of Eastern Christianity, i.e., Orthodoxy. Our People know neither the Serbs nor the Bulgarians; they send their humble donations and their volunteers not to help the Slavs and not to help Slavism. They do this only because they have heard how Orthodox Christians, our brethren, are suffering at the hands of the Turks, the "godless Agarians," for the faith of Christ. That is why—and that is the only reason—this whole movement of the People began this year. The present and future destinies of Orthodox Christianity make up the entire idea of the Russian People; in this is their service to Christ, and in this their eagerness to accomplish some great deed for Christ. This eagerness is genuine and magnificent; it has been unstoppable since times of old; perhaps it will never stop. And that is a most important fact about the character of our People and our state. The Old Believers of Moscow equipped and donated a whole field hospital (and an excellent one), which they sent to Serbia; yet they knew full well that the Serbs were not Old Believers but people like ourselves with whom they are not in accord on matters of religion. An incident such as this showed clearly the notion of the future, ultimate fate of Orthodox Christianity, remote though it well may be, and the hope of a future union of all Eastern Christians. And in helping the Christians against the Turks, the oppressors of Christianity, the Old Believers indicated that they considered the Serbs just such genuine Christians as they themselves are—or Christians of the future, at least—despite some temporary differences. In that sense, this donation even has historic significance, inspiring comforting thoughts and confirming in part my statement that in the fate of Christianity is also contained the whole aim of the Russian People, despite the fact that they are temporarily disunited by certain chimerical differences of religion. There can be no disputing the fact that among the People there has even been fixed and consolidated the belief that the whole of Russia exists only in order to serve Christ and to protect *all* of the Orthodox of the world from the unbeliever. If this thought is not directly expressed by every one of the People, then I assert that large numbers of the People will express it quite consciously, and these large numbers unquestionably have an influence on the rest. Thus one may state plainly that this thought is almost a *conscious* one in the whole of our People and not merely something cloaked in Popular sentiment. And so, in this sense alone is the Eastern Question intelligible to the Russian People. That is the most important fact.

But if such is the case, the view of the Eastern Question ought to become much more clearly defined for all of us. Russia's strength lies in her People and their spirit and not merely in her education, for example, or her wealth, enlightenment, and so on, as is the case in certain European states which have, through decrepitude and loss of their vital national idea, become entirely artificial and even somehow unnatural. I think that this will be true for a long time to come. But if the People understand the Slavic question, and the Eastern Question generally, only in terms of the fate of Orthodoxy, then it follows that the cause is not merely an accidental, passing one, nor merely a superficial political one, but touches on the very essence of the Russian People; this means that it is an eternal cause that will remain until its ultimate resolution. Russia, in this sense, can no longer renounce her movement to the East and cannot change her aims, for then she would be renouncing herself. And if, temporarily, following circumstances, this question did—and certainly had to—sometimes assume a different orientation; if there were times when we had to and even wanted to yield to circumstances and curb our aspirations—still, this question as a whole and as the essence of the very life of the Russian People must certainly sometime achieve its principal aim, that is, the union of all the Orthodox families in Christ and in brotherhood and with no more distinction between the Slavs and other Orthodox nationalities. This union may not be a political one at all. The specific Slavic question, in its narrow sense, and the political question, in its narrow sense (i.e., the seas, straits, Constantinople, etc.) will resolve themselves in the course of this process in the way least in discord with the solution of the main and fundamental issue. Thus, I repeat, from this Popular standpoint the whole question takes on solidity and permanence.

In this respect, Europe, which has no comprehension whatever of our national ideals (measuring them by her own standard, that is, and crediting us only with greed for new territory, violence, and conquest) at the same time understands the essence of the matter very clearly.

But for Europe what matters is certainly not that we will now not seize territory and that we promise not to conquer anyone: what is much more important for her is the fact that, as before and as always, we are adamant in our determination to help the Slavs and have no intention of abandoning that help. And if this should happen even now, and we do come to the aid of the Slavs, then we, in the eyes of Europe, will be laying down another stone in that fortress which we supposedly are gradually erecting against her in the East; of this the whole of Europe is convinced. For in helping the Slavs we are at the same time continuing to instill and strengthen the Slavs' faith in Russia and her power, and more and more are making them accustomed to regard Russia as their sun, the center of the whole of the Slavic world and even of the whole of the East. And, in Europe's eyes, the strengthening of this notion is something that could lead us to conquests, despite all the concessions that Russia is honorably and justly prepared to make in order to soothe Europe. Europe realizes only too well that this *planting of an idea* contains the whole essence of the cause at the moment, and that it is not merely a matter of material acquisitions in the Balkan peninsula. Europe also realizes that Russian policy as well regards all this most clearly as the essence of its aim. And if such is the case, then how can she, Europe, not be afraid? That is why Europe would like to take the Slavs under her protection by any means she can, to steal them away from us, as it were, and if possible to turn them against Russia and the Russians for ever. That is why she would have liked the Treaty of Paris to continue for as long as possible. That is also the source of all these projects about the Belgians, the European gendarmerie, and so on. Oh, anything, as long as it is not the Russians, as long as it somehow hides Russia from the eyes and the thoughts of the Slavs and even erases her from their memory! And that is where the matter stands at present.

4. A Short Comment on "Pondering Peter"

Recently there has been a good deal of talk of how the heated summer raptures of our educated classes were followed by a distinct chill, mistrust, cynicism, and even anger. Aside from certain very definite opponents of our Slavic movement, I think that all the others can be grouped into two general categories. The first category we may call the *Judaizers*. They rattle on about the damage that war can cause in an economic sense; they frighten us with bank failures, a drop in the exchange rate, a decline in trade, and even our military weakness—not only with respect to Europe but even with respect to the Turks, forgetting that the Turkish bashibazouk, who tortures the unarmed and the defenseless and who beheads dead bodies, is—in the words of the Russian proverb—"a brave lad against a sheep, but a sheep against a brave lad." The truth of this will certainly be borne out. What exactly do the Judaizers want? The answer is clear: in the first place, and principally, they found it difficult to keep sitting in their comfortable seats. But without entering into this moral aspect of the matter, let me note the second thing: the complete and utter lack of any historical and national understanding of the task that lies ahead. They regard the matter as if it were some passing little whim that can be ended whenever we feel like it: "You've had a chance to kick up your heels," they seem to be saying, "but that's enough. Let's get back to business now." Stock-exchange business, of course.

The second category are the *Europeanizers*, our same old Europeanizing movement again. From this side we still hear the most "radical" questions: "What use are the Slavs to us, and why should we love them? Why should we go off to war for them? In pursuing some useless cause, will we not damage our own development, our schools? In pursuing the cause of nationality, will we not set back the cause of universality? Will we not, finally, arouse religious fanaticism in Russia?" And so on and so forth. In short, although these questions may be radical ones, they have long been worn out. The principal thing here is our old, outmoded, senile, and historical fear of the bold notion that Russia might possibly act independently. At one time this whole lot were liberals and progressives and were considered as such; but their historical moment has passed, and now it is difficult to imagine anything more retrograde. Meanwhile, in their blissful stagnation in the ideas of the 1830s and 1840s they continue to regard themselves as being in the forefront of things.

Formerly they were regarded as democrats; now one simply can't conceive of anyone more squeamishly aristocratic in their attitude to the People. Some may say that they have only condemned the dark side of our People; but the point is that in condemning the dark side they have also belittled all that is bright, and one can even say that it was precisely in the bright side that they saw darkness. They have not managed to make out what is bright and what is dark here! And in truth, if one looks closely into all the views of our Europeanizing intelligentsia, then one can conceive of nothing more harmful to the healthy, just, and independent development of the Russian People.

And all this is done with complete, sincere innocence. Oh, of course they love the People, but . . . in their own fashion. And what does it matter that someday everything in Russia will be consolidated and made clear? Before that happens some great events may come to pass and catch our intelligentsia by surprise. Then might it not be too late? The proverb says, "Catch Peter in the morning; if he ponders an hour his thoughts will turn sour." It's a rough sort of proverb and not a very elegant expression, but there is truth in it. Wouldn't the same thing happen to the Russian Europeanizing individual as to Peter late in the day? Hasn't he perhaps been pondering things too long? The point is just that something of this sort has, it seems, already begun to happen. . . .

And yet for me it is almost axiomatic that all our Russian disunities and dissociations have been founded from the very beginning only on misunderstandings, the crudest sort of misunderstandings, with nothing of real substance in them. The worst of it is that it will be a long time yet before each and every one of us realizes that. This, too, is one of our most interesting topics.

Notes

The following notes are intended to provide the English-speaking reader with at least minimal background information about references in the text. The most important source is provided by the voluminous and quite excellent annotations included in the USSR Academy of Sciences' thirty-volume edition of Dostoevsky's *Complete Works*, F. M. Dostoevsky, *Polnoe sobranie sochinenii v tridstati tomakh* (Leningrad: Nauka, 1972–88), abbreviated hereafter as *PSS*. However, these notes are based on a set of assumptions that are not always applicable to nonspecialist readers in the West: Soviet readers do need not to be told about Belinsky or Nekrasov, for example, whereas the Western reader might. Thus, I have not provided a complete translation of the notes in *PSS* but have used them, rather, as a guide. I have attempted to check independently each reference derived from this source, but this has not always been possible: many of the nineteenth-century Russian newspapers Dostoevsky read so avidly are not available in North America and are difficult to access even in the Soviet Union. Additional material was derived from specific works cited in the notes themselves, and from the works of individual writers whom Dostoevsky mentions in the *Diary*. The sources listed below were repeatedly consulted.

All dates mentioned in the notes are old style (o.s.), i.e., twelve days behind the Gregorian calendar, unless otherwise indicated.

Sources

Baedeker, Karl. *Russia, with Teheran, Port Arthur, and Peking: Handbook for Travellers*. Leipzig: Karl Baedeker, 1914.

Bol'shaia entsiklopediia [Great encyclopedia]. Ed. S. N. Iuzhakov. 22 vols. St. Petersburg: Prosveshchenie, 1896.

Bol'shaia sovetskaia entsiklopediia [Great Soviet encyclopedia]. Ed. O. Iu. Shmidt. 65 vols. Moscow: Sovetskaia entsiklopediia, 1926–47.

Bol'shaia sovetskaia entsiklopediia [Great Soviet encyclopedia]. 3d ed. Ed.
    A. M. Prokorov. 30 vols. Moscow: Sovetskaia entsiklopediia, 1970–
    78.
Dostoevskaia, A. G. *Vospominaniia* [Memoirs]. Moscow: Khudozhestven-
    naia literatura, 1971.
Encyclopaedia Britannica. 11th ed. 29 vols. Cambridge: Cambridge Uni-
    versity Press, 1910–11.
Encyclopaedia Britannica. 14th ed. 24 vols. Chicago, London, and Toronto:
    William Benton, 1958.
New Encyclopaedia Britannica. 15th ed. 32 vols. Chicago: Encyclopaedia
    Britannica, 1987.
Entsiklopedicheskii slovar' [Encyclopedic dictionary]. 82 vols. St. Peters-
    burg: Brokgauz and Efron, 1890–1904.
Entsiklopedicheskii slovar' [Encyclopedic dictionary]. 58 vols. St. Petersburg
    and Moscow: Granat, 1910–40.
Frank, Joseph. *Dostoevsky: The Seeds of Revolt,* 1821–1849. Princeton,
    N.J.: Princeton University Press, 1976.
———. *Dostoevsky: The Years of Ordeal,* 1850–1859. Princeton, N.J.:
    Princeton University Press, 1983.
———. *Dostoevsky: The Stir of Liberation,* 1860–1865. Princeton, N.J.:
    Princeton University Press, 1986.
Der Grosse Brockhaus. 15 vols. Wiesbaden: F. A. Brockhaus, 1977–81.
Grossman, Leonid. *Seminarii po Dostoevskomu: Materialy, bibliografiia i
    kommentarii* [Seminars on Dostoevsky: Source materials, bibliog-
    raphy, commentaries]. Moscow and Petrograd: Gos. Izdatel'stvo,
    1922.
———. *Zhizn' i trudy F. M. Dostoevskogo: Biografiia v datakh i dokumentakh*
    [The life and works of F. M. Dostoevsky: A biography in dates and
    documents]. Moscow and Leningrad: Academia, 1935.
Guedalla, Philip. *The Second Empire.* London: Hodder and Stoughton,
    1932.
Istoriia Moskvy [The history of Moscow]. 6 vols. Moscow: AN SSSR,
    1952–59.
Istoriia russkoi literatury XIX veka [A history of Russian literature of the
    nineteenth century]. Ed. D. N. Ovsianiko-Kulikovsky. 5 vols. Mos-
    cow: Mir, 1908–10.
Kratkaia literaturnaia entsiklopediia [Short literary encyclopedia]. Ed. A.
    A. Surkov. 9 vols. Moscow: Sovetskaia entsiklopedia, 1962–78.
Mochulsky, Konstantin. *Dostoevsky: His Life and Work.* Trans. and intro.
    by Michael Minihan. Princeton, N.J.: Princeton University Press,
    1967.
Modern Encyclopedia of Russian and Soviet History. Ed. Joseph L. Wie-
    czynski. Gulf Breeze, Fla.: Academic International Press, 1976–.
Modern Encyclopedia of Russian and Soviet Literature. Ed. Harry B. Weber.
    Gulf Breeze, Fla.: Academic International Press, 1977–.
Nechaeva, V. S. *Zhurnal M. M. i F. M. Dostoevskikh "Vremia," 1861–*

1863 [M. M. and F. M. Dostoevsky's journal "Time," 1861–1863].
Moscow: Nauka, 1972.

——. *Zhurnal M. M. i F. M. Dostoevskikh "Epokha," 1864–1865* [M.
M. and F. M. Dostoevsky's journal "Epoch," 1864–1865]. Moscow:
Nauka, 1975.

Ocherki istorii Leningrada [Outlines of the history of Leningrad]. Ed. M. P.
Viatkin et al. 7 vols. Moscow and Leningrad: AN SSSR, 1955–89.

Petrovich, Michael Boro. *A History of Modern Serbia, 1804–1918.* 2 vols.
New York: Harcourt, Brace, Jovanovich, 1976.

Abbreviations

BV   *Birzhevye vedomosti* [The Stock Exchange News]—liberal daily
D   *Delo* [The Cause]—radical monthly
DP   *Dnevnik pisatelia* [A Writer's Diary]
E   *Epokha* [The Epoch]—St. Petersburg monthly edited by Dostoev-
      sky (1864–65)
G   *Golos* [The Voice]—St. Petersburg daily, moderately liberal
Gr   *Grazhdanin* [The Citizen]—conservative weekly edited by Dos-
      toevsky (1873)
MV   *Moskovskie vedomosti* [Moscow News]—conservative daily
NV   *Novoe vremia* [New Times]—leading St. Petersburg daily
OZ   *Otechestvennye zapiski* [Notes of the Fatherland]—monthly, edited
      by N. N. Nekrasov and M. Saltykov-Shchedrin (1868–84)
PG   *Peterburgskaia gazeta* [The Petersburg Gazette]—popular daily
RM   *Russkii mir* [The Russian World]—conservative daily
RV   *Russkii vestnik* [The Russian Messenger]—conservative monthly; a
      leading literary journal of the nineteenth century
S   *Sovremennik* [The Contemporary]—radical monthly, edited by N.
      Chernyshevsky and N. Dobroliubov (1856–62)
SV   *Sankt-Peterburgskie vedomosti* [St. Petersburg News]—conservative
      daily
V   *Vremia* [Time]—monthly, edited by F. M. and M. M. Dostoevsky
      (1861–63)
VE   *Vestnik Evropy* [The European Messenger]—liberal monthly
Z   *Zaria* [Dawn] — neo-Slavophile monthly

1873.1: Introduction

The Citizen: Dostoevsky's appointment as editor of *Gr* was confirmed by
the Main Administration of Press Affairs on December 20, 1872. His
tenure as editor began on January 1, 1873.

Chinese emperor: *MV,* no. 315, December 13, 1872, carried an account
of the elaborate ceremonies accompanying the wedding of the emperor
of China, T'ung-Chi, which took place on October 16, 1872.

Meshchersky, Vladimir Petrovich, prince (1839–1914), publisher, political
figure, and extreme conservative.

Bismarck: Meshchersky's novel *Odin iz nashikh Bismarkov* [One of our Bismarcks] was appearing in *Gr* in 1872–73.

Moscow News: *MV* was published by the conservative M. N. Katkov (1818–87), who frequently wrote its editorials.

The Voice: G was published by A. A. Kraevsky (1810–99) and frequently exchanged barbs with *Gr.*

From the Other Shore: Dostoevsky met Alexander Herzen (1812–70), writer, journalist, political thinker, and nineteenth-century Russia's most famous political emigré, in London in July 1862. Herzen's *S togo berega* [From the other shore] (1850) conveys his disillusionment after the failure of the European revolutions of 1848.

Pogodin, Mikhail Petrovich (1800–75), Russian historian, journalist, and panslavist. His article on Herzen appeared in *Z*, no. 2, 1870.

Belinsky, Vissarion (1811–48), nineteenth-century Russia's most famous literary critic. Herzen relates this story in *Byloe i dumy* [My past and thoughts], pt. 2, chap. 16. Belinsky's article, "Russkaia literatura v 1841 godu" [Russian literature in 1841] appeared in *OZ*, no. 1, 1842.

1873.2: Old People

That story: Dostoevsky first met Belinsky in early June 1845. Belinsky had heaped lavish praise on Dostoevsky's first work, *Bednye liudi* [Poor folk]. (See also notes to January 1877, 2.3.)

Proudhon, Pierre Joseph (1809–65), French socialist and political writer. Herzen contributed to Proudhon's newspaper *La Voix du peuple*, 1849–50. He describes his visit to the Paris barricades during the 1848 revolution in *My Past and Thoughts*, pt. 5, chap. 35.

appeal to Russian revolutionaries: Herzen's appeal, "Russkim ofitseram v Pol'she" [To Russian officers in Poland] (1862) urged liberal-minded Russian officers to ally themselves with Polish rebels, in the hope that this would both help the Poles and extend the uprising to Russia. He later admitted that this had been an error.

Belinsky's father was a naval doctor.

The Internationale: The International Working Men's Association was founded in 1864 by Marx and Engels. The proclamation Dostoevsky quotes here, however, came from M. A. Bakunin's organization, L'Alliance de la Démocratie Socialiste, and dates from 1869.

Renan, Ernest (1823–92), French philosopher and orientalist. His *Vie de Jésus* (1863) depicts Jesus as a purely human preacher of noble moral teachings.

one of Belinsky's friends: Belinsky's friend, apparently, was Vasily Petrovich Botkin (1811–69), writer, critic, and translator. The novice writer was likely Ivan Turgenev.

Sand, George (1804–76), pseudonym of Amandine Lucile Aurore Dudevant, French novelist. Her novels propounded utopian and Christian socialism and enjoyed great popularity in Russia. Etienne Cabet (1788–1856), French utopian socialist, founder of a utopian colony in Nauvoo,

Illinois. Pierre Leroux (1798–1871), French philosopher and utopian socialist whose notions of Christian socialism had a strong influence on George Sand. (See also notes to June 1876, 1.2.)

Feuerbach, Ludwig Andreas (1804–72), German philosopher. His *Das Wesen des Christentums* (1841) attempts to humanize theology and views God as a projection of man's nature.

Strauss, David Friedrich (1808–74), German theologian-philosopher. His *Leben Jesu* (1835) criticized Christian dogma and denied the historical basis of the supernatural events related in the Gospels; it was a popular "forbidden book" in Russia.

Mme. Högg kept a pension for women in Geneva and was active in the women's movement.

The Nikolaevsky railway, built 1843–51, linked Moscow and St. Petersburg.

The wives of the Decembrists: The women, Mme. Muravieva, Mme. Annenkova, and Mme. Fonvizina, arranged the meeting with Dostoevsky and later interceded with the prison authorities on behalf of him and other convicted members of the Petrashevsky Circle. (See also notes to January 1876, 3.2, and July–August 1876, 4.2.)

1873.3: Environment

new (just) courts: In 1864 occurred a major reform of the Russian judicial system, one of the main features of which was the institution of trial by jury.

I was in prison: Dostoevsky was sentenced to four years of hard labor, followed by a term of Siberian exile, on December 22, 1849; his period of hard labor ended on February 15, 1854.

Not long ago: Dostoevsky lived in Europe from April 1867 to July 1871.

The woman's story: The trial of the peasant N. A. Saiapin, accused of abusing his wife, occurred in the Tambov circuit court on September 30, 1872.

hang by the heels: The daughter's plight, as described by Dostoevsky, roused a group of Moscow ladies to take steps to have her sent to a trade school in Moscow.

1873.4: Something Personal

Kovalevsky, Egor Petrovich (1811–68), explorer, writer, and statesman. Dostoevsky knew him during the former's tenure as president of the Literary Fund, an organization to assist writers in need. Dostoevsky served as secretary of the fund from 1863 to 1865.

Crime and Punishment was serialized in *RV,* beginning in January 1866.

One of these magazines: The publishers were M. M. Stasiulevich (1826–1911), who edited *RV* beginning in 1866, and the poet N. N. Nekrasov (1821–77), coeditor of *S,* which was closed by the government in April 1866. Nekrasov was one of the first readers of Dostoevsky's *Poor Folk* in 1845; he had high praise for the work, but their later relationship, which Dostoevsky describes in detail in *DP,* December 1877. 2.1-2.4, was often difficult. (See also notes to chapter 5.)

"... a dressing-down": The author of the review of the first part of *Crime and Punishment,* which appeared in *S,* nos. 2 and 3, 1866, was G. Z. Eliseev. He sharply criticized Dostoevsky for attacking students in the novel.

Chernyshevsky, Nikolai Gavrilovich (1828-89), journalist, social thinker, and a major figure in the revolutionary movement of the 1860s. In 1862 he was arrested for revolutionary activities. After a rigged trial, he was sentenced to a prison term followed by exile for life. He was considered a martyr by many.

'The Crocodile': Dostoevsky's story "Krokodil" [The crocodile] appeared in *E,* no. 2, 1865.

Bulgarin, Faddei Venediktovich (1789-1859), Russian writer, journalist, and publisher of *Severnaia pchela* [The Northern Bee], a conservative newspaper. Bulgarin was notorious for his denunciations of writers to the secret police of Nicholas I.

my return from Siberia: Dostoevsky seems to have erred here, since he returned to St. Petersburg from his exile in December 1859. Chernyshevksy's account of the meeting, which differs in some details from Dostoevsky's, places it in late May 1862 (see N. G. Chernyshevsky, *Polnoe sobranie sochinenii* [Complete collected works], Moscow: Khudozhestvennaia literatura, 1939-50, vol. 1, p. 777). N. G. Rozenblium maintains that the meeting took place shortly after the series of major fires in St. Petersburg in May 1862, most probably on May 30 or 31 (*Literaturnoe nasledstvo* 86: *F. M. Dostoevsky: novye materialy i issledovaniia* [Literary legacy, 86: F. M. Dostoevsky: New material and research], Moscow: Nauka, 1973, pp. 39-40.)

"To the Young Generation": The proclamation "K molodomu pokoleniiu" [To the young generation] appeared in September 1861. It was the product of Chernyshevsky, N. V. Shelgunov, and M. L. Mikhailov. Dotoevsky may have had in mind the proclamation "Molodaia Rossiia" [Young Russia], which appeared in May 1862. "Young Russia" was written by P. G. Zaichnevsky and was much more revolutionary in tone than the other proclamations of the time.

Chernyshevsky's arrest: Arrested on July 7, 1862, Chernyshevsky spent nearly two years in prison in St. Petersburg before being exiled to Siberia, where he remained until 1883.

The Arcade [*passazh*]: A popular shopping area off Nevsky Prospect.

The Voice: G, no. 93, April 3, 1865, noted: "Although Mr. F. Dostoevsky will not take our advice, of course, we still would suggest that he break off this most tactless story at Chapter Four. Rumors which are extremely detrimental to the reputation of *The Epoch* and to Mr. Dostoevsky himself are already circulating about the story."

Strakhov, Nikolai Nikolaevich (1828-96), Russian philosopher and literary critic, coeditor of Dostoevsky's *V* and, to some extent, his philosophical mentor.

Andrei Aleksandrovich Kraevsky: See notes to 1873.1.

"Notes of a Madman" [Zapiski sumasshedshego] (1835), story by Nikolai Gogol; "God" [Bog] (1784), ode by G. R. Derzhavin; *Yury Miloslavsky, or the Russians in 1612* [Iurii Miloslavskii, ili Russkie v 1612 godu] (1829), novel by M. N. Zagoskin; Afanasy Afanasievich Fet (1820–92), Russian lyric poet; Ivan Fedorovich Gorbunov (1831–95), Russian actor, writer, and storyteller.

critical article on . . . *What Is To Be Done?*: V. S. Nechaeva (in *Zhurnal M. M. i F. M. Dostoevskikh "Epokha," 1864–1865* [Moscow: Nauka, 1975], pp. 209–10) points out that no such review appeared in *E*, although Strakhov had written one. Dostoevsky decided against publishing it; after *E* ceased publication, Strakhov's review appeared in *Biblioteka dlia chteniia* [Library for Reading], nos. 7–8, 1865.

1873.5: Vlas

"Vlas," by N. N. Nekrasov, appeared in *S*, no. 6, 1855. Dostoevsky's relationship to Nekrasov underwent many changes. Nekrasov was one of the first readers to heap high praise on Dostoevsky's first work, *Poor People*. In the 1860s and 1870s, however, Nekrasov was solidly in the radical camp. Dostoevsky continued to admire Nekrasov as a poet but had strong ideological disagreements with him. (See also December 1877, 2.1–2.4.)

verses about the barge-haulers' songs: Nekrasov's "On the Volga" [Na Volge] appeared in *S*, no. 1, 1861. The poem describes the hard lot of the barge-haulers and suggests that they should not simply accept it passively.

this remarkable tale: The exact source of Dostoevsky's story is unknown, but the motif of the desecration of the Eucharist is not uncommon in Russian folklore.

"new people": A phrase used most notably by N. G. Chernyshevsky to describe the young generation of radicals he depicts in his novel *What Is to Be Done?* [Chto delat'?] (1863).

Mr. Ostrovsky's tempter: Ostrovsky, Aleksandr Nikolaevich (1823–86), Russian dramatist. His comedy *Don't Live as You Choose* [Ne tak zhivi kak khochetsia] (1855) has a character, Eremka, who leads the play's hero astray.

On February 19, 1862, the Edict of Emancipation of the serfs was signed.

"fledglings from Peter's nest": This metaphor appears in Pushkin's poem "Poltava" (1828). Dostoevsky has in mind the educated classes that originated after the reforms of Peter the Great.

1873.6: Bobok

my portrait: A portrait of Dostoevsky, by V. G. Perov, was exhibited in the Academy of Arts in early 1873. A commentator in *G*, no. 14, 1873, noted: "This is a portrait of a man exhausted by a serious ailment."

Collegiate Councilor: Rank of the 6th class, equivalent to the rank of colonel in the army. (See also notes to October 1876, 2.3.)

the smell, the smell!: Dostoevsky's narrator makes an untranslatable pun here: *dukh* (spirit), which colloquially can mean "smell," and *dukhovnyi*, "ecclesiastic."

people trained as engineers: As in Dostoevsky's novel *The Devils* [Besy] (1871), where Kirillov, an engineer, is involved in a political conspiracy and has developed philosophical ideas.

Moscow Exhibition: In the summer of 1872 a polytechnical exhibition commemorating the 200th anniversary of birth of Peter I was held in Moscow.

bread crumbs on the ground: M. M. Bakhtin's explanation: "bread may be crumbled and left on the earth: this is a planting of the seed, an act of fecundation. It must not be left on the floor, since that is infertile." (M. M. Bakhtin, *Problemy poetiki Dostoevskogo*, 3d ed. (Moscow: Khudozhestvennaia literatura, 1972), p. 238.

Suvorin's *Almanac*: A. S. Suvorin, *Russkii kalendar' na 1872 god* (St. Petersburg, 1872). A reference book and compilation of facts about Russia; the fourth section dealt with popular customs and beliefs.

Your Excellency: An official in the civil service of the third and fourth ranks, equivalent to a lieutenant- or major-general in the army, would be addressed as "Your Excellency" [*vashe prevoskhoditel'stvo*] and, although not a military man, would be called a general nonetheless, particularly by those attempting to flatter him.

"Rest, beloved ashes...": *Pokoisia, milyi priakh, do radostnogo utra!* was the epitaph on the grave of the Russian writer and historian N. M. Karamzin (1766–1826), and was frequently reused.

Court Councilor: 7th rank, equivalent to lieutenant-colonel in the army.

forty-day memorial: Memorial prayers [*sorokoviny, sorochiny, sorokoust*] were said forty days after a death. It was popularly believed that during these forty days the soul of the deceased was in torment.

rice porridge: A porridge of rice or wheat with honey [*kut'ia*], a symbol of resurrection, was customarily eaten after the funeral.

Actual Privy Councilor: 2d rank, equivalent to general in the army.

The Vale of Jehoshaphat was considered the site at which the Last Judgment would take place (Joel 3:12).

Ekk, Vladimir Egorovich (1818–75), professor and well-known physician.

Botkin, Sergei Petrovich (1832–89), eminent physician and scholar, one of the finest diagnosticians of his day.

State Councilor: A rank of the 5th class, equivalent to the rank between that of colonel and major-general in the army.

Lebeziatnikov is also the name of an obsequious character in *Crime and Punishment*. The name suggests the verb *lebezit'*, "to fawn upon someone, ingratiate oneself."

Bobok means "bean."

1873.7: A Troubled Countenance

"The Sealed Angel": Leskov, Nikolai Semenovich (1828–95), Russian writer. His story "Zapechatlennyi angel" [The sealed angel] appeared in *RV*, no. 1, 1873. Nekrasov's "Kniaginia M. N. Volkonskaia" [Princess M. N. Volkonskaia] appeared in *OZ*, no. 1, 1873. Mikhail Evgrafovich Saltykov-Shchedrin (1826–89), Russian satirist. The second sketch of his "Blagonamerennye rechi" [Loyal speeches] likewise appeared in *OZ*, no. 1, 1873.

Skabichevsky, Aleksandr Mikhailovich (1838–1910), Russian critic. His "Drama v Evrope i u nas" [Drama in Europe and Russia] appeared in *OZ*, no. 1, 1873. N.M.: Nikolai Konstantinovich Mikhailovsky (1842–1904), journalist, literary critic, sociologist, and theoretician of the Populist movement.

Patriarch Nikon: Nikita Minin (1605–81), Patriarch of Moscow and All Russia. His liturgical reforms provoked the "great schism" in the Orthodox church. The icons in question thus would have been revered by the Dissenters because they had been consecrated before the schism.

Deacon Akhilla, in Leskov's novel *Soboriane* [Cathedral folk] (1872) spends much of his time "doing battle with evil," which he personifies as the Devil. Akhilla dies after he attacks what he assumes is the Devil himself, falls into an icy canal, and eventually dies of exposure.

new sect of Stundists: The Stundists were a Protestant religious sect that appeared in southern Russia in the late 1860s; their origins were linked to German settlers in that area.

costs us so dearly: The relatively large portion of the Russian budget that derived from the tax on alcohol was a topic in the Russian press; Dostoevsky comments on this problem in 1873.11.

1873.8: A Half-Letter from "A Certain Person"

"a certain person": The author here is therefore the same fictional character who narrated "Bobok" (1873.6). Later in the *Diary* another character, "the paradoxicalist," makes more than one appearance.

my supposed literary enemies: Prominent among Dostoevsky's literary "enemies" here are N. K. Mikhailovsky, who in *OZ*, no. 1, 1873, had taken issue with Dostoevsky's suggestion, made in 1873.2, that socialism was necessarily atheistic and revolutionary. Socialists, Mikhailovsky argues, have no uniform views on religious matters; "Socialism in Russia," he stated, "is conservative." Another "enemy," V. P. Burenin, had written a critical review of *The Devils* (*SV*, nos. 6 and 13, 1873). Throughout much of 1872, *OZ* and *SV* had also carried on a public quarrel between Mikhailovsky and Burenin. Burenin is one of the prime targets of "A Certain Person's" abuse, but his letter is also directed generally at the rancorous polemics and personal attacks that had been common among journals and journalists since the 1860s. A few excerpts from one of

Burenin's attacks on Mikhailovsky show that "A Certain Person's" portrayal of this literary squabble is not unduly exaggerated: "Tell me, Mr. Mikhailovsky, are you feeling all right? Do you now think that you have crushed me like a bedbug? What's now being spattered, after your reading of this column—is it my 'bedbuggish blood' or tears of impotent fury squeezed from your tender soul . . . ? . . . From here I can see Mr. Mikhailovsky, his face now red, now pale, struck with fear and heartache as he casts his eye over these opening remarks. . . . In despair he pulls his hair, and a horrible thought runs through his mind: 'My God, this Z. [Burenin] wants to make me out a madman in front of my readers . . .'" (*SV*, no. 205, 1872).

Dear old Krylov: Krylov, Ivan Andreevich (1769?-1844), Russian fabulist; many of his fables are frequently quoted.

Palkin's: A tavern on the corner of Nevsky and Liteiny Prospects.

"I fear amidst war's strident clamor": The verse comes from Pushkin's "Iz Gafiza" [From Hafiz] (1829).

Berg's Theater in St. Petersburg staged mainly light entertainment.

Antropka appears at the end of Turgenev's story "Pevtsy" [Singers] (1850).

Dussault's: A fashionable restaurant on St. Petersburg's Bolshaia Morskaia Street.

the last day of Carnival: The last Sunday before Lent was traditionally the day upon which one sought forgiveness of one's acquaintances.

1873.9: Apropos of the Exhibition

the exhibition: Some hundred paintings and sculptures were exhibited in March 1873 at the Academy of Arts in St. Petersburg.

Our Own Folk: Ostrovsky's comedy *Svoi liudi sochtemsia* [Our own folk, we'll settle it] was published in 1850 and first performed in 1861.

a Frenchman who knew not a word of Russian: Louis Viardot's translations of five stories by Gogol, *Nouvelles russes*, appeared in Paris in 1845.

Viardot's translation of *Don Quixote* appeared in 1836.

"Three Portraits": Turgenev's story "Tri portreta" [Three portraits] was published in 1846.

Pushkin's "Pikovaia dama" [Queen of spades] (1834) was translated by Paul de Julvecourt and published in Paris in 1843; a translation by Prosper Merimée appeared in 1849. *Kapitanskaia dochka* [The captain's daughter] (1836) was translated by Turgenev and Viardot and appeared in 1853.

"This barren landscape . . .": line from the poem by F. I. Tiutchev, "Eti bednye seleniia" [These poor villages] (1855).

Kuindzhi, Arkhip Ivanovich (1842-1910). His painting *Na ostrove Valaame* [On the Island of Valaam] (1873) was the first work to bring him some fame as a painter. See V. S. Manin, *Arkhip Ivanovich Kuindzhi i ego shkola* [Arkhip Ivanovich Kuindzhi and his school] (Leningrad: Khudozhnik RFSFR, 1987), plate 14.

resettlement of Circassians: Dostoevsky probably has in mind Petr Nikolaevich Gruzinsky's *Ostavlenie gortsami aulov pri priblizhenii russkikh voisk* [The mountaineers abandon their villages at the approach of Russian forces] (1872).

Makovsky, Vladimir Egorovich (1846-1920), *Liubiteli solov'ev* [Nightingale fanciers] (1872-73). See *Russia: The Land, The People. Russian Painting 1850-1910* (Washington, D.C.: Smithsonian Institution, 1986), p. 59.

Then we see a game of cards: The painting Dostoevsky probably has in mind is *Kosinta Ahvenanmaalla* [In a Cabin on Åland], by the Finnish painter Karl Emanuel Jansson (1846-74).

Perov, Vasilii Grigorevich (1832-82) *Okhotniki na privale* (1871). See Vladimir Leniashin, *Vasilii Grigorevich Perov* (Leningrad: Khudozhnik RFSFR, 1987), plate 79.

Makovsky's *Pridvornye psalomshchiki na klirose* [Court singers in the choir stalls] (1870). See E. V. Zhuravleva, *Vladimir Egorovich Makovskii, 1846-1920* (Moscow: Iskusstvo, 1972), pp. 26-27.

Patriarchs: i.e., prior to Peter the Great's reform of 1720, which ended the patriarchate and brought the church effectively under government control.

"Affli-i-cted!": In chapter 1 of Leskov's novel *Cathedral Folk* (see note to 1873.7), Deacon Akhilla is so carried away by his solo part in the anthem "And by sorrows afflicted" that he goes on repeating "afflicted, afflicted" long after the rest of the choir have finished.

Hood, Thomas (1799-1845), English poet. His "Song of the Shirt" (1843) is a poem of social protest against the exploitation of women's work.

two latest poems by Nekrasov: The poems are "Kniaginia Trubetskaia" [Princess Trubetskaia], *OZ*, no. 4, 1872, and "Kniaginia M. N. Volkonskaia" [Princess M. N. Volkonskaia], *OZ*, no. 1, 1873, published under the common title *Russkie zhenshchiny* [Russian women]. They deal with the Decembrists' wives (see notes to July-August 1876, 4.2).

Repin, Ilia Efimovich (1844-1930). His *Burlaki na Volge* [Barge-haulers on the Volga] (1870-73) was the most discussed painting at the Exhibition. See O. A. Liaskovskaia, *Il'ia Efimovich Repin: zhizn i tvorchestvo* [Ilia Efimovich Repin: Life and work] (Moscow: Iskusstvo, 1982), p. 59.

stuffed with porridge: Dostoevsky may have taken this detail from Leskov's *Cathedral Folk*, which had appeared in *RV,* nos. 4-7, 1872.

Bronnikov, Fedor Andreevich (1827-1902). His painting *Gimn pifagoreitsev voskhodiashchemu solntsu* [The hymn of the Pythagoreans to the rising sun] (1869) was in the pseudoclassical academic style.

Ge, Nikolai Nikolaevich (1831-94). His painting *Petr I doprashivaet tsarevicha Alekseia Petrovicha v Petergofe* [Peter I interrogates the tsarevich Aleksei Petrovich at Peterhof] (1871) was among those exhibited (see *Nikolai Ivanovich Ge* [Moscow: Iskusstvo, 1978], plate 31). His earlier *Tainaia vecheria* [The Last Supper] (1863) was extremely controversial because of what many considered a mundane treatment of an event having profound religious significance. See V. Porudominskii, *Nikolai Ge* (Moscow: Iskusstvo, 1970) p. 32, plate 1.

1873.10: An Impersonator

Kastorsky is the alias used here by N. S. Leskov, whose major novel, *Cathedral Folk,* portrayed Russian clergymen. Dostoevsky pretends to be unaware of the real identity of the writer.

Nedolin, M. A.: Minor writer who published a number of stories in 1872–77.

The novel *Zapiski prichetnika* [Notes of a psalm-reader], by Marko Vovchok [M. A. Markovich], appeared in *OZ*, nos. 9–12, 1869, and nos. 10–11, 1870.

The choristers in Makovsky's painting are wearing dark soutanes and pelerines, as had been the practice since Peter the Great, who borrowed the costume from the Poles.

Dmitry Donskoi (1350–89), Grand Duke of Muscovy; Yaroslav the Wise (978–1054), Grand Duke of Kiev.

The verse is from N. M. Yazykov, "Komu, o Gospodi! dostupny tvoi Sionski vysoty?" [Who, O Lord, may lodge in Thy heights of Zion?] (1830), which is based on Psalm 15.

Mount Athos: A peninsula in northeastern Greece, a center of Orthodox monasticism and frequent place of pilgrimage for Russians.

bewilderment: At the end of part 5 of Leskov's novel *Na nozhakh* [At daggers drawn] (1870–71) the scene suddenly and inexplicably shifts to Moldavia.

"Bring him back!": Inaccurate quotation from the end of act 2 of Gogol's play *Zhenit'ba* [The Marriage] (1842).

Pushkin's epigram "Sapozhnik. Pritcha" [The shoemaker: A fable] (1829)

The Russian World: Leskov was a regular contributor to *RM* in the early 1870s; the newspaper published a number of flattering references to his work.

1873.11: Dreams and Musings

drunkenness: *Gr,* like many other Russian newspapers in 1872–73, carried a number of articles on the problem of widespread drunkenness among the peasantry and on means to combat the abuse of alcohol.

In Gogol's "Notes of a Madman" the main character, Poprishchin, comments on current Spanish politics and ends by imagining himself king of Spain.

Pypin, Aleksandr Nikolaevich (1833–1904), Russian critic, literary historian, and folklorist. In parts 5 and 6 of his "Kharakteristiki literaturynykh mnenii ot dvadtsatykh do piatidesiatykh godov. Istoricheskie ocherki" [Characteristics of Russian literary opinions from the 1820s to the 1850s: a historical sketch] (*VE*, nos. 11 and 12, 1872), Pypin took the Slavophiles to task for their "romantic patriotism" and idealization of traditional Russian life. He argued that "to become independent of Western civilization and to rise above it, to 'make Western enlightenment conform to our principles,' as Kireevsky demanded, we must first acquire the strength to do so; we must absorb and transform the content of

"all the impressions of existence . . .": A paraphrase of lines from Pushkin's poem "Demon" [The demon] (1823).

January 1876.1.3: The Christmas Party at the Artists' Club. Children Who Think and Children Who Are Helped Along. A "Gluttonous Boy." "Oui" Girls. Jostling Raw Youths. A Moscow Captain in a Hurry

"gluttonous boy": Pushkin, *Eugene Onegin* (1825-33), "The Travels of Onegin."

Noblemen's Club: *PG* of January 3, 1876, carried an item describing a fistfight between two merchants in the Noblemen's Club and a disturbance caused by a drunken army officer at a ball.

Skvoznik-Dmukhanovskys: Characters from Gogol's *The Inspector-General.* Skvoznik-Dmukhanovsky is mayor of the town, Derzhimorda is a policeman; both are portrayed as crude Russian types.

high-society balls: In act 3 of Gogol's *Dead Souls,* Khlestakov boasts that he has attended a society ball in Petersburg where a watermelon costing 700 rubles was served.

Hypocrisy: A maxim from François de la Rochefoucauld, *Réflexions ou sentences et maximes morales* (1665): "L'hypocrisie est un hommage que le vice rend à la vertu."

January 1876, 1.4: The Golden Age in Your Pocket

Piron, Alexis (1689-1773). French poet, renowned for his epigrams and witty ripostes.

January 1876, 2.1: The Boy with His Hand Out

". . . and pitilessly": A paraphrase of lines from N. A. Nekrasov's poem "Detstvo" [Childhood] (1844), one portion of which describes a peasant boy being forced to drink vodka by his elders.

January 1876, 2.2: The Boy at Christ's Christmas Party

As noted by G. M. Fridlender ("Sviatochnyi rasskaz Dostoevskogo i ballada Riukkerta" [Dostoevsky's Christmas Story and F. Rückert's Ballad], in *Mezhdunarodnye sviazi russkoi literatury* [Russian literature's international links] [Moscow-Leningrad: AN SSSR, 1963], pp. 370-90), Dostoevsky borrowed the basis for this story from the ballad of the German poet Friedrich Rückert (1788-1866), "Des fremden Kindes heiliger Christs" (1816).

famine: A series of poor harvests in Samara Province between 1871 and 1873 led to a disastrous famine.

All the more: i.e., as Dostoevsky promised in his "Announcement," above.

January 1876, 2.3: A Colony of Young Offenders. Dark Individuals. The Transformation of Blemished Souls into Immaculate Ones. Measures Acknowledged as Most Expedient Thereto. Little and Bold Friends of Mankind.

Powder Works: Dostoevsky, accompanied by the lawyer and writer A. F. Koni, visited the colony on December 27, 1875.

P. A. R——sky: Rovinsky, Pavel Apollonovich (1831–1916), ethnographer, traveler, and journalist. His accounts of his travels in Mongolia and Serbia appeared in *VE* in the early 1870s.

The "Lithuanian Castle," located at the corner of the Moika and Nikolsky canals in St. Petersburg, housed a prison that held both adults and (until 1875) juveniles.

all our schools: The educational reforms of 1864 virtually abolished corporal punishment in schools.

Sevastopol Tales: L. N. Tolstoy, "Sevastopol v dekabre 1854"; "Sevastopol v mae 1855"; "Sevastopol v avguste 1855" [Sevastopol in December 1854; Sevastopol in May 1855; Sevastopol in August 1855] (1855–56); *Vechera na khutore bliz Dikanki* [Evenings on a farm near Dikanka] (1831), Nikolai Gogol's first collection of stories; M. Iu. Lermontov, *Pesnia pro tsaria Ivana Vasil'evicha, molodogo oprichnika i udalogo kuptsa Kalashnikova* [The tale of Kalashnikov] (1838). Aleksei Vasilevich Kolstov (1808–42), Russian poet who wrote verse in a folk style.

the duck: Dostoevsky refers to the visual method of education favored by some "progressive" teachers. The pupils were asked, for example, why a duck had feathers and were gradually led to deduce the reason.

"he who labors": A paraphrase of Matthew 10:10: "For the workman is worthy of his meat...."

Potugin, a character from Turgenev's novel *Dym* [Smoke] (1867). In chapter 14, he argues forcefully that Russia has made no real contribution to world civilization and expresses views that are strongly Westernizing.

January 1876, 3.1: The Russian Society for the Protection of Animals. The Government Courier. Demon-Vodka. The Itch for Debauch and Vorobev. From the End or from the Beginning?

The Russian Society for the Protection of Animals was founded on October 4, 1865, in St. Petersburg; branches were later established in other centers. Its president through the first decade of its existence was Prince A. A. Suvorov-Ryminsky (1804–82). In 1871 the society's efforts helped pass a law levying a fine of up to ten rubles for cruel treatment of domestic animals.

Pushkin had died: Dostoevsky errs here: Pushkin died on January 29, 1837.

flogging: After 1861, specified civil and criminal offenses committed by peasants had been tried in rural district (*volostnoi*) courts, whose members were chosen from among the peasants themselves. Flogging was frequently chosen as a punishment in such courts.

railway disaster: On December 24, 1875, a train carrying army recruits on the line between Elisavetgrad (now Kirovgrad) and Odessa derailed, killing sixty-six and injuring fifty-four. The subsequent inquiry revealed widespread shortcomings in the administration of the railway line. In July of 1873, A. S. Suvorin (see note to January 1876, 1.1), writing in *SV*, no. 199, reported that Golubev, manager of the Orel-Vitebsk railway, had expelled the passengers from a first-class compartment that he wanted for his own use. Golubev denied this accusation and eventually sued Suvorin for slander. The case was not heard until September 1874.

penknife: The incident, which took place on January 5, 1876, was widely reported in the press.

January 1876, 3.2: Spiritualism. Something about Devils. The Extraordinary Cleverness of Devils, If Only These Are Devils

The Decembrists were the group of young men, mostly army officers, who attempted a coup on December 14, 1825. Five were executed, many others exiled to Siberia for long terms.

Annenkov, Ivan Aleksandrovich (1802–78), Russian army officer, Decembrist, and memoirist. *Les Mémoires d'un maître d'armes* (1840), by Alexandre Dumas-père, was based very loosely on the experiences of a French fencing master, Grisier, who had given fencing lessons to Annenkov in the 1820s.

Muravev-Apostol, Matvei Ivanovich (1793–1886), brother of S. I. Muravev-Apostol, one of the five Decembrists who were executed. Petr Nikolaevich Svistunov (1803–89). Mikhail Aleksandrovich Nazimov (1800–88), exiled 1825–56.

devils and spiritualism: Spiritualism was frequently discussed in the Russian press in the 1870s. Seances, with table-turning and attempts to communicate with spirits, were not an uncommon form of entertainment in some social circles; the emperor Alexander II himself had seances conducted in the Winter Palace. Among the leading proponents of spiritualism were A. N. Aksakov (1832–1903) and N. P. Vagner (1829–1907). (For Vagner, see also notes to December 1876, 2.2). The noted chemist D. I. Mendeleev was instrumental in organizing a Scholarly Commission, in which he participated, to study spiritualism. The commission attended a number of seances and exposed fraudulent practices by several mediums.

Eddy, Horatio, and Eddy, William, brothers who owned a small farm in the township of Chittenden, Vermont. Various psychic phenomena occurring at their homestead aroused considerable interest in the 1870s. Dostoevsky combines their name with Harriet Beecher Stowe's *Uncle*

Tom's Cabin, a novel widely known in Russia. See Sir Arthur Conan Doyle, *The History of Spiritualism* (London: Cassell, 1926), 1: 259ff.

Gogol: *G,* no. 6, January 6, 1876, reported that a respected Moscow intellectual (whom the newspaper did not identify) had become a medium and had claimed that Gogol had dictated to him portions of volume 2 of *Dead Souls* from the manuscript Gogol had burned. A number of people in Moscow had seen portions of the manuscript, and some of them agreed that its style did indeed resemble Gogol's.

"Who can be likened . . . ?": Dostoevsky here combines two verses from the Book of Revelations, chapter 13, verse 4: ". . . Who is like unto this beast?" and chapter 13, verse 13: ". . . and he doeth great wonders, so that he maketh fire to come down from heaven on the earth in the sight of man." The same verses are quoted by his Grand Inquisitor in *The Brothers Karamazov,* bk. 2, pt. 5, chap. 5.

the pope himself: Dostoevsky has in mind Bismarck's conflict with the Catholic church during the 1870s, which was partly prompted by the declaration of papal infallibility of 1870 (see also notes to March 1876, 1.5). His *Kulturkampf* aimed at limiting the power of the Catholic church and making it subservient to the state. The Jesuits were expelled from Germany, and a number of priests and bishops were imprisoned. In his encyclical of February 5 (n.s.), 1875, Pope Pius IX excommunicated German Catholics who opposed the notion of papal infallibility and accepted teaching positions from the state.

Crookes and Olcott: Crookes, William (1832–1919), noted English chemist. He became interested in making a scientific study of spiritualism and, after seances with a medium, concluded that a certain "psychic force" actually did exist. Henry Steel Olcott (1832–1907), American lawyer and journalist, cofounder (with Mme. Blavatsky) of the Theosophical Society. In 1874 he was sent by the New York *Daily Graphic* to write a series of articles about the psychic powers of the brothers Eddy.

Ivan Filippovich: Dostoevsky here apparently combines the names of two figures from the Flagellant sect, Ivan Timofeevich Suslov and Danila Fillipovich. The name may also reflect the Moscow "prophet" Ivan Iakovlevich Koreisha (1780–1861), whom Dostoevsky portrays as Semen Iakovlevich in his novel *The Devils.*

The Tuileries Palace was burned on orders of the Paris Commune during fighting in the Paris revolution of 1871.

Polonsky, Iakov Petrovich (1819–98), Russian poet. His poem "Starye i novye dukhi" [Old spirits and new] appeared in December 1875 and contrasted the "new spirits" that caused tables to turn with the old ones that had inspired humanity for centuries.

January 1876, 3.3: A Word Apropos of My Biography

Mr. V. Z.: The author of the articles on Dostoevsky and his brother, Mikhail, was Vladimir Rafailovich Zotov (1821–78), writer, journalist, and historian of literature. Zotov's article is often very critical of Dostoevsky's writings.

1822: Dostoevsky himself errs here. He was born on October 30, 1821.

February 1876, 1.1: On the Fact That We Are All Good People. How Russian Society Resembles Marshal MacMahon

I don't hate children: *PG*, no. 24, February 4, 1876, commented that Dostoevsky's remarks about suicides among young people (see January 1876, 1.1) revealed his lack of understanding of the younger generation and that his description of the Christmas party in the Artists' Club (January 1876, 1.3) abused young and old alike. The same issue of *PG* reprinted "The Boy at Christ's Christmas Party" (January 1876, 2.2), however. Other press reactions to the January *Diary* were generally positive.

Pechorin is the cynical, manipulative hero of Mikhail Lermontov's *A Hero of Our Time* [Geroi nashego vremeni], 1840–41. In a climactic duel scene in the novel, he shoots Grushnitsky, a rival for a woman.

Silvio, hero of Alexander Pushkin's short story "The Shot" [Vystrel], 1831.

MacMahon, Marie Edmé Patrice Maurice de, Duke of Magenta (1808–93), French marshal and president of the French republic, 1873–79.

"J'y suis et j'y reste!": "I am here and here I will remain." Phrase uttered by Marshal (then General) MacMahon when his troops captured the Malakoff redoubt in Sevastopol during the Crimean War. The seizure of this strongpoint, on September 8, 1855 (n.s.), marked the fall of the city and the effective end of the war.

February 1876, 1.2: On Love of the People. An Essential Contract with the People

Slavic Committees were founded in St. Petersburg in 1856 and in Moscow in 1858 with the aim of promoting education, culture, and religion in non-Russian Slavic countries. The committees subsequently took on a more political and panslavist role and helped to rally Russian support for the Serbs in their uprising against Turkish rule. K. S. Aksakov (1817–60), writer, memoirist, and one of the founders of the Slavophile school; he was an active member of the Moscow Slavic Committee during the first years of its existence. *Fraternal Aid* [Bratskaia pomoch' postradavshim semeistvam Bosnii i Gertsogoviny], an anthology published to raise funds to aid families displaced by the Slavic uprising against the Turks in Bosnia and Herzegovina, was put out by the St. Petersburg section of the committee in 1876. Aksakov's article, "O sovremennom cheloveke" [On contemporary man], argued that successful communal living demanded a high degree of education or development [*obrazovanie*] and that the Russian peasants had achieved this through years of participation in their peasant commune, the *mir*.

Sergei of Radonezh, Saint (c. 1321–92), founder of the Trinity Monastery (located near present-day Zagorsk). St. Sergei was also noted for his efforts in consolidating the power of the Duchy of Moscow and for promoting the unity of Russian duchies before the Tatar threat. Saint Theodosius of Pechersk (d. 1074), founder of the Kiev Crypt Monastery. Saint Tikhon of Zadonsk (1724–83), Bishop of Voronezh and Elets, and one of the prototypes for Zosima in *The Brothers Karamazov*.

Belkin: Pushkin's collection of five short stories, *Povesti Belkina* [The tales of Belkin] (1831) is narrated by Ivan Petrovich Belkin, an artless, good-natured character who had been held up by the critic Apollon Grigorev as a typically humble Russian type.

Oblomov (1859), novel by Ivan Goncharov. *A Nest of Gentlefolk* [Dvorianskoe gnezdo] (1859), novel by Ivan Turgenev.

February 1876, 1.3: The Peasant Marey

I'll tell you a story: According to the memoirs of Dostoevsky's younger brother, Andrei, Marey was an actual personage.

The Pole M——cki: The Polish revolutionary Aleksandr Mirecki was an exile in Omsk while Dostoevsky was serving his term of hard labor there. The conversation he describes probably took place in April 1851. He also figures in Dostoevsky's *Notes from the House of the Dead*.

Gazin likewise appears in *Notes from the House of the Dead*.

February 1876, 2.1: Apropos of the Kroneberg Case

Kroneberg case: Stanislav Leonidovich Kronenberg (the name appeared in newspaper accounts as Kroneberg, the form Dostoevsky uses) was tried on January 23 and 24, 1876, for physically abusing his daughter, Maria.

V. D. Spasovich: See notes to 1873.11. He was appointed by the court to defend Kronenberg. Spasovich was a well-known liberal who took part in a number of important trials; he is also one of the prototypes for the lawyer Fetiukovich in *The Brothers Karamazov*.

February 1876, 2.2: Something on Lawyers in General. My Naive and Hasty Assumptions. Something on Talented People in General and in Particular

Minister of the Imperial Court: In June 1873, Dostoevsky, as editor of *Gr*, was brought to trial for having published an article that included remarks made by the emperor, Alexander II, but that had not been cleared by the palace censor. Dostoevsky's lawyer, V. P. Gaevsky, argued that, by law, permission from the Minister of the Imperial Court was required only for quotations that contained expressions of the emperor's will.

Somewhere in Gogol: In chapter 10 of *Dead Souls*, Nozdrev, questioned by the townspeople about Chichikov, tells them spectacular lies, which even they have difficulty believing.

Thackeray: In *Pendennis* (1850), chapter 34, the narrator says about the writer Mr. Wagg: "He liked to make his *entrée* into a drawing-room with a laugh, and, when he went away at night, to leave a joke exploding behind him."

"one spares . . .": For the sake of a witty word one spares not even one's father." Russian proverb.

". . . beast that roars . . .": Aleksandr Pushkin, "Ekho" [Echo] (1831).

Lamartine, Alphonse Marie Louis de (1790–1869), French poet, statesman, and man of letters. During the February revolution of 1848 he was chosen as one of the five members of the executive committee. Although his political career was brief and without lasting influence, his eloquent speeches often pacified Parisians. His *Harmonies poétiques et religieuses* appeared in 1830, his *Histoire des Girondistes* in 1847.

February 1876, 2.5: The Pillars of Hercules

"for they bind . . .": Matthew 23:4.

February 1876, 2.6: The Family and Our Sacred Ideals. A Concluding Note about a Certain Modern School

legal profession: The Russian legal profession, in the same sense that it existed in Europe, only came into being with the legal reform of 1864.

March 1876, 1.1: How True Is the Notion That "The Ideals May Be Base so Long as the Reality Is Good"?

Gamma: Pseudonym of G. K. Gradovsky. His column was entitled "The Leaflet" [Listok].

"they may take the odd bribe . . .": A quotation from I. A. Krylov's fable "Muzykanty" [The Musicians] (1808).

March 1876, 1.2: A Hundred-Year-Old Woman

a lady told me: The lady was Dostoevsky's wife, Anna, as noted in Grossman, *Seminarii po Dostoevskomu*, p. 64.

One of the buildings on Nikolaevsky Street (now Marat Street) housed the facility where *DP* was printed.

March 1876, 1.3: Dissociation

"things I have seen . . .": Again, as promised in his "Announcement," which precedes January 1876.

Dobroliubov, Nikolai Aleksandrovich (1836–61), literary critic and, during his brief life, one of the leading figures among the radicals of the 1860s.

a certain manuscript: The manuscript was the work of Nikolai Pavlovich

Peterson (1844–1919), a one-time revolutionary who became a disciple of the Russian philosopher Nikolai Fedorov. Peterson introduced Fedorov's ideas to Dostoevsky (and to Tolstoy). He had spent six months in prison for his revolutionary activities.

March 1876, 1.4: Musings about Europe

everyone . . . is talking about peace now: Many Russian newspapers saw the decline in tension between Great Britain and Russia (relations had grown strained due to British fears of Russian incursion into India), the improvement in relations between France and Germany, and the establishment of a conservative republic in France as symptoms of new stability in Europe. In January 1876, Austria, Great Britain, Germany, France, Italy, and Russia jointly urged Turkey to institute reforms to ease the lot of Christians in Herzegovinia and Bosnia (the "Andrássy Note": see notes to April 1876, 2.1); Turkey agreed, provided the rebels put down their arms.

five-billion contribution: Under the terms of the Treaty of Frankfurt, which ended the Franco-Prussian War (March 1, 1871), France was compelled to pay Germany an indemnity of five billion francs.

The "senior line" (the Bourbons) were deposed by the Revolution of 1830. Their hopes to a return to power were partially based on support from the Catholic church.

The "junior line" (the Orleans Dynasty) held power in France from 1830 to 1848.

March 1876, 1.5: An Expired Force and the Forces of the Future

Pope Pius IX was eighty-three years old at the time of writing; he died in 1878.

this enormous decision: Dostoevsky refers to the dogma of papal infallibility, accepted by the Vatican Council of July 18, 1870.

the gates of Rome: Italian troops entered Rome in September 1870; the city and the Papal States subsequently became a part of Italy. Pius IX refused to accept the situation and withdrew into the Vatican.

Julian (Flavius Claudius Julianus) (c. 331–63), called Julian the Apostate, emperor of Rome, A.D. 361–63. He attempted to restore paganism as the official religion.

in a novel: In part 2, chapter 8 ("Ivan Tsarevich") of *The Devils* (1871), Dostoevsky's archconspirator Peter Verkhovensky says: "Do you know, I have been thinking of delivering up the world to the Pope. Let him come forth, barefoot, and show himself to the mob, saying: 'See what they have brought me to!' and they will all rush to follow him, even the army. The Pope on top, with us all around him, and beneath us— Shigalyov's system. All we need is for the *Internationale* to come to an agreement with the Pope; and so it will."

For Bismarck and Catholicism, see notes to January 1876, 3.2.

March 1876, 2.1: Don Carlos and Sir Watkin. More Signs of "The Beginning of the End"

Carlos, Don (Carlos Maria de los Dolores) (1848–1909), Prince of Bourbon, claimant, as Don Carlos VII, to the Spanish throne. After the defeat that ended the Second Carlist War, he fled to France. The French republican government refused to give him refuge, and, on March 4, 1876, he was received in England.

Kupernik, Lev Abramovich (1845–1905), lawyer and journalist. On February 5, 1876, he created an incident by threatening the manager of a coaching station and then firing several shots at a coachman to urge him to drive faster.

Chambord, Henri Charles Ferdinand Marie Dieudonne, Comte de (1820–83), claimant, as Henry V, to the French throne. One of his conditions for accepting the throne was the abandonment of the republican tricolor and the return of the white banner of the Bourbons as flag of France.

Heinrich Heine, in chapter 16 of his *Reisebilder*, describes this reaction to the passage. Near the end of *Don Quixote* (pt. 2, chap. 64), Don Quixote encounters the Knight of the White Moon (who in fact is the bachelor Sansón Carrasco); Carrasco defeats Quixote in a duel and forces him to return to his [Quixote's] native village for a year. Heine (and Dostoevsky) apparently confuses this episode with an earlier one (pt. 1, chap. 46), in which the Don is bound while asleep and imprisoned in a cage after a brawl over the "helmet of Mambrino," a brass basin the Don had taken from an itinerant barber.

The Carlists' siege of Bilbao was broken by the republicans in May 1874, and they were forced to retreat. However, on June 27 the general commanding the republican forces, Manuel de la Concha, was killed in battle; the demoralized republican army was subsequently pushed back toward Madrid by the Carlists who, however, missed their opportunity to take the city. The republicans rallied, and on December 30, 1875, Carlos's cousin, Alphonso XII, was proclaimed king.

Watkin, Sir Edward William (1819–1901), British statesman and railway manager.

"guest's" rude reception: Sir Edward's letter appeared in the *London Times* of March 7, 1876. Dostoevsky's translated text is incomplete and differs somewhat from the original English text that appeared in the *Times;* it is included, as it provides the basis for Dostoevsky's remarks. The complete portion of the letter reads as follows: "At the moment we touched the platform some gentlemen cheered, and Don Carlos raised his cap, while a flag, belonging to the Independent Order of Oddfellows, flapped round in the wind, showing a device of Charity protecting children, with the motto—"Remember the widows and orphans!" The effect was electrical, and certainly the crowd groaned; but it was rather a groan of pain than one of anger—a groan which did credit to the human emotions of the people, and did not discredit their manners. As Don Carlos had, I found, suffered from sea-sickness, I offered him an invalid carriage in place of the saloon in which he was first seated, which he accepted, and during the moment of transfer I sent across the rails to beg that no further manifestation should be made, and I am thankful to say that from that moment no sound which could be fairly interpreted as insulting was uttered, though as the train rapidly left the station, some marks of displeasure witnessed the regret of all present that the blinds of the carriage had been, as I thought needlessly, drawn down. While regretting that anything should have occurred to give, even to the most ungenerous, an excuse for complaint, I feel bound to say that no other people in the world, assembled for a joyful day and suddenly confronted by the chief actor in a bloody patricidal war, would have shown so much courtesy and forebearance as was exhibited by the vast majority on Saturday at Folkestone." Sir Edward was writing in reply to a *Times* report of March 6 indicating that Don Carlos had been "insulted by an unmannerly crowd" when he arrived at Folkestone.

Sébastiani, Horace François Bastien, Count (1771-1851), French marshal and diplomat, Minister of Foreign Affairs of France, 1830-32.

Dobell, Sydney Thompson (1824-74), English poet and critic. The passage quoted appears in his book, *Thoughts on Art, Philosophy and Religion: Selected from the Unpublished Papers of Sydney Dobell* (London: Smith, Elder & Co., 1876), pp. 154-55. The italics are Dostoevsky's.

"There is no God . . .": Dostoevsky probably has in mind Voltaire's famous saying: "If God did not exist, He would have to be invented."

". . . amid the waves": Saltykov-Shchedrin, "Dlia sleduiushchikh nomerov 'Svistka'. . ." [For subsequent issues of "The Whistle . . ."], *Svistok* [The Whistle], no. 9, 1863. This same piece also contains a sarcastic reference to the incident between Shchapov and Mikhail Dostoevsky (see April 1876, 2.4).

one observer: The observer, as indicated in Dostoevsky's notebooks, was K. P. Pobedonostsev.

"love and sorrow": The passage quoted can be found in *A Raw Youth*, pt. 3, chap. 7, sec. iii.

March 1876, 2.2: Lord Radstock

Radstock, Baron Granville Augustus William Waldegrave (1831-1913), English preacher and evangelist. Radstock visited Russia several times between 1874 and 1876. His evangelistic efforts had considerable success among the upper levels of St. Petersburg society. A group called the Pashkovists, after one of the group's leaders, V. A. Pashkov, continued to propagate Radstock's evangelical Christianity.

Tatarinova, Ekaterina Filippovna (1783-1856). In the second decade of the nineteenth century she founded a "spiritual union" of members of the Flagellant and Castrate sects that met in the Mikhailov ("Engineers'") Castle in Petersburg. Rumors circulated of their ecstatic rites.

Templars, The Knights Templars, or Poor Knights of Christ and of the Temple of Solomon, a medieval military order. The Masons of the Enlightenment considered the Templars their predecessors.

inspiration from on high: A report in *Gr*, no. 12, March 21, 1876, described prayer meetings among society ladies in which "some began throwing themselves down on divan cushions, gasping for breath, seeking there the inspiration of Christ's spirit. . . ."

March 1876, 2.3: A Word or Two about the Report of the Scholarly Commission on Spiritualistic Phenomena

home of Mr. Aksakov: The report appeared in *G*, no. 85, March 25, 1876. For Aksakov see notes to January 1876, 3.2.

March 1876, 2.5: On Yury Samarin

Samarin, Iurii Fedorovich (1819-76), Slavophile writer and historian who played an active role in the planning and implementation of the emancipation of the serfs.

Vasilchikov, Victor Illarionovich, Prince (1820-78), general and minister of war, 1858-60.

April 1876, 1.1: The Ideals of a Stagnant, Vegetative Life. Kulaks and Bloodsuckers. Superior People Who Drive Russia Forward

Avseenko, Vasilii Grigorevich (1842-1913), writer and critic. Avseenko's article takes issue with Dostoevsky's assertion (in *DP*, February 1876, 1.2) that Russian writers took their ideals from the peasants: "despite Mr. Dostoevsky's opinion, the main task of our literature, particularly in the period from 1830 to 1860, was to assimilate West-European ideals, common ideals, the ideas of civilization, law, justice, and humaneness—all the things that were lacking in our Russian life and our Russian People" (p. 366). One could not expect salvation from the peasants, as Dostoevsky suggests: "We believe, to the contrary, that the Russian minority with European education has absorbed all that is vital and moral from the stagnant culture of the People; that educated minority must now refine these principles in the crucible of its own culture" (p. 376).

Fadeev, Rostislav Andreevich (1824-83), general, military publicist. In the 1870s Fadeev was a leading figure in the "party" of the conservative gentry. His book, *Russkoe obshchestvo v nastoiashchem i budushchem (Chem nam byt'?)* [Russian society in the present and in the future (What are we to be?)] (St. Petersburg, 1874), argued that the Russian gentry were a valuable national resource, created at the cost of the development of other social classes, and that the gentry's position should be strengthened in order to bring stability to Russian life.

April 1876, 1.2: Minor Cultural Types. Damaged People

Pisemsky, Aleksei Feofilaktovich (1821-81), novelist and dramatist, who frequently wrote on peasant themes. Avseenko's review of Pisemsky's dramas (in *RV,* no. 10, 1874) complained that Russian drama since Gogol had largely ignored the life of the educated classes. He called for less of the "artistic element," by which he meant the vivid depiction of distinctive, usually comic types, and for more intellectual content.

Ostrovsky: See note to 1873.5. Most of his plays are set in a distinctly Russian merchant milieu.

The Mihailovsky Theater (now the Leningrad Maly Theater of Opera and Ballet) was favored by members of Petersburg high society and by foreign residents of the city. It presented performances by touring foreign theater companies.

Liubim Tortsov is a character from Ostrovsky's comedy *Bednost' ne porok* [Poverty is no vice] (1853).

Woe from Wit: Gore ot uma (1824), play by Aleksandr Griboedov. Avseenko regards it as the only Russian play having a hero, Chatsky, who expresses the concerns of the educated classes.

Avseenko's *Mlechnyi put'* [The Milky Way] appeared in *RV* from October to December 1875; after a three-month interruption, it continued from April to June 1876.

Juvenals: A quotation from N. F. Shcherbina's poem "Fiziologiia 'Novogo Poeta.' Fel'eton v stikhakh" [The physiology of 'The New Poet': A feuilleton in verse] (1853).

Bolshoi Morskoi Street (now Herzen Street) was in a very fashionable area of St. Petersburg.

"perish separately": Dostoevsky paraphrases his remarks from February 1876, 1.2.

nothing at all worth preserving: One of the gentlemen is probably N. K. Mikhailovsky, writing in *OZ,* no. 12, 1875: "In *Notes of the Fatherland* we have shown many times that . . . European conservatism is utterly unthinkable in Russia because our conservatives have nothing to conserve. . . ."

April 1876, 1.3: Confusion and Inaccuracy in the Points at Issue

Ivan IV (Ivan the Terrible) (1530–84) was unable to seize a permanent Russian outlet on the Baltic during the Livonian War.

Potugin: See note to January 1876, 2.3.

Family Chronicle: Aksakov, Sergei Timofeevich (1791–1859), writer and memoirist. The episode mentioned occurs not in his *Family Chronicle* [Semeinaia khronika] but in his *Memoirs* [Vospominaniia] (1856), in the chapter entitled "High School: The First Period" [Gimnaziia. Period pervyy].

wooden plank: An icon. There were a number of superstitions and taboos associated with Friday, the day of Christ's crucifixion. Saints Florus and Laurus were much revered by Russian peasants.

April 1876, 1.4: The Beneficent Swiss Who Liberates a Russian Peasant

"count's lackeys": One could acquire the status of a nobleman (and with it, at least before 1861, the right to own serfs) by advancing through the civil or military hierarchy to a specific rank. During the nineteenth century this rank was raised from the eighth to the fourth.

Turgenev: Ivan Petrovich Lavretsky's biography is related in chapters 8 through 11 of *A Nest of Gentlefolk* [Dvorianskoe gnezdo] (1859).

Anton Goremyka (1847), short novel by D. V. Grigorovich that concerns the difficult life of a peasant serf.

Baltic Provinces: Serfs in the three Baltic Provinces (Estland, Lifland, and Kurland) were liberated between 1816 and 1819 but were not given land. They rented it from the landowners or worked it for wages.

Guizot, François Pierre Guillaume (1787–1874), French historian and statesman.

April 1876, 2.1: Something on Political Questions

Everyone is talking: The prime political topic of the day was the "Eastern Question," the term used to describe the whole range of problems connected with the disintegration of the Turkish empire in the nineteenth century. The treaty of Kuchuk Kainardji (1774) contained a clause in which Turkey promised to protect the Christian religion within its empire and permitted Russia to make representations "in favor of the new church in Constantinople, and of those who carry on its services." Apart from her interest in the Orthodox Slavs of the Balkans, Russia had a long-standing political interest in the straits that provided her access to the Mediterranean. Austria saw Turkish power declining only to be replaced by Russian influence; Great Britain, likewise, saw her communications with India threatened by the advance of Russia. Both states saw the advantage of maintaining the Ottoman Empire. Russia's defeat in the Crimean War and the peace terms set out in the Treaty of Paris (1856) seemed to resolve the Eastern Question in favor of Austria, Great Britain, France, and Turkey: Russia lost territorial gains in Bessarabia; she was not permitted to maintain naval forces in the Black Sea, which was made neutral. With the collapse of France in 1870, however, Russia denounced the Black Sea clauses of the Treaty of Paris. In July 1875, the Christian Slavs of Herzegovina rose up against Turkish rule. On December 30, 1875, Russia, Germany, and Austro-Hungary, fearful of a wider war in the Balkans, agreed on a joint note, which they presented to Turkey. This "Andrássy Note" urged Turkey to give equal status before the law to the Christian and Muslim subjects and to institute various administrative reforms in Bosnia-Herzegovina. The revolt in the Balkans continued to spread, however. Serbia armed and gave command of its forces to the Russian general Cherniaev. On May 13 the emperors of Russia, Germany, and Austro-Hungary signed the Berlin Memorandum, which proposed the enforcement of a two months' armistice. Great Britain refused to support the memorandum. (See also notes to June 1876, 2.3.) The "three chancellors," A. M. Gorchakov, Russia's foreign minister, Bismarck, and Andrássy of Austria, planned a meeting in Berlin (which took place on May 11-13 n.s.) to discuss the Balkan question.

Rodich, Gavro (1813-90), baron, viceregent of Dalmatia. Baron Rodich had been sent by the European powers to negotiate a truce with the Herzegovinian insurgents. Russian newspapers reported that Rodich, in his talks with the insurgents in April 1876, had stated that Russia was too weak to offer them any aid. The insurgents agreed to lay down their arms provided Turkey would institute a number of reforms in Herzegovina; Turkey refused to agree to a truce, however. Russian newspapers subsequently wrote of the increasing possibility of war in the Balkans.

general crusade against Russia: During the Polish rebellion of 1863, the governments of England and France sent diplomatic notes to Russia demanding that the Polish question be brought to a European congress and insisting that Russia institute reforms in her Polish territories; Russia rejected these demands.

explosion all over Europe: Russia was at war with Turkey in 1828-29. Russia's suppression of the Polish uprising of 1830-31 aroused considerable sympathy for the Poles in Europe but brought them no real material help. Russia's acquistions in Central Asia (the Khanate of Kokanda was annexed in February 1876) caused some alarm in England, as Russian expansion was seen to threaten British interests in India.

April 1876, 2.2: A Paradoxicalist

of the sort that Europe made of us in 1863: See notes to April 1876, 2.1.

April 1876, 2.3: Just a Bit More about Spiritualism

back in February: On February 13, 1876, Dostoevsky attended a seance at the home of A. N. Aksakov, where the English medium, Mrs. Claire, demonstrated her capacities.

Mendeleev's first lecture took place on April 24, 1876. (See also the notes to January 1876, 3.2.)

"crinoline springs": In G, no. 101, April 12, 1876, Vagner (see notes to January 1876, 3.2) noted that during the seance his foot touched "something long and springy" under the table; he described this as a "crinoline spring." When he looked under the table he saw "something white, like the end of a spring, flashing under the skirt of Mrs. Claire."

Solianoi Gorodok: The account appeared in NV, no. 56, April 26, 1876.

Rachinsky, Sergei Aleksandrovich (1833-1902), botanist and educator. In an article published in RV (no. 5, 1875), he proposed a purely mechanical explanation for phenomena observed at seances.

Mendeleev's second lecture took place on April 25, 1876. For Suvorin, see notes to January 1876, 1.1. Petr Dmitrievich Boborykin (1836-1921),

Russian novelist. Both Suvorin and Boborykin had written newspaper articles on spiritualism.

April 1876, 2.4: On Behalf of One Deceased

Mikhail Mikhailovich: Dostoevsky's wife, Anna, notes: "I recall how indignant Fedor Mikhailovich was as he read to me the excerpt from *New Times* and how passionately he spoke of his brother and refuted the allegations that had been raised against him. Fedor Mikhailovich always recalled Mikhail Mikhailovich with the most tender feeling. He loved him more than any other of his blood relatives, perhaps because he had grown up with him and shared his ideas as a youth" (quoted in Grossman, *Seminarii po Dostoevskomu*, pp. 64-65). The article is an obituary of Afanasii Prokof'evich Shchapov (1830-76), historian and journalist, exiled in 1864 for his activities in support of the revolutionary movement. The obituary appeared first in *D*, no. 4, 1876. Dostoevsky's brother, Mikhail Mikhailovich, provided the financing for the brothers' journalistic activities, acted as business manager, and also contributed articles. (See also notes to March 1876, 2.1.)

"The Runners": Shchapov's article, "Zemstvo i raskol. Beguny" [The *Zemstvo* and the sectarians: The runners] appeared in *V,* October-November 1862.

Time had a brilliant success: *V* was quite successful; its maximum circulation was over four thousand.

money in advance: V. S. Nechaeva (*Zhurnal M. M. i F. M. Dostoevskikh "Vremia"* [Moscow: Nauka, 1972], p. 47) notes that Shchapov did in fact receive an advance from Mikhail Dostoevsky.

In 1849: Mikhail Dostoevsky was arrested on May 6, 1849, and released on June 25.

secret society: Fedor Dostoevsky became involved with two of the more extreme members of the Petrashevsky Circle, N. A. Speshnev (1821-82) and S. F. Durov (1816-69). Mikhail disapproved of some of the radical proposals discussed in Durov's group, notably a proposal to obtain a lithograph and use it to reproduce articles exposing the shortcomings of the government.

Gagarin, Pavel Pavlovich (1789-1872), senator; member and factual head of the commission investigating the Petrashevsky case.

May 1876, 1.1: From a Private Letter

The Kairova case: Vasilii Aleksandrovich Velikanov, manager of a theatrical company in Orenburg, had gone bankrupt in the spring of 1875. Leaving his wife, an actress in his company, in Orenburg, Velikanov traveled to St. Petersburg with his mistress, Anastasia Kairova, who was also an actress in his company; they hoped to find work in the theaters of the capital. Velikanov's wife arrived in St. Petersburg at the end of June and found her husband and his mistress at a suburban summer cottage. She announced that she intended to remain with her husband, and

Kairova at first gave way and moved to the city. On the night of July 7/8, however, Kairova returned to the cottage and inflicted several razor cuts, which did not prove fatal, on Mrs. Velikanova's throat. The case came to trial on April 2, 1876; Kairova was acquitted. Russian newspapers commented extensively on the case; many of them regarded it as a test of the relatively new system of trial by jury.

May 1876, 1.2: A New Regional Voice

The First Step: Pervyi shag: Provintsial'nyi literaturnyi sbornik (Kazan', 1876). The anthology contains fiction, ethnographical and historical studies, and literary criticism by writers from the Kazan-Volga region.

"... no fourth Rome": The notion that Moscow was the Third Rome stems from the fifteenth century and was particularly fostered by the fall of Constantinople in 1453, which marked the end of the "second" (Byzantine) Roman empire. The idea that Moscow had inherited the political and spiritual authority of Byzantium also strengthened Moscow's claim to dominance over its city-state rivals.

May 1876, 1.3: The Court and Mrs. Kairova

Jack of Hearts: The name of a band of Moscow hooligans, many of whom were from gentry families. An investigation into crimes committed by the band was being conducted in 1876.

Utin, Evgenii Isakovich (1843–94), liberal lawyer and frequent contributor to *VE*.

May 1876, 1.5: The Defense Attorney and Velikanova

Arbenin, Byronic hero of Mikhail Lermontov's play, *Maskarad* [Masquerade] (1835/1842). Convinced, wrongly, of his wife Nina's infidelity, he abuses her verbally and eventually poisons her.

six-year-old stepdaughter: Dostoevsky writes of this case in detail in *DP*, October 1876, 1.1.

"She loved much ...": Luke 7:47: "Her sins, which are many, are forgiven; for she loved much...."

May 1876, 2.1: Something about a Certain Building. Some Appropriate Thoughts

Dostoevsky visited the Foundling Home on April 28, 1876; his wife's cousin, Mikhail Nikolaevich Snitkin, was employed there as a pediatrician.

Betskoi, Ivan Ivanovich (1704–95), educational reformer, who, in the eighteenth century, established the first foundling homes in Moscow and St. Petersburg.

gets into the water and chokes: A sixteen-year-old girl, Bogomolova, was accused of having murdered her newborn infant on November 1, 1875.

She was acquitted after a trial in March 1876. Dostoevsky parodies portions of her testimony here.

"Why does the duck have feathers?": See note to January 1876, 2.3.

May 1876, 2.2: One Inappropriate Thought

New Times: The letter was published in *NV,* no. 85 (May 26, 1876).

paid her dues to progress: Midwifery was one of the few professions open to women at the time; radical young women in particular chose it as a career.

May 1876, 2.3: A Democratic Spirit, for Certain. Women

Shchapov's wife: Olga Ivanovna Shchapova (née Zhemchuzhnikova) met Shchapov (see note to April 1876, 2.4) when he was gravely ill and about to be exiled. Against the wishes of her family, she married him and shared the hardships of his exile for ten years.

June 1876, 1.1: The Death of George Sand

Sand, George (1804–76), pseudonym of Amandine Lucile Aurore Dudevant, French novelist.

Potugins: See note to January 1876, 2.3.

au poète allemand: Schiller was made an honorary citizen of the French republic on August 26, 1792.

Zhukovsky, Vasily Andreevich (1873–52), Russian early romantic poet and translator.

June 1876, 1.2: A Few Words about George Sand

all the rest . . . was strictly suppressed: In the years following the European revolutions of 1848 a very strict censorship was imposed upon Russia in the hope of keeping out new Western ideas that might threaten the social order.

Metternich-Winneburg, Clemens Wenzel Lothar, Prince (1773–1859), Austrian statesman, diplomatist, and chancellor, 1821–48. He followed a largely reactionary policy in order to combat the forces of revolution.

The verse is from "Sovremennaia pesnia" [Contemporary song] (1836) of Denis Davydov (1784–1839), Russian poet and soldier, hero of the War of 1812: Thiers, Louis Adolf (1797–1877), French statesman and historian; Rabaut Saint-Etienne, Jean-Paul (1743–93), French revolutionary, executed in December 1793; Mirabeau, Honoré Gabriel Riqueti, Comte de (1749–91), French statesman and orator.

Magnitsky, Mikhail Leontevich (1778–1855), curator of the Kazan educational district, notorious careerist and reactionary. In 1819 he recommended that Kazan University be closed and its building destroyed because of the institution's "godlessness."

Liprandi, Ivan Petrovich (1790–1880), official in the Ministry of Internal Affairs who managed the police observation of the Petrashevsky Circle and was active in the investigation of the affair.

Senkovsky, Osip Ivanovich (1800–58), journalist, critic, and humorist. His reviews of contemporary writers display cynicism and contempt.

Bulgarin, Faddei: See notes to 1873.4.

Yegor is a Russian form of George.

Leroux, Pierre (1798–1871), French philosopher and utopian socialist whose notions of Christian socialism had a strong influence on George Sand. Alexandre Auguste Ledru-Rollin (1807–74), French lawyer and politician, minister of the interior in the provisional government following the 1848 revolution. *Severnaia pchela* [The Northern Bee], no. 109, May 17, 1848, carried an account of orgies involving, among others, George Sand and Ledru-Rollin, which supposedly took place at the French Ministry of the Interior. Standard biographies of George Sand make no mention of these, however.

middle of the thirties: George Sand's first work to be translated was her novel *Indiana* (1832), which appeared in Russian in 1833.

L'Uscoque (1838), novel.

Balzac's significance: Grigorovich notes in his memoirs that on one occasion Belinsky furiously attacked Balzac as a "petty-bourgeois" writer and that the critic reserved particular scorn for Balzac's *Eugénie Grandet* (which Dostoevsky had translated into Russian in 1843) (D. V. Grigorovich, *Literaturnye vospominaniia* [Moscow: Goslitizdat, 1961], pp. 87–88).

Venetian tales: *La Dernière Aldini* (1837–38), novel. Dostoevsky translated the novel into Russian in 1844, only to learn that a Russian translation already existed.

Jeanne (1844), novel.

"La Marquise" (1832), short tale.

"no name other than His": paraphrase of Acts 4:12: "Neither is there salvation in any other; for there is no other name under heaven given among men, whereby we must be saved."

June 1876, 2.1: My Paradox

tussle with Europe: Russian newspapers wrote of the growing possibility of war between Turkey and her restive possessions, Serbia and Montenegro. Serbia in fact declared war on Turkey on June 30 (n.s.). Russian involvement in the Balkans, which in turn could lead to conflict with the other European powers, was raised as a possibility. (See also notes to April 1876, 2.1.)

"kvasnik" and "zipunnik": The words derive from "kvas," a traditional Russian fermented drink, and "zipun," a peasant coat of rough homespun material; they imply crude and specifically Russian qualities.

Grigorev, Apollon Aleksandrovich (1822–64), Russian critic, philosopher, and poet, one of Dostoevsky's ideological mentors. His remarks about Belinsky appeared in *V*, no. 2, 1861, p. 89.

June 1876, 2.2: Deduction from My Paradox

Gagarin, Ivan Sergeevich, Prince (1814–82), Russian diplomat. Gagarin converted to Roman Catholicism in 1842 and entered the Jesuit order the following year; this made him ineligible to return to Russia. He spent the remainder of his life mainly in France, where he taught and published scholarly works.

June 1876. 2.3: The Eastern Question

they will have no success: While conservative newspapers such as *NV* raised the possibility of war, more liberal papers such as *G, BV,* and *SV* advised prudence and wrote of the necessity of preserving the peace. They argued that Serbia should seek a diplomatic solution to the dispute. After Serbia's declaration of war on Turkey on June 30, 1876 (n.s.), some liberal newspapers adopted a more militant policy.

Batory, Stefan (István Báthory) (1533–86), king of Poland and prince of Transylvania. The episode of Ivan IV's embassy to Stefan Batory is related in Karamzin's *Istoriia gosudarstva Rossiiskogo,* vol. 9, chap. 5.

Milan of Serbia (Milan Obrenović IV) (1854–1901), Grand Duke of Serbia, 1868–82; king of Serbia (as Milan I), 1882–89). Nicholas of Montenegro (1841–1921), Grand Duke of Montenegro; king of Montenegro, 1910–18. Serbia declared war on Turkey on June 30, 1876 (n.s.); Montenegro, on July 2, (n.s.).

bashibazouks and Circassians: The Berlin Congress of the three chancellors (see note to February 1876, 2.1) produced the "Berlin Memorandum," which demanded that Turkey cease all military operations against the insurgent Slavs for a period of two months and that she, Turkey, institute reforms in Bosnia and Herzegovina. France and Italy supported the memorandum; England, however, refused to sign it. The Russian press saw this as a hostile act on the part of England. Turkish nationalists demanded that Turkey refuse to comply with the conditions of the memorandum. The Turkish Sultan Abd-ul-Aziz was deposed on May 30 (n.s.); the new Sultan, Murad IV, was easily exploited by Moslem extremists. Because of the shift of power in Turkey, the European powers decided to delay delivery of the Berlin Memorandum. An uprising that broke out in Bulgaria in April was put down by Turkish forces (bashibazouks, or irregulars, noted for their cruelty and lack of discipline, and Circassians who had emigrated to Turkey after the Russian conquest of the Caucasus), who committed a number of atrocities.

three monarchs: Alexander II had meetings with Wilhelm I of Germany and Franz Josef I of Austria in June 1876.

"the sick man": i.e., Turkey.

England's prime minister: On June 26 (n.s.) Prime Minister Benjamin Disraeli, replying to a question in Parliament about Turkish atrocities in Bulgaria, noted that "they appear to have been begun by strangers entering the country and burning the villages without reference to religion or race. . . . The persons, who are called Bashi-Bazouks and Circassians, are persons who had settled in the country and had a stake in it" (*Hansard's Parliamentary Debates, Third Series* [London: Cornelius Bond, 1876], 230: 425). These remarks were widely reported in the Russian press.

June 1876, 2.4: The Utopian Conception of History

Diary: See February 1876, 1.2.

document concocted by Poles: Charles-Louis Lesur (1770–1849), French writer, publicist, and an official in Napoleon's Foreign Ministry, describes a secret "document" outlining Russian plans for expansion in Europe, which included the expulsion of the Turks from Europe and the seizure of Constantinople. The document was his own invention and formed part of a campaign of anti-Russian propaganda. See his *Des progrès de la puissance russe depuis son origin jusqu'au commencement du XIX siècle* (Paris, 1812). The "testament" was subsequently republished a number of times.

Tsargrad: Here Dostoevsky uses the traditional Russian name (which is also akin to the name used in several other Slavic languages) for Constantinople—literally, "the tsar's city." He thereby suggests its significance in Russian history and, perhaps, even Russia's claim to it (see notes on the notion of Moscow as the Third Rome, May 1876, 1.2). Constantinople/Tsargrad was a holy city for medieval Russians and a common place of pilgrimage.

capital of Slavdom: The possibility of a Slavic federation whose capital would be Constantinople was raised a number of times in the nineteenth century but was set forth in detail by the Russian publicist and ideologist of panslavism, N. Ia. Danilevsky (1822–85), in his *Rossiia i Evropa* [Russia and Europe] (St. Petersburg, 1871). The Slavic peoples, Danilevsky argued, should turn away from Europeanism and pursue national goals, the first of which was to resolve the Eastern Question through seizure of Constantinople. War with Europe would ensue, and Russia would unite the Slavs under her leadership. The capital of this panslavic union would be Constantinople (Tsargrad), which Danilevsky envisaged as becoming the common property of all the Slavic peoples, belonging to no one of them. Dostoevsky read Danilevsky with great interest, but later (see *DP*, November 1877, 3.1) expressed his disagreement with him, arguing that Constantinople must belong to the Russians.

Ivan III (1440–1505), grand duke of Muscovy. His conquests consolidated Moscow's dominance over other Russian city-states and established a strong centralized power. After his marriage to Sofia Paleologa, niece of the last Byzantine emperor, he adopted the Byzantine double-headed eagle and many of the trappings of the Byzantine court. The notion of Russia as heir to Byzantium (see note to May 1876, 1.2) was strengthened during his reign.

June 1876, 2.5: About Women Again

Piedmont: The reference is to its central role in the uniting of Italy. Serbia was sometimes called "the Piedmont of the Balkans" because of its efforts to lead the movement to overthrow Turkish rule.

Cherniaev, Mikhail Grigor'evich (1828–98), lieutenant-general, publisher, panslavist. His newspaper, *RM*, was the first Russian publication to support the insurgents in the Balkans. In April 1876 Cherniaev arrived in Serbia without official Russian approval; he was warmly welcomed in Belgrade and subsequently took command of the main Serbian army. Although Emperor Alexander II disapproved strongly of Cherniaev's actions, his failure to renounce the general publicly led the Serbs to believe that the Russian government secretly supported him.

Slavic Committee: See note to February 1876, 1.2.

church of the Serbian community: The service was held on June 28, 1876.

a young girl: The girl was Sofia Efimovna Lure (1858–189?), identified by Anna Dostoevskaia as the daughter of a wealthy banker from Minsk (Grossman, *Seminarii po Dostoevskomu*, p. 65). Dostoevsky publishes a portion of a letter from her in *DP*, March 1877, 3.1. She in fact conceded to the wishes of her family and did not go to Serbia.

July-August 1876, 1.1: Going Abroad. Something about Russians in Railway Carriages

Ems: Dostoevsky left St. Petersburg on July 5, 1876, to spend the summer in Bad-Ems, a fashionable German resort noted for its mineral springs.

The verse is from K. F. Ryleev's "Peter the Great in Ostrogozhsk" [Petr Velikii v Ostrogozhske] (1823).

"desolation" of the region: *MV*, no. 174, July 10, 1876.

July-August 1876, 1.2: Something on Petersburg Baden-Badenism

article in the *Stock-Exchange News*: *BV*, no. 182, July 4, 1876, in an article by "Bukva" (I. F. Vasilevsky), accused Dostoevsky of political naiveté for his views on the Eastern Question (*DP*, June 1876, 2.3, 2.4).

Ivan III: See note to June 1876, 2.4. Russian historical claims to Byzantium developed after the fall of that city to the Turks in 1453 and were strengthened by the doctrine of Moscow as the Third Rome (see note to May 1876, 1.2).

July-August 1876, 1.3: On the Pugnacity of the Germans

Saxon troops: Dostoevsky and his wife lived in Dresden from early August 1869 to July 5, 1871, during which time the victorious German armies returned from France.

The German Suburb: In the seventeenth century, foreigners (whom the Russians referred to as "Germans") were forbidden to live inside the walls of Moscow. In 1652 Tsar Alexis set aside an area some three miles northeast of the Kremlin, in which foreign residents created their own European town. See Robert K. Massie, *Peter the Great: His Life and World* (New York: Alfred A. Knopf, 1980), pp. 110–11.

The Voice: *G*, no. 200, June 21, 1876, suggested that this anti-Russian campaign was the work of the German government.

July-August 1876, 1.4: The Very Last Word of Civilization

Khlestakov and Skvoznik-Dmukhanovsky are characters from Gogol's play *The Inspector-General;* in act 4, Skvoznik-Dmukhanovsky tells Khlestakov that a woman who complained to him of being flogged by the police was lying: "She flogged herself."

wipe France: In the spring of 1875 Bismarck hoped to attack France once more so as not to allow her to recover from the defeat Germany inflicted during the war of 1870-71. A strident anti-French campaign was carried out by the German press. Alexander II visited Berlin in May 1875, and is credited by some historians for helping to improve German-French relations.

July-August 1876, 2.1: Idealist-Cynics

Granovsky, Timofei Nikolaevich (1813-55), Russian historian and social thinker. The article, "Vostochnyi vopros s russkoi tochki zreniia 1855 goda" [The Eastern Question from the Russian point of view of 1855], was reprinted several times and was attributed to Granovsky; its author in fact was B. N. Chicherin (1828-1904), Russian philosopher and historian. Granovsky was the major prototype for Dostoevsky's Stepan Trofimovich Verkhovensky in *The Devils.*

dispute with the Hungarians: In 1849, Nicholas I sent Russian troops to Hungary to help Austria put down the uprising of Hungarians fighting for their independence.

July-August 1876, 2.2: Should One Be Ashamed of Being an Idealist?

holy war: One of the immediate causes of the Crimean War was the question of Christian rights in the Holy Land, then under Turkish rule, and of who was to be entrusted with the keys to the temple of Bethlehem.

"...idyllic way of life": Dostoevsky here quotes Avseenko's remarks, which were discussed in *DP,* April 1876, 1.1.

Kireev, Nikolai Alekseevich (1841-76). A former soldier, Kireev was an active member of St. Petersburg's Slavic Committee. He traveled to the Balkans on behalf of the committee to assess the prospects for an uprising against the Turks. He took command of a detachment of Bulgarian volunteers in Serbia and, conspicuously dressed in a white uniform, led them into an attack on a Turkish position. He was killed by Turkish fire on July 6 and his body seized and mutilated by the Turks. Kireev's death became a powerful symbol to rally support for the Serbian cause.

"And though he fell": A verse from K. D. Ryleev's "Volynskii" (1822).

Areopagus: In Acts 17:22-34, Paul's statement about the raising of the dead is met with disbelief by the members of the Court of Areopagus in Athens. "However, some men joined him and became believers, including Dionysius, a member of the Court of Areopagus; also a woman named Damaris, and others besides" (verse 34).

July-August 1876, 2.3: The Germans and Labor. Inexplicable Tricks. On Wit

"And if you give a poor man . . .": A paraphrase of Matthew 10:41: "And whosoever shall give to drink unto one of these little ones a cup of cold water only in the name of a disciple, verily I say unto you, he shall in no wise lose his reward."

July-August 1876, 3.1: Russian or French?

"Wunderfrau": A Munich woman named Hohenester earned this nickname for her renown as a healer.

Lahn: The river on which Bad-Ems is situated.

Turgenev: The scene occurs in Turgenev's *Smoke*, chapter 5.

July-August 1876, 3.2: What Language Should a Future Person of Consequence Speak?

novels of peasant life: Dostoevsky refers to D. V. Grigorovich (see note to April 1876, 1.4). Grigorovich was educated in French by his mother and grandmother and subsequently studied in a boarding school where French was the working language; he learned Russian from family servants and peasants. Dostoevsky, a fellow student at the Engineering School in 1838, provided him with a list of Russian novels, the first he had read in that language.

Arina Rodionovna: Pushkin, like Grigorovich, was educated largely in French and made his first acquaintance with Russian from servants. In later life, during a period of exile at his family estate, Mikhailovskoe, he absorbed the language and folktales of his childhood nurse, Arina Rodionovna.

"three whales": In Russian folk belief, the world is supported on the backs of three whales.

M. Viardot: See note to 1873.9. Viardot's collaborator in the translation was Ivan Turgenev.

Archpriest Avvakum: Avvakum Petrovich (1620?–1682), archpriest and central figure in the great schism in the Orthodox Church. His *Life* [Zhitie] (1672–75) is noted for its direct and colorful language, which often reflects the spoken idiom of the day.

classical reform: See notes to 1873.16.

teachers who are Czechs: The increased stress on classical languages in the reformed education system resulted in a shortage of native-born teachers of Latin and Greek; teachers from central Europe were hired to fill the gap.

The letter "yat'," the thirtieth in the Russian alphabet until a reform of orthography in 1917–18, had historically represented a distinct sound; subsequently, its pronunciation in the literary language changed to coincide with that of the letter "ye" (pronounced as in the English word "yet"), by which it was replaced. Until the reform of orthography, many spelling errors resulted from the confusion of these two letters.

July-August 1876, 4.1: What Effects the Cure When Taking the Waters: The Water or the *Bon Ton?*

Doctor Hirschorn's: A. Iu. Girshgorn, *Ems i tselebnye ego istochniki. Deistvie ix na zdorovyi i bol'noi organizm, primenenie v razlichnykh bolezniakh, pravila upotrebleniia vod, i t.d.* [Ems and its healing springs. Their effect on the sound and on the unhealthy organism, their applicability to various illnesses, procedures for the use of the waters, etc.] (St. Petersburg, 1874).

Pechorin: See note to February 1876, 1.1. "Kavkazskii plennik" [Captive of the Caucasus] (1822), poem by A. S. Pushkin.

the verses: Matthew 6:28-30.

July-August 1876, 4.2: One on Whom Modern Woman Has Shown Favor

For Granovsky, see note to July-August, 2.1. The pamphlet on women was by N. N. Strakhov, *The Woman Question: John Stuart Mill "On the Subjection of Women"* [Zhenskii vopros. Razbor sochineniia Dzhona Stiuarta Millia "O poodchinenii zhenshchiny"] (St. Petersburg, 1871). Strakhov here argued against equal rights for women.

The author must be a bachelor: Strakhov was in fact a bachelor.

Tatiana: heroine of Pushkin's *Eugene Onegin;* she remains faithful to her husband despite her love for Onegin.

A number of wives of Decembrists sentenced to a lifetime of Siberian exile decided to share their husbands' fate, thereby giving up their wealth, social position, and right to return to European Russia. (Nekrasov's "Russian Women" [see notes to 1873.9] concerns two such wives.)

Kreuznach: Bad Kreuznach, city on the River Nahe, now in Rheinland-Westphalia; a popular spa.

July-August 1876, 4.3: Children's Secrets

"Whoever lacked the wit": A. S. Griboedov, *Woe from Wit,* act 3, scene 3.

Sonechka: In his *Gospoda Molchaliny* [The Messrs. Molchalin] (1874), the satirist M. E. Saltykov-Shchedrin provided an ironic continuation of the life of Chatsky, hero of *Woe from Wit.* Here Chatsky marries the heroine, Sofia (Sonechka), but because of his poor knowledge of the law, he writes a will in which he unintentionally disinherits her.

Articles de Paris: Small articles, mainly those connected with the fashion industry, that were made in Paris and were valuable exports. They helped pay the war reparations imposed by Germany under the Treaty of Frankfurt of 1871.

Dumas, Alexandre (Dumas-fils) (1824-95), French dramatist and novelist. His *L'Homme-femme. Réponse à M. Henri d'Ideville* (1872) advises married couples to have only one child, after which the wife should simply be a mistress to her husband.

Gavroche: Urchin from Victor Hugo's *Les Misérables*.

In Emile Zola's *Le Ventre de Paris* (1873), chapter 3, the teacher Charvet lives in a "free marriage" with Clémence: "Depuis plus de dix ans, Clémence et lui vivaient martialement, sur des bases débattues, selon un contrat strictement observé de part et d'autre."

July-August 1876, 4.4: The Land and Children

Clovis (466–511), king of the Franks and founder of the Frankish monarchy.

Potugins: See note to January 1876, 2.3.

memoirs of a certain Russian landowner: The book in question was *Zapiski Ivana Dmitrievicha Iakushkina* [Notes of Ivan Dmitrievich Iakushkin] (London, 1862). Iakushkin, who was involved in the Decembrist movement, offered his peasants their freedom, but without land, in 1819. He taught serf children to read and write (not singing, as Dostoevsky states) so as to allow them to be trained in trades.

July-August 1876, 4.5: An Odd Summer for Russia

'Down with Cherniaev': Cherniaev: See note to June 1876, 2.5. After a few initial victories in late June, his Serbians suffered several defeats at the hands of the Turks and were compelled to retreat. On July 25, 1876 (August 6 n.s.), however, he was appointed commander-in-chief of the Serbian army. Again, after a few initial successes, his armies were forced into retreat. Russian newspapers carried reports of Serbian hostility toward Cherniaev and of deep division in Belgrade as to whether the war should be continued or a peace negotiated with Turkey. Some Serbs viewed Cherniaev as a megalomaniac who was ready to sacrifice Serbian lives in order to further his ambitions. The Russian voluteers also included some adventurers and ne'er-do-wells; their rowdy behavior in the cafes of Belgrade also fueled Serbian resentment.

"Emburdened...": From F. I. Tiutchev's poem "Eti bednye selen-'ia..." ["These poor villages..."] (1855).

September 1876, 1.1: *Piccola Bestia*

Dostoevsky and his wife lived in Florence from November 1868 to August 1869, during which time this incident occurred (Grossman, *Seminarii po Dostoevskomu*, p. 65).

Semipalatinsk: After he completed his term of hard labor in 1854, Dostoevsky spent five years serving in the army in Siberia, initially as a private soldier at Semipalatinsk.

Kuzma Prutkov: Pseudonym of A. K. Tolstoy, Vladimir Aleksei, and Aleksandr Zhemchuzhnikov, who produced nonsense verses, ridiculous aphorisms, plays, and parodies. In the fable "Konduktor i tarantul" a tarantula that has crept into a coach is killed by the conductor because it has not paid its fare.

Beaconsfield, Benjamin Disraeli, Earl of (1804–81), British statesman and man of letters, prime minister of Great Britain, 1874–80. Disraeli at first appeared not to take seriously the reports of Turkish atrocities in Bulgaria, expressing skepticism about newspaper accounts of torture and the imprisonment of ten thousand persons: "In fact, I doubt whether there is prison accommodation for so many, or that torture has been practised on a great scale among an Oriental people who seldom, I believe, resort to torture, but generally terminate their connection with culprits in a more expeditious manner" (George Earle Buckle, *The Life of Benjamin Disraeli, Earl of Beaconsfield* [London: John Murray, 1920], 6:43). The fact that members of the House of Commons took this remark as a joke was used by Disraeli's opponents to prove the prime minister's cynicism. On July 31 (n.s.) Disraeli dismissed reports of Turkish atrocities in Bulgaria as "coffee-house babble." He later claimed that the documents initially available to him had in fact justified his playing down the atrocities (Robert Blake, *Disraeli* [London: Eyre and Spottiswoode, 1966], p. 593). *NV,* September 14, carried a portion of a dispatch from the Vienna correspondent of the London *Times* which claimed that many of the Russian volunteers in Serbia were Slavophile or social-democratic extremists who, once organized into military units, might return home to present a real danger to the Russian stability.

war . . . is a dishonorable one: In a speech delivered on September 20 (n.s.), Disraeli described the conflict in the Balkans as "this outrageous and wicked war, for of all the wars that were ever waged there never was a war less justifiable than the war made by Servia against the Porte. . . . Not only every principle of international law, not only every principle of public morality, but every principle of honour was outraged" (*The Times,* September 21, 1876).

chef-d'oeuvre: Some Russian newspapers charged that Turkey would not have undertaken the massacre of Bulgarian civilians without the certainty of British support.

'magnanimity . . . never disinterested': Dostoevsky quotes here some phrases from the pamphlet he discusses in *DP,* July–August, 2.1.

Tuileries: See notes to January 1876, 3.2.

Kireev: See note to July–August 1876, 2.2. Raevsky, Nikolai Nikolaevich (1839–76), Russian colonel, killed in battle in Serbia on August 20, 1876.

September 1876, 1.2: Words, Words, Words!

"Administrative autonomy": A cease-fire was in effect in the Balkans for the period September 17–24 (n.s), but Turkey refused Serbia's proposal to continue the truce. The European powers, attempting to resolve the conflict in the Balkans by diplomatic means, proposed a return to the situation that had existed prior to hostilities as well as administrative autonomy for Bulgaria and the areas in which the uprising occurred. Some Russian newspapers supported this move.

September 1876, 1.3: Schemes and More Schemes

"unnatural thing": *NV*, no. 196, September 14, 1876, proposed such a solution.

Tory party: Gladstone and the British Liberal party, opposing the Conservatives' support of Turkey, played on the horrors of Turkish atrocities and proposed supporting the Slavs in the Balkans. Gladstone's pamphlet, "The Bulgarian Horrors and the Question of the East" (September 1876), helped to rouse anti-Turkish feeling in Britain.

elsewhere: Dostoevsky commented briefly on anti-Russian feelings among the Serbs in *DP*, July-August 1876, 4.5.

Ionian islands: In 1864 Britain abandoned her protectorate of the Ionian islands and ceded them to Greece, in accordance with the wishes of the inhabitants.

September 1876, 1.4: Dressing Gowns and Soap

Turkey . . . pushed back into Asia: Russian newspapers in 1876 carried various reports of proposals, originating mainly from Gladstone and the British Liberal party, of expelling the Turks from Europe.

The siege and capture of Kazan by Ivan IV (Ivan the Terrible) in 1552 marked the defeat of the last remnant of the Tatar Horde and the end of Tatar (Mongol) power in European Russia.

Karamzin (see notes to 1873.6) described the taking of Kazan in his *History of the Russian State*, vol. 8, chap. 4.

September 1876, 2.1: Outmoded People

The European Messenger: The article, by L. A. Polonsky, appeared in *VE*, no. 9, pp. 351–54.

September 1876, 2.2: Kifomokievism

Kifomokievism: in chapter 11 of Gogol's *Dead Souls*, his character Kifa Mokievich is described as one whose "existence was taken up more with cerebration. . . ." The character has come to symbolize idle speculation on utterly trivial matters.

shariah: the system of Islamic duties—legal, ethical, and religious—that governs both private life and criminal law. The title "caliph" implied both temporal and spiritual rule.

September 1876, 2.3: Continuation of the Preceding

"*questioning feelings*": The word used, *sysk*, suggests not only "questioning" but "investigation" and "searching," and was commonly used in connection with the struggle of the authorities against the revolutionary movement.

a factual event: In the summer of 1876 some Russian newspapers carried reports of disturbances among the Moslem population of the Caucasus and of the presence of Turkish agitators in the Crimea; other Russian newspapers discounted these reports.

Stundists: See notes to 1873.7.

krestianstvo: The Russian word for Christianity is *khristianstvo*, and for peasantry, *krest'ianstvo*. The two words have a common Greek origin.

September 1876, 2.4: Fears and Apprehensions

communiqués in 1863: See notes to April 1876, 2.1.

North American battleship: In July 1866, an American diplomatic mission, headed by G. V. Fox, arrived in St. Petersburg on board the monitor *Miantonomo*. The purpose of the mission was to congratulate Emperor Alexander II on his escape from an assassination attempt in April and to express gratitude for Russian support during the civil war. The American visitors traveled widely in Russia and were lavishly entertained. Thomas A. Bailey, *America Faces Russia: Russian-American Relations from Early Times to Our Day* (Gloucester, Mass.: Peter Smith, 1964), pp. 96–99.

Candiots: In 1866 the Greek population of Crete (then Candia) rose up against Turkish rule; a widespread campaign took place in Russia to collect money to aid the insurgents (Candiots), who were of the Greek Orthodox faith.

Petersburg and Moscow: The Slavic Committee (see notes to June 1876, 2.5), in May 1867, organized a congress in Moscow that aroused widespread interest in Russia toward the other Slavic nations. A number of leading writers from these nations participated.

liberation of Italy: In July 1858, Count Cavour (1810–61), prime minister of Piedmont, concluded a secret agreement with Napoleon III whereby both states would declare war on Austria and expel her from Italy; subsequently, a North Italian state would be formed. In exchange for her help, France was to receive Savoy and the county of Nice. Napoleon was reluctant to see a united Italy, however, and he concluded a separate armistice with Austria.

"Jamais!": In the autumn of 1867, with Garibaldi's troops at the gates of Rome, the French intervened to defend the Holy See. France's foreign minister, Eugène Rouher, declared in the Chamber of Deputies on December 5 (n.s.): "Au nom du gouvernement français, l'Italie ne s'emparera pas de Rome! Jamais, jamais la France ne supportera cette violence à son honneur et à la catholicité" ["In the name of the French government, Italy will not take possession of Rome! Never, never will France tolerate this violence to her honor and her catholicity"]. Quoted in Philip Guedalla, *The Second Empire* (London: Hodder and Stoughton, 1932), p. 297.

The Hungarians: The author of the article notes that a number of Hungarians joined the forces of Garibaldi to fight for the liberation of Italy, "despite the fact that they were not fellow countrymen of the people whom they went off to help" (*VE* 5 [September 1876]: 352). Hungary supported maintaining the integrity of the Ottoman empire and opposed the possibility of independent Slavic states near her borders.

September 1876, 2.5: Postscript

Jack of Hearts: See notes to May 1876, 1.3.

October 1876, 1.1: A Case That Is Not as Simple as It Seems

survived in good health: See May 1876, 1.5. Dostoevsky discusses this case again in December 1877, 1.1–1.6.

October 1876, 1.2: A Few Remarks about Simplicity and Simplification

Meshchansky Street: According to Dostoevsky's wife, the incident he describes was an actual one (Grossman, *Seminarii po Dostoevskomu*, p. 65). The period he refers to, 1862–63, marked a high point in the influence of radical and utilitarian doctrines.

Pushkin: In the 1860s, the radical critics V. A. Zaitsev (1842–82) and D. I. Pisarev (1840–68), basing their thesis on utilitarian principles, argued that a pair of boots were of more value to humanity than the entire works of Shakespeare or Pushkin.

October 1876, 1.3: Two Suicides

one of our writers: The writer is Mikhail Evgrafovich Saltykov-Shchedrin (1826–89), then an editor of *OZ*, which wanted to publish something by Dostoevsky.

Molchalin, a character from Griboedov's play *Woe from Wit*. (See also the notes to April 1876, 1.2.) Saltykov-Shchedrin recast Molchalin in his satirical cycle *The Messrs. Molchalin* (1874). (See also notes to July–August 1876, 4.3.)

daughter of one very well-known Russian emigré: The girl was Elizaveta Aleksandrovna Herzen, daughter of Alexander Herzen (see note to 1873.1), who committed suicide in Florence at the age of seventeen. The suicide note Dostoevsky quotes here is an abbreviated paraphrase of the original. The original also does not contain the phrase "Ce n'est pas chic!" This, apparently, was a comment made by Konstantin Pobedonostsev, who wrote to Dostoevsky about the suicide, and which the latter assumed to be part of Miss Herzen's note.

a suicide in the city: One such report was carried in *NV*, no. 215, October 3, 1876. The girl served as a prototype of the heroine of "The Meek One" (*DP*, November 1876).

October 1876, 1.4: The Sentence

suicide *out of boredom:* An acquaintance of Dostoevsky's, the writer L. Kh. Khokhriakova (1838-1900), stated that Dostoevsky admitted that this was not a genuine suicide note but his own creation (L. Simonova [L. Kh. Kokhriakova], "Iz vospominanii o Fedore Mikhailoviche Dostoevskom" [From my recollections of F. M. Dostoevsky], *Tserkovno-obshchestvennyi vestnik* [The Clerical and Social Messenger], no. 18, February 1881).

October 1876, 2.1: A New Phase in the Eastern Question

defeat of Cherniaev: On October 17, 1876, at Djunis, the Turks inflicted a decisive defeat on Cherniaev's army, effectively crushing the Serbian and Montenegrin forces.

Suvorov, Aleksandr Vasil'evich (1729-1800), Russian field marshal. During a campaign against the French revolutionary armies in Italy in 1799, he led his army out of French encirclement on a retreat through the passes of the Alps.

words of the tsar: After Cherniaev's defeat, Prince Milan of Serbia appealed to Alexander II for assistance. On October 19, Russia presented Turkey with an ultimatum, threatening to break off diplomatic relations if Turkey did not suspend hostilities against the Serbs for a period of up to two months. Turkey quickly yielded, and discussions on how to resolve the situation ensued; Russia suggested a conference of the major powers.

Hungarians: *NV,* no. 234, October 22, 1876, quoted Hungarian sources that claimed Russia was hesitating to take action in the Balkans out of fear of Hungary.

1853 marked the beginning of the Crimean War.

Bulgaria and the Slavs: The truce arranged in late October was between the Turks and the Serbs but did not extend to the Bulgarians and other Slavs involved in the conflict. In October, Russian newspapers carried accounts of massacres of Bulgarian civilians.

Stock Exchange News: BV, no. 291, October 21, 1876, carried a strong criticism of Cherniaev's activities in Serbia. Coming to Cherniaev's defense, *PG* (no. 208, October 22, 1876) suggested that readers show their disagreement with the views of *BV.*

"schools, for example ...": G, no. 277, October 7, 1876, suggested that Russia's domestic development, not foreign war, ought to be her prime concern; the practice of making donations to a common cause was a good one, but funds raised thereby should be devoted to Russian schools, roads, and medical services rather than to the Slavs.

New Times: NV, no. 236, October 24, 1876, carried a strong defense of Russian volunteers in Serbia, noting that they were motivated by noble feelings of brotherhood, not by personal gain or wish for glory.

Ilya Muromets: One of the principal heroes of the traditional *bylina* or Russian epic song.

October 1876, 2.2: Cherniaev

The English, as a matter of policy: In later September and early October, several Russian newspapers reported that some Russians in Belgrade were undermining Cherniaev's efforts and causing dissension between him and the Serbs; *NV*, no. 215, October 3, 1876, noted that the British and Greek consuls in Belgrade were actively working against Russian interests.

The item appeared in *MV*, no. 270, October 22, 1876.

October 1876, 2.3: The Best People

a German name: In 1722 Peter the Great instituted the "Table of Ranks," a hierarchy of fourteen categories of civil servants and military officers. He thus abolished, in theory at least, the previous tradition of aristocratic privilege, since henceforth all who served were expected to begin at the bottom of the hierarchy and advance by their own merit. Even one of humble birth could acquire the status of gentry by attaining a certain rank.

October 1876, 2.4: On the Same Topic

Ostrovsky's characters: See notes to 1873.5.

Ovsiannikov: In 1876, Stepan Tarasovich Ovsiannikov, a wealthy St. Petersburg flour-mill owner, was convicted of arson and sentenced to exile in Siberia. Russian peasants traditionally gave alms to convicts being transported to prison or exile.

"this young school...": Quoted from February 1876, 2.6.

Strusberg, B. Henry (1823-84), German railway entrepreneur. Strusberg had contracted to build a railway line in Russia. By bribing two of the directors of the Moscow Commercial Loan Bank, he obtained a loan of seven million rubles, using worthless papers as security. Strusberg went bankrupt and in turn caused the failure of the Moscow Bank. His trial took place in Moscow in October 1876.

Landau was one of the bank directors whom Strusberg bribed.

Shumakher, Danila Danilovich, mayor of Moscow, 1874-76. He was a member of the Moscow Commercial Loan Bank's advisory board and was accused of using information gained through his position to recover his own deposits when the bank was about to fail. His sentence, which was only proclaimed after this issue of the *Diary* appeared, was in fact one month's imprisonment. (See *Istoriia Moskvy* [Moscow: AN SSSR, 1952-59], 4: 500-501.)

A father—an old soldier—: *G*, no. 285, October 15, 1876, carried an account of this retired soldier.

November 1876: Author's Foreword

his last moment of life: Victor Hugo's *Last Day of a Condemned Man* [*Le Dernière Jour d'un condamné*] is a first-person "confession" written by the hero. It ends with his description of the sound of the footsteps of those coming to take him to be executed. In his preface to the first edition of the story, Hugo also attempted to explain its origins: "There are two ways of accounting for the existence of the ensuing work. Either there really has been found a roll of papers on which were inscribed, exactly as they came, the last thoughts of a condemned prisoner; or else there has been an author, a dreamer, occupied in observing nature for the advantage of society, who, having been seized with those forcible ideas, could not rest until he had given them the tangible form of a volume."

November 1876, 1.1: Who Was I and Who Was She?

"'I am a part of that whole...'": A paraphrase of Mephistopheles's remark in Goethe's *Faust*, part 1, scene 2:

> ...Ein Teil von jener Kraft,
> Die stets das Böse will, und stets das Gute Schafft.

November 1876, 1.3: The Noblest of Men, but I Don't Believe It Myself

"'The first impressions of existence'": An inaccurate quotation from Pushkin's poem "The Demon" [Demon] (1823).

November 1876, 1.4: Plans and More Plans

The Pursuit of Happiness [Pogonia za schast'em] (1876), a play by Petr Ilych Iurkevich; *The Singing Birds* [Ptitsy pevchie] (1868), an operetta by Jacques Offenbach, more commonly known as *La Périchole*.
John Stuart Mill noted: "If we consider the works of women in modern times, and compare them with those of men, either in the literary or the artistic department, such inferiority as may be observed resolves itself essentially into one thing: but that is a most material one: deficiency of originality" (*The Subjection of Women* [Cambridge, Mass.: MIT Press, 1970], p. 69).

November 1876, 1.5: The Meek One Rebels

the Viazemsky house: A notorious lodging in the slums of St. Petersburg whose horrors were thus described in *G*, no. 298, October 28, 1876: "One can say without exaggeration that this house is the breeding ground and receptacle of every form of vice of which a human, oppressed by poverty and ignorance, is capable."

November 1876, 2.3: I Understand All Too Well

Gil Blas: In book 7, chapter 4 of Alain René Le Sage's novel, *L'Histoire de Gil Blas de Santillane* (1715-35), the archbishop of Grenada asks Gil

Blas for his honest opinion on a sermon the archbishop has delivered; when Gil Blas offers some very tactful criticism, the archbishop dismisses him.

November 1876, 2.4: I Was Only Five Minutes Late

"hero of the Russian epic": The narrator uses here the word *bogatyr'*, the exceptionally strong and courageous hero of the traditional Russian epic poems, the *byliny*.

is it not a corpse?: The image of the dead sun may derive from Revelations 6:12: "and lo, there was a great earthquake, and the sun became black as sackcloth of hair, and the moon became as blood." P. V. Bekedin, in "Povest' 'Krotkaia' (K istolkovaniiu obraza mertvogo solntsa)" [The tale "The Meek One": Toward an interpretation of the image of the dead sun], *Dostoevskii: materialy i issledovaniia* (Leningrad: Nauka, 1987), 7: 102–24, suggests some other possible sources, including Shakespeare and Goethe.

December 1876, 1.1: More about a Case That Is Not as Simple as It Seems

the woman Kirilova: *G*, no. 255, September 15, 1876, reported that on August 2, 1873, Anna Kirilova, a twenty-seven-year-old St. Petersburg woman, had killed her lover, Semen Malevsky, when she found another woman in his bedroom. On November 2 she was acquitted; spectators in the court applauded the verdict.

one very fortunate circumstance: An official in the Ministry of Justice who had read Dostoevsky's October *Diary* urged Dostoevsky to convince Kornilova to submit an appeal for clemency and helped him arrange a meeting with her.

Article 693 stipulated that witnesses to a crime, participants in it, jurors, and judges could not be summoned as expert witnesses. Kornilova's sentence was quashed because one person was examined both as a witness and as an expert.

looking out to see: Because of a typographical error in the newspaper report of the incident, Dostoevsky mistakenly states that Kornilova looked out at the girl after pushing her; in fact, she did not look out the window but went directly to the police station. Dostoevsky describes the scene correctly in *DP*, December 1877, 1.4.

December 1876, 1.2: A Belated Moral

Several of my friends: Khokhriakova (see note to October 1876, 1.4) states that when she suggested that this note itself might prompt someone to suicide, Dostoevsky became quite alarmed and was anxious to correct any misunderstanding the note may have caused.

weekly *Recreation*: The article appeared in the humor magazine *Razvlechenie* [Recreation], no. 51, December 14, 1876.

December 1876, 1.4: A Few Words about Young People

facts set forth in *The Moscow News*: On December 6, 1876, a group composed mainly of students demonstrated in Kazan Square in St. Petersburg. This was the first demonstration inspired by the newly organized revolutionary group *Zemlia i Volia* [Land and Freedom]. "On 6th December the red banner of *Zemlya i Volya* appeared for a moment on the Square of Our Lady of Kazan in St. Petersburg, during the workers' and students' demonstration, as if to announce the quick progress they had made during the previous months" (Franco Venturi, *Roots of Revolution* [New York: Grosset and Dunlap, 1966], p. 569). Several newspapers, including *G*, no. 343, December 12, 1876, suggested that the demonstration was a product of Western, or even Turkish, intrigues.

December 1876, 1.5: On Suicide and Arrogance

"No man shall hate his flesh": Quotation from Ephesians 5:29: "For no man ever yet hated his own flesh. . . ."
competent member: The lawyer and writer A. F. Koni (1844–1927) provided Dostoevsky with these suicide notes.

December 1876, 2.1: A Story from the Lives of Children

mother and her twelve-year-old daughter: As Dostoevsky's wife notes (in Grossman, *Seminarii po Dostoevskomu*, p. 66), the mother was L. Kh. Khokhriakova. (See also notes to October 1876, 1.4.)
Gostiny Dvor: A large block of shops in central St. Petersburg.
The Arcade: See notes to 1873.4.

December 1876, 2.2: An Explanation Regarding My Participation in the Forthcoming Publication of the Magazine *Light*

Vagner, Nikolai Petrovich (1829–1907), Russian zoologist, writer, and publisher. The announcement of his magazine that appeared in *DP* listed Dostoevsky as one of its contributors. He did not have any links with the magazine, however. (See also note to January 1876, 3.2.)

December 1876, 2.3: Where Does the Matter Stand at the Moment?

"godless Agarians": In Russian folklore, this was the name given to Arabs or Saracens, who were seen as mortal foes of Christendom. The name derives from Hagar, whose son, Ishmael, is the biblical ancestor of the twelve nomadic tribes (Genesis 25:12–18).
The Treaty of Paris (1856) ended the Crimean War. Its terms guaranteed the territorial integrity of Turkey and deprived Russia of her acquisitions around the mouth of the Danube and in southern Bessarabia. The Black Sea was made neutral, and neither Russia nor Turkey was allowed a

naval presence there. Russian diplomacy subsequently attempted to have these harsh terms lifted. In 1871 Russian warships were again allowed in the Black Sea. (See also notes to February 1876, 2.1.)

European gendarmerie: The Constantinople Conference—held from December 23, 1876, to January 20, 1877 (n.s.), in an attempt to find a peaceful solution to the Eastern Question—discussed, among other proposals, the possible provision of a detachment of Belgian or Italian troops to supervise the truce, and the implementation of proposed reforms among the Christian population in Turkey's Balkan possessions.